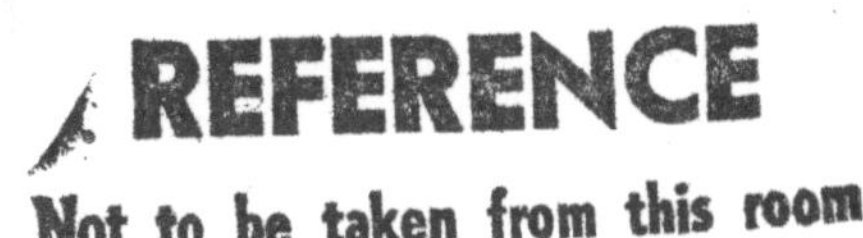

★★★★★★★★★★★★★★★★★★★★★★★★★★★

ALMANAC OF AMERICAN PRESIDENTS

FROM 1789 TO THE PRESENT

An Original Compendium Of Facts And Anecdotes About Politics And The Presidency In The United States Of America

EDITED BY THOMAS L. CONNELLY
AND MICHAEL D. SENECAL
A Manly Book

New York • Oxford

Almanac of American Presidents

Facts On File, Inc.
460 Park Avenue South
New York NY 10016
USA

Facts On File Limited
Collins Street
Oxford OX4 1XJ
United Kingdom

Library of Congress Cataloging-in-Publication Data

Almanac of American presidents : from 1789 to the present : an original compendium of facts and anecdotes about politics and the presidency in the United States of America / edited by Thomas L. Connelly and Michael D. Senecal.
p. cm.
"A Manly book."
Includes bibliographical references (p.) and index.
ISBN 0-8160-2219-4
1. Presidents—United States. 2. United States—Politics and government. I. Connelly, Thomas Lawrence. II. Senecal, Michael D.
E176.1.A584 1991
973'.0992—dc20 91-18895

British CIP data available on request from Facts On File.

Jacket design by Ellie Nigretto
Manufactured by the Maple-Vail Book Manufacturing Group
Printed in the United States of America

10 9 8 7 6 5 4 3 2 1

This book is printed on acid-free paper.

Professor Thomas L. Connelly died shortly before the completion of this volume. The work was completed in accordance with his plan.

Contents

Foreword

In his memoirs, Harry S Truman observed that "no one who has not had the responsibility can really understand what it is like to be President, not even his closest aides or members of his immediate family. There is no end to the chain of responsibility that binds him, and he is never allowed to forget that he is President." Few men and no women have had the opportunity to dispute him, yet history reveals that the presidency may be more comprehensible, though no less fascinating, than President Truman suggests, due to a simple fact basic to the democratic nature of the office: the responsibilities the presidents bear are the concentrated duties and concerns of the people they represent; the presidents are what the Americans they represent boil down to.

The American presidency is a remarkably telling expression of national character. Distressing and gratifying as it has sometimes been, Americans are almost always rewarded with the kind of leadership they deserve, because they elect a leader in their own image, or in the image they most admire, which is just as significant. The president mirrors faithfully the collective aspirations, abilities, shortcomings, and obsessions of the electorate he represents. He faces the nation's challenges for us and with us.

The purpose of this book is to provide views of the presidents, and, collaterally, of our American heritage, from various perspectives: to see our chief executives as heroes and as villains, as experienced leaders and as tyros, as campaigners and decision makers; to consider the nature of their education, the women they married, the houses they lived in, the mistakes they made, and how they spent their dotage. Candid or posed pictures reveal their own extra-verbal truth, and so pictures are a key element in this examination of the presidency. For readers whose curiosity is aroused by material in this book, a full complement of books for research and further reading are cited.

The contributors for this volume, scholars in the field of American history, have used the best source material available to compile an almanac that does not neglect the role of humor and irony in the too-often ponderous history of presidential leadership. Though the authors of this work relate the major events in the presidents' lives and careers, they have also endeavoured to express the human qualities of our chief executives, which serve to remind us of our kinship with them.

The American presidency is one of the most demanding and humbling jobs any person has been asked to undertake. This book describes the people who were bold enough to accept the challenge, how they fared, and, if you read between the lines, what that record says about our national character.

–T.L.C./M.D.S.

Acknowledgments

This book was produced by Manly, Inc.

Production coordinator is James W. Hipp. Systems manager is Charles D. Brower. Photography editors are Edward Scott and Timothy Lundy. Permissions editor is Jean W. Ross. Layout and graphics supervisor is Penney L. Haughton. Copyediting supervisor is Bill Adams. Typesetting supervisor is Kathleen M. Flanagan. Information systems analyst is George F. Dodge. Charles Lee Egleston is editorial associate. The production staff includes Rowena Betts, Polly Brown, Reginald A. Bullock, Teresa Chaney, Patricia Coate, Sarah A. Estes, Robert Fowler, Mary L. Goodwin, Ellen McCracken, Kathy Lawler Merlette, Laura Garren Moore, John Myrick, Pamela D. Norton, Cathy J. Reese, Laurrè Sinckler-Reeder, Maxine K. Smalls, and Betsy L. Weinberg.

Walter W. Ross and Timothy D. Tebalt did library research at the Thomas Cooper Library of the University of South Carolina with the assistance of the following librarians: Gwen Baxter, Daniel Boice, Faye Chadwell, Jo Cottingham, Cathy Eckman, Rhonda Felder, Gary Geer, David L. Haggard, Jens Holley, Jackie Kinder, Thomas Marcil, Laurie Preston, Jean Rhyne, Carol Tobin, Virginia Weathers, and Connie Widney.

ALMANAC OF AMERICAN PRESIDENTS

Where They Lived: Homes of the Eighteenth- and Nineteenth-Century Presidents

by KATHERINE H. RICHARDSON

The eighteenth- and nineteenth-century presidents came from diverse walks of life and from widely varied pasts. Their birthplaces and later homes reveal much about their personal lives as well as the social and economic origins of the nation as a whole. From Washington's Mount Vernon, exemplary of Virginia plantation society in its heyday, and the modest New England saltbox homes of the Adams family of Quincy, Massachusetts, to the Gothic Revival style of William McKinley's Canton, Ohio, residence, the presidential homes illustrate architectural history and symbolize the diversity of American society.

To the American people the presidential homes are shrines. Many are run as house museums, sometimes open only by appointment at the owner's convenience; some remain completely private residences. The National Park Service maintains others. Many no longer stand, though illustrations and photographs remain. Others are forgotten. Americans have always been a mobile people, and the families of the presidents have proven no exception. The homes that survive are important apart from their significance as social history because they help the people attach a sense of place to the highest office in the land.

A survey of the homes of the eighteenth- and nineteenth-century presidents also underscores the importance of historical preservation in the United States. In some presidential homes personal possessions have never been removed. In others the buildings have been restored and the rooms re-created with period pieces, giving an approximation of the past. Where preservation-minded people have not tried or have tried and failed, there is a void.

GEORGE WASHINGTON

George Washington was born on February 22, 1732, at Popes Creek Plantation on the Potomac River, thirty-eight miles east of Fredericksburg, Virginia. He lived there for the first three-and-a-half years of his life, then the family moved to another site on the Potomac, Little Hunting Creek, later known as Mount Vernon. The house at Popes Creek, known as Wakefield, burned in 1779 and was never replaced, though thirty-six years later Washington's adopted son George Washington Parke Custis marked its location with a stone tablet, which has since disappeared. The foundation of the original home, now preserved, indicates that it was a U-shaped structure containing at least nine rooms.

In 1930-1931 the Wakefield National Memorial Association, which purchased a then-moribund Popes Creek from the federal government in 1923, constructed the George Washington Memorial House there. Built of clay brick (of local origin) to resemble a typical Virginia plantation home of the mid eighteenth century, the Memorial

West front of George Washington's Mount Vernon, on the Potomac River in Virginia. Washington first moved to the site of Mount Vernon, then known as Little Hunting Creek, when he was three-and-a-half years old.

House features period furnishings (including a dining room table believed to be original to Popes Creek), a kitchen located on the site of the original, and a typical plantation garden. The Wakefield National Memorial Association transferred the refurbished site back to the federal government in time for the celebration of Washington's birth bicentennial in 1932. A Colonial Farm established there in 1968 recreates the rural life of the period. Administered by the National Park Service, the George Washington Birthplace National Monument at Popes Creek Plantation is open to the public daily except Christmas and New Year's Day.

After their 1735 move, young Washington and his family spent four years at Little Hunting Creek before moving again, to the Ferry Farm on the Rappahannock River near Fredericksburg. After his father died in 1743, Washington spent some of the remainder of his youth at Popes Creek, which his half-brother Augustine, Jr., inherited. Little Hunting Creek, the choicer site, went to another half-brother, Lawrence, and Washington went to live there when he was sixteen. Two years after Lawrence's death in 1752 Washington acquired that plantation, then known as Mount Vernon, securing a release from Lawrence's widow. He would call Mount Vernon

---

No estate in United America is more pleasantly situated than this [Mount Vernon]. It lies in a high, dry and healthy Country 300 miles by water from the Sea . . . on one of the finest Rivers in the World. . . . It is situated in a latitude between the extremes of heat and cold, and is the same distance by land and water, with good roads and the best navigation (to and) from the Federal City, Alexandria and George Town; distant from the first twelve, from the second nine, and from the last sixteen miles.

—Letter of George Washington to Arthur Young, December 12, 1793

---

home for the rest of his life.

The original Mount Vernon was a one-and-a-half-story hall-and-parlor house, typical of the Virginia tidewater area and built by Washington's father in 1740. After he acquired the home, Washington, first a major then a colonel in the Virginia militia, spent little time there until he resigned his commission in 1758 to serve in the Virginia House of Burgesses. At that time he also courted Martha Custis, whom he married the next year. In preparation for her arrival he began the work of designing and constructing a second story for Mount Vernon. Acting as his own architect, he continued to revise and expand the structure throughout his career, adding a handsome columned piazza to the east front in 1777 and overseeing final details of construction during his "retirement" from 1783 to 1787.

Certain details are particularly interesting. Likely seeking the appearance of an English stone house, Washington "rusticated" the boards of the siding of Mount Vernon to give them the appearance of stone. The boards were beveled and sand was applied to the painted surfaces. On a more symbolic level, he topped the cupola, the final construction project, with a weather vane styled as a dove of peace.

Mount Vernon remained in the hands of family after the deaths of Washington in 1799 and Martha Washington in 1802. The family unsuccessfully tried to sell the estate to the federal government in 1848. Only the efforts of the Mount Vernon Ladies' Association, founded by Ann Pamela Cunningham of Columbia, South Carolina, in 1853, saved the home and grounds. In 1858 the association purchased the plantation from the family for two hundred thousand dollars.

Cunningham, the force behind the movement to save Mount Vernon from the ravages of time, is largely responsible for the establishment of the historic preservation movement in the United States.

The home and grounds, still under the care of the Mount Vernon Ladies' Association, are open to the public year-round.

JOHN ADAMS AND JOHN QUINCY ADAMS

John Adams was born on October 30, 1735, in Braintree (later known as Quincy), Massachusetts. Three houses in the town are associated with the family. The first, the John Adams Birthplace, stands at 133 Franklin Street. A saltbox house of traditional New England design, it originally contained four rooms and a massive central chimney; soon after it was built in the late seventeenth century it was enlarged by the addition of a "lean-to" in back that provided four more rooms and almost doubled its size. Once a farm complex, the property supported a barn and outbuildings until the 1880s.

As an adult John Adams lived and raised his family at 141 Franklin Street in another saltbox house also enlarged by the addition of a lean-to. Known as the John Quincy Adams Birthplace, the house first served as the site of the elder John's law office. His son, the sixth president, was born there on July 11, 1767, and spent much of his childhood there (between European trips with his diplomat-father). Both the John Adams Birthplace and the John Quincy Adams Birthplace are maintained by the city of Quincy and are open to the public from April to October.

In 1787, while serving as American minister to England, John Adams purchased a home that he named Peacefield on what later became known as Adams Street. The family called the place Old House. Constructed in 1731, Old House underwent extensive renovation and expansion after Adams returned to the States in 1788 and during his terms as vice-president and president. After his presidency he retired to Old House, and John Quincy Adams later used it as a summer home. The family donated the house to the federal government in

BIRTHDATES AND BIRTHPLACES OF THE PRESIDENTS

GEORGE WASHINGTON
February 22, 1732
Westmoreland County, Virginia

JOHN ADAMS
October 30, 1735
Braintree, Massachusetts

THOMAS JEFFERSON
April 13, 1743
Goochland County, Virginia

JAMES MADISON
March 16, 1751
Port Conway, Virginia

JAMES MONROE
April 28, 1758
Westmoreland County, Virginia

JOHN QUINCY ADAMS
July 11, 1767
Braintree, Massachusetts

ANDREW JACKSON
March 15, 1767
Waxhaw Region, North/South Carolina

MARTIN VAN BUREN
December 5, 1782
Kinderhook, New York

WILLIAM HENRY HARRISON
February 9, 1773
Charles City County, Virginia

JOHN TYLER
March 29, 1790
Charles City County, Virginia

JAMES K. POLK
November 2, 1795
Mecklenburg County, North Carolina

ZACHARY TAYLOR
November 24, 1784
Orange County, Virginia

MILLARD FILLMORE
January 7, 1800
Locke Township,
New York

FRANKLIN PIERCE
November 23, 1804
Hillsborough County, New Hampshire

JAMES BUCHANAN
April 23, 1791
Cove Gap, Pennsylvania

ABRAHAM LINCOLN
February 12, 1809
Hodgenville, Kentucky

ANDREW JOHNSON
December 29, 1808
Raleigh, North Carolina

ULYSSES S. GRANT
April 27, 1822
Point Pleasant, Ohio

RUTHERFORD B. HAYES
October 4, 1822
Delaware, Ohio

JAMES A. GARFIELD
November 19, 1831
Orange, Ohio

CHESTER A. ARTHUR
October 5, 1829
North Fairfield, Vermont

GROVER CLEVELAND
March 18, 1837
Caldwell, New Jersey

BENJAMIN HARRISON
August 20, 1833
North Bend, Ohio

WILLIAM MCKINLEY
January 29, 1843
Niles, Ohio

THEODORE ROOSEVELT
October 27, 1858
New York, New York

WILLIAM HOWARD TAFT
September 15, 1857
Cincinnati, Ohio

WOODROW WILSON
December 28, 1856
Staunton, Virginia

WARREN G. HARDING
November 2, 1865
Corsica, Ohio

CALVIN COOLIDGE
July 4, 1872
Plymouth, Vermont

HERBERT HOOVER
August 10/11, 1874
West Branch, Iowa

FRANKLIN D. ROOSEVELT
January 30, 1882
Hyde Park, New York

HARRY S TRUMAN
May 8, 1884
Lamar, Missouri

DWIGHT D. EISENHOWER
October 14, 1890
Denison, Texas

JOHN F. KENNEDY
May 29, 1917
Brookline, Massachusetts

LYNDON B. JOHNSON
August 27, 1908
near Stonewall, Texas

RICHARD M. NIXON
January 9, 1913
Yorba Linda, California

GERALD R. FORD
July 14, 1913
Omaha, Nebraska

JIMMY CARTER
October 1, 1924
Plains, Georgia

RONALD REAGAN
February 6, 1911
Tampico, Illinois

GEORGE BUSH
June 12, 1924
Milton, Massachusetts

MASSACHUSETTS FARM BOY

In his native Braintree, Massachusetts, John Adams enjoyed a typical Massachusetts farm boy's childhood. Though the future president's father was a town leader—a militiaman, a church deacon, and a selectman—in early-eighteenth-century Braintree those honors were more ideal than material. The Adams homestead, biographer Page Smith writes, "stood close by the coast road, upright and unadorned, forthrightly rectangular, entirely functional, with only such grace as simplicity might give it." Still, riches abounded, for Braintree was young Adams's "range." After chores and school, he roamed all over the surrounding countryside, "until he knew by heart every pond, creek and swamp, every fold, hill, inlet and indentation, and, venturing farther, every island within a skiff 's range."

1946; it is filled with Adams family furnishings, which recall the family's wide travels. Administered by the National Park Service as the Adams Historical Site, the home and grounds are open to the public during the vacation season.

THOMAS JEFFERSON

The second member of the Virginia presidential dynasty was born on April 13, 1743, at the plantation Shadwell in Gouchland (later Albemarle) County, Virginia, near Charlottesville. Upon his father's death in 1757 he inherited Shadwell and the family home. The house burned in 1770, and Jefferson moved to nearby Monticello (the name means "little mountain" in Italian), where he had already constructed a temporary residence and had begun building his mansion.

The original Monticello was very different from the one that stands today. Basing the design of the home upon the ideas of Venetian architect Andrea Palladio and Britishers James Gibbs and Robert Morris, Jefferson planned a Classical Revival mansion for the leveled top of the little mountain. Much of the material that went into the building—the foundation stones, the bricks and timbers, the nails, even some of the hardware—came from local sources and was fabricated on site. A surviving drawing by Jefferson shows a structure about half the size of the later Monticello, featuring a two-story portico supported by two tiers of columns, Tuscan on the lower level and Ionic on the upper, but the second tier was probably never erected. Triglyphs decorated the stringcourse separating the first and second stories. The main parlor on the first floor supported a large library on the second. The visiting Marquis de Chastelleux described the home in 1782: "The house, of which Mr. Jefferson is the architect and often one of the workmen, is rather elegant, and in the Italian taste, though not without fault; . . . We may safely aver, that Mr. Jefferson is the first American who has consulted the fine arts to know how to shelter himself from the weather."

Martha Skelton, Jefferson's wife of ten years, died in 1782, and he left the United States to serve as a minister to France in 1784, ending Monticello's first period. Jefferson learned much about the great estates of Europe during his five-year sojourn abroad and returned home anxious to implement new ideas in the design of Monticello. From 1789, the year he assumed the position of first U.S. secretary of state, to 1808, the last full year of his second presidential term, he (and his large contingent of slaves and servants) completely reconstructed the home, making it probably the premier example of Neoclassical architecture in the country.

The second Monticello serves as both a tribute to Jefferson's sense of classicism and his inventiveness. He traced the design for the west front and dome

Thomas Jefferson's Monticello, near Charlottesville, Virginia (photograph by Edwin S. Roseberry)

to the Temple of Vesta through Palladio and, true to the form, placed Doric columns on the exterior of the building and Ionic in the interior. He also ingeniously hid the dome-room stairways in corners, removing the need for a central passage, and partially buried the outbuildings to hide them from view.

Building Monticello also gave Jefferson his greatest chance to tinker, and that perhaps is what the public notices most about the home. He designed a weather vane that could be read indoors and built a clock with double faces. A wine connoisseur, he built dumbwaiters that simultaneously brought bottles from the cellar and returned the empties. He placed his bed in an alcove separating a study from the bedroom proper; in the bedroom he kept a reclining writing chair with a swivel seat for easy entry and exit. He paid great attention to the grounds as well, using them to showcase interesting imported plants and to perform experiments.

All my wishes end, where I hope my days will end, at Monticello. Too many scenes of happiness mingle themselves with all the recollections of my native woods and fields, to suffer them to be supplanted in my affection by any other.

—Letter of Thomas Jefferson to Dr. George Gilmer, August 12, 1787

In 1831, five years after Jefferson's death, the family sold Monticello, and over the years the estate fell into disuse. In 1923 the Thomas Jefferson Memorial Foundation purchased it and spent years restoring the house and grounds, the latter to Jefferson's original specifications as recorded in plantation records. In the house reside many original and period furnishings. In 1952 the foundation began offering Monticello for year-round public view, and it quickly established itself as one of America's best-attended public monuments.

JAMES MADISON

Montpelier, situated about 110 miles from Washington, D.C., in Orange County, Virginia, was always home to James Madison. He was born on March 16, 1751, in the home of his maternal grandparents at Port Conway in King George County, but the family soon returned to the small wood home built on the Orange County site. Madison's father began construction of the plantation house during Madison's childhood; four years after his 1794 marriage Madison began modernizing the aging home. In 1809, as he was beginning the first of his two presidential terms, he commissioned William Thornton and Benjamin Latrobe to remodel Montpelier. They added a single-story wing to each side and changed the exterior walls from brick to Virginia limestone. The Classical Revival mansion displays dentil molding around the cornice and a semicircular fanlight on the portico.

Montpelier has been acquired by the National Trust for Historic Preservation and will be opened as a house museum.

JAMES MONROE

James Monroe, the last of the first generation of Virginia presidents, was born on April 28, 1758, in a frame house that stood in Westmoreland County, Virginia, near Colonial Beach. The structure is no longer extant, but recent archaeological explorations have revealed that the Monroe family lived considerably above the subsistence level analysts have often alleged. Evidence indicates that the future president's father owned as many as eight slaves at the time of his death and also worked as a carpenter. Several decorative stoneware pieces unearthed at the site attest to the family's "middle-class" status. The Monroe birthplace site is presently maintained by the Westmoreland County Board of Supervisors.

The first house Monroe lived in as an adult was "on the hill" in Fredericksburg, Virginia, where he practiced law beginning in 1786. His law office on Charles Street has been maintained as a historic shrine under the aegis of the James Monroe Memorial Foundation. Also in 1786 Monroe married Elizabeth Kortwright, and shortly thereafter he and his wife moved to Charlottesville and purchased a farmhouse and eight hundred acres of land. That house is now part of the University of Virginia, on the arcade in the old part of campus. It is known as Monroe House.

In 1795 Monroe purchased a plantation, Ash Lawn, near Thomas Jefferson's Monticello in Albemarle County. Jefferson arranged details of the construction of the farmhouse according to Monroe's plans while Monroe was serving on a diplomatic mission to France. The present home at Ash Lawn, claimed to have been Monroe's, is a simple side-gabled frame dwelling with an interior chimney and a tin roof. On the basis of the Monroe-Jefferson correspondence regarding plans for the home, experts speculate that the surviving structure is not the house for which Jefferson directed construction. Monroe's plans have not survived. The existing home and grounds are administered by Monroe's alma mater, the College of William and Mary.

In Washington, D.C., during his term as President James Madison's secretary of state from 1811 to 1817, Monroe owned the home at 2017 I Street, N.W., a three-and-a-half-story Adam style brick structure. Each story is divided by a stringcourse and each symmetrically placed window features a lintel and keystone. A semicircular fanlight and sidelights frame the door.

After his presidential terms from 1817 to 1825, Monroe retired to Oak Hill near Leesburg, Virginia. The house was built upon land Monroe inherited from his father-in-law. The Palladian home was designed by Thomas Jefferson and built by James Hoban, who designed the White House. Monroe lived at Oak Hill from 1825 until 1831, when he was forced to sell it due to his precarious financial situation. The house still stands, but it is privately owned.

Monroe lived the rest of his life with his daughter at the corner of Prince and Marion Streets in New York City.

ANDREW JACKSON

Andrew Jackson, the first of a new breed of populist presidents, grew up in the frontier regions of southern colonial America. He was born on March 15, 1767, in the Waxhaw district along the border between North and South Carolina. The exact site of his birth remains unknown, and none of the homes of his youth in South Carolina, North Carolina, and Tennessee survive. In 1792 Jackson and his wife Rachel (whom he married the previous year) built a log cabin at Poplar Grove, Tennessee, outside Nashville. A few years later they moved to Hunter's Hill, where they built another house and opened a general store. When forced to sell the home because of financial difficulties in 1804, the couple moved to a one-and-a-half-story log cabin at Jackson's new plantation, the Hermitage, about twelve miles from Nashville. The original cabin measured only twenty-four by twenty-six feet, though a later addition enlarged it somewhat. There Jackson—lawyer, politician, and military man—entertained presidents and statesmen and resided with his wife for fifteen years.

In 1819 Jackson erected a two-story, brick hall-and-parlor house on the site. The unpretentious structure, probably designed by the future president, featured a modest, four-column porch that made life in the hot summers easier. Aside from the use of brick, the first Hermitage adhered closely to the nearly universal design of plantation homes of the period. Jackson was evidently satisfied. While he was serving in Washington, D.C., as U.S. senator in 1823, he wrote, "How often does my thoughts lead me back to The Hermitage. There in private life, surrounded by a few friends, would be a paradise compared to the best situation here; and if once more there it would take a writ of *habeas corpus* to remove me into public life again."

LET'S SETTLE IT LIKE MEN

The birthplace of Andrew Jackson remains in dispute. Jackson's father, native Irish Andrew Jackson, died shortly before his son was born in 1767, and his wife, Elizabeth "Betty" Hutchinson Jackson, moved in with her sister, Jane Crawford, in present-day Lancaster County; but some contend that enroute to the Crawford house Mrs. Jackson stopped in what is now Union County, North Carolina, to visit another sister and suddenly went into labor there. For his part Jackson always claimed a South Carolina origin, but, not unexpectedly, the two counties contested the issue. In 1979 officials decided to resolve the dispute in an appropriately Jacksonian way: by a duel of sorts, but with less permanent results than Jackson's shooting matches. Now the Lancaster County and Union County high school football teams compete every year in the "Old Hickory Football Classic." The victorious county wins the right to claim Jackson as a native son and to house a stoneware bust of the president in its courthouse—until the next game.

No one had to issue such a writ after he won the presidency on his second try in 1828. After the victory, but without his beloved wife, who died shortly after the election, Jackson made plans to enlarge the Hermitage. The remodeling was finished by 1831, after which fire gutted the mansion. In 1834 Jackson ordered the house rebuilt using the surviving walls and foundation. The result was the Classical Revival home that survives to the present.

After Jackson's death on June 8, 1845, the Hermitage passed into the hands of his adopted son and namesake, who ran it into the ground. In 1886 the state of Tennessee, under Governor Andrew Johnson, purchased the estate, but the home and grounds continued to deteriorate. In 1889 the Ladies' Hermitage Associates, led by Amy Jackson, the wife of one of the president's grandsons, became the caretaker of the Hermitage. The association retains custody of the mansion and opens it to the public every day except Christmas.

MARTIN VAN BUREN

Martin Van Buren was born on December 5, 1782, in Kinderhook, New York, the son of a farmer and tavern keeper. None of the houses of his youth or his early career survive. In 1840, after his defeat in a bid for a second presidential term, he purchased a two-hundred-acre estate in Kinderhook he named Lindenwald. The original home, a brick Adam style mansion, was constructed in 1797 by the Van Ness family. Van Buren transformed Lindenwald into an Italianate villa, hiring Richard Upjohn to add a wing that incorporated a soaring tower. Upjohn also added a front gable, a front porch, and dormer windows. Extensive interior renovations, including the removal of a central staircase to make way for a great dining hall, completed the project. When Van Buren died in 1862 the property was sold out of the family and the furnishings dispersed.

Twentieth-century owners obscured Van Buren's Italianate fenestrations by constructing a quasi-southern, antebellum-style, two-story porch with columns on the front facade. Lindenwald tells its story well, displaying vestiges of all its major alterations. Located between Kinderhook and Stuyvesant Falls on the Hudson River, it is administered by the National Park Service.

WILLIAM HENRY HARRISON

William Henry Harrison's boyhood home, Berkeley Plantation, where he was born on February 9, 1773, had served as the family seat since before 1725. The original Harrison house, a two-and-a-half-story brick Georgian mansion, was built between 1725 and 1726 and stands near the James River between Richmond and Williamsburg, Virginia. Harrison sold the estate to his brother and moved west after accepting a commission as ensign in the First U.S. Infantry Regiment in 1791. He would later become governor of the Northwest Territory and would never return to live on the East Coast. The restored house is privately owned and open to the public every day except December 25.

In 1795 Harrison eloped with the daughter of Ohio landowner John Cleves Symmes. The couple made their home in North Bend, Indiana, first living in a two-story log cabin. Around the cabin core Harrison built additions, and the augmented structure became known as Big House. With its central section and "flankers," it eventually somewhat resembled Palladian style construction. Big House supported the claim that Harrison lived in a log cabin; the story aided his presidential campaign in 1840. Big House burned in 1858, seventeen years after Harrison's death; his grandson Benjamin, the twenty-third president, was born in Big House in 1833.

In 1804, four years after his appointment as territorial governor of Indiana, Harrison built his mansion, Grouseland, in the Indiana capital, Vincennes. The two-and-a-half-story brick house contained thirteen rooms and was built to resemble his ancestral home in Virginia. But it was more than a home; it was a fortress. Vincennes was a frontier community, and the danger of Indian attack was real. Grouseland's outer walls were eighteen inches thick and featured slits through which guns were aimed. The attic windows were designed for sharpshooters and the house windows reinforced with double shutters. A powder magazine in the cellar supplied the guns, and a trapdoor on the second floor led to a first-floor hiding closet. An

Birthplace of William Henry Harrison, near Charles City, Virginia. Harrison moved to Ohio as an eighteen-year-old army ensign in 1791 (photograph by Taylor Lewis and Associates).

underground passage ran from the house to an outbuilding.

Grouseland served as a place to live and work as well. The first floor of the mansion contained a Council Chamber where Harrison conducted territorial business and entertained guests. The dining room was well appointed in the understated frontier style of the day. Portraits of Harrison by Rembrandt Peale and of his son's wife, Jane Findley Harrison, grace the walls of the home.

In 1814, after resigning his second army commission, Harrison moved back to Big House, where he lived until he assumed the presidency for one month in 1841. The Daughters of the American Revolution saved the mansion from destruction in 1909 and opened it as a house museum in 1911.

JOHN TYLER

John Tyler, the sixth Virginia native to hold the presidential office, was born at Greenway Plantation in Charles City County on March 29, 1790. Greenway's one-and-a-half-story frame house, built in about 1750, is a National style dwelling typical of the prerevolutionary tidewater South. The home is privately owned and is not open to the public.

Tyler's better known home is the plantation near Richmond, Virginia, that he purchased as president in 1842. When he acquired Sherwood Forest, as he called it, thinking himself a sort of outlaw president at the time, the plantation supported a modest frame house built in about 1790. He enlarged the house and added a colonnade to the old kitchen. The improvements resulted in an incredibly long structure of some three hundred feet. Without considering the extensions to the kitchen and the office, Sherwood Forest appears basically a Georgian style house with a central block and two wings.

About two years after the death of his first wife, Letitia Christian, and two and a half years after purchasing Sherwood Forest, Tyler married Julia Gardner, and the new couple outfitted their plan-

The house . . . is neat and beautiful and in all the arrangements I am very much gratified. The house when we arrived was vacated and opened to us by the servants. Some bedrooms were in order, but I went immediately into the preparation of my own particular one. . . . I defy you to find so sweet a bedroom or chamber in every respect as mine! *I assure you Mama my house outside and in is very elegant and quite becoming "a President's Lady."*

—Letter of Julia Tyler, John Tyler's second wife, to her mother upon arriving at the Tyler plantation after the completion of her husband's presidential term, March 9, 1845

tation in style. The Tylers also entertained enthusiastically, as the testimony of Mrs. Tyler's sister indicates: "We danced incessantly until one o'clock when the first supper was announced. . . . The mottoes and confectionary were of the most expensive kind—candied fruits, ices, etc. in abundance. This over we danced again until three, when the second supper was announced. . . . Such turkeys and such saddles of mutton! the fat on the former three inches thick—there was venison, wild duck, etc. etc. Champagne flowed unceasingly—of the nicest kind."

The house remains in the hands of the family virtually as Tyler left it. It is operated by Historic Sherwood Forest Corporation as a house museum and is open by appointment. The grounds are accessible to the public all year.

JAMES K. POLK

The eleventh president was born near Pineville, Mecklenburg County, North Carolina, on November 2, 1795. A one-and-a-half-story "two-pen" log house of the German style, believed to be similar to the original, has been constructed on the site. The reconstruction is operated by the North Carolina Museum of History and is open to the public every day except Thanksgiving, Christmas Eve, and Christmas Day.

In 1816, when Polk was away at the University of North Carolina, his family moved to Columbia, Tennessee, where they built a modest Federal style house of handmade brick. The first floor of the restored home contains an entrance hall, double parlors, and a museum that was originally a porch. Many of the furnishings displayed were used by the Polk family in the White House, and the home also features portraits of the president and his wife, Sarah Childress, by G. P. A. Healy. The Polk ancestral home is now operated as a house museum and is open to the public every day except Christmas.

When Polk retired from the presidency in 1849, he moved back to Nashville, Tennessee, where he had spent much of his adult life in politics, to a home he called Polk Place. He died there only three months after leaving office. His wife remained at Polk Place until her death in 1891, and then, contrary to the instructions of Polk's will, the house was demolished.

ZACHARY TAYLOR

A "small log cabin, about twelve feet square," on Muddy Fork of Bluegrass Creek in Orange County, Virginia, was the November 24, 1784, birthplace of Zachary Taylor. The family had stopped at the home of relatives while en route to new quarters in Springfield, Kentucky, where they had acquired four hundred acres. That parcel soon grew into a ten-thousand-acre tract. Springfield was a prosperous settlement, and Taylor's father, John, was able to build a large brick house for his family in 1790. The three-story brick hall-and-parlor home stands at 5608 Apache Road. It is in private hands.

Zachary Taylor joined the army in 1808, beginning a period of four decades during which he moved to posts throughout the United States. His wife, Margaret "Peggy" Smith Taylor, patiently endured the life of an army wife and bore six children.

During the demobilization after the

Replica of the birthplace of Millard Fillmore, Moravia, New York

War of 1812 Taylor and his family returned to Springfield and a three-hundred-acre farm given to them by Taylor's father. But the calm of pastoral life disagreed with the former soldier, and he went back to the service in 1816. He maintained a connection to the soil during his army career, however, by buying and selling land. By 1832 he had moved his family's permanent residence to Louisiana. In 1842 he purchased a 1,923-acre plantation called Cypress Grove located about ten miles south of Rodney, Mississippi. He intended it to be his retirement home, but after the Mexican War the family retired to a place known as Spanish Cottage, in Baton Rouge along the Mississippi River. The simple-frame, gable-ended home at Spanish Cottage had four rooms and a central chimney. Wide verandas encircled the one-story structure. Taylor's wife had the cottage remodeled and planted an extensive kitchen garden. Taylor remained at Spanish Cottage for only about a year, however. A national hero after his war exploits in Mexico, he accepted the presidential nomination of the Whig party in 1848 and took up residence in the White House after winning the election. He died in office in 1850. Spanish Cottage is no longer extant.

MILLARD FILLMORE

Another of the log cabin presidents was Millard Fillmore, born at Locke Township (later Summerhill), New York, on January 7, 1800. Fillmore's father, Nathaniel, had purchased the land sight unseen in 1799. Located in the Finger Lakes region of the Alleghenies, the place, as Fillmore recalled as an adult, was "high and cold" and "one of the poorest in the region." The family moved on to the village of Semipronious, New York, and rented a farm one mile east of Skaneateles Lake, then moved to Montville and then East Aurora, New York. East Aurora was near Buffalo, where Fillmore made his home as an adult.

Though the actual boyhood cabins and homes no longer stand, a reproduction of the Fillmore birthplace is located in Fillmore State Park in Monrovia. It is open to the public during the vacation season.

In 1826 Fillmore married Abigail Powers and built a two-story wooden home a few houses down the street from his East Aurora law offices. The home featured a pillared front porch and a single-story kitchen in the rear. Around the kitchen Fillmore's wife planted a large rose garden and an herb garden. The family was living there when Fillmore won election to the New York state assembly in 1828. The house, in private hands, still stands in East Aurora.

Fillmore moved his home and law practice to Buffalo in 1830. He and Abigail acquired a six-room, hall-and-parlor, clapboard home on Franklin Street near the center of town. Fillmore retired to the Franklin Street home after his presidential term, but without his beloved wife, who died of pneumonia three weeks after his inauguration. He remembered, "It does not seem like home . . . the light of the house is gone."

The former president remarried in 1858 and moved. After serving as a hotel for a time, the Franklin Street home was demolished. Fillmore and his new wife, Carolina McIntosh, purchased the Hollister Mansion on Niagara Square in Buffalo. Fillmore renamed the residence Gothick House, correctly describing its architectural style. He wrote of it, "My own house is the most comfortable place I can find . . . and my wife and library . . . the most charming society."

Fillmore lived in Gothick House until he died in 1874. In 1929 the home was torn down to make way for a hotel.

FRANKLIN PIERCE

The fourteenth president was born on November 23, 1804, in a log cabin in Hillsborough County, New Hampshire. Six weeks later his father, Benjamin Pierce, moved the family to their new home, which had been under construction for some time. That house, known as the Pierce Homestead, still stands in Hillsborough. The Georgian frame house reflected the growing wealth of the Pierces. It featured hand-stenciled cornices, imported wallpaper, and a second-floor sitting room. Gardens around the house and a fish pond in front gave the grounds an elegant look. Pierce went away to college, then moved back to Hillsborough and set up law offices across the street from the home. He lived in it until his marriage. The Pierce Homestead is presently administered by the State Recreation Division of New Hampshire and is open to the public.

When Pierce married Jane Appleton in 1834, he and his wife set up housekeeping in a Hillsborough home purchased from Pierce's brother-in-law. While Pierce served as a U.S. senator he lived in Washington boardinghouses; his wife often stayed with relatives. She was unhappy living the political life and convinced her husband to resign his Senate seat in 1842. That year the family purchased a two-and-a-half-story frame house on Montgomery Street in Concord, New Hampshire. Two of their sons died while the family lived in that house, and they sold it in 1847, while Pierce fought in the Mexican War. In the years before Pierce went to the White House the couple shared a Main Street home with friends and purchased sixty nearby acres for future construction. They never built on that property.

After the conclusion of Pierce's presidential term in 1857 he and his wife traveled before settling back in Concord at a residence on South Main Street they constructed while they were still living in the White House. Known as the Second Empire Mansion, the home had a stucco finish, a concave mansard roof, bracketed cornices, and paired windows over the main entrance—quite the height of style for the day. A wide hall flanked by a parlor, a sitting room, and a dining room occupied the first floor. Upstairs were five bedrooms.

In 1863 Pierce's wife died in the Second Empire Mansion. Thereafter Pierce spent more and more of his time at a seashore cottage at New Hampshire's Little Boar's Head. But he died in 1869 at the house in town, now a private residence that can be toured by appointment.

JAMES BUCHANAN

James Buchanan's April 23, 1791, birthplace, a log cabin in Cove Gap, Pennsylvania, now stands at Mercersburg Academy in Mercersburg, Pennsylvania, and is furnished with period pieces as a house museum. When Buchanan was five the family moved to a two-story brick home in the town proper. Buchanan's father ran a general store out of the same building. That home does not survive.

After he graduated from Dickinson College in 1809, Buchanan studied law. He was admitted to the Pennsylvania bar in 1812. He purchased a tavern in Lancaster, Pennsylvania, transformed it into his office and residence, and from there embarked on his long and distinguished political career that culminated in a frustrating presidential term on the eve of the Civil War.

In 1848, while he served as James K. Polk's secretary of state, Buchanan purchased a mansion known as Wheatland, which sat on a twenty-two-acre estate outside Lancaster. A two-and-a-half-story hall-and-parlor design, the house featured a one-story entrance porch and symmetrically placed windows and dormers. It is a curious blend of Greek Revival and Dutch Colonial influences, which are especially evident in the gables of the central portion of the house.

Presently maintained as a house museum, Wheatland is located at 1120 Marietta Avenue in Lancaster. The restorers have had an easy time furnishing the home authentically, because the rooms were sketched and described in 1857, the year Buchanan assumed the presidency. Many of the furnishings in the house are original, including the Venetian blinds and oilcloth floor coverings.

At Wheatland, Buchanan raised his orphaned nephew and niece, Henry and Harriet Lane. Harriet served as White House hostess during Buchanan's term. After his presidency Buchanan happily retired to the peace and quiet of his home, where he died in 1868.

ABRAHAM LINCOLN

Controversy has long surrounded the log cabin enshrined on a hill in Hodgenville, Kentucky. Experts question whether the cabin is actually the site of Lincoln's February 12, 1809, birth. The National Park Service, administrator of the hilltop site, perpetuates the birth story, but in their files another story casts doubt on the park's public interpretation.

Abraham's father, Thomas Lincoln, did not hold clear title to the land near Hodgenville on which he had settled.

Tom Lincoln, his wife, boy, and girl, had arrived on a claim at Little Pigeon Creek, without a horse or a cow, without a house, with a piece of land under their feet and the wintery sky high over. Naked they had come into the world; almost naked they came to Little Pigeon Creek, Indiana.

The whole family pitched in and built a pole-shed or "half-faced camp." On a slope of ground stood two trees about fourteen feet apart, east and west. These formed the two strong cornerposts of a sort of cabin with three sides, the fourth side open, facing south. The sides and the roof were covered with poles, branches, brush, dried grass, mud; chinks were stuffed where the wind or rain was trying to come through. At the open side a log fire was kept burning night and day. In the two far corners inside the camp were beds of dry leaves on the ground. To these the sleepers brought their blankets and bearskins.

Here they lived a year.

—*Carl Sandburg,* Abraham Lincoln: The Prairie Years *(1926)*

Traditional Lincoln birthplace, housed since 1911 in a memorial building near Hodgenville, Kentucky. In all likelihood, however, the true Lincoln birthplace had nearly completely deteriorated by the time of Lincoln's election to the presidency.

When the person holding the lien on the property sued in 1811, the court put the land up for sale and the Lincolns moved ten miles away. At the Hodgenville farm, the story goes, they had constructed a log cabin "in the vicinity of a knoll by the spring" that later became known as Sinking Spring. Some time after the Lincolns left, a family named Jackson built a new cabin within fifteen feet of the Lincoln home, which by then had fallen into disrepair. The two cabins stood next to each other for years, according to the testimony of others living in the area. In 1860, the year of Lincoln's election to the presidency, the Jackson cabin was dismantled and moved to a nearby farm. The Lincoln cabin continued to decay until the site contained only the chimney stones, two fruit trees, and a path.

Richard Crail (sometimes Creal), a Hodgenville neighbor of the Lincolns, acquired the old Lincoln property in 1867. His son, Judge John C. Creal, sold the one-hundred-ten-acre tract to A. W. Dennett of New York in 1894; in 1895 Dennett had the Jackson cabin dismantled and brought back to the Lincoln/Crail farm, billing it as the birthplace of Abraham Lincoln. Several times Dennett dismantled the Jackson cabin and toured the country with it. In 1911 it was enshrined in the Memorial Building at what would become the Abraham Lincoln Birthplace National Historic Site.

To make matters worse, the National Park Service tore down the two-story Crail log home, which stood near the highway at the entrance to the birthplace park, because tourists passing by kept mistaking it for the "real" Lincoln cabin. Ironically, that was probably constructed nearer to the time of the Lincoln cabin than the Jackson cabin.

In 1816 the Lincoln family left Kentucky and moved to a farm near Little Pigeon Creek outside of Gentryville, Indiana. There they built an eighteen-by-twenty-foot log cabin with a sleeping loft and a mud and stick chimney. At Little Pigeon Creek Lincoln's mother, Nancy Hanks, died of "milk sickness," and a stepmother, Sarah Johnston, came to raise the children.

Sarah coaxed Thomas Lincoln to add practical and civilized touches to the crude Indiana cabin. Soon it had glass windows and a working door, and a plank floor replaced the original dirt surface. Sarah's furniture from home added the final touches to the finest cabin Lincoln's parents ever inhabited.

Lincoln grew to maturity at the Little Pigeon Creek farm, learning to read and write with the encouragement of Sarah and to the perplexity of his father. He helped illiterate neighbors write letters and also read aloud to his family while lying on his back with his feet propped against the wall. Even at an early age Lincoln delighted in humor, some of it directed against his log cabin home. By some accounts, once he had a neighbor child walk in mud and then hoisted the child upside down and had him walk on the ceiling, leaving mysterious footprints.

The Lincoln home in Indiana stood until about 1891. A replica can be viewed at the Lincoln Living Historical Farm at Lincoln City, Indiana.

After the Lincolns moved to Illinois in 1830, Abe left to begin life on his own. He ended up in New Salem, Illinois, where he spent six years working as a storekeeper, postmaster, surveyor, and handyman. He moved from place to place in town, usually boarding with families who needed the extra income. When he clerked in stores, he often bunked in the back rooms.

In 1837 Lincoln moved to Springfield, which became the Illinois capital that same year. Not until 1844, after his marriage to Mary Todd, did Lincoln purchase a home. Built in 1839, that house, located on the corner of Eighth and Jackson Streets, was originally owned by the minister who married the couple. In 1856 Lincoln had the one-and-a-half-story Greek Revival structure enlarged to two full stories. Unoccupied after the Lincolns left for Washington in 1861, the home was restored by the National Park Service and is open to the public as the Lincoln Home National Historic Site.

ANDREW JOHNSON

A tiny, two-story clapboard house with a gambrel roof in Raleigh, North Carolina, was the modest birthplace of Andrew Johnson. He was born there on December 29, 1808, to a landless porter, Jacob Johnson, and his wife, Polly. Jacob died after rescuing a group of drunken men from drowning, leaving his wife and children to make it on their own. The family sank into even deeper poverty than they had experienced when Jacob was living. Andrew Johnson never attended school. Polly bound him and his brother out to a tailor in 1822, and in the two years before the boys ran away from their apprenticeship they learned the trade. The future president ended up in Carthage, North Carolina, where he made a living as a tailor. He then moved to Laurens, South Carolina, for a time before moving back to Raleigh briefly. In 1826 he left Raleigh with his mother and stepfather and settled in Greeneville, Tennessee. Casso's Inn, where he lived during the Raleigh sojourn, was moved to Pullen Park in the city, where it remains open to the public as a commemoration to Johnson.

In Greeneville, Johnson lived for a brief time with his parents; then he set up a shop of his own. He married Eliza McCardle in 1827; the couple resided in the back room of the two-room shop. In 1831 they purchased a home and shop on Water Street. By then Johnson's political career had solidified. The shop became a center of Tennessee politics in the 1840s.

In 1851 the Johnsons, far away from the poverty of their early years, purchased a two-story brick Georgian home on Main Street. It featured a central gable flanked by symmetrically placed

Point Pleasant, Ohio, birthplace of Ulysses S. Grant (courtesy of the Ohio Historical Society)

windows and became known as the "Homestead" to the Johnson family. Eliza Johnson planned a large, pleasant garden in the rear, and her husband enjoyed working in it for relaxation.

Johnson was living in the Main Street home when in 1864 he was elected vice-president for Abraham Lincoln's second term. The home fell into disrepair during Johnson's tenure as vice-president and president, falling into the hands of Confederate forces, then Union forces during the Civil War. It was used as a brothel during his presidency. After he completed his presidential term in 1869 he and his wife returned to the home and remodeled it by adding a second story and verandas to the rear.

After Johnson's death in 1875, his daughter "Victorianized" the home, adding gables, a metal roof, and wooden pediments over the windows. In 1921 the state of Tennessee purchased the original Water Street tailor shop. Later it and the Main Street home, restored to its original style, were incorporated by the National Park Service into the Andrew Johnson National Historic Site, which remains open to the public.

ULYSSES S. GRANT

Ulysses S. Grant was born in Point Pleasant, Ohio, on April 27, 1822, in a small, one-story frame house constructed in 1817. The design of the house was based on the hall-and-parlor plan so common during the Early National Period. The birthplace remains open to the public from April to November.

Grant's father, a tanner and leather merchant, moved his brood to Georgetown, Ohio, when Ulysses was two. The future president spent his boyhood in Georgetown in a house on Cross Street built by his father. Grant entered the U.S. Military Academy in 1839 and graduated in 1843, twenty-first in a class of thirty-nine. He was assigned to the infantry at Jefferson Barracks, Missouri. There he met his wife, Julia Dent; they were married in 1848 after Grant served in the Mexican War.

During the next six years Grant and

his wife and growing family were shuttled around from barracks to barracks in standard military fashion. In 1854 the officer resigned from the service and moved the family to a farm in St. Louis, Missouri. Besides working the farm, Grant sold real estate and firewood and tried bill collecting, none of which he did very well. On the property he built a two-story log house that he called Hardscrabble; after he achieved fame it was moved several times, ending up on the Anheuser-Busch estate near St. Louis. It is not open to the public.

The Grants moved to Galena, Illinois, in 1858, and Grant clerked in his father's leather goods store until he reenlisted in the army at the beginning of the Civil War. He rose to command the Union armies by 1864 and in 1865 returned to Galena a national hero. Three houses were offered to the Grant family as gifts from an admiring public. The family first lived in a large brick house built for them by the people of Galena. An Italianate mansion, it remains almost as the Grants left it when they moved to Philadelphia later in 1865. The house is located on Bouthillier Street in Galena and is open to the public.

The Philadelphia home was purchased and furnished by the Union Club of that city for thirty thousand dollars. Since the home was too far removed from Washington, the Grants decided to move to the capital for the Christmas of 1865. The Washington town house they inhabited was Julia's love. It featured two elegant drawing rooms, spectacular chandeliers, and a library. The Grants lived there when the Union hero was offered the Republican nomination for president in 1868. Upon his election, Grant wanted to sell the town house, but Julia refused. He remarked, "Very well. . . . I will send word that my *wife* will not *let me* sell the house."

During and after the presidential years the Grants summered at Long Branch on the New Jersey shore. The house there blended several architectural styles. It sported nine dormers, an encircling two-story porch, and a widow's walk on top.

After Grant's retirement from the White House he and Julia traveled extensively. Grant wrote, "I have no home but must establish one. I do not know where." New York was his first choice, where once again admirers promised to purchase a house, a four-story brownstone located at 3 East 66th Street. It was filled with souvenirs of the Grants' travels and Victorian clutter. A second-floor library looked out on Central Park. There Grant, ill with throat cancer, penned most of his *Personal Memoirs*.

When his illness advanced, Grant was offered the use of a two-story wooden cottage at Mount McGregor in the foothills of the Adirondack Mountains near Saratoga Springs, New York. He sat there on the broad veranda, waved to passersby, and finished the final pages of his life story before succumbing to the cancer on July 23, 1885. The cottage on the New Jersey shore still stands and is open to the public.

RUTHERFORD B. HAYES

The nineteenth president was born in Delaware, Ohio, on October 4, 1822, three months after his father's death

---

We were well provided with all that was necessary and our red-brick house, built fronting on the street, was as grand as the houses of our neighbors. I do not know that Fanny or myself ever envied the condition or possessions of our friends, except, perhaps, the picture and story books which Mr. Pettibone, the leading lawyer of the village, gave his children. And after Uncle Birchard went into business we were well supplied with everything of that sort by him.

—Diary and Letters of Rutherford Birchard Hayes *(1922)*

Photograph of the North Fairfield, Vermont, birthplace of Chester Arthur taken before the home was destroyed and a replica built on the site (courtesy of the Vermont Development Commission)

from typhoid fever. Unlike the families of some other fatherless presidents, Hayes's family was not destitute. They lived in a plain brick house with a long wooden addition in the rear. Sophia, Hayes's widowed mother, received aid from her wealthy brother, Sardis Birchard, who acted virtually as a surrogate father to Rutherford and put him through college and law school. The Hayes birthplace is no longer extant.

Hayes became a successful lawyer. He married Lucy Webb in 1852 and purchased a small three-story home on Sixth Street in Cincinnati, where the couple raised eight children. After serving in the Civil War, Hayes returned to his law practice. He won election to Congress in 1864 and became governor of Ohio in 1867, serving three terms in that office.

In the meantime, Hayes's Uncle Sardis was building an estate near what would become Fremont, Ohio. Known as Spiegel Grove, the place subsequently became the Hayes home, as Sardis left it to the family in his will.

Hayes added extensively to the home, originally a two-and-a-half-story brick structure with gables and a wide veranda on three sides. The renovated house resembled a sprawling Victorian mansion of indeterminable style. It featured a cupola and a towerlike semicircular addition on the side. The family returned to Spiegel Grove, Hayes's "obscure and happy home in the pleasant grove at Fremont," after the conclusion of Hayes's presidential term in 1881.

Spiegel Grove still contains many of the Hayeses' possessions and furnishings and is open for tours by appointment.

JAMES A. GARFIELD

James A. Garfield, born on November 19, 1831, in Orange, Ohio, was the last of the log cabin presidents. As a child he was a quick learner and a hard worker who consistently led his school classes. After graduating with highest honors from Williams College in 1856 he settled in Hiram, Ohio, and acquired a teaching position at Hiram Eclectic Institute. Soon he took the position of president of that institution. He married Lucretia Rudolph in 1858. They spent their first years together in a boardinghouse near the Hiram campus. Then they purchased a small two-story frame house across the street from the Institute.

In 1859 Garfield became a state senator. He served in the Civil War for two years, and then won election to the U.S. House of Representatives in late 1862. He served for seventeen years in the House. The Garfields built a house in Washington that looked out on Franklin Square. During the construction of the house Garfield wrote to his wife, "I go every day to the little spot of earth where we are planting a home. . . . How sweet it would be when all our little darlings should be happy and safe sheltered under its roof."

In 1876 Garfield decided he should own a home "where my boys can learn to work and where I can get some exercise, where I can touch the earth and get some strength from it." He purchased a one-hundred-sixty-acre farm near Mentor, Ohio. "Here is my love of a farm revived in me," he commented. Though the farm was "shabby, neglected . . . with a sagging, one-and-a-half story frame house hard beside a reeking pigsty and several slowly collapsing barns," Garfield got what he wanted. From those humble beginnings he transformed the place into his haven. Newspaper reporters named it Lawnfield. The renovated farm featured a three-story mansion, fine barns, and picket fences. The house had a central gable, a one-story porch across the front, and plentiful "gingerbread" in the eaves and gables.

Garfield died at the hand of an assassin four months after he assumed the presidency in 1881. Lawnfield is maintained as a house museum and is open to the public from May through October.

GOOD TIMING

In May 1830 the congregation of the Fairfield, Vermont, Baptist Church divided into two separate bodies, and Rev. William Arthur was retained as pastor of the North Fairfield parish. While the North Fairfield congregation constructed a parsonage, Rev. Arthur lived in a log cabin on the outskirts of town. Work on the Fairfield parsonage progressed slowly using the volunteer labor of farmer-parishioners. The parish held a ceremony when the scaffolding for the new parsonage was completed. As biographer George F. Howe recounts, townspeople were scandalized by the antics of a local youth who before the celebration bounded into the rafters of the church and shouted:

> This is a shell
> It looks like Hell
> Wrought out of crooked wood
> But I'll bet a curse
> Were it ten times worse
> Baptists would call it good.

The Arthurs moved in just in time to celebrate the birth of their fifth child—a boy, Chester, named after the doctor attending the birth.

CHESTER A. ARTHUR

A small, National style frame house in North Fairfield, Vermont, was the October 5, 1829, birthplace of Chester A. Arthur. Though it no longer stands, a replica has been constructed on the site. The place provided only temporary residence for the Arthur family. As a boy Chester resided in at least eight homes, because his father, a Baptist minister, traveled from one parsonage to another. One of the churches he served was located in Greenwich, New York, and the parsonage still stands on Woodlawn Avenue, though it has been moved from its original location.

ALL WORK AND NO PLAY

For John Scott Harrison, son of William Henry Harrison and father of Benjamin Harrison, farming was a hard life. He was constantly in debt and once wrote to a relative that a mutual friend had "advised me to sell my farm and come to the city to live,—sell my farm, I really would, but what could I do in the city? I could not feed myself much less my children. Besides I am miserable enough here and I should be more so there." As a child, future president Benjamin Harrison worked hard and played hard without much knowledge of his father's troubles. Benjamin loved to hunt, fish, and swim, and, in the words of early biographer Lew Wallace, "very frequently . . . assisted the negro who served the household in the capacity of cook; he carried wood and water for him, and helped him wash the dishes that he might better secure his company in a bout of fishing or hunting."

After he married Ellen Herndon in 1859, Chester Arthur moved to New York City to take up the full-time practice of law. For a time before the Civil War, he and his wife lived with her mother in lower Manhattan. After the war the Arthurs purchased a row house at 123 Lexington Avenue. The home contained several large parlors, in which the couple entertained frequent guests. Law offices occupied the street-level section.

Arthur died twenty months after leaving the presidency in 1885. The Lexington Avenue house remains in private hands.

GROVER CLEVELAND

Stephen Grover Cleveland was born on March 18, 1837, in the Presbyterian parsonage in Caldwell, New Jersey. Constructed in 1837, the house was "rather extravagant, gabled." It still stands and is open for tours. From Caldwell, the Cleveland family, eleven strong, moved to Fayetteville, New York, to a three-story parsonage that featured a stone-clad first floor and clapboard upper stories. Then the family moved to Clinton, New York. Neither of those homes survives.

As a young man Cleveland struck out for Cleveland, Ohio, stopping along the way in Buffalo, New York, to visit an uncle. He liked what he saw and went no further. He spent thirty years there, living in rented rooms and hotels. The bachelor became mayor of Buffalo in 1882 and three years later took office as president of the United States. In a White House wedding in 1886, he married Frances Folsom, the daughter of a longtime friend. Before their marriage he had purchased a home three miles from the White House in Georgetown Heights. The stone house had two-story porches that wrapped around its red roof. It was known varyingly as "Oak View" and "Red Top."

Back in New York after his first round as president, the Clevelands purchased a home at 816 Madison Avenue. That Gothic style four-story brownstone featured rounded arches and a square tower. The couple later moved to 12 West 51st Street in New York. From 1891 to 1904 they summered in a two-story wooden cottage known as Gray Gables at Cape Cod, Massachusetts.

In 1897 Cleveland retired after his second presidential term and moved with his wife to Princeton, New Jersey, where he had close ties with the college's faculty. The Clevelands purchased an estate, Westland, in Princeton. The home, patterned after the colonial governor's mansion in Princeton, is no longer extant.

BENJAMIN HARRISON

Benjamin Harrison was born on August 20, 1833, in Big House, the home of his grandfather, William Henry Harrison.

His boyhood home was known as The Point and was located in North Bend, Ohio. It occupied six hundred acres on a peninsula between the Ohio and Big Miami Rivers.

Harrison married Caroline Lavinia Scott in 1853 and moved to Indianapolis, where he developed a thriving law practice. He and his wife lived in a "sagging, three-room shack" on Vermont Street. As his law practice grew, Harrison changed the family's residence to a two-story wooden house on North New Jersey Street. In 1862 they moved to a home on the corner of North Street and North Alabama Street. It has been described as an "old-fashioned affair with a radically sloped roof, a dormer jutting off the second-floor front, and a pillared half-circle portico."

The Harrisons packed their belongings again in 1874. Their last home was located on a lot purchased seven years before at 1230 North Delaware Street. It was, and remains, an Italianate style, sixteen-room, red brick mansion. The rooms were vast, the chandeliers sparkling, and the draperies sumptuous. Harrison died there in 1901; the home is still filled with the family's belongings and memorabilia and is open to the public.

WILLIAM MCKINLEY

William McKinley was born the seventh of nine children in Niles, Ohio, on January 29, 1843. His father was an ironmaker who moved his family to Poland, Ohio, when McKinley was a boy. The future president entered military service in 1861 and reached the rank of brevet major by the end of the Civil War. He went on to study law and established a practice in Canton, Ohio.

McKinley and his wife, Ida Saxton, lived on Canton's North Market Street in a Gothic Revival home given to them as a wedding present. They sold the house in 1871 and repurchased it in 1899 after leasing it for several years. From the front porch of the North Market Street house McKinley accepted the Republican nomination for president in 1896. He died in office in 1901, the victim of an assassin's bullet. The family home fell into decay, and it was torn down in the 1930s to make way for a hospital.

HOMES OF THE TWENTIETH-CENTURY PRESIDENTS OPEN TO THE PUBLIC

THEODORE ROOSEVELT
Theodore Roosevelt Birthplace
28 East 20th Street, New York, NY

Sagamore Hill
Cove Neck Road, Oyster Bay, NY

WILLIAM HOWARD TAFT
Taft House
2038 Auburn Avenue
Cincinnati, OH

WOODROW WILSON
Wilson Birthplace
Greenville Avenue
Staunton, VA

Wilson Boyhood Home
1705 Hampton Street
Columbia, SC

Wilson Retirement Home
2340 S Street
Washington, DC

WARREN G. HARDING
Harding Home and Museum
380 Mount Vernon Avenue
Marion, OH

CALVIN COOLIDGE
Coolidge Birthplace
State Highway 25
Plymouth, VT

HERBERT HOOVER
Hoover Birthplace
Downey Street
West Branch, IA

Minthorn House (boyhood home)
River Street
Newberg, OR

FRANKLIN D. ROOSEVELT
Franklin Roosevelt Birthplace
State Highway 9
Hyde Park, NY

Roosevelt Cottage
Campobello Island
New Brunswick, Canada

HARRY S TRUMAN
Truman Birthplace
U.S. 71
Lamar, MO

DWIGHT D. EISENHOWER
Eisenhower Birthplace
Denison, TX

Eisenhower Boyhood Home
Eisenhower Center
Southeast Fourth Street
Abilene, TX

JOHN F. KENNEDY
Kennedy Birthplace
83 Beals Street
Brookline, MA

LYNDON B. JOHNSON
Johnson Boyhood Home
Johnson City, TX

LBJ Ranch
Accessible by tour bus departing from LBJ State Park, U.S. 290
Near Johnson City, TX

Educating the Presidents

by EDWARD D. C. CAMPBELL, JR.

In civics class students are taught that they can all aspire to the presidency. True enough in theory, but the odds are close to incalculable. Students can aspire much more realistically to win a million-dollar lottery one day. But even though only forty Caucasian men have been elected president, they exhibit an array of qualifications that would baffle the most astute oddsmakers. Their educational experiences exhibit certain similarities, such as the preponderance of law-trained presidents in the nineteenth century, but the presidential schoolboys have experienced diverse pre-chief-executive training. The differences in the educational lives of the presidents are as indicative of the character of American democracy as the commonalities. In the eighteenth and nineteenth centuries American society presented few possibilities for professional advancement—the law, the military, medicine, and the clergy—and law training became the avenue for advancement among the politically minded. But the training that helped create the ambition to move into politics could be as formal as that of the Adamses of Harvard College or as slapdash as that of Andrew Johnson, unread until adulthood. The electorate also elevated military heroes—Washington, Jackson, Harrison, Taylor—who owed their positions in no small part to good fortune. In the twentieth century solid credentials assumed greater significance; still, Harry Truman assumed the presidency in 1945—and won his own term in 1948—without so much as a day in college. Warren Harding and Lyndon Johnson worked as schoolteachers after local-college educations; Harding also ran a newspaper; and Truman went into business as a haberdasher. George Bush graduated from Yale University and surprised his family by moving to Texas and entering the oil business. No school for the presidency trains America's leaders. Ambition and luck seem to matter most.

WASHINGTON: RESPECT FOR LEARNING

That George Washington "was not a scholar was certain. That he was too illiterate, unread, unlearned for his station and reputation is equally past dispute," John Adams huffily observed. Washington had little formal education. He learned his first lessons from his parents, Augustine and Mary Ball Washington, and later from his elder half brother, Lawrence, at Mount Vernon. There is also sketchy evidence that as a young boy Washington may have studied with a tutor and later for a brief time attended a local Virginia school. But his father's death in 1743 quashed any hopes that he might attend school abroad like his half brothers. In any case, he probably enjoyed no more than seven or eight years of schooling, and, except for mathematical principles, especially trigonometry, Washington possessed little more than an elementary education by age fourteen or fifteen—although not for lack of effort. As a surveyor he was a keen draftsman, enjoyed mapmaking and formulating numerical tables, and in his sometimes detailed correspondence attempted to refine a "pictorial quality."

In short, Washington at an early age exhibited a respect for learning. His biographer James Thomas Flexner judged Washington's careful compilation of 110 maxims under the title "Rules of Civility and Decent Behavior in Company and Conversation" as "justly the best known of George's authentic

Harvard College, engraving by Paul Revere, 1767. Harvard has graduated more presidents than any other institution: John Adams in 1755, his son, John Quincy Adams, in 1787, Theodore Roosevelt in 1880, Franklin Delano Roosevelt in 1903, and John F. Kennedy in 1940 (American Antiquarian Society).

childhood activities." He was also a keen reader and frequently made notes on what he had acquired or completed, once, for example, writing that he had received a book on "the reign of King John, and in the *Spectator* read to No. 143." And although when building his library in later years he was sure to stress the practical—ordering volumes on military history, agriculture, and biography— he also made sure he kept up with the era's less austere books, such as *Tom Jones* and *Peregrine Pickle*. He was never so bold, however, as to deny his formal schooling had been abbreviated. Instead, he frankly recognized his "defective education" and duly noted that Virginia's College of William and Mary "has ever been in my view an object of veneration." After all, he freely admitted, "a knowledge of books is the basis" upon which the knowledge earned from experience "is to be built."

Washington nevertheless learned much from his surroundings and profited from his mistakes. "Errors," he wrote, "once discovered are more than half amended." He thus taught himself from his own readings, from his experiences—as a surveyor and junior militia officer, for instance—and especially from his observations. His associations, for example, with the Fairfax family at Belvoir, adjacent to Mount Vernon, brought him into contact with the best customs and manners of English culture. Adams's assessment, therefore, was in large part overstated. As Washington himself remarked, "Some men will gain as much experience in the course of three or four years as some will in ten or a dozen."

There is nothing which can better deserve your patronage than the promotion of Science and Literature. Knowledge is in every country the surest basis of public happiness. In one in which the measures of government receive their impression so immediately from the sense of the Community as in ours it is proportionably essential.

—George Washington, First Annual Message to Congress, January 8, 1790

JOHN ADAMS: PURITAN SCHOLAR

Adams, on the other hand, completed a rigorous scholastic education. The eldest son of John and Susanna Boylston Adams was first taught to read by his father and then in Dame Belcher's primary school. Although she had little education herself, Dame Belcher taught the local children basic skills as well as a good bit of Puritan doctrine. Their *New England Primer* for the letter "A" reminded students that "In Adam's fall/ We sinned all," and so on through "Zebediah served the Lord." Young John Adams was next placed under the care of Joseph Cleverly, an Episcopalian and 1733 graduate of Harvard who unfortunately for his pupils found teaching a considerable chore. Adams quickly tired of school and declared he preferred farming to studying, to which his father supposedly replied, "Aye, but I don't like it so well, so you shall go to school." The son returned but bristled under his tutor's uninspired efforts until at age fourteen he confronted the senior Adams with his displeasure. Within a day John Adams was instead the pupil of Joseph Marsh, an adept and challenging teacher. After a year of hard work Adams fulfilled his father's wish that he be admitted to Harvard.

Harvard in 1750 was presided over by Edward Holyoke, class of 1705, a political liberal, a strict disciplinarian, and a "man of noble commanding presence" who demanded much of the students. In this he was aided greatly by the college's schedule. Adams attended morning prayers at six, followed by a spartan breakfast usually of "bread, biscuit and milk," then a lecture at eight, with the rest of the morning given to study and recitation. A lunch of mutton or beef washed down with beer and cider preceded more study, more prayers at five, and a meager supper at seven-thirty. All were in bed by nine. John Adams's tutor that first year was Joseph Mayhew, who introduced his pupils to the complexities of logic, physics, Greek, Latin, and rhetoric—the last, the "art of speaking and writing with elegance," receiving special attention. Amid all that Adams also confronted Harvard's student traditions: he was prohibited from wearing a hat in the college yard, always removed his cap in the presence of seniors, and when not in study periods generally served at the beck and call of upperclassmen, always ready to retrieve "batts, balls, and foot-balls for the use of the students."

As a sophomore, Adams added natural philosophy to his course work; as a junior, geography, metaphysics, and moral philosophy; and as a senior, mathematics and geometry. Small wonder the tutors openly feared that students might take to drink, "abominable lasciviousness," or, worse, the "atrocious crime . . . of fornication." Adams instead took solace in a "love of books" and "fondness for study" that, he admitted, "dissipated all my inclinations for sports" and even "for the society of the ladies." Instead, he joined several of his fellows to discuss "any new publications, or any poetry or dramatic compositions, that might fall in their way." Thus four years passed. Graduation in 1755 was as usual a festive, public affair. While outside the meetinghouse farmers, laborers, beggars, prostitutes, and innumerable merchants celebrated the day, inside dignitaries and students listened as the class's most distinguished scholars—Adams included—delivered theses in Latin. Adams was evidently impressive, for immediately after the festivities he was employed, at age nineteen, as schoolmaster of Worcester.

He believed, however, that his education was not quite complete and for a time considered the ministry, but he soon despaired of the "frigidity of John Calvin." Optimistically rationalizing that since "the study of and practice of law . . . does not dissolve the obligations of morality or of religion," he instead took up his new studies under lawyer James Putnam. Three years later, in November 1758, he was presented for admission to the bar in Boston. Whatever his activity, however, he always gratefully acknowledged to his education, especially its classical foundation. Writing his son, John Quincy, he remarked that translating the ancients soothed the cares of business. "You will find it," he insisted, "the most delightful employment you ever engaged in" and one in which you will "have learned more wisdom . . . than from five hundred volumes of the trash that is commonly read."

JEFFERSON: CLASSICIST

Thomas Jefferson, too, was drawn to

But why am I dosing you with these Antediluvian topics? Because I am glad to have some one to whom they are familiar, and who will not receive them as if dropped from the moon. Our post-revolutionary youth are born under happier stars than you or I were..They acquire all learning in their mothers' womb, and bring it into the world ready-made. The information of books is no longer necessary; and all knowledge which is not innate, is in contempt, or neglect at least.

—Letter of Thomas Jefferson to John Adams, July 5, 1814

the classics and then law. As a child Jefferson spent six years at Tuckahoe plantation along the James River, several miles west of the present site of Richmond. There his father, Peter Jefferson, as guardian of his "dear and loving friend" William Randolph's children and estate, had moved his family and soon thereafter employed a tutor to hold an "English school" in a small building in the plantation yard. Jefferson was then five. From age nine to thirteen, after his family had returned to its home at Shadwell in Goochland (now Albemarle) County, he boarded with and attended the Latin school of the Reverend William Douglas, a Goochland clergyman. Jefferson was, however, little inspired by a teacher he regarded as but "a superficial Latinist, less instructed in Greek."

After his father's death in 1757 Jefferson at age fourteen enrolled in the Albemarle County school of the Reverend James Maury. Twelve miles from Shadwell, the clergyman's log school was still far enough away that Jefferson had to board, although he was at least allowed weekend visits home. But the young man this time did not care. His relationship with his mother was at best uncertain, and his remarkable teacher was, as Jefferson himself commented, "a correct classical scholar." For two years he read Greek and Roman authors and, better still, had access to his teacher's personal library of more than four hundred volumes—Jefferson's admiration for books was set. At the same time he mastered the rudiments of the violin. By then he was also ready for college. To a guardian he argued his case: "by going to the College I shall get a more universal Acquaintance, which may hereafter be serviceable to me."

Just under seventeen, Jefferson enrolled in the spring of 1760 at the College of William and Mary in Williamsburg. To his "great good fortune," Dr. William Small, of Scotland, took note of the new student. "He, most happily for me, became soon attached to me and made me his daily companion," Jefferson wrote. Of the seven-member faculty, Small was unique. "It is a highly significant fact," Jefferson's preeminent biographer Dumas Malone wrote of this period, "that the early teacher who did most to fix the destinies of [Jefferson's] life was the only layman in the faculty of the College." It was Small who first introduced young Jefferson to the wonders of the Enlightenment, the tenets that, the student recollected, revealed glimpses "of the expansion of science and of the system of things in which we are placed."

William and Mary was then an institution of no more than one hundred pupils divided among four schools: an Indian school, a school of philosophy (Jefferson's), a school of grammar, and one of divinity. Dr. Small taught moral and natural philosophy, ethics, rhetoric, and belles lettres and perhaps just as important introduced his student to the lawyer George Wythe and Virginia governor Francis Fauquier. Jefferson completed his college studies in two years but not without welcome distraction. By 1762 he was at times more interested in love than books, admitting that Rebecca Burwell, the sister of a fellow student, brought to mind "so lively an image" that "I shall think of her too often I fear for my peace of mind." And he was one of six members of the secret Flat Hat Club—a student gathering, he confessed, of "no useful object."

Like Washington, Jefferson learned perhaps as much from his associations. After he began studying law under Wythe's tutelage, Jefferson joined Small, Wythe, and Fauquier for frequent dinners at which "he heard more good sense, more rational and philosophical conversations, than in all my life besides." Wythe by himself imparted much, too. His student, however, was more inclined to learn on his own. After he gained admittance to the bar, Jefferson admitted that "the placing of a youth to study with an attorney was rather a prejudice than a help." The lawyer had his own tasks, while the "only help a youth wants is to be directed what books to read, and in what order to read them." Wythe did that, instructing his pupil to embark upon the ponderous seventeenth-century compendium *Coke upon Littleton* as well as numerous other studies.

Jefferson, as he would throughout his life, also read on his own. His 1774 notations, later published as *A Summary View of the Rights of British America,* furnish a glimpse of his early studies. His selective readings for "Politicks, Trade" listed eight titles, including Locke's *Treatises on Government,* Montesquieu's *Spirit of Laws,* and Algernon Sidney's *Discourses Concerning Government.* Such a "diffusion of knowledge among the people," Jefferson wrote in 1786, guaranteed the surest "foundation [that] can be devised for the preservation of freedom."

NO TIME FOR FUN

Several months before he entered the College of William and Mary in the spring of 1760, Thomas Jefferson weighed the advantages of additional education. He could think of several reasons to enter college: first, "as long as I stay at the Mountains [at the family home, Shadwell] the Loss of one fourth of my Time is inevitable, by Company's being here and detaining me from School"; second, his absence, besides allowing him to avoid so many visitors, would "lessen the Expenses of the Estate in House-Keeping"; and, finally, going away would provide him with "a more universal Acquaintance, which may hereafter be serviceable to me." Moreover, Jefferson realized he might "pursue my Studies in the Greek and Latin as well there as here, and likewise learn something of the Mathematics."

MADISON: HOMESPUN AMERICAN

From his own educational experiences, James Madison would have agreed. As a child Madison had access to his father's library at Montpelier in Orange County, Virginia, but what he may have learned from such volumes as Floxer on *Cold Bathing* can only be guessed. At age eleven his more formal education began when he enrolled in Donald Robertson's boarding school, located on the Mattapony River, four miles from Dunkirk, Virginia. There "Jamie" (as Robertson called him) remained five years, studying English, Greek, Latin, and basic Spanish and French—the last, thanks to his Scots teacher, forever after spoken with a distinctive burr. Madison also had the chance to read Locke, Montesquieu, Montaigne, as well as *The Spectator.* He evidently read Robertson's copy of Fontenelle's *Plurality of Worlds,* too. In his copybook survives a doodled human face centered in a Copernican solar system.

Madison returned home in September 1767 and for two years studied with his siblings' tutor, Thomas Martin, an Anglican cleric and a recent graduate of the College of New Jersey (Princeton). Martin no doubt had some influence in Madison's decision not to attend the staunchly Anglican College of William and Mary in Williamsburg but rather to enroll at Princeton, then under the

THREE YEARS' CONFINEMENT

In June 1769 James Madison with two companions and a slave, Sawney, set off on horseback through Fredericksburg, Georgetown, and Philadelphia to the College of New Jersey at Princeton. Arriving in August, Madison enrolled early and wrote of his pleasure at "the prospect before me of three years [*sic*] confinement." He sent Sawney home burdened with several errands, a few books, and a pamphlet on the founding of the college, which, Madison commented to his family, "perhaps may divert you." In his next letter home, perhaps thinking his family might be disturbed at his welcome "prospect," the young Madison promised to watch his expenses.

presidency of John Witherspoon, a Scotsman who strongly opposed British attempts to control the colonies' churches. Madison, therefore, left Virginia for school elsewhere.

The college's course work included the expected Greek, Latin, mathematics, and natural philosophy, and a new subject—the Law of Nature and of Nations, which, Madison's biographer Irving Brant believed, "laid the groundwork for a lifelong devotion to public law." Perhaps as instructive was the president's advice to his students: "Lads, ne'er do ye speak unless ye ha' something to say, and when ye are done, be sure and leave off." Madison and his classmates Philip Freneau and Hugh Henry Brackenridge, as members of the American Whig, one of the college's two verbose literary groups, had ample occasion to heed it.

Madison completed the four-year course work in only two, but with considerable effort. His sleep, he wrote, "was reduced for some weeks to less than five hours in the twenty-four." Not all the strain, however, was from study. Madison's fellow students had reacted angrily to the Stamp Act of 1765 and the Townshend Acts of 1767. In July 1770 he wrote his father that whereas protesting merchants in Boston and other ports had ceased importing British goods, he found deplorable "the base conduct of the merchants in New York in breaking through their spirited resolutions not to import." That September, twenty-two seniors, in support of the Boston embargo, wore homespun American rather than British broadcloth for their graduation. Madison graduated a year later but chose to remain at Princeton, engrossed "in miscellaneous studies; but not without a reference to the profession of law." In truth, he was weighing whether to pursue law or theology, but finally decided upon the former as the "principles and modes of government are too important to be disregarded by an inquisitive mind."

MONROE: STUDENT PROTESTER

Like Madison, James Monroe's college years were interrupted with political strife. Born in Westmoreland County, Virginia, Monroe in 1769, at age eleven, entered the Campbelltown academy—considered the colony's finest school. There under the rigorous guidance of the school's founder, the Reverend Archibald Campbell, Monroe so excelled at Latin and mathematics that he was able to enter the College of William and Mary in 1774 at age sixteen. He had hoped for a European education, but political conditions dictated a safer course—and a less distinguished one. The Williamsburg college was by then not as notable as it might have been, but at least Monroe and his fifteen-year-old Stafford County roommate, John F. Mercer, could observe the considerable social and political whirl.

By 1774 there was time for little else. The House of Burgesses had refused Governor Dunmore's order to dissolve and issued a call that by the next year resulted in the First Continental Congress. Then in April 1775 the governor seized a store of gunpowder belonging to the town of Williamsburg. Only at the last instant was Dunmore able to forestall a threatened counterattack. All this aroused the students—including Monroe—to action, even to purchasing and keeping muskets in their rooms and drilling openly on the college lawn. Monroe was also one of seven students who presented the faculty with a petition accusing Maria Driggs, the "Mistress of the College," with rudeness, neglect, and with selling college stores to the government. But when confronted Monroe surprisingly recanted, confessing "that he had never read the petition and consequently could not undertake to prove a single article."

Perhaps it was the heat of the moment that had encouraged Monroe to participate at all. In any case, when aroused the next time, he took an even more dangerous stand. On June 24, 1775, he joined a group of twenty-four men in a surprise attack on the Governor's Palace from which they looted some five hundred swords and muskets for the Williamsburg militia. Monroe was the youngest member of the raiding party. He remained a student for nearly a year longer, but at last in the spring of 1776 he and his roommate Mercer abandoned their studies and enlisted in the 3d Virginia Infantry. It was not until 1781 that he returned to academic pursuits, this time following what he believed would best qualify him for public office. Jefferson assisted by forwarding books on law as well as some forty volumes of parliamentary debates. Within the year Monroe was elected to the Virginia legislature, within another to Congress.

JOHN QUINCY ADAMS: FORTUNATE SON

Revolution played as large a part in the education of John Quincy Adams as well. As a boy he accompanied his uncle Sam Adams several times to Boston Common to see the hated British redcoats; a company of militia on its way to Lexington camped near his Braintree home; and with his mother he climbed Penn's Hill on June 17, 1775, to see the fight at Bunker Hill. The war also closed his school. He thus began his formal studies under the guidance of his father's law clerk, John Thaxter, and by ten was already widely read. But it was with John Adams's appointment to a diplomatic mission abroad that his real education began. Not yet eleven, he boarded the frigate *Boston* with his father for the perilous voyage to France: the ship for two days outraced a pursuing British squadron and days later captured a British privateer.

Once safely in Paris, "Mr. Johnny" entered a private boarding school at Passy to study French, Latin, and the gentlemanly arts of fencing, dancing, and drawing. There he was also attracted to the theater, especially the children's Theatre des Petits Comedians in the nearby Bois de Boulogne. With his father he returned home briefly in

SCHOOL OF POLITICS

John Quincy Adams benefited greatly from accompanying his father on his diplomatic missions to Europe. Visiting England in 1783 and again in 1784, the young Adams heeded his father's instructions to attend debates in the House of Commons, where he could learn much by observing the leading figures' oratorical skills. "Mr. Pitt," the student remarked of his favorite British politician, "is upon the whole the best and most pleasing speaker of them all. He has much grace in speaking and has an admirable choice of words." Charles James Fox, on the other hand, he found "speaks with such an amazing heat and rapidity that he often gets embarrassed and stammers some time before he can express himself." Adams tried to model himself on the former.

ALWAYS GOOD FOR A LAUGH

Andrew Jackson studied law by copying various documents and poring over law books. How much he learned is, however, only conjecture. He also ran errands, even cleaned the office. And despite his choice of profession he was well known in Salisbury, North Carolina, for his wild ways. While supposedly reading law he was frequently away on drunken sprees—"parties of pleasure"; he spent his apprenticeship, one town resident noted, "more in the stable than in the office." He enjoyed practical jokes such as moving outhouses. Worse, placed in charge of a Christmas dance, he invited the town prostitutes, a mother and her daughter, to the affair. Not knowing the invitation was a joke, they appeared dressed in their finest attire to the citizens' shock and the two women's utter embarrassment.

1779 only to learn that the elder Adams was immediately ordered back abroad. Before the year was out he and his father crossed the Atlantic again, this time with his brother Charles, age nine. As John Adams moved from post to post, twelve-year-old John Quincy studied again at Passy, then in 1780 attended school in Amsterdam and in 1781 lectures at the University of Leiden. When Francis Dana of Boston, a family friend, was appointed minister to Russia, the young Adams went as his secretary, crossing Germany and the Baltic states to St. Petersburg and returning fourteen months later by way of Finland and Sweden. For a while he resumed his studies at The Hague but was soon called back to Paris where he served as his father's secretary from 1783 to 1785 and had frequent occasion to enjoy the company of his father's fellow diplomatic commissioners, Benjamin Franklin and Thomas Jefferson, and the Marquis de Lafayette.

On John Adams's appointment to London, his son at last returned to America, entered Harvard as a junior sophister, and graduated in 1787 at age twenty-one. He then studied law with Theophilius Parsons, later chief justice of Massachusetts, and was admitted to the bar in July 1790. It was Europe, however, that cemented his education. John Quincy Adams's biographer Samuel Flagg Bemis points out that it was while there that Adams learned Dutch, French, and some Spanish; there that he read widely in Greek and Roman history as well as French and English literature; and—most important—there that he so closely observed the amenities and complex protocol of diplomatic and political life.

JACKSON: A FRONTIER EDUCATION

Andrew Jackson's youth and education were so different from the others' as to be of another world altogether. Yet he was also the last of the revolutionary generation directly influenced by the fight for independence. Named for his father, who died only weeks before his birth, Jackson grew up in the Waxhaw region straddling North and South Carolina. His mother, Elizabeth Hutchinson, had hopes her son might one day enter the ministry and so enrolled him first in the local academy of Dr. William Humphries, where he learned to read, write, and "cast accounts," and later in that of James White Stephenson, a Presbyterian cleric. But Jackson learned relatively little. His foremost biographer, Robert V. Remini, points out that as an adult Jackson still "knew next to nothing" of history or political science, nothing of mathematics or natural science, and little of grammar and spelling—he "could write a single word or name four different ways on the same page."

The Revolution in its first years little affected Jackson's education, but by 1780—after the fall of Charleston—bands of British soldiers and American guerrillas were terrorizing the countryside in brutal raids. Jackson first lost his oldest brother, Hugh (likely by heatstroke), to the local campaigns, and Jackson himself in August 1780, at age thirteen, took part in the battle of Hanging Rock. It was after another engagement that Jackson and his brother Robert were captured and the former badly wounded by a saber blow. Robert died soon after their release. Within months his mother died too.

Jackson eventually worked in a saddler's shop, moved to Charleston at fifteen, then at seventeen left for Salisbury, North Carolina. There for two years he studied law with Spruce McCay, an attorney of some note. How much law he learned is questionable; much of his time was spent in copying legal papers, cleaning the office, running errands, and generally gaining a reputation as "the most roaring, rollicking, game-cocking, horse-racing, card-playing, mischievous fellow that ever lived in Salisbury." Jackson, however, remained with McCay until 1786, when he moved to the law office of Col. John Stokes. Within another six months, in September 1787, he was, despite his considerable reputation and quick temper, deemed a man of "unblemished moral character" and authorized to practice law.

"It is while we are young," Thomas Jefferson once remarked, "that the habit of industry is formed. If not then, it never is afterwards." As youths, Jackson and Washington acquired their "habit" more by experience than by formal education, though Washington by self-motivation eventually made up for much of his early educational misfortunes. Jackson, however, never read much besides religious tracts and the Bible; he was purported to have read *The Vicar of Wakefield,* perhaps the only secular book he ever read cover to cover. The Adamses, father and son, Jefferson, Madison, and Monroe, on the other hand, all benefited from a rigorous education as well as unique early experiences. The Adamses attended Harvard, Jefferson and Monroe the College of William and Mary, and Madison the school at Princeton; all but Washington eventually studied law.

VAN BUREN: VILLAGE SCHOOL

Jackson and his successor, Martin Van Buren, likewise a self-made man, more than their urbane and cultured predecessors, symbolized the raw new republic. Van Buren was the third child of Maria Hoes and Abraham Van Buren, a farmer and tavern keeper in Kinderhook, New York, near Albany. Young Martin Van Buren attended the village's rundown, one-room academy and was fortunate in two respects: he had a conscientious schoolmaster, David B. Warden, and his family, determined that he escape his father's lot, allowed him to remain in school until he was fifteen. He learned a little Latin, sufficient grammar and rhetoric, and especially that he had to control "a disposition ardent, hasty, and impetuous."

He did well enough that his family was able to place him under the care of a local lawyer, Francis Sylvester. For four years he studied the complexities of New York law, tended his mentor's brother's store, and entered politics—at seventeen helping to secure a townsman's nomination to Congress. He also began poring over Republican pamphlets—a risky business in his benefactor's Federalist household. After frequent "tho' slight bickering" over their respective political beliefs, he and his teacher parted company. In 1801 Van Buren joined the almost clientless but highly political law office of John P. Van Ness, a recently elected congressman and a supporter of Aaron Burr, and in 1803 returned home to open an office with his half brother and further his own political ambitions. Still, years later, Van Buren lamented that he did not have the time to learn more. "How often," Van Buren recollected, "have I felt the necessity of a regular course of reading to enable me to maintain the reputation I had acquired and to sustain me in my conflicts with able and better educated men."

William Henry Harrison: College, but No Degree

William Henry Harrison, who served as ninth president for only a month before he died from pneumonia, was the son of Benjamin Harrison, a signer of the Declaration of Independence. Raised at Berkeley plantation along the James River in Charles City County, Virginia, Harrison was apparently first educated at home. In 1787 he enrolled at Hampden-Sydney College, eighty-five miles west of Richmond. Unfortunately, little record of his short time there survives except a bill for his room and another for a doctor, but as students were to "be acquainted with the English Grammar, Caesar's Commentaries, Sallust, Virgil, and the Roman Antiquities," he evidently arrived prepared. He was also a member of the Union Society, a debating club. In 1790, at his father's insistence, he left without a degree to study medicine first with Dr. Andrew Leiper in Richmond and within months with the famous Dr. Benjamin Rush in Philadelphia. But he disliked medicine intensely, and with the death of his father and the lure of Indian warfare in the Ohio Valley, he entered the army in August 1791.

Tyler: States' Rights Training

John Tyler came from a no less privileged background. Reared, like Harrison, in Charles City County, Tyler's father in time served as governor, speaker of the Virginia House of Delegates, and as a judge. Little, however, is known of Tyler's education before 1802, when at twelve he entered the preparatory school of the College of William and Mary. In 1806 his name first appeared on the roll of the college-level students, although he may well have started a year earlier. He studied the usual classical texts, history, and English literature but was also introduced to political

---

Your letter of the 23d instant is now before me, and, although it is somewhat short, yet it certainly deserves an answer. Before I proceed to express to you the pleasure it gave me, I must point out to you two errors into which you have fallen. The river Rhone *is spelt with an* h, *but not so with James* Roane. *You turned him into a river by your mode of spelling his name. And you say that "this is a great letter to be sent* a *150 miles." Thus you conclude your letter. Now the* a *is out of place, and cannot be the antecedent to "miles." You would say* a mile, *but not* a miles. *I mention this to make you more attentive to your grammar. . . .*

To write with facility requires practice.

—Letter of John Tyler to Mary Tyler, his daughter, April 28, 1830

---

economy and Adam Smith's *Inquiry into the Nature and Causes of the Wealth of Nations*, a work that influenced Tyler forever after. At age seventeen he graduated, returned home, and began studying law with his father and then in Richmond with Edmund Randolph, who had served as Washington's attorney general.

Tyler had, however, absorbed the states' rights philosophies of both his father and his William and Mary teachers and thus found Randolph's Federalist principles awkward and confining, even frightening. "He proposed a supreme central government," John Tyler recollected, "with a supreme executive, a supreme legislature, and a supreme judiciary, and a power in Congress to veto state laws." Admitted to the bar in 1809 and at twenty-one elected to the Virginia House of Delegates, he was, though, soon enough able to foster his own views.

Polk: Mature Student

More than the others, James K. Polk reveled in his education. He needed it—it was an escape from physical debility. Sick and unable to participate in the rough-and-tumble life of the Tennessee frontier, Polk found in education a means to verify his worth. His father, fearing for his son's weak constitution, first apprenticed him to a Columbia, Tennessee, storekeeper. Jim Polk lasted only a few weeks before his parent relented and sent him in July 1813, at almost eighteen, to a small academy just outside town. Older than the other students, an abysmal speller, and with little education of any sort, Polk at first must have seemed an odd pupil. He soon, though, took to "the usual course of latin authors, part of [the] greek testament and a few of the dialogues of Lucian." Impressed, his father agreed to yet another year of school, this time sending his son fifty miles away to a small academy near Murfreesboro.

At the end of the second year both father and son were impressed enough again by the latter's progress to consider college. And since Sam Polk's patron and cousin, Col. William Polk, was a leading trustee of the University of North Carolina at Chapel Hill, the choice was evident. In January 1816, at twenty-one years old, James Polk entered as a sophomore. Tuition was ten, later fifteen, dollars a term. The university, also twenty-one, was still struggling under the inept administration of the Reverend Robert Chapman and with only a small faculty—one professor and a single senior and two junior tutors. The community had not grown much either: Chapel Hill was just down the "Grand Avenue" from the campus and boasted two stores, a tavern, and thirteen houses.

Still, Polk was excited to be there. Students awoke at six o'clock, went to chapel twice a day, attended lectures and gave recitations most of the day, and at eight in the winter, nine in the summer, were called to study. All this was capped at the end of each term by public examinations by the faculty and trustees. Polk studied the usual Greek and Roman texts, mathematics the next year, and moral and natural philosophy his final year. Throughout each term were the unremitting drills in English grammar. Besides all that, he was a member and later twice president of the Dialectic Society, one of two campus "literary" groups. A few of Polk's papers and lectures survive from the society's meetings. Given his frontier Tennessee upbringing, his fellow students could not have been surprised, for instance, that Polk found Alexander Hamilton a dangerous man, one "accustomed to cringe to the despots of Europe." Polk was, in fact, already an intense nationalist.

By May 1818—only five years after he had entered his first formal school—James K. Polk graduated from college. He was close to collapse and never recovered his health. His father arrived in late July to accompany him home, and even then he was still too weak for the trip. It was not until October that he was strong enough. Nevertheless, he was determined to enter politics and knew full well that the legal profession provided the best avenue. He studied law in the Nashville office of the remarkable Felix Grundy, a skilled criminal lawyer, and in 1820 was admitted to the bar. He then returned home where "his thorough academical preparation [and] his accurate knowledge of the law" quickly earned him "full employment." Three years later he entered the Tennessee legislature.

TAYLOR: NOT MUCH SCHOOLING

Zachary Taylor also emerged from a frontier upbringing and like Jackson lacked academic polish. Born in Orange County, Virginia, Taylor grew up in Jefferson County, Kentucky. There his father, Richard Taylor, entered him in the Louisville school of Elisha Ayer, an itinerant Connecticut schoolmaster, and later in another taught by the innovative Irish-born classical scholar Kean O'Hara. Still, Taylor's biographer K. Jack Bauer remarks, the student learned relatively little. As an adult his spelling remained atrocious, his gram-

Bowdoin College in 1821, three years before Franklin Pierce graduated. Two of Pierce's classmates were Nathaniel Hawthorne, a lifelong friend, and Henry Wadsworth Longfellow (courtesy of the Bowdoin College Collection).

mar bad, and "his hand was that of a near illiterate." At some point, perhaps alarmed at his own poor education, Taylor found a considerable appreciation for learning. As a military commander, for example, he always ensured that his soldiers' children received satisfactory schooling. The call to a military career came early, perhaps heightened by his father's Revolutionary War service and his eldest brother William's securing an officer's commission. Thus when the U.S. government, alarmed by developments abroad, decided in the spring of 1808 to expand the army by eight regiments, Taylor saw his chance. He received his first lieutenant's commission on May 3, 1808; there his practical education began, his academic education ended.

FILLMORE: PART-TIME STUDENT

Millard Fillmore—harshly described by some as a "handsome, dignified man of no great abilities"—more than Jackson, Van Buren, or even Polk, could point to humble beginnings. He was, in fact, one of the few significant nineteenth-century politicians who could honestly say he had been born in a log cabin. Born in 1800 in Cayuga County, New York, Fillmore as a boy labored on the family farm, then as an apprentice in a cloth-dressing and carding mill. Wanting more, he bought out his apprenticeship and enrolled as a part-time student in a New Hope, New York, academy while continuing to work at the textile mill. In 1819, thanks to his father, Fillmore secured work as a law clerk. For several years he worked in Montvale and later, when the family moved, in Buffalo. He also taught school to supplement his small income. In 1823 he was admitted to the bar in Erie County; five years later he won election to the state legislature on the Anti-Masonic party ticket.

PIERCE: AN EARLY LACK OF DISCIPLINE

Franklin Pierce grew up in Hillsborough County, New Hampshire, the son of Anna Kendrick and Benjamin Pierce, a staunch anti-Federalist, militia general, Revolutionary War veteran, and county sheriff. Both parents were intent on their children's education, and young Franklin Pierce was soon packed off to the Hancock Academy. There he became homesick and one morning simply walked home. His father duly listened to his son's pleas, cordially invited him to join the family at dinner, and afterward without a word got in his chaise and began driving his son back toward the town of Hancock. Some way down the road he stopped, ordered his son down, and left him there to make his own way through a drenching rain back to school. Even so inspired, Pierce would need more tutoring at the Francestown Academy in the spring of 1820 to merit college admission.

Benjamin Pierce had hoped to send his son to Dartmouth, but its Federalist leanings convinced him that the more democratic Bowdoin College in Brunswick, Maine, was the better choice. Bowdoin, when Pierce arrived, had only three buildings: two rectangular brick halls and an unpainted, unheated chapel that doubled as the college library, such as it was. The library was open only for an hour a day, no student could borrow books more than once in three weeks, and freshmen were restricted to a single book each visit. No matter. Pierce was excited, "exuberant" in fact. He was, he remarked, "far away from my home without restraint except such as the government of a college imposed." The college, however, attempted to forestall such emotions with considerable discipline. "No student," the faculty declared, "shall eat or drink in any tavern unless in company with his parent or guardian, nor attend any theatrical entertainment or any idle show . . . not play at cards, billiards, or any game of hazard . . . nor go shooting or fishing."

So challenged, many of Pierce's eighteen freshman classmates did their best to circumvent the rules. Pierce especially succeeded. He frequented the tavern, missed classes, and generally avoided as much work as possible so that by the beginning of his third year he ranked at the bottom of his class. On learning his class standing, he at first pouted and swore never to reenter a classroom. Fortunately, his more serious friends—including Nathaniel Hawthorne—provided a better example. Chastened, Pierce then began a regimen of rising at four and retiring at midnight in a desperate effort to catch up. Under strenuous protest he even gave up a midyear vacation to teach in a country school. He also captained a military company, the Bowdoin Cadets, and joined the more politically radical of two campus literary societies. By graduation, Pierce had moved from last to fifth place in his class. On August 31, 1824, probably somewhat to his surprise, Pierce joined his classmates bedecked in "silk robes borrowed from neighboring clergy, president and professors in like array." Redirected, he studied law in Portsmouth, New Hampshire, and Northampton, Massachusetts, before admittance to the Hillsborough County bar in 1827 and election to the New Hampshire General Court in 1829.

IT'S ONLY MONEY

For Franklin Pierce to attend Bowdoin College in the early 1820s his father paid eight dollars for each of three terms a year; other small fees for damages, use of the library, catalogues, and materials; and such fines as his son might receive for "neglect of forensics," absence from class, or various other improprieties. Pierce was, for instance, fined fifty cents for "sitting in an improper posture in chapel." Room and board totaled about two dollars per week. All that came to about two hundred dollars a year—no small sum when the young Pierce was at the same time trying to see just how many recitations he could cut and still get by without expulsion.

BUCHANAN: ROUGH GOING

James Buchanan, too, was sorely distracted in college. For the first fourteen years of his life he was his parents' only son. As one biographer remarked, Buchanan by then "must have been obnoxiously conceited and self-assured." The young James Buchanan learned his first lessons at the Old Stone Academy in Mercersburg, Pennsylvania, and while tending his father's store. There he developed a passion for fiscal exactitude.

Years later, one story goes, he refused a check for fifteen thousand dollars—because of a ten-cent error.

At age sixteen he entered Dickinson College in Carlisle, Pennsylvania, intent not on a career in the ministry—as his mother wanted—but in law—learning the skills of acquisition and contract that his father encouraged. Buchanan initially worked hard, but soon discovered that there were quicker, more enjoyable ways to make a mark with his classmates. "To be a sober, plodding industrious youth was to incur the ridicule of the mass of the students." Instead, he reasoned, why not partake of "every sort of extravagance and mischief." He succeeded too well. At the college's Fourth of July celebration in 1808 he had already bolted down sixteen toasts before the general drinking even began.

Somehow he managed to keep up with his studies. Retribution, however, was soon to come. Lolling at home before returning for his second year, Buchanan learned he had been expelled for his excessive conduct. Badly shaken, the student was able to return only after a "gentle lecture" from the college's trustee president (fortunately, a family friend). Buchanan did his work and by September 1809 was judged "prepared to receive" his degree. The faculty, though, refused to award the conceited upstart the academic honors he believed he deserved. And as they feared, Buchanan reacted in character. His father, however, defused the situation by pointing out that the family was sorry that James was to receive no honors, particularly since the decision was made "by the professors who are acknowledged by the world to be the best judges of the students under their care." Though properly put in his place, Buchanan would later write that he left "feeling but little attachment towards the Alma Mater." For the next three years he studied law in Lancaster, passed the bar in 1812, and within only three years was bringing in more than eleven thousand dollars a year.

I am not a master of language; I have not a fine education; I am not capable of entering into a disquisition of dialectics, as I believe you call it; but I do not believe the language I employed [in a previous debate in Springfield] bears any such construction as Judge Douglas puts upon it.

—Abraham Lincoln, in debate with Stephen A. Douglas, Chicago, July 10, 1858

LINCOLN: HIS OWN BEST TEACHER

Abraham Lincoln's law partner, William H. Herndon, pointed out that Lincoln "never seemed to care to own or collect books." Robert T. Lincoln, on the other hand, recollected that he could "not remember ever seeing [his father] without a book in his hand." The truth rests somewhere between. Poetry enthused him. Indeed, among the oldest samples of Lincoln's handwriting are bits of poetic doggerel such as "Abraham Lincoln/his hand and pen/he will be good/god knows When." He was also, his son recalled, especially "devoted" to Shakespeare and Milton as well as to the melancholy themes of Robert Burns. Lincoln, of course, knew the Bible and also read works by Thomas Paine, several technical works on surveying, and occasionally biographies, particularly of Revolutionary War figures. And after serving in Congress he laboriously "studied and nearly mastered the Six-books of Euclid." He also read law. In fact, his legal education, he was always anxious to point out, came with little direction. He read William Blackstone's *Commentaries* and borrowed what else he needed.

Lincoln, however, always considered himself "uneducated," his learning "defective." He had, after all, little classroom learning beyond rude "A.B.C. schools." In New Salem, Illinois, his class work "did not amount to one year." Lincoln still grappled with grammar at twenty-three. His, though, was a practical education, and mostly self-taught.

Moreover, simply to grasp a book's main points was often "the main thing." Lincoln scholar Mark E. Neely, Jr., recounts that at the Hampton Roads Peace Conference R. M. T. Hunter informed President Lincoln that King Charles I had bargained with rebels. Lincoln is said to have responded, "All I distinctly recollect about the case of Charles I, is, that he lost his head in the end." Lincoln was also keen enough to assess biographies of noted Americans as "not only misleading, but false." He was far, though, from being anti-intellectual. Instead, as a contemporary remembered, he tackled learning as "a business not a pleasure," a practical exercise undertaken more "in reference to special questions and not with a view to laying in a general store of knowledge."

Among my earliest recollections I remember how, when a mere child, I used to get irritated when anybody talked to me in a way I could not understand. . . . I can remember going to my little bedroom, after hearing the neighbors talk of an evening with my father . . . and spending no small part of the night walking up and down, and trying to make out what was the exact meaning of their, to me, dark phrases.

—Letter of Abraham Lincoln to J. P. Gulliver, March 10, 1860

ANDREW JOHNSON: HIS WIFE'S STUDENT

Andrew Johnson possessed even less education. His father died when Johnson was three, and his mother, a desperately poor washerwoman, could not afford to send her sons to school. She instead apprenticed them both to a Raleigh, North Carolina, tailor. Andrew Johnson, then thirteen, was bound over until his twenty-first birthday. As the days were long and the work difficult, many tailors traditionally had someone read to their workers, and so Johnson listened to Dr. William G. Hill (in such moments as the physician could spare) read the orations of Burke, Fox, Pitt, and other British statesmen. At the same time, Johnson desperately attempted to teach himself to read—at first apparently memorizing words by sight.

Unfortunately, their master was a harsh one, and in June 1824 Johnson and his brother Bill escaped, moving from town to town picking up whatever tailoring work they could. Eventually they returned to Raleigh, where their former employer made sure they found no work. Johnson then traveled to Columbia, Tennessee, where he earned employment with the town tailor, James Shelton. Years later, when Johnson was president, Mrs. Shelton claimed she had taught her husband's young employee to read. "She did not," Johnson answered. But, he added, "I have not denied it. I am glad to give her all the pleasure that I can, for she was a mother to me."

Johnson returned to North Carolina to retrieve his still-destitute mother and stepfather and in time settled with them in Greeneville in East Tennessee, where he wed the seventeen-year-old Eliza McCardle. Johnson in the bargain perhaps also gained a teacher: stories persist that it was his wife who taught him to read and write. At age eighteen he filled his account book with his new knowledge, scrawling over the page "And," then "Andrew," and finally "Andrew Johnson." While he worked in his tailor's shop he often sat cross-legged in front of a book, usually of Thomas Jefferson's messages to Congress or the earl of Chatham's speeches to Parliament. Then, every Friday, he walked four miles to participate in the student debates at Greeneville College and, when they were discontinued, four miles in the other direction to Tusculum College.

His shop gradually became a gathering place for like-minded young men, those who were poorly educated but aware of their opportunities and especially aware of their subservient status among the planter elite. When these dis-

A TIME AND A PLACE FOR EVERYTHING

The interest Ulysses S. Grant showed in literature, dating from his years at West Point, did not extend to literary talkers. He told his wife, Julia Dent Grant, about attending a dinner party at which his host, a college president, "at once began talking of books, mentioning one or two familiar names, and I—well, I looked as though if I had read that particular book I had forgotten it. After a while, he made some allusion to a character of Dickens. I was equally ignorant of poor little Oliver." The scheme worked to perfection, for soon enough "the old gentleman gave me up, and I enjoyed the rest of the evening."

gruntled citizens decided to do something at last, they engineered the election of three of their own—including Johnson—to the town council in 1829. The next year Johnson was reelected, in 1831 elected yet again, and after that voted mayor. In 1832, at age twenty-three and never having attended school, a grateful Andrew Johnson was appointed a trustee of the nearby Rhea Academy.

GRANT: A LOVE OF LITERATURE

Ulysses S. Grant attended two local Georgetown, Ohio, schools, for a time an academy in Maysville, and later a school in Ripley. His father, Jesse Grant, was by and large self-taught, and several historians have therefore surmised that higher education offered his son a unique opportunity to succeed. The general's preeminent biographer, William S. McFeely, points out that the elder Grant treasured no such hopes for his other children, preferring that his sons enter business and that his daughters remain home. Indeed, Jesse Grant appears to have admired his other children's practicality and fretted over the future president's incompetence. Thus, for Jesse Grant and his untalented offspring West Point may well have represented a prestigious—and free—alternative to entering a business world both knew the young man would never master. For Ulysses himself, it was an opportunity to leave Ohio.

He arrived at the United States Military Academy in 1839, age seventeen. To his credit, Grant found the usually difficult first year on the Hudson more "wearisome and uninteresting" than onerous. More impressive perhaps, Grant passed his entrance examinations "without difficulty, very much to [his] surprise." And although he "never succeeded," he said, "in getting squarely at either end of my class," he nevertheless by his second year ranked tenth in his class of fifty-three. He once even admitted that "on the whole I like the place very much." "The fact is," he forthrightly added, "if a man graduates here he safe fer life." Grant was, though, not particularly happy.

The courses were frequently too abstract to interest him. And those taught by the excitable Dennis Hart Mahan—a devout disciple of the Swiss military theorist Antoine Henri Jomini—were often only a vehicle to announce again and again the glories of Napoleon. Mahan was, in fact, president of the academy's Napoleon Club, which included some of West Point's most promising cadets. Grant never joined. He also balked at the military mindset and began to believe that the "military life had no charms for me." To escape, he read books and in his *Memoirs* recalled that he "devoted more time to these than to books relating to the course of studies. Much of the time, I am sorry to say, was devoted to novels, but not," he added, "those of a trashy sort." He also turned to art. Guided by Robert Walter Weir, the academy's drawing master from 1834 to 1876, Grant painted and sketched scenes of the Old World and the American West.

Thus Grant spent his four years, completing his course work while seeking whatever solace he could in literature and art. Many years later, while president, he wrote that the day he left public office would be "the happiest of my life, except possibly the day I left West Point[,] a place I felt I had been at always and that my stay had no end." When he graduated in June 1843, West Point's best horseman failed to earn a commission in the cavalry. His disillusion was complete. Assigned to the infantry, Lieutenant Grant left school planning to resign as soon as his required tour of duty ended.

HAYES: SKEPTIC

Rutherford B. Hayes was more enthralled with his college experiences. His widowed and overprotective mother, Sophia Birchard Hayes, first taught him to read and write. Only after considerable hesitation did she allow him to attend first an academy in Norwalk, Ohio, and then a private school in Middletown, Connecticut, where as a leader of "The Cobwebbs," a secret society, he led his fellow students in all manner of pranks and youthful drinking. Young Hayes dreamed of next going to Yale, but practical considerations intruded. His uncle, Sardis Birchard, agreed to fund a less elite education, and so Hayes enrolled at Kenyon College in Gambier, Ohio, not so far from his home.

Kenyon in the fall of 1838 stressed discipline, course work worthy of future gentlemen, and Christian ethics. Hayes was not, however, so swayed by the last. After a revival during his first year, he wrote that "there are now but ten in the whole college who are not changed." "*I am among the ten as yet,*" he boasted. In fact, he proved enormously popular and led his fellows in all types of fun. Hunting, for example, was not allowed, and "we were forbidden to have any guns," he recalled. But Hayes "always had two." Cooking in the rooms was forbidden, too, but Hayes had "considerable of a reputation" for preparing surreptitious meals. One incident brought a fiery sermon after a tutor apprehended several "rascals" cooking, "all dripping . . . with sweat and gravy and thoughts on clandestine enjoyment."

Rutherford B. Hayes in 1845, the year he graduated from Harvard Law School (Library of Congress)

Hayes had his serious side. He participated, for example, in the Philomathesian Society's student debates and declamations. The society's activities were by then so rife with the issue of slavery that students "upon both sides carried arms, ready for attack or defense." Many of Kenyon's southern undergraduates formed their own philosophical society, Nu Pi Kappa. By 1840, though, the association was in danger of disbanding for want of southern members. It was Hayes who proposed ending the two societies' exclusive, sectional membership, a characteristic stance that earned him considerable fame as a "first-rate fellow." By his 1842 graduation, at age twenty, Hayes in the opinion of the faculty had "attained the highest grade. His delinquincies are as follows: 0, 0, 0."

COLLEGES ATTENDED BY THE PRESIDENTS

JOHN ADAMS: Harvard College, Bachelor of Arts, 1755

THOMAS JEFFERSON: College of William and Mary, Bachelor of Arts, 1762

JAMES MADISON: College of New Jersey (Princeton), Bachelor of Arts, 1771

JAMES MONROE: College of William and Mary, 1774-1776 (no degree)

JOHN QUINCY ADAMS: Harvard College, Bachelor of Arts, 1787

WILLIAM HENRY HARRISON: Hampden-Sydney College, 1787-1790 (no degree)

JOHN TYLER: College of William and Mary, Bachelor of Arts, 1807

JAMES K. POLK: University of North Carolina, Bachelor of Arts, 1818

FRANKLIN PIERCE: Bowdoin College, Bachelor of Arts, 1824

JAMES BUCHANAN: Dickinson College, Bachelor of Arts, 1809

ULYSSES S. GRANT: U.S. Military Academy, graduated, 1843

RUTHERFORD B. HAYES: Kenyon College, Bachelor of Arts, 1842; Harvard Law School, Bachelor of Laws, 1845

JAMES A. GARFIELD: Williams College, Bachelor of Arts, 1856

CHESTER A. ARTHUR: Union College, Bachelor of Arts, 1848

BENJAMIN HARRISON: Miami University, Bachelor of Arts, 1852

WILLIAM MCKINLEY: Allegheny College, 1860 (no degree)

THEODORE ROOSEVELT: Harvard College, Bachelor of Arts, 1880; Columbia Law School, 1880-1881 (no degree)

WILLIAM HOWARD TAFT: Yale College, Bachelor of Arts, 1878; Cincinnati Law School, Bachelor of Laws, 1880

WOODROW WILSON: Davidson College, 1873-1874 (no degree); College of New Jersey (Princeton), Bachelor of Arts, 1879; University of Virginia Law School, 1879-1880 (no degree); Johns Hopkins University, Doctor of Philosophy, 1886

WARREN G. HARDING: Ohio Central College, Bachelor of Science, 1882

CALVIN COOLIDGE: Amherst College, Bachelor of Arts, 1895

HERBERT HOOVER: Stanford University, Bachelor of Arts, 1895

FRANKLIN D. ROOSEVELT: Harvard University, Bachelor of Arts, 1903; Columbia Law School, 1903-1905 (no degree)

DWIGHT D. EISENHOWER: U.S. Military Academy, graduated, 1915

JOHN F. KENNEDY: Princeton University, 1935 (no degree); Harvard University, Bachelor of Science, 1940; Stanford University Graduate School of Business Administration, 1940 (no degree)

LYNDON B. JOHNSON: Southwest Texas State Teachers College, Bachelor of Science, 1930

RICHARD M. NIXON: Whittier College, Bachelor of Arts, 1934; Duke University Law School, Bachelor of Laws, 1937

GERALD R. FORD: University of Michigan, Bachelor of Arts, 1935; Yale University Law School, Bachelor of Laws, 1941

JIMMY CARTER: Georgia Southwestern College, 1941-1942 (no degree); U.S. Naval Academy, Bachelor of Science, 1946

RONALD REAGAN: Eureka College, Bachelor of Arts, 1932

GEORGE BUSH: Yale University, Bachelor of Science, 1948

At first he had believed he "would like to be a farmer," then a doctor, but he soon admitted that "cutting up people" was more than he could handle. For a short time he even considered the ministry. At last, though, he decided upon law. On August 22, 1843, after several months in a Columbus, Ohio, law office, he entered the "middle class" in law at Harvard, where he studied under the conservative Supreme Court justice Joseph Story and Simon Greenleaf. The curriculum was rigorous and included all the "great orations" plus French, German, Greek, Latin, and the standard law texts. Small wonder, he thought, "I am now as dull and stupid as an ass!" Hayes originally planned to stay only two twenty-week terms but eventually decided to finish a third and thereby earn a bachelor of arts degree. He graduated on January 17, 1845. With considerable relief, he declared, "Now I shall begin to *live!*"

Impartial suffrage secures . . . popular education. Nothing has given the careful observer of events in the South more gratification than the progress which is there going on in the establishment of schools. . . . The ignorance of the masses, whites as well as blacks, is one of the most discouraging features of Southern society. If congressional reconstruction succeeds, there will be free schools for all.

—Rutherford B. Hayes, gubernatorial campaign speech, Lebanon, Ohio, August 5, 1867

GARFIELD: STUDENT, TEACHER

James A. Garfield—the last president to be born in the proverbial American log cabin—grew up in Cuyahoga County, Ohio, as one of four children raised by a widowed mother amid grinding hardship. By 1861, at age thirty, Garfield had by grit and some chance acquired a basic education, worked as a canal boy and carpenter, for several years attended the Western Reserve Eclectic Institute (later Hiram College), and as a member of the class of 1856 worked his way into and through Williams College. By the eve of the Civil War he had served as a teacher and principal of the institute at Hiram. By the time he was elected president he had also been a minister in the Disciples of Christ and a professor of ancient languages. He was, in short, a self-made man. As his predecessor, Rutherford B. Hayes, put it, "The boy on the tow path has become in truth the scholar and the gentleman by his own unaided work."

ARTHUR: POPULAR

His successor, Chester A. Arthur, born at Fairfield, Franklin County, Vermont, in 1830, first attended a village school. After the family moved to Schenectady, New York, he spent a winter at the local lyceum honing his skills for entry to the town's Union College. When he entered as a sophomore in September 1845, Union offered an array of up-to-date programs, but, perhaps influenced by his cleric father's knowledge of Latin, Greek, and Hebrew, "Chet" Arthur chose a traditional classical curriculum. The routine was classical as well, with breakfast and prayers at six-thirty and strictly enforced evening study periods. Arthur also taught school in nearby Schaghticoke during the winter breaks to earn money. He was remembered by his classmates as "genial and very sociable," traits that surfaced in one of his class sketches, "A brief Universal history from the Deluge to the present time." Since Moses was the only one, Arthur postulated, to survive the Great Flood, he then

> set his son Nebudchadnezzar [*sic*] to build Solomon's temple. In the course of which happened the confusion of languages, and this was the cause why the temple was left unfinished. About this period Alexander the Great after a siege of some months, took the tower of Babel by storm, and put all the inhabitants to the sword. But soon after

> he was attacked with vertigo, and fell into the bullrushes, where he was found by Pharoah's daughter, and taken care of.

There was fun outside the classroom as well. The college records testify to several fines for missing chapel and the usual exuberant student breakage. He was also caught for twice carving his name on the college buildings and, still better, once throwing the college bell into the Erie Canal. Even so, he was a member of Phi Beta Kappa. After graduating in the top third of his class, he returned to teach school for a while in Schaghticoke, spent a short time at the new State and National Law School in Ballston Spa, New York, then in 1851 worked as a principal of a North Pownal, Vermont, academy so small it fit within a church basement. By 1852 he was teaching at yet another school—but also studying law in his spare time. By the Civil War Chester Arthur had risen from a fifteen-dollar-a-month teaching post to a successful New York practice.

In the autumn of 1886 Harvard College, celebrating its 250th birthday, invited the President to attend with Mrs. Cleveland and receive an honorary degree. He accepted the invitation but refused the degree. . . . "My disinclination to receive the degree," he wrote [Secretary of the Interior William C.] Endicott, "is based upon a feeling which I cannot stifle and which I hope may be humored without any suspicion of lack of appreciation or churlishness.

—*Allan Nevins,* Grover Cleveland: A Study in Courage *(1934)*

CLEVELAND: ON HIS OWN

The son of a Yale-educated preacher, Grover Cleveland was the fifth of nine children. But Richard Cleveland was never able to care for so many on his small salary. When he died, he left his offspring little means to acquire an education. Sixteen-year-old Grover Cleveland turned to work, grasping schooling only when he could, and for a year taught at the New York Institute for the Blind. Hating it, he abandoned his job and moved west to Buffalo, where a wealthy uncle, Lewis P. Allen, found him a position in a respected local law firm. In 1859, after four years of study, Cleveland was admitted to the bar. He spent the next twenty-three years as a capable lawyer, content in his work and little suspecting the pinnacle that awaited him.

BENJAMIN HARRISON: A BUDGET EDUCATION

Benjamin Harrison weathered the usual country schoolteachers as well as a series of tutors. First was Miss Harriet Root, a preacher's daughter who for years served as the family nurse and then as teacher in the log-cabin schoolhouse. When Harrison was president, she remembered that "Ben was the brightest of the family, and even when five years old was determined to go ahead in everything. He was much ahead of his older brother, Irvin, but I held him back at the mother's request." She was followed in turn by three others, including Joseph Porter, who remained with the Harrison family for many years and recommended that young Ben attend one "of the yankee colleges." Young Harrison also had access to his grandfather William Henry Harrison's library, filled with history and biography—but no fiction. Benjamin Harrison, so family legend has it, supposedly never read a novel.

Still hoping to attend Harvard or Yale, Harrison next attended Farmers' College, more a preparatory school than a college, where he developed a fondness for "forbidden" cucumbers and "long" cigars. While there he also struck up an acquaintance with one of his teachers, the Reverend Dr. John W. Scott. His frequent visits to the Scott home were, however, more to see the professor's "charming and loveable, petite and a little plump" daughter Caroline than his learned teacher. By the time young Ben was seventeen, his father, John Scott Harrison, had no money for an expensive eastern education and decided instead to send his son to the "Yale of the West"—Miami University at Oxford, Ohio. Benjamin Harrison enrolled as a junior in the autumn of 1850. The school fostered the usual strict habits, but students often gathered in one another's rooms to escape their teachers' supervision. Harrison's roommate, John Anderson, remembered it as a time

> when we sat together in our room at Oxford . . . "gowned and slippered" . . . your book in hand . . . picking your nose or gazing at the chance coal in the little stove . . . thinking of—I won't say who—perhaps Doctor Scott . . . with frowning brow descanting on Saylor's latest meanness . . . or "in costume" dreading the intended bath . . . [or outside] bowling on the green . . . or strolling along the river bank at evening.

Benjamin Harrison during his term at Miami University in Oxford, Ohio, from 1850 to 1852 (Library of Congress)

Anderson, of course, knew it was not Dr. Scott of whom his friend thought. Indeed, just across the street from the campus was the new Oxford Female Institute—and "Carrie" Scott as well. In time they became secretly engaged. Harrison had other successes. He was elected president of the students' Union Literary Society and was only the nineteenth member of the Phi Delta Theta fraternity, founded at Miami University in 1848. (Remarkably, at his death in 1901 Harrison was still the only president who had been a fraternity member.) Harrison graduated in June 1852 and for the next two years read law in the offices of Storer and Gwynne in Cincinnati. In 1854 he settled in Indianapolis.

MCKINLEY: "ALWAYS STUDYING"

William McKinley grew up in a Niles, Ohio, household eager to read. Although little educated themselves, his parents, Nancy Allison and William McKinley, Sr., purchased books and subscribed to leading magazines they expected all six children to read. Both also appreciated the opportunities classroom education afforded. Mrs. McKinley recollected that she placed her children "in school just as early as they could go alone to the teacher, and kept them at it. I did not allow them to stay away." Their son William first attended the local school. As the Mexican War was then drawing to a close, the children especially enjoyed playing at military drill, complete with paper hats, wooden swords, and even a worthy foe. Their teacher Alva Sanford they dubbed "Santa Anna."

The elder McKinley eventually sought an even better school and at some considerable inconvenience to his business in 1852 moved the family to Poland, Ohio, and its Methodist Episcopal academy, or high school. There William McKinley joined the debating society and was soon found "always study-

Avoid the dangerous tendency of the times toward superficial knowledge, which accepts shallow rather than real acquirement. . . . Exact knowledge is the requirement of the hour. Luck will not last. It may help you once, but you cannot count on it. It is not permanent.

—*Address of William McKinley to a group of schoolchildren,* Speeches and Addresses of William McKinley *(1893)*

ing, studying, studying all the time." In 1860, with money borrowed from his mother, he enrolled in Allegheny College in Meadville, Pennsylvania, at age seventeen. Illness, or more likely a lack of enough money, forced him to return home in the winter of 1860. For a while he worked in the Poland post office, then at eighteen taught school at twenty-five dollars a month. With the outbreak of the Civil War he enlisted as a private in the Twenty-third Ohio Volunteer Infantry under Rutherford B. Hayes. After mustering out as a brevet major, he read law in a Mahoning County, Ohio, law office and for less than a year in the Albany Law School. In 1867 he opened his own office in Canton, where he maintained a home the rest of his life. Only two years later he was elected the local prosecuting attorney. Long after, McKinley advised a group of schoolchildren that "exact knowledge is the requirement of the hour. Luck will not last. It may help you once, but you cannot count on it. It is not permanent."

One of McKinley's successors, Woodrow Wilson, carried vivid memories of the Civil War, particularly its prisons and hospitals. But Wilson was just a boy of eight when the war ended. William McKinley's memories of the conflict were sharper. Mustered out as a major, he had the better claim to being the last president of the Civil War generation. He also symbolized the end of an era, the last president of the nineteenth century. He was also the last of a remarkable group. Of the nation's first twenty-four chief executives, from Washington's inauguration in April 1789 to McKinley's assassination in September 1901, eighteen were educated as lawyers. For many of them, politics was always the goal; law was simply the means to get there despite radically varied backgrounds, economic resources, and social ties. Only six chose a different profession. With no political ambitions at first, Washington, Harrison, Taylor, and Grant chose a military career; Andrew Johnson worked as a tailor, Garfield as a teacher. Their followers were not as diverse in background, but far more so in the professions for which they were educated.

THEODORE ROOSEVELT: MANY INTERESTS

As a sickly, asthmatic child, Theodore Roosevelt was educated primarily at home and on travels abroad. The son of patrician parents, Theodore and Martha (Bulloch) Roosevelt, young "Teedie" was educated at home by a succession of private tutors, including his aunt Annie Bulloch. It was then, too, that Roosevelt developed his interest in books and especially natural history. He once for days dragged around a volume filled with detailed pictures of all sorts of wildlife and begged any adult to conjure up stories to match what he saw. Soon after his well-to-do family moved into their newly built New York City mansion, young Roosevelt had his own natural history museum in the garret. His last tutor was the eminent Arthur Hamilton Cutler. Charged with Roosevelt's final preparations for entering Harvard, Cutler found his student at "every leisure moment" with "the last novel, some English classic, or some abstruse book on Natural History in his hand."

In July 1875, at age seventeen, Roosevelt passed Harvard's preliminary entrance examinations. "Is it not splendid," he rejoiced. "I passed in all the eight subjects I tried." He arrived at Cambridge in the fall of 1876, choosing his new friends carefully, checking their "antecedents" and gravitating more toward the "gentleman-sort," especially the Boston Brahmins. "On this very account," he wrote home, "I have avoided being very intimate with the New York fellows." He also immediately shunned the dormitories and for four years rented an elaborately decorated room nearby. Still, he tried not overly to offend and was popular. By the time he left he was a member of Harvard's most prestigious clubs: the Dicky, the Hasty Pudding, and the Porcellian, perhaps the most exclusive undergraduate club in the country. As one biographer described him, "he was 'queer,' he was 'crazy,' he was 'a bundle of eccentricities,' but he was wholly interesting."

Besides attending classes, he boxed, kept up with his bodybuilding, took dancing classes, hunted in the nearby woods, organized a whist club, followed the football team (The Yale players, he wrote, "seem to be a much more scrubby set than ours"), and continued his amateur scientific pursuits, dissecting and mounting so many specimens that his room soon looked like a zoo. He was equally engrossed in his studies. An intense young man, he was not especially brilliant but "an average B man . . . not in any way distinguished." And when compared to his other classmates, his writing, while "to the point," did not have their "air of cultivation." Nevertheless, he was elected to Phi Beta Kappa. In July 1877 his first printed work, *The Summer Birds of the Adirondacks*, appeared. His father was impressed enough to promise funds to support his son's career as a natural historian.

When his father died prematurely in 1878, however, Roosevelt's career plans received a considerable jolt. He graduated from Harvard in 1880 not sure what he was to do next. As did so many of his social position, he decided upon the study of law and duly enrolled at Columbia Law School. Although he claimed to "like the law school work very much," it held no future for him. He turned back to writing and in 1882 published *The Naval War of 1812*. He was twenty-four. The book, a strongly anti-Jeffersonian cry for military preparedness, launched his career as a free-lance historian. Having inherited some two hundred thousand from his father, Roosevelt could afford it. His only fear was that he might be forced to join "these small men who do most of the historic teaching in the colleges." Roosevelt began work, as Richard Hofstadter wrote, as one of an "American underground of frustrated aristocrats." By reason of family connection, intellect, and education, such men felt alienated from the more aggressive sources of considerable commercial—and political—power. Roosevelt lost little time in entering the fight.

At Sagamore Hill we love a great many things—birds and trees and books, and all things beautiful, and horses and rifles and children and hard work and the joy of life. . . . The books are everywhere. . . . The gun room at the top of the house . . . contains more books than any of the other rooms; and they are particularly delightful books to browse among, just because they have not much relevance to one another.

—Theodore Roosevelt: An Autobiography *(1913)*

TAFT: UNDER PRESSURE

William Howard Taft had far fewer educational opportunities than Roosevelt, although his parents, Louise and Alphonso Taft, were obsessed with their five children's achievements. His mother monitored every detail of his early schooling; his father oversaw his college and law school years. Driven by his parents and also by his irreverent peers—who called the already heavy Taft "Lub" or "Lubber"—as a boy he studied incessantly. One of his Cincinnati schoolmates recalled him as a "heavyweight. . . , who buckled to it for the best there was in him." But Taft later confessed that "one of the great and many defects of my character is my inability to do anything far in advance." By whatever method, in 1874, at age sixteen, he graduated second in his Woodward High School class.

At Yale he worked hard and by "steady, ponderous work" again finished second in his class. He wanted to try out for football, maybe even rowing, but his father forbade it. When Taft received the coveted invitation to join Yale's secret society, Skull and Bones, his father again said no. The elder Taft, a lawyer, also dictated that his son pursue a career in law. Taft returned home and attended the Cincinnati Law School, graduating in 1880. Pushed relentlessly since childhood, Taft later remarked that his father had "been a kind of guardian angel" whose drive for his son's success had "been so strong and intense as to bring it." Taft suspected that at his father's death he would "cease to have the luck which has followed me thus far." Perhaps, but Taft reached the presidency without previous election to any executive or legislative office.

WILSON: ACADEMIC

Woodrow Wilson's father was probably equally as crucial to his son's education, but in a far different manner. As a minister, Joseph Ruggles Wilson moved his family with some frequency, from his son's Staunton, Virginia, birthplace to Augusta, Georgia, and then to Columbia, South Carolina, in 1870. Unsure of the local schools, his father taught Wilson his first scholastic and moral lessons. The latter were obviously of paramount importance, for Thomas Woodrow Wilson did not master the alphabet until he was nine and did not read until age eleven. Once able, though, he had access to the household's array of English literature and periodicals such as the *Nation* and the *Edinburgh Review*. Wilson also absorbed much from his southern experience. As a child he witnessed the Civil War's considerable human cost to great effect: "I yield to no one precedence in love for the South," he exclaimed in 1880. "But *because* I love the South, I rejoice in the failure of the Confederacy."

Wilson eventually attended an Augusta, Georgia, academy run by a former Confederate officer and then a somewhat better school in Columbia. In neither did he make much of a mark. As one classmate recalled, he was "extremely dignified" and "not like the other boys. He had a queer way of going off by himself." Throughout much of his youth Wilson wrestled with his religious convictions—so much so that when in the fall of 1873 he left for North Carolina's Davidson College the family assumed he was to study for the ministry. There Wilson evidently opened up somewhat: he joined the debating club, played second base on the baseball team, and was at least variously viewed as "witty, genial, superior, but languid." He was nevertheless still plagued by a crisis of faith, noting at age seventeen how little time he had "spent in the fear of God," as opposed to time "spent in the service of the devil." He began to turn his ambitions from the ministry to politics.

Wilson spent only the 1873-1874 year at Davidson and returned home, by then in Wilmington, North Carolina, to prepare for entry to Princeton. In the autumn of 1875 as an eighteen-year-old freshman he at first found the work difficult, but "everyone soon began to look upon him as one of the most original and superior men in the college." Wilson avoided the theological students with which the college abounded and gravitated instead toward the wealthier and more worldly of his classmates. And except for several "quite bitter" sectional debates, he got along well with his fellows, joining prestigious debating, literary, and dining clubs, becoming a rabid booster of the athletic teams, and by his senior year editing the student newspaper, the *Princetonian*. He also de-

Woodrow Wilson (standing third from right) and his Alligator Club cohorts at the College of New Jersey in Princeton, circa 1879 (Library of Congress)

cided that law was the best route to a political career: "I entered the one because I thought it would lead to the other." Indeed, Wilson was already dreaming, even writing out cards as "Thomas Woodrow Wilson Senator from Virginia." He also completed his first major essay, "Cabinet Government in the United States," accepted by Henry Cabot Lodge for publication in the August 1879 *International Review*.

That fall he enrolled as a law student at the University of Virginia. His professor, the nationally known legal scholar Johnn Barbee Minor, was, Wilson thought, "a *perfect* teacher." But the grind of a legal education eventually discouraged him. Charlottesville, he concluded, was "a splendid place for the education of the *mind*, but no sort of place for the education of the *man*." He left the university after a year, returned briefly in the fall of 1880, and withdrew again in December. Home again, he completed two more articles, this time for publication in the *New York Evening Post*. As a practical measure he gained admittance to the Georgia bar and with a partner opened an office in Atlanta, but his heart was hardly in it, and within a short time his father was sending money to sustain him.

After only four months he decided to enter the graduate program in history at Baltimore's Johns Hopkins University. For the next two years he studied under Herbert Baxter Adams and Richard T. Ely. He chafed, though, at their methods. Adams, Wilson found, shunned the sweeping interpretations "of history as it furnishes object-lessons for the present." Instead, the professor emphasized "accurate details"—"the precise day of the month on which Cicero cut his eye-teeth." Confronted by Wilson's objections, Adams eventually bowed to his student's frustrations. The result was Wilson's first book, *Congressio-*

THE ROAD NOT TAKEN

Woodrow Wilson studied law at the University of Virginia with the renowned John Barbee Minor. "One cannot expect," the exacting Minor warned, "to gorge himself with law as a Boa Constrictor does with masses of food, and then digest it afterwards." Wilson, not known for his study habits as an undergraduate, adapted to the demanding curriculum briefly. At the end of his first semester, in December 1879, he waxed philosophical to a classmate: "I have, of course, no idea of abandoning this study because of its few unpleasant features. Any one would prove himself a fool, to be sincerely pitied by all wise men, who should expect to find any work that is worth doing easily done, accomplished without pain or worry." By the end of the first year, however, the pain and worry had become burdensome. Wilson left school, tried practicing law without a degree for a time, but by September 1883, intent on becoming a college professor, enrolled as a graduate student at Johns Hopkins University.

nal Government, completed with little original research and without even observing sessions of Congress.

With the book's publication planned for January 1885, Wilson decided in the fall of 1884 that two years of graduate work were enough. He was by then engaged to Ellen Louise Axson and eager to be married and earning an income. And although he realized "that a degree would render me a little more *marketable*," he also knew that his "mental and physical health . . . would be jeopardized by a forced march through fourteen thousand pages of dry reading." He left for a teaching position at Bryn Mawr College. The next year, however, he returned at Adams's encouragement, completed special examinations, and submitted *Congressional Government* as his dissertation. In May 1886 he received his degree. To his wife, he wrote, "I won the degree for *you*." His degree led him to the governorship of New Jersey and the White House—by way of Bryn Mawr, Wesleyan University, and Princeton (where he served as president).

HARDING: WITHOUT MUCH EFFORT

Warren G. Harding enjoyed no such educational opportunities. Raised in Caledonia, Ohio, the son of physicians, he worked hard. A sister remembered him at fourteen laboring during school vacations. "He was large and strong," she remembered, "and we thought him able to carry out anything he would undertake." He also learned from his labors. As his biographer Randolph Downes pointed out, Harding's heroes were "the hard-driving men who did things, rather than the merchants who sold things, or the teachers who thought things." The sawmill owner, Harding believed, "was an inspiration," the blacksmith "the captain of industry of the village." A formal education seemed tame in comparison.

His father, George Tryon Harding, never quite knew how his son completed school: "He studied his lessons, I don't know when. I never caught him at it and it used to worry me." A boyhood friend agreed: "Nobody ever saw him at hard study, but he shone at recitations." In 1880 Harding, not quite fifteen, went off to school. A two-year institution, Ohio Central College was by then struggling to remain open—within only two years, in fact, it was a school for the blind. Harding worked his way through, edited the campus newspaper, the *Spectator*, with Frank Harris, but was otherwise unimpressed by what the school offered. Harding later wrote that by the time he graduated in 1882 the school was "more like an academy and normal school" than a college. He was known as a "bear" in debate, history, and literature but struggled with mathematics. Harding would "sit down with his face to the wall, head in hands and soak it up. Then when he was through, he would jump up with a yell and shout, 'Now, darn it, I've got you,' and slam the book against the wall."

After leaving Ohio Central he taught a single term in a schoolhouse near Marion, Ohio. He detested the experience: "I will never teach again without better (a good deal better too) wages, and an advanced school." He next tried law. He hated it easily as much and recalled that only by "lashing his feet to the top of a desk" was he able to work in the Marion County office. He much preferred to read other fare, especially "the Dare-Devil Dick kind of thing, but, of course, we had to read them on the sly." Harding was occasionally drawn to some more serious works, such as books on Alexander Hamilton, a "passion" since boyhood. Years later as an owner of the *Marion Daily Star* he looked back on his education as generally a poor one. As a United States senator he criticized his hometown, too. To a New York audience he lamented that Caledonia had "dreamers" aplenty, "but the creative forces and constructive leadership were lacking."

COOLIDGE: "GETTING BY"

Calvin Coolidge grew up in rural Vermont, labored on the family farm, and tended the family store in Plymouth Notch. In 1877, at age five, he entered the local school, a stone building crude but typical of its time and place. Twenty-three children between five and eighteen years old gathered on rough spruce-board seats around a wood-burning stove. Coolidge at thirteen passed the school examination, a somewhat less than singular distinction. His sister passed at age twelve. He was, though, never very much taken with books. His mother (who died in 1884) introduced him to Scott and Tennyson, but he forever regarded books as a chore, as only a means to an end.

Calvin Coolidge at Amherst College, where he was a student from 1891 to 1895

In 1886, like his grandfather, father, and mother before him, he entered Black River Academy, a Baptist-sponsored "finishing school" of about 125 students in nearby Ludlow. During his first year he studied algebra, English grammar, government, and Latin, the next year adding American literature, ancient history, geometry, rhetoric, and both French and Greek. He obviously needed the work. In a letter to his sister during his first year he remarked of a lecture that he had "a half ticket which cost 50 cts they are illustrated by the magic lantern including scenes in all the wonderland of the world." He no doubt improved, for when he graduated in 1890 his principal encouraged Coolidge to consider attending Amherst College.

Coolidge, sick with the flu and perhaps overly nervous, failed the entrance examination. His father, however, agreed to his attending St. Johnsbury Academy, considered the state's best preparatory school. More important, the school was empowered to issue students a college entrance certificate. After a two-month review, Coolidge had his ticket, thus bypassing a second entrance exam, and entered Amherst. When Coolidge arrived in 1891, most of Amherst's 336 students were the sons of doctors, lawyers, ministers, and teachers. In such company the new arrival had to admit, "I don't seem to get acquainted very fast." He could have tried harder. Although he was asked to give a few orations, he took no interest in athletics, church, the local YMCA, or clubs. He only gained access to a fraternity in his last term, and then only with the considerable aid of a friend who insisted that to get one pledge the fraternity had to take the other. He was, in the local vernacular, "getting by." He did in his junior year publish a story, "Margaret's Mist," in the campus *Literary Monthly*. "While speaking," Coolidge wrote, "[Margaret] had moved towards the pool, and with her eyes still fixed upon the man she had loved, she plunged beneath its eddies. The black water closing over her buried the sorrowing maiden forever beneath its bosom." It was his only published fiction.

Going away to school was my first great adventure in life. I shall never forget the impression it made on me. It was so deep and remains so vivid that whenever I have started out on a new enterprise a like feeling always returns to me. It was the same when I went to college, when I left home to enter the law, when I began a public career in Boston, and when I started for Washington to become Vice-President and finally when I was called to the White House.

—Autobiography of Calvin Coolidge *(1929)*

In his first two years Coolidge took Greek for five terms, Latin for four, French, German, and Italian for three. He added mathematics (with differential and integral calculus) for five, with rhetoric and physics for two. In the former he received an A, in the latter a D; otherwise his grades were mediocre. In his last two years his grades were far better. In a class with the future jurist Harlan Stone, Coolidge studied history for five terms with Anson D. Morse, a tall, gaunt man completely obsessed with civic responsibility. Even more influential was the eccentric Charles E. Garman, a secretive philosophy professor his students "looked upon . . . as a man who walked with God." From him Coolidge learned to "weigh the evidence" and to "carry all questions back to fundamental principles." But as Donald R. McCoy, one of his biographers, points out, Coolidge learned too little from Garman "to cover the complexities of the society over which Coolidge was later to reign as President."

Coolidge graduated cum laude in June 1895 with a 78.71 average. He had written his father that he might return to the Plymouth Notch store or perhaps attend a Boston or New York law school. "I do not see," he claimed, "as I have much of any preference now but may have later." In truth, he did. He had already decided upon the law and so perhaps was only giving his father a chance to express a preference. John Calvin Coolidge, however, was supportive: he knew the benefits law might bring. Even without having read the law, the elder Coolidge at one time or another was a tax collector, a town selectman, state legislator, school commissioner, and a constable. Within only months after leaving Amherst, Coolidge on the advice of a friend entered a Northampton, Massachusetts, law office. In June 1887 he was admitted to the bar. With eight hundred dollars from a small inheritance and his savings, Coolidge bought books and furniture, rented a Northampton office, and in February 1898 opened his practice.

HOOVER: LAB RAT

Raised in the Quaker faith, Herbert Hoover spent his first eleven years in the small town of West Branch, Iowa. "Birdie" Hoover was an average student, although good at mathematics, and to his teacher a "mischievous, laughing boy." After his father's death in 1880 and his mother's in 1884, Hoover and his brother Tad and sister May were separated. For a year "Bert" remained in Iowa and then—with two dimes in his pocket—was sent to Newberg, Oregon, to the home of his uncle, Dr. John Minthorn. Tad eventually joined him, and together they attended the Friends Pacific Academy (later George Fox College), "about the same as a good High School" in the opinion of their uncle. Dr. Minthorn in 1888, when Hoover was not quite fourteen, moved to Salem to open a real estate office.

In Salem, Hoover continued to study, but at night. By day he worked in his uncle's busy Oregon Land Company office. "In all this," Dr. Minthorn recalled, "Bert was a factor and could at any time give information about any detail." For the company "he gave all his time from early morning until late at night." In the evenings Hoover used his small inheritance to attend a local polytechnic and business school. Years later, he recollected that during the same period a local spinster and his Quaker Sunday school teacher together introduced him to the works of Charles Dickens (especially to *David Copperfield*, a favorite) and Sir Walter Scott.

By the time the three children were reunited in 1888, Dr. Minthorn wanted fourteen-year-old Hoover to enter a Quaker college, perhaps Haverford or Earlham. Two respected Quakers, one a mining engineer, the other a mathematician, suggested a new California school instead. Leland Stanford's university had its advantages, especially that it was then tuition-free and desperately needed students. Unfortunately, however, Hoover had never finished high school and failed all but one of the entrance examinations. In June 1891, at sixteen, he completed a summer of tutoring, passed his mathematics examination, received a "condition" in English, and entered Stanford's "pioneer" class. He later commented that he "happened to be the first boy to sleep in the Men's Dormitory before the university was formally opened—and so may be said to be its first student."

Although he took courses in history, French, German (which he failed), and philosophy, he preferred geology. As for the others, he had the "disconcerting habit," one friend remembered, of

SHAKY START

Herbert Hoover's undergraduate classmates at Stanford University would not have predicted a presidential future for him. A faculty wife described him as "always blunt, almost to the point of utter tactlessness." With his friends, however, his tactlessness took on a fun-loving character. He recorded an account of one memorable trip to Yosemite, during which he and his friends delighted in making the life of a local restaurateur miserable: "And even now you may hear of those 7 college boys who ate so valliently [*sic*] that day. For it is one of the legends of the valley. The proprietor," he added, "is now bankrupt and at [the] Stockton Insane Asylum."

His demeanor in the classroom was in keeping with his extracurricular shenanigans. In the year following his Yosemite trip, "having run Athletics" during the previous semester, he found himself with two conditional grades, no credit for the first term's works, and carrying twenty-three credit hours of course work to catch up.

Years later, Hoover allied himself repeatedly with his alma mater. He served as a trustee, helped found Stanford's business school, and donated one hundred thousand dollars for a student union, desperately needed for students—like Hoover—who had not chosen to join fraternities.

starting a course "and then, if he found it unpromising as a contribution to the special education in which he was interested, he would simply drop out of the class without consultation or permission." He probably believed he had no time to waste. Hoover started a campus laundry business, sold it at a profit, and by his sophomore term was looking for still another enterprise. He told a classmate he was going into the baggage business, was working "awful hard" at making money, and had "worked up 300000000000 schemes for making more."

In 1894 Hoover was elected class treasurer and by that spring was student treasurer. It was an unpaid office. Hoover, not surprisingly, was "in favor of the Treas. receiving a salary myself." Nevertheless, the position led to other opportunities. By the time he left office the student-body debt was cleared, and he was earning money booking lectures, concerts, even athletic events. He arranged Stanford's first football game with the University of California at Berkeley, scheduled extra baseball games and track meets, and saw the proceeds go to build a new grandstand, diamond, and track.

Geology, though, was his chief interest. Hoover as a student assistant "practically lived in the geology laboratory." He also worked as a typist for John Branner, chairman of the Department of Geology and Mining. It was Branner who influenced Hoover to change his major from engineering to geology. (Lou Henry, a fellow geology major, later married Hoover.) In May 1895 Hoover graduated with an A.B. He was twenty and had originally hoped to spend a year studying mining geology at either Johns Hopkins or Columbia, but he needed a job more. He had spent his summers working for the United States Geological Survey, but a hoped-for job there never materialized. Recalling Professor Branner's admonition to his students to try their hand at mine work at least once, Hoover did. He started as a laborer at $1.50 to $2.50 a day, seven days a week, on the ten-hour night shift.

FRANKLIN D. ROOSEVELT: STUDENT JOURNALIST

When Franklin D. Roosevelt arrived at Groton in 1896, at age fourteen, he was entering his first full year in any school. As a child, Roosevelt had been taught by first a German, then a Swiss governess. The former eventually left and entered a sanitarium, and the latter married. Roosevelt as an adult always enjoyed pointing out that he had driven one to insanity and the other to wedlock. He did attend at least one elementary school—but for only six months. On a family trip abroad, his mother placed him in a small German Volksschule, one Sara Delano Roosevelt found "very amusing," but also one she doubted could teach her only child very much. Young Franklin wrote that "I go to the public school with a lot of little mickies, and we have German reading, German dictation, the history of Siegfried, and arithmetic."

Groton provided an altogether different life. As a freshman, young FDR lived in a six-by-ten-foot cubicle into which were crammed a bed, a bureau, a chair, and but a single domestic item—a small rug. At least by the second year a student moved to somewhat better quarters. "You have no idea," Roosevelt wrote in the fall of 1898, "how nice it is to have a study, and do just as you like." Cold showers preceded breakfast, which preceded two equally plain meals. Finally freed for a meal outside the school's confines, Roosevelt revealed that the "food tasted perfectly delicious," especially after "sausages or sausage-croquettes for the last three days."

Educated alone, and as an only child, Roosevelt at first experienced some awkward moments in adjusting to his classmates. To make matters worse, he was entering two years late and was thus one of only two new boys in his class. In his first year, he proudly wrote, "I have not had any blackmarks or latenesses yet." Indeed, the next year he won the Punctuality Prize. But by the end of his first year he slowly began to realize what might please a parent did little to ingratiate him to his rowdier classmates. Soon enough he could write that "I have served off my first black-mark today, and I am very glad I got it." Thereafter he toed a fine line between too few, which would endanger his standing among his classmates, and too many, which only earned trips to the headmaster's office. He also tried out for baseball, crew, and football. In his last year he managed the baseball team. His mother was delighted; he was not—it was, he said, a "thankless task."

Groton when Roosevelt arrived was under the headmastership of the remarkable Endicott Peabody, a man much taken with the social gospel. "If some Groton boys do not enter political life and do something for our land," he repeatedly preached, "it won't be because they have not been urged." His faculty was equally strong-minded. Sherrard Billings, known as "Mr. B." or simply "Beebs," took Roosevelt on his clerical duties about the neighboring countryside. Amory Gardner, "Uncle Billy Wag," a magnificent showman, taught Greek. "I can learn better & quicker with him than anyone else," Roosevelt wrote. The new student took the usual Greek, Latin, French, and German, also English, sacred studies, and some science, but little social studies. A course in American history was not even offered. And the class in political economy did Roosevelt little good thirty years later. In his notebook, he wrote: "Gold is stable, silver is unstable, therefore gold is the only suitable standard of value."

His last year was his best. Roosevelt was a "full-fledged dormitory prefect" (as was at least half his class), and he enjoyed the larger room and the responsibilities the office carried. Of his charges he commented: "All is confusion and Babel; the new infants are like the sands of the sea." He also did well at his studies and at his graduation in June 1899 received the Latin Prize. (Such work had perhaps compelled him that spring to purchase his first pince-nez. The rector remarked of his stay that he had "been a thoroughly faithful scholar & a most satisfactory member of this school throughout his course. I part with Franklin with reluctance." Like his cousin Theodore Roosevelt before him, he was bound for Harvard.

FDR's biographer Frank Freidel has written that "at Groton, Roosevelt learned to get along with his contempo-

NO LADIES' MAN

While a student at Groton, Franklin D. Roosevelt carefully avoided escorting particular young ladies to campus or holiday dances. His letters refer unflatteringly to female acquaintances: he called one lady an "awful pill"; another acquaintance he nicknamed "Brat"; and another, "Elephantine." In a letter to his mother, Roosevelt hoped that she "would think up some decent partner for me, so that I can get somebody early, and not get palmed off on some ice-cart." By the winter of 1903-1904, however, he had fallen in love with his distant cousin Eleanor Roosevelt, whom he had known since childhood. A Harvard classmate recalled that "Franklin had no serious affair with any girl, which was remarkable in view of his exuberance. In the back of his mind there was always Eleanor as an ideal." Once she became accustomed to the idea of her son's marriage, his mother rationalized that the news "probably surprised us only because he had never been in any sense a ladies' man. I don't believe I ever remember hearing him talk about girls or even a girl."

Harry S Truman in the seventh grade, 1898 (courtesy of the Harry S Truman Library)

raries; at Harvard he learned to lead them." Not in athletics, however. Again, he tried out for practically every sport, but he only made one of the scrub football teams and the intramural crew. He did manage an acceptance from the Freshman Glee Club but rose no further. Elective or appointed office was a different matter. From a field of sixty-eight candidates Roosevelt was chosen as one of five new editors of the student paper, the *Crimson*. He was elected to Alpha Delta Phi—the Fly Club—and served as its head librarian; he was also on the library committee for both the new Harvard Union and the Hasty Pudding Club. And he joined the Harvard Republican Club—mostly as a gesture of support for cousin Theodore. Thanks in large part to his Groton course work, he completed his degree requirements within three years. He graduated in June 1903, but as the new editor in chief of the *Crimson* he returned the next fall and enrolled as a candidate for a master of arts degree. Although he took "four or five history and Economics courses," he had no intention of completing the work. For one thing, he was completely devoted to the newspaper—and by the winter of 1903-1904 devoted as well to his cousin Eleanor Roosevelt.

Just like his other cousin, when his fourth year at Harvard came to an end FDR had no idea what he might do next. At least Theodore Roosevelt by the same age had written a naval history of the War of 1812. He, on the other hand, had only his Crimson editorials. Franklin Roosevelt was to spend the next three years at Columbia Law School and another three as a law clerk. His fiancée Eleanor rightly commented: "He will not find himself altogether happy with the law he is studying at Columbia unless he is able to get a broad human contact through it." Unenthused and preoccupied with the city itself and his forthcoming marriage, Roosevelt did not even take the trouble to finish his degree. In 1927 he corrected a biographical sketch with the observation: "I wish you would change the LL.B. after my name to LL.D. of which I hold two!" Roosevelt later defended his choice by declaring, "You know you don't learn law at the best of our law schools. You learn how to think." His biographer Friedel retorted that there is little evidence he learned either there.

TRUMAN: NO COLLEGE

The oldest of three children raised in Grandview and Independence, Missouri, Harry S. Truman benefited from a far different, and an extremely abbreviated, education. His mother, Martha Ellen Young Truman, instilled in her son a lifelong appreciation for books, and by age five he could read. He particularly enjoyed histories. Years later, Truman remembered "reading all the books obtainable in the Independence and Kansas City libraries on history and government from Egypt to U.S.A." He started formal schooling at age eight and had tackled Appleton's *First Reader* before promotion to the second grade. By then, however, he and his brother

Vivian were striken with diphtheria. "My arms, legs and throat were of no use," Truman recalled in an autobiography, "but I recovered and went back to school and skipped the third grade."

After completing his junior high years he transferred to the local high school, in 1901 inaugurated a school paper, the *Gleam*, and graduated in May 1901. Truman had hoped "there would be some chance for more education," but hard times and poor eyesight prevented his securing a coveted appointment to West Point. He went to work first as a timekeeper on a railroad construction job, next "wrapping singles" for the *Kansas City Star*, then by 1903 was employed as a bank clerk. Two years later, with "some of the boys in the bank," he joined a local military unit. It was not West Point, but it was a beginning. He had always believed a citizen should know something about business, or farming, or the army, "so I started my grass roots military education by joining a National Guard Battery, June 14, 1905." It was an inauspicious beginning. His grandmother, Truman recalled, was hardly taken with his new uniform: "She said, 'Harry this is the first time since 1863 that a blue uniform has been in this house. Don't bring it here again.' I didn't."

EISENHOWER: ATHLETE-STUDENT

Dwight D. Eisenhower's first uniform also came as something of a surprise to his family. Born in Denison, Texas, and raised in Abilene, Kansas, David Dwight (his mother, Ida Stover Eisenhower, later reversed the names) attended the nearby Lincoln School through the first six grades and then the Garfield School across the tracks on the better side of town. "Little Ike" (his brother Edgar was first called "Ike," then later "Big Ike," to distinguish him from his younger sibling) also worked after school at the Belle Springs Creamery, where his father was employed as a mechanic. He did well at Abilene High School, played football and baseball

> *My success in compiling a staggering catalogue of demerits was largely due to a lack of motivation in almost everything other than athletics, except for the simple and stark resolve to get a college education. I didn't think of myself as either a scholar whose position would depend on the knowledge he had acquired in school, or as a military figure whose professional career might be seriously affected by his academic or disciplinary record. I suspect, instead, that I probably looked with distaste on classmates whose days and nights were haunted by fear of demerits and low grades.*
>
> —*Dwight D. Eisenhower,* At Ease: Stories I Tell to Friends *(1967)*

with enthusiasm if not brilliance, and in 1909 finished at the top of his class. Eisenhower, however, had no real idea what he wanted to do next, where he wanted to go, or what he wanted to study.

A friend, Everett E. ("Swede") Hazlett, Jr., the son of an affluent local physician, had received an appointment to the United States Naval Academy and encouraged Eisenhower to come, too. Eisenhower's parents were disappointed, in fact dismayed, at the idea of a military career. His high school classmates had predicted that Eisenhower would become a professor of history at Yale. Eisenhower nevertheless returned to his high school for additional courses, studied with Hazlett, and in October 1910 took the entrance examinations. He scored 87.5 out of a possible 100. The appointment, however, was to West Point—past his twentieth birthday, he was ineligible for Annapolis.

Eisenhower arrived at West Point with few expectations—except that he at last excel in athletics. By his second year his ambition seemed fulfilled; he played halfback so well that several sports writers predicted he might eventually be named All-America. But a knee injury in a game against Carlisle (led by Jim Thorpe) and another injury against

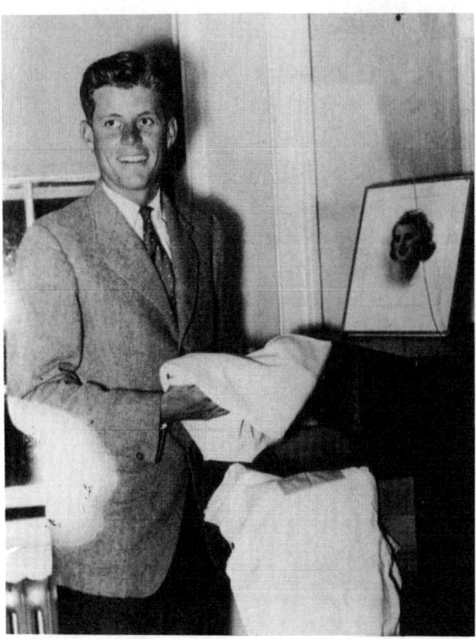

Harvard freshman John F. Kennedy, 1936 (courtesy of Pictorial Parade*)*

Tufts the next week ended any hopes he would be a football star. Wanting to participate somehow, he became a cheerleader and a junior-varsity coach. Otherwise, he essentially became just another cadet among the many. Eisenhower never sought cadet rank, served as a private for years, and only near the end of his West Point career was named color sergeant. In his 1915 graduating class of 164, he ranked ninety-fifth in conduct and sixty-first in class performance—the bottom of the top third. He was, his friend Hazlett remarked that spring, "generally liked and admired." By September, he was serving as a second lieutenant in the Nineteenth Infantry at Fort Sam Houston, San Antonio, Texas. In 1930, age forty, he was still a major. In 1939, as a new lieutenant colonel, he calculated that he might make full colonel by 1950.

KENNEDY: A SECULAR EDUCATION

John F. Kennedy, though raised in a devout Catholic family, and except for an abbreviated year at Canterbury, in New Milford, Connecticut, never attended a

Our progress as a nation can be no swifter than our progress in education. Our requirements for world leadership, our hopes for economic growth and the demands of citizenship itself in an era such as this all require the maximum development of every young American's capacity.

—John F. Kennedy, Special Message to Congress on Education, February 20, 1961

Catholic school. His father, Joseph P. Kennedy, opposed parochial schools and instead favored the secular schools' broader education. His second son therefore attended a succession of prestigious preparatory schools—the Dexter School in Brookline, Massachusetts, then New York's Riverdale Country Day School, Canterbury, and finally Choate in Wallingford, Connecticut. His older brother and father's pride, Joseph P. Kennedy, Jr., was already at Choate. The brothers had also attended the Dexter School together. "Jack's grades," a biographer has remarked, "were average (Joe's were superior); he failed to make the varsity football squad (Joe was a star)." Jack Kennedy did, however, for two years serve as business manager of the yearbook and was on the cheering squad.

When Kennedy finished Choate in 1935 at age eighteen his father expected him to follow his brother again, this time to Harvard. Kennedy insisted instead on Princeton. It was only a partial and temporary victory. Again like his brother before him, Kennedy at his father's insistence was dispatched for a summer of study at the London School of Economics under the respected social theorist Harold Laski. While Joe, as usual, had done well, Jack was rushed home with an attack of jaundice. He did, though, enroll that fall at Princeton, but by December he was ill again and never returned. Once he had recovered, he enrolled at Harvard—as his father had wished.

His first two years in Cambridge were unexceptional. He missed making the varsity football team, played for the scrubs, then injured his back severely. He did do well at swimming and with his brother Joe won the intercollegiate sailing title. As for his grades, during his first two years he maintained an average barely above a C. But after a summer in Europe in 1937, his interest in history increased. More important, as one of his father's "experiments" to see whether he might be suited to a diplomatic career, the twenty-two-year-old Kennedy spent six months during his junior year as an office boy in the American embassies in London and Paris. Two days after Germany and Britain went to war, his father also sent him to Glasgow to assist the American survivors of the torpedoed liner *Athenia*.

He returned to Harvard with a new perspective and graduated in June 1940. His senior thesis, "Appeasement at Munich," earned magna cum laude honors. Quickly published by a new firm in search of books, and with a new title suggested by Arthur Krock of the *New York Times*, *Why England Slept* was a remarkable first effort. A *New York Times* reviewer commented that Kennedy's call for military preparedness "ought to be weighed carefully in this country." It was hardly, though, the usual senior paper. Both Krock and Henry R. Luce, the editor of *Time*, had assisted with the prose, and Kennedy's father had arranged meetings for his son with Winston Churchill, Secretary of State Cordell Hull, Harold Ickes, and the duke and duchess of Kent, as well as many other American and English figures.

Undecided about what to do next, Kennedy at first considered entering Yale Law School. He instead enrolled in the graduate business program at Stanford University but left after six months on a tour of South America. In October 1940, while still away, he learned he "had become No. 18 on [the] Palo Alto, Calif., draft board rolls." After rejections from both the army and navy because of his weak back and the inauguration of a considerable strengthening program, he received a navy commission in September 1941.

LYNDON JOHNSON: AMBITIOUS

Lyndon B. Johnson was by then already a congressman. Born near Johnson City, Texas, to Rebekah Baines and Sam Ealy Johnson, Jr., he grew up between parents pulling him between different values and ambitions. Deeply affected by his father's financial problems and equally determined to avoid them, Johnson at fifteen graduated from his Johnson City high school as valedictorian of a six-member class. Confused as to his next step and having no money to do much else, he worked his way to California taking odd jobs as a car washer, an elevator operator, and a handyman. "Up and down the Pacific coast I tramped," he recalled years later, "washing dishes, waiting on tables, doing farm work when it was available and growing thinner and more homesick." A cousin in Los Angeles took him in for a while. He returned home and took a job on a local road crew shoveling gravel, pushing a wheelbarrow, and partaking in "a reasonable amount of helling around on Saturday nights."

Many months of that convinced him to attend college. Johnson's mother remembered his returning home after an especially rough day to declare he was "sick of working just with my hands"; he was "ready to try working with my brain." He hitchhiked to Southwest Texas State Teachers College in San Marcos, worked for a time in the college president's office (thanks to his father) and as a part-time janitor, studied history, joined the school debate team, and wrote for the student paper. Needing money, he took a year off to teach school in Cotulla, Texas, a small, destitute Mexican-American community. After graduating in 1930, he returned to teaching (this time in Houston), but

Richard M. Nixon, Whittier High School, 1927-1930 (courtesy of Whittier College)

soon saw a better chance. He became assistant to Richard M. Kleberg, a newly elected Texas congressman. By December 1931, at only twenty-three, he was a congressman's aide in Washington, D.C.

NIXON: ALL-AROUND HONORS

Richard M. Nixon grew up in Yorba Linda and Whittier, California, the first of Hannah Milhous and Frank Nixon's four sons. Eager to learn, he read newspapers rather than children's books. At seventeen Nixon graduated from Whittier High School with the Harvard Award as "best all-around student." He could not, though, for a moment consider an expensive education in the East and so instead chose Whittier College, a school dedicated to Quaker ideals. There Nixon played football for his first year, then sat on the bench for three more, was elected president of his freshman class, student vice-president his second year, and president in his fourth. He was also associate editor of the college paper and repeatedly won honors as a debater. He perhaps earned as much notoriety for founding the Orthogonians, or "square shooters." As a Quaker institution, Whittier had neither the fraternities and sororities nor the drinking and dining clubs of secular schools. Whittier did, though, have the Franklins—a snobbish collection of the school's most affluent students who sported black-tie attire at campus events. Nixon's group, on the other hand, adopted loose sweaters and open collars. Their organization's symbol was a square, the corners signifying "Beans, Brawn, Brains, and Bowels."

Graduating second in his class, Nixon won a scholarship in 1934 to the Duke University Law School. One of forty-four students, most of whom were also there on scholarship, Nixon had to maintain at least a B average. "I'm scared," he admitted. "I counted thirty-two Phi Beta Kappas in my class. I don't believe I can stay up in that group." And as the school reduced the number of scholarship students in both the second and third years, Nixon was forced to work doubly hard: "I'll never learn the law. There's just too much of it." He worked as a research assistant, managed

A GOOD BENCHMAN

Richard M. Nixon had ample experience in college to prepare him for two terms as Dwight D. Eisenhower's vice president. As a football player at Whittier College Nixon was, his coach recalled, "a second-string man. . . . Weeks would go by and he wouldn't even play a minute, but he'd hardly ever miss practice, and he worked hard. He was wonderful for morale, because he'd sit there and cheer the rest of the guys, and tell them how well they'd played. To sit on a bench for four years isn't easy." A teammate added that "he was always talking it up. That's why the coach let him hang around, I guess."

to make do on thirty-five dollars a month from home, and in 1937 finished third in his class. But he failed to secure the offer he wanted from a prestigious eastern firm and returned to Whittier to practice law.

FORD: LAW OR FOOTBALL

Gerald Ford's path to college and law school was somewhat different. He attended the University of Michigan on a football scholarship but still continued working part-time to pay his way. Upon graduation in 1935 he had a chance to play professional football for the Detroit Lions or the Green Bay Packers but instead chose to attend law school. He at first preferred to stay in Ann Arbor, but the offer to coach Yale's boxing and freshman football teams provided the financial assistance he needed. Before starting work, though, he had to take boxing lessons himself. Wisely, even then he only "boxed the lightweights and coached the heavyweights." Because he had never formally been accepted to Yale's law school, Ford in 1935 began as a conditional student. With his busy work schedule and with little money he took nearly six years of part-time course work to complete his studies. In June 1941 he returned to Michigan to open a law office.

CARTER: NAVAL ACADEMY

When Jimmy Carter completed high school in 1941 he had long hoped to attend the U.S. Naval Academy. With the world already at war and American entry expected soon, appointments to Annapolis or West Point were, however, especially difficult to win. At seventeen, he was told to wait and use the time to bone up on math and science. For a year Carter enrolled at Georgia Southwestern College in Americus, near his home in Plains, then transferred to the Georgia Institute of Technology as a naval ROTC cadet. The following year, 1943, he was accepted at Annapolis. "The academy requirements were stringent,"

Jimmy Carter while a student at Georgia Southwestern College in Americus, Georgia, 1942 (courtesy of the Carter family)

Carter recalled, but even in wartime some customs remained. The midshipmen, he remembered, "learned how to dance from professional instructors—without girls. Fox trot, waltz, samba, and rhumba were required subjects." He graduated in 1946, fifty-ninth in a class of 820. With the war over he was first assigned to a converted battleship. It was not a good start: "I became most disillusioned with the Navy, and the military in general, and probably would have resigned had not I and all Annapolis graduates been serving 'at the pleasure of the President.' "

REAGAN: EXTRACURRICULAR TALENTS

Born in 1911, Ronald Reagan while growing up moved from Tampico to Galesburg to Chicago to Monmouth to Dixon, Illinois. After completing high

Ronald Reagan (standing, third from left) and the Eureka College dramatic society. Reagan graduated in 1932 eager to try a show business career (courtesy of Eureka College).

school at age seventeen he entered Eureka College, a small, morally conservative institution operated by the Disciples of Christ. The school had always been "perpetually broke," with professors sometimes going for months without pay and its suppliers having to accept produce from the college's farm in payment for goods. Reagan majored in economics but was an undistinguished student, preferring to participate in campus theater productions, football, and other student activities; he was a reporter for the school paper and eventually class president. Reagan also participated in a student strike that led to the eventual dismissal of the college's puritanical president. When he graduated in 1932, one of only forty-five students still left in the senior class, he was eager to try show business. In the midst of the Great Depression he knew, though, that "Broadway and Hollywood were as inaccessible as outer space." He decided to try radio instead.

BUSH: YALE OILMAN

That George Bush after attending Yale entered the oil business is in many ways representative of his twentieth-century predecessors as president. Whereas eighteen of the nation's first twenty-four chief executives were lawyers, since McKinley's term there have been only four—Taft, Coolidge, Nixon, and Ford. Of those sixteen presidents elected since 1900, five others—Theodore Roosevelt, Wilson, Harding, Franklin Roosevelt, and Kennedy—at least studied or for a time seriously considered law. Still, they as part of the majority—twelve of sixteen—chose other careers. Of all the nation's forty presidents, in fact, barely more than half, or twenty-two, embarked on the profession of law. Considering that in the late eighteenth and throughout the nineteenth century law provided one of the best means to personal and political success—and that for many it did not require a college education—it is perhaps not surprising that the proportion is so much higher for the earlier than for the later period. Six—Washington, William Henry Harrison, Zachary Taylor, Grant, Eisenhower, and Carter—entered the profession of arms. Including Andrew Jackson, though first trained as a lawyer, the total is seven. Of all forty, only nine did not attend college: Washington, Jackson, Van Buren, Taylor, Fillmore, Lincoln, Johnson, Cleveland, and Truman. Warren Harding completed only a two-year degree. Five—John and John Quincy Adams, Theodore and Franklin Roosevelt, and John F. Kennedy—attended Harvard. Three—Jefferson, Monroe, and Tyler—completed their studies at the College of William and Mary. Two each graduated from Princeton (Madison and Wilson) and West Point (Grant and Eisenhower).

Family Ties: Facts About First Families

by THOMAS L. CONNELLY

President Chester Arthur once remarked, "I may be president of the United States, but my private life is nobody's damned business." A noble sentiment, but few Americans agree. The president wins the election, but the whole family takes office. The wife assumes the role of First Lady; in the early years that meant little more than having to fulfill the social responsibilities of White House hostess, but the wives of the modern presidents are expected to be active social advocates and political advisers as well, ill-prepared though they may be. The president's children become news fodder. If they make mistakes the whole country hears about it; if they do well their success is attributed to family influence. National attention has curious effects on mothers, fathers, brothers, sisters, and other presidential relatives. Sometimes the antics of family members add exasperating complications to the chief executive's life. The presidency is a lonely job in which the chief executive often experiences the isolation that only ultimate decision makers can know, yet he has traditionally found mixed comfort in the assurance of the Psalmist that God setteth the solitary in families.

GEORGE WASHINGTON

On January 6, 1759, George Washington married Martha Dandridge Custis at her estate northwest of Williamsburg, Virginia. She was the widow of John Parke Custis, who died in 1757, leaving her with two children, a daughter and a son. The daughter, Martha Parke Custis, died at the age of thirteen. Only the son, John Parke Custis, survived to adulthood.

George Washington never adopted John Custis but treated him as a ward. He served as one of Washington's aides-de-camp in the American Revolution and died not long after the war. Two of Custis's four children survived infancy, and after his death they were sent to Mount Vernon to live with George and Martha. One of the children was named George Washington Parke Custis. After the death of Martha in 1802 George Washington Parke Custis inherited the land along the Potomac River that now includes the Arlington National Cemetery and Fort Meyer. In 1804 Custis began construction of the Arlington mansion. His only surviving child, Mary, married Robert E. Lee there in 1831.

JOHN ADAMS

John Adams married Abigail Smith at the home of the bride's parents in Weymouth, Massachusetts, on October 25, 1764. The couple had five children, of whom four survived to adulthood. The eldest son, John Quincy, won election to the presidency in 1825. John Adams and John Quincy Adams are the only father-and-son pair to become president.

John Quincy Adams was the first of three Adams sons to attend Harvard College. The second son, Charles, became a lawyer in New York City after graduation. He died from alcoholism at the age of thirty. A third son, Thomas

Portrait by Edward Savage of George and Martha Washington and Martha's children by her first marriage, John Parke and Martha Parke Custis. The Custis daughter died at the age of thirteen, but the son grew up to serve as aide-de-camp to General Washington during the American Revolution (Andrew Mellon Collection, National Gallery of Art).

Boylston, became a lawyer and a Massachusetts state judge. He died in debt, also after a lifetime of excessive drinking. The daughter and eldest child, Abigail "Nabby," married William Stephens Smith, who served as U.S. representative from New York from 1813 to 1815.

THOMAS JEFFERSON

Thomas Jefferson and Martha Wayles Skelton, widow of Bathurst Skelton, married on January 1, 1772, at the estate of the bride's father in Charles City County, Virginia. Jefferson thus became the second president to marry a widow. Martha Skelton had a son by her first marriage. He died in 1771 when he was only four. Martha died in 1782, aged only thirty-three, and Jefferson never married again.

Equally tragic were the fates of most of the six children of Thomas and Martha Jefferson. Only two girls out of five girls and a boy survived to adulthood, and one of those, Mary, died in 1804 at the age of twenty-five. The other, Martha, survived her father, who died in 1826, by ten years. She served Jefferson as White House hostess during his terms as president.

JAMES MADISON

James Madison married Dorothea Payne Todd on September 15, 1794, in what became Jefferson County, West Virginia. Known as Dolley, she had married John Todd in 1790, but he died in a Virginia yellow fever epidemic in 1793. Dolley's first husband and her father had both been devout Quakers, and when she married Madison she was expelled from the Society of Friends.

Dolley won lasting fame for her vivacious command of Washington society during her husband's presidential terms. After retiring to his Virginia es-

Elizabeth Kortright Monroe, wife of the fifth president (Library of Congress)

tate in 1817, she returned to Washington after his death in 1836 and resumed her place in the capital's social circuit, but the financial strain of that life-style, combined with the demands of her spendthrift son from her first marriage, forced her first to sell her husband's papers (to Congress) and then his estate before she died in 1849.

James and Dolley Madison had no children of their own.

JAMES MONROE

On February 17, 1786, James Monroe married Elizabeth Kortright in New York City. .The Monroes had three children,—two daughters and a son. The son died in infancy.

The elder daughter, Eliza Kortright, was educated in France at the school of a former lady-in-waiting to Marie Antoinette and in her youth was quick to remind others of her lofty status. She married George Hay, the Virginia lawyer who prosecuted Aaron Burr, and often substituted for her ailing mother as White House hostess. In that capacity she refused to call on the wives of the diplomatic corps in Washington, alienating official society. After the deaths of her father and husband she moved to Paris, converted to Catholicism, and lived in a convent. Her death date is unknown.

The younger daughter, Maria Hester, moved to the White House after finishing her education and was married there in 1820, in the first wedding held in the presidential residence. Her husband, first cousin Samuel L. Gouverneur, never got along with sister-in-law Eliza. Former President Monroe moved to the Gouverneurs' New York City residence after the death of his wife in 1830.

I begin to think very seriously of the duty incumbent upon all good citizens to have a family. If you think this is the language of a convert, perhaps you will enquire how he became so? I am not yet prepared to answer that.

—Letter of John Quincy Adams to Abigail Adams, his mother, March 30, 1786

JOHN QUINCY ADAMS

John Quincy Adams married Louisa Catherine Johnson on July 26, 1797, in London, where she was born. The future couple met in Nantes, France, when she was four and he was twelve and traveling through the country with his diplomat-father. They met again, after she had grown up a bit, when John Adams was serving as U.S. consul in London from 1785 to 1788. First John Quincy wanted to escort her older sister, then he set his sights on Louisa.

By the time her husband won the presidency in 1825, Louisa Adams had come to the opinion—shared by others less intimate—that Adams men were rather too reserved to be tolerated for long. Nevertheless, she remained a devoted mother to her three surviving children and, in Adams's words, "a faithful and affectionate wife."

The couple's eldest son, George Washington, suffered a tragic fate. A Harvard graduate, he became a Massachusetts attorney and served as a member of the state legislature. A failed personal relationship evidently left him emotionally unstable and a heavy drinker. In April 1829 he boarded a steamer, the *Benjamin Franklin,* in Rhode Island. Near New York City, officials discovered that he apparently had either jumped or had fallen into the ocean. Several weeks later his body washed up on the shore of Long Island Sound.

The second son, John II, was expelled from Harvard during his senior year for taking part in a student riot. Then he studied law under his father and became the president's secretary in 1825. In 1828 he got into a celebrated dispute with a Washington newspaperman who had been critical of President Adams. After John II had insulted the newspaperman, Russell Jarvis, at a party, Jarvis challenged the president's son to a duel. When John II refused the challenge, Jarvis accosted him in the Capitol Rotunda, yanking his nose and slapping his face. President Adams sent a message to Congress requesting legislation securing "official avenues of exchange" to prevent such contacts.

After his father lost his bid for a second term, John II ran a Washington flour mill owned by the ousted politician, but he died in 1834, five years after his older brother's sudden ending.

The future of the youngest son, Charles Francis Adams, was much brighter. Also a Harvard graduate, he served in the U.S. House of Representatives from 1859 to 1861. During the American Civil War he performed brilliantly as American minister to Great Britain. He nearly beat Horace Greeley for the Liberal Republican presidential nomination in 1872.

Louisa Catherine Adams, circa 1801, about four years after her marriage to John Quincy Adams (courtesy of Fanny C. Mason)

ANDREW JACKSON

Andrew Jackson was the first president to marry a divorcée, Rachel Donelson Robards, in Natchez, Mississippi, in August 1771. Rachel Jackson died in December 1828, shortly before her husband's inauguration as president. She is the only president's wife who died after her husband's election but before his inauguration.

The couple had no natural children. Due to their poor finances and ill health, her brother and his wife allowed them to adopt one of their children, an infant they named Andrew Jackson, Jr. The adopted son proved a failure. Fond of drinking and dalliances with women, he was also a poor businessman and a heavy spender, running up huge debts. The young Jackson, heir to the Jackson estate, The Hermitage, sold the property in 1856 to the state of Tennessee for fifty thousand dollars. Even that sum covered only half his indebtedness.

MARTIN VAN BUREN

Martin Van Buren married childhood sweetheart Hanna Hoes on February 21, 1807, in Catskill, New York. Hanna Van Buren died in Albany, New York, in 1819 at the age of thirty-five. Van Buren survived his wife by forty-three years and never married again.

The Van Burens had four children—

all sons. The eldest, Abraham, graduated from West Point and was a career army officer. He served as his father's private secretary during his presidential term. The second son, John, was a lawyer and secretary of the American legation in London while his father served as minister-designate to Great Britain. He served as a U.S. representative from New York beginning in 1841, winning prominence for his abolitionist stance. The third son, Martin, Jr., served as an aide to his father and died in Europe. The fourth, Smith Thompson, drafted some of the president's speeches and edited his papers. His second marriage was to a niece of Washington Irving.

WILLIAM HENRY HARRISON

William Henry Harrison married Anna Tuthill Symmes on November 25, 1795, in North Bend, Ohio. They had nine children who survived to adulthood—more than any other presidential couple. Their fifth son, John Scott, was the father of future president Benjamin Harrison. William Henry Harrison and Benjamin Harrison are the only grandfather-and-grandson pair to become president.

John Scott was an Ohio farmer who served in the U.S. House of Representatives. He is best known by the circumstances of his death. He died of unknown causes in 1878 and was buried in a family plot in North Bend, Ohio. A few days previously the body of a young nephew recently buried was stolen from the cemetery. Since it was common practice for medical colleges to obtain cadavers by unscrupulous means, family members went to search for the nephew's body. They never found it, but at the Ohio Medical College in Cincinnati they did find the body of John Scott Harrison. It had been stolen without the family's knowledge while they were on the hunt for the nephew.

Tragedy encompassed the other male Harrison children after they grew up. When President William Henry Harrison died in 1841, only one of his five sons—John Scott—was still alive. The eldest son, John Cleves, died of typhoid fever at the age of thirty-four, not long after a court had ruled him guilty of embezzlement. He had secreted away thousands of dollars while working for a federal land office in the Indiana Territory. Another son, William Henry Harrison, Jr., died in his thirties of alcoholism. His wife served as White House hostess during her father-in-law's one-month presidential term. Benjamin, the fourth son, was wounded in 1836 during the war for Texas independence and died four years later. The youngest, Carter Bassett, practiced law until he died at twenty-eight.

The Harrisons' female children like-

ONE PRESIDENT—TWO FIRST LADIES

John Tyler was the first president to experience the death of a first wife and marriage to a second during his presidential term. As a twenty-three-year-old he married Letitia Christian in 1813. In 1839 Letitia suffered a stroke that made her an invalid. On September 9, 1842, during her husband's second year in the presidency, she suffered another stroke and died the next day. Tyler had been introduced to Julia Gardiner at a White House reception early in 1842. In January 1843 Tyler and Julia began courting, to the consternation and amusement of some of Tyler's friends. The president was fifty-three, and Julia, only twenty-three, was the object of many younger men's desires. She turned down the president's first marriage proposal in February, but Tyler persisted, and Julia finally accepted his offer. They married in New York City on June 26, 1844, and Julia served as First Lady until Tyler left the presidency the next year.

wise were not long-lived. Elizabeth "Betsey" Bassett died at fifty, Lucy Singleton at twenty-six, Mary Symmes at thirty-one, and Anna Tuthill, the youngest, at thirty-two. All the Harrisons' sons and daughters married—once only in each case.

JOHN TYLER

John Tyler had more children—fifteen—than any other president, but he had to marry twice to reach that figure. On March 29, 1813, he married Letitia Christian in New Kent County, Virginia. They had eight children—five daughters and three sons—seven of whom survived to adulthood. Letitia was first lady for only seventeen months after Tyler took office in April 1841. She had previously suffered a stroke and was paralyzed. During those seventeen months she appeared in public at the White House only once, at the marriage of her daughter, Elizabeth. Meanwhile, Pricilla Tyler, wife of Robert Tyler, the president's eldest son, served as official hostess at the White House. Letitia died in 1842, the first wife of a president to die in the White House.

Tyler married again on June 26, 1844, in the next-to-last year of his presidential term, to Julia Gardiner, a native of New York who was thirty years younger than the president. With Julia, Tyler began another family, which grew to include five sons and two daughters.

The births of the Tyler children were dispersed over a wide period. The first, Mary, was born in 1815, and the last, Pearl, in 1860. Pearl Tyler Ellis lived until 1947, 157 years after the birth of her father.

JAMES K. POLK

On January 1, 1824, James K. Polk married Sarah Childress in Murfreesboro, Tennessee. She survived the president by forty-two years, dying in 1891. The Polks had no children.

Sarah Polk was a woman unusually well educated for her time. She attended the Moravian Female Academy

Julia Gardiner Tyler, John Tyler's second wife and mother of seven of his fourteen children

in Salem, North Carolina, and met her future husband when they shared a tutor. After Polk won election to Congress in 1825, she quickly adapted to social and political life in Washington. She banned dancing and hard liquor in the White House. She retired to Nashville, Tennessee, with her husband in 1849 and supported the Confederacy during the Civil War.

ZACHARY TAYLOR

Zachary Taylor married Margaret Macall Smith on June 21, 1810, in Louisville, Kentucky. She survived her husband by two years and died in 1852 in Mississippi at the age of sixty-three.

The Taylors had six children—five daughters and a son. Two of the children achieved a level of distinction. The second daughter, Sarah, married Jefferson Davis, later president of the Confederate States of America. Three months after the marriage she died of malaria at the age of twenty-one. Taylor, a military man, had been adamant

A HAPPY MARRIAGE

Log-cabin-born Millard Fillmore came from rather too humble circumstances to impress his bride-to-be Abigail Powers's family without some convincing. After Fillmore, by then a twenty-five-year-old lawyer in East Aurora, New York, popped the question in 1825, one of Abigail's sisters wrote her, "I was as much surprised to hear of his visit as yourself. . . . Why did you not inform me more particularly how he appeared to you and whether you think him improved in etiquette, and how much Mr. and Mrs. Powers [Abigail's brother and sister-in-law] was [*sic*] pleased with him, and what remarks they made of him." The couple married in February 1826. When in late 1829 Fillmore left for Albany to serve in his first term as a New York assemblyman, Abigail wrote a touching series of letters to him, including this one, dated January 19, 1830: "I am now alone and having laid our little son on the bed to sleep, employ a few minutes in writing, having again perused your *affectionate* favor, and to return thanks to kind Providence for so tender a friend. Though I regret the loss of your society more than I can express, I am far happier in having you at the distance with an assurance that you love me, than I should be in your society, doubting your affections. . . ."

against the marriage: "I will be damned if another daughter of mine will marry into the Army. I know enough of the family life of officers." At one point Taylor and Davis considered a duel. The couple continued to court secretly, and Taylor and his wife did not attend the wedding.

The Taylors' only son, Richard, became a Confederate general and distinguished himself in combat with the Army of Northern Virginia. Later he won promotion to the rank of lieutenant general and in May 1865 surrendered all Confederate forces in Alabama, Mississippi, and eastern Louisiana.

MILLARD FILLMORE

Millard Fillmore married Abigail Powers in Moravia, New York, on February 5, 1826. They had two children, a son and a daughter. Abigail died in Washington in 1853, the last year of her husband's presidency. Fillmore remarried in 1858, to Caroline Carmichael McIntosh, a widow from Albany, New York. The second Fillmore marriage produced no children.

FRANKLIN PIERCE

Franklin Pierce married Jane Means Appleton on November 19, 1834, in Amherst, New Hampshire. The Pierces had three sons, but all died under tragic circumstances before they reached adulthood. One lived only three days, and a second died at the age of four. The third, Benjamin, died in a railroad accident at the age of eleven, about two months before Pierce's inauguration as president. The death of their last child brought severe hardship to the Pierces. Their son had been the only fatality in the accident. Pierce's wife came to the conclusion that "Bennie" had been taken so that her husband would experience no distractions as president. Pierce interpreted the death as punishment for his sins and refused to swear the presidential oath on the Bible at his inauguration. Instead, he raised his right hand and affirmed the oath.

JAMES BUCHANAN

James Buchanan is the only president who remained a bachelor all his life. He had no children.

ABRAHAM LINCOLN

Abraham Lincoln married Mary Ann Todd in Springfield, Illinois, on No-

THE BACHELOR PRESIDENT

During the summer of 1819, lawyer James Buchanan of Lancaster became engaged to Ann Coleman, the daughter of a wealthy Pennsylvania iron manufacturer who was one of America's first millionaires. Ann's parents doubted the propriety of the prospective marriage. Her father, a trustee of Buchanan's alma mater, Dickinson College, questioned whether or not it was wise for Ann to marry a man who once had been dismissed from the university for poor performance and lack of discipline.

Buchanan had little time to worry about Coleman's misgivings, for the financial panic of 1819 made his law practice busier than it had ever been. As autumn turned into winter he neglected his courting. Rumors swept the "teacup" set in Lancaster that the attorney was actually more in love with the Coleman fortune than with Ann Coleman. Ann herself grew suspicious and questioned her fiancé's motives in a letter to him. Then another complication arose.

On the way home from a business trip, Buchanan visited the wife of an associate and met her unmarried sister. Lancaster gossip mongers conveyed that episode to Ann. She was so angry that Buchanan should visit another lady before seeing her that she wrote him a letter releasing him from their engagement. Ann's mother convinced her depressed daughter to visit Philadelphia, hoping the change of scenery would do her good. Buchanan busied himself with a particularly trying law case. Five days after Ann's departure Buchanan received word that she had died at her sister's home in Philadelphia. Rumors that Ann had committed suicide swept Lancaster, and the Colemans could express nothing but bitter hatred toward her former suitor. Mr. Coleman refused even to open Buchanan's letter requesting permission to walk as a mourner at Ann's funeral. In part the letter read: "It is now no time for an explanation, but the time will come when you will discover that she, as well as I, have been much abused. . . . I may sustain the shock of her death, but I feel that happiness has fled from me forever."

vember 4, 1842. She survived her husband by seventeen years, dying in 1882 at the age of sixty-three.

The Lincolns had four sons. The eldest, Robert Todd, was the only one to survive to maturity. He was born in 1843 and died in 1926. Robert Lincoln became secretary of war in the cabinets of James A. Garfield and Chester A. Arthur. Later he served as minister to Great Britain in the Benjamin Harrison administration, and then he became president of the Pullman Company.

The second son, Edward, was born in 1846 but lived less than four years. The third, William, known as "Willie," was ten when Lincoln was elected president, but he died of pneumonia in 1863 at eleven, becoming the only president's child to die in the White House. Thomas, the youngest, known as "Tad," became the object of his father's greatest affection after the death of Willie. He died of diphtheria in 1871 at the age of eighteen.

ANDREW JOHNSON

Andrew Johnson and Eliza McCardle were married in Greenville, Tennessee, on May 17, 1827. He was eighteen and she was sixteen. Johnson was a tailor who once had been an indentured servant before fleeing his master. Eliza taught him how to read and write.

The Johnsons had five children. The eldest, Martha, was married to David Patterson, U.S. senator from Tennessee during the Civil War. The second child, Charles, became a Union surgeon during the war and died under unusual cir-

Abraham Lincoln and son Thomas, February 9, 1864. "Tad," the youngest of four Lincoln sons, became the third to die as a youth when he succumbed to diptheria in 1871, aged eighteen (Ostendorf Collection).

cumstances in 1863: some reports indicate that he was killed when he was thrown from a horse, others indicate he committed suicide. The third son, Robert, became a colonel in the Union infantry and died of alcoholism in 1869, the last year of his father's presidential service. The youngest Johnson child, Andrew Johnson, Jr., became a journalist and died at the age of twenty-seven.

ULYSSES S. GRANT

Ulysses S. Grant married Julia Boggs Dent in St. Louis, Missouri, on August 22, 1848. She was a cousin of James Longstreet, later a prominent general in the Confederate army. Ulysses and Julia Grant had four children.

The Grants' eldest son, Frederick Dent, was nineteen when his father entered the White House. Too young to fight in the Civil War, he graduated from West Point in 1871. Later he held a curious assortment of positions—minister to Austria-Hungary under President Benjamin Harrison, police commissioner of New York City, and eventually the rank of major general in the U.S. Army. Ulysses S. Grant, Jr., nicknamed "Buck," was a graduate of Harvard and the Columbia Law School. He became a prominent attorney in New York City until his death in 1929. The third child, Ellen Wrenshall, was married twice, first to a British diplomat in a White House ceremony. After the death of her first husband in 1890 she was forced to petition the U.S. Congress for return of her citizenship. Jesse Root, the youngest Grant child, enjoyed a long career as an engineer and died in 1934.

RUTHERFORD B. HAYES

Rutherford B. Hayes and Lucy Ware Webb were married in Cincinnati, Ohio, on December 30, 1852. They had four sons and a daughter who survived infancy.

The eldest Hayes child, Sardis Birchard, became a Toledo, Ohio, real estate and tax attorney. The second, James Webb, became a presidential secretary during his father's term. He served in Cuba, Puerto Rico, and the Philippines during the Spanish-American War and was awarded the Congressional Medal of Honor for his exploits. Later he became a general's aide during the Boxer Rebellion and served in European brigades before the United States officially entered World War I. The only Hayes daughter, Frances "Fanny," was the first president's child to survive to the 1950s. She married a future U.S. Naval Academy instructor. The final surviving Hayes child, Scott Russell, participated in the first White House egg roll, sponsored by his mother. He became a New York railroad executive.

JAMES A. GARFIELD

James A. Garfield and Lucretia Rudolph married in Hiram, Ohio, on

Ulysses S. Grant and family in 1868, at about the time the general received the Republican presidential nomination (left to right): Julia, Grant's wife; Ellen, the third child; Jesse, the youngest; "Buck," the second child; and Frederick, the oldest.

November 11, 1858. They had seven children, five sons and two daughters, of whom five lived to adulthood. Garfield and his wife met at Geauga Seminary in Chester, Ohio. She went on to teach school while he studied at Williams College. They got married two years after he graduated. Lucretia Garfield took a keen interest in White House history when she became first lady. She intended to oversee a restoration of the residence but contracted malaria before she could start the project. Her husband was assassinated while journeying to visit his sick wife.

The two oldest Garfield boys enjoyed political prominence rivaling that of their father. The eldest, Harry Augustus, became a lawyer and then a college professor and president of Williams College. He served as chairman of the price committee of the U.S. Food Administration during World War I, earning the Distinguished Service Medal for his efforts. The second son, James Rudolph, also became a lawyer, then he served in the Ohio state senate, on the U.S. Civil Service Commission, in the U.S. Department of Commerce and Labor, and as secretary of the interior. He worked for the Red Cross during World War I. He witnessed his father's 1881 assassination.

The third Garfield child, Mary, married her father's presidential secretary. The fourth, Irvin McDowell, became a

U.S. Representative James A. Garfield and daughter "Molly," one of five Garfield children, several years before Garfield assumed the presidency in 1881 (Library of Congress)

lawyer like his older brothers and also a corporate director. The youngest, Abram, was an architect.

CHESTER A. ARTHUR

Chester A. Arthur married Ellen Lewis Herndon in New York City on October 25, 1859. She died in 1880, slightly more than a year and a half after Arthur succeeded his assassinated predecessor. The Arthurs had two sons and a daughter. One son did not survive infancy. The second son, Chester Alan II, attended Princeton and graduated from the law school at Columbia University. Young Alan established himself as a playboy in Washington circles, and the reputation eventually spread to Europe, where he took long and frequent sojourns. Due to his family's wealth he was able to live a life of luxury as a sportsman and art connoisseur. He died in 1937.

GROVER CLEVELAND

On June 2, 1886, President Grover Cleveland married Frances Folsom in the White House. Cleveland is the only president who was married in the presidential residence. Frances Cleveland survived the president by thirty-nine years. The couple had three daughters and two sons.

The eldest child, Ruth, died in 1904 at the age of thirteen. Immensely popular with the Washington press, she quickly earned the nickname "Baby Ruth." In 1921 the Curtiss Candy Company named a candy bar after her.

The president was busy. At the appointed time he put on his overcoat, and stood waiting. Minute after minute passed; finally, concluding that he would teach her a lesson in punctuality, he threw off his coat and gloves, resolved that he would not go driving that day. Presently he heard her [his wife's] voice at the foot of the stairs. "Come along," she cried, "I am ready now." "And what do you suppose I did?" asked the President. "Why, I got up, put on my coat and gloves again, and went driving."

—*Allan Nevins,* Grover Cleveland: A Study in Courage *(1932)*

BENJAMIN HARRISON

Benjamin Harrison, grandson of the ninth president, married Caroline Lavinia Scott in Oxford, Ohio, on October 20, 1853. She died in the White House in 1892. The couple had a daughter and a son. Harrison married a second time in 1896, to Mary Dimmick. They had a daughter. Harrison's second wife survived her husband by forty-six years and died in New York City in 1948.

Benjamin and Caroline Harrison's son, Russell Benjamin, worked as a mint assayer, raised livestock, and published a newspaper. He became his father's secretary during his presidential term and later served in the Spanish-American War. After the war he became a lawyer and Indiana state politician. The Harrisons' daughter, Mary

Scott, performed hostess duties at the White House and married a future vice-president of the General Electric Company. Benjamin and Mary Harrison's daughter, Elizabeth, married the grand-nephew of Ohio politician James G. Blaine.

WILLIAM MCKINLEY

On January 25, 1871, William McKinley married Ida Saxton in Canton, Ohio. The couple had two daughters, both of whom died in infancy.

Ida McKinley suffered from epilepsy. Her husband displayed a caring understanding of the problem throughout their marriage, dissolving the awkwardness caused by her sometimes public seizures with firm patience. The wife of vice-president Garret Hobart often performed White House hosting duties. McKinley was the third president to be assassinated, and Ida McKinley, broken by his death, could not attend her husband's funeral. She died in 1907.

THEODORE ROOSEVELT

Theodore Roosevelt married Alice Hathaway Lee in Brookline, Massachusetts, on October 27, 1880. They had one child, Alice Lee. Roosevelt's wife died in 1884 at the age of twenty-two. His mother died on the same day in the same house. Roosevelt married again, on December 2, 1886, to Edith Kermit Carow, in London. They had four sons and a daughter. Edith Roosevelt died in 1948.

Roosevelt's first child has been his most celebrated. She married Ohio representative Nicholas Longworth and became the grande dame of Washington society. Her barbed wit was well known. She once described 1948 Republican presidential candidate Thomas Dewey as resembling the small figure atop a wedding cake. Alice Longworth died in 1980.

Three sons from Roosevelt's second marriage died in wartime, Quentin during World War I and Theodore, Jr., and Kermit during World War II. Quentin served in the army air corps and was shot down by German air fighters over France. Both Theodore, Jr., and Kermit died of natural causes during their wartime service. The other two children also contributed service in wartime: Ethel as a nurse at the American Ambulance Hospital in Paris during World War I and Archibald as an army officer in both world wars.

A TRAGIC DAY

New York assemblyman Theodore Roosevelt was a happy man on the eve of Valentine's Day 1884. On the House floor in Albany he accepted the congratulations of many of his colleagues, having just received a telegram that his wife, Alice, had given birth to a girl the day before. The telegram reported that Alice was "only fairly well" but gave no sign of the impending double disaster.

Several hours later Roosevelt received the worst news of his life. Alice, stricken with Bright's disease, was dying. And "Mittie," Roosevelt's mother, was dying of acute typhoid fever.

By the time Roosevelt arrived home at half past ten that night, his wife, semicomatose, could barely recognize him. In a bedroom downstairs Mittie was in the last stages of her illness. Roosevelt spent hours holding his dying wife, "in a vain effort," biographer Edmund Morris recounts, "to impart some of his own superabundant vitality." At three in the morning on Valentine's Day he went downstairs to say goodbye to his mother. Back upstairs, he watched the morning dawn with Alice still in his arms. At two in the afternoon, she died.

In his diary for February 14, 1884, Roosevelt wrote, "The light has gone out of my life."

Theodore Roosevelt, his second wife, Edith, and their five children: Quentin, Ethel, Kermit, Theodore, Jr., and Archie

WILLIAM HOWARD TAFT

William Howard Taft married Helen Herron in Cincinnati, Ohio, on June 19, 1886. She is the only first lady who also was the wife of the chief justice of the Supreme Court. William and Helen Taft had two sons and a daughter.

The most famous Taft child was Robert Taft, known as "Mr. Republican," who served as U.S. senator from Ohio from 1939 to 1953. He narrowly lost the Republican presidential nomination to Dwight D. Eisenhower in 1952. Helen Herron, the second child, took a Ph.D. in history from Yale and served as a history professor and as president of Bryn Mawr College. Charles Phelps became a lawyer and local Cincinnati politician. He lost the 1952 race for governor of Ohio.

WOODROW WILSON

Woodrow Wilson married Ellen Louise Axon in Savannah, Georgia, on June 24, 1885. Ellen Wilson died in the White House in 1914 at the age of fifty-four, the last first lady to die in the presidential mansion. Wilson married Edith Bolling Galt in Washington on December 18, 1915. She died in 1961.

The three Wilson daughters by the president's first marriage followed widely divergent paths. Margaret became attracted to eastern religion and died in India in 1944. Jessie became active in Democratic politics, delivering the nomination speech for presidential candidate Alfred Smith in 1928. Eleanor married and divorced William G. McAdoo, Wilson's secretary of the Treasury until 1918.

WARREN G. HARDING

Warren G. Harding married divorcée Florence DeWolfe in Marion, Ohio, on July 8, 1891. She had been married previously, at nineteen years of age, to Henry DeWolfe, by whom she had a son. When her father discovered her affection for Harding, he warned her not to marry into "the black blooded Harding family," but she did it anyway. Florence Harding was deeply interested in astrology. Shortly before the 1920 presidential election she visited a Washington clairvoyant who predicted that her husband would win the election but would then die in office.

Warren and Florence Harding had no children. To Nan Britton, the object of one of Harding's extramarital affairs, was born in 1919 a daughter named Elizabeth.

CALVIN COOLIDGE

Calvin Coolidge married Grace Anna Goodhue in Burlington, Vermont, on October 4, 1905. Grace Coolidge survived her husband by fourteen years and died in Northhampton, Massachusetts, in 1957.

The Coolidges had two sons. The eldest, John, graduated from Amherst College and pursued a business career in Connecticut. The younger, Calvin, Jr., died at the age of sixteen while his father was president. During a tennis match on the White House court he stumbled and stubbed his toe. The toe became infected, and he died of blood poisoning.

Grace and Calvin Coolidge with their two sons, John (left), the older, and Calvin, Jr., who died of an infection during his father's presidency (Library of Congress)

ONE PRESIDENT— TWO FIRST LADIES

Woodrow Wilson was the second president to experience the death of his first wife and marriage to a second during his presidency. Wilson married Ellen Axson on June 24, 1885, and she died on August 6, 1914, during the president's first term. Wilson's cousin Helen introduced Edith Gault to the president at the White House in March 1915. He proposed in May and she accepted in July. They kept their plans secret until October. Rumors of the engagement circulated, however, causing a scandal that prompted Wilson to offer to withdraw the proposal. Edith refused to be cowed by the scandalmongers, and the couple was married at the bride's Washington home on December 18, 1915.

HERBERT HOOVER

Herbert Hoover married Lou Henry in Monterey, California, on February 10, 1889. Lou Hoover died in 1944. Her husband survived her by twenty years. The Hoovers had two sons, both born in London while Hoover worked there as an engineeer.

The eldest son, Herbert, Jr., gradu-

Franklin Delano Roosevelt, "emperor" of the New Deal, surrounded by family and friends (including his wife, Eleanor, to his immediate right) at his fifty-second birthday party, the White House, January 30, 1934 (courtesy of the Franklin D. Roosevelt Library)

ated from Stanford University and received a graduate degree in geology from Harvard. He became a celebrated inventor, particularly of devices designed to detect oil deposits beneath the surface of the earth. During World War II he developed several instruments to test the proficiency of military aircraft.

The younger son, Allan, also graduated from Stanford and received a graduate degree from Harvard. Allan became the manager of his father's ranch in California.

FRANKLIN D. ROOSEVELT

Franklin D. Roosevelt married Anna Eleanor Roosevelt in New York City on March 17, 1905. The couple had a daughter and five sons. One of the sons died in infancy. Eleanor Roosevelt survived her husband by seventeen years and died in 1962.

The saga of the Roosevelt sons provides proof of the lesson that the children of famous parents come under intense public scrutiny. Despite whatever success they might achieve on their own, others usually attribute it to the parents' fame.

The eldest Roosevelt son, James, had a brief career in Massachusetts politics after graduation from the law school of Boston University. He abandoned politics after enduring criticism that he was attempting to capitalize on his famous father's name. In the mid 1930s he became president of a corporation that planned to manufacture industrial alcohol. He left that position, too, after political opponents of his father raged that the younger Roosevelt intended to use the father's name to further the company.

After serving as a marine colonel and winning the Silver Star in World War II, James Roosevelt entered politics in Cali-

FDR'S CHILDREN

Franklin Roosevelt once remarked, "One of the worst things in the world is being the child of a president. It's a terrible life they lead." Anna, James, and Elliot Roosevelt would have agreed. When Anna's husband, John Boettiger, was named publisher of the *Seattle Post-Intelligencer,* press observers accused the Hearst-owned newspaper of attempting to win presidential favor. James endured criticism of his big-money insurance deals and for working with Joseph Kennedy to "corner" the market for imported Scotch once the prohibition repeal went into effect. Elliot's connections to the airline industry and a chain of Texas radio stations were deemed too cozy by the press. "Jimmy" apparently saw some truth on the accusations of his critics. "Possibly I should have been sufficiently mature and considerate enough of father's position to have withdrawn from the insurance business entirely," he later commented. "But I was young, ambitious, spoiled—in the sense of having been conditioned to require a good deal of spending money—so I went ahead in pursuit of what seemed to be the easiest solution."

In domestic life as well the Roosevelt children experienced more than their share of difficulty. In total they were married seventeen times. Elliot proved especially difficult. Even as his father was preparing to be inaugurated, Elliot left his wife and children and announced plans to marry again immediately after the divorce was final. But the parents steered clear of their children's problems, offering support but not marching orders. Roosevelt himself suggested, "I believe that a politician should be judged on politics." First Lady Eleanor explained, "They were not really rooted in any particular home and were seeking to establish homes of their own."

fornia. He lost a race for governor of California but then served several terms in the U.S. House of Representatives.

Other Roosevelt sons endured criticism and bad luck. Elliott was commissioned a captain in the army air corps prior to World War II. He won several decorations, including the Distinguished Flying Cross and the French *Croix de Guerre*. Still, he could not satisfy critics of the family. A storm of protest developed in Congress when he was nominated to the rank of brigadier general. More scorn erupted in 1945, when three servicemen returning home were "bumped" from a cargo flight because the space was needed for a crate containing Roosevelt's dog. The animal was being shipped to his wife in California.

Franklin, Jr., who became a New York attorney after graduation from the University of Virginia law school, experienced the barbs of political and gossip columnists because he got married four times. Like his brother James, Franklin, Jr., served in the U.S. House and was defeated in an effort to win election as governor—not of California, but of New York.

Three things can ruin a man if you want to know what I believe. One's power, one's money, and one's women. . . . A man who is not loyal to his family, to his wife and his mother and his sisters can be ruined if he has a complex in that direction. If he has the right woman as a partner, he never has any trouble. But if he has the wrong one or if he's mixed up with a bunch of whores, why, then he's in a hell of a fix.

—*Merle Miller,* Plain Speaking: An Oral Biography of Harry S. Truman *(1973)*

HARRY S TRUMAN

Harry S Truman married Elizabeth "Bess" Wallace in Independence, Missouri, on June 28, 1919. They had one daughter, Margaret, who married journalist Clifton Daniels after a partly successful singing career. She became an author of mystery novels and has also published well-received biographies of her father (1973) and mother (1986).

DWIGHT D. EISENHOWER

On July 1, 1916, Dwight D. Eisenhower married Marie "Mamie" Geneva Doud in Denver, Colorado. The couple had two sons, one of whom, Dwight Doug, died of scarlet fever at the age of three. The other, John, graduated from West Point in 1944 and served as a staff officer in the European theater in the latter stages of World War II. He remained a professional soldier until his retirement in the 1960s. One of John Eisenhower's sons, David, married Julie Nixon, the daughter of his grandfather's vice-president.

JOHN F. KENNEDY

John F. Kennedy and Jacqueline Lee Bouvier were married on September 12, 1953, in Newport, Rhode Island. They had a daughter and two sons. One of the sons, Patrick, lived for only two days after his birth in 1963. The eldest child, Caroline, was six when her father was assassinated in 1963. She entered the publishing business after her graduation from Radcliffe College and then in 1987 married a designer. John, Jr., graduated from Brown University and the New York University law school. He made headlines in 1988 when he was voted "sexiest man alive" by *People* magazine. He made the newspapers again in 1990, when he failed the New York bar exam for the second time.

Jackie Kennedy married Greek oil tycoon Aristotle Onassis in 1968. He died in 1975. That year she became an editor for the Doubleday publishing company in New York.

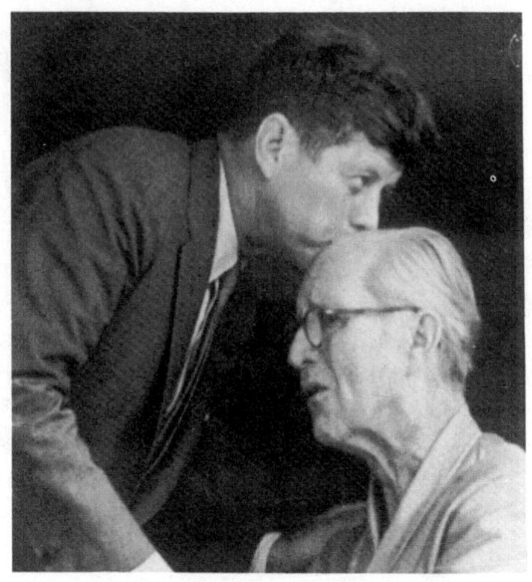

John F. Kennedy and his father, Joseph P. Kennedy, Cape Cod, summer 1963 (courtesy of the John F. Kennedy Library)

LYNDON B. JOHNSON

Lyndon B. Johnson married Claudia Alta "Lady Bird" Taylor on November 17, 1934, in San Antonio, Texas. The couple had two daughters, Lynda Bird and Luci Baines. Lynda Bird married Charles Robb, later governor of Virginia, in a White House ceremony in 1967. Luci Baines married and divorced Patrick Nugent, then married investment banker Ian Turpin and settled in Toronto, Canada.

Lady Bird retired with her husband to their Texas ranch after he refused to run for another presidential term in 1968. Since his death in 1973 she has worked as chairman of the LBJ Company, a radio and cable television enterprise, as a board member of the LBJ Library, as a regent of the University of Texas, and as a member of the National Parks Advisory Board. In 1988 she moved to Austin, Texas.

RICHARD M. NIXON

On June 21, 1940, Richard M. Nixon married Thelma Catherine "Pat" Ryan in Riverside, California. They had two daughters, Patricia and Julie. Patricia married Edward Cox in a White House Rose Garden ceremony in 1971. Julie

Dwight D. Eisenhower's grandson, David, and David's wife, Julie Nixon Eisenhower, defending Julie's father during the Watergate scandal (courtesy of the Nixon Presidential Materials Project)

married David Eisenhower, grandson of the former president, in 1968. She lives in Pennsylvania and has edited and authored several books, including a well-regarded biography of her mother, *Pat Nixon: The Untold Story* (1986).

Richard and Pat Nixon retired to San Clemente, California, then New York and New Jersey, after Nixon's resignation from the presidency in 1973.

GERALD R. FORD

Gerald R. Ford and Elizabeth Anne "Betty" Bloomer were married in Grand Rapids, Michigan, on October 15, 1948. They had three sons and a daughter. The eldest, Michael Gerald, became a seminary student and then a Christian activist. In 1981 he was appointed student affairs director at Wake Forest University. The second child, John ("Jack") worked as a ranger at Yellowstone National Park while his father was president and became an assistant to the editor of *Outside* magazine and then copublisher of a California newspaper. The third child, Steven, has become an actor, working most recently as a regular on the soap opera "The Young and the Restless." The fourth, Susan, is a photographer. She married one of Gerald Ford's secret service agents.

Betty Ford won the admiration of many Americans for her outspokenness on topics of social concern during her husband's presidential term. She also undoubtedly saved many lives as a result of her forthright commentary on her own operation for breast cancer. After that episode she sought treatment for alcohol and drug abuse and later founded the Betty Ford Clinic for drug and alcohol dependents.

JIMMY CARTER

Jimmy Carter married Eleanor Rosalynn Smith in Plains, Georgia, on July 7, 1946. He was twenty-one and an ensign in the U.S. Navy; she was eighteen and about to become a student of interior decorating at Georgia Southwestern College in Americus, Georgia. Jimmy and Rosalynn Carter had four children—three sons and a daughter.

The eldest son, John ("Jack") earned degrees in nuclear physics and law and then became a lawyer before accepting a position on the Chicago Board of Trade. The second son, James "Chip," worked in his father's peanut business and then founded his own corporate consulting firm based in Decatur, Georgia. The third son, Jeffery, studied city planning and urban geography. He founded a computer consulting firm in 1978. The daughter, Amy, much younger than the other Carter children, won notoriety for giving advice to her father on issues of national prominence during his presidential term. Later, while attending the University of Massachusetts, she was arrested several times for protesting the university's investments in South Africa and on-campus CIA recruitment. While at Massachusetts she became acquainted with activist Abbie Hoffman, then she transferred to Brown University. Brown dismissed her because of poor grades in 1987.

RONALD REAGAN

Ronald Reagan, the first president to be divorced, married actress Jane Wyman in Hollywood, California, on January 26, 1940. The couple had one natural child, Maureen, and adopted a son, Michael. As an adult Maureen became active in the California Republican party, unsuccessfully running for governor of the state in 1982. She wrote an account of her childhood entitled *First Father, First Daughter* in 1989. Michael's business career has been varied and at times unsuccessful. He has met with much success as a professional speedboat racer. His childhood account, published in 1988, is entitled *On the Outside Looking In.*

Ronald Reagan and Jane Wyman divorced in 1948, and Reagan married actress Nancy Davis in the San Fernando Valley on March 4, 1952. They had two children, a daughter and a son. The daughter, Patti, has worked as an actress and has authored a best-selling novel, loosely based on her family, entitled *Home Front* (1986). The son, Ronald, studied ballet and became a television journalist and entertainer.

Nancy and Ronald Reagan retired to California after Reagan's terms as president.

GEORGE BUSH

George Bush married Barbara Pierce on January 6, 1945, in Rye, New York. He was a navy lieutenant on leave; she dropped out of Smith College to marry him. The couple had four sons and a daughter who survived childhood; their first child, Robin, died of leukemia at the age of four.

The Bushes' oldest surviving child, George, served in Vietnam as a pilot for the Texas National Guard. After the war he graduated from Yale University and then from Harvard Business School, with an M.B.A. In 1978 he ran for a U.S. House seat from Texas but was defeated. He formed an oil and gas exploration firm but sold his interest in the business to campaign for his father's presidential bid in 1987-1988. The family's second son, "Jeb," became a bank executive and later a real estate developer based in Miami, Florida. The third son, Neil, founded an oil and gas exploration firm in Denver, Colorado. In 1990 he was implicated in the savings and loan scandal for accepting loans from a savings and loan for which he served as a director. The fourth son, Marvin, worked as a Wall Street investment consultant before founding his own investment firm in 1986. The youngest Bush child, daughter Dorothy, has worked as a travel agent, a caterer, and a bookkeeper for her husband's construction firm in Maine.

Odd Jobs: Occupations of the Presidents Before They Were President

by THOMAS L. CONNELLY

It is interesting to speculate how pre-presidential jobs might have affected America's chief executives. Lawyers, soldiers, surveyors, and teachers; a peanut farmer, a tailor, and a mail room clerk; even an actor has sprung forward to the nation's highest office. A pattern of anything more precise than diversity is hard to discern. Some presidents performed well in their first jobs, showing their potential early on; others were driven into the political arena because they were unable to measure up elsewhere. Some learned to work hard as a result of early struggles; others were born into wealth and seemed preordained. But talent and virtue have not been exclusively the possessions of the presidents of modest origins, incompetence and vice not solely flaws in the wealthy. How much job training has to do with presidential success is open to question: some of the most solidly prepared chief executives ended up botching their presidencies, while some with lackluster records confounded the experts and turned in good terms. The only constants are that it takes work to become president and that no job can truly prepare a person to hold the office. Still, no one, not even the farmer or the actor, has entered the presidency without sound experience.

WASHINGTON: ALL BUSINESS

In 1749 seventeen-year-old George Washington received his license as a land surveyor from the College of William and Mary and was appointed official surveyor of newly formed Culpepper County, Virginia. The practical skills of surveyors brought important order to the tobacco-growing business, and the college-granted license carried a status not unlike the similarly practical American business school degree of the late twentieth century. Washington learned the trade, using a set of instruments that had belonged to his father, during an expedition the previous year chartering the western estate of Virginia proprietor Lord Fairfax in the Shenandoah Valley. He worked three years as a professional surveyor, purchasing more than a few of the land tracts he mapped.

Washington relinquished the job in 1752 upon accepting an appointment by Virginia governor Robert Dinwiddie as district adjutant of the state with the rank of major. He was twenty years old. By that time he had purchased or had inherited some five thousand acres of land and was well on his way to achieving leadership among Virginia farmers.

Washington put his surveying skills to use again in 1770 during his service as a member of the Virginia House of Burgesses, when he led an expedition to the Ohio country to inspect and claim tens of thousands of acres of land for himself and those who served under him during the French and Indian War. Biographer James T. Flexner quotes a later remark of Washington regarding the lucrative land claim: "I might add without much arrogance," wrote the former military hero, "that if it had not been for my unremitted attention to every favorable circumstance, not a single acre of land would ever have been obtained."

Portrait of John Adams by Benjamin Blyth, 1766. Adams was admitted to the Massachusetts bar in 1758 and by the time he sat for Blyth was among Boston's leading attorneys (courtesy of the Massachusetts Historical Society)

The first president entered politics as a member of his colony's House of Burgesses in 1759. Service in the First and Second Continental Congresses in 1774 and 1775 culminated in his appointment in the latter year as commander in chief of the Continental Army. He "retired" in 1783 and then helped lead the American transition to strong federal government as the nation's first president.

JOHN ADAMS: SCHOOLMASTER

John Adams was twenty when he graduated from Harvard College in 1755 and took a job as a schoolteacher in Worcester, Massachusetts. He intended to live the academic life only temporarily and studied law under James Putnam of Worcester while he worked. Adams considered teaching a broadening experience, however, recording in his diary for March 15, 1756, that "my little school, like the great world, is made up of Kings, Politicians, Divines, L.D., Fops, Buffoons, Fiddlers, Sycophants, Fools, Coxcombs, chimney sweepers, and every other character drawn in history or seen in the world." But law and public life held greater attractions. He gained admission to the Massachusetts bar in 1758 and moved back to his hometown, Braintree, Massachusetts.

While Adams built his law practice he continued to find other work. All Braintree males who could contribute were expected to perform some kind of public service, and in 1761 Adams was appointed road surveyor for Braintree, though he had no experience in the job. He also served as a selectman for the town before his first notable legal case—he succeeded in having charges dropped against future patriot John Hancock for allegedly smuggling wine into Boston Harbor—made him a public figure. A distinguished career as a diplomat and vice-president followed before he assumed the presidency.

JEFFERSON: BORN LEADER

Thomas Jefferson inherited Shadwell, his father's one-thousand-acre estate, in 1757, at the age of fourteen. He graduated from the College of William and Mary in Williamsburg at nineteen, and then embarked on a five-year law apprenticeship (a long time by the standards of the day) under George Wythe, who also trained future chief justice John Marshall and future U.S. senator Henry Clay. He was admitted to the Virginia bar in 1767. Jefferson practiced law and managed Shadwell until his election to the House of Burgesses in 1769. Service in the Continental Congress—and the June 1776 charge of drafting the Declaration of American Independence—secured him a place of prominence in Virginia and the nation.

MADISON: A LIFE IN POLITICS

After twenty-year-old James Madison graduated from the College of New Jersey in September 1771 (he remained at the college for six months after graduation, studying Hebrew and ethics), he did not know what to do with himself. He took up the study of law without enthusiasm and entered public life, first as a member of the Orange County Committee of Safety, which his father chaired, then as a colonel in the Virginia militia (he saw no active military duty during the Revolution), then as a delegate to the Virginia Constitutional Convention of 1776. In October 1776 he won a seat in the Virginia House of Delegates. A long and fruitful political career followed.

MONROE: JEFFERSONIAN NATIONALIST

When the American Revolution broke out, the fourth of the Virginia presidents was a seventeen-year-old student at the College of William and Mary in Williamsburg. He left school in March 1776 to join the army, gaining a commission as a lieutenant under Col. Hugh Mercer in the Third Virginia Regiment. The regiment joined the New York headquarters of Gen. George Washington in September. Monroe fought in the battles of Harlem, White Plains, and Trenton during the remainder of the year and was wounded in the Christmas-night Trenton fight.

Monroe resigned from the army in 1778 and returned to Williamsburg to try to raise his own regiment. Unsuccessful in the attempt, he began his long association with then-governor Thomas Jefferson in 1780, when Jefferson appointed him military commissioner of the state and also accepted him as a law student. He read law with Jefferson until 1783, meanwhile winning a seat on the Virginia Council of State in 1782. He served in the Continental Congress from 1783 to 1786, was admitted to the Virginia bar in the latter year, and practiced law in Fredericksburg until 1790. A member of the 1788 Virginia ratifying convention, he voted against the Constitution. He took a vacant seat in the U.S. Senate by appointment in 1790. Service as a U.S. diplomat, Virginia governor, and U.S. secretary of state followed.

JOHN QUINCY ADAMS: PRODIGY

The future sixth president grew up in one of the leading families of Massachusetts politics at one of the most exciting times in American history. As a member of the Massachusetts legislature, his father, the second president, helped lead his colony into revolutionary conflict with England. John Quincy Adams and his mother, Abigail Adams, watched the Battle of Bunker Hill from a nearby high spot. When John Adams accepted the position of minister to France in 1778, John Quincy followed him to Europe and the world of diplomacy, where he remained, except for a brief return in 1779, for seven years. Because he fluently spoke French, the language of the Russian court, in 1781 the fourteen-year-old left school for the Russian capital of St. Petersburg to serve for a year as secretary to Francis Dana, the American minister to Russia. After that he spent some time with his father, then serving as ambassador to the Netherlands, at The Hague.

I have been accustomed all my life to plain dealing and candor, and am not sufficiently versed in the art of political swindling to be prepared for negotiating with an European Minister of State. In other words, besides numerous other deficiencies of which on this occasion I am strongly sensible, I have not the experience *which the proper performance of the duty would require.*

—Letter of John Quincy Adams, U.S. minister to the Netherlands, to his parents, John and Abigail Adams, December 29, 1795

Adams graduated from Harvard in 1787, gained admission to the Massachusetts bar in 1790, and entered diplomatic service in 1794 when President George Washington appointed him American minister to the Netherlands, a position for which his fluent Dutch

Engraving of Andrew Jackson from a portrait painted about 1804, during Jackson's last year of service as judge of the Tennessee Superior Court (Tennessee State Library)

made him particularly suited. In 1797 Washington appointed him minister to Portugal, but before he arrived in Lisbon he learned that his father, the new president, had changed the appointment to Prussia. Adams served in Prussia until the end of his father's administration, then returned to Massachusetts and a seat in the state senate.

JACKSON: A NEW KIND OF PRESIDENT

The first six presidents lived and worked with the privileged classes in their states—Washington, Jefferson, Madison, and Monroe among the plantation elite of Virginia, and the Adamses among the leading citizens of Puritan Massachusetts. Andrew Jackson experienced an entirely different kind of occupational upbringing. His election to the presidency signified the empowerment of a newly representative American electorate and helped prove for many that in the New World a man's merit really did mean more than his station.

His first job was with the military. Jackson was born in the Waxhaw region along the border between North and South Carolina and in 1780, at the age of thirteen, joined the Continental Army in South Carolina as an orderly. He and a brother, Robert, were taken prisoner by the British the following year. The harsh treatment they received at the hands of their captors earned the British the future president's lifelong enmity. When Jackson refused to clean the boots of a British officer, the officer struck him with a sword and left permanent scars. In April 1781, after two weeks in captivity, the brothers were released from a Camden, South Carolina, prisoner-of-war camp, where both had contracted smallpox. Robert died later in the month. Jackson's other brother, Hugh, had died in 1779 during the battle of Stone Ferry, and his mother died in November 1781 while nursing American captives on British prison ships in Charleston. Jackson's father had died before his birth, so the American Revolution left him an orphan.

Jackson lived with two uncles in Charleston after the war. In 1783 he received a legacy of some $300 to $400 from a grandfather who died in Northern Ireland. He gambled that away in Charleston, returned chastened to Waxhaw, and ended up in Salisbury, North Carolina, determined to make something of himself. He began the study of law in December 1784 and was admitted to the North Carolina bar in November 1787. In 1788 he moved to Nashville, Tennessee, and became the prosecuting attorney for the western district of that territory. Jackson served as a delegate to the convention that drafted a constitution for the new state of Tennessee in 1796. He became Tennessee's first U.S. representative in 1796, a Tennessee senator in 1797, and judge of the Tennessee Superior Court in 1798. Then he embarked on the military career that made him presidential material.

YOUTHFUL NONPARTISAN

Martin Van Buren began the study of law at "not more than fifteen or sixteen" years of age and had already taken business in his hometown of Kinderhook by the time of his 1803 admission to the New York bar. At the very beginning of his career he decided to avoid involvement in local party battles, which were manifested in the rivalry between two leading Kinderhook families—the Silvesters on the side of the Federalists, and the Van Nesses on the side of the Democratic-Republicans: the shrewd youth hoped to attract the legal business of both groups.

Complicating Van Buren's strategy of objectivity, however, was the fact that he read for the bar exam in the law office of one of the Silvesters and experienced constant pressure to take the Federalist side in Kinderhook society. He remembered in his "Autobiography" (first published in 1918) that when he refused to participate in a celebration following a Federalist electoral victory, Cornelius Silvester, the brother of his law teacher, "for more than an hour occupied himself in presenting the reasons which ought to induce me to adopt the politicks of the Federal party, and solicited me to do so with a degree of earnestness and obvious concern for my welfare which I could not but respect." Van Buren listened to the argument and politely replied that his course "could not be changed."

VAN BUREN: CAREER POLITICIAN

Martin Van Buren spent his life in politics. Admitted to the New York bar in 1803, at twenty-five years of age, he succeeded his half-brother as surrogate for Columbia County, New York, in 1808. He became a New York state senator in 1812, a U.S. senator in 1821, and governor of New York in 1829. He left the governorship after serving only three months to take the position of secretary of state in Andrew Jackson's presidential administration. He resigned that position as part of a Jackson cabinet shake-up in 1831, which resolved the "petticoat war" over the social status of former barmaid Peggy Eaton, the wife of Jackson's secretary of war. Grateful for Van Buren's support in the matter, Jackson made Van Buren his vice-president in 1833.

WILLIAM HENRY HARRISON: MEDICAL SCHOOL DROPOUT

Under the strong guidance of his father, the ninth president started planning a medical career when he was still a teenager. His studies at Hampden-Sydney College were premedical in nature. In 1790 the seventeen-year-old became an apprentice to Dr. Andrew Leiper of Richmond, Virginia. In 1791 he journeyed to the University of Pennsylvania Medical School, where he studied under Dr. Benjamin Rush. But Harrison did not want to be a doctor. Soon after he arrived in Philadelphia he received the news of his father's death, left school, and joined the army.

Harrison spent the next seven years in the service, then entered politics in his adopted Indiana. Stints as governor of the Northwest Territory and as territorial delegate to the U.S. House of Representatives were followed by a twelve-year tenure as governor of newly formed Indiana Territory beginning in 1800. Harrison became a national hero in the Indian wars of the region toward the end of his service as governor, joined the regular army for the War of 1812, then entered politics again as U.S. representative from Ohio beginning in 1816. Terms as a state senator, U.S. senator, and U.S. minister to Colombia fol-

Engraving from a portrait by John Wesley Jarvis of John Tyler, governor of Virginia from 1825 to 1827

lowed. He missed in his first try for the presidency in 1836 but won a brief chance at the top job in 1840—he died of pneumonia a month after his inauguration.

TYLER: A NEW GENERATION IN VIRGINIA

John Tyler took up where his great Virginia predecessors left off. He enjoyed the privileges of upper-class southern living, entered the legal profession, and assumed a seat in his state's House of Delegates in 1811 at age twenty-one. He became a U.S. representative in 1816, a state representative again in 1823, governor of Virginia in 1825, and a U.S. senator in 1827. One more term as a member of the House of Delegates beginning in 1838 preceded his brief elevation to the vice-presidency.

POLK: CAREER JACKSONIAN

Like so many of the early presidents, James K. Polk's path to the presidency seems inexorable in retrospect. But Polk was the first dark horse to win the nomination of his party, and without the help of Andrew Jackson, whose policies Polk had strongly supported as a leader in the House of Representatives, he never would have made it.

All along the eleventh president held political ambitions. His studies at the University of North Carolina prepared him to read law, and he became clerk of the Tennessee Senate in 1819, when he was twenty-four. Election to the state house of representatives in 1823 followed. In 1825 Polk won election to the U.S. House. Ten years later he became Speaker. Throughout his long House career he faithfully supported Jackson, the political leader of his state. Controversy back home led to Polk's resignation in 1839 and his election to the governorship of Tennessee later that year. His political career appeared over after his defeat for reelection in 1841 and another defeat in 1843. But a deadlocked Democratic National Convention and the counsel of Old Hickory resulted in his nomination to national candidacy in 1844.

TAYLOR: HERO OF THE MEXICAN WAR

President Polk's greatest achievement in the eyes of his Democratic party contemporaries was the conquest of Mexico. Ironically, that military victory elevated to the presidency a career soldier loyal to the other party, the Whigs. Zachary Taylor, "Old Rough and Ready," joined the U.S. Army in 1808, when he was twenty-four (having already served two years in the Kentucky militia) and left its service in 1848 ranked as a major general and revered by his soldiers and the people for his victory over Mexican general Santa Anna at Buena Vista. The Whigs, led by Henry Clay and Daniel Webster, knew from their previous experience with William Henry Harrison that Taylor's record as a military hero far outweighed the somewhat disturbing fact that he had never voted in a presidential elec-

Engraving from a portrait by Charles Fenderich of Tennessee governor James K. Polk, who served as governor from 1839 to 1841 and lost two successive reelection bids before winning election to the presidency (Library of Congress).

tion and could demonstrate no clear allegiance to Whig principles.

FILLMORE: TRULY A LOG CABIN PRESIDENT

Millard Fillmore was born in a log cabin in the wilderness of New York State. A fourteen-year-old in a poor farm family, he took his first job as an apprentice to a cloth dresser, but he was ill-treated and left—"tearful and terrorized," he later wrote—after four months. At fifteen he was apprenticed to a wool carder. When the village of New Hope, New York, opened a circulating library, seventeen-year-old Fillmore discovered the joys of self-education. In town he also met his future wife, Abigail Powers, the daughter of a local minister. She expanded his horizons.

Meanwhile Fillmore's father convinced a lawyer to accept young Millard as a temporary clerk in his firm if the boy could obtain a leave of absence from his wool-carding apprenticeship, which he did. That taste of the legal profession convinced Fillmore that much lay beyond his narrow focus, but his father had arranged only a two-month stay. Fillmore was surprised to receive an offer from the lawyer to read law in his office if he could remove his apprentice's obligation, and he took a three-month job as a schoolteacher in 1818 in order to purchase the remaining time of his apprenticeship. In 1823 he began his legal practice. In 1829 he won election as an Anti-Mason to the New York state assembly. He entered national service as a Whig U.S. representative beginning in 1833. Though Fillmore had experienced little formal education, in 1846 he became chancellor of the University of Buffalo. He left the House to become comptroller of New York in 1848, then entered the vice-presidency in the Taylor administration in 1849. Taylor's death opened the door of the president's office in 1850.

PIERCE: NEW HAMPSHIRE NATIONALIST

Franklin Pierce's father, Benjamin Pierce, was a leader in New Hampshire political society and once a governor of the state. Not surprisingly, his son followed a career path meant to establish himself as his father's successor. After a shaky start at Bowdoin College, Pierce read law under a succession of promi-

---

His first case was a failure, and perhaps a somewhat marked one. But it is remembered that this defeat, however mortifying at the moment, did serve to make him aware of the latent resources of the mind, the full command of which he was far from having yet attained. To a friend, an older practitioner, who addressed him with some expression of condolence and encouragement, Pierce replied, "I do not need that. I will try nine hundred and ninety-nine cases, if clients continue to trust me, and if I fail just as I have today, I will try a thousandth. I shall live to argue cases in this court house in a manner that will mortify neither myself nor my friends."

—*Nathaniel Hawthorne,* Life of Franklin Pierce *(1852)*

---

nent members of the profession: first with John Burnham of Hillsborough, New Hampshire, the Pierces' hometown; then with future Supreme Court justice Levi Woodbury; then with Samuel Howe; and finally with Edmund Parker. Pierce was finally admitted to the New Hampshire bar at the age of twenty-three in September 1827.

Soon afterward he entered politics. Pierce served as a representative in the New Hampshire state legislature beginning in 1829; he took the position of Speaker of the House in 1831. He won election to the U.S. House of Representatives in 1832 and served from 1833 to 1837. From there he moved on to the Senate. For several reasons, including his wife's opposition to his political career, he resigned his Senate seat in 1842. Returning to the practice of law in his new home of Concord, New Hampshire, he worked as chairman of the state Democratic party for the election of James K. Polk as president, and subsequently became New Hampshire's U.S. district attorney. During the Mexican War Pierce served honorably, then came his successful dark horse presidential candidacy and his tenure as leader of a nation headed toward war. Pierce's attempt to satisfy the "slave power" in Congress by supporting passage of the Kansas-Nebraska Act demonstrated his fidelity to the idea of Union but made him an object of scorn in his hometown and his state.

BUCHANAN: CHANCE POLITICIAN

The fifteenth president entered politics largely in an effort to escape the grief caused by the death of his one true love. Anne Colman's December 1819 demise came after the couple broke their engagement after a quarrel that remains a mystery to historians. Buchanan had been practicing law in Lancaster, Pennsylvania, since his admission to the Pennsylvania bar at the age of twenty in 1812 and had even served a term in the Pennsylvania state house from 1815 to 1816; with the need for the economic stability of a law practice removed and the need for the distractions of politics established, he consented to run for Congress. He entered the U.S. House of Representatives in 1821 and served until President Andrew Jackson appointed him U.S. minister to Russia at the end of 1831. Back from Russia in 1833, he was elected U.S. senator in 1834. When James K. Polk entered the presidency, Buchanan took the position of Polk's secretary of state. He spent some leisure years after he lost the Democratic presidential nomination in 1848, then became President Franklin Pierce's minister to Great Britain in 1853. With the decline of Pierce's popularity as a result of his support of the Kansas-Nebraska Act, Buchanan emerged as a top contender for the Democratic presidential nomination in 1856. He accepted the call and won the election.

LINCOLN: SELF-MADE MAN

America's greatest chief executive was by all standard measures also the most inappropriate figure to reach the position. Abraham Lincoln enjoyed few of the advantages of life and scuttled around from job to job during much of his early career. Only with great effort he entered into a successful law practice, after which he inhabited the political periphery in his home state of Illinois until events no one could have predicted made him the best man for the worst job in the nation. On the other hand, the failures in Lincoln's career have been overemphasized. He was never really out of politics. And when the nation reached its time of crisis, the voters chose him to be president.

Lincoln stepped out on his own as a nineteen-year-old flatboat entrepreneur in 1828, making money by floating produce and other goods down the Mississippi River to New Orleans. Life on the Mississippi revealed the tragedy of slavery for the first time to the free-soil midwesterner. He settled in New Salem, Illinois, in 1831 and became a clerk in a general store, earning fifteen dollars a month plus the opportunity to sleep in the rear of the building. His boss closed down the store, and Lincoln enlisted in the Illinois militia, serving as a captain in the Black Hawk war and shedding blood, he later remembered, only to the mosquitoes. He came back to New Salem after his brief military service and became part owner of a general store that failed.

Meanwhile he made his first run for political office, carrying ninety-two percent of the hometown vote in a districtwide race for the Illinois state legislature in which he finished eighth overall. Appointed in 1833 by President Andrew Jackson to the position of postmaster of New Salem, he supplemented his fifty-five-dollar monthly income by performing odd jobs such as splitting rails and working as a mill hand. Later he recalled that he split rails only so he would never again have to split rails, but his down-home industriousness provided an attractive political image. With little formal education, he also began the study of law.

A supporter of Henry Clay from the beginning of his political career, Lincoln won election to the Illinois legislature in 1834 and won reelection in 1836, 1838, and 1840. He gained admission to the Illinois bar in 1836 and moved to Springfield, Illinois, in 1837, where he steadily built a law practice that proved especially lucrative after he lost his fourth bid for reelection to the legislature in 1842. During the years away from politics from 1842 to 1846 he solidified his image as a leader in his community and his state.

Lincoln entered the U.S. House of Representatives in 1847 as a Clay Whig opposed to the Mexican War. He then declined to run for another term and turned down offers to serve as secretary and governor of the Oregon Territory. By the early 1850s he was one of the leading lawyers in his state and a respected fount of political wisdom. He won another term as a state legislator in 1854 but resigned immediately to run unsuccessfully for the U.S. Senate. He formed his mature views on the slavery question after the Whig party disintegrated over the Kansas-Nebraska issue, and he joined the Republican party in 1856. He was nominated by the Illinois legislature (but not by the Republican party) for vice-president in 1856 and campaigned for the Republicans that year. He ran in a losing effort against Stephen Douglas for the Senate in 1858 in a contest that produced the most highly regarded series of debates in American political history, and then accepted the call of his new party in 1860.

ANDREW JOHNSON: TAILOR'S APPRENTICE

Even by comparison with his low-born predecessors Andrew Jackson, Millard Fillmore, and Abraham Lincoln, Andrew Johnson had an unpromising beginning. When he was fourteen he and his brother signed on as tailor's apprentices in Raleigh, North Carolina. Two years later the harshly treated boys broke their contract. The tailor offered a bounty for their return, indicating his estimate of the future president's promise: "Ran away from the Subscriber, on the night of the 15th instant, two apprentice boys legally bound, named William and Andrew Johnson. . . . I will pay the above Reward [ten dollars] to any person who will deliver said apprentices to me in Raleigh, or I will give the above Reward for Andrew Johnson alone." The boys got away.

By the age of seventeen Andrew Johnson had tailored in Laurens, South Carolina, and Greeneville, Tennessee. Johnson set up a tailor shop there as well. He got married at eighteen (his wife helped him learn how to read) and at twenty became an alderman in his adopted hometown. Two years later, in 1830, he was elected mayor, and he occupied that office until 1833. His Greeneville tailor shop had by that time become a sort of local political center. Johnson supported the populist program of President Andrew Jackson and

Andrew Johnson's tailor shop in Greeneville, Tennessee, which served as a center for local politics after Johnson's election as mayor of Greeneville in 1830 (National Archives)

won election to Tennessee's legislature in 1835. Defeated for reelection in 1837 because of his opposition to internal improvements, he won another term in 1839. He took a seat in the state senate in 1841 and a seat in the U.S. House of Representatives in 1843. Representative Johnson became Governor Johnson in 1853 and Senator Johnson in 1857. He was the only U.S. senator from a seceded state to retain his seat during the Civil War. President Abraham Lincoln made him military governor of reconstructing Tennessee in 1862 and chose him as his running mate on the Union-Republican presidential ticket in 1864. Johnson served as vice-president only about a month before Lincoln's death elevated him to the presidency.

GRANT: FAILED SOLDIER

Ulysses S. Grant was an aimless seventeen-year-old when he entered the U.S. Military Academy in 1839. He did average work there, and the army refused his request to enter the cavalry upon graduation. Instead, Second Lieutenant Grant became an infantry commander and shuttled from one unexciting post to another. A drinking incident forced him out of the service in 1854.

Grant tried farming near St. Louis, Missouri, without much success. By 1856 the family was so destitute that Grant resorted to selling firewood on the streets of the city. He finally sold the farm in 1858 and formed a real estate partnership that was as unsuccessful as his other pursuits.

At the end of his rope, Grant moved to Galena, Illinois, in 1860 to work as a clerk in his father's leather goods store. When the Civil War broke out he enlisted in the Illinois Infantry. He rose with great speed to command all the Union armies by 1864, emerged from the war America's greatest hero, and attained the presidency in 1869.

HAYES: OHIO LAWYER

A college and law school graduate, twenty-three-year-old Rutherford B.

Hayes was admitted to the Ohio bar in 1845 and established himself as a Cincinnati lawyer with a growing practice by 1849. He was appointed a city solicitor in 1858, served in the Civil War with distinction, and emerged from the war a major general and a local hero. Before he left uniform in 1865 he won election to the U.S. House of Representatives. Then came the governorship of his state, an office he occupied for a term from 1868 to 1872 and a partial term from 1876 to 1877. He resigned from his second gubernatorial term after he won a disputed election to the presidency.

Representative James A. Garfield, Republican presidential nominee, June 10, 1880 (Smithsonian Institution)

GARFIELD: OHIO LAWYER

James A. Garfield taught school before he became a lawyer and entered politics. A twenty-four-year-old in 1856, he took a position as instructor in classical languages at Hiram Eclectic Institute, an institution he attended and taught at previously. The next year he took the position of president of the institute, an office he held until the beginning of the Civil War. He also served as a state senator from 1859 to 1861. Meanwhile he read law and was admitted to the Ohio bar in 1860.

After two years of distinguished service in the Civil War, Garfield entered the U.S. House of Representatives. He made a career of his House service, leaving office only to campaign for the presidency in 1880. Garfield started on a promising presidential term before an assassin shot him in July 1881. He died the following September.

ARTHUR: UNLIKELY REFORMER

Like his slain predecessor Garfield, Chester A. Arthur worked in education for a short time after he graduated from college. But brief stays as principal at North Pownall Academy in Vermont from 1851 to 1852 and at Cohoes Academy in New York from 1852 to 1853 proved unsatisfying, so after admission to the New York bar in 1854 the twenty-four-year-old future president joined a New York City law firm. He left his growing practice to serve in the military during the Civil War and after the war rose to become a force in Republican party politics in the state of New York. He worked as counsel to the New York City Tax Commission in 1869 and 1870 and then in 1871 was appointed collector of the Port of New York, a lucrative post that introduced Arthur to the attractions of machine politics as orchestrated by New York senator Roscoe P. Conkling. The collector was expected to reserve a portion of available jobs for Republican party patrons and to acquiesce to various salary kickback schemes. New president Rutherford B. Hayes decided to take on the "spoilsmen" and demanded the resignation of Arthur, among other of Conkling's lieutenants. When Arthur refused to leave his post quietly, Hayes suspended him, and he returned to the practice of law in New York.

Arthur became the Republican vice-presidential nominee to please the con-

HE SPARED THE ROD

Chester Arthur, teacher and principal at North Pownal Academy in Vermont from 1851 to 1852, was in the habit of requiring his students to recite bits of memorized verse before examination-day assemblages of parents gathered to measure their children's progress. As one of those examination-day recitals approached, bashful eight-year-old student Asa Stillman, pleaded with his teacher for a reprieve; he was under the impression that students were supposed to compose the poetry they recited and lacked the confidence to try. On the day before the examination Arthur asked him to stay after school. Asa expected "to receive the full benefit of the birch rod." Instead, Arthur asked, "Don't you think you can speak a piece tomorrow?"

"I haven't one," Asa replied.

"Will you learn one if I write it down for you?"

"I'd try, but I can't read writing well enough."

"Then I'll print it for you":

Pray, how shall I a little lad
 In speaking make a figure?
You are but jesting, I'm afraid,
 Do wait until I get bigger.
But since you wish to hear my part,
 And urge me to begin it,
I'll strive for praise with all my art,
 Though small my chance to win it.

The next day Asa successfully recited his poem to the praise of parents and teacher.

In 1883, after Arthur became president of the United States, Asa Stillman told a reporter his story and also revealed that in gratitude for Arthur's kindness he had named his son Chester Arthur Stillman.

servative Stalwart wing of the party. He served as vice-president for only six and a half months. Observers believed his accession to the chief executive's office hailed the beginning of a dark cycle in national politics. But Arthur proved equal to the tasks of the presidency.

CLEVELAND: NEW YORK LAWYER

After the death of his father forced an end to his formal education at the age of sixteen, Grover Cleveland worked as a clerk and teacher for the New York Institute for the Blind in 1853 and 1854. He decided to seek his fortune in Cleveland, Ohio, but on the way the future president stopped at an uncle's house in Buffalo, New York, liked what he saw, and cut short his journey. He helped his uncle, editor for the *American Shorthorn Handbook*, while he studied law. Admitted to the New York bar in 1859, he took his first public job in 1871 as sheriff of Erie County, New York. One of his tasks as sheriff was to act as public executioner—Cleveland personally hanged two men convicted of murder.

Increasingly prominent in Buffalo legal circles and state politics, Cleveland won a term as Buffalo mayor in 1882 and then was elected governor of New York in 1883. The Democratic nomination for president came in 1884. Defeated by Benjamin Harrison in his bid for reelection to the presidency in 1888,

Grover Cleveland, mayor of Buffalo, New York, in 1882 (courtesy of the Firestone Library, Princeton University)

Cleveland became the only man to win nonconsecutive presidential terms when he returned Harrison's favor in 1892.

BENJAMIN HARRISON: INDIANA LAWYER

After graduating from Miami University in Ohio in 1852, nineteen-year-old Benjamin Harrison, grandson of the ninth president, studied law and was admitted to the Indiana bar in 1854. Before the Civil War he was already prominent in Indiana Republican politics. He served as his state's supreme court reporter in 1861 and 1862 before entering military service; after the war he resumed his reporter's job and his law practice. At the state convention he lost the 1872 Republican gubernatorial nomination to Thomas Browne.

Harrison's political rise occurred after he became chairman of the Indiana delegation to the 1880 Republican national convention. The Indiana legislature elected him U.S. senator after James A. Garfield assumed the presidency. His own nomination to the Republican presidential ticket came in 1888.

MCKINLEY: OHIO LAWYER

William McKinley was admitted to the Ohio bar in 1867 at the age of twenty-four and immediately began his rise in local and state politics. He served as Stark County, Ohio, prosecutor from 1869 to 1871, resumed his private law practice, then won election to the U.S. House of Representatives in 1876. He lost his 1882 reelection bid, then won another term in the House in 1885. A term as Ohio governor from 1892 to 1896 preceded his election to the presidency.

As with all other forms of work, so on the round-up, a man of ordinary power, who nevertheless does not shirk things because they are disagreeable or irksome, soon earns his place. There were crack riders and ropers who, just because they felt such overweening pride in their own prowess, were not really very valuable men.

—Theodore Roosevelt: An Autobiography *(1918)*

THEODORE ROOSEVELT: RANCHER

Of all the presidents Theodore Roosevelt enjoyed the richest and most diverse prepresidential career. After displaying an interest in natural history during his Harvard years, Roosevelt entered Columbia Law School in 1880. He dropped out as a twenty-three-year-old in 1881 to run for the New York state assembly. Roosevelt served three one-year terms and seemed headed for a prominent political career when his wife and mother died, throwing him into a depression. He headed for the Dakota territory and life as a cattle rancher. For a while he served as deputy sheriff of Billings County in what later became the state of Montana. Back in New York City in the summer of 1886, he ran for New York mayor in the fall, lost, and turned his full attention to writing, publishing biographies of Thomas Hart Benton (1886) and Gouverneur Morris

PRINCETON PROGRESSIVE

In 1902 Woodrow Wilson took over the presidency of Princeton University and promptly initiated a modernization program. First he convinced the administration to discard the lecture-hall method of teaching in favor of the "preceptorial" concept: instructors guided the reading of small groups of students instead of lecturing to large groups. He also reorganized departments and the curriculum.

He met with opposition, however, in his effort to abolish the social eating clubs then popular on the Princeton campus. He proposed to replace the cliquish eating clubs with dining halls in which students of all classes could gather for meals. "We are not seeking to form better clubs," he said of his suggestion, "but academic communities. We are making a university, not devising a method of social pleasure." Princeton alumni and the Board of Trustees rejected the plan, on the grounds that Wilson had acted dictatorially in making the proposal and also because they thought abolishing the eating clubs would "destroy the spirit of Princeton."

(1888) and the second in a series of books on wilderness life (1888). In 1889 he gained an appointment as a member of the U.S. Civil Service Commission from President Benjamin Harrison, for whom he had campaigned in 1888.

Roosevelt took the job of president of the New York City Police Board in 1895 and attacked the city's chronic problem of corruption with what he had by then shown to be his characteristic vigor. Terms as assistant U.S. secretary of the navy from 1897 to 1898 and governor of New York from 1898 to 1900 preceded his nomination to the vice-presidency. President William McKinley's 1901 assassination put "that damned cowboy" (as Senator Mark Hanna called him) in the White House, at forty-two the youngest man ever to occupy the presidency (John F. Kennedy, forty-three, was the youngest elected president).

TAFT: JUDICIAL CAREER

William Howard Taft worked as a courthouse reporter for the *Cincinnati Commercial* during his law school days from 1878 to 1880. After his admission to the New York bar later in 1880 the twenty-three-year-old took advantage of his father's political connections to become assistant prosecutor of Hamilton County, Ohio, in 1881 and 1882 and collector of internal revenue in Ohio's First District from 1882 to 1883. He started a law partnership after that, then served as Hamilton County assistant solicitor from 1885 to 1886. He served as judge of the Cincinnati Superior Court from 1887 to 1890, U.S. solicitor general from 1890 to 1892, and judge of the Sixth U.S. Circuit Court from 1892 to 1900. From 1896 to 1900 he also served as professor of law and dean of the University of Cincinnati Law School.

Taft got into politics first as commissioner and then as governor-general of the Philippines. He left the latter job in 1904 to become U.S. secretary of war under President Theodore Roosevelt. Roosevelt handpicked Taft as his successor in 1908.

WILSON: PROFESSOR AND COLLEGE PRESIDENT

Woodrow Wilson was a sickly student. Poor health forced him at the age of eighteen to leave Davidson College in 1874, after one year. He ended up graduating with the College of (Princeton) New Jersey's class of 1879 and entered the University of Virginia Law School. But he found law studies a bore and a chore and dropped out, again for health reasons, after one year. He continued to study law on his own, however, and gained admission to the Virginia bar in

Warren G. Harding, one-term teacher at the White Schoolhouse, Marion, Ohio, 1882

1882, but he found the law unfulfilling. So, he enrolled as a graduate student at Baltimore's Johns Hopkins University in 1883 and took a teaching position at Bryn Mawr College in 1885. He also earned his Ph.D. in history from Johns Hopkins that year.

In 1888 Wilson moved from Bryn Mawr to Wesleyan University, where aside from his teaching duties he also coached the football team. In 1890 he took a position as professor of jurisprudence and political economy at Princeton. In 1902 he became president of the university. Progressive Democrats in New Jersey pushed the university president to run for the governorship of the state in 1910, and he won. Nomination to the Democratic presidential ticket and victory in November 1912 followed.

HARDING: NEWSPAPERMAN

Warren G. Harding's first job after graduation from college in 1882 was as a teacher at the White Schoolhouse in Marion, Ohio. The twenty-one-year-old found teaching entirely too challenging considering the poor salary and moved after one term into positions more worthy of his talents—first into an insurance salesman's job, then a reporter's position at the *Marion Mirror*. In 1884 Harding and two partners purchased the *Marion Star*, which became Harding's personal sounding board.

The publisher first entered politics at the state level, winning two terms as Ohio state senator from 1899 to 1903. A term as lieutenant governor of Ohio came next, after which Harding went home to his newspaper. A term in the U.S. Senate beginning in 1915 put him in a position to emerge as a dark horse presidential candidate in 1920. With the possible exception of George Washington, Harding may be the only president who won election because his supporters thought he looked like a president.

Do the day's work. If it be to protect the rights of the weak, whoever objects, do it. If it be to help a powerful corporation better serve the people, whatever the opposition, do that. Expect to be called a stand-patter, but don't be a stand-patter. Don't hesitate to be as revolutionary as science. Don't hesitate to be as reactionary as the multiplication table. Don't expect to build up the weak by pulling down the strong. Don't hurry to legislate. Give administration a chance to catch up with legislation.

—Calvin Coolidge, Massachusetts state senator, 1914

COOLIDGE: SMOOTH RISE

After graduating from Amherst College in 1895, twenty-five-year-old Calvin Coolidge studied law for two years and was admitted to the Massachusetts bar in 1897. He served on the Northampton, Massachusetts, City Council from 1899 to 1900, as city solicitor from 1900 to 1902, as Hampshire County clerk of courts briefly in 1903, and as chairman of Northampton's Republican party in 1904. He ran unsuccessfully for a seat on the Northampton School Board in 1905.

Herbert Hoover during his initial stint as a mining engineer, in Coolgardie, Australia, from 1896 to 1899 (Berton W. Crandell Photograph Collection)

Coolidge followed two one-year terms as a member of the Massachusetts General Court in 1907 and 1908 with two single-year terms as Northampton's mayor in 1910 and 1911. He became a state senator in 1912 and lieutenant governor in 1916. The governorship followed in 1919 and the vice-presidency of the United States in 1921.

HOOVER: MINING ENGINEER, HUMANITARIAN

The gap between Herbert Hoover's success before he assumed the presidency and his seeming failure as chief executive is wider than any other president's. After graduating from Stanford University as part of its first class in 1895, Hoover embarked upon a career in mining, first as a laborer and then as an office worker. In 1896, aged twenty-four, he accepted a position as a mining engineer with Bewick, Moreing & Company and moved to Coolgardie, Australia, charged with inspecting and evaluating the firm's potential purchases. He was transferred to China in 1899 to do the same job and then returned to Australia in 1902. Before he left mining he spent time in India, South Africa, Russia, and other countries as well.

Hoover first entered public service in 1914 as head of the American Relief Committee, responsible for assisting the thousands of Americans left stranded by the outbreak of hostilities in Europe. Among many other positions, he became chairman of the Commission for the Relief of Belgium in 1914, U.S. food administrator in 1917, U.S. director-general for the relief and reconstruction of Europe in 1918, and director of the American Relief Administration in 1919. Also in 1919 he founded the Hoover Institution on War, Revolution, and Peace at Stanford University.

Considered for the Republican presidential nomination in 1920, Hoover settled for the position of secretary of commerce in the administrations of Presidents Harding and Coolidge. By the end of Coolidge's term no one in Hoover's party seriously challenged him for the top spot. He assumed the presidency in triumph in 1929 and left it in disgrace in 1933.

FRANKLIN D. ROOSEVELT: PATRICIAN, HUMANITARIAN

Franklin D. Roosevelt was admitted to the New York bar in 1907 before he graduated from Columbia Law School. He practiced law with the New York firm of Carter, Ledyard, and Milburn until 1911, when he was elected a New York state senator. His support of the progressive program in New York politics gained him the attention of president-elect Woodrow Wilson, who made him assistant U.S. secretary of the navy in the Wilson administration. In 1920 he resigned that position to run unsuccessfully for vice-president on the Democratic ticket with James M. Cox.

After the defeat he reentered the law profession with the firm of Emmet, Marvin, and Roosevelt and then was struck down by polio in 1921. His speech nominating Alf Landon for president at the 1924 Democratic national convention marked his coming-out after three years of grueling therapy. After the convention he worked as a lawyer in partnership with D. Basil O'Conner. He nominated Landon for president again in 1928.

The year 1928 also brought Roosevelt's own political resurgence. He won the Democratic nomination for governor of New York and a narrow victory in the general election. As a Depression-era governor he enacted many of the programs—farm credit relief, unemployment insurance, a reduced working week, workmen's compensation programs—that made his New Deal presidency so politically successful. He went into the 1932 Democratic convention as the front-runner for the presidential nomination and overwhelmingly defeated Herbert Hoover to win the presidency. He spent the rest of his life as the nation's leader.

TRUMAN: WINDING ROAD

Harry S Truman took a winding road to the presidency. He graduated from an Independence, Missouri, high school as a seventeen-year-old in 1901, took a job as a timekeeper for a railroad contractor, left that for a position in the mailroom of the *Kansas City Star* newspaper, left that to become a Kansas City bank clerk, and left that to work as a bank bookkeeper. In 1905, in his second year as a bookkeeper, he joined the Missouri National Guard and served until 1911. In 1906 he left bank work to run his father's farm near Grandview, Missouri, where he remained until he reenlisted in the Guard in May 1917.

Truman's National Guard unit was nationalized, and he went to France. He first saw action in September 1918 and reputedly fired one of the last shots of World War I on November 11.

THE HARD SELL

After gaining his discharge from the army in 1919, Harry Truman and his former canteen sergeant, Eddie Jacobson, opened a haberdashery in Kansas City, Missouri. Truman scraped together his share of the capital—$15,000—mostly from loans. During the first two years, the business thrived, grossing $70,000 in the first year.

Eddie Jacobson outshone his partner at selling. After he became president, Truman loved to tell the story of how Jacobson sold "a big Swedish fellow" some underwear. When the Swede asked for a set of heavy underwear, Jacobson showed him the heaviest the partners had in stock. The customer said it was not heavy enough. So Jacobson looked around on the shelves and found a set of exactly the same weight but of a different color. He explained, "These will cost you a couple of dollars more. I didn't know you wanted to pay that much." Truman remembered being unable to keep a straight face and had to walk to the back of the store to keep out of sight as the Swede happily handed over the money.

After the war Truman went back to Kansas City and established a haberdashery that went out of business during the recession of 1922. At about that time he won election as judge of Jackson County, Missouri. He sold automobile club memberships between 1924, when he was defeated in a reelection bid, and 1926, when he was elected Jackson County's presiding judge. While he was a judge Truman served as president of the Greater Kansas City Plan Association beginning in 1930 and reemployment director for the Federal Emergency Relief Administration beginning in 1933.

Elected to the U.S. Senate in 1935,

Truman pledged to support the New Deal, which he did while remaining free of the corruption that tainted Missouri's Democratic party boss, Thomas J. Pendergast, the man who made it all possible for Truman. In the Senate he gained a reputation for integrity, attracting attention during World War II by exposing billions in waste through an investigation of army procurement procedures. President Roosevelt wanted him for the vice-presidency in 1944, and Truman accepted knowing full well that the president might not make it through his fourth term.

EISENHOWER: THE NEW GRANT

America's greatest military leader experienced little of the glories of military life until the crisis of war brought out the best in him. Dwight D. Eisenhower left the military in 1948 lauded as the hero of the Western world and assumed the largely honorary position of president of Columbia University. In 1951 he took the position of supreme commander of the North Atlantic Treaty Organization. He could have had either presidential nomination in 1952 but felt more a Republican than a Democrat. His two-term presidency, unlike the tenure of another national military hero nearly a century earlier, was often successful and notably free of scandal.

KENNEDY: HIS FATHER'S SON

Like all of Joseph Kennedy's sons, John F. Kennedy lived in large part to please his father, a self-made millionaire frustrated by his own political ambitions. The son, after a brief career as a journalist upon his discharge from the navy, won election to the U.S. House of Representatives in 1947 and the U.S. Senate in 1953. A narrow presidential victory over Richard M. Nixon in 1960 culminated his seemingly effortless rise. He joked after the election that his father did not buy a single vote more than was necessary.

LYNDON B. JOHNSON: AMBITIOUS AND IDEALISTIC

The slain Kennedy's successor always resented the ease with which the Kennedy brothers found their success. Johnson had to work much harder. Who got his hands dirtier is open to debate.

Johnson struggled to get his college education and took his first real job, teaching in 1928-1929 at a predominantly Mexican-American school in Cotulla, Texas, to help pay for college extension courses he took there. After his 1930 graduation he taught school in Pearsall, Texas, and Houston, Texas, before leaving the educational field in 1931 to serve as U.S. senator Richard M. Kleberg's secretary. He entered public service as Texas director of the National Youth Administration from 1935 to 1937, then he ran successfully as a Roosevelt loyalist for a seat in the U.S. House of Representatives. He was defeated in a bid for the U.S. Senate in 1941 but came back to win a suspicious victory on his second try in 1948.

In the Senate Johnson emerged as a leader of the southern liberal wing of the Democratic party and became Senate majority leader in 1955. In his position as majority leader he pushed, first gently, then forcefully, for the passage of the first civil rights acts in twentieth-century national politics. He also supported President Dwight Eisenhower's internationalist foreign policy and emerged as a strong advocate of a national space program. He finished second to Kennedy for the Democratic presidential nomination in 1960 and accepted the second spot on the ticket. Johnson completed the term of the assassinated Kennedy and won a landslide victory in the next election.

NIXON: DETERMINED

Richard M. Nixon passed the California bar exam in 1937 and practiced law as a member of the firm of Wingert and Bewley and then with Bewley, Knoop, and Nixon until he joined the military

Gerald R. Ford during his summer as a ranger at Yellowstone National Park, 1936 (National Park Service)

in World War II. In 1940 he and partners started a frozen orange juice company that failed within two years.

After serving in Washington, D.C., with the Office of Price Administration for a few months in 1942, Nixon grew disillusioned with the inefficiency of government bureaucracy and joined the navy. He left the service in 1946 and ran successfully for the U.S. House of Representatives, where he remained until he won a seat in the U.S. Senate in 1950. Two years later Republican presidential nominee Dwight D. Eisenhower wanted someone young and conservative from the West as his running mate.

Nixon lost the presidency in 1960 in a close race with John F. Kennedy. When he lost a race for governor of California two years later he promised the press, "You won't have Dick Nixon to kick around anymore." But he came back in 1968 to win the first of two presidential terms.

FORD: STEADY SUBSTITUTE

Beginning in 1941 Gerald R. Ford practiced law in Grand Rapids, Michigan, until he enlisted in the U.S. Army for World War II. He went back to the law in 1946 and then won a seat in the U.S. House of Representatives in 1949. There he remained, as minority leader after 1965, until Nixon called him to the vice-presidency in 1973.

CARTER: POLITICAL NOVICE

Jimmy Carter started out in the navy from 1946 to 1953 before leaving the service to take over his late father's peanut farm in his hometown of Plains, Georgia. He entered politics as a Georgia state senator in 1963, won reelection in 1965, but then lost to the notorious Lester Maddox in the 1966 gubernatorial primary. He won the governorship on his second try in 1970, adopting an uncharacteristically conservative stance to upset his moderate opponent. In 1974 he became the first Democrat to declare his candidacy for the 1976 presidential nomination.

REAGAN: POLITICAL NOVICE

Ronald Reagan lived a life in show business until he became governor of California in 1967. He started as a radio announcer in Davenport, Iowa, in 1932, then moved to the sports beat in Des Moines. In 1937 he went to Hollywood and got into movies, starring in several memorable films, including *Knute Rockne—All American*, *Kings Row*, and *Bedtime for Bonzo*. His first job in politics was as president of the Screen Actors Guild from 1947 to 1952 and from 1959 to 1960. He was a liberal Democrat who campaigned for Helen Douglas against Richard Nixon in the 1950 California Senate race, but he switched to the Republicans in 1962.

Reagan drew plaudits for his per-

Ronald Reagan, sportscaster at WHO in Des Moines, Iowa, from 1935 until he left for Hollywood in 1937 (the White House)

formance in support of Barry Goldwater during the 1964 presidential election campaign, and the notices convinced him to take his friends' advice and run for governor of California in 1966. He did, and he won, and then he won reelection in 1970. He barely lost the 1976 Republican presidential nomination to incumbent Gerald R. Ford but came back to defeat George Bush in 1980.

BUSH: POLITICAL EXPERT

George Bush entered the presidency in 1989 with more political and governmental experience than his two predecessors had combined. The forty-first president left Yale University in 1948 for Texas and the oil business. As a Texan he became active in the Republican party, serving as Harris County chairman in 1963 and 1964 and running unsuccessfully for the U.S. Senate in 1964. He won a seat in the U.S. House of Representatives in 1966 and was reelected in 1968. After he lost another bid for the Senate in 1970, President Richard M. Nixon made him ambassador to the United Nations in 1971. He went from that job to the chairmanship of the Republican National Committee in 1973, which was a difficult year for Republicans in national politics. He became U.S. liaison in China in 1974 and director of the Central Intelligence Agency in 1976. He started running for the 1980 Republican presidential nomination after Jimmy Carter assumed office in 1977. But when the time came he agreed to accept the second spot on the Republican ticket in favor of Ronald Reagan.

Military Careers of the Presidents

by PHILIP COCKRELL

From the time of our revolutionary beginnings, wars of varying magnitude have had a major impact on American life, and, accordingly, twenty-nine of the forty U.S. presidents have also served in the armed forces—twenty-three in the army (one in the U.S. Army Air Forces) and six in the navy. All of the twenty-two who have served in army ground forces won election to the presidency before 1960; all of the navy men have been elected since then.

Most of the military presidents spent their years of service in citizen volunteer forces, militia, or reserves. Only George Washington, William Henry Harrison, Zachary Taylor, Ulysses S. Grant, Dwight D. Eisenhower, and Jimmy Carter can be considered "professional" soldiers. Only two presidents, Ulysses S. Grant and Dwight D. Eisenhower, graduated from the U.S. Military Academy at West Point, and only Jimmy Carter has earned a Naval Academy ring.

Of the eight presidents who have seen military service since the invention of the airplane, only one, Ronald Reagan, has served in the air force. Reagan's duties in the U.S. Army Air Force during World War II did not involve flying, however. Reagan's vice-president, George Bush, the only aviator to become president, served in the navy.

Twelve presidents have risen to the ranks of general. Dwight D. Eisenhower is the only president to have held the nation's highest military rank, five-star general of the army, and Ulysses S. Grant rose to the rank of four-star general (at the time the highest rank attainable). George Washington is the only president to have resigned from service with the rank of three-star lieutenant general. Six presidents, Andrew Jackson, William Henry Harrison, Zachary Taylor, Andrew Johnson, Rutherford B. Hayes, and James A. Garfield, held the rank of two-star major general. Three presidents, Franklin Pierce, Chester A. Arthur, and Benjamin Harrison, served as one-star brigadier generals.

George Washington and Dwight D. Eisenhower are the only presidents who have commanded allied as well as American forces. Washington commanded French troops that fought in conjunction with the Continental army during the American Revolution, and Eisenhower directed troops of many nations as commander in chief of Allied Expeditionary Forces in Europe in World War II and later as supreme commander of the North Atlantic Treaty Organization.

WASHINGTON: SYMBOL FOR A NATION

The first president possessed a truly commanding presence. George Washington was elected president because of his service as commander in chief of the Continental army during the American Revolution. His military career began years earlier, when his home state, Virginia, was still a colony. He became a major in the Virginia militia in 1752 and resigned in 1755 over what he considered to be the insubordination of lesser-ranked British regulars in his command. Later that year, however, he accepted a position as aide-de-camp to British general Edward Braddock, leading a heroic retreat of colonial forces during a campaign against French and

Mezzotint of a portrait of Gen. George Washington by Charles Willson Peale, 1780

Indians in which Braddock was killed.

Washington's service in the Continental army was extensive though not often tactically successful. His first year of campaigning saw one disaster after another. His ragtag army simply could not fight toe-to-toe with the British and win. The only American victory in 1776 came on Christmas night, when Washington's forces crossed the ice-laden Delaware River under cover of darkness and surprised a Hessian garrison in the town of Trenton, New Jersey.

The long privation of the winter at Valley Forge in 1777-1778 nearly wiped out the memory of success for Washington's soldiers. Those who survived that horrible camp emerged tougher and better trained. Still, final victory was years away.

The Battle of Yorktown finally secured the liberty of the American colonies from Great Britain in October 1781. Cornwallis, the British general, could not face his defeat and left his second in command to surrender his sword. That officer attempted to surrender to French general Rochambeau, but Rochambeau respectfully refused to accept the sword and pointed to Washington, indicating the victory belonged to the Americans. While Washington had seldom displayed tactical genius or inspiring battlefield command, he did supply something irreplaceable to the American cause. The infant nation possessed few symbols to which an army and a people could express loyalty. Washington provided an unflinching symbol of American liberty to which all Americans could flock in difficult times. While others faded from the scene, Washington remained steady. His constant devotion to the Revolution did much to keep the army and the nation together.

The army as usual is without pay and a great part of the soldiery without shirts; and the patience of them is equally threadbare—it seems to be a matter of small consequence to those at a distance. In truth if one were to hazard an opinion for them on this subject, it would be that, the army having contracted a habit of living without money, it would be injurious to it to introduce other customs.

—Letter of Gen. George Washington to John Augustine Washington, January 16, 1783

Washington won few battlefield victories, but he was never totally defeated. His tenacity won independence for his country and made him its first president.

JOHN ADAMS: NO MILITARY MAN

By his own admission John Adams was no military man. He was content to let others do the fighting while he worked in the political and diplomatic arenas. The future second president did participate in his local Massachusetts militia during his college days, but he was not very faithful to the drills and left after a short time.

MADISON: WILLING, BUT NOT ABLE

During the early days of the American Revolution, James Madison assisted his father, a lieutenant colonel in the local Orange County, Virginia, militia, in procuring and distributing arms and supplies. The younger Madison was himself commissioned a militia colonel in October 1775, but due to poor health he saw no field service in the revolution.

MONROE: LOYAL SUBORDINATE

The future fifth president dropped out of college to join the Continental army in March 1776. In September 1775 he had commissioned a lieutenant under Col. Hugh Mercer in the 3d Virginia Regiment, which joined Gen. George Washington's headquarters, at the time located on the outskirts of New York City, in September. Monroe and the Third Virginia saw action in the battles of Harlem, White Plains, and Trenton. During the Christmas-night battle for Trenton, Monroe caught a bullet in the shoulder as he was leading troops in a charge down the town's main street. His bravery under fire earned him a promotion to the rank of captain.

Monroe hoped to gain a commission in the Continental army, but he remained assigned to Virginia militia units. He was attached to the staff of the Earl of Stirling during the campaigns of 1777-1778 and saw action at Brandywine, Germantown, and Monmouth. Late in 1778 he resigned his militia commission, but back home he was unable to raise the necessary men to form the Continental army regiment he had hoped to lead.

Under those strange circumstances Monroe found himself out of the fight, so he returned to law school. When British troops threatened Virginia in 1781, Gov. Thomas Jefferson appointed him military commissioner of Virginia with the rank of lieutenant colonel. He gathered intelligence on Cornwallis's forces and also explored the possibility of forming a southern army to fight the British general. The American victory over Cornwallis at Yorktown signaled the end of Monroe's military career. He again returned to law school, and this time he finished his studies.

JACKSON: FRONTIER SOLDIER

"Old Hickory" was thirteen when he joined the Continental army in July 1789 as a messenger boy. He was present at the Battle of Hanging Rock, South Carolina, in which a British regiment was destroyed by guerrillas commanded by Thomas Sumter. In reprisal for that defeat British troops began raiding frontier homes in an effort to capture the partisans. In one of those raids young Jackson was taken prisoner. The treatment he claimed to have received in captivity earned the British his lifelong enmity.

Jackson next saw military service during the War of 1812. As soon as he heard of the breakout of hostilities with Britain he offered the services of his twenty-five-hundred-man Tennessee militia to federal authorities. Tennessee governor William Blount commissioned Jackson a major general of U.S. volunteers, and the new commander marched his force off to Mississippi.

Jackson had understood that he was to take his men to Natchez, where they would be mustered into federal service, but when they arrived Gen. James Wilkinson ordered Jackson to demobilize the unit and send the men back to Tennessee. Jackson bluntly refused and led the unit back to Nashville as a military force. The toughness, discipline, and spartan military values he displayed on the march home earned him the nickname "Old Hickory."

On September 24, 1813, Governor Blount requested Jackson's assistance in dealing with Britain's Creek Indian allies. The Indians had been encouraged by British success and had massacred 250 people (including women and children) at Fort Mims in the Mississippi Territory. Jackson took command of the volunteer forces at Fayetteville, Tennessee, on October 7, 1813, and set

"Old Hickory," 1819 portrait of Gen. Andrew Jackson by John Vanderlyn (New York City Hall)

off after the Indians.

Jackson's forces first attacked the Creeks at Talladega (later part of Alabama) and thoroughly defeated them. Jackson continued the campaign in January, but his volunteers fought poorly and were beaten at Emuckfaw, Enotachopoo Creek, and Calibee Creek. Jackson was not at all pleased and set about whipping his command into fighting shape. By March his methods had drastically improved the militia. Proof came on March 27, when Jackson defeated a combined Creek and Cherokee force at Horseshoe Bend, Alabama. That battle, which killed nearly 850 Indians, ended the Creek War.

In recognition of his efforts the federal government issued Jackson a commission as a brigadier general in the U.S. Army in May 1814. About two weeks later, following the resignation of William Henry Harrison, Jackson was promoted to major general and given command of the VII Military District consisting of western Tennessee, Louisiana, and the Mississippi Territory.

> *Never, my dear, have I seen such a crowd. . . . All the troops arriving to the strains of military music & of the cannons. . . . more than 12000 people of whom 8000 were armed. . . . Tomorrow they will crown the General; twelve young girls will strew his path with flowers. . . . They are practicing at Mme. Floriant's.*
>
> *—Letter of Pierre Favrot, citizen of New Orleans, to his wife concerning the city's reception of Gen. Andrew Jackson, January 21, 1815*

Jackson assumed his new duties with zeal. He had learned he would be facing his old nemesis, the British, and he did not wait for the enemy to attack. Instead, he took a sizable force into Spain's Florida territory and laid siege to the British-garrisoned fortress at Pensacola (Spain and Great Britain were allies). Jackson had no orders to take offensive action in Spanish territory, but he deemed the operation of high military importance, so he marched. When Pensacola fell, the British lost a fort, but, more important, they lost the confidence of their Spanish and Indian allies in the region.

Jackson had little chance to savor his success at Pensacola. British plans to attack New Orleans forced Old Hickory to put his men on the march to defend the port city. On December 23, 1814, Jackson learned that British troops had landed two weeks earlier at Lake Borgne. He had not had time to organize his defenses but believed the British were not expecting much resistance. To hide the weakness of his defense Jackson decided to attack. His assault caught the British by surprise and forced them to halt their advance on New Orleans.

The British did not renew their attack until January 8, 1815. Jackson used the interlude to fortify positions along the Rodriguez Canal just outside the city. The defenses covered an open field

Currier lithograph of Gen. William Henry Harrison, hero of the Battle of Tippecanoe, prepared for Harrison's presidential campaign in 1840 (Library of Congress)

approximately two hundred yards wide. The British marched out of the woods in good Continental order and Jackson's frontiersmen riddled their advance, giving the United States its most decisive victory in the war. The Battle of New Orleans made Jackson a national hero. Ironically, the battle was fought almost two weeks after the Treaty of Ghent officially ended the war.

Jackson continued his military service until 1821. In 1817-1818 he fought in the First Seminole War in Florida, then he served as Florida's military governor for a few months in 1821. He resigned from the army in October 1821 and entered politics.

WILLIAM HENRY HARRISON: INDIAN FIGHTER

William Henry Harrison began his military career in August 1791 when he left medical studies to join the 1st U.S. Regiment of Infantry. He was commissioned in Philadelphia as an ensign and left for duty in the Ohio Valley.

Harrison arrived at Fort Washington on the Ohio River just as word reached the post that the expedition of Gen. Arthur St. Clair had been destroyed by Indians near the headwaters of the Wabash River. Harrison was not discouraged by the somber news and soon impressed his commanders with his businesslike attention to duty. He soon won promotion to lieutenant and was assigned as an aide-de-camp to Gen. "Mad" Anthony Wayne. His service during the Battle of Fallen Timbers in August 1794, in which Wayne's force decisively defeated a force of eight hundred Indians under Little Turtle, earned him a captaincy and the command of Fort Washington by the end of 1795.

Harrison soon discovered that peacetime army life was much less adventurous. He found himself attracted to the commercial life of the towns and villages of the Northwest Territory. On the first of June in 1798 he resigned his army commission, and later that month President John Adams appointed him territorial secretary.

GOOD LUCK-BAD LUCK

At the battlefield of Tippecanoe in 1811, Gen. William Henry Harrison benefited from the most fickle of battlefield fates—luck. Harrison's Indian foes, the Shawnee, knew that the general rode a light-colored gray mare. But in the violence of the predawn attack, Harrison's usual mount bolted in fear, forcing the general to take another horse, a black stallion. One of Harrison's lieutenants, Col. Abraham Owen of Kentucky, had the misfortune of owning a gray mare, on which he rode at Harrison's side. In the confusion the Shawnee mistook Owen for Harrison and killed the unlucky colonel.

After Harrison's stint as territorial secretary and as a nonvoting member of the U.S. Congress earned him a presidential appointment as governor of the Indiana Territory in May 1800. His attempts as governor to engineer good relations between Indians and white settlers earned Harrison the goodwill and trust of most of the Indian chiefs of the region. Agreements including the Sac and Fox Treaty of 1804 and the Treaty of Fort Wayne of 1809 also opened millions of acres of formerly Indian lands to white settlement. However, remote white settlements faced a constant threat of attack from Indian groups who refused to take part in the treaty process.

The Shawnee tribe, led by brothers named Tecumseh and the Prophet, most prominently opposed white settlement of the Northwest. The brothers stirred up discontent in other tribes and plagued the Harrison governorship for years. Harrison also had to weather threats from outside. British agents saw an advantage in creating havoc on the American frontier and supported the Shawnee brothers. The presence of British agents among the Indians and worsening relations between Great Britain and the United States, mostly over the issue of freedom of the seas, increased the possibility of Indian war in the Northwest. Fearing hostilities, Harrison called up the Indiana militia. But when no crisis developed in the territory, Harrison dismissed the volunteers and hoped for continuing peaceful relations with the Indians.

For a few years the frontier was quiet, but after the 1809 ratification of the Treaty of Fort Wayne, in which friendly Indians ceded further territory to white settlement, the Shawnee, led by the Prophet and Tecumseh, began to agitate for war. A series of conferences between the Shawnee leaders and Harrison succeeded only in solidifying their resolve–Harrison for continued white settlement, the Shawnee for a return of all treaty lands to the Indians. Attacks on white settlements increased, and Harrison again called up the militia, up to that time a military force in name only, and began serious training. After another unsuccessful conference between Harrison and Tecumseh in July 1811, the governor believed that conflict between the two sides was almost inevitable. In September he and the militia, numbering some 950 men, departed Vincennes, the Indiana capital, and established a military post, Fort Harrison, three miles north of Terre Haute, on the Wabash River about halfway between Prophetstown and Vincennes. Harrison's march was intended to give strength to the treaty and to dissuade the Prophet from further violence. Harrison was acting under congressional order to convince the Prophet to disperse and to cease violence. If that was unsuccessful, Harrison was ordered to disperse him.

I pray you to recollect that I was a soldier from my earliest youth; that there are principles recognized in that profession which everyone belonging to it is bound to defend, which he may not on any occasion surrender or abandon without dishonor. For his friend a true soldier will willingly part with his wealth; in his defense shed his blood or lose his life, but his right to command he will give up to no one. On such an issue "he will cavil for the ninth part of a hair."

—*Letter of William Henry Harrison [campaigning for the presidency] published in* Niles' Register, *November 15, 1834*

By the end of October the militia completed construction of Fort Harrison and were ready to march. The force arrived near Prophetstown on November 6, where Harrison met with a representative of the Prophet, Chief White Horse, and informed him that hostilities could be avoided if the Prophet met the known demands. White Horse proposed a council for the following day, to which Harrison

PRESIDENTIAL MILITARY SERVICE
WAR BY WAR

AMERICAN REVOLUTION
George Washington, James Madison, James Monroe, Andrew Jackson

WAR OF 1812
Andrew Jackson, William Henry Harrison, John Tyler, Zachary Taylor

MEXICAN WAR
Zachary Taylor, Millard Fillmore, Franklin Pierce, Ulysses S. Grant

CIVIL WAR
Andrew Johnson, Ulysses S. Grant, Rutherford B. Hayes, James A. Garfield, Chester A. Arthur, Benjamin Harrison, William McKinley

SPANISH-AMERICAN WAR
Theodore Roosevelt

WORLD WAR I
Harry S Truman, Dwight D. Eisenhower

WORLD WAR II
Dwight D. Eisenhower, John F. Kennedy, Lyndon B. Johnson, Richard M. Nixon, Gerald R. Ford, Ronald Reagan, George Bush

AMERICAN INDIAN CAMPAIGNS
George Washington, Andrew Jackson, William Henry Harrison, Zachary Taylor, Abraham Lincoln

agreed. Harrison moved his force to the west of Prophetstown and laid out a camp on the banks of the Tippecanoe Creek. He ordered his men to sleep with their weapons at the ready. Just before dawn the Shawnee attacked. It was a wild and bloody fight, but with daylight the militia gained the upper hand and put the Indians to flight. Harrison moved his force into Prophetstown the day after the battle and found it deserted. His men searched the village and discovered a cache of British gunpowder and muskets, many still in their wrappings. The Americans torched the village and began their triumphant march back to Vincennes. Harrison had a new nickname–"Old Tippecanoe"–that subsequently served him well in the political arena.

Harrison's military career was far from over, however. Upon the U.S. declaration of war against Great Britain on June 18, 1812, he resigned his governorship. In September he received a commission as a brigadier general in the U.S. Army and took command of American forces in the Northwest. He was responsible for protecting the frontier against Indian attack while formulating a plan to recapture the fort at Detroit, which had been lost to the British by American general William Hull in the summer.

By late in the fall sixty-five hundred of a projected ten-thousand-man army had been collected, and Harrison, though doubtful about his chances for success in a winter campaign, set off for Detroit. He hoped frozen ground in the swamps south of the city and a frozen Lake Erie would aid his advance while at the same time immobilizing the British forces and naval flotilla. After an abortive advance, Harrison retired to quarters at Forts Meigs and Stephenson and was instructed by the government in Washington to delay the attack on Detroit until American naval supremacy on Lake Erie could be established. In March, Harrison won promotion to major general. While encamped at Fort Meigs a portion of his army fought off two British assaults in May 1813. Then, in September, after American commodore Oliver Perry's spectacular victory over the British fleet on Lake Erie, Harrison successfully recaptured Detroit.

The objective accomplished, the Americans gave chase up the Thames River after the remaining British forces. They caught up with the enemy near Moraviantown after a few days' march. Harrison and his troops emerged completely victorious in the brief battle that followed. The victory also yielded unexpected results for Harrison. The British force at Moraviantown had contained Indian units commanded by Tecumseh, Harrison's old Shawnee nemesis. During the battle Tecumseh had led his warriors in a charge at the American line and had been shot down. Harrison's greatest threat to peace in the northwestern frontier had been removed.

At a peak of success, Harrison's military career came to an end. In November 1814 he resigned his commission and assumed membership on several U.S. government Indian commissions. The commissions negotiated a series of peace treaties with some of the Indian tribes remaining in the region. In 1816 he won election to the U.S. House of Representatives representing Ohio.

TYLER: LOYAL SOLDIER

John Tyler saw very little military service. During the War of 1812, to aid in the defense of Richmond, Virginia, he raised a militia company called the Charles City Rifles and served as its captain. When the British threat to Richmond faded in 1813 the Rifles disbanded, without seeing action.

TAYLOR: CAREER MAN

Zachary Taylor enjoyed a lengthy and mostly successful military career before he assumed the presidency in 1851. He got his first taste of the military life as he grew up in Louisville, Kentucky. His father, a Revolutionary War hero, often spun wartime tales around the family hearth.

Taylor's personal introduction to the military came as a result of the threefold increase in American manpower authorized by the U.S. Congress in response to the June 1807 impressment affair involving the HMS *Leopard* and the USS *Chesapeake*. He took advantage of the expansion, receiving a commission as a first lieutenant in the 7th Infantry Regiment in May 1808. He then settled into the grind of peacetime service, managing well enough to earn promotion to captain in November 1810. He still held that rank when war with Great Britain broke out in June 1812.

Taylor was assigned to defend Fort Harrison in the Indiana Territory, much of which was still hostile Indian country. Upon his arrival at the fort, Taylor was astonished to find it garrisoned by only fifty men. The majority of the local men had marched off with Gen. William Henry Harrison to retake Fort Detroit from the British. The Indians soon tested the small garrison's mettle. One night in September 1812 a large Indian force attacked Fort Harrison and managed to set part of it ablaze. Taylor and the garrison desperately fought off the Indians and saved the fort and the nearby town of Vincennes. For his part in directing the successful defense effort Taylor won promotion to the rank of brevet major.

The future twelfth president spent much of the rest of the War of 1812 protecting settlers from Indians and assisting regular army units when needed, but he saw almost no further fighting.

The years of peace that followed the war found Taylor moving from one distant army post to another. Gradually he rose in rank until he made it to colonel shortly before the start of the Black Hawk War in the Illinois Territory in April 1832. He saw only limited action in that conflict, which culminated in the Battle of the Bad Axe in Wisconsin in August, but he was successful enough to broaden his reputation as an Indian campaigner.

Following the Black Hawk War Taylor served in Kentucky and Missouri until November 1837, when he was sent to Florida to pacify the Seminole Indians. In what became known as the Second Seminole War, Taylor and a mixed force of regulars and volunteers moved against the Indians, who had retreated into the interior of the territory and constructed defenses on the banks of Lake Okeechobee. Taylor pushed his force, numbering slightly more than a thousand, through swamps toward the Indian encampment, hoping that a show of force would compel the Seminoles to surrender without a fight. That stratagem only hardened the Indians' resolve. The Americans reached the Seminole camp on Christmas day 1837 only to find it abandoned, but with the campfires still burning. Taylor's scouts did not have to look far to find the Seminoles, who were holding a strong position about a mile from the camp.

Though some of his advisers warned against it, Colonel Taylor determined to take the Indian position in a frontal attack. The battle cost both sides dearly, but it forced the badly battered Seminoles into a retreat and went a long way toward establishing American supremacy in Florida, a task never quite accomplished during Taylor's tenure. Though he was severely criticized by some for his handling of the Battle of Okeechobee, the political power of Taylor's Washington friends soon silenced his detractors. In May 1838 Taylor, then a brevet brigadier general, took command of all U.S. forces in Florida, a post he held until

Portrait of "Old Rough and Ready," Gen. Zachary Taylor, by Joseph H. Bush (the White House)

May 1840. After an extensive leisure tour of the eastern United States he took command of the army's Second Department, Western Division, based at Fort Smith, Arkansas; and in June 1844 he accepted command of the First Department, Western Division, based at Fort Jesup, Louisiana.

Events in Texas soon started to influence Taylor's orders. On June 15, 1845, he received orders to occupy a position "on or near the Rio Grande." The orders went on to say that Taylor was to limit his action to the defense of Texas unless war broke out with Mexico. He was somewhat taken aback since Mexico claimed the Rio Grande, but army commander Winfield Scott designed the order to strengthen the American claim to the northern shore of the river.

Taylor broadly interpreted his orders and set up camp in undisputed territory north of the Neuces River. Diplomatic efforts to settle the controversy over the

U.S. boundary with Mexico proved fruitless, and on January 13, 1846, President James K. Polk ordered Taylor to cross the Neuces and proceed to the Rio Grande. Sooner or later an incident was bound to take place, but it occurred much later than Polk or Taylor expected. In part, Taylor's efforts to appear nonthreatening to Mexican forces encamped on the southern shore of the river caused the delay in action. Nevertheless, on April 25, 1846, a Mexican patrol crossed the river and attacked one of Taylor's patrols. That inconclusive skirmish precipitated the Mexican War and the greatest American territorial acquisition since the Louisiana Purchase.

Taylor took his force into Mexico and early in May quickly won two battles, Palo Alto and Resaca de la Palma. On June 29 he was breveted to major general. He then began extensive operations against the Mexican forces, winning a decisive battle at Monterrey in September. Not all of Taylor's military decisions were politically popular. His decision to allow Gen. Pedro de Ampudia's Mexican force to retreat for a period of eight weeks brought Taylor much criticism in Washington. In November, President James K. Polk ordered Gen. Winfield Scott to Mexico, where he took command of much of Taylor's army. Scott would go on to strike against Veracruz and Mexico City while Taylor was supposed to remain in a defensive position. Disobeying orders, in February 1847 Taylor took an exposed position at Buena Vista and met the attack of twenty thousand Mexican soldiers under Gen. Antonio Lopez de Santa Anna. The Mexicans outnumbered the Americans four to one, but Taylor's superior artillery won the battle. After that victory he took command of all American forces in northern Mexico until November 1847, when he left the country, ostensibly to go into retirement in Baton Rouge, Louisiana. In June 1848 he won the Whig nomination for president.

FILLMORE: STAYED HOME

Millard Fillmore's military career was briefer and more inconspicuous than his presidency. During the Mexican War he commanded a corps of the New York Home Guard, a collection of men who filled the places of the active New York militia units that went to fight in Mexico. Fillmore's service in the Home Guard lasted a few months.

PIERCE: BRAVE, BUT UNLUCKY

Motivated by news of the U.S. declaration of war against Mexico, Franklin Pierce began his military service as a private in the Concord, New Hampshire, militia in May 1846. Political considerations nearly ended his military career before it began. In September, President James K. Polk offered Private Pierce, also the U.S. district attorney for New Hampshire and a prominent state politician, the position of U.S. attorney general, but Pierce declined the nomination and prepared to go to war.

He remained in New Hampshire as an enlisted man through 1846, then in February 1847 took a commission as a colonel of infantry in the U.S. Army, assigned to recruit a New England regiment to go to Mexico. That job took less than a month and earned the new soldier a further promotion, to brigadier general.

Training the new command, the 9th Regiment of Infantry, took up the month of April 1847. Then the force sailed for Mexico, a voyage taking the better part of two months. In Mexico, a shortage of mules kept Pierce from moving to the front until the Battle of Contreras on August 19. During the battle Pierce injured his knee when his horse threw him. He refused to leave the battle and continued to lead his troops until the fight was finished. He reinjured the knee the following day at Churubusco but again refused to leave his men.

Mexican general Antonio Lopez de Santa Anna asked for an armistice as a result of the American victories in those battles. American general Winfield Scott appointed Pierce to the armistice commission as the general's representative, but the commission was unable to secure a lasting peace. Hostilities resumed on September 7.

General Scott began the campaign to take Mexico City. Pierce hoped to participate in the campaign, but the age-old Mexican ally, "Montezuma's revenge," laid him low. The end of the fighting in Mexico also brought the end of Pierce's military career. He sailed for home in December 1847 and arrived in Concord to a hero's welcome. His Mexican service gained Pierce considerable support in the presidential campaign of 1852, in which he was commonly referred to as "the general."

BUCHANAN: PRIVATE VOLUNTEER

The fifteenth president holds the distinction of being the last president to have served in the War of 1812—which is the only fact that makes his service significant. Buchanan was a young man of twenty-three when he volunteered his service to the Shippen's Company of Lancaster County, Pennsylvania, in August 1814. The company was neither a regular U.S. force nor an arm of the state militia. Instead, it was a small group of men who privately responded to the British burning of Washington by taking up arms. The company marched to Baltimore and offered its services to Maj. Charles Sterret Ridgley of the Third U.S. Cavalry. The major had no serious use for the untrained group, but seized the opportunity to take what advantage he could of their willingness to serve by asking for volunteers to undertake a secret mission—rounding up horses for his regular cavalry troops. Buchanan was one of ten volunteers; but before the would-be horse thieves departed, the British threat dissipated, and the Shippen's Company returned to Lancaster.

DO AS I SAY

In local militia companies of the antebellum period soldiers commonly elected their officers from among the ranks, often with the result that the responsibility of command was given to men unfamiliar with even the most common of army maneuvers. When Abraham Lincoln enlisted in the militia in 1832 to fight in the Black Hawk War, his colleagues made him captain. Lincoln had almost no knowledge of military routine and had to learn as he went along.

On maneuvers one day, his company encountered a fence running along its line of march. Lincoln had deployed his troops in "line-abreast" formation and would have to convert to single-column formation to move them through the narrow fence gate. As Lincoln remembered, "I could not for the life of me remember the proper word of command for getting my company endwise. Finally, as we came near I shouted 'This company is dismissed for two minutes, when it will fall in again on the other side of the gate.' "

LINCOLN: LOTS OF MARCHING

When the United States entered into one of its numerous Indian wars, this one against the Black Hawk tribe of the Illinois Territory in April 1832, Abraham Lincoln responded to the territorial governor's call for volunteers.

Lincoln was only one of many from his district to heed the government's call for volunteers. As was often the case in the nineteenth century, militia units elected their leaders, and the men with Lincoln elected him their captain. The company moved to join other troops, among them Col. Zachary Taylor's command, near the Rock River. There Lincoln and his men were sworn into federal service for a period of thirty days.

Lincoln saw only limited action against the Black Hawks. He also twice met with reprimand, once for failing to restrain his men from stealing army liquor and another time for discharging a weapon in camp. When the thirty-day term for federal service expired, he reenlisted as a private for an additional twenty days of service, then reenlisted for another thirty days. He participated in the unsuccessful effort to locate Chief Black Hawk in what became southern Wisconsin before he was mustered out in July without seeing action. Lincoln later recalled that his election as captain of his militia company brought him the most satisfying honor of his life. He also once joked that the only blood he shed for his country was to mosquitoes.

ANDREW JOHNSON: SOUTHERN UNIONIST

Andrew Johnson saw limited military service during the Civil War. A U.S. senator from Tennessee at the outbreak of the war, Johnson remained in the senate when his home state seceded from the Union. He was the only senator from a seceded state to do so. Johnson's loyalty was repaid in early 1862, when most of Tennessee fell to the Union. On March 4 Johnson was given the rank of brigadier general of U.S. Volunteers and appointed military governor of the state.

In that role he formed a provisional state government loyal to the Union and raised many troops for federal service. Throughout the next two years he actively pursued the cause of the Union, resigning his commission and the military governorship only after his election to the vice-presidency in 1864. (See chapter 15: Presidents and the Civil War.)

GRANT: FROM WEST POINT TO THE WHITE HOUSE

Ulysses S. Grant has the distinction of being the first West Point graduate elected to the presidency. He graduated in July 1843, three years before he was called upon to apply his training in the

---

My inclination is to whip the rebellion into submission, preserving all constitutional rights. If it cannot be whipped in any other way than through a war against slavery, let it come to that legitimately. If it is necessary that slavery should fall that the Republic may continue its existence, let slavery go. But that portion of the press that advocates the beginning of such a war now, are as great enemies to their country as if they were open and avowed secessionists.

—*Letter of Gen. Ulysses S. Grant to Jesse Grant, his brother, November 27, 1861*

Mexican War. A second lieutenant, he was attached to Gen. Zachary Taylor's force when the May 1846 incident on the Rio Grande occurred, precipitating the conflict. Taylor had left Lieutenant Grant's regiment in quarters on the Neuces River before marching to the Rio Grande; Grant's regiment followed after the outbreak of hostilities.

Grant saw extensive action during the Mexican conflict. He served with Taylor's troops throughout 1846 and assisted in the capture of Monterrey in September. He was transferred, along with most of Taylor's troops, to Gen. Winfield Scott's command in early 1847. Scott had been chosen to lead the assault on Mexico City via Veracruz. Grant landed at Veracruz on March 29 and fought bravely in the battles that captured the city.

The future Union army commander continued to serve in the front lines in Mexico, taking part in the Battles of Cerro Cordo, Churubusco, and Molino del Rey. His bravery under fire and his inspirational leadership earned him a promotion to brevet first lieutenant shortly before the Battle of Chapultepec.

The Battle of Chapultepec, fought on September 13, decided the fate of Mexico City. It was one of the fiercest battles of the war, and again Grant distinguished himself. The following day

Mexico City surrendered. Random skirmishing still occurred from time to time, but for the most part the heavy fighting was done. Grant remained in Mexico until July 1848, when he was transferred to Pascagoula, Mississippi.

The rigors of peacetime service took a heavy toll on Grant. By then a captain, he soon became tired of the long periods of separation from his wife and children and the poor army pay. During this period he began to drink excessively. In August 1854, during one of Grant's binges, Col. Robert C. Buchanan, Grant's commander, found him drunk in public. Grant either had to resign his commission or face court martial; he chose the former.

The coming of the Civil War spurred Grant to reapply for his commission. During the course of the war he rose from the rank of colonel in the 21st Illinois Infantry to the command of all Union armies, in the process making a fundamental contribution to the preservation of the Union and establishing for himself a prominent place in his nation's history. (See chapter 15: Presidents and the Civil War.)

HAYES: BUCKEYE SOLDIER

Rutherford B. Hayes served with the 23d Ohio Volunteer Infantry during the Civil War, rising from the rank of major in June 1861 to the rank of brevet major general by the time he resigned the service on June 8, 1865. (See chapter 15: Presidents and the Civil War.)

GARFIELD: STAFF OFFICER

During the Civil War, James A. Garfield served in the 42d Regiment of the Ohio Volunteers as a lieutenant colonel and then a colonel from August to November 1861. In December he was given command of the Eighteenth Brigade of the Army of Ohio, winning promotion to brigadier general in January 1862. He served as chief of staff under Maj. Gen. William Rosecrans, commander of the Army of the Cumberland, and gained the rank of major general. Garfield resigned his commission to take a seat in the U.S. House of Representatives in December 1863. (See chapter 15: Presidents and the Civil War.)

ARTHUR: POLITICIAN-SOLDIER

Chester A. Arthur served in the New York state militia from February 1858 to December 1862, serving first as brigade judge advocate and later as state quartermaster general. He resigned his commission to resume his law practice in New York City. (See chapter 15: Presidents and the Civil War.)

CLEVELAND: DRAFT EVADER

Drafted into Union service in 1863, Grover Cleveland hired a substitute under the terms of the federal Conscription Act of that year.

BENJAMIN HARRISON: HOOSIER SOLDIER

The grandson of war hero and president William Henry Harrison saw Civil War action with the 70th Indiana Infantry Regiment from July 1862 to June 1865, rising meteorically from second lieutenant to brigadier general. (See chapter 15: Presidents and the Civil War.)

MCKINLEY: ROSE THROUGH THE RANKS

During the Civil War, William McKinley served with the 23d Ohio Volunteer Infantry Regiment from June 1861 to July 1865, rising from the rank of private to brevet major by the time he was mustered out. (See chapter 15: Presidents and the Civil War.)

ROOSEVELT: ROUGH RIDER

"Teddy" Roosevelt believed strongly in the manly virtues. He had grown up admiring members of his father's family who had fought for the Union in the Civil War, and his mother instructed young Theodore in the cavalier traditions of her southern relatives. Roosevelt loved hunting and the strenuous outdoor life. When his wife and mother

The "Rough Rider," Lt. Col. Theodore Roosevelt, posing with troops after the Battle of San Juan Hill, Cuba, July 1898 (Library of Congress)

died on the same day in 1884, he left his native New York for life as a Dakota rancher. Although something of a "dude" rancher, his full-steam-ahead approach soon earned him the admiration of his cattle hands.

When war broke out between the United States and Spain in April 1898, he resigned his position as assistant secretary of the navy and went west to recruit cattle-ranching friends for the war effort and volunteered the new unit's services to the U.S. government. It was mustered into the army as the First Volunteer Cavalry Regiment, but it quickly became known as the "Rough Riders." Roosevelt was commissioned a lieutenant colonel, second in command of his unit. The regiment trained in San Antonio, Texas, and moved to Tampa, Florida, to prepare for invasion of Cuba. Roosevelt was promoted to full colonel and led the troopers onshore on June 22, 1898.

Roosevelt went to Cuba to get a taste of combat, and he got just that on July 1, on the day American troops encountered the only real Spanish resistance of the entire war when they advanced on a series of blockhouses on San Juan Hill. Contrary to the legend, Roosevelt and the Rough Riders did not actually charge up the hill. Instead, the unit advanced up Kettle Hill (adjacent to San Juan Hill) on foot. Later, for the photographers, they rode their horses to the top. Still, in later life Roosevelt considered his battle experience one of his proudest moments.

During World War I, Roosevelt offered to raise another volunteer force, but President Woodrow Wilson denied his request.

TRUMAN: TOUGH OLD CUSS

Harry S Truman's military experience began when he joined Battery B of the Missouri National Guard in June 1905. He was one of the unit's charter members, and the artillery training he received with the battery proved useful later. Truman left the service of the National Guard in 1911, but when the United States entered World War I, he returned to the Guard and was made a first lieutenant in Battery F of the Second Missouri Field Artillery. His unit was federalized on August 5, 1917, and became the 129th Field Artillery of the 35th Infantry Division. Truman and his men were sent to the artillery school at Fort Sill, Oklahoma, for training.

Six months later the 129th was on the troopship *George Washington* headed for France. En route Truman learned of his promotion to captain, and upon arrival he took command of Battery D, of the 129th. Truman first saw combat on September 6, 1918, in the Vosges Mountains in France. Two weeks later the U.S. Army launched the Battle of St. Mihiel, and Battery D was in the thick of the fight, pounding German positions around the clock and opening gaps in the German lines for the American infantry.

Truman continued to find himself near the action. Pausing just long enough to regroup, the Americans

THE MEMORY OF BATTLE

Theodore Roosevelt never forgot his baptism under fire at the Battles of Kettle Hill and San Juan Hill during the Spanish-American War. "I would rather have led that charge [up San Juan Hill] and earned my colonelcy than served three terms in the United States Senate," he said afterward. "It makes me feel as though I could now leave something to my children which will serve as an apology for having existed."

Some of Roosevelt's stories, however, such as his lurid descriptions of dead Spanish in their trenches, were received with skepticism. Although Roosevelt had indeed acted bravely during the conflict, observers had difficulty believing he was as much of a hero as he claimed to be. "It is astonishing," he commented, "what a limited area of vision and experience one has in the hurly-burly of battle."

Roosevelt also provided a convincing explanation of the disparate numbers of American to Spanish casualties during the Battle for San Juan Hill. (The Americans lost 1,385 soldiers to only 215 for the Spanish.) "It would have been very extraordinary if the reverse were the case, for we did the charging; and to carry earthworks on foot with dismounted cavalry, when these earth works are held by unbroken infantry armed with the best modern rifles, is a serious task."

launched the Meuse-Argonne Offensive on September 26. Truman's guns were among those that sounded the beginning of the attack, and as before, the artillery supported the infantry throughout the battle. After the Meuse-Argonne Offensive only the coming of the Armistice halted the American advance. Reputedly Truman's guns fired the last shots of the war, at 10:45 A.M. on November 11, fifteen minutes before the Armistice went into effect.

As was the case with many American soldiers, Truman did not return to the United States until well after the conclusion of hostilities. The future president was mustered out of service as a major of artillery in May 1919.

EISENHOWER: SOLDIER-PRESIDENT

Dwight D. Eisenhower was one of the few professional soldiers to become president.

The future thirty-fourth president entered the United States Military Academy in 1911. His class was later called "the class the stars fell on" because so many of its members rose to generalships.

Eisenhower graduated in 1915 in the middle of his class, was commissioned a second lieutenant, and took his first assignment with the 19th Infantry Regiment at Fort Sam Houston, Texas. He became a first lieutenant in July 1916 and a captain in May 1917. As with most career officers, his early years in the service presented an array of out-of-the-way posts and days filled with paperwork. World War I seemed to promise salvation, but Eisenhower never made it to France. He repeatedly requested combat duty but the War Department assigned him the task of training others to fight. He first went to Oglethorpe, Georgia, and then to Fort Leavenworth, Kansas, to instruct officer candidates. While at Leavenworth he took time to learn about tanks in the army's first tank school. His next orders sent him to Camp Meade, Maryland, where he was attached to the 65th Engineer Battalion, from which the army created the 301st Tank Battalion, Heavy. Eisenhower thought he might see combat with his new unit, but the army admired his organizational skills more than his fighting spirit and made him Commander of the

Tank Corps Training Center at Camp Colt, Pennsylvania. Tanks were an invention of World War I, and though they were unpopular with many of the older soldiers, the young officers, among them George S. Patton and Eisenhower, saw that the armored monsters would fundamentally change battle tactics. Both published articles on the future use of tanks that contradicted standard Army doctrine. Both were sternly warned to stop publishing and conform. Eisenhower did as he was told but still quietly disagreed.

After temporary wartime promotions, Eisenhower reassumed his captain's rank on June 30, 1920. A few days later he was promoted to major, the rank he would hold for the next sixteen years. Though lacking sympathy for official Army tank doctrine, Eisenhower

Harry S Truman during World War I (Library of Congress)

remained an instructor at the Infantry Tank School at Camp Meade until 1922. He was then transferred to Camp Gaillard in the Panama Canal Zone to serve as executive officer for Gen. Fox Conner in the 20th Infantry Brigade. In fall 1924 he went back to Fort Meade to coach its football team. He was unhappy in that duty, but he was even more disturbed by his next assignment as a recruiter in Colorado. That duty was cut short in August 1925 when Ike reported to the Command and General Staff School at Fort Leavenworth, Kansas, in 1925. Much of the curriculum was tedious, but Eisenhower mastered the material anyway and graduated at the top of his class of 245. That ranking earned him an appointment to the Army War College in 1928. Again he excelled in his studies, and he drew the notice of many of his instructors, most of whom were professionals of command rank.

With excellent recommendations from both the Command and General Staff School and the Army War College on his record, Eisenhower then accepted a series of postings to command staffs. In 1929 he went to Washington

EARLY HELL

One of the lesser-known battles of World War I, the "Battle of Who Run," involved Harry Truman's Battery D. Truman's boys had fired hundreds of poison-gas shells at their German enemy, but the unperturbed Germans sighted the guns of Battery D and commenced a highly accurate and devastating counter-battery fire. Truman's first sergeant, believing the battle was lost, gave the order to abandon the guns. Out of nowhere it seemed, Truman appeared, flailing his arms, giving orders, swearing as only he could. He used all of his powerful presence to rally his men and save the guns. The regimental chaplin later recalled that Truman's verbosity seemed much more fearful than the German shells: "It took the skin right off the ears of those boys." Chastened, Truman's soldiers limbered their guns, and moved them out of the way of the German fire.

to serve as special assistant to the assistant secretary of war, a post he held until 1932. Then he served on the staff of the army chief-of-staff, Douglas MacArthur, from 1932 to 1934. When MacArthur left for the Philippines in 1934 he took Major Eisenhower with him. Eisenhower served as MacArthur's senior military assistant in the Philippines until 1939. In 1936 he was promoted to lieutenant colonel. Eisenhower's years in the Philippines were unpleasant, but he gained valuable experience in budget cutting and other governmental operations. War broke out in Europe just as his Pacific tour was ending, and he returned to the States as executive officer of the 15th Regiment of the 3d Infantry Division, based at Fort Lewis, Washington. In November 1940 he became chief of staff to infantry commander Gen. Charles Thompson at Fort Lewis. Ike's advancements continued. In March 1941 there was a promotion to colonel and reassignment as chief of staff for Gen. Kenyan A. Joyce, commander of the IX Army Corps. In June came a transfer to Fort Sam Houston, Texas, and assignment as chief of staff to III Corps commander Gen. Walter Krueger. In September he got his coveted first star.

On December 7, 1941, Japanese forces attacked the U.S. base at Pearl Harbor, Hawaii, and brought the Americans into World War II. The U.S. Army quickly mobilized for war, and soon Eisenhower found himself in the middle of it. He was summoned to Washington by army chief of staff Gen. George Marshall to coordinate planning for the defense of the Southwest Pacific. In February 1942 Eisenhower was made head of the War Plans Division in the War Department. Slightly more than a month later he was promoted to major general and given the job of chief of the Operations Division of the War Department General Staff. He held that post for only a short time, however, leaving for London in June to assume the duties of commanding officer of the European Theater. In July he was made a lieutenant general.

SMALL CONSOLATION

In early 1943 Dwight D. Eisenhower received promotion to four-star full general just as the Battle of Kasserine Pass, one of the first between U.S. forces and the German army, was getting underway. In that battle Americans took a bloody beating before driving the Germans back. Almost two years later, in December 1944, Eisenhower received his fifth star and promotion to America's highest military rank, general of the army. That promotion also occurred at the same time as a major German attack, the Battle of the Bulge. Again American troops took a beating before they were able to stabilize their lines and launch a successful counterattack. Reflecting on the circumstances of his promotions years later, Eisenhower said, "I came to feel it was fortunate that no higher rank could be conferred. There was no promotion worth such battles."

Less than six months after the European posting, Eisenhower helped plan and execute the Allied invasion of North Africa. That mission culminated in the surrender of all Axis forces in Africa, a feat that earned the admiration of President Franklin D. Roosevelt and British prime minister Winston Churchill. In February 1943 Ike was made a full general, at the time the highest rank in the U.S. Army and one usually reserved for the chief of staff. In December he was made supreme commander of Allied Expeditionary Forces. That job put all the armies of the western allies under his personal command.

The new commander had no time to stop and ponder the significance of his office. He had orders to carry out, issued by the combined chiefs of staff.

Gen. Dwight D. Eisenhower, supreme commander of Allied Expeditionary Forces, with U.S. paratroopers preparing for the D day invasion of France, June 6, 1944

The orders were simple and direct: "You will enter the continent of Europe and, in conjunction with the other United Nations, undertake operations aimed at the heart of Germany and the destruction of her armed forces."

A full year of planning, training, and preparatory actions went into the Allied invasion of Normandy on D day, June 6, 1944, a day on which the free world held its breath. If the landings in northern France were thrown back, Europe might forever remain under the Nazi boot. The invasion, code-named Operation Overlord, was the largest amphibious military operation ever undertaken. Eisenhower commanded some 3 million troops, 1,750,000 of them Americans. On D day 175,000 troops landed on five French beaches along a sixty-mile stretch. On four beaches the forces quickly overcame initial resistance, but on Omaha Beach the German defenders came very close to wrecking the plan. As late as mid morning the assault troops were still pinned on the beach. Individual acts of courage overcame the stubborn defense, and by nightfall all the landing areas were cleared of resistance and the armies were moving inland. Eisenhower could announce to a waiting world that the Allies had returned to Europe.

The next month saw heavy fighting, but slowly the Allied advantage in men and materiel began to tell on the Germans. In late July, Eisenhower and the American army launched Operation Cobra and the British opened Operation Goodwood. The combined operation broke the back of the German army in France, and the Germans began a retreat toward their own border. By the end of August the Allies had liberated

Paris, and by December they stood on the German frontier.

A week before Christmas 1944, Hitler began a last-ditch offensive that he hoped would bring about a negotiated peace. Initially successful, the Battle of the Bulge ended in a crushing German defeat and opened the way into the heart of the Nazi nation. The coming of spring in 1945 brought the death knell of Nazism. With Russian tanks sweeping down the streets of Berlin, Germany surrendered on May 7.

Eisenhower's stellar service in World War II made him an international hero. Following the war he accepted the post of U.S. Army chief of staff, which he resigned in 1948 to assume the presidency of Columbia University. Beginning in 1950 he served as supreme commander to the new North Atlantic Treaty Organization. He resigned that post to accept the Republican party nomination for president in July 1952.

I learned that there is a priority of procedure in preparing for and carrying forward great tasks that the leader ignores at his peril. People close to a respected or liked commander fear he is losing his stature and urge the "squelching" of a Montgomery or a Bradley or a Patton; the seizing of the limelight in order to personalize the whole campaign for the troops and the public. But obviously in the hurly-burly of a military campaign—or a political effort—loyal, effective subordinates are mandatory.

—Letter of President Dwight D. Eisenhower to speechwriter Emmet John Hughes, December 10, 1953

KENNEDY: NAVY MAN

John F. Kennedy was commissioned an ensign in the U.S. Navy in October 1941. He received training as a patrol-torpedo (PT) boat commander. The PT boats were made mostly of plywood, and besides the torpedos they carried light anti-aircraft guns. They were very fast but also quite vulnerable to enemy fire.

In March 1943 Kennedy received orders to command a PT boat in the South Pacific. He was promoted to lieutenant (junior grade) and assigned the boat PT-109. After several months of relatively uneventful patrols, Kennedy and his crew became casualties of war. On the night of August 3, PT-109 was rammed and sunk by the Japanese destroyer *Amagiri.*

Kennedy gathered the survivors onto the floating forward part of the boat, where they remained until it too began to sink. He then led his crew on a four-hour swim to a nearby island. One of the crew members was too gravely wounded to swim on his own, so Kennedy towed him to the island. During the next few days the crew moved from one island to another until they were discovered by friendly natives, who took a message carved on a coconut shell from Kennedy to U.S. personnel. Shortly thereafter came rescue. Kennedy was awarded the Purple Heart, the Marine Medal, and the Navy Medal for his actions. He returned to the United States with malaria and back injuries suffered during the ordeal. He saw no more combat before his discharge in April 1945.

JOHNSON: OPPORTUNIST

Lyndon B. Johnson's naval service during World War II was, to say the least, extremely limited, yet it earned him a Silver Star for gallantry.

Two days after the Japanese attack on Pearl Harbor, Johnson, a U.S. representative from Texas, took a commission as a lieutenant commander in the navy. His motivation for doing so had as much to do with politics as it did with patriotism. Johnson's rank made him eligible for command, but his health disqualified him. Disturbed by the inequity, he went to a friend for help. The friend happened to be the president of the United States, and, as happened to many who entered the service but were

Lt. (jg) Richard M. Nixon (third from left), South Pacific, circa 1943

not fit for duty, Franklin Roosevelt gave Johnson a mission to the South Pacific as a "presidential inspector."

Johnson's arrival in Australia alerted politically sensitive Douglas MacArthur, commander of the Allied effort in the South Pacific. MacArthur believed that if he showed Johnson proper courtesy, the congressman might prove sympathetic to the general's concerns once he returned to the states.

In the meantime, Johnson found himself frustrated by the Japanese. They had run rampant in the South Pacific, leaving the Allies in control of only the southern part of New Guinea, Australia, New Zealand, and a few scattered islands. There was precious little for Johnson to inspect that lay outside the realm of comfortable Australia. But when Johnson got wind of a bombing mission directed at Lae, an island held by the Japanese, he persuaded MacArthur to arrange a place on one of the bombers for him. What happened next is not clear. According to some, Johnson's plane was ambushed by Japanese fighters; in the subsequent firefight the American plane lost an engine and had its fuselage holed and several crewmen wounded. This version goes on to relate how Johnson leapt to an abandoned gun and took part in the defense of the damaged bomber until it returned home. Other, less glamorous accounts indicate that the plane aborted its mission because of engine trouble before even seeing the enemy. The truth probably lies somewhere in between. In any case, MacArthur heard both versions and believed the former, reasoning that decorating the congressman should pay dividends. In later years MacArthur claimed that had he known Johnson would one day become president, he would have awarded him the Congressional Medal of Honor.

Johnson's days in the South Pacific were numbered. Shortly after his adventure President Roosevelt ordered all congressmen in the services to return to their duties in Washington. Much in the manner of Theodore Roosevelt, Johnson had seen his combat. He returned to Washington destined never to wear a military uniform again.

NIXON: REAR AREA SAILOR

A minority of those who served in World War II actually saw combat. Richard M. Nixon's service was therefore typical. On June 15, 1942, Nixon received a commission as a lieutenant (junior grade) in the naval reserve. He trained for service in naval aviation, not as a flyer, but as a staff officer. During the course of the war he performed valuable staff service in rear areas, overseeing military air transport. He held posts in the United States and overseas. His only combat assignment occurred in the Solomon Islands in June 1943, where he was attached to the headquarters squadron of Marine Air Group 25.

Nixon remained in the South Pacific for a year, returning to the United States in 1944 to take a position with the Bureau of Aeronautics, Navy Department. In that job he worked as a liaison officer between the navy and civilian contractors. Unlike most other presidential veterans, Nixon's military service outlasted the war. He was promoted to lieutenant commander in October 1945 and discharged in March 1946.

FORD: NAVY VOLUNTEER

The thirty-eighth president was a navy veteran of World War II. He joined the service as an ensign shortly after the Japanese attack on Pearl Harbor. He did not spend much time in the States, serving on the aircraft carrier USS *Monterey* for much of his forty-seven months of duty. Ford served as assistant navigator, gunnery division officer, and athletic director on the carrier. He never personally took the fight to the enemy, but the *Monterey* took part in enough campaigning to earn him ten battle stars. Ford left the navy at the end of the war with the rank of lieutenant commander.

THE MOST DANGEROUS SLIP

During his presidency Gerald Ford had the embarrassing misfortune of occasionally losing his footing in public places. He acquired a reputation for clumsiness—physical and verbal—that probably contributed to his defeat in the 1976 presidential race against Jimmy Carter. In his memoirs, however, Ford recalled a much more dangerous slip than any that occurred while he was president.

In the navy during World War II, Ford was assigned to the light aircraft carrier the U.S.S. *Monterey* during 1944. In December of that year the *Monterey* weathered a severe typhoon in the area of the Philippine Islands. During the storm Ford ventured out on the flight deck to investigate the smell of smoke. He lost his footing and began rolling down the heaving deck toward the edge and the frothy sea beyond. Just as he rolled over the lip of the deck he managed to twist his body and land on a catwalk just below. Had his desperate maneuver been unsuccessful, Ford would have been spared later embarrassment.

CARTER: SUBMARINER

Jimmy Carter's military service began in 1943 when he was appointed to the United States Naval Academy at Annapolis. He is the only president to have graduated from the Naval Academy and is one of the few presidents whose military service occurred mostly in peacetime.

Carter graduated in the top ten percent of the class of 1946 and was first assigned to work in battleships. He wanted to serve in submarines, however, and he got his wish in 1948 aboard the U.S.S. *Pomfret.* Carter's service during the next few years involved cruises and training missions until word of the navy's infant nuclear submarine program attracted the highly competitive officer. His good service record, excellent academic background, and ambition had been duly noted, and Carter won assignment to the elite program in 1952. He served as senior officer during the precommission service of the U.S.S. *Sea Wolf,* the second American nuclear sub. Then the navy sent him to Union College to do graduate work in engineering and physics.

At that point tragedy struck. Carter's father died in July 1953, and the young officer decided that his duty to his family outweighed his duty to the navy. He resigned his commission and returned to his hometown of Plains, Georgia, to work in the family peanut business.

REAGAN: STARRING ROLE

When World War II broke out, American industry quickly mobilized. Hollywood was no exception, and like many other Americans, actor Ronald Reagan offered his know-how to the country. He was one of many film stars who joined the military during the conflict. The War Department recognized that war propaganda made by the stars could have a morale-boosting effect on the nation. Reagan joined the U.S. Army Air Force's motion picture unit and worked on many propaganda films, including *Memphis Belle, Target Zero, This Is the Army,* and *Japanese Zero.*

BUSH: COMBAT PILOT

George Bush began his military career in Boston on his eighteenth birthday in June 1942. He was assigned to naval aviation training in North Carolina and received his pilot's wings before his nineteenth birthday. He went on to advanced pilot training in 1943 and learned to fly Grumman TBF Avenger torpedo bombers from aircraft carriers. After training he was attached to the air wing of the U.S.S. *San Jacinto* and went to the Pacific.

Bush saw action almost immediately upon arriving in the combat theater. Then his war took a turn for the worse. His craft was hit by antiaircraft fire during a bombing run on September 2, 1944. He held the faltering plane on course until the run was completed, ordered the crew to bail out, and abandoned the aircraft. He was rescued by an American submarine, but none of the other crew survived. For his efforts he earned the Distinguished Flying Cross.

Bush returned to his ship and continued to fly. He went home after completing fifty-eight combat missions and remained in the service until the end of the war.

Presidents in Congress

by MILES S. RICHARDS

When Lyndon B. Johnson assumed the presidency in November 1963, he found drafts of "New Frontier" legislative proposals on his desk. His slain predecessor, John F. Kennedy, had shelved many pieces of legislation because of an obdurate Congress. Despite the fact that Kennedy had served on Capitol Hill for nearly fifteen years, he enjoyed little rapport with the key lawmakers. Political sages attributed the curious situation to the fact that JFK had not worked hard enough during his years in Congress to cement binding ties with his colleagues. Kennedy had simply never been interested in being a congressional insider; his administration paid the price for that mistake.

In contrast, Johnson entered the Oval Office following an eminent career in both houses of Congress (especially in the Senate) where he had built an imposing base of support. The quintessential political power broker, Johnson had mastered the congressional way of doing things. Many in Congress owed him favors. Accordingly, by the summer of 1964 he managed to overcome conservative opposition and secure passage of many of the Kennedy administration's proposals. After his resounding electoral triumph later that year, LBJ initiated another string of legislative victories to construct his own social reform edifice known as the "Great Society." Johnson's mastery over Congress ended in 1967, when his Vietnam War policy cost him the support of congressional liberals.

Many argue that Johnson was on his way to a great presidency prior to the drastic military escalation in Southeast Asia in 1965. His success in the domestic sphere is usually attributed to his intimate knowledge of institutional procedures on Capitol Hill. That analysis implies that Johnson's long congressional tenure served as a necessary prerequisite to the Great Society. But another twentieth-century president who enjoyed a superb legislative track record was Franklin D. Roosevelt. For much of his fifteen-year presidency FDR played Congress like a virtuoso, but he never served as much as a day there. The same may be said for other effective presidents of the modern era, such as Theodore Roosevelt, Woodrow Wilson, and Ronald Reagan.

Still, twenty-four of George Washington's successors served in Congress before entering the White House. Interestingly, comparatively few of them enjoyed especially notable congressional careers. Many powerful legislators infected with the presidential bug never managed to convince the voters that they were worthy of the presidency. That list includes such renowned solons as Henry Clay, John C. Calhoun, James G. Blaine, William Jennings Bryan, and Robert A. Taft. To watch less-distinguished colleagues succeed where they had failed must have pained them considerably. Some influential men of Capitol Hill, though, have managed to satisfy their presidential ambitions.

MADISON: HOUSE, 1789-1797

The first president to emerge from the congressional ranks was James Madison of Virginia, prominent in official circles as a leader at the Constitutional Convention in 1787 and an author, with Alexander Hamilton and John Jay, of *The Federalist*, a series of essays arguing for the ratification of the Constitution. His career in the House of Representatives from 1789 to 1797 had its ups and

Representative James Madison, portrait by Charles Willson Peale, 1792 (courtesy of the Thomas Gilcrease Institute)

downs. President Washington relied heavily upon Madison's advice early in his first term. The congressman also introduced and steered to passage the Bill of Rights, the first ten amendments to the Constitution and the cornerstones of American democracy, ratified in 1791.

But in 1792 Madison's opposition to the nationalism of Washington's secretary of the Treasury, Alexander Hamilton, cost him much of his influence in Congress and with the president. Madison considered the Hamiltonian economic program—its advocacy of a national debt, a federally chartered central bank, and federal support for internal improvements—dangerous to the interests of the states. When he realized that Hamilton had Washington's ear, he commenced his break with the president. His friend, Secretary of State Thomas Jefferson, joined him in opposing the administration's economic policy; subsequently, Jefferson and Madison stood together in opposition to the president on a whole range of foreign and domestic matters. Madison became the congressional leader of a dissident minority allied with Jefferson, known as the Democratic-Republicans. Arrayed against them were the partisans of Washington and Hamilton, styled the Federalists.

After John Adams, the incumbent vice-president, won election as Washington's successor in 1796, Madison resigned his House seat to return to Virginia and help organize the Jeffersonians as a national political force. Madison returned to the District of Columbia in 1801 as President Jefferson's secretary of state. In 1808 Madison was elected president in his own right, serving for two terms.

JOHN QUINCY ADAMS: SENATE, 1803-1808 HOUSE, 1831-1848

John Quincy Adams of Massachusetts, son of President John Adams, compiled a distinguished record of public service before assuming the presidency himself in 1825. His stint in the Senate from 1803 to 1808, however, was among the low points of his public career. In 1802 the Massachusetts General Court elected Adams, who called himself a Federalist, to a six-year term. But the senator, a born maverick, soon emerged at odds with prevailing political sentiments in his state. He consistently refused to heed the instructions of the Federalist-dominated state legislature that elected him. A dedicated nationalist, he deeply opposed the growing regionalism and disunionism of many New England Federalists; moreover, he was disgusted by their pro-British attitudes, especially since the Royal Navy continually plundered American shipping on the high seas. As his term progressed, Adams increasingly supported Jefferson. He was the only Federalist in either house to support Jefferson's Louisiana Purchase, and he also repeatedly voted in favor of the president's second-term embargo of American trade with Britain and France, a highly unpopular action in New England merchant society. By then he barely spoke to most of his Federalist colleagues. As a kind of final insult, the Massachusetts General Court elected his senatorial successor in June 1808, a full nine months before his term was to expire. Rather than serve the remainder, he resigned shortly thereafter. New president James Madison appointed Adams U.S. minister to Russia in 1809, inaugurating a period of brilliant diplomatic activity for the former senator, culminating in his appointment as President James Monroe's secretary of state in 1817.

After his controversial election to the presidency in 1824, Adams suffered through a stormy term. The congressional supporters of his rival, Andrew Jackson, who lost the election, waged a ceaseless campaign of obstruction. The Jacksonians thwarted virtually all the president's initiatives. In 1828, following a fierce campaign, Jackson decisively beat Adams. But the resilient Adams was not meant for a life of political retirement.

Contrary to custom, the former president stood for election to the House of Representatives in 1831, and he served for the next seventeen years with distinction. Observers considered him nominally a member of the Whig party, but the redoubtable Adams insisted he was nonpartisan. To the despair of Henry Clay and other Whigs, Adams occasionally voted with the Jacksonians.

Adams was renowned as a master of parliamentary debate, and his colleagues came to call him "Old Man Eloquent." During his last years he became more outspoken in his opposition to slavery, especially regarding its spread into the western territories. He strongly opposed the annexation of Texas on those grounds, and he viewed the Mexican War as an immoral conflict created by the "Southern slave power." In early February 1848 Adams was about to join a floor debate over a military appropriation bill when he suffered a fatal stroke. Appropriately, "Old Man. Eloquent" died in the chamber where he had experienced some of his most glorious political triumphs.

Now I hope you never appear in the Senate with a beard two days old, or otherwise make what is called a shabby appearance. Seriously I think a man's usefulness in society depends much upon his personal appearance. I do not wish a Senator to dress like a beau, but I want him to conform so far to the fashion, as not to incur the character of singularity, nor give occasion to the world to ask what kind of mother he had or to charge upon a wife negligence or inattention when she is guiltless.

—Letter of Abigail Adams to Senator John Quincy Adams, her son, circa 1803

TYLER:
HOUSE, 1816-1821
SENATE, 1827-1836

During the two decades after he left the presidency, John Quincy Adams did not enjoy especially amiable relations with his presidential successors. Oddly, John Tyler of Virginia proved the main exception. Although the two seldom agreed on political issues, their cordial relationship dated from 1819, during Tyler's service in the House of Representatives. The Virginian first entered Congress in 1816. Quickly he won recognition as a firm upholder of Jeffersonian Republicanism and the states' rights tradition. Throughout his congressional career Tyler's colleagues respected his skill as a debater. He was deeply involved in the fierce House debates over the admission of Missouri into the Union as a slave state in 1819. He also outspokenly advocated annexing Florida from Spain. But he never assumed an apologist's stance regarding slavery as an institution. He seemed destined for a long career in the lower chamber when he resigned his seat in 1821 because of ill health.

After concentrating on state politics

> OLD ENEMIES
>
> In 1823 the Tennessee General Assembly elected Gen. Andrew Jackson to the U.S. Senate, mainly to promote his presidential prospects in the coming year. In the Senate chamber Jackson was assigned a desk in the third row near the center aisle, next to the redoubtable Thomas Hart Benton of Missouri. The two men had last met more than a decade before under less than cordial circumstances. On September 4, 1813, they had been involved in a ferocious brawl in Talbot's Tavern in Nashville, Tennessee, that included assorted other distinguished politicians of the state. Jesse Benton, Thomas's brother, nearly shot Jackson to death during the melee. Fearing retribution from Jackson's circle, Thomas Benton fled to Missouri, where he became a leading citizen. Rather than renew the battle, the old enemies chose to shake hands when they met on the Senate floor. Benton loyally supported Jackson when the latter became president in 1829.

for five years, Tyler returned to the national scene in 1826, when the Virginia General Assembly elected him to the Senate. Initially, Senator Tyler stood with the Jacksonians, and in 1828 he actively worked for "Old Hickory" in the presidential campaign. Prior to 1831 Tyler was a loyal Democrat who appeared to enjoy President Jackson's marked confidence. But Tyler also respected Vice-President John C. Calhoun and supported the South Carolinian when he broke with Jackson in early 1830 over the nullification issue. During the nullification crisis Jackson's hardline attitude toward the secessionist movement in South Carolina appalled Tyler, one of the few southerners in Congress who supported South Carolina consistently during its confrontation with the administration. The nationalist strain in Jacksonianism convinced Tyler that Jackson was not the ideological heir to Thomas Jefferson he had believed he was. After 1833 Tyler openly opposed the Jacksonians.

In the mid 1830s coalescing Whig opposition in Congress gathered sufficient strength to secure a brief hegemony in both houses. In 1835 Tyler was elected president pro tempore of the Senate as a Whig. But by 1836 it seemed obvious that the Democrats were resurging in many states, including Virginia. Tyler resigned his Senate seat that year rather than vote to expunge a resolution censuring Jackson for his veto of a bill to recharter the Bank of the United States.

Tyler spent two years in the Virginia House of Delegates and then won the Whig nomination to the vice-presidency in 1840. President William Henry Harrison's death one month after assuming office brought "His Accidency" the head job. President Tyler never enjoyed much clout on Capitol Hill, however, especially after he broke with Henry Clay and the Whigs over the issue of re-establishing the Bank of the United States in 1841. The majority of Democrats in Congress, however, were not prepared to support him either, despite his numerous conciliatory gestures. Realizing that he had little political influence, in 1844 Tyler declined to seek another presidential term in order to enhance the prospects of the Democratic nominee, James K. Polk of Tennessee.

POLK: HOUSE, 1825-1839

Unlike John Tyler, President James K. Polk enjoyed considerable leverage with congressional Democrats. Also, he had a thorough knowledge of the legislative branch from his many years in the House of Representatives. A protégé of Andrew Jackson, Polk quickly established himself as a vocal advocate of the Jacksonian viewpoint after his election to the lower house in 1824. His criticism of the "bargain" that elevated John Quincy Adams to the presidency gained him Adams's lifelong enmity. But the attacks assured Polk of much influence when Jackson took power in 1829.

Polk served as one of the Jackson administration's floor leaders in the House of Representatives, and he had great say in determining committee assignments. He was Jackson's point man during the fierce legislative debates over the rechartering of the Bank of the United States. Moreover, as chairman of the House Ways and Means Committee Polk helped manage the withdrawal of federal funds from the bank. His partisanship earned Polk the sobriquet "Young Hickory." In 1835 the Democratic majority elected Polk to the post of Speaker of the House. He was a strong Speaker, cast in the mold of Henry Clay.

In 1837 Polk dutifully supported Jackson's anointed successor, Martin Van Buren, although he did not regard the new president especially fondly. Polk's full influence could not bolster the fortunes of Van Buren and the Democrats in the face of a severe depression that commenced soon after the new president assumed office. Polk accurately foresaw that his party would lose control of both the executive and legislative branches in the elections of 1840. He was willing, therefore, to give up his "safe" House seat in 1839 to run successfully for the governorship of Tennessee.

An aged Andrew Jackson persuaded Governor Polk to accept the presidential nomination of the Democratic party in 1844. Throughout his campaign against the Whig nominee, Henry Clay, Polk promised to serve only one term if elected. He also pledged to annex California as a free state, to settle the Pacific Northwest boundary dispute with Great Britain, to initiate tariff reform, and to create an Independent Treasury System. During his term Polk accomplished all those goals while waging a winning

Portrait of Representative James K. Polk by Ralph E. W. Earl, circa 1830s (courtesy of the Sam Polk House, Polk Memorial Association)

war for Mexico's North American territory. Harry Truman once stated of Polk: "A great president. He said exactly what he was going to do and did it." Throughout his presidency Polk retained majority support in Congress. His notable presidential success depended upon his early experience in Congress.

PIERCE:
HOUSE, 1833-1837
SENATE, 1837-1842

Contrary to common opinion, Franklin Pierce was not a political lightweight, especially during his congressional years. Prior to election to the House of Representatives in 1832 he led the Democrats in the New Hampshire General Assembly. Once in the lower federal chamber he gained a reputation for partisanship rivaling even that of James K. Polk. Pierce never voted for a major piece of legislation not sanctioned by the Democratic leadership. That practice continued when he entered the Senate in 1837.

Although conscientious in his official duties, Pierce also liked to be sociable.

That tendency encouraged him to drink upon occasion. Many of his congressional drinking companions were southern congressmen, such as Senator Jefferson Davis of Mississippi. Since his closest friends in Washington held slaves, Pierce tended to sympathize with the proslavery viewpoint. Proslavery politics reinforced a Negrophobic attitude quite pronounced in Pierce.

In 1842, after nearly a decade in Congress, Pierce resigned his senatorial seat to return to private life. In 1846 he enlisted in the Mexican War and emerged from that conflict a brigadier general. His war record gained the dark-horse Democratic candidate enough votes to elect him president in 1852.

Despite Pierce's best efforts, the slave question continued to increase in national importance during his presidential term. The president exerted little leverage with northern antislavery elements in Congress who viewed him as a foil of the slave power after the passage of the Kansas-Nebraska Act in 1854. Moreover, since most of Pierce's former congressional colleagues had long since retired from politics, he could rely on only a few personally loyal members for support. In March 1857 an embittered Pierce, abandoned by a split Democratic party, gladly departed for home.

BUCHANAN: HOUSE, 1821-1831 SENATE, 1835-1845

Pierce's successor, Democrat James Buchanan of Pennsylvania, soon found himself in a similar situation. His many critics viewed him as an apologist for the slave interest and an unabashed opportunist. That reputation had plagued him since his earliest days in Congress.

Buchanan first won election to the House in 1820 as a Federalist. But as he observed the rising strength of Jackson in Pennsylvania, Buchanan endorsed that presidential drive in 1824. When the House of Representatives decided the deadlocked election, Buchanan reveled in his role as an electoral "fixer." Some alleged that he offered bribes to congressmen on behalf of his candidate. Although he hotly denied the charges, Buchanan never regained Jackson's complete trust.

Representative Buchanan stood with the Jacksonians in opposition to the Adams administration. Despite his good voting record, Jackson did not include Buchanan among his inner circle. After his presidential victory in 1828, Jackson pointedly declined to acknowledge Buchanan's efforts on his behalf. He also saw to it that Buchanan's Pennsylvania rivals received the benefits of federal patronage.

Fortunately, Buchanan's congressional associates held him in higher esteem. In 1829 he was selected chairman of the House Judiciary Committee. As chairman he spearheaded the unsuccessful effort to impeach federal judge James H. Peck on bribery charges. On a more positive note, Buchanan blocked a move by some ardent states' rights advocates to pass a constitutional amendment that would have stripped the Supreme Court of appellate jurisdiction based on writ of error. That responsible move gained him the criticism of many powerful Democrats. Generally, Buchanan faithfully upheld the Jacksonian viewpoint during his congressional career. In 1831 he resigned his seat when Jackson appointed him minister to Russia.

After his return from Russia in early 1835, Buchanan learned that the Pennsylvania General Assembly had elected him to fill an unexpired term in the Senate; he won election in his own right in 1836. He later maintained that the senatorial interlude provided the most satisfying period of his official career. He was considered one of the mainstays of the Democratic party in the upper chamber. Unlike Jackson, Martin Van Buren frequently consulted with Buchanan on policy matters, including the dispensation of patronage in Pennsylvania. In 1839 Buchanan refused Van Buren's request to join the cabinet as attorney general.

Certain southerners, especially Senator William R. King of Alabama, acted as Buchanan's close political allies during his Senate years. Through their influence Buchanan came to loath the abolitionists, yet he always claimed opposition to slavery. He was among the few prominent Democratic lawmakers who regularly met with John Tyler during his presidential term. Buchanan reluctantly left the Senate in 1845 to join the Polk administration as secretary of state.

LINCOLN: HOUSE, 1847-1849

In December 1847, during Polk's eventful presidential term, future president Abraham Lincoln made his quiet debut in the House of Representatives. Lincoln, a Whig representing the seventh district in Illinois, drew only scarce notice from his colleagues when he took his seat, even though he had enjoyed a lucrative law practice in the Illinois capital of Springfield and had played an influential role in the State's Whig party since 1838. The crisis of the Mexican War left little time for freshman introductions.

Although Jacksonian democracy was popular in Illinois, Lincoln had long identified with the Whiggish political creed of Henry Clay. Although he was not especially vocal concerning the slavery issue, in Washington he shared quarters at the Spriggs Boarding House with Representative Joshua Giddings of Ohio, a longtime antislavery Whig. In later years Lincoln credited Giddings with influencing him to adopt a more forthright stand against the "peculiar institution." On the issues of the tariff and internal improvements Lincoln remained loyal to established Whig positions. He gave a speech on the House floor upholding the Whig doctrine that the federal government had a role to play in funding internal improvements. Conceding the Democratic argument that such public construction projects inevitably wasted funds, Lincoln remarked, "The rule . . . is not whether it has any evil in it; but whether it has more evil than good. There are few things in life wholly evil or wholly good."

Earliest-known photograph of Abraham Lincoln, taken shortly after his election to the U.S. House in 1846 (Library of Congress)

Lincoln performed the routine work of a congressional first-termer with diligence. He rarely missed a roll call and performed full shares of the labor on two committees—the Postal Committee and the Committee on War Department Expenditures. Along with many other Whigs, he spoke out strongly against U.S. policy in the Mexican War.

Lincoln always maintained that he enjoyed his service in Congress. But he declined to seek a second term, claiming his family begged him to return home to Springfield. In spite of that public reason, insiders claimed that he retired because he realized that his opponents had enough votes to defeat him in the next election. During the final months of his term Lincoln spent much of his time campaigning in various eastern states for the victorious Whig presidential candidate, Zachary Taylor. The lame duck representative remained in Washington to watch Taylor replace Polk in the White House.

ANDREW JOHNSON: HOUSE, 1843-1853 SENATE, 1857-1862, 1875

Buchanan turned over the White House to Abraham Lincoln in March 1861 as the last of the line of Jacksonian Democrats to serve as president. Lincoln's advent commenced an almost unbroken succession of Republican regimes in the remainder of the nineteenth century. Ironically, Lincoln's immediate successor, Andrew Johnson of Tennessee, considered himself a Jacksonian of the old school. In 1864 Johnson took his place on the presidential ticket to broaden the Lincoln administration's appeal to independent northern voters, including ex-Democrats. But he never officially joined the Republican party. During his turbulent congressional career, prior to the Civil War, "Andy" Johnson had acted as a fiery Democratic partisan.

He first took office in the House in 1843, in a national electoral sweep that assured Democratic control of Congress. But because he refused to defer to established leaders in the House Democratic caucus, publically disagreeing with remarks made by majority leader John W. Davis, he missed out on choice committee assignments. Johnson always claimed he was a self-made man who followed his personal dictates. Party leaders rarely included him in inner councils on legislative strategy. It was no secret that President Polk would have gladly seen Johnson retired to private life. Periodically the bellicose representative criticized Polk's handling of the Mexican War. But Andy's East Tennessee constituents routinely dispatched their "maverick tribune" back to the fight.

In most votes Johnson remained true to his Jacksonian roots. He advocated fiscal retrenchment and limited government in many aspects of American national life. In the 1840s he repeatedly voted against the establishment of the Smithsonian Institution. He paid lip service to the southern position on slavery but made it clear that he was not prepared to dissolve the Union to protect the "peculiar institution." As a friend of the working man Johnson consistently sought to open western public lands to yeomen farmers and workers. Despite many attempts at passage his homestead bills remained buried in committee. Finally, in 1853 political enemies in the Tennessee General Assembly managed to gerrymander his district, forcing him from his seat.

Senator Andrew Johnson, circa 1857 (Smithsonian Institution)

In 1856, after a term as Tennessee governor, Johnson won election to the Senate. During his years in the upper chamber his course remained familiar. Increasingly, he distanced himself from his southern colleagues on the slavery question. He reiterated his Unionism and vowed to oppose the powers behind secession. He also continued his crusade to enact homestead legislation, without much luck before 1862.

In 1861 Johnson was the only southern congressman who refused to resign his seat and endorse the Confederacy when his state seceded. In April he actually fled detention in Tennessee in order to return to Washington. He remained in the Senate, a symbolic figure, until 1862 when President Lincoln appointed him military governor of occupied Tennessee. He won the vice-presidency in 1864 and became president one month after Lincoln's second inauguration.

Johnson might have renounced politics forever when he left the presidency in March 1869. He had barely escaped conviction on impeachment charges in the politically charged atmosphere of 1868; most in Congress considered him irrelevant after that. He continued to espouse the archaic Jacksonian political creed, but the Tennessee General Assembly elected him to the Senate again in 1874. Perhaps the assembly did it out of pure sentiment, but he regarded it as a vindication. Along with John Quincy Adams, Johnson is the only former president to return to Congress. His triumph was short-lived, though, because he died in July 1875, four months after taking his seat.

GARFIELD: HOUSE, 1863-1880

The Republican presidents of the late-nineteenth century were not generally known as seasoned legislative veterans. The primary exception is James A. Garfield of Ohio. In the 1850s Garfield was a prominent Ohio Republican. A pro-Union man, he volunteered in 1861 for duty as a colonel in the Forty-second Ohio Infantry. He was promoted to brigadier general after the Battle of Shiloh in 1862; subsequently he became a major general for his gallantry under fire at Chickamauga. In 1863 he resigned his commission to take a House seat he won in a special election. He spent his next seventeen years in Congress.

Whether it costs me my head or not these men shall all know that I am not to be scared or driven in regard to any vote I give in the House. . . . The fact is many of these men want a Representative they can own and carry around in their pantaloons pocket. They shall certainly know that I am not a piece of merchandise subject to their caprices and wishes.

—Letter of Representative James A. Garfield to Harmond Austin regarding Garfield's dispute with supporters of a high tariff on iron, January 31, 1870

Initially he affiliated himself with the Radical Republicans, but by 1870 he had moderated his hard-line attitude toward the defeated Confederates. In financial matters Garfield supported the retirement of greenback currency and the resumption of U.S. Treasury specie payments. In 1873 Garfield helped sponsor legislation demonetizing silver. In inflationist circles that measure came to be called the "Crime of '73." Throughout the fierce public debates over the bill Garfield never wavered from his "hard money" position.

The members of the House respected Garfield as a hard worker. He championed the cause of northern Civil War veterans, facilitating the passage of a myriad of military pension bills. During the Gilded Age he maintained a reputation as an honest legislator. He generally steered a clear path between the rival Republican patronage factions, the Stalwarts and the Half Breeds. But he was a friend of the latter group's leader, Senator James G. Blaine of Maine. Periodically Garfield endorsed the cause of civil service reform. On the special presidential electoral commission in 1877, he voted for Republican Rutherford B. Hayes over Democrat Samuel Tilden.

By the late 1870s Garfield was minority whip of the Republican membership in the lower house. In 1878 he unsuccessfully challenged Speaker of the House Samuel Randall of Pennsylvania

William McKinley, early in his congressional career

for his chair. In 1880 the Ohio General Assembly elected him to the Senate. But that July a deadlocked Republican convention nominated him as a compromise presidential choice over Ulysses S. Grant, Blaine, and John Sherman. Chester A. Arthur of New York ran with Garfield on the Republican ticket, which won comfortably in the fall election.

McKinley: House, 1877-1883, 1885-1891

A second congressional insider of the late-nineteenth century who entered the White House was another Ohioan, William McKinley. Like so many Republican politicians of his era, McKinley served as an officer in the Union army during the Civil War. He was first elected to the House of Representatives in 1877, as a good friend of fellow soldier President Rutherford B. Hayes. McKinley, therefore, got his wish to sit on the Ways and Means Committee. From his earliest years in Congress, McKinley developed an expertise on the tariff issue. A staunch protectionist, he gained the friendship both of industrial magnates and trade union leaders. But he depleted the good will of the latter group by strongly opposing the passage of eight-hour workday bills.

On most policy questions McKinley supported well-established Republican positions. On occasion he wavered on the currency question by speaking in favor of free silver. His fiercest debates with the Democratic opposition occurred whenever the Democrats attempted to legislate tariff reductions.

By 1885 McKinley ranked first in Republican seniority on the Ways and Means Committee. With ready access to the various Republican presidential administrations, he contributed a great deal in the formulation of congressional legislative strategies. After the Republicans regained control of the lower house in 1888, McKinley sought the Speaker's nomination, but he lost to Thomas R. Reed of Maine. McKinley's biggest booster was future House Speaker Joseph G. Cannon of Illinois.

In 1890 McKinley led the winning fight for the passage of the highly protectionist McKinley Tariff Bill. In the congressional elections that fall the Democrats hotly campaigned against the tariff, which they considered the primary reason for the subsequent downturn in the national economy. McKinley's usually faithful constituents finally voted him out over the issue.

The resilient McKinley was destined for greater things. In 1892, under the management of Cleveland industrialist Mark Hanna, he won the governorship of Ohio. Hanna then carefully groomed him for a successful run for the presidency in 1896.

THE TWENTIETH CENTURY

Several twentieth-century presidents came from the ranks of Congress, but

THE FIRST KENNEDY-NIXON DEBATE

John F. Kennedy and Richard M. Nixon first squared off in debate not on television during the presidential campaign of 1960, but in front of a small audience in McKeesport, Pennsylvania, in 1947. McKeesport's Junto Club asked the local congressman, Frank Buchanan, to select two of the more articulate younger members of the House of Representatives to attend a club meeting and debate the merits of the pending Taft-Hartley labor bill, a subject of keen interest in industrial Pennsylvania. Buchanan asked Kennedy and Nixon, and they both accepted. The pair had become friendly during their brief time in the House, and on April 21 they rode the train together from Washington to the meeting in McKeesport. About two hundred Junto members listened to the Democrat Kennedy oppose passage of the bill and the Republican Nixon support it. Most of the observers were impressed with Kennedy's wit and charm and viewed Nixon as a relatively humorless man. Of course, since most of the audience sympathized with Kennedy's position, he had an easier time making jokes. After the debate the congressmen enjoyed dinner with an assortment of local politicians and boarded the evening train back to Washington. As they departed a prescient local politico was heard to remark, "Those two boys are real comers."

only two—Lyndon Johnson and Gerald Ford—truly distinguished themselves in the legislative branch. The others—Warren Harding, Harry S Truman, John Kennedy, Richard Nixon, and George Bush—served relatively undistinguished terms. Harding missed more than two-thirds of Senate roll calls during his term from 1915 to 1921. Truman's faithful support of Franklin Roosevelt's New Deal and wartime policies in the Senate beginning in 1935 won him the vice-presidential nomination on the ticket with Roosevelt in 1944. Kennedy served in the House from 1947 to 1953 and in the Senate from 1953 until the assumption of his presidency, compiling a solid if unspectacular record. Nixon entered the House in the same year as Kennedy, quickly rose to prominence as a staunch anticommunist, vaulted to the Senate in 1951, and entered the executive branch as Dwight D. Eisenhower's vice-president in 1953. Bush served two quiet terms in the House from 1967 to 1971 and left to run unsuccessfully for the Senate. Johnson, on the other hand, spent much of his senatorial career as the leader of the Democrats; Ford played the same role for the Republicans in the House.

LYNDON B. JOHNSON: HOUSE, 1937-1949 SENATE, 1949-1961

Undeniably, Lyndon Johnson was the first true legislative insider to occupy the Oval Office after McKinley. Moreover, no previous president was so integral to the congressional system as the Texan. He first entered the halls of Congress as aide to Representative Richard Kleberg in 1931. He developed a reputation as a "fixer" and also gained the favorable notice of another key Texas legislator, Speaker Sam Rayburn. In 1936 Johnson won election to the House in his own right.

Johnson always knew how to win the friendship of the powerful. Political columnist Drew Pearson once noted that he first encountered Johnson in March 1937, carrying Rayburn's suitcase into Washington's Willard Hotel. Because of his faithful support of the New Deal, Johnson became one of Franklin Roosevelt's favorite congressmen. He also worked extremely hard, securing, for example, a disproportionate amount of Rural Electrification Administration aid for his native West Texas. But critics have also noted that Johnson also helped the influential oil lobby in his Capitol Hill years.

Lyndon B. Johnson as Senate majority leader, 1957-1961 (courtesy of AP/Wide World Photos)

In 1940 Johnson made a run for the Senate against the colorful governor W. Lee O'Daniel, but he lost in a close contest. A quirk in the electoral laws of Texas permitted him to run simultaneously for his House seat, which he won. In 1948 Johnson again ran for the Senate against Coke Stevenson, winning by a margin of less than one hundred votes. Many doubted the honesty of that election. The episode gained him the dubious label "Landslide Lyndon."

During the waning years of the Truman presidency Johnson emerged as one of the most influential Senate Democrats. Despite Truman's misgivings Johnson became majority whip in 1951. The next year the Republicans regained control of the upper house and the White House, and Johnson took on the job of minority leader. He enjoyed cordial relations with President Dwight D. Eisenhower and helped forge a bipartisan foreign policy consensus. Although he disliked the excesses of McCarthyism, he worked hard at cultivating an anticommunist image.

> *Very early in my Congressional career, a senior member took me aside and said that as a representative, I could choose one of two alternatives. I could spend most of my time in my office attending to the problems of constituents and providing service to the district, or I could spend my time on the floor of the House listening to the debate, mastering parliamentary procedures and getting to know the other members personally. I could not do both. Since I had a good staff to handle constituent problems, I elected to spend time on the floor. That's how I got to know Richard Nixon.*
>
> *Gerald R. Ford,* A Time to Heal *(1979)*

With the Democratic resurgence in the Senate in 1956 the Texan finally secured the cherished job of majority leader. After a halfhearted run for the Democratic presidential nomination in 1956, Johnson set his sights on the White House in 1960. With bitterness he watched the glamorous John Kennedy secure the nomination. Johnson was probably as surprised as anyone when the victorious Kennedy offered him the vice-presidential job.

FORD: HOUSE, 1949-1973

President Johnson often made snide remarks about former associates in Congress. He reserved many scornful observations for Representative Gerald R. Ford of Michigan. Johnson once declared that he doubted whether "Jerry Ford could actually walk and chew gum at the same time." Ford's reputation as an intellectual lightweight dogged him throughout his career, especially after he succeeded the disgraced Richard M. Nixon as president in 1974. Ford, though, had enjoyed a notable career in the House by that time.

TRICKY DICK

Richard Nixon's opponent in the 1946 race for the 12th congressional district seat in California was incumbent Jerry Voorhis, a New Deal liberal. Nixon defeated Voorhis by portraying him as a communist sympathizer, once even distributing a pink sheet summarizing Voorhis's prolabor voting record. Dick Tuck, a Voorhis campaign worker, decided never to let the congressman forget his shady tactics. He decided to dedicate himself to making life miserable for Nixon in future elections. In his 1950 Senate race against Democrat Helen Gahagan Douglas, Nixon employed the same negative strategy, even the same pink-sheet ploy. But this time Douglas—and Tuck—gave as good as they got. At a campaign stop in Sacramento, Tuck arranged to have Nixon's train pull away from the station before Nixon finished giving his speech. Observers enjoyed watching the irate candidate bleat curses at his aides. It was Tuck who convinced Douglas to call her opponent "Tricky Dick," a nickname that followed Nixon for the rest of his career. Tuck also devised scathing anti-Nixon posters, including one featuring an unflattering portrait of Nixon accompanied by the question: "Would you buy a used car from this man?" Nixon had the last laugh, however. He defeated Douglas, and she never returned to politics.

He first won election to Congress in 1948. A committed conservative, he faithfully voted against the Truman Fair Deal. In 1952 he initially supported Robert Taft's presidential candidacy, but he easily switched his loyalty to Eisenhower when the time came. During the Eisenhower presidency Ford acted as the quintessential legislative "foot soldier." In later years he could not recall ever bucking the Republican leadership on a key vote. Invariably, critics cited this loyalty as evidence that Ford was an unthinking "party hack." In retrospect, Ford regretted that he had not challenged the reckless ploys of Senator Joe McCarthy.

Following the election of 1964 House Republicans decided on a leadership change. They wanted to replace their aged leaders with younger members still committed to the party's traditional tenets. In January 1965 Ford became minority leader in the House. During the years prior to Nixon's election to the presidency in 1968, he served as one of the Republicans' most prominent national spokesmen. At no time, for example, did he waver from his hawkish stance on the war in Southeast Asia.

Ford was also President Nixon's loyal deputy in the lower chamber. He never cast a vote that opposed the interests of the administration. But Ford's partisan inclinations periodically caused him to undertake dubious projects. In 1970 Nixon grew enraged when the Senate refused to confirm two conservative appointees to the Supreme Court. In retaliation he convinced Ford to initiate impeachment proceedings against liberal Justice William Douglas on the grounds of judicial impropriety. By the spring of 1971 colleagues convinced Ford to abandon the blatant gambit.

Predictably, after the Watergate break-in in 1972 Ford defended Nixon even as calls for the president's impeachment increased. In November 1973 Nixon selected him to succeed the disgraced Spiro Agnew as vice-president.

Unfortunately, President Ford's well-meaning pardon of Nixon in the autumn of 1974 doomed his own electoral chances in 1976. He in essence became a caretaker president in the last two years of his term. His personal integrity, though, restored a great deal of legitimacy to the Oval Office after the misdeeds of the Nixon years.

When reviewing the congressional careers of the presidents few generalizations can be established. Clearly the most outstanding legislative power brokers were James K. Polk, James A. Garfield, and Lyndon B. Johnson. Yet experts judge only the first a successful president. An assassin's bullet precluded the success of Garfield. The bitter military stalemate in Southeast Asia ruined Lyndon Johnson. Most of the others were competent lawmakers but only average presidents. Franklin Pierce and James Buchanan failed in the eyes of their contemporaries. In spite of the advantages, being a legislative insider does not automatically result in White House success.

The Camp Meetings of American Politics: Presidential Nominating Conventions

by MILES S. RICHARDS

American presidential campaigns have traditionally served as quadrennial national jamborees. The party nominating conventions, held invariably during the summer months, have provided many of the most exciting highlights in the process. The star-spangled maneuverings of the convention partisans can be highly entertaining. Among the colorful happenings, though, party members often make decisions that profoundly affect the history of the nation.

THE COLLEGE AND THE CAUCUSES

The framers of the American Constitution would probably view the modern presidential election process with disdain. Distrustful of full democracy, they set up an "Electoral College" system in which a conclave of presidential electors selected by the state legislatures judiciously studied the merits of the worthiest candidates and picked a winner. The framers envisioned the procedure as an eminently dignified affair, much like a parish council assembling to fill a pastoral vacancy. But the Electoral College option worked well only in the case of George Washington. By the election of 1796 conflicts between two emerging parties, the Federalists and the Democratic-Republicans, rendered the original concept moribund. That year John Adams, the Federalist candidate, defeated Democratic-Republican Thomas Jefferson in a close contest. Jefferson's second-place finish put him (and the opposition interest) in the vice-presidential chair.

After the election of Jefferson in the "Revolution of 1800," congressional party caucuses emerged as the preferred mode of presidential candidate selection. Another Jeffersonian innovation involved the nomination of "favorite sons" by the state legislatures. During the heyday of the "Virginia Dynasty" from 1800 to 1824 both of those alternatives were utilized.

In 1808 and 1812 New England Federalists convened conventions to discuss potential presidential nominees, but they were informal, nonbinding gatherings of regional party leaders. The concept of a party nominating convention had entered the public arena, however.

THE BEGINNINGS OF THE CONVENTION SYSTEM

The election of 1824 went a long way toward fostering the notion among the people that the party caucus was an undemocratic way to select a nominee. But the Jacksonians, defeated by an overcrowded field and some purported back-room maneuvering in 1824, were not the first to hold nominating conventions. The convention innovation, ironically, was the work of some of Old Hickory's political opposition. Strangely, the apparent murder of an obscure western New York State bricklayer, William Morgan, in 1826 started the process.

Morgan, an erstwhile Mason, disappeared about the time he was to publish an exposé on the secret order. Many believed he had been killed by his former associates. A wave of anti-Masonic sentiment swept through the Northeast after word of the deed spread. By 1829 enemies of the Masons had organized politically in ten states. Since President Andrew Jackson was a devoted Scottish Rite Mason, the new aggregation bore him little love. Most members of the new Anti-Masonic party opposed the tenets of Jacksonian Democracy anyway. In September 1831, 116 Anti-Masons representing ten states gathered in Baltimore, Maryland, to nominate a presidential candidate for the election of 1832.

After some wrangling, they selected constitutional lawyer William Wirt of Virginia. Never more than a special interest, the Anti-Masons did not do well in the polls that year. But their concept of a national convention found favor with others. In February 1832 the main anti-Jackson party, the National Republicans, made up mostly of the old Henry Clay-John Quincy Adams faction of the Democratic-Republicans that won with Adams in the election of 1824, nominated Clay to oppose Jackson. Clay was unable to make much headway against the president in 1832. In fact, since Wirt subscribed to an activist concept of national government similar to Clay's, the Anti-Masonic "third party" hurt the Kentuckian more than it did the president.

DEMOCRATS AND WHIGS

Before the 1836 election, opponents of Jacksonianism organized formally as the Whig party, but in the election they relied on state legislatures to nominate regional presidential candidates, believing that throwing the election into the House of Representatives presented their only hope of keeping Jackson's anointed successor, Martin Van Buren, out of office. The party of Jackson—the Democrats—met in convention in Baltimore in May 1835 to nominate Van Buren in an affair modest by subsequent standards.

HARRISON DEFEATS CLAY

The first full-blown convention extravaganza occurred in December 1839 when the Whigs convened in Harrisburg, Pennsylvania. Several outstanding candidates vied for the nomination. As usual, Clay was a leading candidate, but he had acquired too many enemies within his party, especially among Anti-Masons. Some thought his long record of prominent service made him an easy target for the Democrats. Those desiring a "Stop Clay" movement, though, were vexed when Daniel Webster of Massachusetts refused to run in opposition. A boomlet for Senator Willie P. Mangum of North Carolina among southern Whigs fizzled. A faction of New Yorkers led by the wily Thurlow Weed promoted the cause of Gen. Winfield Scott, but Clay sensed that Scott was a stalking-horse for his real rival, William Henry Harrison, who had gained lasting popularity in the Old Northwest for his victory over the Shawnee Indians at the Battle of Tippecanoe in 1811.

The convention delegates bolstered Harrison's candidacy when they voted to require the state delegations to vote as units for a favored contender. This "unitary" setup hurt Clay because he had minority support in several key delegations and hoped to gather votes in each successive ballot. A candidate needed two-thirds of the total vote to win the nomination. The 1839 Whig convention also introduced the practice of placing the candidates' names in nomination with rousing orations and "spontaneous" floor demonstrations. During the outburst for Clay a group of his supporters from western Pennsylvania rolled a huge leather ball down the center aisle. "Clay's Juggernaut" exhorted the convention to "keep the ball rolling."

In the first roll call Clay tallied 103 votes, Harrison 94, and Scott 57. That balance continued through six more ballots, but during the seventh roll call Harrison's floor manager, Thaddeus Stevens of Pennsylvania, secured Weed's promise that Scott's delegates would bolt to Harrison the next time around, securing the nomination for "Tippecanoe." A bitter Clay refused to allow his supporters to nominate a candidate for vice-president.

After much discussion the convention delegates agreed by acclamation to nominate John Tyler of Virginia for the second spot on the ticket. During the concluding rally convention members chanted "Tippecanoe and Tyler Too." A disillusioned Clay supporter quipped, "There was a rhyme, but no reason in it." The phrase had a lilt to it though, and it helped the Whigs to their first presidential victory.

DARK HORSE FOR THE DEMOCRATS

After President Harrison's unexpected death in April 1841, Tyler moved into the presidency. His bitter feud with Clay and the Whigs over the issue of creating a third Bank of the United States in 1841 badly divided the party, and the breach had not healed by campaign time in 1844. The Democrats were not exactly a "band of brothers" either. Former president Martin Van Buren was anxious to reverse his decisive defeat of 1840, but he opposed the annexation of Texas, making him unacceptable to southern Democrats. His chief rival for the 1844 nomination was Senator Lewis Cass of Michigan, who had the reputation of being a dull campaigner. Despite receiving some discreet hints from President Tyler, few Democrats were inclined to accept him into the fold. John C. Calhoun of South Carolina announced his availability, but only hard-core southern sectionalists had much use for him. Many of the southerners preferred Senator James Buchanan of Pennsylvania. Aside from Tyler and Calhoun he was the only potential candidate who advocated the prompt annexation of Texas.

The aged, infirm Andrew Jackson initially stayed aloof from the intrigue. But he was not satisfied with the main contenders, including his longtime friend and former vice-president, Van Buren. Old Hickory feared that none of the Democrats under discussion could best the probable Whig candidate, Clay. Jackson wanted a strong nominee who would take a solid stand in favor of Texas annexation but who would also appeal to northern Democrats, who had to satisfy the antislavery elements of their constituencies. As the Democratic Convention convened in Baltimore in late May 1844, most of the delegates still were unaware of Jackson's preference. Senator Robert J. Walker of Mississippi kept in touch with the former president and promised to convey his choice to the convention.

After considerable deliberation Jackson settled on a veteran Jacksonian, Governor James K. Polk of Tennessee. He fit the criteria in all respects, and Jackson's nephew, Andrew Jackson Donelson, journeyed eastward with a letter for Walker. Donelson arrived in Baltimore to find the convention deadlocked. Van Buren had led on the first ballot, but Cass, Buchanan, and Van Buren's former vice-president Richard M. Johnson of Kentucky steadily eroded his margin until Cass led on the fifth ballot. Through seven ballots, however, no candidate could gain the two-thirds majority necessary to win. Emotions were so heated on the floor that a series of brawls erupted. Prior to the eighth ballot Walker dramatically read Jackson's message to the assembly, and a truly spontaneous demonstration broke out for Polk. Van Buren's floor manager, Senator Thomas Hart Benton of Missouri, vainly protested that Polk had already agreed to serve as "Little Van's" running mate.

Polk's entry signified the end for every candidate except Martin Van Buren. On the ninth ballot Van Buren's support declined enough so that Polk easily gained nomination. Polk was the

Contenders for the Republican presidential nomination portrayed in Harper's Weekly, *May 12, 1860*

first true "dark horse" to secure a presidential nomination. After a spirited campaign he defeated Clay in the general election, and he went on to enjoy a successful presidency. Historians consider him the most effective president between Andrew Jackson and Abraham Lincoln.

LINCOLN DEFEATS SEWARD

That Abraham Lincoln would be the choice of the Republicans in 1860 was far from certain. Despite his growing national reputation, most Republican loyalists preferred giving the nomination to William Seward of New York, the Republicans' most visible politician during the party's coalescence in the late 1850s. Longtime power broker Thurlow Weed directed Seward's campaign. He arranged for a large contingent of New Yorkers to attend the convention in Chicago to lead the cheers for Seward. For several days prior to the May 16 opening session those worthies paraded around the city led by a famous exboxer, Tom Heenan, and accompanied by a brass band. Governor A. G. Curtin of Pennsylvania hailed Seward as the "Toast of the Northeast." But astute observers realized that Seward was not an especially inspired campaigner and that he was too closely associated with abolitionism to command mainstream appeal.

As the delegates filed into the "Wigwam" in Chicago, a concerted stop-Seward drive got under way. Maryland judge David Davis and Senator Lyman Trumbull of Illinois headed Lincoln's forces, and they knew that Seward commanded only lukewarm support in several key state delegations. Several contingents had come to the convention pledged to support "favorite son" candidates. Other contenders had their followers, but the issue was between Lincoln and Seward.

Lincoln was fortunate that the convention met in his home state. His supporters found it possible to pack the convention galleries with Lincoln partisans. The Seward camp was outraged when they learned that Davis had facilitated the printing of extra seating passes favorable to the Lincolnites. The fact that convention chairman George Ashmun had come down in favor of Lincoln became known only after the convention commenced.

By and large the 466 delegates agreed on the myriad of antislavery planks in the platform. But trouble arose over a plank that called for a tightening of Federal immigration and naturalization laws. To placate Republican nativists Seward had not opposed the provision. German-speaking delegates (the Dutch Bloc), led by Republican insider Carl Schurz of Wisconsin, immediately defected to Lincoln.

Clearly Lincoln had some savvy floor operators handling his campaign. Ohio senator Benjamin Wade secured the bloc vote of Pennsylvania by promising that state's political boss, Senator Simon Cameron, a cabinet slot in the future Lincoln administration. Trumbull convinced venerable Supreme Court justice John McLean to second Lincoln's nomination. But all attempts to woo the third major candidate, Senator Salmon Chase of Ohio, met with failure.

A wild floor demonstration followed the placing of Lincoln's name in nomination. Inside, the convention roared for the "Rail Splitter," while a large throng of supporters demonstrated in the streets around the "Wigwam." Seward's subsequent demonstration seemed tame by comparison. Lincoln's followers hooted constantly during the speeches extolling Seward's virtues.

Although reeling, Seward's floor managers kept their ranks together for the first two ballots. But after Chase bowed out just prior to the third roll call, they realized Lincoln would triumph. He went on, of course, to win the election. Seward ably served in the Lincoln administration as secretary of state.

A NECESSARY ALLIANCE

In 1876 the Republicans were approaching a crucial electoral interlude. They had already lost their long-standing control of Congress, and their hold on the White House was shaky. No clear-cut presidential nominee had appeared. Although his administration had been badly tainted by scandal, President U. S. Grant retained his personal popularity. Congressional barons such as Senators Roscoe Conkling of New York and Oliver P. Morton of Indiana advocated that Grant run for a third term. The president was receptive, but many state party leaders forcefully opposed the prospect. Conkling and his "Stalwart" faction proposed Morton as an alternate candidate.

Rutherford B. Hayes, Republican presidential nominee in 1876

Senator James G. Blaine of Maine should have been the front-runner for the nomination. He was an able legislator and a fine public speaker. But his reputation for influence peddling with corporate (mostly railroad) lobbyists made him unpopular with the reformist element of his party. Before the convention, for example, in a confidential letter to a railroad executive, Blaine had advised him "to burn these letters." When the missive leaked to the press the sena-

A BROKERS' CONVENTION

In June 1880 the Republican party experienced an almost textbook example of a "brokers' convention." Out of a large field, party barons meeting in Chicago selected Representative James A. Garfield of Ohio as the presidential nominee. Long an influential member of the House, Garfield stepped in as a "dark-horse" candidate when "Half Breed" supporters of James G. Blaine of Maine switched their votes to prevent Ulysses S. Grant's "Stalwart" supporters from gaining a third presidential nomination for the Civil War hero.

To placate the disappointed Stalwarts, the convention nominated Chester A. Arthur of New York to the vice-presidency, but not without a fight. Republican reformers considered Arthur the personification of the party hack. Desperate, delegates proposed several other candidates. The most interesting alternative to Arthur was former senator Blanche K. Bruce of Mississippi. Bruce was an African-American who had represented Mississippi in the Senate during the early 1870s. He was the last of his race to sit in the upper house of Congress until 1966. An able lawyer, he had impressed many of his political colleagues greatly; if he had been born white, some believed, he would have enjoyed a long and distinguished senatorial career. Exactly why Senator William Windom of Minnesota placed Bruce's name in nomination remains a mystery, and Bruce received only about a dozen votes in subsequent ballots, but he was the first African-American to be nominated to the vice-presidency. (Nearly a century passed before one of the two major parties—the Democrats this time—proposed the nomination of another African-American: Julian Bond of Georgia.)

After much complaining the delegates agreed on Arthur. Upon Garfield's assassination Arthur ascended to the presidency, where he served an unexpectedly honorable tenure. One of Arthur's first acts as president was to nominate Blanche Bruce as registrar of the U.S. Treasury.

tor was styled "Burn the Letters" Blaine. Through his associates in the "Half-breed" faction, though, Blaine still commanded considerable clout with many of the delegates who gathered at the convention hall in Cincinnati, Ohio, in June 1876.

Republican reformers were pushing the candidacy of Secretary of the Treasury Benjamin Bristow of Kentucky, but party regulars considered him a loser. Among a group of compromise choices Governor Rutherford B. Hayes of Ohio looked the most promising. Hayes showed interest and had put out feelers.

Among the nominating speeches, Col. Robert Ingersoll's oration for Blaine was the most notable. While denouncing the Democratic "rebels" he extolled Blaine as a "Plumed Knight" who fought for all patriotic Americans. Blaine's detractors in the galleries jeered: "James G. Blaine—the Continental Liar from the State of Maine." But a Blaine bandwagon got rolling just as the initial ballot commenced. Suddenly, the house lights literally went out.

Anti-Blaine operatives had gone down to the basement of the convention hall and shut off the gas supply to force an early adjournment for the day. As session chairman Senator John Sherman of Ohio moved to adjourn, Blaine's floor leader, Representative Joseph G. Cannon of Illinois, rushed toward the podium, cursing. The enraged Cannon had to be restrained from attacking Sherman. Despite fierce protests from the Blaine camp, the delegates dispersed. Throughout the evening a coalition of Blaine's enemies worked to agree on someone else.

After the first ballot the next day, which Blaine led, Conkling airily admitted that Morton was a "dead duck" and would soon withdraw. There was no chance that Conkling would back the Plumed Knight. But Conkling and the Stalwarts would not endorse Benjamin Bristow either. Bristow's chief henchman, Carl Schurz, made contact with Governor Hayes's spokesman, Ohio representative James A. Garfield. During a short break before the fifth ballot, Bristow's 113 delegates joined the growing movement to draft Hayes. Then Conkling led the majority of Morton's contingent into the Hayes camp. That curious alliance of reformers and domestic reactionaries on the seventh ballot secured the 378 votes Hayes needed. A bitter Blaine was convinced that a vicious conspiracy had deprived him of his rightful prize. But Hayes's "Ohio Gang" had pursued a quiet and effective strategy. The nominee selected Blaine's good friend Representative William A. Wheeler of New York as his running mate. After a hotly disputed election the Hayes-Wheeler ticket took power in March 1877.

BIG BILL TAFT

When he ran for president in 1904, Theodore Roosevelt promised, probably to his eternal regret, not to seek another term in 1908. Republicans worried about their ability to nominate a worthy successor. They gratefully accepted the president's choice—Secretary of War William Howard Taft of Ohio. But the affable "Big Bill" was not much of a campaigner. At the June party convention in Chicago, partisans tried to whip up enthusiasm for Taft with catchy slogans such as "The Only One to Fill the Bill is Taft." Delegates also warbled campy songs, including this favorite:

> B- I- double L Bill!
> Good, old honest Bill!
> He's the Bill to start each mill
> And we'll have him, yes we will!
> He'll get in for the next four years
> Let's all give him three hearty cheers!
> B- I- double L Bill!
> That's no counterfeit Bill!

The role of such lyrics in Taft's solid defeat of his Democratic rival, William Jennings Bryan, is open to debate.

WILSON, WITH BRYAN'S HELP

The 1912 Democratic National Convention, held in Baltimore, was a colorful affair that featured dramatic episodes as well as moments of low comedy. That year the Republicans were divided between incumbent president William Howard Taft and his predecessor, Theodore Roosevelt, and the Democrats sensed victory. Accordingly, many party regulars were determined to grant the nomination to a veteran Democratic wheelhorse, Speaker of the House James B. "Champ" Clark of Missouri. Although he had a distinctly provincial manner and was no oratorical dynamo, "Old Hound Dawg" Clark enjoyed support in every section of the country. Representative Oscar W. Underwood of Alabama, with a conservative support base in the Deep South, was also a contender. Progressive Democrats of the Northeast gathered around Governor Woodrow Wilson of New Jersey, but certain party insiders thought that Wilson, a former president of Princeton University, was a sanctimonious prig. Several state governors emerged as favorite sons, but they were an unexceptional lot. As the Democrats assembled in late June, Clark possessed nearly 500 delegate votes; he needed 726 to win the nomination.

As the first session opened on June 24, 1912, it seemed that Clark would roll to an easy victory. He had the fervent support of the powerful press baron William Randolph Hearst, and various Democratic elder statesmen, including New York judge Alton B. Par-

Theodore Roosevelt and William Howard Taft on Taft's inauguration day, March 4, 1909

ker (the 1904 nominee), had endorsed him. President Samuel Gompers of the American Federation of Labor (AFL) was also in Champ's corner. Speaker Clark's trusted lieutenant, Governor Ollie James of Kentucky, had been appointed the permanent chairman of the convention. But William Jennings Bryan was destined to be the "joker in the deck" in 1912.

Although the Democrats had run Bryan in three presidential elections, in 1912 he was an ordinary delegate from Nebraska. He had endorsed the front-runner earlier in the year, but Clark had kept his distance from the "Great Commoner." The repeated snubs of the Clark camp had deeply offended Bryan, and he went to Baltimore determined "to kick up a dust."

At the opening session Bryan tried to thwart a public tribute to his old rival, Parker, but Clark's supporters shouted him down. Soon Bryan was making a nuisance of himself by disputing the wording of several platform planks. Then he offered a resolution that the convention deny the nomination to any candidate tied to the interests of Wall Street. After great uproar and confusion the declaration was adopted. The complacent Clark entourage did not consider Bryan's antics a serious threat to their candidate.

Through the first ten ballots Clark retained a large lead, but he could not reach the required two-thirds majority. The Underwood and Wilson managers agreed to stand together against Clark. A despondent Wilson had sent a message to his manager, William McCombs, stating his intention to withdraw. McCombs chose to ignore the note and ordered his aides to keep the Wilson delegates intact. Even that canny political hand did not anticipate Bryan's next move.

Just before the eleventh ballot Tammany boss Charles Murphy delivered New York's votes to Clark. The roll call was delayed an hour while the Missouri delegation, believing it was all over, led a floor parade for Clark. At that point Bryan demanded that he be given the chance to explain his upcoming vote. Despite the jeers and catcalls of the Clark crowd, Bryan started for the rostrum. Chairman James and Clark's floor leader, Joseph Folk, had foolishly assented to Bryan's request. Only Judge Parker seemed to sense impending disaster.

After waiting out the hecklers, Bryan roundly denounced Clark's alliance with Murphy and Tammany Hall. He declared that he could not support a candidate who agreed to act as a foil for Murphy and Hearst. He would switch his vote to Wilson. Folk was stunned to learn that the entire Nebraska delegation planned to follow Bryan's example. Gompers and his AFL associates were also going over to Wilson. Many old Bryan Democrats had been looking for an excuse to dump the Missourian. From that moment it was downhill for Clark. To the end of his life Clark was convinced that Bryan had created havoc in 1912 to secure a fourth presidential

Woodrow Wilson accepting the 1912 Democratic presidential nomination from the front porch of his Princeton, New Jersey, home, August 7, 1912

nomination for himself. Hearst, who loathed both Wilson and Bryan, heartily seconded Clark's bitter sentiment.

With Bryan now "running point," the Wilsonians gained reinforcements. Various favorite-son votes went into Wilson's column. But the Clark forces fought on and sought an alliance with Underwood. For five days the Democrats sweated through a myriad of roll calls. On the forty-fifth ballot Underwood's lieutenants quit and most of their charges went over to Wilson, who now controlled 633 votes. Only the California and Missouri delegations and a smattering of votes from other states remained with Clark. On the forty-seventh ballot Governor John Burke of North Dakota moved that the nomination of Wilson be made unanimous. Aided by the Republican split, Wilson won the national election that fall; he enjoyed one of the more effective presidencies of the twentieth century.

EISENHOWER AND THE UNCOMMITTED

Probably the last dramatic convention occurred in July 1952 when Ohio senator Robert A. Taft battled Dwight D. Eisenhower for the Republican nomination at the International Amphitheater in Chicago. Taft had been actively campaigning since September 1951. It was his intention to return the party to what he considered true conservative Republicanism. To his cause rallied the Republican "Old Guard," which longed to undo the "big government" policies created by President Franklin D. Roosevelt. Taft's message might have sounded good to small-town elements in the Midwest, but mainstream party moderates of the Northeast wanted no part of "Mr. Republican." They knew that most Americans had little interest in dismantling the New Deal. Those Republican "realists," led by former New York governor Thomas E. Dewey and Henry Cabot Lodge of Massachu-

Vice-President John Nance Garner's David-and-Goliath contest with Franklin D. Roosevelt for the 1940 Democratic presidential nomination turned out differently than the biblical version (Library of Congress)

setts, sought an alternative.

The shopworn Harold Stassen of Minnesota was available, but by 1952 many viewed him as a marginal figure. Governor Earl Warren of California expressed interest, yet his appeal was mostly limited to the West Coast. Most insiders guessed that Warren was really after the vice-presidential spot. A brief boomlet for Gen. Douglas MacArthur failed to stir much emotion. Dewey and Lodge had decided that war hero Eisenhower was the man to stop Taft. Ike was serving in Europe as the supreme commander of the multinational defense forces of the North Atlantic Treaty Organization (NATO). A nominal Republican, he enjoyed popularity that transcended party lines. The general acted coy while the draft movement gathered strength, especially after publisher Henry R. Luce joined the effort. In February 1952 Eisenhower allowed his name to be entered in the New Hampshire primary.

The results of the early primaries were inconclusive, and Taft fattened his lead in the delegate count. Taft had secured the votes of token Republican organizations in the Deep South, but a Republican resurgence in that region still lay a decade in the future. The selections of those skeleton groupings were irregular at best and easy targets for concerted challenge efforts at the convention. By May 1952 Taft felt his position was secure, although Illinois senator Everett M. Dirksen warned him that he "heard noises around the edges."

Eisenhower resigned a NATO commander and returned home to proclaim in June that he was a "No Deal Man." To Taft's dismay Eisenhower made stunning headway with uncommitted delegates. As the convention convened on July 7, Taft still led, but Eisenhower was closing the gap. At the credentials committee meetings the Eisenhower forces began winning disputed southern seats. Many of those challenges carried over to the actual convention sessions. Convention chairman Joseph Martin was hard-pressed to keep order as the debates became bitter. At one point an angry Dirksen, pointing at Dewey in the New York delegation, denounced him for twice leading the Republicans to defeat as the presidential nominee.

THIRD-TERM STRATEGY

In 1940 a substantial group of anti-New Deal Democrats attempted to hold President Franklin Roosevelt to his alleged promise not to seek a third term. Vice-President John Nance Garner of Texas announced his desire to win the nomination, and Senator Harry Byrd of Virginia was also waiting in the wings. But Roosevelt had no intention of vacating the Oval Office. With the world war raging, spokesmen for the Roosevelt administration warned that it was unwise to "swap horses in midstream."

Roosevelt and his advisers adopted the position that the president was the helpless victim of overwhelming public demand that he seek a third term. When the Democratic convention convened in Chicago that July, Harry Hopkins, Roosevelt's closest aide, had a plan to ensure his boss's "draft." On the night of the nominations, Chicago sewers superintendent Thomas McGarry hid in the basement of the hall with a microphone hooked to the convention's speaker system. On cue, the "Voice from the Sewers" dutifully bellowed "We Want Roosevelt" for more than twenty minutes. Meanwhile, groups of strategically placed party workers took up the chant, setting off a turbulent floor demonstration in favor of the nomination, which was humbly accepted.

After most of the contested seats were settled in Eisenhower's favor, the Taft camp learned that Stassen's votes were also going to the general. Clearly the Eisenhower floor leaders were far more effective than Taft's operatives. The large uncommitted Pennsylvania and Michigan delegations also leaned toward Eisenhower. Taft had depended far too heavily on old-time regulars and organizations that were no match for the sophisticated team working for Eisenhower. During Eisenhower's floor demonstration the slogan "I Like Ike" was introduced to the American voting public.

On the first ballot Eisenhower emerged with 595 votes—just nine short of the majority needed to win. Although Taft's delegates pledged to stay loyal, his inner circle knew the cause was lost. Virtually every previously uncommitted vote went to Eisenhower. Senator John Bricker of Ohio sorrowfully moved that the nomination be made unanimous.

To Governor Warren's chagrin, he was not the Californian Eisenhower named to the vice-presidential spot. Desiring some youth, Eisenhower and his advisers tapped the up-and-coming Senator Richard M. Nixon, then thirty-nine years of age. Senator Taft was angered that one of his supporters had not been named in Nixon's stead. But he prudently endorsed the ticket, which went on to win in the fall. Eight years of "I Like Ike" followed.

In most respects the 1952 convention served as a watershed in American electoral history. It was the last conclave that featured some suspense regarding the ultimate nominee. The intense national grass-roots organizing effort by the Eisenhower team pointed to a new trend. The process was refined in 1960 by the campaign organization created for the Democratic candidacy of Massachusetts senator John F. Kennedy.

REPUBLICAN CONSERVATIVES AND MODERATES

Since 1952 presidential nominating conventions have tended to be pro forma events designed to ratify decisions made in state party caucuses and presidential primaries. Delegates arrive at the meeting places already knowing who they will nominate. Still, the modern conclaves remain important because they often serve as backdrops for social and political developments having lasting implications. The Republican National Convention held in San Francisco in

THE LAST LAUGH

The Democratic National Convention that gathered in Philadelphia in July 1948 was anything but a jolly affair. The delegates battled furiously over much of the platform, all with the knowledge that their candidate, Harry Truman, trailed in the polls. The party faithful were in need of a good laugh—and they got it on the final night of the convention.

Prior to President Truman's nomination acceptance speech, the inimitable Mrs. Emma Guffey Miller of Pennsylvania, a longtime party wheelhorse, was scheduled to address the convention on the topic of world peace. A host of pigeons was brought onstage in two large hampers; they were going to be released as "doves of peace" when the "Old Gray Mare," as Mrs. Miller was known, gave her speech. When the time came, however, the birds refused to budge, and convention workers were obliged to heave them into the air by hand. Once airborne, the disoriented pigeons circled drunkenly looking for roosts. Many "buzzed" the convention floor before heading for the main stage, where Truman and other dignitaries were seated. Some of the birds flapped about in the rafters while others clung to the draperies.

When House Speaker Sam Rayburn, the convention chairman, tried to restore the howling delegates to order, a pigeon landed on his bald head. To the delight of the spectators, at intervals the brave bird returned to "Rayburn's Roost" during the remainder of the evening. Mrs. Miller gave her worried convention colleagues more than peace—she gave them peace of mind. And Truman got the last laugh—nearly universally picked to lose the general election, he won.

July 1964 served as just such a backdrop.

After Richard Nixon's defeat in his race with John Kennedy in 1960, moderate and conservative factions of the Republican party began to compete for control of the national party apparatus. Although Nixon wanted another chance in 1964, moderates of the Northeast and Midwest preferred a standard bearer who would remain true to the middle-of-the-road traditions of such candidates as Alf Landon and Thomas Dewey. Governor Nelson Rockefeller seemed to some of them to fill the bill, but others judged the scion of great wealth as too aloof to win the hearts of the voters. Henry Cabot Lodge and Governor George Romney of Michigan were often mentioned as alternatives.

The conservative wing of the party, which gained much of its support in the states of the Deep South, the Plains, and the Far West, rejected all of those candidates. Since the death of Robert Taft in 1954, Republican conservatism had undergone a distinct transformation. The "New Right" of the 1960s remained anticommunist, but it abandoned the isolationism of Taft. On the domestic side it was not content merely with railing against "big government"; the new breed wanted actually to dismantle the New Deal's legacy of regulatory agencies and social welfare administrations. Moderate regulars were dismayed at the growing fervor of Republican conservatives and at the increasing influence within the party of such ultra-right conservatives as the John Birch Society. Everett Dirksen remarked, "These boys seem to have taken the Mau Mau Oath—in a serious way." The conservatives preferred Senator Barry Goldwater of Arizona as their candidate.

During the primary season, Goldwater, aided by an extremely efficient campaign organization, trounced the competition. By late spring only Rockefeller remained as a serious contender. Once Goldwater won the California primary in June, however, his nomination be-

Presidential nominee Dwight D. Eisenhower and Ohio senator Robert Taft, Eisenhower's chief rival for the nomination, at the Republican National Convention, Chicago, July 1952

came a foregone conclusion. A final "Stop Goldwater" effort coalesced around Governor William Scranton of Pennsylvania, but going into the convention Goldwater had enough delegates to win a first-ballot nomination.

Although Goldwater personally tried to befriend his disappointed moderate opponents in the Republican party, many of his supporters wanted to humiliate their longtime rivals. An ugly mood prevailed during much of the remaining convention. In floor speeches Goldwater spokesmen openly scorned such party stalwarts as Dewey and Senator George Aiken of Vermont. The conservative majority loudly rejected a series of resolutions sponsored by moderates. On the grounds that they held incomplete press credentials, several reporters, including John Chancellor of NBC, were physically ejected from the convention floor by security marshals.

By far the most memorable scene occurred before the nomination, when the delegates debated the party platform. Rockefeller appeared to argue a moderate plank that denounced political "extremism." When the New Yorker attempted to speak, he was greeted with a wave of abuse from both the floor and the public galleries, which led him to observe, "Ladies and gents, this is still a free country you know." A shaken Dirksen noted that Goldwater's floor leaders made little effort to quiet the aroused crowd. Remorseless television cameras captured all of it.

On the final night of the convention, Goldwater appeared to deliver his acceptance speech. Many hoped he would offer conciliatory remarks to the moderates. He had already selected the fiercely conservative but relatively unknown William E. Miller of New York as his vice-presidential running mate, a bitter pill for the moderates to swallow. After a game Richard Nixon gave an upbeat introduction, Goldwater launched into his speech, which conceded nothing to his opponents. Referring to the platform battle, he defiantly stated: "And let me remind you that extremism in the defense of liberty is no vice, and moderation in the pursuit of justice is no virtue." Supporters such as

Police equipped in riot gear prepare to keep the peace during the 1968 Democratic National Convention.

California delegate Ronald Reagan cheered heartily, but moderate listeners were astonished at the inflammatory tone of the remark. Dwight Eisenhower later asked Goldwater exactly what he meant by the statement.

The bizarre episode did nothing to enhance Goldwater's already remote chance of defeating Lyndon Johnson in the general election. As expected, he lost to the incumbent in a landslide. Conservatives in the Republican party, however, were not as disappointed as they might have been if they had lost the election by running a moderate. Goldwater's nomination signaled that in the Republican party the conservatives were a force to be reckoned with.

CONFLICT OVER VIETNAM

By 1968 the political fortunes of Lyndon Johnson and the Democrats had sharply declined because of the war in Vietnam. The Republicans had their best chance at gaining the presidency since the Eisenhower years. The Republican convention, which convened in Miami, Florida, in July, was a bland affair; Richard Nixon secured the nomination on the first ballot. The Democrats, on the other hand, faced their conclave with great trepidation.

At the beginning of 1968 President Johnson found himself in a difficult position. Most of the Republicans supported his war policies, but many Democrats opposed the war. Certain groups within the party hoped he would not run for reelection, although few were willing to enlist in a "dump Johnson" movement. In the autumn of 1967 the enigmatic Senator Eugene McCarthy of Minnesota had announced his candidacy for the Democratic nomination. Running on an antiwar platform, the droll McCarthy conducted a low-key campaign spurned by political "professionals" but endorsed by an increasing number of voters. McCarthy found his greatest acceptance among the students on the nation's college campuses.

Many so-called experts were shocked when McCarthy upset Johnson in the

New Hampshire primary in late February 1968. Quickly Senator Robert Kennedy of New York entered the race—if the people seemed prepared to accept an antiwar Democrat on the presidential ticket, Kennedy wanted it to be him. Despite the pleas of his supporters, the demoralized Johnson refused to mount an aggressive campaign for the nomination. In fact, he did just the opposite. At the conclusion of a national television address on March 31, Johnson announced, "I do not seek, and will not accept the nomination of my party for another term as your president."

After the Johnson pullout party regulars cast their lot with Vice-President Hubert Humphrey of Minnesota, who pledged to continue the policies of the president. But old John Kennedy loyalists and liberal Democrats scrambled onto the "Bobby Express." A bitter Eugene McCarthy, angry because he had demonstrated the viability of an antiwar candidacy only to see his support migrate to Kennedy, refused to make common cause and faded from contention. He made it clear that he would never graciously accept a Kennedy nomination.

By late May, "Hubert the Happy" led the delegate count, but Kennedy's campaign continued to gain strength. Then tragedy struck. In Los Angeles on June 5, minutes after claiming victory in the California Democratic primary, Senator Kennedy was assassinated. Few of Kennedy's supporters switched to the Humphrey camp. McCarthy regained some of the support he had lost to Kennedy, and other Kennedy supporters started a movement to draft Senator George McGovern of South Dakota—that effort went nowhere. Humphrey continued to secure delegate support in the primaries.

In August the Democratic National Convention convened in Chicago under a cloud of controversy. Mayor Richard Daley had vowed to make the proceedings "secure" from the hordes of antiwar demonstrators that had gathered to protest Humphrey's nomination and had turned much of Chicago into an armed camp. Security was so restrictive in the convention hall itself that critics deemed the proceedings worthy of the Soviet Union. President Johnson remained home in Texas.

A series of tense sessions commenced. The choice of House majority leader Carl Albert as permanent chairman turned out to be a disaster. The diminutive Albert proved volatile and several times became embroiled in undignified verbal exchanges with hecklers. Certainly he did nothing to quiet the turmoil that surfaced during debates over Vietnam policy planks of the platform. Meanwhile, thousands of students and other antiwar protesters milled around in the streets outside the convention hall.

On the evening of the presidential nomination the streets of Chicago exploded. Goaded beyond endurance, police suddenly charged into the protesters with billy clubs swinging. Officers believed Daley had given them permission to quell the demonstrators in any manner they saw fit. Witnesses testified that many of the police used excessive force to disperse the crowds. Observers noted later that some of the most brutal officers hailed from precincts that were notorious for corrupt dealings with organized crime figures.

When word of the riot outside reached the convention hall, commotion erupted among the delegates. As Senator Abraham Ribicoff of Connecticut denounced the Chicago "Gestapo," an enraged Mayor Daley jumped to his feet, cursing. The first ballot of the roll call proceeded with many interruptions. Fistfights broke out between supporters of Humphrey and McCarthy. Humphrey indeed won the nomination on the first ballot, but many in the hall, and outside, believed the prize of the Democratic presidential nomination was tarnished by events. A melancholy Humphrey watched the spectacle from his hotel suite.

On the final day of the convention Humphrey made a gallant and conciliatory acceptance speech, but many delegates gave the speech only cursory attention. His praise of the record of President Johnson brought catcalls. The hopes for the Democratic party in the general election seemed dim. Although experts predicted that Humphrey might be left behind in the election not only by Nixon but also by third-party candidate George Wallace, the resilient vice-president proved a good campaigner and began to close the gap, especially after he became more dovish on the war. Nixon managed a narrow margin.

Since 1968 the primary system has become more entrenched and conventions less exciting. Sometimes, as in the case of Ronald Reagan's 1980 Republican nomination, convention assemblies can supply just the right mood of celebration to legitimize a candidate in the eyes of the nation. In contrast, Jimmy Carter's renomination to the Democratic ticket in 1980 took place in a demoralized atmosphere, hurting Carter's chances in the election. Now that party conventions serve largely as ratification gatherings for electoral decisions made during the primaries, some of the fun and certainly most of the suspense are gone from presidential politics. That is a great pity!

Selling the President and His Party: Presidential Campaign Iconography

by SCOTT DERKS

In the early days of the American Republic the nation had little need for campaign iconography. By means of the Electoral College, men of property handpicked the president, somewhat in the manner of a church selecting a new pastor. The emergence of clearly defined parties during George Washington's second administration altered the mechanics of the process, but politics remained a gentlemen's affair. The missing component in the early American version of democracy was the people. That soon changed. In the beginning, state legislatures selected most of the presidential electors, but after 1800 states gradually allowed their white male citizens to make the choice.

The emergence of Andrew Jackson as a presidential contender in 1824 signaled the arrival of something close to popular democracy in American politics. Jackson was in some ways much like the traditional leaders he supplanted. While he was relatively uneducated, he had become a leading attorney in his state and a national military hero. He was politically sophisticated and accustomed to command. What was indisputably different about Jackson was the rough-hewn image he projected. That image—based in fact—became the central feature of Jackson's campaigns for the presidency; with it he solicited the approval of the new mass of voters upon which his rivals also depended.

Historians characterize the American experience in part as the story of the gradual achievement of popular democracy. The election of Jackson to the presidency in 1828 signaled the completion of the first stage in that process. Ironically, with the attainment of greater democracy has come increased reliance on the image making the Jacksonians successfully pioneered. Political loyalty in the modern sense depends not so much on loyalty to a set of issues as on loyalty to a party and a candidate. The images that establish the identity of a candidate therefore reveal as much about the voters as about the candidate seeking the vote—not always a happy thought.

EARLY NATIONAL ICONOGRAPHY

Since none of the early presidents had to rely on the approval of the people, none of them had to endure the process of campaigning. Since there were no campaigns there was no campaign image making. But commemorative artifacts associated with the early presidents—especially the first president—do exist.

Washington's election inspired the creation of brass, silvered copper, and pewter garment buttons bearing such slogans as "The Majesty of the People" and "E Pluribus Unum." The diaries of several of Washington's contemporaries record that the president actually wore a set of the buttons, probably sporting an eagle-sunburst design, to his inauguration. Hundreds in the inaugural audience wore buttons bearing the slogan "Long Live the President" or the initials

Clothing buttons commemorating the inauguration of George Washington as president, 1789. Members of the inaugural audience reported that at the ceremony Washington wore buttons of a similar type.

"GW" encircled by the first initial of each of the thirteen states. (At that point only eleven had ratified the Constitution.) In addition to the buttons, commemorative tankards bearing Washington's likeness also survive.

Washington's successors—John Adams, Thomas Jefferson, James Madison, and James Monroe—slipped in and out of office without stimulating even the modest outpouring of iconography that Washington inspired. A few items survive, including a leather bridle rosette commemorating the inauguration of John Adams; buttons, mugs, pitchers, and snuffboxes celebrating the ascension of Jefferson (one of the pitcher designs satirizes Jefferson's second-term foreign policy, portraying the president as a cow being tugged in opposite directions by John Bull and Napoleon); and similar items paying tribute to Madison and Monroe, including a handsome transfer pitcher bearing Madison's likeness.

In spite of the fact that during the administrations of Madison and Monroe the party system of Federalists and Democratic-Republicans dissolved, commemorative iconography manufactured during their administrations featured increasingly partisan messages, mostly endorsing the anti-Federalism of the Democratic-Republicans. A patriotic song, "Hail Columbia," that Jeffersonians adapted in 1800 to tout the virtues of their candidate appeared on an 1809 Madison pitcher:

Hail Columbia happy land
Hail ye patriotic band
Who late opposed oppressive laws
And now stand firm in freedom's cause
Rejoice for now the storm is gone
Columbia owns her chosen son
The rights of man shall be our boast
And Jefferson our favorite toast
Republicans behold your chief
He comes to give your fears relief
Now arm'd in virtue firm and true
Looks for support to Heaven and you

As the conflict between the United States and Great Britain heated up, objects critical of the antiwar stance of the Federalists appeared. One such object, an 1813 medal commemorating the in-

Hand-painted banner proclaiming "T. Jefferson President of the United States of America, John Adams no More" (Smithsonian Institution)

auguration of Madison for a second term, bore the slogan, "Protection Against Invasion Is Due from Every Society to the Parts Composing It." That kind of material prepared the way for the virulently partisan campaign iconography that appeared after Jackson's surge to prominence.

HERO OF NEW ORLEANS

The iconography associated with Andrew Jackson's presidential candidacy in 1824 is transitional in nature. In several states the responsibility of selecting presidential electors remained in the hands of legislators; the nation had not yet learned how to gear up for a national campaign at the grass-roots level. Much of the material that survives portrays Jackson as the "Hero of New Orleans" who defeated the British during the War of 1812. Whether or not the pitchers, plates, tokens, and snuffboxes associated with Jackson's first campaign were manufactured before or after the election is a matter of conjecture. The Smithsonian Institution has dated one item, a ceramic crock bearing the slogan "25,000 Majority/GNL Jackson," from 1824, but the crock could as likely have appeared after the election in protest of the "corrupt" result.

After Jackson's defeat in 1824 he immediately began preparing for a rematch with John Quincy Adams. That time small amounts of campaign iconography appeared in its mature form: medals; garment buttons; silk bandannas and ribbons; ceramic pitchers, plates, and vases; copper goods; snuffboxes; combs; whiskey flasks; and other items promoted Jackson as a public personality and presidential candidate. One medal lauded "The Gallant & Successful Defender of New Orleans & Candidate for the Presidency of the United States

Silk bandana (left) and papier-mâché snuff box lauding the "Hero of New Orleans," presidential candidate Andrew Jackson (Smithsonian Institution)

of America." Even so, contemporary accounts of the campaign indicate that people more often employed casual items to whip up enthusiasm. A story circulated that during the War of 1812 General Jackson gave his horse to a wounded soldier and fashioned a hickory walking stick for himself. At public gatherings Old Hickory's supporters planted hickory trees, raised hickory poles, and waved hickory sprigs. More than a few also took a drink or two from whiskey flasks displaying the portrait of their hero.

The campaign items associated with John Quincy Adams lack the focus on popular image that made Jackson material so successful with voters. A clay tile in the Smithsonian Institution promotes Adams as the candidate of "Peece [*sic*]/Liberty/Home/Industry." Thread boxes carried such unimaginative slogans as "Victory for Adams," "Adams and Liberty," "Be Firm for Adams," and "Adams Forever."

Jackson's 1832 campaign for reelection featured iconography similar to that of 1828. Oddly, although Jackson had angered opponents by taking stands against nullification and against rechartering the Second Bank of the United States, ideology remained in the background of the campaign. Only a few items touted Jackson's positions on the issues. One, a medal struck in New York, proclaimed "The Bank Must Perish/the Union Must and Shall Be Preserved." Jackson's opponent, Kentuckian Henry Clay, inspired a few similarly ideological pieces. One token identified him as "The Champion of Republicanism and the American System," and a button bore the slogan "The Champion of Internal Improv[ement]s." Seeking to promote Clay as a statesmanlike alternative to the rustic president, a New York medal maker portrayed the Kentuckian in a Roman toga. Clay, the "Sage of Ashland," claimed his share of the western vote as well, and during the campaign his supporters erected ash poles similar to Jacksonian hickory poles.

DEMOCRATS AND WHIGS

By the time of Jackson's 1828 campaign his supporters were calling themselves "Democrats" or "Democratic-Republicans." Jackson's opponents, led by President John Quincy Adams and Henry Clay, called themselves "National Republicans." After Jackson's reelection, Clay's supporters banded with disaffected Democrats and anti-Jacksonians to form the Whig party, taking their name from the prominent British antiroyalist party of the revolutionary period. In 1836 Jackson's vice-president, Martin Van Buren, ran as the Democratic presidential candidate; the Whigs believed their only hope of preventing a Van Buren victory lay in throwing the election to the House of Representatives, so they ran three regional candidates for president. None of the candidates in 1836 commanded much of the voters' attention. Little iconography associated with the election that year survives.

The Whig party, however, had already shown that they thrived as an opposition force. Upon its formal organization in 1834 the party issued buttons, tokens, and ribbons promoting itself as the successor to the American revolutionists of 1776. Much of the material featured the Whig symbol, a liberty cap on a pole; that symbol had been prominent during the revolutionary period. Slogans promoted the "Whigs of 76 & 34" and claimed the party stood "For the Constitution." After Van Buren's election, moreover, the Whigs proved adept at self-promotion and at satire. Whigs advertised an 1837 convention by issuing ribbons featuring a portrait of George Washington and declaring "The Spirit of 76 Revived in 1837." Criticizing Van Buren's proposal to create a subtreasury system to house federal deposits, they struck medals featuring a jackass braying, "I Follow in the Steps of My Illustrious Predecessor." Whether or not the Whigs could discard their opposition mentality and assume a leadership role remained to be seen.

THE REAL THING

By the time Andrew Jackson started running for president he had accumulated enough life experience to satisfy two ordinary men. His reputation for roughhousing stood him in good stead with his supporters and provided ample material for his opponents' futile attempts to smear him into defeat. One anti-Jackson pamphlet circulated during the campaign of 1828, entitled *Reminiscences; or an Extract from the Catalogue of General Jackson's Youthful Indiscretions, between the ages of Twenty-Three and Sixty,* purported to chronicle fourteen fights, duels, brawls, and shootings in which Jackson had "killed, slashed, and clawed various American citizens." Some of the stories, such as the story of Jackson's incredible duel with Charles Dickinson in which he fired only after Dickinson put a bullet in his chest, were largely true. "I intended to kill him," Jackson remarked afterward. "I would have stood up long enough to kill him if he had put a bullet in my brain."

TIPPECANOE IN 1840

The election of 1840 confirmed the power of the Whigs—and the voters. Finally released from property and tax restrictions, the American electorate was large enough to influence decisively the nature of electioneering. The Whig party was mature enough to imitate the Democratic party of 1828 and nominate for president its own popular war hero, Indianian William Henry Harrison, who gained his fame by defeating the Shawnee Indian confederacy at the Battle of Tippecanoe in 1813. As the election approached, Whigs across the nation raised a call for Harrison (and running mate John Tyler of Virginia): "Tippecanoe and Tyler too." Democrats countered weakly with incumbent Van Buren, wounded politically by the panic and depression that began just after he assumed office in 1837.

Well educated, moderately wealthy, and fond of quoting the Latin classics, Harrison waged one of the most colorful presidential campaigns in American history. Much of the symbolism of the campaign involved log cabins and hard cider, images that, ironically, the Van Burenite press introduced. During the early days of the campaign a commenta-

Presidential candidate "Tippecanoe" Harrison promises the voters "true hospitality" on the cover of an 1841 Whig campaign pamphlet printed in New York. Andrew Jackson judges the product "sour" while Martin Van Buren endeavors to "stop the supply" (Library of Congress).

tor for the *Baltimore Republican* suggested that a barrel of hard cider and a modest pension might induce the elderly Harrison to "sit out the remainder of his days in his log cabin by the side of a 'sea coal' fire, and study moral philosophy." Whigs were quick to turn the comment into a slur against log cabin dwellers who drank hard cider, and Harrison became "The Poor Man's Friend." A variety of log cabin and hard cider campaign items appeared, including songbooks, almanacs, posters and ribbons, and cloth banners. Log cabin glee clubs sang Harrison's praises. Across the land Whigs sponsored raucous parades featuring actual log cabins loaded on wagons; at political rallies, operatives dispensed free hard cider. Those preferring harder stuff might prefer "Old Cabin" whiskey.

Other items recalled Harrison's military exploits. "Tippecanoe" brand shaving soap and tobacco appeared. One ribbon proclaimed, "Washington the father of the country, Harrison a Chip of [*sic*] the old block." Dances such as the Harrison Hoe-Down and the Tippecanoe Quick Step gained afficionados. Glass sandwich plates, china designed for everyday use, and metal tokens appeared at campaign rallies beside brass belt buckles, lacquered wood hairbrushes, and toiletries such as "Tippecanoe Extract," a "delicate perfume for handkerchiefs, gloves, and the hair, leaving a rich and durable fragrance."

The Van Buren camp responded to this deluge by trying to brand Harrison backward, revealing that his name spelled in reverse was "nosirrah," but voters had enough of the old leadership. A strong majority of the nearly two and a half million who voted—80 percent of those eligible—elevated Harrison to office.

Unfortunately the Harrison campaign proved far more exciting than the Harrison presidency. The sixty-eight-year-old former general produced the longest inaugural address on record—more than two hours—and the briefest term of office: he died of pneumonia on April 4, 1841—thirty days after his inauguration.

The broadening of the political franchise under Harrison influenced the style of presidential campaigns for the next fifty years. No campaign would be complete without its souvenirs: almanacs; campaign "songsters"; metal tokens; banners, ribbons, and buttons; paper ballots; flags; plates; glasses; walking canes; colorful paper lanterns; elaborate snuffboxes; and hand-blown whiskey bottles embossed with the candidate's portrait. Campaigns would also become filled with rituals similar to those of the revival meetings people knew and understood. And, in a land that loved celebrations and was learning to love elections, few campaigns would be devoid of social entertainment.

POLK IN 1844

With the theatrics of 1840 still fresh, supporters of 1844 candidates James K. Polk and Henry Clay recognized the need to cement the commitment of the voters to the politics of rural populism. Clay's forces invented the slogan "The Mill Boy of the Slashes" to give their Washington insider appropriate poor-boy roots. Ribbons portrayed Clay as "The Farmer of Ashland," complete with rustic scenes of a farmer plowing his field. The most unusual image created during the campaign was the Clay raccoon. Live raccoons in cages became a fixture at Clay rallies, and ribbons featuring an aggressive raccoon and a cowering Democratic rooster appeared, accompanied by the slogan, "Why Don't you Crow?"

For the first time, buttonlike lapel ornaments featuring the candidates' pictures appeared, along with multicolored lithograph prints of the candidates and their running mates. Legions of immigrant women were employed to hand-color the prints. Pro-Polk silk ribbons supported the annexation of Texas, and Pro-Clay ribbons called for "A Tariff for Protection" and declared Clay "Champion of the American System."

Both Clay and Polk forces staged parades in which huge, decorated balls, floats, and banners were rolled, hauled, and carried from town to town. The ball-rolling phenomenon would disappear in the 1850s—in the contemplative days before the Civil War—only to reappear in later elections with gusto.

TAYLOR IN 1848

Having attempted an issue-oriented campaign and failed in 1844, the Whigs in 1848 recruited another war hero, "Old Rough and Ready," Zachary Taylor. The fact that nobody, including Taylor himself, was quite sure of his positions on the issues made little difference. When a Whig politician first proposed that Taylor run for president, the old general scoffed, "Stop your nonsense and drink your whiskey!" The veteran soldier was such a political novice that he had never even voted for president before he ran in 1848. Evidence hints that he did not vote in that election. Most of the campaign's iconography emphasized "Old Zach's" years in the Mexican War. Eager supporters could own a full-sized, wood-burning stove featuring his likeness; thirty-seven types of whiskey flasks; dozens of bandannas; snuffboxes; cigar cases; razors; song sheets; and tokens. Many items carried the legend, "General Taylor Never Surrenders." Taylor spent most of the campaign at his military post and rarely met the public or made speeches.

The third-party Free Soil ticket, featuring Martin Van Buren in a comeback attempt, produced an innovative new campaign item in 1848. Searching for cheap, mass-produced items to tell their political story, Free Soil advocates transformed the large copper cent in use at the time into a political notice by "muling," or stamping, the words

MUSICAL SATIRE

Music has often served as a means of focusing the affections of voters during a campaign. In 1840, William Henry Harrison, "Old Tippecanoe," was ushered into the White House accompanied by a chorus of derisive ditties contrasting his common-man mystique with incumbent president Martin "Matty" Van Buren's aristocratic manners. For example, Harrison supporters were fond of loading up with a chaw of tobacco and singing:

> Old Tip he wears a homespun coat,
> He has no ruffled shirt-wirt-wirt;
> But Mat he has the golden plate,
> And he's a little squirt-wirt-wirt.

Tobacco juice flew every time the "wirt-wirt" part came around.

"VOTE THE LAND FREE" directly on the coins. As pennies were exchanged from hand to hand, the message spread.

Like Harrison, Taylor died in office, and the party found itself with the presidency but not the man it wanted there. Taylor's successor, vice-president Millard Fillmore, put in an honorable three years but lost his own bid for the Whig nomination in 1852.

PIERCE IN 1852

The election of 1852 pitted two military men—Franklin Pierce and Winfield Scott—who shared many of the same views. Dark horse Pierce did not receive the Democratic nomination until the forty-ninth ballot. Whig efforts to ride another war hero to victory failed, but Scott's candidacy did set the stage for the conversion of northern Whig sentiment to the Republican Party and candidate Abraham Lincoln in 1860. During the 1852 contest Scott campaigned hard to belittle the military record of Pierce; his party published a tiny but slanderous book, only one and a half inches wide, that pejoratively summarized *The Military Services of General Pierce*. The Whigs also attempted to tag Pierce as a "doughface," as a northern man with southern principles. Pierce forces struck back with a widely distributed cartoon that was captioned, "An Available Candidate/The One Qualification of a Whig President."

BUCHANAN IN 1856

A supporter of the Kansas-Nebraska Act (which opened new territory to slavery), Pierce was denied another Democratic nomination in 1856. Moreover, the Whigs had fallen by the wayside, hopelessly divided. A new party—the Republicans—had risen to take the Whigs' place. As befitted the times, campaign literature focused on the issues of slavery and union. Keepsakes advertising the first Republican candidate, John C. Fremont, flooded the market preaching "Free Speech, Free Press, Free Soil, Free Men, Fremont and Victory" and "No More Slave States." The Democrats, behind James Buchanan, used thinly veiled racism and a high-minded devotion to national unity to win southern votes and the election. One pro-Buchanan ribbon distributed throughout the South portrayed fugitive slaves fleeing to Fremont's Rocky Mountains under the caption "Fremont! Free Niggers!" Other ribbons portrayed Buchanan as the champion of national harmony, offering slogans such as "The Union Must Be Preserved" and "Our Union-Our Destiny: In the Lexicon of Buchanan there is [*sic*] no Such Words as North or South." Buchanan also attempted to play on his nickname, "Old Buck," incorporating leaping stags into his campaign material along with pun-filled rhymes:

> We Po'ked 'em in '44
> We Pierced 'em in '52
> And we'll 'Buck 'em in '56.

LINCOLN AND THE REPUBLICANS

The Republicans approached the election of 1860 with excitement and cunning. The Democrats were in disarray. From the beginning of the campaign, election material was everywhere. Fundraising came easily for the Republicans, and their candidate, Abraham Lincoln, could afford to use a new device that had been added to the campaign arsenal. For the first time the likeness of the candidate could be displayed through cheap "ferrotype" photographs. Ferrotype campaign buttons established a new level of campaign iconography during the most critical election of the century.

Torchlight parades, already an exciting staple of campaigning, were taken to new heights as people clambered for an opportunity to be part of Lincoln's railsplitter mystique. Split rails were mandatory decorations at local Republican "wigwams," a weekly campaign letter was dubbed the "Rail Splitter," and Lincoln Clubs began calling themselves Rail Splitters. Some groups even performed a "zig-zag" march in imitation of the appearance of a split-rail fence.

Thousands of ribbons poured into the campaign, many designed locally to honor the "Prince of Rails." During the early days of the contest some of the ribbons and banners spelled Lincoln's first name "Abram" and often proclaimed support for causes the Republicans were attempting to ignore that year. A Massachusetts-based banner, for example, read, "Resistance to Tyrants is Obedience to God." Lincoln campaign iconography established a new level of image making and helped lure former Whigs and disillusioned Democrats to the Republicans' antislavery cause.

While the clean-shaven Lincoln capitalized on his rail-splitter image, John Bell's Constitutional Union campaign was clearly focused on one issue—the preservation of the Union. John C. Breckinridge's southern Democratic effort featured tokens reading "No Submission to the North" and "Our Country and Our Rights," but the direction of the south was not toward the ballot box but away from the Union.

After Lincoln took office, several joke books containing his anecdotes circulated through the nation. Publications such as *Old Abe's Jokes* and *Wit at the White House* increased Lincoln's popularity and extended his image as a common man who loved to laugh.

THE UNION CAMPAIGN OF 1864

In 1864 Lincoln was opposed by Democrat George B. McClellan, the former Union military commander, who ran a peace campaign until Union victories late in the election season sealed victory for the North. Unlike in the 1860 election, Lincoln's image no longer proved the dominant campaign theme: the "Rail Splitter" identity rarely appeared on ferrotypes, tokens, and metal stickpins. The literature of both camps was dominated by the theme "Union and Victory." Still, the often hostile *New York World*, which thought little of the National Union party of Lincoln and his running mate, Andrew Johnson, wrote, "The age of statesmen is gone. The age of rail splitters and tailors, of buffoons, boors and fanatics has succeeded."

> **BEST-CASE SCENARIO**
>
> After Abraham Lincoln was nominated to his second presidential term, a supporter assured the president that he would be reelected unless General Grant took Richmond and decided to run against him. "Well," replied Lincoln, "I feel very much like the man who said he didn't want to die particularly, but if he had to die that was precisely the disease he would like to die of." On the way to Richmond, the Union army stalled outside Petersburg, but Lincoln, bolstered by Union victories elsewhere, easily defeated Democratic presidential challenger George McClellan.

Lurking in the shadow of the campaign was the northern desire to exact revenge against the Democrats for contributing to the nation's slide into war. A poster at a Pennsylvania rally for Lincoln and Johnson welcomed voters with these words: "All Who Desire Peace through Victory over Rebels in Army Against Their Government; All Who Rejoice in the Successes of Grant, Sherman, Sheridan and Farragut; and All who are Opposed to a DISGRACEFUL ARMISTICE with Traitors."

CIVIL WAR HERO IN 1868

Another fighting man, Ulysses S. Grant, was the logical choice of the Republicans in 1868. The first full general since George Washington, Grant was a man the people could trust, the man who had triumphed over the Confederacy. And he was also a man pledged to the slogan, "Let us have peace." Most of the iconography of the Grant campaign reflected that one-dimensional appeal to the voters. Grant's Republican platform stressed that Negro suffrage was only an

YEOMAN SUPPORT

Michigan agriculturalist and part-time poet "Farmer" Reynolds turned to verse to express his commitment to 1868 Republican presidential candidate Ulysses S. Grant. The following submission appeared in the *Grand Rapids Eagle* during the campaign:

I ain't got heaps of larnin'
And I seldom argy well,
But I sorter form opinions
Which I ain't afraid to tell.
So I says it square and open
Without fear small or great,
I stand by the loyal party
And I goes for Ulysses straight.

. . .

I can't explain the taxes
But I've seen the niggers free,
And voting 'gin their master
Is right enough for me.
I ain't a cussed bullhead
To swaller rebel bait,
But I keeps the side of freedom
And I goes for Ulysses straight.

issue in the defeated southern states, leaving the rest of the nation to decide the issue locally. Ribbons proclaimed Grant as "His Country's Friend in the Hour of Danger/Protector of American Liberty." The more devoted of Grant's supporters added a stiff cloth collar to their wardrobes complete with line drawings of both Grant and his running mate, Schuyler Colfax. One of the most unusual Grant campaign trinkets was created in the shape of an army knapsack that opened to reveal a military portrait of the general-turned-candidate.

Personality dominated the election, which Grant won handily over Horatio Seymour, although one haunting issue of the day—the issue of the Democrats' role in the rebellion—did make an appearance. Tokens were issued reading, "Loyalty Shall Govern What Loyalty Has Preserved." As is often the case, locally produced banners addressed the civil rights issue most squarely. One parade in Indiana included an anti-Seymour banner reading "Democracy Sold Out Cheap/Gone Down with Rebel Colors Flying."

During the Grant-Seymour campaign, political cartooning, especially the work of Thomas Nast, also exerted a major influence. The passionate Nast, who also challenged the power of New York political boss William Marcy Tweed on the pages of *Harper's Weekly*, was eager to support the "Man Who Saved the Nation." While Grant's campaign workers told northern voters, "Vote as you shot," Nast attacked Seymour and the Democrats with rapier precision. A typical Nast caricature of Seymour turned the candidate's tufts of hair on either side of his head into a pair of horns—creating a satanic look for the Democrat. After the election results were in, Grant attributed his victory to "the Sword of Sheridan and the Pencil of Thomas Nast." (In 1884, his faith in Grant still strong, Nast was one of the investors financially ruined when the firm of Grant and Ward, in which Grant was partner, failed. Nast lost thirty thousand dollars.)

HAYES IN 1876: A GILDED AGE CAMPAIGN

After Grant had completed eight mediocre and scandal-filled years in office, America endured a disputed election between Republican Rutherford B. Hayes and Democrat Samuel J. Tilden. Termed "His Fraudulency," Hayes won election when an appointed arbitration commission voted along strict party lines despite evidence of fraud on both sides. Hayes established himself as the first in a string of forgettable presidents who nevertheless produced interesting campaign innovations and attracted en thusiastic crowds.

The politics of the Gilded Age depended on close-knit political clubs, stirring election rhetoric, and lots of entertainment. In an era of fervent partisanship, voter turnouts were exceptionally high: the major parties were nearly equal in power, and campaign events were the biggest entertainment events of the day. Before the urbanization of the nation and the evolution of the culture of leisure, Republicans and Democrats provided the people with tension-filled mass meetings, memorable torchlight parades, and massive ox roasts. Railway companies mounted special promotions, reducing fares for eager supporters planning to attend torchlight processions. In many cities parades were combined with massive, outdoor barbecues—creating in many communities the biggest social event of the year.

GARFIELD IN 1880

Republican James A. Garfield was the perfect candidate for his time. Selected as a compromise nominee on the thirtieth ballot, he was a spellbinding orator, a great party man, and a great campaigner. Bandannas, handkerchiefs, and other textiles—largely out of favor for thirty years—appeared in abundance during the campaign. A mechanical lapel pin featured Garfield thumbing his nose at Democratic opponent Winfield S. Hancock, and pin-on ribbons displayed albumin paper and cardboard photographs of both candidates. Hancock promoted his candidacy with a device that combined a rooster and a hand, symbolizing "hand-cock."

Accusations that Garfield was guilty of influence peddling hardly mattered following a decade of turmoil and scandal. During the campaign, stories surfaced that Representative Garfield had accepted a bribe of $329 from a lobbyist anxious to head off an investigation of the powerful Crédit Mobilier railroad construction company. Despite protests by Garfield, including the issue of a thirty-page pamphlet defending himself, the telltale $329 figure was written on rocks, fences, walls, sidewalks, hats, napkins, and on the steps of Garfield's Washington home. In some parts of the country, the parade routes were decorated with the incriminating number.

Currier and Ives banner portraying the 1872 Republican presidential ticket as candidates of the working man

He won the election anyway.

A DEMOCRAT IN 1884

In 1884 both parties believed they had picked a winner and were ready to wage political war, even though the candidates carried considerable baggage into the campaign. The Republican standard-bearer, James G. Blaine, had been accused of business improprieties, and Democrat Grover Cleveland, a bachelor, was rumored to have fathered a child. The Cleveland slogan "A Public Office Is A Public Trust" ridiculed Blaine's wealth and his supposed belief in "The 'Great American' Game of Public Office for Private Gain." One pro-Cleveland campaign flier contrasted the modest look of Blaine's home in 1862 with his mansion in 1876 to demonstrate the profitability of his political life. All the while the Republicans were throwing mud themselves, chanting at rallies, "Ma, Ma, Where's My Pa, Gone to the White House, Ha, Ha, Ha!" to remind

GILDED AGE CAMPAIGN STYLE

No matter how much it had to spend, the well-dressed campaign club of the 1880s employed a variety of commercial sources when preparing for torchlight parades, rallies, and conventions. According to the *Catalogue of the New England Campaign Company,* local political "companies" could be outfitted for a torchlight parade at a cost of from seventy-five cents to five dollars per man. The illustrated *New England* catalogue presented twenty-eight varieties of parade torches, several kinds of campaign uniform, silk American flags featuring the candidate's name ("$2 each for a 30 by 48"), "correct and lifelike portraits of all the candidates," and—new in 1880—campaign balloons called "carrier pigeons." Replacing the unreliable balloons of old, the paper "hot-air" carrier pigeons boasted a more stable design, based on that of balloon pioneers the Montgolfier brothers. The *New England Campaign Company* also offered campaign pole banners, badges, and shirts featuring a removable front "shield" holding the candidate's likeness that could be converted to general use after the campaign.

voters of Cleveland's alleged indiscretion.

Blaine's campaign emphasized his fight for "Good wages, happy homes, and education for our children" and employed the image of the "Bloody Shirt," symbolizing soldiers lost in the Civil War. In support of their "Plumed Knight," Blaine campaigners took torchlight parading to a new level, wearing papier-mâché suits of armor complete with plumes and swords. "Plumed Knight" canes, lapel pins, clothing buttons, ribbons, badges, and medals appeared. Campaign plates and bandanas continued to gain popularity as manufacturing processes became more sophisticated and costs declined. Most featured portraits of the candidates, often surrounded by eagles and other symbols of integrity, a reflection of the recent American centennial and a rising feeling of national unity. Campaign toys were also popular. A miniature scale on which the two candidates could be weighed against each other saw widespread circulation. Presumably Cleveland's portliness helped tip the scales in his favor.

CLEVELAND OUSTED IN 1888

The Cleveland-Benjamin Harrison race of 1888 inspired a variety of campaign gimmicks, including mechanical toys that allowed the face of the candidate to pop out of a chair, glass cologne bottles, and a spring-guided toy featuring Cleveland and Harrison literally wrestling for the presidency. Republican Harrison, the grandson of the eighth president, and vice-presidential nominee Levi Morton attempted to cash in on Harrison's grandfather's 1840 presidential success, coining the slogan, "Tippecanoe and Morton too."

Cleveland's White House marriage to Frances Folsom and the birth of the couple's first child inspired one of the most unusual campaign items of 1888. A diaper displaying the words "Vote for My Daddy" opened to reveal a picture of the proud presidential father. Other unusual items appeared. Cleveland's running mate, Allen G. Thurman, was in the habit of carrying a red bandanna, and Democrats exhorted voters to "Wave High the Red Bandanna." At rallies the party also displayed crossed brooms to symolbize the need to "sweep clean the stables of government." Harrison won the election.

CLEVELAND AGAIN IN IN 1892

For the 1892 Harrison-Cleveland matchup, the *New York Sunday Herald* issued white cotton ribbons to its readers, featuring each contestant riding a

Elaborate poster seeking votes for the party of Jefferson in 1884 (Library of Congress)

rooster—a Democratic party symbol. Harrison's name was stamped onto the lids of cigar boxes, and the department store Myers and Heim of Pennsylvania promised to give away campaign eggs—featuring a pop-up crowing chicken—to anyone who purchased clothing from the store. The Myers and Heim campaign egg was modestly advertised as "The Greatest Campaign Novelty Out." Cleveland defeated Harrison in the rematch.

CELLULOID AND GOLD IN 1896

In 1896 the manufacturing innovation, grassroots party organizing, and big-money deal making of the past two decades culminated in the nation's first modern campaign, pitting Republican William McKinley, champion of business, against the "boy orator," Democrat-Populist William Jennings Bryan. A hotly contested race, the McKinley-Bryan extravaganza served as the launching pad for one of the most important and lasting campaign innovations, the celluloid button. First invented in 1868, in response to a billiard ball manufacturer's offer of ten thousand dollars to anyone who could discover a substitute for ivory, celluloid revolutionized American politics. No other innovation in campaign history gained acceptance more rapidly. First patented by Bostonian Amanda M. Lougee as a clothing button, the modern campaign button found its manufacturing home at the Whitehead and Hoag Company of Newark, New Jersey, where highly colorful, exceptionally durable, photographically accurate images could be produced and distributed for less than a penny apiece. Freed from the limitations of die-struck metals and cast artwork, candidates across the country quickly discovered that only the imagination limited the use of the celluloid button.

Millions of campaign buttons were made for the national standard-bearers

Pro-tariff anti-silver poster from William McKinley's 1896 presidential campaign against Democrat-Populist William Jennings Bryan

in 1896, and for local candidates for sheriff and mayor in towns large and small. Almost overnight the buttons appeared on lapels from coast to coast. Advertisers, of course, did not want to be left out. Items promoting McKinley or Bryan were given out to purchasers of American Pepsin gum and Sweet Caporal [*sic*] and High Admiral cigarettes.

Campaign buttons were not the only innovation of the McKinley-Bryan years. Bryan broke with tradition and traveled some eighteen thousand miles during the campaign, making five or six speeches a day and turning the rear platform of a train into a new kind of campaign icon. His opponent remained at his home in Canton, Ohio, welcoming delegations representing industry, agriculture, the church, and labor on his front porch.

Another campaign development was unleashed by the bimetallism debate of 1896, inspired by Bryan's "Cross of Gold" speech, which won him the nomination. In reaction, the Republicans turned out a swarm of innovative "gold bugs" in support of McKinley's position that gold alone should back U.S. currency. Several types of the mechanical "gold bugs" had wings that unfolded out of the bug's body to reveal pictures of the candidates, and other gold bugs rode bicycles or held "solid money" coins.

A solar eclipse that occurred in the midst of the campaign inspired several campaign buttons featuring the face of McKinley partly covering the face of Bryan. The slogan read, "Eclipse will be total on November 6, 1900." It was a wild election. In the end, the rapidly urbanizing nation believed McKinley's promise of a "Full Dinner Pail" for everyone.

MORE OF THE SAME IN 1900

In 1900 McKinley set the tone for his rematch with Bryan by declaring that the "real issue" was prosperity. The economy was generally solid, and Bryan was doomed. McKinley's running mate in 1900 was New Yorker Theodore Roosevelt, an enemy of political money man Mark Hanna, bankroller of the McKinley campaigns. Hanna, who established the first highly centralized campaign in history, was appalled when "that damned cowboy" was elevated to the presidency following the assassination of McKinley in 1901.

THE ROUGH RIDER

The campaign of 1904 was one of the nation's dullest, but it produced some of its most spectacular items for one reason—the charismatic Rough Rider himself, Teddy Roosevelt. Women sported pins that recalled the glories of San Juan Hill, and men wore club-shaped pins, a symbol of Roosevelt's "Big Stick" brand of diplomacy. Red, white, and blue canes featuring portraits of Roosevelt and running mate Charles Fairbanks appeared along with umbrellas, watch fobs, and bandannas—1904 was the last election in which that staple of the past was used widely. Roosevelt's face and name appeared everywhere: on pencils, noisemakers, cuff and button trays, campaign stamps, pocket watches, cigars, bow ties, aluminum combs, and paperweights. His Democratic opponent, Judge Alton B. Parker, could not compete in personality, campaign gimmickry, or votes, and quickly faded into obscurity after the election.

Reflecting the changing times, the 1904 election ushered in several new campaign items. For the first time campaign watch fobs appeared in profusion, dangling freely from the widely popular and inexpensive pocket watches sold by Sears, Roebuck and Company. Penny postcards, set free from government monopoly by Congress in 1898, debuted as campaign items in 1900 and became a phenomenal success in the elections of 1904 and 1908. They went out of vogue by 1916. Another memorable feature of the 1904 campaign was an item known as "Teddy's Teeth." Facsimilies of the robust outdoorsman's prominent choppers were fixed to mouth horns, allowing campaigners to blow their horns for Teddy while constantly displaying his grin.

A single dinner in the White House in 1901, shortly after McKinley's death, created a more serious campaign issue in 1904. President Roosevelt entertained black educator Booker T. Washington, producing campaign fodder for both Republicans and Democrats. In the North a picture of Washington and Roosevelt portrayed Washington with caucasian features and carried the slogan, "Equality." The picture circulated in the south showing Washington with much darker features. It too carried the slogan "Equality," but its intent was to inflame.

Roosevelt's handpicked successor was "good old honest B-I Double L Bill Taft," a 300-pound Republican with a great mind and horrible political instincts. His opponent was the old warhorse William Jennings Bryan, back for one more race around the country on behalf of populism and the Democrats. With the economy booming, confidence up, and party politics still in vogue, thousands of campaign items appeared. Taft's chubby face peered from color photographs on watch fobs, china dinner plates, postcards, and hundreds of colorful banners. Inspired by the popularity of the invention, street vendors erected full-sized figures of the candidates and played phonograph recordings of their speeches. Inspired voters could then purchase their own records of the "actual words" of Taft and Bryan. Multicolored designs imitating the art nouveau style of Maxfield Parrish took political campaign buttons to an artistic pinnacle not matched until the 1970s. Taft's campaign managers were eager to exploit former president Roosevelt's popularity, issuing buttons that read, "T-ake A-dvice F-rom T-eddy." Bryan's supporters yelled "Down with Trusts" and attacked Taft's ties to Roosevelt with the saying, "The Nation/The State/ No Twilight Zone."

The 1908 campaign also featured feeble but highly visible campaign efforts from both the Socialist and Prohibition parties; both organizations would exert greater influence in the years ahead. The Prohibition party issued thousands of buttons featuring sad-looking children encircled by the words, "Vote Dry for My Sake."

WILSON, TAFT, AND A MOOSE IN 1912

By 1912, Taft's political blunders, the candidacy of Woodrow Wilson—a non-professional politician—and Roosevelt's desire to recapture the presidency—even if it meant a third-party campaign—set the stage for one of the most unusual elections of the twentieth century. After Taft's renomination, Teddy threw his hat into the ring and formed the Progressive party. Wilson became the "Man of the Hour," while incumbent Taft's campaign literature and but-

Postcard advising voters to turn back the threat to Republican prosperity in 1908

tons lamely told voters, "Good Republicans Don't Bolt a Party Ticket." During the campaign the restless Roosevelt's Rough-Rider hat was everywhere; his famous teeth and spectacles reappeared by popular demand, and his declaration, "I feel fit as a bull moose," transformed the name of his party.

Reflecting Roosevelt's personal beliefs, the Progressive party favored woman suffrage. Campaign buttons supporting suffrage displayed a star for each state that allowed women to vote. When Congress passed the nineteenth amendment in 1919, eleven states had already given women voting rights.

On election day 1912 the most successful third-party candidacy in campaign history succeeded only in splitting the Republicans and securing the election of Democrat Wilson.

NO WAR IN 1916

The election of 1916 pitted the incumbent Wilson against a Republican party desperate to remain united. Its candidate was future chief justice Charles Evans Hughes. The raging war in Europe presented one of the key issues of the campaign. Wilson campaign items read "He Kept Us Out of War," "America First," "They Have Kept the Faith," and "Woodrow Wilson's Wisdom Wins Without War." The isolationist tendencies of America were decidedly for allowing Europe to handle its own affairs. When Wilson did commit American troops, he called for "peace without victory." A major portion of his campaign material focused on a nation adjusting to industrialization under the guidance of "The Man of the Eight Hour Day."

The Prohibitionist party produced an all-time record for results in 1916 with former Indiana governor J. Frank Hanly at the head of the ticket. That year the party expanded its platform reforms to include freedom for the Philippines, old-age pensions, federal grain elevators for farm surpluses, a single term for the president, and public ownership of utilities. By 1919 the nation heard the cry of the Prohibitionists and went "dry."

HARDING IN 1920

By 1920, presidential campaigns no longer served as the primary form of mainstream entertainment in American society. Voter turnout was falling, participation in party politics was declining, and the grass-roots enthusiasm for presidential campaigns was fading. The emergence of radio, movie theaters, and automobiles relegated campaign politics to secondary status. Even as the presidential candidates became more visible through increased travel, newsreel coverage, and radio broadcasts, the voting public became even more fascinated by the expanding world around them. World War I had shifted the boundaries of the ordinary man's imagination.

To begin the new decade, Republican senator Warren G. Harding of Ohio was chosen as the presidential nominee on the tenth ballot after three leading contenders became hopelessly deadlocked. It was the last time in this century a Republican national convention selected a favorite son for president. Harding's running mate was Massachusetts governor Calvin Coolidge. Recalling the success of McKinley's stay-at-home campaign and ignoring the "whistle stop" campaign style then in vogue, Harding made most of his speeches from the front porch of his Marion, Ohio, home. He made dozens of talks over the radio that were then turned into phonograph records. Harding's campaign focused on "normalcy"—a welcome change for the nation after four years of "Mr. Wilson's War" and Wilson's efforts in foreign affairs. Early on, the Republicans could smell victory; Democratic challenger James Cox and his running mate, Franklin D. Roosevelt, were given little chance of winning and even less campaign money. The Cox campaign created few presidential items, although it did produce a celebrated icon—the Cox-Roosevelt jugate. Printed in small quantities, the button portraying Cox and Roosevelt became very popular—and expensive—in later years as collectors attempted to link the future four-term president to his first national campaign. Cox campaigned under the banners "Peace with Honor" and "Keep Faith with our Sons, Bring America into The League of Nations" with little impact. Yet his campaign items did reflect one important new trend. As more voters behaved like spectators, campaign items became personal and practical: a pocketknife displayed pictures of Cox and Roosevelt, for example. The reverse side of the knife carried the slogan, "Vote for Cox, He's a Hun, and One Hundred Percent Wilson." Lighted signs and window stickers for the home appeared for the first time that year, and watch fobs and straight razors featuring the candidates disappeared—victims of the growing popularity of wristwatches and safety razors.

COOLIDGE IN 1924

Calvin Coolidge, elevated to the presidency upon the death of Harding in August 1923, became the Republican standard-bearer in 1924—and the man responsible for explaining his predecessor's Tea Pot Dome scandal. Convinced that the Republican scandal would serve as a surefire rallying cry, the Democrats were eager to retake the White House in 1924, unaware that they were about to be ambushed by another modern innovation of campaign politics. At the national Democratic convention, a nasty inner-party struggle between the Ku Klux Klan and Catholic forces was closely followed nationwide—thanks to the radio. Then, when the Democratic party became embroiled in a ten-day stalemate before selecting West Virginia's favorite son John W. Davis on the 103th ballot, the nation grew disenchanted. Despite a campaign emphasizing "Honest Days with Davis," overexposure through excessive media coverage had claimed its first victim.

Aware of America's fascination with its rural roots, Coolidge used the campaign tricks of another era, returning often to his ancestral farm to be photographed. One widely distributed campaign item featured Coolidge, clad in overalls, perched on a hay wagon—still wearing a starched white shirt and polished black shoes. America's love affair with the automobile also spilled into the 1924 campaign with the creation of license-plate attachments and the formation of a Republican "Lincoln tour," composed of a motorcar caravan from city to city. The sayings "Keep Cool with Coolidge" and "Keep Cool-ige" appeared on stamps, pennants, buttons, and signs—many shaped like an electric table fan. The election also saw the ascendancy of the campaign poster, an item that would be printed in extraordinary numbers in future years. Coolidge also appealed to the newly enfranchised women of America, distributing mirrors reading "The lady on the other side is requested to vote for Calvin Coolidge." Cool Cal, the candidate best known for the words he did not utter, was the winner in a walk.

THE GREAT ENGINEER

The election of 1928 was no ordinary contest; it served as a national referendum on religion and the noble experiment of prohibition, argued by two well-known personalities. For the first time since 1912 America experienced a political campaign it could truly get worked up about. The contest matched Catholic Democrat Al Smith against longtime public servant Herbert Hoover. Known as the "Great Engineer," Hoover was considered a wonder boy for his administration of World War I food-relief programs and for his organizational skills as secretary of commerce. During the campaign the economy remained strong and the world peaceful; everyone, it seemed, was optimistic. "The poorhouse is vanishing among us," Hoover declared. "We in America today are nearer to the final triumph over poverty than ever before in the history of the land." Republican campaign items included such frivolous and ironic designs as owl-shaped buttons reading, "Who but Hoover" or "Elect Hoover and Insure Prosperity." Other buttons hinted at the festering issue of the campaign—Smith's religion. Buttons appeared with the slogans, "Hoover/100% American" and "A Christian in the White House." In the South, where voting Democratic was almost a religion in itself, the possibility of electing a Catholic president stirred strong emotions. The slogans "Principle Above Party" and "Another Democrat for Hoover" became rallying cries in parts of the Deep South. An anti-Catholic "whisper" campaign featured handwritten or typewritten items that were passed privately. Many displayed the number "3909-3HT," which when viewed backwards reads "The Pope." Other whisper items carried bigoted "poetry":

> When cotton grows on fig trees,
> And apples hang from the rose,
> When Catholics rule the United States
> And the Jew grows a straight nose,
> When Pope Pius is head of the Ku Klux Klan
> In the land of Uncle Sam,
> Then Al Smith will be President
> And the country won't be worth a damn.

Smith's campaign emphasized the positive. He came from the Lower East Side of New York with slogans such as "America's Biggest Man for America's Biggest Job." Oilcloth spare-tire covers featuring a picture of Smith also appeared (that particular display space idea disappeared by 1936 as automobile manufacturers began placing the fifth tire in the trunk). Hoover sewing needles also appeared, another reflection of the role women were beginning to play in national politics. Book matches bearing the faces of candidates were another innovation of 1928. As wooden matches disappeared from American homes, paper matches carrying advertising took their place.

FDR

By 1932 the optimism of the 1920s had been swept away by unemployment, a failed Wall Street, and broken promises. Hoover, still struggling for solutions, ran against Democrat Franklin D. Roose-

String-operated button from the 1932 presidential campaign (courtesy of McKissick Museum)

velt. Hoover's forces halfheartedly attempted to brand Roosevelt a dangerous radical and endeavored to reassure the public that an economic solution was just around the corner. "Don't Swap Horses/Stand with Hoover" and "Keep Them on the Job" became popular slogans. But it was Roosevelt's incurable optimism, along with his theme song, "Happy Days Are Here Again," that inspired the public and helped a nation cope. Roosevelt's energetic button designs featured the Democratic donkey as a depression buster—kicking away the Republican elephant and hard times. "Get Rid of the White Elephant, Turn Democratic," buttons read; "Roosevelt or Ruin." One mechanical button even allowed the wearer to pull a string so the donkey's feet could fly back and "Kick Out Depression." For a nation looking for relief, Roosevelt was a welcome sign.

During the 1932 campaign Roosevelt also played upon his family name and political heritage with slogans such as "America Calls Another Roosevelt" and (one that linked the programs of both Roosevelts) "A New Deal/A Square Deal." "Roosevelt and Repeal" stickers also appeared, along with a license plate featuring pictures of Roosevelt and his running mate John Nance Garner on each side of a foaming stein of beer. Prohibition had outlived its welcome and both parties were moving toward the "wet" position. The Republicans called for repeal of the prohibition amendment on a state-by-state basis. The Democrats wanted prohibition abolished nationally.

The Republicans swung back at the controversial Roosevelt in 1936 with a platform full of generalities and a likable candidate they thought the entire nation could embrace. Alf Landon of Kansas castigated the New Deal on neckties, pencils, posters, and campaign buttons and tabs. Landon made much of his Kansas heritage, putting sunflowers on nearly everything. But the main focus of his campaign was an attack on Roosevelt's social welfare programs; Landon felt that Roosevelt's reliance on public-policy fixes for the Depression was destroying the American work ethic. Posters reading "Farewell to Alms" and "Willful Waste Makes Woeful Want" appeared along with stickers reading, "Frankenstein D. Roosevelt" and "Americans Cannot Be Bought." The National Republican Council distributed stickers showing Roosevelt arrogantly employing a burning copy of the Constitution to light his cigarette.

Roosevelt forces, warned that the race could be close, responded with "Back on the Rocks with Landon and Knox" and "We Can't Eat Sunflowers/Lose with Landon." The Roosevelt campaign boosted their man as "A Gallant Leader," and buttons proclaimed "He Saved America" and "Man of the House." Hundreds of slogans were created: "Friend of the People," "New Deal Democrat," and "Have Faith in the New Deal for Prosperity" were prominent. An important sign of Roosevelt's influence was the great number of lesser-office candidates who linked their fortune to the president with buttons, slogans and endorsements.

The slogan "We Want Willkie" was heard nationwide as the election of 1940 loomed. A successful New York businessman with a delightful sense of humor, Wendell L. Willkie appeared capable of finally unseating the "imperial president." Since the days of General Grant and his failed third-term attempt in 1880, the no-third-term tradition assumed almost the force of law. Many were shocked that Roosevelt challenged the tradition. Hundreds of comical buttons appeared: "No Man Is Any Good The Third Time," "We Don't Want Eleanor Either," and "Roosevelt Gone With the Wind" addressed the issue. Roosevelt forces answered with "A Third Termer is Better than a Third Rater" and "Willkie for the Millionaires/ Roosevelt for the Millions."

The campaign stimulated a renaissance in political trinketry. An estimated fifty-four million buttons were ordered by the two campaigns, not counting those created by commercial vendors. A self-conscious Willkie button read, "100 Million Buttons Can't Be Wrong." Textiles made a comeback with the appearance of mini-banners and bandannas; cigars, paperweights, ribbons, aluminum bookmarks, pocketknives, thimbles, needle books, and coasters were also prominent. A pair of paper earmuffs supporting Willkie read, "Please Don't Talk 3rd Term." Willkie buttons also called for "No Royal Family" and "No Franklin the First" and referred to election day as "Dethronement Day." Few dealt with America's possible entry into the war in Europe. Jobs and personalities—not war—proved the focus of the campaign.

Four years later war was all the nation was thinking about. In 1944 President Roosevelt ran as the commander in chief and told America it was not right to change horses in midstream. With metal and plastics in short supply on the home front, few resources were devoted to the campaign. "Go 4th to Win the War" summarized the campaign for Roosevelt, while his challengers, New York governor Thomas E. Dewey and Ohio governor John W. Bricker, preached, "Back to Work Quicker with Dewey and Bricker." Items reading "Dewey for President" were answered with "Phooey On Dewey." Neither the issue of fourth term nor Roosevelt's poor health seemed to matter to the voters. Roosevelt was reelected and died in office. Harry Truman, a last-minute choice to replace Henry Wallace as vice-president, became president.

TRUMAN IN 1948

After Gen. Dwight D. Eisenhower refused to accept the Democratic nomination for president in 1948, the party turned in desperation to the incumbent Truman. The nomination of underdog Truman, unwanted yet undaunted, split his party into three factions in 1948. The Dixiecrats booed him and Wallacites sniped at him, but his supporters continued to sing, "I'm Just Wild About Harry." Experts predicted that 1948 would be a Republican year. Tom Dewey, back for a second try, had his "Victory Special" rolling across the nation's rails, going through the motions and emotions of the process of campaigning. "We know the kind of government we have now," Dewey would tell the crowds from the back of the train. "It's tired. It's confused. It's coming apart at the seams. It cannot give this nation what it needs most—what is the real issue of this election—unity." Dewey never mentioned Truman by name, making references instead to the fumbling and weaknesses of "the administration which happens to be in power at the moment." Campaign literature told the voters, "Save What's Left" and asked "Had Enough?"

The combative Truman fought back. Angry that few expected him to win, Truman simply outworked the complacent Dewey. Dewey campaigned six weeks; Truman eight. Dewey covered sixteen thousand miles; Truman, twenty-two thousand. Dewey made 170 speeches; Truman 271. And everywhere Truman went, lifelong Democrats yelled out, "Give 'em Hell, Harry." And he did. When a reporter asked

Truman what he thought about Dewey's deliberate attempt to avoid saying "Truman," the president replied, "That's all of a lot of hooey. And if that rhymes with anything, it's not my fault." Campaign literature for Truman linked his presidency to Roosevelt and the war with slogans such as "Secure the Peace" and "Count Your Blessings." Still, the polls—a campaign feature that had become increasingly important—predicted an easy Republican victory.

Further complications came from a pair of third-party candidates. Strom Thurmond of South Carolina was championing the cause of states' rights and segregation, and Henry Wallace was seeking votes for the Progressives. Each was capable of taking Democratic votes away from Truman. On election day bookies quoted odds of 30-to-1 against Truman. But it was anything but a short night. Only later did it become clear what had happened. The shift to Truman took place in the final days—after the polling stopped. Some people changed their minds after they entered the polling booth. The nation had fallen in love with the spunky underdog who was not afraid to be one of the people.

IKE

The 1952 election signaled the return of an old tradition, the nomination of a war hero, coupled with the onset of a technological development that would change political campaigns forever: television. Increasingly, Americans were leaving politics to the professionals and identifying themselves as independents.

He had turned down an opportunity to run on the Democratic ticket in 1948, but Dwight D. Eisenhower said "yes" to a "draft" campaign championed by the Republicans in 1952. His New Hampshire primary victory over Senator Robert Taft secured his nomination while he was still serving as NATO supreme commander in Europe. Eisenhower's campaign gathered more than a hundred thousand write-in votes on a near-blizzard March election day. Almost

Button from the 1952 campaign (courtesy of McKissick Museum)

overnight the slogan "I like Ike" was on everyone's lips. Eisenhower was unpretentious, good-humored, and capable of convincing the American people that his military experience would make him a good president. Even though the Korean conflict and "red baiting" were national issues, they rarely influenced the campaign. Even the general's military exploits played second fiddle to his affable style.

Eisenhower's opponent in both 1952 and 1956 was Adlai E. Stevenson, who could never find a way to turn the tide against Ike. Stevenson's campaign featured the symbol of a shoe with a hole it its sole, symbolizing the thrift of Stevenson. "Hole In Shoe Clubs" sprang up around the country, and lapel pins in the shape of shoes were issues by the thousands. Buttons reading "The Thinking Man's Candidate" were also issued, but Stevenson, who sought to diminish his "egghead" image, also emphasized his links to Roosevelt and Truman with the slogan "Never Before Has Business Been Better or More People Employed at Higher Wages/Why Change." One of the few war-related items came from the group Kentucky Citizens for Eisenhower-Nixon, which in 1956 issued a flier showing a woman holding a picture of a smiling General Eisenhower. A "comic-book balloon" carried the woman's words: "He went to Korea so my boy didn't have to go."

Television imposed itself on the 1952 campaign in an unusual way: to save the candidacy of vice-president Richard Nixon—who had already acquired the nickname Tricky Dick. In a speech broadcast nationally, Nixon defended himself against accusations that he had received secret supplementary salary payments and gifts from a group of California businessmen. One gift he would never return, he said. That gift was a dog: Checkers. America forgave.

By the time Eisenhower and Stevenson matched up again in 1956, the modern bumper sticker had appeared. A traveling minibillboard of sorts, the back of an automobile rapidly became the place people were most willing to display their political preferences. Bumper stickers superseded metal campaign license plates and window stickers. They also contributed to the decline of campaign buttons.

Refracting "flashers" also winked that year, showing, for example, the phrase "Win With Ike" when tilted one way and Eisenhower's picture when tilted the other. Buttons were larger, the result of more sophisticated manufacturing techniques and the fact that they end up on the clothing of dedicated campaign workers, not the man on the street. Eisenhower's habit of playing golf inspired one satirical bumper sticker that read, "Ben Hogan for President. If We're Going to Have a Golfer, Let's Have a Good One." Even Eisenhower laughed. On election day, America voted for the golfer they knew could also perform as president.

KENNEDY'S THE ONE

Eisenhower's vice-president, Nixon, carried the Republican flag against a young senator from Massachusetts in 1960. It was the type of clash of styles and ideologies that had previously inspired clever campaign materials and creative thematics. But not this time. The Kennedy-Nixon contest featured the Great Debates and the emergence of television as the most powerful campaign force. Almost 120 million Americans watched or listened to at least part of one of the four presidential debates. And many decided to cast their votes for the articulate young Kennedy, based on his television image. Few realized it at the time, but the influence the debates exerted signaled the beginning of a new era. Pinback buttons and other campaign image makers began to take a backseat to the never-blinking eye of the television camera. Nonetheless, in 1960 the candidates' names and faces appeared on eyeglasses, clothes, potholders, and ice cream bars, matchbook covers, ashtrays, neckties, and kitchen sponges.

For the most part, the flamboyant Kennedy's campaign material was plain. The candidate symbolized "Leadership for the '60s" and promised "A Time for Greatness." Nixon's items emphasized continuity, reading "My Pick is Dick," "Click with Dick," and "Experience Counts." The most effective campaign items of the 1960 campaign were Kennedy's PT-109 lapel pins, which commemorated his heroism in the South Pacific during World War II. They became the most prized possessions of the Kennedy campaign. Few items mentioned Kennedy's religion or his Irish roots. Similar to the Smith campaign in 1928, most of the smear sheets were produced outside the Republican campaign and distributed privately. One anti-Kennedy piece was headlined, "Homo Sapiens vs Irish—The Simian Usurpation of the Presidency," written by "Professor Wisdom."

The 1960 election also saw a rise in public cynicism. With the news media growing more sophisticated and more pervasive, thanks to television, the public had access to more information. Often they came away more confused than committed. One prankster lampooned both Nixon and Kennedy with the button, "Prostitutes . . . Vote for Nixon or Kennedy/We don't Care Who Gets In."

In one of the closest races in the nation's history, Kennedy edged out Nixon, but he would not live out his term.

Lyndon Johnson campaign button promising a continuation of the policies of John F. Kennedy in 1964

LBJ

The 1964 election completed the transformation of the grass-roots politics of the 1860s to party-directed campaigning—largely for the benefit of television. At a cost of $100,000, Republican senator Barry Goldwater became the first presidential candidate to purchase national network time prior to his party's convention. Major television advertisements—especially those used by Johnson—became the focus of intense debate. Television coverage of the Republican convention so inflamed the delegates that they threatened to cut the cables. The debate over which was more important—the event itself or the coverage of the event—had begun. Politics could never be the same again.

The right-leaning Goldwater rallied conservative Republicans—but few others—with his famous call to arms, "Extremism in the defense of liberty is no vice, moderation in the pursuit of justice is no virtue." Republican stalwarts claimed, "In Your Heart, You Know He's Right," but 1964 was President Lyndon B. Johnson's year. Johnson turned the 1964 election into a referendum on his "Great Society." Political T-shirts were popular, and some of the best and worst political put-downs in years were circulated. Reacting to Senator Goldwater's cute use of the symbols for gold (Au) and water (H_20), a Johnson button retorted, "$C_5H_4N_4O_3$ on AuH_2O"—"Piss on Goldwater." In response to Goldwater's slogan "In Your Heart, You Know He's Right," Johnson's forces issued buttons reading, "In Your Guts, You Know He's Nuts." Goldwater's forces hammered Johnson's Great Society with the saying, "A New Leech on Life" and advertised "The LBJ Cocktail—America on the Rocks."

While previous campaigns stretched the limits of good taste, in 1964 the limits were abandoned altogether. From Goldwater advocates there was: "Sterilize LBJ—No More Ugly Children"; a license plate showing a pregnant black woman read "I Went All de Way wif LBJ." Six-packs of a soft drink called "Gold Water" and cosmetic soaps promising "4-Year Protection" provided still more humor.

The Vietnam War, which eventually destroyed the Johnson presidency, was rarely mentioned—except by Johnson, who worked hard to convince the nation that Goldwater could not be trusted with military might. A short-lived but highly effective pro-Johnson television commercial implied that Goldwater would use nuclear weapons if he became president. Despite predictions that Johnson would win in a landslide rivaling the lopsided Roosevelt-Landon race of 1936, the president worked around the clock to capture a massive mandate, making as many as twenty-two speeches in a single day.

Poster portraying a regal Richard Nixon running for reelection in 1972

NIXON'S THE ONE

By 1968 the nation was embroiled in a confusing war in Southeast Asia. Several American cities had been burned as the militancy—and the frustration—surrounding the civil rights movement increased. A lightly regarded peace candidate named Eugene McCarthy performed well enough in the snows of the New Hampshire primary to force President Johnson to step out of the race. Candidate Robert Kennedy was assassinated the night he won the Democratic primary in California. Then, with much of America watching on live television, the Democrats nominated Johnson's vice-president, Hubert Humphrey, while Chicago police teargassed, beat, and kicked peace demonstrators gathered outside the convention—not a wonderful way to begin a campaign.

The Republicans called upon Richard Nixon and turned over to him a large treasury, a united Republican party, and a nation at odds with itself. Nixon's campaign items and themes were simple. "Nixon's The One" appeared on a host of objects. Anxious to protect his image, Nixon's campaign workers assured that his appearances were highly controlled events, designed to attract the best possible television exposure. Image was to be the key element in the campaign, despite the constant swirl of controversy.

The wild-card candidate in 1968 was Alabama governor George Wallace, who ran against big government and busing and for "law and order." His slogan, "Stand Up For America," was widespread on bumper stickers, postcards, posters, and license plates.

Humphrey had to fight what had become known as Johnson's war, a deeply divided party, the unified Republicans, and a nation in turmoil. The 1968 race was one of the most issue-oriented campaigns of modern times. Humphrey and running mate Edmund Muskie promised "A Better World," and Humphrey's initials, HHH, appeared on thousands of items, but America wanted a change. Nixon indeed appeared to be the one.

By 1972 Vietnam had become Nixon's war. The Democrats nominated a peace candidate, George McGovern, to oppose Nixon, and cause-related campaign material appeared in astounding profusion. Nixon promised "Peace with Honor," and seemed to know from the outset that the campaign would never be close.

The only thing lasting about Democrat George McGovern's campaign was that it offered some of the most colorful, fanciful, and creative campaign material seen in years. McGovern brought back grass-roots politics for a time, attracting thousands of young people to politics to protest the war, rail against Nixon, and forget to appear at the polls on election day. For twenty-five dollars, donors joined the "McGovern Million Member Club," and a dollar bought a "Buck Nixon/(I Did)" button. Campaign posters and buttons also spoke to the most powerful issue of the day, U.S. involvement in Vietnam: "Come Home & Stop Killing Little Babies." The emerging influence of the environmental movement also played a part in the McGovern magical mystery tour. A button reading "America the Beautiful/ Let's Make It that Way" featured a multicolored rainbow over an idyllic scene.

Nixon's campaign was aimed straight at middle America: jewelry, T-shirts, scarves, suspenders, bubblegum cigars, and thousands of buttons were issued. The popularity of polyester double-knit fabrics also changed political campaign thinking that year. The material proved vulnerable to damage from pin-back buttons and opened the way for the disposable lapel sticker, which had made its debut in 1968. The themes printed on the stickers and buttons were simple: "Re-elect the President," "Four More Years," and "Nixon Now More than Ever." More than any president in history, Nixon capitalized on the word "president" and made it his own. Unlike 1960, when Nixon was referred to as "Dick," the 1968 and 1972 campaigns took the high road, featuring slogans such as "Right On, Mr. President." Nixon's strategy was a huge success. He won the reelection in 1972, but in 1974 he resigned the presidency because of campaign antics at the Watergate Hotel and Nixon's dishonorable cover-up attempts.

Nixon's original vice-president, Spiro Agnew, had already resigned because of accusations of financial misdealing, and Michigan representative Gerald Ford took his place. When Nixon resigned, Ford became the first man in history to become president without winning election either to the vice-presidency or the presidency. Opening a speech shortly after he was sworn in, Ford told the audience, "So much has happened since I received his invitation to speak here today. At that time I was America's first instant Vice President. Today I'm America's first instant President. The United States Marine Corps Band is so confused they don't know whether to play 'Hail to the Chief' or 'You've come a long way, Baby.' "

GRITS 'N' FRITZ IN '76

By the time Ford squared off against challenger Jimmy Carter in 1976, the rules had changed. Indignation over the Watergate affair had ushered in hundreds of new campaign laws, rules, and limitations—including the institutionalization of Political Action Committees (PACs) as a campaign's most important source of money. Jimmy Carter's media director, Gerald Rafshoon, decided that campaign buttons were unnecessary and initially did not order any for the Carter-Mondale race. Only after a chorus of complaints did he relent, purchasing only enough for his campaign workers, believing they were the only people willing to make a personal and visible commitment to candidates anymore. But it did not matter. The common man's candidate, Carter inspired dozens of locally made buttons that spoofed his massive smile and his ownership of a peanut farm. The post-Watergate election reforms had decentralized the designing, ordering, and purchasing of campaign iconography. Dedicated workers purchased their own button machines and turned out their own creations by the dozens. In that way, the legal limits of a candidate's expenditures—mostly intended for television—would not be stretched for buttons or bumper stickers or jewelry or bags of Carter peanuts.

Ford attempted to follow Nixon's lead and use the presidency as his launching pad. Campaign material read, "President Ford in '76" and "He's making us proud again." All the while local campaigners were pumping out buttons reading, "Carter Hasn't Shown Me Anything but His Teeth" and "Will Rogers Never Met Jimmy Carter." Ford also attempted to capitalize on Carter's ill-advised *Playboy* magazine interview, in which he admitted he sometimes lusted in his heart for other women. To

Buttons from the Carter-Mondale campaign, 1976 (courtesy of McKissick Museum)

promote sales the magazine distributed thousands of advertising fliers and buttons announcing, "Carter Talks to Playboy." Ford supporters countered immediately with a play on an old Goldwater slogan: "In His Heart, He Knows Your Wife." But Ford's pardon of Nixon was a ghost that would not go away. The slogans "Remember Watergate/Vote Carter" and "Pardon Me, Gerald" haunted Ford throughout the campaign and contributed to his defeat.

REAGAN

Carter was a better campaigner than president. By the time he took to the campaign trail in 1980 against former actor and California governor Ronald Reagan, Carter had been crippled by internal conflict, cabinet desertions, and a hostage crisis that would not go away. The Carter campaign appeared to be going through the motions, and Carter's supporters lacked the fire and enthusiasm they displayed four years earlier. They issued campaign items reading, "Send Reagan Back to Central Casting" and "Stop Pollution/Nuke the Trees" (a reminder of Reagan's assertion that trees generated more pollution than industry). But the tide shifted. Reagan told voters, "Let's make America great again" and was often shown wearing a Stetson to underscore his western loyalties. More important, the Republican Reagan appealed to the working man. After conceding generations of the blue collar vote to the Democrats, the Republicans finally had a man who could speak to the factory worker. As in past elections, Reagan's ability to control the media and project well on television made him the winning candidate. For a time he was one of the most popular presidents in modern history.

In 1984 Reagan's greatest challenge was dispelling the "age issue," and he used humor at every turn to do it. Reminded that if reelected he would be seventy-eight when he left office, Reagan replied, "Well, Andrew Jackson left the White House at the age of seventy-five and he was still quite vigorous. I know because he told me." In a debate with Democratic challenger Walter Mondale, when a reporter asked the president: "You are already the oldest President in history. . . . Is there any doubt in your mind that you would be able to function in such circumstances?" Reagan replied, "I want you to know that I will not make age an issue in this campaign. I am not going to exploit, for political purposes, my opponent's relative youth and inexperience." Even though he had not answered the question, humor and the power of television scored again. Mondale never recovered. Concerned that his chances for reelection could be damaged by the so-called "gender gap," Reagan concentrated much of his energy and dozens of button designs on women's issues.

Mondale's superbly organized campaign generated many effective items—but they may have hurt him. When labor organizations across the nation cranked out thousands of Mondale buttons and bumper stickers in hopes of electing a pro-labor president, much of the nation grew apprehensive. When the National Organization for Women enthusiastically endorsed Mondale, whose running mate was Geraldine Ferraro, the first woman to run for vice-president on a major party ticket, a nation of middle-of-the-roaders turned back to Reagan.

BUSH IN 1988

The final election of the 1980s pitted Reagan's vice-president George Bush against Massachusetts governor Michael Dukakis. With the economy strong, Bush attempted to conduct his campaign from a position of strength, taking advantage of Reagan's popularity while implying he was more capable of meeting the challenges of foreign affairs and economic stability. The Democrats began and ended the campaign in disarray, unable to cope with a primary system that had become too complex and expensive. Hundreds of items were produced for the campaign, often by local groups, including full-color posters, jogging suits with the candidate's names on the legs, plastic windshield scrapers, and, of course, buttons. Efforts to brand Dukakis an irresponsible liberal took hold early in the campaign, and Bush sailed to victory on the wings of Reagan, television, and a war chest filled with PAC money.

For much of the history of the United States, then, one of the consequences of democracy has been that candidates for political office must sell themselves to win votes. Like everything else in politics, the campaign habit has brought mixed results. George Bush and his advisers went to great lengths to characterize Michael Dukakis as weak and inexperienced, some say unfairly. Experts say that American voters consider weakness and inexperience undesirable presidential traits. But it takes two candidates to hold an election. Could Dukakis have labeled George Bush inexperienced without calling his own perception into question? And Bush's efforts during the campaign to compensate for the press-generated "wimp factor" by talking tough on foreign policy would have made a Dukakis effort to label Bush weak seem like an accusation. Whether they know it explicitly or not, voters gain the assurance that something approaching the truth comes out in political campaigns because the candidates are trying as hard as they can to smear each other without seeming crass. Usually voters vote for the candidate less smeared. The system is not perfect, but most of the time the best man wins.

The Politics of Religion

by RICHARD GAMBLE

Although Article VI of the Constitution forbids any religious test "as a qualification for any office or public trust under the United States," it does not, and cannot, bar the voters from applying such a test at the polls. Whether on the local or national level, whether in the eighteenth century or the twentieth, the American people have repeatedly judged a candidate on the basis of his religion. For good or ill, right or wrong, this has been our practice.

Presidential elections in particular have felt the influence of religion. One historian estimated that religion has played a major role in about one out of every three campaigns. In those races, religion was, if not actually the deciding factor, at least one of those foremost in the rhetoric of the campaign and in the minds of voters. In each case, politics and religion, the meeting of the temporal and spiritual, proved a volatile mix.

ELECTION OF 1800

Thomas Jefferson pleaded in his inaugural address for national unity. He was quick to include a call for a liberal spirit, one allowing citizens to "regulate their own pursuits," including religion. During the campaign he had experienced firsthand the power of religious persuasion when applied to politics, and he feared the factionalism that had set Federalist against Republican.

Jefferson, a longtime deist, faced questions about his faith, or the assumed lack of it, in three presidential races. But the election of 1800 stands out for the intensity of the "religious question." Alexander Hamilton, the prototypical Federalist, championed his own party's candidate, John Adams, more by attacking Jefferson than by inspiring enthusiasm for Adams. He warned that Jefferson was "an atheist, a modern french Philosopher, [and an] overturner of Government." He recommended using any "*legal* and *constitutional* step, to prevent an *atheist* in Religion, and a *fanatic* in politics from getting possession of the helm of State," going so far as to suggest that New York amend its election laws to take the choice of electors out of the hands of the Republican-controlled legislature.

Philosophy looks with an impartial eye on all terrestrial religions, I have examined all, as well as my narrow means and my busy life would allow me; and the result is that the Bible is the best book in the world. It contains more of my little philosophy than all the libraries I have seen, and such parts of it as I cannot reconcile to my little philosophy, I postpone for future investigation.

—*Letter of John Adams to Thomas Jefferson, December 25, 1813*

Throughout the campaign Federalists and Republicans waged a war of words, distributing hundreds of pamphlets, writing countless letters to local editors, and, in the case of the Federalists, even enlisting the help of the clergy.

Primarily the debate raged over Jefferson's comments on religion in his *Notes on Virginia*, in particular the remark most goading to theological and political conservatives that "it does me no injury for my neighbor to say there are twenty gods, or no God." It may well have done him no harm, but the Federalists feared that such thinking would threaten morality, the churches, and the country itself if Jefferson won the election. The Republicans, on the other hand, used Jefferson's tolerance to their advantage. They promised equality for Quaker, Mennonite, Moravian, and Dunker alike and attacked Adams as the friend of an established church and other trappings of monarchy.

Associating Jefferson with the forces of political radicalism and theological infidelity, the Federalist pamphlets accused the Republican candidate in vivid terms. "Can serious and reflecting men look about them and doubt," one queried, "that if Jefferson is elected, and the Jacobins get into authority, that those morals which . . . shield our religion from contempt and profanation, will not be trampled upon and exploded[?]" Jefferson himself mailed to influential friends various tracts defending his views, but he pleaded for anonymity. Even though some concerned members of his own party asked for clarification on key doctrines, he never responded publicly to the charges against him.

The party newspapers rallied to their man in full voice. One Philadelphia journal framed the debate over Jefferson's beliefs in absolute terms: "At the present solemn and momentous epoch, the only question to be asked by every American . . . is 'shall I continue in allegiance to GOD—AND A RELIGIOUS PRESIDENT; or impiously declare for JEFFERSON—AND NO GOD!!?' "

The clergy, generally those from New England, enlisted mainly in the cause of the Federalists and repeated the theme of impending national disaster. A certain Rev. William Lind of New York promised his readers that electing Jefferson would equal a "rebellion against God." Another minister wrote that he feared "the election of Mr. Jefferson, because I believe him to be a confirmed infidel."

THE RIGORS OF WORSHIP

As in most New England small-town communities, the Puritan church played a central role in the social life of John Adams's Braintree, Massachusetts. The dilapidated church building was replaced by a new structure in 1732, three years before Adams was born. The manner of worship in the new facility reflected the changing social structure of the community. In the earlier church women and girls sat on the left of the pulpit; men on the right; and blacks, Indians, and the boys of the town in the gallery above. In the new church the leaders of the community—the "tribal elders," biographer Page Smith writes—had their own pews around the walls of the building. The rest of the women and men sat segregated in the center. Regardless of one's class, the church was a hard place in which to worship. It was almost completely uninsulated and therefore stuffy in the summer and very cold in the winter. During winter services the parishioners commonly brought foot stoves to warm their toes, and, sometimes, a parishioner put it, "Sacramental bread . . . frozen pretty hard . . . rattled sadly as broken into the plates."

ELECTION OF 1828

As has been often noted, the presidential campaign of 1828 really began with Andrew Jackson's loss to John Quincy Adams in the "stolen election" of 1824, a race decided in the House of Representatives amid rumors of a deal between Adams and another minority candidate, Henry Clay. Although Jackson had received a plurality in both popular and electoral votes, none of the candidates garnered the necessary majority. Vowing to oust the offspring of the "corrupt bargain," Jackson's forces immediately set out to capture the White House.

Federalist cartoon depicting Thomas Jefferson—aided by the devil and a bottle of brandy—toppling the federal edifice erected by Presidents George Washington and John Adams

With increasing voter participation—eighteen of the twenty-four states chose electors by popular vote by 1824—the appeal to partisanship was swift and strong. Jackson and Adams went straight for one another's throat as they grappled for voter loyalty. The campaign of 1828 quickly degenerated into mutual character assassination, earning it the reputation as the dirtiest election in American history.

Naturally the subject of religion could not stay out of the brawl for long, especially in the atmosphere of the Second Great Awakening. Moreover, rising Irish and German immigration, the majority of which was Catholic, inflamed religious controversies between Protestants and Catholics. No party dared alienate these potential voters or chanced to appear irreligious to an increasingly evangelical electorate.

Adams, the National Republican candidate, was hounded by a Fourth of July speech he had given in 1821 in which he referred to the Catholic church as a "portentous system of despotism and superstition." His party countered quickly that he had appointed Catholics to key positions during his term, that he had actually attended Catholic churches, and that he had even made donations for erecting new churches. But the tables were turned again when this behavior was assailed as part of a thinly veiled ploy for votes. He was also maligned for being a Unitarian (to be read "heretic" at the time), a Sabbath breaker who traveled on Sundays, and someone a little too fond of gambling, particularly horse racing and billiards. One letter to a Connecticut newspaper urged those of Puritan stock to see to it that Adams met defeat.

Likewise, Jackson's piety was questioned on much the same ground: for allegedly not observing the Sabbath, for being a deist, and for being soft on certain fundamental doctrines. Some of his detractors, though, tried to paint him as *too* religious. Supposedly while governor of Florida he had acted with a despotism worthy of a tyrant by claiming for himself the power to "regulate the due observance of the Sabbath."

Jackson's supporters trumpeted his Presbyterianism, and stories of his leading his troops in prayer abounded. Concerned lest Jackson not appear religious enough, though, Martin Van Buren, a staunch supporter and later Jackson's vice-president, asked a fellow New Yorker to "mention it modestly" in the campaign that the general had "prayers in his own house." The impact of these strategic comments cannot be known for certain, but Jackson did spend the next eight years in the White House.

ELECTION OF 1844

In the middle of three decades of unprecedented immigration to America, the 1840s erupted into intense ethnic and religious conflict between an overwhelmingly Protestant America and a predominantly Catholic tide of Irish and German newcomers. Sympathetically viewed by some and vilified as the "scum and dregs of human nature" by others, these immigrants, particularly the Irish, became part of a divisive political battle waged nationwide. The election of 1844 itself came just months after the great Philadelphia riots between Catholic Irish and nativist Americans over—among other volatile issues—which translation of the Bible to use in public schools.

In order to drive the immigrant vote away from the Whigs, the Democrats portrayed their opponent, Henry Clay, as anti-Catholic and, to hold the Protestant vote, circulated rumors about alleged inconsistencies between his private morality and his religious professions. Some Protestant voters supported Clay for his supposed anti-Catholicism, hoping he would thwart an alleged Jesuit conspiracy to take over America in the name of the papacy.

For a handful of Democrats, their fear of Catholic influence was so strong that they crossed over to the Whigs. But all in all neither party played up anti-Catholicism to the point of driving the potentially powerful block of staunchly Catholic immigrants away from its candidate. Especially in the urban North, immigrants were changing the profile of national politics.

Republican party marching banner appealing to antislavery constituents (Smithsonian Institution)

ELECTION OF 1852

During the campaign of 1852 both major parties came out publicly in favor of the Compromise of 1850, which maintained a balance of power in Congress and pledged the North to enforce the fugitive slave laws. In so doing the Democrats and Whigs temporarily buried the most politically vexing question of the day but consequently left themselves without an issue to rally voters.

The Democratic nominee, Franklin Pierce, was a native of New Hampshire, a state with a long history of anti-Catholic controversy. Pierce's father had served as governor of New Hampshire, connecting him to the so-called anti-Catholic clause of that state's constitution and had earlier voted in favor of John Adams's Alien and Sedition Laws, connecting him with nativism. Not only was the younger Pierce laden with his father's reputation as "a red hot enemy of the Catholics," he himself had failed to support "Catholic Emancipation" when it surfaced during his own tenure as governor. As a New York editor said in a speech in 1852, "When Religious liberty needed a champion Gen. Pierce was found—wanting."

In order to combat this image and to introduce Pierce to the American public (the slogan "Who is Franklin Pierce?" was used to great effect by the Whigs), Pierce's old friend and classmate, Nathaniel Hawthorne, wrote the customary campaign biography. Hawthorne lauded Pierce as a man who "has naturally a strong endowment of religious feeling," but not to the point of bigotry, "no narrowness or illiberality, but a wide-embracing sympathy for the modes of Christian worship, and a reverence for individual belief . . . with which no other has a right to interfere." In a direct counter to the charge of anti-Catholicism, Hawthorne maintained that Pierce had tried to remove New

Both read the same Bible, and pray to the same God; and each invokes his aid against the other. It may seem strange that any men should dare to ask a just God's assistance in wringing their bread from the sweat of other men's faces; but let us judge not that we be not judged. The prayers of both could not be answered; that of neither has been answered fully.

—*Abraham Lincoln, Second Inaugural Address, March 4, 1865*

Hampshire's religious test for office seekers.

The Democrats also went on the offensive, repaying the Whigs in kind with countercharges of anti-Catholicism. Neither party dared offend the blocs of predominantly Catholic Irish and German voters, but each tried tirelessly to associate the other with bigoted, nativist sentiment. Pierce, in the only personal defense he made, even released an old Fourth of July oration in which he had made kind remarks about the role of the foreign-born in the American Revolution. But the issue would not die and even followed him into office. For the sake of his party's reputation, he appointed James Campbell, a Catholic, as postmaster general.

ELECTION OF 1856

The old party loyalties realigned in the 1850s, giving rise to the new Republican party, an amalgam of nativism, antislavery, and nationalist forces united mostly by opposition to the Democrats. Numerous congressmen were swept into office by appealing to anti-immigration and antislavery sentiments, but the Democratic party worked to gain the allegiance of the more than three million immigrants who came to America between 1848 and 1860.

The campaign of 1856 perhaps marked the high tide of anti-Catholicism in American politics. Religious tension was pulling the country apart. The visit of Cardinal Bedini to America in 1854 sparked rioting in the cities he visited and even prompted attempts on his life. Observers predicted that the anti-Catholic novel *Beatrice*, published in 1853, would surpass *Uncle Tom's Cabin* in sales. Deluged by conspiracy theories and impassioned rhetoric, most Americans came to view the Catholic church with deep suspicion. The American party, which received twenty-five percent of the popular vote in 1856, criticized the Roman church as a highly organized, authoritarian, intolerant, and secret body, antithetical to cherished American ideals and supported by the immigrant population. "America," the party declared, "should be governed only by Americans."

Probably the candidate most affected by the religious intensity of the times was John C. Fremont, explorer, military hero, and maverick, the choice of the infant Republican party to face Democrat James Buchanan. Pamphlets with inflammatory titles, such as *Fremont's Romanism Established* and *The Romish Intrigue*, linked the candidate with papist plots. The Democrats spread stories that he was a closet Catholic and that a priest had secretly married him to a certain Jessie Benton. That his father actually was a Catholic and that his niece attended a Catholic school were used to great effect.

One Currier and Ives lithograph from the campaign pictured those who supposedly would profit from Fremont's election. Waiting to speak with him, in a line of radicals that includes abolition, free-love, and woman's rights advocates, stands a priest who reminds Fremont that "we look to You Sir to place the power of the Pope on a firm footing in this country." Fremont reassuringly replies to the group, "You shall all have what you desire—and be sure that the glorious Principles of Popery, Fourierism, Free Love, Womans [*sic*] rights, . . . and above all the Equality of our Colored brethren, shall be maintained. . . ." In other cartoons he was made to carry a cross, identifying him

STATE AND CHURCH

In the summer of 1866, during the furor over federal Reconstruction policy and the pending ratification of the Fourteenth Amendment, President Andrew Johnson went on a speaking tour to drum up support for his program. One of the most unpopular aspects of Johnson's Reconstruction policy, especially in the opinion of Radical Republican congressmen such as Thaddeus Stevens, Wendell Phillips, and Charles Sumner, was his practice of leniency in the matter of pardons for former Confederates. In his speeches, Johnson recounted his own rags-to-riches story and, as biographer Hans I. Trefousse writes, "compared himself to Jesus Christ and explained that like the Savior, he, too, liked to pardon repentant sinners. More and more often remarks along those lines encouraged hecklers in Johnson's audiences. As the tour wore on Johnson began to engage his opponents in a series of embarrassing tirades. The culmination occurred in a speech given in St. Louis on September 8:

> I know I have been . . . abused. . . . And I have been traduced, I have been slandered, I have been maligned, I have been called Judas Iscariot and all that. . . . If I have played the Judas, who has been my Christ that I have played the Judas with? Was it Thad. Stevens? Was it Wendell Phillips? Was it Charles Sumner? (Hisses and cheers.) These are the men that stop and compare themselves to the Savior; and everybody that differs from them . . . is to be denounced as a Judas.

The *Chicago Tribune* called the outburst the "crowning disgrace of a disreputable series."

in the public mind with Rome.

Although his enemies portrayed Fremont as the friend of the Catholic church and he personally opposed nativism, Catholic voters never did support him. To the end of the race he could not outrun the Know-Nothing, nativist image of the Republican party.

ELECTION OF 1876

The religious issues that fueled political controversy in antebellum America survived the Civil War. The Hayes-Tilden election of 1876 witnessed not only the aggravation of deep sectional wounds, but also continued the national debate over Catholicism in American society. The issue before the voters was familiar: religion in the public schools. The question of whose religion should predominate, which had rocked the city of Philadelphia thirty years earlier, was now of national concern.

The Republican platform defended the traditional system of public education as "the bulwark of the American republic." It recommended the passing of a constitutional amendment to forbid the use of "public funds or property for the benefit of any school or institution under sectarian control." The Democratic platform, on the other hand, called the public-school battle a "false issue" contrived by the Republicans to reap the political rewards of sectarian strife. Nevertheless, the Democrats reaffirmed their own commitment to the separation of church and state.

> *I would rather be defeated than make capital out of my religion.*
>
> *—Representative James A. Garfield, presidential campaign speech, Chautauqua, New York, August 8, 1880*

In his letter of acceptance for the Republican nomination, Rutherford B. Hayes embraced his party's position on aid to Catholic schools, saying that "agitation upon this subject is to be apprehended, until, by constitutional amend-

Cartoon by Grant Hamilton, published in the December 27, 1884, issue of The Judge, *depicting Rev. S. D. Burchard, a Republican, recovering from making his "Rum, Romanism, and Rebellion" speech, which helped swing the 1884 presidential election to the Democratic party*

ment, the schools are placed beyond all danger of sectarian control or interference." Republicans denounced the Catholic church repeatedly during the campaign, supposedly with party approval, as a menace to public education. James A. Garfield, later Republican president, quaked at the name of a new trinity: "The combined power of rebellion, Catholicism and whisky." The voters responded with the largest percentage of participation in American history.

ELECTION OF 1884

In 1884 Grover Cleveland became the first Democratic candidate to win election to the White House after the Civil War, defeating his opponent, James G. Blaine, in a very tight race. Only twenty-three thousand votes separated the two men nationwide, with the electoral ballot from the state of New York alone throwing the election to Cleveland. It was a campaign seasoned with scandal and indiscretion, illegitimate children and influence peddling, and it may have reached what one historian called "a new low in standards and practice." Key among the issues may have been religion. Of all the presidential contests in which religion has figured, in this case it may have been decisive.

The two sides threw charges of anti-Catholicism back and forth. Typically, both parties played the issue in two directions simultaneously, depending on the group it wanted to attract. For one constituency the Republicans claimed that Cleveland was anti-Catholic and emphasized the fact that Blaine's mother was Irish-Catholic, while for another they identified themselves with Protestantism and the prohibition movement.

The major blunder came when Blaine, attending a meeting of several hundred Protestant ministers in New

Hon.W.H.Taft,

Cincinnati, Ohio.

Dear Sir:

Some of my friends state that they will vote against you on the ground that you are an Infidel, and that you do not believe in our God. In order that I may answer this accusation, please let me know just how you stand on the subject.

Hon William Howard Taft,

Cincinnati, Ohio.

Sir:–

Beg to ask you "Do you believe in Jesus Christ as your personal Saviour?"

Hope I am worthy of a prompt reply,

Hon.W.H.Taft,

Cincinnati,Ohio.

Dear Sir: Objection is being urged to your election to the presidency on the groundthat you deny the divinity of Jesus Christ.

See inclosed leaflet of H.C.Morrison .

Please state whether you believe or disbelieve the statement of Peter: " Thou art the Christ the son of the living God" Matthew I6_I6.

A sampling of letters criticizing 1908 Republican presidential candidate William Howard Taft for being a Unitarian (Henry F. Pringle, The Life and Times of William Howard Taft, *1964)*

AN "ELEGANT ROW"

After Theodore Roosevelt left the presidency in 1909, he went on an African safari and, on the way home, toured the European capitals. In Rome for an audience with Pope Pius X, Roosevelt involved himself in what he later termed "an elegant row" with the Roman Catholic Church. The Pope sent word that he would not receive Roosevelt unless the former president promised not to visit a group of American Methodist missionaries who had referred to the Pope as "the whore of Babylon." Roosevelt had claimed no intention of visiting the overzealous Protestants, but he informed the Vatican that he would not conform to "any conditions which limit my freedom of conduct." The missionaries were bad, Roosevelt decided, but papal secretary Merry del Val (Roosevelt's Vatican connection) was probably worse: a "furiously bigoted reactionary," he remarked. Roosevelt later testified that in spurning the conditional offer of a papal audience, he had demonstrated "that I feared the most powerful Protestant church just as little as I feared the Roman Catholics."

York City, failed to respond to an insult to Catholic immigrants. One minister's remarks to the crowd included a reference—perhaps not original with him—that the Democratic party was the home of "Rum, Romanism and Rebellion." Somehow Blaine did not notice the comment and to his everlasting regret failed to distance himself from it in his own address to the group. The journalists from Republican papers took note, though, and sent the memorable phrase ringing across the country by telegraph. By the next morning the damage had been done, and Blaine's best efforts to limit the destruction were in vain. For the Democrats the slogan became a badge of honor and a potent weapon against the Republicans. Enough Irish left the Republican party to cost Blaine the election.

ELECTION OF 1908

William Howard Taft was the Republican nominee for president in 1908, the hand-chosen successor to Theodore Roosevelt. He faced Democrat William Jennings Bryan in the Great Commoner's third bid for the White House. Taft had served as Roosevelt's secretary of war, but his previous position as governor-general of the Philippines led to religious troubles for his campaign.

After the United States acquired the Philippines during the Spanish-American War, President William McKinley appointed Taft first as chairman of a committee to set up a government for the islands, and then as governor-general in 1901. After a six-month stay Taft returned to the States, but on his way back to the Philippines he visited Pope Leo XIII in Rome as the representative of the new president, Theodore Roosevelt. The meeting concerned land policy in the Philippines. The United States wanted the Catholic church to return to the farmers land that several orders of friars had appropriated. The negotiations were fruitless, and the orders rejected a U.S. offer to purchase the land, but the fact that Taft had visited a pope proved political dynamite six years later.

Actually Taft got himself into a no-win situation. Protestant publications characterized him as "pro-Catholic" as a result of his dealings with the pope, and rumors circulated that some of his family were actually Catholics. But American Catholics vigorously criticized his Philippine land proposal as antagonistic toward the Church. On another issue, Taft's Unitarianism, especially that church's rejection of the divinity of Jesus, left conservative Protestants cold. On top of that, Jews were being told that

Cartoon published in the November 3, 1928, issue of the pro-Ku Klux Klan periodical Friendship Forum *claiming that the 1928 Democratic presidential candidate, Al Smith, would be a servant of the Catholic Church (courtesy of the New York State Library)*

Taft had made insulting remarks toward them during a recent visit to Russia.

Bryan worked hard to keep Catholics loyal to the Democratic party. Although a fundamentalist Presbyterian, he appointed Catholics to key positions on his campaign staff. In the end, though, Bryan met defeat for the third and final time, and some of his supporters quickly blamed the Catholic church, which they claimed had conspired with Wall Street and the Republican party to elect Taft.

ELECTION OF 1928

Perhaps the most notorious election involving the "Catholic question" was the campaign of 1928 between Herbert Hoover and Alfred E. Smith. Smith had lost his bid for the Democratic nomination in 1924, but he was a very popular governor of New York, a progressive who fought hard for improved working conditions. As a result, he returned in 1928 to capture his party's prize, the first Roman Catholic in any major party ever to do so. His was the classic immigrant success story: a poor altar boy grew up to become governor of his state and then candidate for his country's highest office.

Smith entered the campaign with two major liabilities: his stand on Prohibition and his Catholicism. He had compiled a solid reform record, but he came out in favor of at least a modification of the Volstead Act if not the repeal of Prohibition itself. To many Progressives this was heresy. Even that voice of religious ecumenism and liberalism, the *Christian Century*, gave its support to Hoover in order to remain faithful to the doctrine of Prohibition.

Smith's Catholicism, though, gave

him even more trouble. Many Protestants believed that a Catholic in the nation's highest office threatened cherished American institutions. Anti-Smith literature amounting to an estimated ten million pamphlets and posters promised ruin for America if Smith were elected. William Allen White, a prominent Republican columnist, wrote that beyond the specifics of Smith's religion and his position on alcohol was the general belief among Middle America that "the whole Puritan civilization which had built a sturdy, orderly nation is threatened by Smith."

Among protests against Smith's election was an article in the *Atlantic Monthly* of April 1927. The author contended that Roman Catholicism placed itself above the state and was therefore "irreconcilable" with the Constitution. In other words, Smith, if a consistent Catholic, would have to put his church before his oath of office. Smith's reply in the following issue was prepared with the help of the distinguished World War I chaplain, Father Francis Duffy. The candidate pointed out that any faithful Episcopalian would have the same theoretical conflict with the state, and that in his years as governor he had not had such trouble. He concluded the reply with a restatement of his belief in the separation of church and state, in freedom of conscience, and in the support of the public schools, a topic stirred by his state's assistance to parochial schools.

To his credit, Hoover refused to make much of the religious issue. In one of his few comments on the subject, he said that anti-Catholic bigotries "give violence to every instinct I possess." The election, though, came in a Republican year at the end of a Republican decade. As one wag quipped at the time, the Republicans could have run a monkey and still won.

ELECTION OF 1960

The campaign of 1960 was one of the tightest of the twentieth century. On election day the voters split almost precisely in half, with a margin of only 118,000 ballots separating Senator John F. Kennedy from Vice-President Richard M. Nixon. Issues ranging from foreign policy to race relations divided the nation, but the issue most frequently raised before the voters was the matter of Kennedy's religion.

Kennedy began his political career in 1946 representing a predominantly Catholic district in Massachusetts. A Catholic himself, and an Irish-Catholic at that, his religion was at first a political asset. But in his Senate race in 1952 he faced speculation over a possible conflict of interest between his church and his office. He affirmed a position then that he found himself repeating years later: "The responsibility of the office-holder is to make decisions on these questions [specific federal policies] on the basis of the general welfare as he sees it, even if such a decision is not in accord with the prevailing Catholic opinion." In effect he sought to relieve the minds of Protestant voters by promising to be a bad Catholic—at least that is how the Catholic press saw it. Some writers criticized Kennedy for putting his political interests above fidelity to his church.

In 1956 Kennedy lost a chance for the vice-presidential spot on the Democratic ticket under Adlai Stevenson, but he gained exposure and certainly benefited by not running on a losing team. By the late 1950s, he was ready to run for president. The off-year elections in 1958 brought the total number of Catholic governors up to eight, the number of Catholic senators to a dozen, and Catholic representatives to ninety-one. Catholic politicians had come a long way, and the opportunity looked better than ever for a Catholic presidential nominee.

During the primaries, though, Kennedy faced familiar questions from the public and the press. In the key Wisconsin and West Virginia primaries, the newspapers played up the religious debate. As he had a few years before, Kennedy vowed that he did not and would

Evangelist Billy Graham with President John F. Kennedy, the first Catholic American chief executive (photograph by Abbie Rowe; courtesy of the John F. Kennedy Library)

not "take orders from any Pope, any Cardinal, any Bishop or any priest." Believing that the issue crowded out more important and substantive matters, Kennedy objected to the emphasis given to the religion issue. In an article for *Look* magazine, echoing Al Smith's response written under similar circumstances in 1927, Kennedy reaffirmed his commitment to the separation of church and state and his loyalty to the Constitution.

Kennedy won his party's nomination, and the religious debate spread to the nation at large. In a Washington speech before the American Society of Newspaper Editors, he repeated his oft-stated views on the relationship between church and state, denied that he was bound by the pronouncements of the pope, and said that he did not favor public aid for parochial schools. He brought the same defense deep into the Bible Belt in an address to the Houston Ministers Association, hoping to allay fears and keep the "Solid South" solidly Democratic.

As in so many previous campaigns involving religious issues, the race brought down a deluge of written and spoken words. An estimated twenty million pieces of campaign literature flooded the country. As part of this rhetorical tide, some of Nixon's supporters wanted him to play on the Catholic controversy, and a few of Kennedy's backers suggested that he turn the tables with talk of "bigotry," but neither candidate, especially toward the end of the race, made much of the issue, each having more to lose than gain.

Religion influenced the election in several ways. It may have brought some conservative Democrats, who had earlier crossed over to vote for Eisenhower, back into the fold. But movement in the opposite direction of more than four million Protestant Democrats, especially in the Midwest, who voted for Nixon, largely counteracted that movement. To return the favor, though, many Protestants went the other way to vote for Kennedy. Nationwide, Kennedy received eighty percent of the Catholic vote, but whether his religion decided the election is impossible to know.

Cartoon from the presidential campaign of 1976. To the consternation of a scandal-weary Republican elephant, born-again candidate Jimmy Carter and the Democratic party have sprouted angel's wings (cartoon by Hugh Haynie; courtesy of the Louisville Courier-Journal*).*

ELECTION OF 1976

George Gallup called 1976 the "year of the Evangelical." Conservative Protestants had emerged in the late 1970s as a significant force in American politics. Invigorated with a revived activism, they worked to regenerate politically an afflicted America, a nation which had suffered through Vietnam and Watergate and seemed, at least to them, to be wallowing in a spiritual malaise.

The Democratic candidate was a former one-term governor from Georgia, James E. "Jimmy" Carter, who cultivated a folksy image as an outsider in Washington who could clean up the mess. To a country that still felt shamed by a dishonest president, he promised integrity, saying, "I will never lie to you." To many evangelicals in particular, the fact that he was a born-again Southern Baptist meant that he was "one of us" and the right man for the hour.

In an interesting reversal of Catholic-Protestant confrontations in presidential politics, though, Carter's affiliation with evangelical Christians hurt his chances among Catholic voters. Indeed, some Catholic leadership openly spoke against him. Rev. Andrew Greeley said that Catholics "should be afraid of the Carter-Mondale ticket." "Carter represents," he continued, "the old tradition of Southern populism, which was fundamentally and often viciously anti-Catholic." Moreover, on the abortion issue, many Catholics felt more at home with the Republican party's platform against abortion and supported its candidate, Gerald Ford. Ford even advertised in Catholic periodicals to encourage the trend.

Carter's evangelical ties also hurt him among Jews. Since the Southern Baptist church held to the traditional Protestant belief in Jesus as the Messiah and in the sure damnation of those who rejected him, some Jews suggested that Jewish members of Carter's campaign staff should resign.

Even some evangelicals eventually abandoned Carter over what they saw as inconsistencies in his beliefs. The most notorious example, which became a political albatross for Carter, was his interview with *Playboy* magazine. The vehicle of the comments was problematic enough for evangelicals, but Carter's free admission that he had "looked upon a lot of women with lust" and had therefore "committed adultery in my heart many times" was a little more than they could bear. It was an honest enough admission, but a little too honest for politics.

Overall, Carter's religion lost him votes from among Catholics, Jews, and some evangelicals. Nevertheless, it did gain him some ground among Protestants, and he carried the election.

RELIGIOUS AFFILIATIONS OF THE PRESIDENTS

George Washington	Episcopalian
John Adams	Unitarian
Thomas Jefferson	Deist
James Madison	Episcopalian
James Monroe	Episcopalian
John Quincy Adams	Unitarian
Andrew Jackson	Presbyterian
Martin Van Buren	Dutch Reformed
William Henry Harrison	Episcopalian
John Tyler	Episcopalian
James K. Polk	Methodist
Zachary Taylor	Episcopalian
Millard Fillmore	Unitarian
Franklin Pierce	Episcopalian
James Buchanan	Presbyterian
Abraham Lincoln	None
Andrew Johnson	None
Ulysses S. Grant	Methodist
Rutherford B. Hayes	Methodist
James A. Garfield	Disciples of Christ
Chester Arthur	Episcopalian
Grover Cleveland	Presbyterian
Benjamin Harrison	Presbyterian
William McKinley	Methodist
Theodore Roosevelt	Dutch Reformed
William Howard Taft	Unitarian
Woodrow Wilson	Presbyterian
Warren G. Harding	Baptist
Calvin Coolidge	Congregationalist
Herbert Hoover	Quaker
Franklin D. Roosevelt	Episcopalian
Harry S Truman	Baptist
Dwight D. Eisenhower	Presbyterian
John F. Kennedy	Roman Catholic
Lyndon B. Johnson	Disciples of Christ
Richard M. Nixon	Quaker
Gerald R. Ford	Episcopalian
Jimmy Carter	Baptist
Ronald Reagan	Disciples of Christ
George Bush	Episcopalian

Critical Presidential Elections

by THOMAS L. CONNELLY

American presidential elections have frequently riveted the attention of the nation. On a personal level, skillfully managed elections can achieve all the effects of melodrama, as the fates of the candidates, who take on heroic and sometimes tragic characteristics, are predicted, analyzed, and then played out. Issues that are at any other time soporific take on heightened significance. The electorate ingeniously, if not soberly, confronts with varying degrees of enthusiasm the cyclic responsibility of determining the fate of the candidates, the viability of their parties, the resolution of great issues, and even the course of world affairs. Each election has special significance, which is sometimes dulled by the perspective of history. The survey that follows describes some of the elections that have retained over time some of the luster ascribed to them by contemporary pundits.

ELECTION OF 1800

Thomas Jefferson called the election of 1800 "as real a revolution in the principles of our government as that of 1776 was in its form," and he does not appear to have exaggerated. The election confirmed the emergence of a two-party system in American politics, a development that must have seemed ironic to some Federalists and Democratic-Republicans because most of them had believed with George Washington that the appearance of parties would do more harm than good. Washington commanded respect enough to engineer unanimous presidential victories in 1789 and 1792, but during the presidency of Washington's successor, John Adams, political factions began warring openly. Adams and the Federalists had led the nation into an undeclared naval war with France and in the process expressed an activist concept of government that Vice-President Thomas Jefferson and the Democratic-Republicans thought contradicted democratic principles.

In 1789 most observers tended to view popular government in terms of the republicanism of their classical forebears. Many questioned whether a "large-state" democracy, such as the one they were forming, could contain a diverse set of interests and still remain viable. Along with a set of conservative constitutional restrictions on democracy, they erected a "federal" structure—a system of interlocking national, state, and local governmental jurisdictions—and a system of "checks and balances" between executive, legislative, and judicial branches of the national government in hopes of frustrating power-hungry politicians. They hoped Congress could contain rival interests without dividing itself into parties.

But in the 1790s partisanship developed anyway. Two cabinet members in the Washington administration represented the opposing ideologies. Secretary of the Treasury Alexander Hamilton, the philosophical leader of the administration, the man Washington listened to more than anyone else, headed one camp—the Federalists. Thomas Jefferson opposed Hamilton and headed the other—the Democratic-Republicans.

The Federalists believed in a strong central government. They feared the threat of the majority interest against the status quo and favored limiting control of the government to property own-

By Yesterday's Mails.

Highly Important and Intereſting.

PENNSYLVANIA. PHILAD. FEB. 14.

BY EXPRESS.

WASHINGTON, Feb. 11, half paſt 3, afternoon.

" ACCORDING to the rule of proceedings eſtabliſhed by the Houſe, they proceeded to the Senate Chamber, where (by Mr. *Nicholas* and Mr. *Rutledge*, the tellers on the part of the Houſe, and Mr. *Wells* on the part of the Senate) the votes were counted and the reſult declared by the Vice-Preſident, as follow :—

For THOMAS JEFFERSON,	73
AARON BURR,	73
JOHN ADAMS,	65
C. C. PINCKNEY,	64
JOHN JAY,	1

The tellers declared there was ſome informality in the votes of *Georgia*, but believing them to be the true votes, reported them as ſuch.

The Vice-Preſident then, in purſuance of the duty enjoined upon him, declared, that *Thomas Jefferſon* and *Aaron Burr* being equal in the number of Votes, it remained for the Houſe of Repreſentatives to determine the choice.

The two Houſes then ſeparated, and the Houſe of Repreſentatives returned to their chamber, where ſeats had been previouſly prepared for the members of the Senate. A call of the members of the Houſe, arranged according to States, was then made; upon which it appeared, that every member was preſent except Gen. *Sumpter*, who is unwell, and unable to attend. Mr. *Nicholſon* of *Maryland*, was alſo unwell but attended and had a bed prepared for him in one of the committee rooms, to which place the ballot box was carried to him, by the tellers appointed on the part of the State.

The mode of balloting was this—each State had a ballot box in which the members belonging to it, having previouſly appointed a teller, put the votes of the State; the teller on the part of the United States, having then counted the votes, duplicates of the reſult were put by him into two general ballot boxes—Tellers being nominated by each State for the purpoſe of examining the general ballot boxes, they were divided into two parts, of whom one examined one of the general ballot boxes, and the other examining the other.—Upon comparing the reſult and finding them to agree, the votes were ſtated to the Speaker who declared them to the Houſe.

The firſt ballot was 8 States for JEFFERSON, 6 for BURR, and 2 divided.

Which reſult continues to be the ſame, although they have already balloted ſeven times. A motion was made about half an hour ſince, to repeat the ballot in one hour, and was agreed to. The balloting is to recommence at the expiration of that time. Some of the members have gone to their lodgings to dine, and others are taking refreſhments in the Committee Rooms.

As there will be no poſſibility of aſcertaining what will be the event of the choice to be made by the Houſe for ſome time to come, it is not improbable that the balloting will continue for ſome days. *Yours, &c.*

" 3 o'clock A. M. Two ballots have been taken ſince:—The ſame reſult.—Ballot to be repeated again at 4 o'clock." [*Thus far our Correſpondent.*]

At the requeſt of the Speaker the mail was detained until 4, on Thurſday morning, that the members might have an opportunity of communicating theſe proceedings.

The ballot which was to take place at 4, made the TWENTY-FIRST eſſay of the Houſe to come to a deciſion.

News of a deadlocked presidential election from "Yesterday's Mails," Columbian Centinel, *February 21, 1801*

ers, whom they considered the rightful leaders of society. They also supported close ties between the national government and the business and manufacturing classes, believing that federal support of business created conditions by which everyone could achieve greater prosperity. They favored the creation of a national bank and a national debt structure (the latter to assure the loyalty of the nation's creditor class), the establishment of federal support for internal improvements such as roads and canals, and aid for the promotion of manufacturing in the form of a protective tariff. They held little sympathy for the interests of the agricultural segment of society, or for the interests of westerners, artisans, or indentured servants.

Jefferson, secretary of state under Washington until 1795, and the Democratic-Republicans broke with the administration over Hamilton's Federalist program. The Jeffersonians believed that federal support of one set of interests at the expense of all others was antidemocratic; consequently, they opposed all forms of specialized federal aid. They also championed—or at least they said they did—the interests of farmers and the working class, who had enjoyed little previous governmental support. By 1796 the Federalists and the Democratic-Republicans faced each other for control of the executive branch, and Adams defeated Jefferson in a close election.

In 1800 Adams and Jefferson again faced each other. During that campaign (such as it was) the Federalist press attempted to smear Jefferson as a dangerous radical and atheist, warning that his election would lead to the same violent excess that marked the French Revolution. They also blunted the other party's attacks against themselves. Under the terms of the Sedition Act of 1798 the government prosecuted what it considered the libelous or treasonous activities of the Democratic-Republican press.

Because several new states had been added to the Union since the last election, expanding western power, and the policies of the stuffy Adams had aroused much public dissatisfaction, the Democratic-Republicans defeated the Federalists. But Jefferson and Aaron Burr of New York tied in electoral votes, throwing the election into the House of Representatives. Several ballots in the House of Representatives were taken before Jefferson finally defeated Burr. Ironically, Hamilton, who could have used his influence to oust Jefferson, supported his bitter rival over Burr. Hamilton preferred Jefferson, a man of character and accomplishment, over the opportunistic and unscrupulous Burr.

The travail over the selection of the president in the Electoral College brought a change in the constitutional system. In 1804 the nation ratified the Twelfth Amendment, providing for separate balloting in the Electoral College for president and vice-president.

ELECTION OF 1824

The election of 1800 marked the beginning of the end of the Federalist party. It never again summoned the support necessary to elect one of its presidential candidates. Thomas Jefferson won a second term as president in 1804, defeating South Carolinian Charles C. Pinckney; Jefferson's longtime friend and colleague James Madison defeated Pinckney in 1808 and New Yorker DeWitt Clinton in 1812. The last Federalist to run for president, Rufus King of New York, lost to the third straight Democratic-Republican president from Virginia, James Monroe, in 1816. In 1820, with the Federalist party only a memory, Monroe ran unopposed for a second term.

The Federalist party disappeared as a national political force because it was unable to alter its program to accommodate changing conditions. Traditionally pro-British and promerchant, it had opposed Jefferson's and Madison's efforts to embargo British trade during the years leading up to the War of 1812, and then when war broke out the party refused to lead the New England states it controlled into the conflict. Some Federalists openly espoused secessionism during the war, a fact that alienated the party from the rest of the country. The party also failed to acknowledge the emergence of a strong western interest in the United States. Controversies over the protective tariff and federal support for internal improvements and a new kind of democratized idealism in politics stood waiting to be exploited by the right candidate.

Just because the Federalists declined did not mean that the country was no longer divided by political issues. In fact, the country was more divided than ever during the years leading up to the election of 1824. The divisions ran along regional lines and centered largely on the issues of the tariff and internal improvements. Four major candidates, each espousing a distinct position and calling himself a Democratic-Republican, ran for president that year. Henry Clay of Kentucky, Speaker of the House, proposed his "American System," which attracted westerners who wanted to develop a home market for their surplus agricultural products, to increase their frontier region's connection to the outside world through federally sponsored roads and canals, and to protect their infant manufacturing sector by means of a high tariff. Secretary of State John Quincy Adams of Massachusetts, the son of the second president, supported a tariff to protect New England's industries but balked at the notion that taxes from the New England region, which boasted the best transportation system in the country at the time, should go west to build roads and canals. Although he tried not to say much about it, Secretary of the Treasury William Crawford of Georgia believed, along with most southerners, that a too-

Detail from "A Foot Race," 1824 cartoon by David Claypoole. John Quincy Adams has edged ahead of William Crawford and Andrew Jackson in the race for the presidency (courtesy of the New-York Historical Society).

high tariff would hurt his predominantly agricultural region, which obtained many of its manufactured goods from Europe in exchange for cotton. Senator Andrew Jackson of Tennessee was perhaps the most politically sagacious of the four. Following the advice of his friends, he said little about the issues, concentrating instead on promoting his status as the hero of the Battle of New Orleans during the War of 1812. Mainly he touted himself as a Jeffersonian traditionalist.

Long a political insider and next to Jackson the candidate most vague on the issues, Crawford stood as the front-runner to succeed Monroe as late as the beginning of 1823. Two factors contributed to his downfall, both beyond his control. One was the stroke he suffered in September of that year. The other was the decision by some members of Congress to call a caucus to nominate him for president. No caucus was called in 1820, and thus it was assumed that none would be needed in 1824. The move on Crawford's behalf served only to exacerbate political differences that no one could have known would end up creating another party system out of the remnants of the old. Clay, Adams, and Jackson all were nominated by state legislatures and an occasional state-based nominating convention; party trappings remained absent in their cases, and they took exception to the affront of a congressional caucus.

Meanwhile, probably to the disbelief of the others, Jackson gathered strength. Not only westerners but also southerners, rural midwesterners, and a smattering of the growing class of lower-income urban voters found Old Hickory a refreshing change. By the time of the election he was the most popular of all the contestants, winning 99 electoral votes and about 43 percent of the popular vote. Adams finished second with 84 electoral votes, Clay third with 41, and Crawford fourth with 37. Jackson's tally fell short of the electoral majority needed for victory, and the decision fell to the House of Representatives.

Neither Adams nor Clay could stomach the neophyte Jackson as the nation's leader. Kentuckian Clay especially resented the sudden loss of much of his western support to the upstart. The two veterans quickly established a working friendship that resulted in the transfer of Clay's support to Adams in the first House ballot. New president Adams made Clay his secretary of state. Jackson cried, "The Judas of the West has closed the contract and will receive the thirty pieces of silver." He and his growing army of supporters vowed to avenge the "corrupt bargain" of 1824.

ELECTION OF 1828

After his loss Jackson immediately geared up for 1828. The Adams presidency—to some extent compromised by the bargain with Clay but also hampered by the president's own disagreeable personality—never got off the ground. Former Crawford supporters, including New Yorker Martin Van Buren and his Albany Regency, fell in behind Jackson; John C. Calhoun led the South in the same direction; Clay grew isolated in his own section of the country; and Adams, a political professional four years earlier, seemed to be in over his head. Adams supporters, who by the time of the election were calling themselves National-Republicans, resorted to cheap character attacks as decision day approached; the Jacksonians, who were calling themselves Democratic-Republicans or Democrats, counted on the support of most of the country outside Adams's native New England. The result was a Jackson landslide. Old Hickory won the electoral tally by a score of 178 to 83; an electorate greatly expanded from that of four years earlier gave him nearly 650,000 popular votes to Adams's 500,000.

United behind a candidate, not a series of issues, the Jackson voters represented the realization of a greater American democracy than the one envisioned by the nation's founders. But it was a democracy more of image than substance. Jackson settled into the presidency determined to create an organization to perpetuate the power he had gathered. He had attracted the support of both protariff and antitariff voters, old Federalists and old Jeffersonians, former Clay men and former Adams men, and a lot of voters who had never voted before in their lives. He would commit his party to a program, mostly a systematic opposition to the nationalism of the American System, and he would employ the negative power of the presidency (the veto) in a way that attracted charges that he was a despot. But he subordinated policy to power politics so skillfully that his supporters never realized that they disagreed with one other.

ELECTION OF 1844

The Democrats met in convention for the first time in 1832 to endorse Jackson, who had already been nominated by a host of state legislatures, for a second presidential term, and to nominate his running mate, Martin Van Buren. The National-Republicans had convened in late 1831 to nominate Henry Clay for president and John Sargent of Pennsylvania for vice-president. Jackson won the election easily. Before the next election the National Republicans banded with other anti-Jackson forces—including former Jacksonians who opposed Old Hickory's veto of the bill to recharter the Second Bank of the United States, old Anti-Masons, and southerners who resented Jackson's weak tariff stance—to form the Whig party. In 1836 the Whigs ran regional candidates in hopes of throwing the election to the House of Representatives, but Jackson's handpicked Democratic nominee Van Buren bested the lot. In 1840 the Whigs did the image-

Presidential candidates Henry Clay and James Polk as "Political Cockfighters," lithograph by James Baillie, 1844

conscious Democrats one better, getting behind the hero of Tippecanoe, William Henry Harrison, to defeat Van Buren's reelection bid. Harrison's quick demise in effect gave the presidency back to the Democrats in the person of states' rights Jeffersonian Whig John Tyler of Virginia.

By the time the 1844 contest approached, the forces that would crumble the second two-party system had already emerged. The slavery issue caught the nation's attention in modified form: on April 21, 1836, an army of Texans under Sam Houston defeated Mexican general Santa Anna's forces at the Battle of San Jacinto. Texas became an independent republic, wrote a constitution, and voted in favor of annexation to the United States.

The desire of the Texans for annexation became the number one political issue in the United States because the admission of Texas guaranteed the admission of another slave state to the Union. Jackson managed to avoid the question. Although Van Buren believed that state governments should decide questions of slavery, he sided with northerners in opposition to annexation because territorial expansion threatened to emphasize sectional differences. Many of Harrison's Whigs opposed annexation for the same reasons, but successor Tyler, a Whig in name only, supported Texas admission. In 1843 the Senate rejected a treaty formulated by his administration that would have annexed Texas.

Many supported annexation not because they wanted to expand the reach of slavery, but because they feared the consequences of an independent Texas on American foreign policy. In particular they feared rising British influence in Texas affairs. Britain saw great promise in having Texas remain a separate republic. A permanent, independent Texas could provide cotton for English mills and also serve as a barrier to further American western expansion.

Near the end of his term in office, President Tyler remained determined to annex Texas. He asked that Congress agree to the annexation in the form of a joint resolution, which required only a majority vote in both houses to gain approval. In February 1845 Congress narrowly passed such a resolution. Tyler signed the measure on March 1, three days before the inauguration of his successor, Democrat James K. Polk.

Polk, the first "dark horse" nominee of a major American political party, did not come to the convention with strong credentials as a winner. After his service in the House of Representatives (he served as Speaker of the House from 1835 to 1839) and one term as Tennessee governor he had been defeated in two successive attempts to win the governorship again. What he did possess was the blessing of Jackson.

Polk needed more than Jackson's blessing to win the contest with Clay. He needed the counteracting effects of a strong third party, the Liberty party, the first American antislavery party. The Liberty party nominated abolitionist James G. Birney for the presidency; although Birney could not gather enough votes to carry even one state, he cost Clay enough northern Whig votes to swing the election to Polk. If Clay had won New York, a state where Birney did particularly well, he would have won the presidency. But Polk won New York and the top prize.

Polk's election brought an important turn in American politics. The national government committed itself totally to a program of national expansion. Texas voted for admission to the Union soon after Polk went to Washington. In 1846 the president signed a treaty with Great Britain fixing the boundary of the Oregon territory and laying the groundwork for the future admission of the states of Washington and Oregon. Most important, the president led the nation into a war with Mexico and in 1848 claimed northern Mexican territory from Texas to the Pacific Ocean for the United States. Democratic expansionism realized what was grandly called America's "Manifest Destiny."

ELECTION OF 1860

With the addition of the territories of the South and West the question of slavery's expansion became hotter. In 1848 another third party, the Free Soil party, ran Martin Van Buren and took antislavery votes from Democratic nominee Lewis Cass; Whig Zachary Taylor, vague and inexperienced but a slaveholder and military hero, won the presidency. In 1852 Democrat Franklin Pierce, a New Hampshire Yankee who nevertheless took a nationalist stance with regard to slavery, defeated Whig party candidate Winfield Scott, another hero of the Mexican war. Then the Whigs collapsed, the Republicans rose to take their place, and the Civil War changed the nation forever.

The seeds of the collapse of the two-party system of Whigs and Democrats were sowed during the administration of James Monroe some forty years earlier. In 1819 the Missouri Territory applied for admission to the Union as a slave state. To maintain a balance between free and slave states in the Senate, Congress admitted the free state of Maine along with Missouri and established guidelines to restrict slavery's expansion by prohibiting slavery in Louisiana Purchase territories north of the southern boundary of Missouri.

When the U.S. victory in the Mexican War presented new opportunities for slavery's expansion in the late 1840s, congressional politicians led by Henry Clay worked out what became known as the Compromise of 1850. They admitted California as a free state, organized the territories of New Mexico and Utah without mentioning slavery, prohibited the slave trade in the District of Columbia, passed a more stringent fugitive slave law, and settled Texas boundary claims. Soon after, however, westward expansion into the Louisiana Purchase territories west and north of Missouri threatened the 1820 compromise. The controversy began with a debate over the eastern terminus of a proposed

Crowd gathering before Abraham Lincoln's first presidential inauguration, Washington, D.C., March 4, 1861

transcontinental railroad. Congress had considered several routes. Democratic Senator Stephen A. Douglas of Illinois, considered a bright presidential prospect, strove to obtain acceptance of Chicago as the terminus.

Douglas's unwitting subsequent actions ruined his chances of becoming president and helped force the nation into a tragic Civil War. To gain southern support for his northern terminus proposal Douglas proposed the organization of the territories of Kansas and Nebraska without mentioning the Missouri Compromise's prohibition of slavery. The Kansas-Nebraska Act, passed in 1854, in effect repealed the Compromise in those areas. According to the act the principle of "popular sovereignty"—based on the right of new states to decide for themselves whether or not to admit slavery—would prevail instead. Many northern Democrats and most northern Whigs would not accept popular sovereignty as a basis for settling the territorial expansion question.

The Kansas-Nebraska Act finished the second American party system. Most members of the Democratic party fell in behind popular sovereignty as the only solution to a nasty problem. The Whigs were not so lucky. That party was unable to mount a candidate in the presidential election of 1856. During the balloting many southern Whigs stayed home, and most of the rest voted for the Democratic candidate, James Buchanan of Pennsylvania, who had been out of the country during the furor over Kansas-Nebraska and was therefore unharmed by the controversy. At first northern Whigs joined either the Free Soil or Know-Nothing party. The latter was a "nativist" anomaly without much to say except that it wanted to restrict German and Irish immigration to the United States. But by the time of the election many northern Whigs thought they had found a solution to their dilemma: the Republican party.

The Republican party had been organized in 1854 as the first openly sectional political grouping in the history of the United States. Calling on the Constitution for its authority, it dedicated itself to the prohibition of slavery's expansion into the territories, which, the party held, were controlled by the federal government and thus subject to federal law. Furthermore, the Republicans supported many traditional Whig principles established by Henry Clay's American System, including federal support for internal improvements and industry and a strong federal role in finance. As 1856 neared the Republicans attracted increasing numbers of former northern Whigs, Know-Nothing nativists, and Liberty and Free Soil antislavery elements to their cause. The Republican presidential candidate in 1856, John Fremont of California, did extremely well in a losing effort, winning more than one-third of the popular vote nationwide. Very few southerners, however, voted for the Republican candidate. And enough northern Democrats voted for Buchanan to win the election for the party of Jackson.

Meanwhile Douglas struggled to contain the expansion issue within the confines of the Democratic party. Civil war broke out in Kansas in 1856 between groups favoring and opposing slavery. To placate northern Democrats who were angry over Douglas's support for popular sovereignty in Kansas and Nebraska, Douglas opposed the Lecompton slavery constitution (named for the town in which it was written) as the basis for the admission of Kansas into the Union. That opposition cost him the support of southern Democrats. President Buchanan pressed for the admission of Kansas under Lecompton, but Republicans and northern Democrats combined to block the effort. (Kansas was finally admitted to the Union as a free state in 1861, after the southern states had seceded.)

While the Kansas debate raged, the Supreme Court announced the Dred Scott decision in 1857. That decision established the principles that black people were not American citizens and therefore were not entitled to equal justice under the law and that property in slaves carried the same status as any other form of property. The second principle refuted the Republican contention that the Constitution established the right of the federal government to restrict slavery to the states. Moreover, it meant that even if the citizens of a new state wanted to prohibit slavery they could not do so, undermining Douglas's popular sovereignty position. The country waited to hear Douglas's feelings concerning Dred Scott.

The nation got its chance to hear Douglas in 1858, when he ran for reelection to the Senate against Republican challenger Abraham Lincoln, a former supporter of the Whig party and Henry Clay and a longtime behind-the-scenes power in Illinois politics. Lincoln was not only a shrewd politician but also a talented stump speaker and a formidable rival to Douglas. He had joined the Republicans in response to the passage of the Kansas-Nebraska Act. The combatants squared off in a series of seven debates—the most famous and politically sophisticated debates in American political history, a series of debates that interested the entire nation. At the second debate, which took place in Freeport, Illinois, Lincoln "trapped" Douglas by asking him if he thought the Dred Scott declaration of the equal rights of slave property destroyed the popular sovereignty position. In reply Douglas enunciated what became known as the "Freeport Doctrine," in which he held that regardless of the federal government's position regarding slave property, the institution required local public support to succeed. For example, Douglas continued, a city or state might pass a so-called "personal liberty law," making it unlawful to deprive a black person accused of escaping slavery of his liberty without due process of law: a jury trial. The jury could then set the black person free even if he really was a slave and everybody knew it. Although Douglas won the race against Lincoln for the Senate, the Freeport Doctrine finished him in the South and ended the Democratic party's hope for a nationwide resolution to the slavery question. Lincoln's unequivocal rejection of the Dred Scott decision and of the idea of popular sovereignty put him in a strong position to take over leadership of the Republicans in 1860.

The Democrats collapsed at their nominating convention in April 1860. Southerners demanded firm proslavery and pro-Dred Scott planks in the party platform in return for the nomination of Douglas; when they did not get them, they walked out. The rump nominated Douglas, and the southern wing nominated Buchanan's vice-president, John C. Breckinridge. A group of former southern Whigs calling themselves the Constitutional Union party nominated John Bell of Tennessee, who pledged little except adherence to the Constitution. The Republicans nominated Lincoln and held their ground against the expansion of slavery and against Dred Scott.

The campaign degenerated into a sectional battle. Douglas ran against Lincoln in the North, and Breckinridge and Bell fought it out in the South. Lincoln won less than 40 percent of the total popular vote but shut out Douglas in electoral votes in every northern state except one; that showing proved sufficient to hold off Breckinridge in the South by a margin of more than one hundred electoral votes. During the lame duck period of Buchanan's presidency seven southern states seceded from the Union; when president Lincoln authorized the resupply of besieged Fort Sumter, South Carolina, in April 1861, and Confederate troops fired on it, four other states left the Union. A northern army was routed by the "rebels" at Bull Run, Virginia, in June. Lincoln called for more volunteers.

ELECTION OF 1876

The election of 1876 was one of the closest in the nation's history. Americans had become weary of the Reconstruction administrations of President Ulysses S. Grant. Financial scandals implicating many in the administration who were close to Grant had tarnished the president's image as a hero of the Civil War. In addition, many Americans sympathized with the South, parts of which still labored under the burden of federal military occupation.

Grant hoped for a third term as president, but the two-term tradition went against him. Instead the Republicans nominated Rutherford B. Hayes of Ohio. Hayes bore an image of respectability, crucial at a time when Americans wanted more than politics as usual. A former member of the U.S. House of Representatives and a three-term governor of his state, Hayes had served with distinction in the Civil War, rising to the rank of major general. He had long championed the liberal ideals of the Republican party. In 1875 an Ohio state convention named him a favorite son presidential candidate, and in June 1876 the Republican national convention at Cincinnati, Ohio, made the nomination official. Meanwhile, in St. Louis, the Democrats nominated Governor Samuel J. Tilden of New York.

Tilden barely won the popular vote and gained 184 undisputed electoral votes. Hayes gained 166 undisputed electoral votes. A total of 185 electoral votes were needed to win a majority, so the election turned on the remaining ballots. The votes of three southern states—South Carolina, Louisiana, and Florida—and one electoral vote from Oregon were confused. The problem in the Deep South states was that, as usual, the Republican party had relied on recently enfranchised black voters for votes and had practiced fraud to get them. The Democrats, as usual, resorted to intimidation and violence to keep blacks away from the polls. In

After an Electoral Commission declared Republican Rutherford B. Hayes the winner of the 1876 presidential election, cartoonist Thomas Nast's Republican elephant moaned, "Another such victory and I am undone" (Harper's Weekly, *March 24, 1877).*

Florida the Republican-controlled election commission tossed out an apparent majority for Tilden and gave the state to Hayes. In South Carolina Hayes appeared to carry the popular vote, though the state also apparently elected a Democrat, Wade Hampton, governor. In Louisiana the Republican election commission tossed out the votes of whole parishes if any evidence of irregularity appeared, changing a Tilden victory into a Hayes victory. Consequently, in each state electors from both parties cast ballots for their respective candidates. Congress had to decide which sets of electoral votes were the real ones.

The Constitution stipulated that the president of the Senate should "open all the certificates, and the votes shall then be counted" in the presence of both houses. The question was whether that clause gave the presiding officer the power to make a determination in disputed cases. Most experts doubted that the writers of the Constitution meant that. But if the consent of both houses was required to decide in the disputed cases, then a problem arose. The Democrats controlled the House and the Republicans controlled the Senate. No one could see agreement on the horizon in that circumstance.

Finally a joint congressional committee decided to appoint a special fifteen-member Electoral Commission consisting of three Republican and two Democratic senators, three Democratic and two Republican representatives, and four Supreme Court justices, two from each party, who were to select an impartial fifth justice. The members of the joint committee understood tacitly that the impartial fifth justice would be David Davis of Illinois, who, it was thought, would act impartially.

The day the bill creating the Electoral Commission passed the House of Representatives, news arrived that the Illinois senate appointed Judge Davis to the U.S. Senate, rendering him ineligible for service. The four justices instead chose Joseph P. Bradley, considered the most impartial of the remaining justices.

When Congress assembled to count the Electoral College votes on February 1, 1877, objections were raised in the cases of the votes from the three southern states, throwing the decision in those cases to the commission. In the first case, Florida, the commission voted eight to seven that it was not competent to consider whether or not the returns reported on that day were gained legally or illegally. That made the outcome of the election moot. Since the "regular" electoral votes were the votes submitted by the Republican-controlled election commissions in each of the three states, the Electoral Commission voted to accept those votes in all three cases. The commission also awarded the disputed Oregon vote to Hayes. He won the election with a total of 185 electoral votes to Tilden's 184.

Hayes might not have won had not a deal been struck with southern members of the Democratic party. The Democratic House of Representatives acquiesced in the electoral vote counts because of assurances given by the Hayes camp that the Republican president would work hard to reconcile the South with the North. In return for the presidency, Hayes would withdraw federal troops from South Carolina and Louisiana, favor a program of federal aid for education and internal improvements in the South, and offer at least one cabinet post to a southern conservative. Tilden's supporters thought that was at least as much as they could expect from their own man. The "Compromise of 1877" signaled the formal end of the Reconstruction Era.

ELECTION OF 1896

With the end of Reconstruction, the United States devoted its attention to a more traditional American occupation than the achievement of racial justice: the pursuit of economic progress. After the Civil War the North embarked upon an unprecedented period of social and economic transformation. The process of industrialization and urbanization begun before the war began again with renewed vigor. Each year thousands of the nation's farmers moved to the cities to take factory jobs. Increasing numbers of immigrants—millions from areas in southern and eastern Europe—crowded into the cities with them. Agriculture continued to expand along with business, and a burgeoning railroad network linked both farmers and manufacturers to their markets, forming the basis for a truly national and even international commerce. Meanwhile, the South struggled with the dual problem of rebuilding its shattered infrastructure while learning to cope with the new legal status of its former slave contingent. Gradually the antebellum South's staple agricultural system adjusted itself; the "crop-lien" setup that emerged trapped many former slaves—and landless whites—in a cycle of poverty and increasing debt.

For the most part, national politics remained aloof, content with establishing a laissez-faire atmosphere conducive to business expansion. The presidents compiled a lackluster record. Hayes's successor, Republican James A. Garfield, died at the hand of an assassin before he had a chance to demonstrate his effectiveness. Garfield's replacement, Chester Arthur, previously a steadfast organization man, in 1883 signed a bill creating a U.S. Civil Service Commission, starting the process that eventually removed a chief occupation of American presidents: disposing of government offices to the party faithful. From 1885 to 1897 Democrat Grover Cleveland and Republican Benjamin Harrison exchanged the presidency between them. Cleveland oversaw the creation of the nation's first federal regulatory agency, the Interstate Commerce Commission, charged with enforcing a fair system of railroad rates; and Harrison signed the Sherman Anti-Trust bill, establishing the position of the federal government in favor of limiting business monopolies. While majorities in both parties favored high tariffs, the Republicans sought to enact barriers to "protect" American industry; most Democrats contented themselves with establishing tariffs for revenue purposes only.

In 1893 Cleveland started his second term as president in good position: he had decisively defeated Harrison's reelection bid, and the Democrats controlled both houses of Congress. A few months after he entered office, however, the Panic of 1893 swept the nation, throwing hundreds of thousands out of work, forcing thousands of banks and businesses out of operation, and dropping already-depressed agricultural prices to near-catastrophic lows. Unrest that had been building behind the scenes spilled onto the stage of national debate.

The question that dominated politics during Cleveland's second term and in the election campaign of 1896 involved the nature of American money. Responding to the desires of the nation's banking and business establishment and to increases in the price of silver that had made it unprofitable to coin, President Ulysses S. Grant signed a "coinage bill" into law in 1873, establishing the currency on the basis of a "gold standard." The advent of the gold standard not only removed the federal government from the silver business, it also tended to limit the amount of currency in circulation because the law tied the amount of bank note issues to scarce gold reserves. The discovery that same year of new silver deposits in Nevada, combined with a decline in the European market for silver, caused the price of silver to decrease until minting it would again realize a profit. Consequently, in 1878 Congress authorized a federal silver purchase and coinage program. Silver prices nevertheless continued to decline, prompting Congress to increase the government's purchases in 1890. Responding to the Panic of 1893, however, "monometallist" congressional forces—Democratic and Republican—returned the country to the gold standard late in the year, with President Cleveland's blessing. That move brought the issue of "free silver" to the forefront of national politics.

The reason federal silver policy became such a divisive issue in the 1890s was because disaffected agrarian and laboring elements in society increasingly saw "bimetallism" as a solution to their problems. Agriculturalists—especially independent western farmers but also many in the chronically depressed South—viewed currency expansion as a way to increase incomes stunted by overproduction and a lack of new markets. Wage earners saw inflation as a way to convert laborers into capitalists, circumventing the seemingly entrenched and self-aggrandizing "elite" already operating. A third party—the Populists—had been organized in 1890 to further the demand for "free and unlimited" silver coinage and to advocate a host of other reforms of agriculture, labor, and industry. After the United States returned to the gold standard in 1893, however, the Democratic party became the focus of the debate between conservatives and advocates of silver coinage. President Cleveland stood with the "sound-money men" of his party, while "silverites" led by Missouri representative Richard P. "Silver Dick" Bland and Nebraskan William Jennings Bryan worked to convert the party to their cause.

Though it housed a substantial minority of free-silver advocates, the Republican party nominated Ohio conservative William McKinley for president in 1896. McKinley had based his career on support for a protective tariff

Chief Justice Melville Weston Fuller administering the presidential oath to William McKinley, March 4, 1897. Outgoing president Grover Cleveland stands alongside (Library of Congress).

and hoped to mute debate on the silver issue by focusing on the tariff issue during the campaign. In the Democratic party, however, the story was different. Cleveland's apparent inability to deal with the depression that stemmed from the Panic of 1893 intensified calls for currency inflation in the South and West. Silverites charged that an eastern banker elite sought to maintain control of the party at the expense of the masses of farmers and laboring men who supplied it with votes. Cleveland paid little heed to the shift in sentiment, more than once stating that he believed Democrats would never accept the demand for free silver. At the party convention in July 1896, however, silverites controlled the floor.

As the convention got under way, several Democrats vied for the presidential nomination. Bland, the most consistent supporter of free silver in the party and coauthor of the original silver-purchase act of 1878, lacked charisma and had a Catholic wife, disqualifying him. Bryan, the eventual nominee, had emerged as an electrifying orator and passionate free-silver advocate in the eighteen months preceding the convention, but experts considered the thirty-six-year-old former House member too green to lead the fight. Only after he stunned delegates with an evangelical address in defense of the platform plank favoring free silver—his famous "Cross of Gold" speech—did the party turn to him. The Populist party, resentful though it was that the Democrats had "stolen" the silver issue and most of the rest of the Populist platform, also nominated the Nebraskan for president.

As a result, the election of 1896 pitted sound-money advocates directly against the silverites. McKinley, a traditionalist, ran the usual "front-porch" campaign of the day, receiving supporters at his Ohio home and asking voters to consult his record to determine his political positions. Bryan, on the other hand, ran more of a crusade than a campaign. In defiance of tradition, he took to the road to trumpet his call for free silver, traveling thousands of miles and sometimes making dozens of speeches a day. Unfortunately for him, he was unable to maintain the focus of the debate. Republicans charged that Bryan was a disguised socialist, too closely connected to the Populist party to be trusted. The Populists, they argued, not only wanted to remove the incentive to do business by inflating the currency, they also favored increasing the government's role in business by nationalizing railroads and utilities and enacting legislation favorable to labor unions—positions Bryan never held.

McKinley won the election with more than seven million votes, 51 percent of the total, to Bryan's six and a half million. In the electoral college, McKinley won 271 votes to Bryan's 176. McKinley took the states of the industrial Northeast and the crucial states of the Midwest, while Bryan won the votes of the South and Far West. Farmers in the midwestern states of Ohio, Indiana, and Illinois might have supported Bryan and swung the election his way, but they had been less damaged by the panic than the farmers of the Plains states and the South and also enjoyed closer economic links with the East. Lucky for the Republicans, as McKinley took office the effects of the panic and depression wore off, new businesses began forming, and farmers across the nation experienced a price-level rise. Although Bryan would participate in two later presidential campaigns, never again would supporters of free silver coinage command as much public attention as in 1896.

ELECTION OF 1912

Although William Jennings Bryan's Populist-infused presidential campaign of 1896 met with failure, in the early years of the twentieth century Populist-inspired ideology—in an expanded, "progressive" version—increasingly found a home in the platforms of the major parties. Continued rapid industrialization and urbanization of the East and Midwest, fueled by a dramatic influx of "new" immigrants from southern and eastern Europe, had exacerbated the problems associated with progress, and in both parties a modernized group of political leaders sensitive to the restive public's demand for action grew in strength at both the state and national levels. Progressives shouldered Populist demands for the regulation of nationwide industries such as the railroads and for legislation to ease the burdens of the working class and fashioned a critique of American society that called for comprehensive reform in both politics and economics. In the election of 1912 the progressive "insurgency" reached its national apex.

In 1900 McKinley and Bryan again vied for the presidency. McKinley promised to "let well enough alone," while Bryan railed against U.S. imperialism, the growing power of trusts and "special privilege," and supporters of the gold standard. McKinley won handily, in most states by greater margins than in the election of 1896. He even took Bryan's home state of Nebraska. The stage appeared set for a calm four-year act, but McKinley's assassination in September 1901 brought Theodore Roosevelt to the presidency.

The sagacious Roosevelt proved more receptive to the progressives in the Republican party than McKinley and his conservative supporters. In 1902 he ordered the Department of Justice to bring an antitrust suit against the Northern Securities Company—the first such suit inaugurated under the terms of the Sherman Anti-Trust Act of 1890—and also mediated a strike of the United Mine Workers labor union, threatening to order federal seizure of the mines if recalcitrant owners refused to concede some of the workers' demands. Running against conservative Democrat Alton B. Parker, Roosevelt easily won election to his own term as president in 1904. A host of progressive reforms followed. Prompted by public furor stemming from "muckraker"

Outgoing president William Howard Taft escorting Woodrow Wilson to his inauguration, March 4, 1913

Upton Sinclair's 1905 novel *The Jungle*, in 1906 Roosevelt signed the Meat Inspection Act. That same year he signed the Pure Food and Drug Act and also the Hepburn Act, which gave the federal government increased power to enforce the provisions of the Interstate Commerce Act of 1887. Roosevelt also won federal approval of the concept of workmen's compensation, signing a law requiring employers in the District of Columbia to compensate their injured workers.

Just when progressive Republicans appeared headed for permanent leadership of their party, the Panic of 1907 brought reform to a halt. President Roosevelt pledged not to interfere with the recovery efforts of J. P. Morgan and his coterie of New York financiers, who "pooled" their assets to bail out threatened financial institutions. The combined effects of Roosevelt's "radicalism" and the panic brought conservatives to the forefront of the party once again, and with Roosevelt's support they nominated William Howard Taft for the presidency in 1908. In the general election Taft easily defeated William Jennings Bryan, who fell short of the presidency for the third time.

Although Taft's actions as president perhaps should have encouraged the progressives in his party (his administration enacted more "progressive" measures in four years than Roosevelt did in seven), by 1911 he was in danger of losing his chance at renomination. Stymied by the Republican "old guard" in Congress and repelled by Taft's political clumsiness and his natural identification with conservatism, progressive legislators backed Wisconsin senator Robert M. LaFollette for the presidency. Roosevelt was also growing increasingly dissatisfied with Taft, mostly a result of Roosevelt's longing for another term but also because he was growing increasingly convinced that the country needed more radical reform than Taft was prepared to support. In February 1912 Roosevelt announced his intention to run against Taft, effectively killing the LaFollette candidacy.

In the first presidential campaign in which direct primaries for delegate selection were extensively used, Roosevelt trounced Taft by a nearly two-to-one primary margin and went to the Republican convention the leader in delegates. At the convention the old guard banded together and awarded Taft nearly all the contested delegates, and with them the nomination. The progressives walked out. An embittered Roosevelt announced the formation of a third party, the National Progressives, and accepted its presidential nomination. The Republicans had split.

On the Democratic side, House Speaker Champ Clark of Missouri entered the convention the front-runner and delegate leader. Woodrow Wilson, then merely a one-term New Jersey governor who won his office with the support of the conservatives of his state, stood as the party's second choice. The convention polled more than forty ballots before deciding on Wilson. William Jennings Bryan, chairman of the Nebraska delegation in 1912, transferred Nebraska's votes to Wilson on the eleventh ballot, preventing Clark from winning on that ballot and setting up a classic "smoke-filled room" decision.

Taft campaigned little for the presidency. Roosevelt toured the country, presenting the specific and comprehensive program of the National Progressives, which the candidate dubbed the "New Freedom." Wilson ran a conservative campaign in which he tried to steer clear of the more controversial issues raised by the energetic Roosevelt, who favored direct primaries for nominations to all state and national offices, direct election of U.S. senators, woman suffrage, campaign reform legislation, a national system of occupational safety standards, a program of workmen's compensation insurance, the prohibition of child labor, currency reform, inheritance and income taxes, and a host of other unprecedented measures.

Try as he might, Roosevelt was unable to overcome the split in the Republican ranks in the general election. The majority of the progressives in the Republican party refused to abandon the "system" to support Taft's rival. Wilson polled more than six million popular votes to Roosevelt's four million; Taft finished third with almost three and a half million votes. Wilson trounced his opposition in the Electoral College, winning 435 votes to 88 for Roosevelt and only eight for Taft.

Although Republican and Democratic progressives might not have realized it at the time, in Wilson they gained a president who, if not temperamentally suited to support progressivism, was at least politically wise enough to sense the turning of the tide in favor of national reform. In his first term he compiled a truly impressive record of support for measures for which Roosevelt had argued in favor during the campaign.

ELECTION OF 1932

After Wilson won reelection in 1916, he and his party were forced to deal with an increasingly insistent war emergency. After campaigning as the president "who kept us out of war," Wilson asked Congress for a declaration of war a month after his second term began. American "doughboys" helped defeat Germany in Europe, and Wilson spent the remainder of his presidency struggling, in Europe, to obtain the cooperation of the victors in the establishment of a new political order on the Continent and, at home, the cooperation of Congress in the establishment of the United States as a world power with global responsibilities. Americans grew tired of contentiousness in politics; the Senate rejected Wilson's bid for American participation in the new League of Nations, and voters elected Republican Warren G. Harding to the presidency in 1920.

Harding and his successor Calvin Coolidge guided the country back to its laissez-faire roots. The United States

Herbert Hoover and Franklin Delano Roosevelt on their way to Roosevelt's inauguration as president, March 4, 1933

embarked upon another spectacular period of postwar economic expansion. That all was not well, however, became clear after Republican Herbert Hoover took over for Coolidge in 1929; after domestic stock markets crashed in September 1929 the nation sank into the worst depression in its history. The combined effects of overproduction and underconsumption brought America dangerously close to economic collapse and set the stage for a renewal of reform as the election of 1932 approached. During his term Hoover made a series of largely ineffective attempts to halt the country's economic slide and then, demoralized, accepted another Republican presidential nomination and prepared to campaign against New York governor Franklin D. Roosevelt, the Democrats' strongest candidate since Wilson.

Roosevelt entered the campaign of 1932 with the strongest progressive credentials of any presidential candidate since Theodore Roosevelt, his distant relative. He served as assistant secretary of the navy under President Woodrow Wilson, fell victim to polio in 1921, and reemerged on the political scene by winning election as New York's governor in 1928. As governor he worked unceasingly to bring his state out of the Depression, easing credit to farmers pressed hard by mounting debt, creating a model unemployment relief administration, and supporting legislation reducing the workweek and extending the protections of workmen's compensation insurance. He also campaigned, unsuccessfully, for the implementation of a works project to harness the power of the St. Lawrence River. Roosevelt announced his candidacy for the Democratic presidential nomination in early 1932, emerged as the delegate leader

Harry Truman exulting over the early edition of the Chicago Tribune *for November 3, 1948 (courtesy of ACME/Bettman Archive)*

during the primary season, and locked up the nomination on the fourth convention ballot.

Hoover never had a chance for victory. Seemingly unaware of the gravity of the situation the country faced, the Republican candidate gamely attempted to adhere to party principles forbidding extensive government intervention in national economic affairs. For his part, Roosevelt vaguely pledged a "new deal" for the American people. He won almost 23 million popular votes to Hoover's 16 million, and 472 electoral votes to Hoover's 59.

Roosevelt went on to become one of the most beloved political leaders in American history. While the New Deal exerted only a limited effect on the nation's economic troubles in the 1930s, the programs of Roosevelt's administrations brought the influence of the federal government into the lives of millions of Americans who previously had no connection to it. A third-term and then a fourth-term winner, Roosevelt also helped push the United States into political and economic leadership of the world's democracies during World War II. In the 1950s and 1960s no American politician—Republican or Democrat—could favor extensively revising Roosevelt's policies and expect to win national success.

ELECTION OF 1948

Roosevelt's death after serving only three months of his fourth term elevated Harry S Truman to the presidency. A little-known senator from Missouri before Roosevelt made him the Democratic vice-presidential candidate in 1944, Truman entered the presidency as World War II drew to a close, just as the United States was beginning its struggle with the Soviet Union to control the political and economic context of postwar world development. Roosevelt had supplied Truman with only cursory briefings concerning his strategy for securing the postwar world order; moreover, the feisty Truman possessed little of the diplomatic subtlety of his predecessor. Soon Americans found themselves embroiled in a cold war with the Soviet Union every bit as threatening as the hostility that produced the hot war against Germany and Japan. The fact that after 1949 (when the Soviets acquired the bomb) the United States and the Soviet Union stood capable of destroying each other with nuclear weapons only made the conflict more acute.

As president, Truman had to concern himself with more than diplomacy. The task of overseeing the conversion of the United States from a wartime to a peacetime economy appeared every bit as daunting. Pent-up consumer demand produced debilitating inflation in the years immediately after the war. Unemployment remained a manageable problem, but labor unions, tired of making patriotic concessions, instigated the most extensive series of labor stoppages in American history in 1946 and 1947. In terms of politics, the end of the war had the effect of boosting conservatism at the expense of New Deal liberalism, and Truman found it next to impossible to secure support for his domestic agenda: an extension of Roosevelt's New Deal program that Truman dubbed the "Fair Deal."

As the election of 1948 approached, Truman appeared doomed to defeat. The Republican party nominated New York governor Thomas E. Dewey for president; southern Democrats dissatisfied with Truman's unstinting support for a comprehensive federal civil rights policy formed a third party based on the principle of states' rights and nominated South Carolina governor J. Strom Thurmond. Liberal Democrat Henry A. Wallace, vice-president during Franklin Roosevelt's third presidential term, opposed Truman's rough handling of the Soviet Union, and Wallace accepted the presidential nomination of another third party, the Progressives. Truman appeared hemmed in by opposition from the regular Republicans and by quasi-Democratic opponents on the right and on the left.

Truman responded to those challenges with characteristic vigor. He called the Republican-dominated Congress into special session to give them another chance to enact his Fair Deal; when they failed to act, he denounced the Republican party and its "do-nothing" legislators. While Dewey placidly waited for what seemed a sure victory, Truman campaigned across the nation, both for his Fair Deal and against the Republicans and his other opponents.

The electorate responded by granting Truman the biggest upset victory in the history of American national politics. Truman won more than 24 million popular votes, 49.5 percent of the total, to Dewey's 22 million. Thurmond and Wallace gathered slightly more than one million votes each. Truman won 303 electoral votes, Dewey 189, and Thurmond—his support confined to the Deep South—39. Liberal Democrats emerged from the election in a position of greater strength and enacted some, but not all, of Truman's domestic program, including legislation that raised the minimum wage, expanded the Social Security System, and inaugurated a federally sponsored program of housing construction. Due to the onset of the Korean War in 1950, Truman left the presidency in 1953 as unpopular as any twentieth-century president, but his victory in the election of 1948 remained a moment of supreme triumph.

ELECTION OF 1960

The election of 1960 was important for many reasons. John F. Kennedy, at forty-three the youngest man ever elected to the presidency, replaced Dwight D. Eisenhower, the oldest man to occupy the White House up to that time. Kennedy's opponent, Richard Nixon, was only forty-seven. As the new president pointed out in his inaugural

Truman, 1960 (courtesy of UPI)

address, a torch had been "passed to a new generation of Americans—born in this century, tempered by war, disciplined by a hard and bitter peace, proud of our ancient heritage—and unwilling to witness or permit the slow undoing of those human rights to which this Nation has always been committed, and to which we are committed today at home and around the world." The election brought other important developments. For the first and only time two incumbent U.S. senators, Kennedy and Lyndon B. Johnson, were nominated for president and vice-president on the same party ticket. Kennedy remains the only incumbent Democratic senator and the only Catholic ever elected to the presidency.

The election was also important because it signaled the arrival of television as a critical element in the presidential selection process. Republican nominee Richard M. Nixon may have lost the election simply because Kennedy's superior performance in a series of four televised debates favorably impressed the public. Though neither candidate possessed particularly strong credentials for the presidency, in the beginning the public perceived Nixon, the incumbent vice-president, as more experienced. But in the debates Kennedy appeared at least as knowledgeable and sophisticated as Nixon, who was only four years older, and considerably less nervous and more handsome, which reassured Americans who wanted to vote for the more inspirational figure, the hero of PT-109 with the glamorous wife.

Nixon had his faults. During his few years in the House and Senate before assuming the vice-presidency he acquired the moniker "Tricky Dick" for his underhanded campaigning style. Even after he became vice-president some in the Republican party considered him a political liability because he tended toward viciousness. A few of Eisenhower's advisers suggested that the president drop Nixon from the reelection ticket, but Eisenhower refused to do so, and Nixon served out his second term. As far as the vice-president's obvious aspirations for the presidency were concerned, though, both his reputation and history were against him. The last incumbent vice-president to win election to the presidency was Martin Van Buren in 1836.

Democratic nominee Kennedy, glamorous war hero though he was, also appeared a weak choice. He had a lackluster record in Congress, especially on the question of civil rights, where he might have led the nation. Mostly he voted cautiously and kept his plans to himself, making few close friends among his colleagues.

The vagaries of politics and national life, however, gave Kennedy advantages over and above his good looks. Eisenhower had appeared a father figure to Americans. He probably would have won a third term if he had wanted to run and the Constitution allowed it. But Eisenhower was unable to transfer his personal popularity to other Republicans. The president had won strong support from Democrats in both his presidential victories, and the Democrats scored big in the off-year congressional elections of 1958. The president did not do his vice-president any good when during a press conference a reporter asked him to name a program or policy to which Nixon had made an important contribution. "Give me a week and I'll think of one," Eisenhower quipped.

Moreover, the nation was ready for a change. Historian Arthur Schlesinger, Jr., has suggested that American history moves in cycles of liberalism and conservatism. All indicators suggested that the Eisenhower years were conservative. Modern Americans remember the 1950s as the decade that introduced the society of the suburban consumer and a television-oriented youth culture. Critics charged that the nation was enjoying an "Eisenhower siesta." The president did little to stir things up, preferring to react to events as they occurred. Meanwhile, America's great rival, the Soviet Union, seemed to make huge advances. The Soviets produced their own hydrogen bomb and, as the launching of the Sputnik satellite proved, developed an impressive intercontinental ballistic missile even before the United States. Observers wondered if the United States had lost the sense of purpose that brought it through the crises of the Depression and World War II.

As the Schlesinger theory suggests, perhaps the nation was ready for a pick-me-up. Kennedy projected a strong militaristic image that indicated he was a man of action. If he did not actually appeal to the idealism that would characterize the later 1960s, he did suggest youth and vigor. Demographers could prove that the nation was young; the youthful Kennedy called for innovation in proclaiming his "New Frontier."

Kennedy defeated Nixon by the slimmest of margins, only slightly more than 100,000 votes out of more than 68 million cast. His record as the nation's chief executive, like his record in Congress, turned out to be lackluster. But the elevation of Kennedy marked the beginnings of a shift in national mood from the conservatism of the Eisenhower years to the liberalism of the years of Lyndon B. Johnson. After Kennedy's assassination on November 22, 1963, the nation dedicated itself to meeting the challenges the late president set out to accomplish. Johnson's browbeating compelled Congress to implement an impressive set of social welfare measures in the mid 1960s, creating what Johnson called the "Great Society."

ELECTION OF 1980

After years of discouragement and upheaval in national politics, the United States secured a needed boost in 1980. The Great Society had brought tragedy as well as triumph to American life. Ambitiously, President Johnson asked the nation to commit itself as strongly to promoting freedom abroad as at home, and by the last years of the 1960s one

President Jimmy Carter and President-elect Ronald Reagan conferring at the White House, November 20, 1980 (photograph by Frank Johnson; Washington Post*)*

of the consequences of that commitment—the Vietnam War—had turned into a bloody stalemate, creating a tremendous upsurge of opposition in the nation. Johnson's reform program stalled, and in early 1968, facing challenges from antiwar Democrats, he withdrew as a candidate for reelection.

Johnson's successor, Republican Richard M. Nixon, entered office after Kennedy's younger brother, Robert F. Kennedy—the leading presidential candidate among Americans who opposed the war—was assassinated. Nixon ended the war after a four-year program of "Vietnamization" and aerial bombing. After winning reelection by a landslide in 1972, Nixon found himself embroiled in a political scandal—Watergate—that forced him out of office in 1974. His replacement, Gerald R. Ford, lost his bid for the presidency in 1976 to political outsider Jimmy Carter, known previously only to those few who followed gubernatorial politics in the state of Georgia.

Carter's presidency, which began in an atmosphere of renewal, ended in failure. Something of a novice in national affairs, he proved unable to attract sufficient congressional support to enact his policies. His inexperienced team presided over a nation beset by rising unemployment and inflation and crippled by declining world influence. Events spiraled out of control. In 1979 Iranian students and revolutionists inspired by the rise of Islamic fundamentalist leader Ayatollah Khomeini occupied the American embassy in Iran and took several dozen Americans hostage. The hostage crisis dominated the final year and a half of Carter's presidency, which saw the president's popularity steadily decline in the polls. Iran released the hostages on the day Carter's successor, Ronald Reagan, took office.

In spite of his unconventional résumé, the new president seemed to embody a style of leadership for which Americans had been searching: tough, steady, traditional. A former movie actor and two-term governor of California, Reagan promised a change in the relationship of the American government to its people. During the campaign he promised simultaneously to cut individual and corporate income taxes, to increase the defense budget, and to balance the budget and reduce inflation. Critics, including Carter, pointed out that Reagan's goals appeared mutually exclusive, but many Americans found the candidate's forthrightness and optimism irresistible. On election day Reagan won more than 43 million popular votes to Carter's 35 million and 489 electoral votes to Carter's 49. Carter carried only six states and the District of Columbia.

Reagan saw his tax-cut proposal enacted and also presided over the largest peacetime military buildup in American history. A Federal Reserve tight-money policy reduced inflation (creating a serious recession in 1982) and unemployment declined, but Reagan was unable to convince Congress to reduce federal spending enough to balance the budget. The American deficit soared to the trillion-dollar level. Reagan's get-tough foreign policy endured some shaky moments, especially after investigators uncovered a clandestine system to supply Contra forces in Nicaragua with weapons purchased with funds obtained through secret arms sales to the Iranian government. But as Reagan's term drew to a close in 1989 the United States appeared economically and politically stronger than at any period in its recent history. While Reagan did not accomplish all he set out to accomplish, a powerful majority of Americans judged his administration a success by overwhelmingly electing his vice-president, George Bush, to the presidency. As Communist governments dissolved in Eastern Europe, America appeared ready to face the challenges of the 1990s.

The Official Residences

by ROBERT B. BENNETT, JR.

In the first years of the American republic, before completion of the public buildings of the "federal city," New York City and then Philadelphia served as the nation's capital. The two sessions of the first Congress convened in New York. During the second congressional session, on July 16, 1790, President George Washington signed into law an act establishing a permanent capital on the Potomac River in Virginia, effective the first Monday of December 1800, and moving the temporary capital to Philadelphia. Washington lived in several homes in the temporary capitals. But he was not the only president to reside in two capital cities; his successor, John Adams, moved from Philadelphia to the federal city, known to all but the first president as Washington, on November 1, 1800, four months before the completion of his single term. He was thus the first president to reside in what later became known as the White House.

Arriving in New York City on April 23, 1789, George and Martha Washington moved into the Walter Franklin House at the corner of Cherry Street and Franklin Square. President Washington had written a request for lodgings to his friend Representative James Madison on March 30:

> I take the liberty of requesting a favor of you to engage lodgings for me previous to my arrival. Mr. Lear, who has lived with me three years as a private secretary, will accompany or precede me in the stage; and Colonel Humphreys, I presume, will be of my party. On the subject of lodgings, I will frankly declare to you, that I mean to go into none but hired ones. If these cannot be had tolerably convenient (for I shall not be nice about them), I would take rooms in the most decent tavern till a house can be provided for the more permanent reception of the President. I have already declined a very polite and pressing invitation from the Governor [of New York, DeWitt Clinton] to lodge at his house, till a place could be prepared for me; after which, should any other offer of a similar nature be made, there should be no propriety in my acceptance of it.

Mrs. Samuel Osgood, whose husband, a representative with Madison in the new Congress, was one of two deputed by Madison to select the presidential residence, owned the Franklin House, a bequeathal from her first husband's estate. Previously the residence of presidents of the Continental Congress, the home was one of the largest and finest in the city. It stood three stories tall, and large windows let in ample light. A heavy brass knocker garnished the single-paneled door on the main Cherry Street entrance. A vestibule on the Franklin Street side formed the other entrance.

To prepare for the presidential occupant, Congress allocated eight thousand dollars to Mr. Osgood to repair and refurnish the residence. Much excitement surrounded the city's reception of the new national leader, as a letter written by a niece of Walter Franklin attests:

> Great rejoicing in New York on the arrival of General Washington. . . . Previous to his coming, Uncle Walter's house in Cherry Street was taken for him, and every room furnished in the most elegant manner. Aunt Osgood and Lady Duer had the whole man-

The modern White House (photograph by George Mobley; courtesy of the National Geographic Society)

> agement of it. I went the morning before the General's arrival to look at it. The best of furniture in every room, and the greatest quantity of plate and china I ever saw; the whole of the first and second stories is papered, and the floors covered with the richest kind of Turkey and Wilton carpets. The house did honor to my aunts and Lady Kitty; they spared no pains nor expense on it. Thou must know that Uncle Osgood and Duer were appointed to Procure a house and furnish it. Accordingly they pitched on their wives as being likely to do it better. I have not yet done, my dear. Is thee not almost tired?. . . There is scarcely anything talked about now but General Washington and the Palace.

The "palace" had been rendered in the Adams style, created by British architect Robert Adams and especially popular in New England from 1760 to 1820. The home's low roofline, nearly hidden from view by a balustrade, was a characteristic Adams style feature.

The Washingtons lived in Franklin House until February 23, 1790. Sadly, the home was demolished in 1856 to make room for new construction. The site, near that of the publishing house of Harper, is marked by a bronze tablet embedded in a pier of the Brooklyn Bridge. From the Franklin House the presidential family moved into a larger place, the Macomb Mansion, built in 1786 by Alexander Macomb, a prominent merchant of high political influence. Macomb's son and namesake became a major general in the U.S. Army.

Experts dispute the exact location of the Macomb Mansion, but the best estimates place it at 39 Broadway. Set back slightly from the sidewalk, the home reached an imposing four stories from

James Hoban's final drawing of the north face of the presidential residence in the federal city, October 1793 (courtesy of the Maryland Historical Society)

a raised brick basement. It featured a projecting entrance pavilion accentuated by palladian windows on the two floors directly above it. A balcony over the rear center entrance gave a view of the Hudson River and the shores of New Jersey. Washington had stables built there at his own expense and also purchased a few household items from the previous occupant, De Moustier, French minister to the United States, including a large pair of drawing-room mirrors and a combination bookcase and writing desk. A ground-floor room looking onto Broadway held the presidential office. In that office Washington signed the bill creating the federal district.

The issue of a permanent national capital had come to a head when the New York assembly authorized the construction of a permanent presidential mansion in New York City. New Yorker Alexander Hamilton, Washington's secretary of the Treasury and a proponent of a strong national government, sold the idea to the assembly as part of a complicated scheme to secure federal assumption of the states' revolutionary war debts. Using the New York assembly's authorization as a bargaining chip, Hamilton convinced Secretary of State Thomas Jefferson of Virginia, emerging as a leading opponent of Hamilton's nationalist policies, to accede to assumption in return for the relocation of the permanent capital in the South. The principals drew up the bill, and the president, a supporter of both assumption and a southern capital, signed it and got his family ready to move to Philadelphia.

Washington wanted to leave New York with a minimum of fanfare, but news of his August 30 departure leaked out. A parade and booming artillery fire accompanied the president and his entourage as they made their way through crowded streets to the ferry at Paulus Point.

The Macomb Mansion continued to house the American political elite in New York until it became a hotel. Known for many years as Bunker's Mansion House, southerners often visited the fashionable stop.

On the way to Mount Vernon, where the president would spend a brief period before relocating, Washington and family stopped in Philadelphia to inspect their new accommodations. In a letter to his secretary Lear dated September 2, 1790, Washington made these observations concerning the new home:

South view of the White House; daguerreotype by John Plumbe, Jr., circa 1846 (Library of Congress)

> The house of Mr. Robert Morris had, previous to my arrival, been taken by the corporation [the City Corporation of Philadelphia] for my residence. It was the best they could get. It is, I believe, the best single house in the city. Yet without additions it is inadequate to the commodious accommodation of my family. These additions I believe will be made. . . . The intention of the addition . . . is to provide a servant's hall, and one or two lodging rooms for the servants. There are good stables, but for twelve horses only, and a coach-house which will hold all my carriages.

Banker Robert Morris, described by contemporaries as openhanded and openhearted, had served as the financier of the American Revolution. After the war he became a Pennsylvania senator, and he played an instrumental role in relocating the temporary capital to Philadelphia. The original building on the site, constructed by Pennsylvania governor Richard Penn, had been inhabited by Benedict Arnold when General Washington left him in command of Continental troops in Philadelphia in 1778. When the British occupied Philadelphia, Gen. William Howe quartered there. Then a fire largely destroyed the residence in 1780. Morris purchased the site in 1785 and renovated it into his principal domicile.

As he had in New York, Washington insisted on paying the rent for his Philadelphia quarters. The City Corporation of Philadelphia offered to pay the fees in hopes of enticing Washington to work toward retaining the capital in that city. The president was annoyed at that, as an excerpt from a letter to Lear before leaving from Mount Vernon conveys:

> I am, I must confess, exceedingly unwilling to go into any house without

> first knowing on what terms I do it; and wish that this sentiment could be again hinted in delicate terms to the parties concerned with me. I cannot, if there are no latent motives which govern in this case, see any difficulty in the business.

Morris set the rent at three thousand dollars a year, and Washington paid it.

The Morris House was a three-story structure built in the Georgian style, a style that dominated American architecture from 1700 to 1780. The home's symmetrical facade, its center entrance with projecting pediment, and its interior double chimneys at each gable end provide evidence of the Georgian style. A garden wall flanked the facade on both sides.

The first floor of the home featured two dining rooms, one for domestics and one for dignitaries. The thirty-foot-long state dining room was located to the rear of the building and boasted a bow window Washington designed himself to create interplay between the room and the garden. The steward and his wife resided on the entrance floor, and the closets in their room served as pantries because there were none in the dining room. The president's family occupied the second floor. Martha Washington had a private study and two drawing rooms that extended from the front to the rear of the house. The president's office was located on the third floor. On April 22, 1793, Washington issued a proclamation of American neutrality in France's war with Britain, the most important presidential action that took place in the Morris House.

During the summer months following the issuance of the neutrality proclamation, a yellow fever epidemic forced the president and his family, and most of the rest of Philadelphia including the departments of both the federal and Pennsylvania state governments, to nearby Germantown. There Washington stayed in the furnished home of Col. Isaac Franks, a former officer in the Continental army. Franks's home, built in the Georgian style, was erected in 1772 by David Deshler, a merchant from Heidelberg, Germany. Forced to find other accommodations during the Washingtons' sojourn, Franks charged the president rent equal to the sum of Franks's expenses plus damages. The presidential party reported a lost flatiron and four broken plates and consumed three of Franks's ducks, a bushel of his potatoes, and a hundredweight of hay. The rent total came to $131.36. Washington returned to Philadelphia when Congress went into session on October 28.

Meanwhile, in 1791 Washington had selected Frenchman Pierre L'Enfant to lay the design for the permanent capital, to be located under federal jurisdiction in a political creation called the District of Columbia. In his modesty the first president could never bring himself to refer to the place as "Washington City." L'Enfant's plan was based on a grid, crisscrossed with diagonal avenues, with circles or squares at every major axis. The open circles and squares would hold parks with fountains and statues commemorating each of the states. L'Enfant reserved one of the axes, an eighty-acre parcel at the edge of the Potomac, for the executive mansion.

The commissioners in charge of overseeing the construction of the District of Columbia conducted a contest to determine who would design the executive mansion. Several architects submitted entries. An anonymous submission, labeled simply "A.Z.," attracted little attention from the judges; no record of the commissioners' comments on it remains extant. Later it was discovered that the "A.Z." plan was Thomas Jefferson's. The entry that attracted the most attention was James Hoban's. Hoban, an Irishman who immigrated to South Carolina, was one of the most influential American architects of his time. Many of his buildings still stand, in such cities as Charleston and Columbia. The South Carolina Statehouse in

The White House draped in mourning after the death of President James A. Garfield, September 1881 (courtesy of the Rutherford B. Hayes Presidential Center)

Columbia is of Hoban's design. In his design for the executive mansion Hoban intended to evoke the appearance and feeling of a contemporary European country gentleman's home, an astute strategy considering the mores of Virginia plantation society. He may have lifted the scheme from a design book published by English architect and designer James Gibbs. The initial plan proposed a three-story building that stretched 160 feet in the front. Hoban won the contest and a gold medal, for which he opted instead of a five-hundred-dollar cash prize.

Although Jefferson's plan did not win, it is interesting for what it indicates about that great American. The design echoes that of Monticello, classical in influence, with a dome that lends majesty to the structure, making the eye travel vertically. Hoban's plan created a more informal yet dignified appearance based on a well-proportioned horizontal rhythm.

Workers laid the cornerstone for the executive mansion on October 12, 1792, the Columbian tricentennial. To some the action seemed too great a leap of faith, for the first auction of Washington City lots, held at Gadsby's tavern in nearby Alexandria, conveyed only thirty parcels. Washington City had not started out all that well. The president was able to convince one of his friends, Col. John Tayloe, to purchase a lot within walking distance of the proposed mansion. There Tayloe would build the stately Octagon House, designed by William Thornton, who designed the Capitol.

The slow sale of Washington City lots and modest cash advances made by the governments of Virginia and Maryland financed the construction of the federal city's public buildings. Growing hostility between Hamilton and Jefferson made federal funding of public buildings a very delicate matter. Hoban's ambitious initial plan for the executive mansion projected a total cost of £77,900, or $400,000. The president persuaded Hoban to scale down the project by removing the third story. Aside from providing relief from financial pressure, Washington justified the scaling-down on the grounds that the president of the republic should reside in a relatively modest structure. But he looked toward the future as well:

> It was always my idea (and if I am not mistaken Mr. Hoban coincided in the

Domestic staff of the White House, May 1877 (courtesy of the Hayes Presidential Center)

> propriety and practicality of it) that the building should be so arranged that only part of it should be erected for the present; and that upon such a plan as to make the part so erected an entire building and to admit of an addition in the future as circumstances might render proper, without hurting but rather adding to the beauty and magnificence of the whole as an original.

Hoban imported a contract-free labor force, mostly German, to work sporadically on the mansion project as funds trickled in. A provision in the act establishing the district prohibited the direct employment by the federal government of slaves in the construction of public buildings. But contractors were free to do so, and did. The federal city took shape slowly, during both of Washington's presidential terms and on into the term of Adams.

A nation of just more than five million honored the official opening of the nation's capital when John and Abigail Adams arrived by coach from Philadelphia on June 3, 1800. A 136-member executive staff conveyed the records of the government on a more comfortable ocean voyage. The president's house was nearing completion, but a twenty-five-thousand-dollar appropriation from Congress to furnish it was hardly noticeable. The presidential couple looked over the home with shared disapproval and drove to Mount Vernon to visit Martha Washington, widowed for almost a year.

The Adamses returned to Washington on November 1, two weeks before the first Congress met for its initial session at the permanent capital. They were used to the comforts of the Morris House in Philadelphia and were about to enter a rather more spartan environment, as Abigail conveyed in a letter to her daughter:

> You must keep all this to yourself, and when asked how I like it, say that I

The White House family kitchen, circa 1890

write you the situation is beautiful, which is true. The house is made habitable, but there is not a single apartment finished. . . . We have not the least fence, yard, or other convenience, without, and the great unfinished audience room [the East Room] I make a drying room of, to hang up clothes in. The principal stairs are not up, and will not be this winter. Six chambers are made comfortable; two are occupied by the president and Mr. Shaw [the Reverend John Shaw, Abigail's brother-in-law and the president's secretary]; two lower rooms, one for a common parlor, and one for a levee room. Upstairs there is the oval room, which is designed for the drawing room, and has the crimson furniture in it. It is a very handsome room now; but when completed, it will be beautiful. If the twelve years, in which this place has been considered as the future seat of government, had been improved, as they would have been if in New England, very many of the present inconveniences would have been removed. It is a beautiful spot, capable of every improvement, and the more I view it, the more I am delighted with it.

The second president and his wife spent just more than a month in the new capital. They held a New Year's Day reception in the mansion and then returned home to Braintree, Massachusetts, to await the inauguration of Thomas Jefferson as the next president. A century and a half later, President Franklin D. Roosevelt requested that a prayer John Adams gave at one of the first dinners held in the executive mansion be carved into the mantle of the State Dining Room:

> I pray to Heaven to bestow the best of Blessings on this House and all that shall hereafter inhabit it. May none but wise Men ever rule under this roof.

Thomas Jefferson managed to make the mansion a more livable place, but at the pain of great expense. The bleak and drafty house merely reflected the condition of Washington City at the time. The area had a swampy character. When Jefferson took office only forty buildings stood completed in the city.

President Herbert Hoover speaking to a conference of humanitarian organizations in the White House Rose Garden, 1932 (Library of Congress)

Domestic animals roamed freely in the unpaved streets. Prominent investors such as Colonel Tayloe chose to live in less malarious environments.

Jefferson, a man of highly refined tastes, quickly embarked on an effort to make the president's house, which he called "big enough for two emperors, one Pope and the Grand Lama," a showcase of the American nation. During his two terms he spent ten thousand dollars on wine alone. He improved the grounds, terracing them and planting trees and gardens, and worked closely with architect Benjamin Latrobe to improve the building itself. Latrobe added porticos to both facades and revised the floor plan several times.

All of Jefferson's revisions went up in smoke on the night of August 24, 1814, when invading British troops burned much of the capital, including the presidential mansion. President James Madison and his wife Dolley spent the rest of the term in John Tayloe's Octagon House, and reconstruction of the mansion got under way. The exterior walls of the building had been badly burned, and much of the interior was unusable. Hoban, the original designer, won the appointment as reconstruction architect.

Although some evidence indicates that the term "White House" dates from the period before the destruction of the presidential residence, the most reliable story dates the name after the restoration. Since the outside surfaces of the building were so badly charred, Hoban applied white paint to cover the stained surfaces. The new appearance of the place quickly caught the public's fancy. Theodore Roosevelt was the first president to acknowledge the general public use of the term, when he included it on his personal stationery.

The next major alteration in the design of the White House came in 1824, during the administration of James Monroe. A semicircular Ionic portico and curving double stair were added to the building's south elevation. Along with the portico and stair, fluted Ionic pilasters were applied between each window opening on the south, east, and west elevations. With those additions also came a shift in front-rear orientation. Jefferson and most everybody else had not liked the oversized and imposing north entrance foyer, and the 1824 changes made the south side the front of the house. Despite the construction of a north portico in 1829, the public continued to enter on the south side, through French doors into the Blue Room, until the time of the Lincoln administration. In modern times, dignitaries and heads of state enter through the Pennsylvania Avenue (north) side, and everyone else enters from the south.

By the time of the Civil War the once-cavernous mansion became so cramped with offices that bureaucracy began to intrude on the living quarters. The problem worsened with every passing decade. Late-nineteenth-century first ladies privately complained about their overstuffed quarters. Each successive administration made plans to expand the building, but none pushed hard enough to woo Congress into allocating funds. For part of his presidency Grover Cleveland actually lived in a house in the suburbs and commuted to work every day.

Benjamin Harrison's first wife, Caroline, was the first of the first ladies to complain openly about the increasingly decrepit state of the White House. She initially proposed relocating the presidential residence. That plan went against tradition and never had a chance. Then she suggested adding large wings to the facades of the existing mansion, but experts claimed that would have compromised the historical integrity of the building's design. Caroline Harrison's ideas fell on deaf congressional ears, but Congress did grant the White House funds for interior renovations, electrification, and rat extermination.

Teddy Roosevelt, a president who knew what he wanted and how to get it, proved a more formidable proponent of White House renovation. He went on the offensive to improve the building by listing the occasions when the damp and drafty place actually made presidents ill or killed them. Andrew Jackson's lung problems, the result of too much youthful dueling, always worsened when he stayed in the White House, Roosevelt claimed. William Henry Harrison contracted pneumonia on inauguration day; the swampy Washington residence aggravated his condition, and he died as a result. Substandard White House plumbing probably contributed to Zachary Taylor's demise. Presidential family members were always getting sick. Roosevelt also complained that the building was so structurally unsound that it creaked and shook in frightening ways.

Congress listened, and allocated funds to renovate and redesign the White House. The construction of an Executive Office Building as a west wing expanded office space. Roosevelt's order to the architect read:

> Discover the design and the intention of the original builders and make it comfortable by modern standards. . . . It is a good thing to preserve such buildings as historic monuments which keep alive our sense of continuity with the nation's past.

The architects completely redesigned the first floor of the original building. They also placed steel beams and installed electrical wiring. Several rooms in the home were refurnished and renovated.

The condition of the house still left something to be desired. When Calvin Coolidge and family moved in, the Department of Public Buildings warned him that the roof slates needed major repair and some of the roof timbers had decayed to an advanced state. Coolidge, characteristically, was undismayed. He retorted, "I presume there are plenty of others who would be willing to take the risk of living under that roof." He had old attic spaces converted into guest

White House renovation during the presidency of Harry S Truman, circa 1949-1952 (photograph by Abbie Rowe; National Park Service)

rooms and service areas, constructed a sun deck, and had the third floor fireproofed. Those improvements placed the integrity of the structure at serious risk. Steel trusses firmly supported the third floor, but the weight of those members and the structures they supported fell on the old wooden beams of the second floor. Structures are designed to support double or triple the weight placed on them. By 1948 the safety factor in some areas of the White House was less than one. The place could have collapsed.

The problems manifested their symptoms. Theodore Roosevelt's children often prowled around unused nooks and crannies of the residence and heard more than their share of the house's creaks and groans, giving rise to haunted house legends told by the fun-loving president. But by the time Harry Truman and family moved in, the house presented a serious danger. Truman White House documents make such comments as, "President Truman became concerned because of a noticeable vibration in the floors of his study." The East Room chandeliers tinkled—without the help of a breeze. Truman ordered a commission to make a stress inquiry of the building.

The initial stabilization estimate came to one and a half million dollars. A congressional commission rejected the plan and appointed a cost-finding commission to help the president locate priorities, and their renovation estimate amounted to more than five million dollars. Clarence Cannon, chairman of the House Appropriations Committee, suggested that the entire building be razed and rebuilt, saving one million of the cost-finding estimate. That process would be easier than excavating a twenty-five-foot cavity under the building to make room for concrete footings and structural members. But Cannon could not take the pressure of being known as the man who would destroy the White House, so he backed down.

The final Truman plan called for the removal of the entire White House interior down to the bare walls. During the course of the four-year project, workers restructured and braced the insides to make them last. The house was fireproofed, rewired, repiped, air-conditioned, wired for television cameras, and equipped with modern conveniences. It was also supplied with the state-of-the-art communications and command-and-control equipment necessary to make it a proper headquarters for the leader of the Western world. The Truman White House is the White House that will survive into the twenty-first century.

More modest but just as dramatic from the point of view of architectural aficionados was Truman's decision to construct a second-story balcony inside the colonnade of the south portico. He wanted to be able to catch the breeze on stuffy Washington summer days. His proposal did not go unopposed. The Fine Arts Commission argued that the balcony would interrupt the vertical line created by the two-story colonnade. Truman's side asserted that Georgian homes of contemporary design often featured similar balconies. The Fine Arts Commission had the power to disagree but not to prevent the construction, so the balcony went up. The plates that printed twenty-dollar bills were changed to match.

To finalize the renovation, Truman embarked on a campaign to fill the White House with antiques reminiscent of past administrations. He requested five hundred thousand dollars to accomplish the refurnishing, but Congress gave him only fifty thousand. Fifteen years later Jacqueline Kennedy continued toward Truman's goal of making the White House representative of the nation's architectural and stylistic past. Centerpieces of her effort to solicit significant antiques to furnish the home were her televised tour of the home and the 1962 publication of a book, *A Tour of the White House With Mrs. John Kennedy*.

Historic public buildings are subject to the whims and wants of their temporary tenants, and the White House is no exception. It is more a four-year hotel than it is a home, and its successive sets of residents have changed it as they have wished. Perhaps something of the strength of the American nation is embodied in the resilience of the house. It tolerates much but still maintains its lofty status as a preeminent symbol of American nationhood.

What Happened During the Terms of the Presidents

by THOMAS L. CONNELLY

For two hundred years American presidents have helped the nation and the world make history. The list of events occurring during the administrations of the chief executives stretches from the age of horse power to the age of nuclear power, from the time of the creation of our government and the Bill of Rights to the establishment of the United States as a dominant world power. Under the Constitution the national government has continually increased in size and scope, and the president has assumed the position of leader of the world's democracies. Every president, no matter how significant in his own time, has lived in an era of great change.

The following is a highly selective list of events that occurred during the terms of the chief executives.

GEORGE WASHINGTON

1789

April 30: Inauguration of Washington as the first president.

June 1: Washington signs the first act of Congress, prescribing oaths of allegiance for members of Congress, federal officers, and state officials.

July 27: Washington signs an act establishing the Department of Foreign Affairs. Congress changes the name to Department of State on September 15.

August 7: Washington signs an act establishing the Department of War.

September 2: Washington signs an act establishing the Department of the Treasury.

September 24: Washington signs the Judiciary Act, providing for a six-member Supreme Court, circuit and federal district courts, and an office of attorney general.

1790

May 29: Rhode Island, the last of the original thirteen colonies, ratifies the Constitution.

1791

March 4: Vermont is admitted to the Union as the fourteenth state.

December 15: Congress declares ratified the first ten amendments to the Constitution—known as the Bill of Rights.

1792

June 1: Kentucky is admitted to the Union as the fifteenth state.

1793

March 4: Washington is inaugurated to his second term as president.

July 31: Thomas Jefferson resigns as secretary of state effective December 31.

August 1: Washington asks the government of France to recall its ambassador to the United States, Edmond Charles Genet. Genet had authorized the use of American ports to dispatch privateers.

1794

June 5: Washington signs the Neu-

Left: The inauguration of George Washington, New York City, April 30, 1789 (Library of Congress); right: "A New Display of the United States," engraving by Amos Doolittle, 1799 (Library of Congress)

trality Act, prohibiting the enlistment of U.S. citizens into foreign military service and the fitting out of foreign armed vessels in American ports.

August 7: Washington issues a proclamation ordering the Whiskey Rebellion tax insurgents of western Pennsylvania to disperse. On September 25, Washington sends fifteen thousand militiamen to the region to suppress the rebellion. No military action is required.

November 19: Jay's Treaty is concluded between the United States and Great Britain. The agreement provides for the withdrawal of British forces in the American Northwest but does not guarantee American neutral rights on the seas. The Senate ratifies the treaty on June 24, 1795.

December 1: Alexander Hamilton resigns as secretary of the Treasury effective January 31, 1795.

1796

June 1: Tennessee is admitted to the Union as the sixteenth state.

September 17: Washington publishes his farewell address in Philadelphia's *American Daily Advertiser* for September 19.

JOHN ADAMS

1797

March 4: Inauguration of Adams as the second president.

1798

January 8: Congress declares ratified the eleventh amendment to the Constitution, prohibiting a citizen of one state from suing another state.

March 19: After the failure of maritime negotiations with France, Adams issues an order authorizing the arming of American merchant vessels, beginning the period of the "quasi-war" with France, which lasts until 1800.

May 3: Adams signs an act establishing the Department of the Navy.

June 18: Adams signs the first of four acts known as the Alien and Sedition

Left: Thomas Jefferson, portrait by Rembrandt Peale, 1805; right: President James Madison, portrait by James Wood, 1817

Acts. The acts extend the period of naturalization from five years to fourteen; give the president authority to arrest, imprison, or deport aliens regarded as dangerous to public safety; and define and set penalties for the crime of sedition.

1800
November 1: Adams and the federal government move to Washington, D.C.

THOMAS JEFFERSON

1801
March 4: Inauguration of Jefferson as the third president.

1803
January 18: Jefferson proposes that Congress fund an exploration of North America to the western ocean. The Lewis and Clark expedition leaves St. Louis in May 1804 and returns two-and-a-half years later after an eight-thousand-mile journey to the mouth of the Columbia River.

March 1: Ohio is admitted to the Union as the seventeenth state.

May 2: The Louisiana Purchase Treaty is concluded between the United States and France, more than doubling the size of the United States. The Senate ratifies the treaty on October 20.

1804
July 11: Alexander Hamilton is killed in a duel with Vice-President Aaron Burr in Weehawken, New Jersey.

September 25: Congress declares ratified the twelfth amendment to the Constitution, providing for the separate election of the president and the vice-president in the Electoral College.

1805
March 4: Jefferson is inaugurated to his second term as president.

1807
March 2: Jefferson signs an act banning the slave trade as of January 1, 1808.

December 22: Jefferson signs the first Embargo Act, beginning a period of restricted trade with Great Britain and France that continues in the administration of James Madison.

JAMES MADISON

1809

March 4: Inauguration of Madison as the fourth president.

1812

April 30: Louisiana is admitted to the Union as the eighteenth state.

June 19: Congress declares war on Great Britain, beginning the War of 1812. Madison's June 1 war message cites British impressment of American seamen and British violation of American neutral rights and territorial waters as grounds for the conflict.

1813

March 4: Madison is inaugurated to his second term as president.

1814

August 24-25: British forces burn the public buildings of Washington, D.C., including the White House and the Capitol.

December 24: The Treaty of Ghent is concluded between the United States and Great Britain, ending the War of 1812. The treaty restores the status quo without addressing the maritime problems that started the war. The Senate ratifies the treaty on February 15, 1815. On January 8, 1815, Gen. Andrew Jackson scores a spectacular American victory over the British at New Orleans.

1816

December 11: Indiana is admitted to the Union as the nineteenth state.

JAMES MONROE

1817

March 4: Inauguration of Monroe as the fifth president.

December 10: Mississippi is admitted to the Union as the twentieth state.

1818

December 3: Illinois is admitted to the Union as the twenty-first state.

1819

December 14: Alabama is admitted to the Union as the twenty-second state.

Panic of 1819: An overextension of bank credit occurs in 1815 as a result of the issue of U.S. Treasury notes to finance the War of 1812. Beginning in 1817 the Second Bank of the United States implements a program to retire the Treasury notes, precipitating the nation's first great economic depression. By 1819 the contraction reaches crisis proportions.

1820

March 3: Monroe signs the Missouri Compromise Act. The compromise permits the admission of Missouri to the Union as a slave state and Maine to the Union as a free state and prohibits the establishment of slavery in Louisiana Purchase territories north of the southern boundary of Missouri.

March 15: Maine is admitted to the Union as the twenty-third state.

1821

March 5: Monroe is inaugurated to his second term as president.

August 10: Missouri is admitted to the Union as the twenty-fourth state.

1823

December 2: Monroe sends his State of the Union Address to Congress. In the address he promulgates the Monroe Doctrine, resolving the intent of the United States to defend the nations of the Western Hemisphere against European interference.

Left: President James Monroe, portrait by Rembrandt Peale (James Monroe Museum and Memorial Library); right: John Quincy Adams, portrait by Thomas Sully, 1825 (Cochran Collection, Philpse Manor State Historical Site)

JOHN QUINCY ADAMS

1825

March 4: Inauguration of Adams as the sixth president.

1828

May 19: Adams signs the Tariff Act, establishing a high protective tariff viewed in the predominantly agricultural South as a "Tariff of Abominations." In December, Vice-President John C. Calhoun of South Carolina issues his famous *South Carolina Exposition and Protest,* in which he advances the principle of state nullification of federal laws.

ANDREW JACKSON

1829

March 4: Inauguration of Jackson as the seventh president.

1832

July 10: Jackson vetoes a bill to recharter the Second Bank of the United States, establishing the veto as a powerful executive policy instrument and prompting a "bank war" that results in the redistribution of public funds in a set of state-chartered "pet" banks and later the establishment of an Independent Treasury System.

July 14: Jackson signs a tariff act that lowers some of the duties levied in the "Tariff of Abominations" of 1828.

November 27: The South Carolina legislature nullifies the tariff acts of 1828 and 1832, enforcing the ordinance of a state convention declaring the laws inoperative within its boundaries and therefore not subject to federal enforcement. On December 10 Jackson issues a proclamation to the people of South Carolina in which he declares nullification an "impractical absurdity." Vice-President Calhoun resigns on December 28. On March 2, 1833, Jackson signs a compromise tariff act and a "force bill"

Left: President Andrew Jackson, portrait by R. E. W. Earl, 1835; right: President Martin Van Buren

authorizing the use of the military to enforce tariff legislation. South Carolina nullifies its nullification acts.

1833
March 4: Jackson is inaugurated to his second term as president.

1834
June 30: Jackson signs an act establishing the Department of Indian Affairs. During the Jackson administration Indian tribes abandoned or were forced out of some 100 million acres of tribal lands and settled farther west.

1836
March 1: Texas declares itself an independent republic.

June 15: Arkansas is admitted to the Union as the twenty-fifth state.

July 11: Jackson issues the "Specie Circular" requiring the payment of gold or silver for public land.

1837
January 26: Michigan is admitted to the Union as the twenty-sixth state.

March 3: The United States recognizes the Republic of Texas.

MARTIN VAN BUREN

1837
March 4: Inauguration of Van Buren as the eighth president.

May 10: The suspension of specie payments by several New York banks prompts the Panic of 1837, the nation's second great economic depression, which in the agricultural South and West lasted until 1843. The panic, exacerbated by the redistribution of federal funds in state "pet" banks during the Jackson administration, cripples Van Buren's presidency.

WILLIAM HENRY HARRISON

1841
March 4: Inauguration of Harrison as the ninth president.

April 4: Harrison dies of pneumonia.

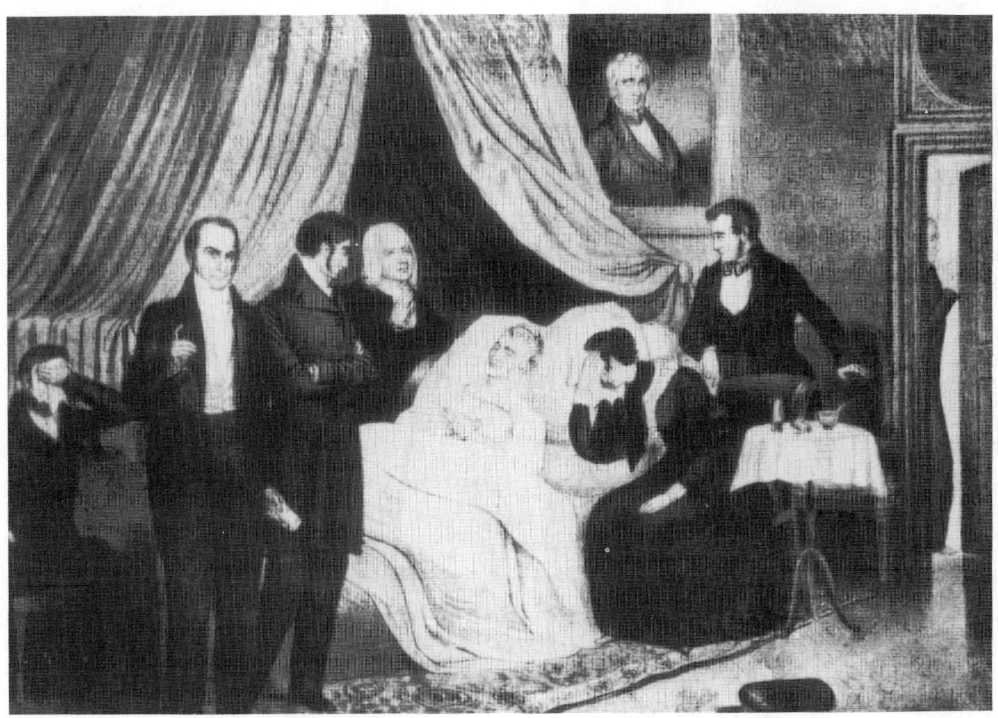

"The Death of Harrison," 1841 lithograph by Nathaniel Currier

He is the first president to die in office.

JOHN TYLER

1841

April 6: Inauguration of Tyler as the tenth president.

August 16, September 9: Tyler vetoes two bills to establish a Third Bank of the United States, prompting the resignation of his entire cabinet except Secretary of State Daniel Webster and alienating Tyler from the Whig party.

1842

August 20: The Senate ratifies the Webster-Ashburton Treaty establishing the boundary between Maine and Canada.

1845

March 1: Tyler signs a joint congressional resolution calling for the annexation of the Republic of Texas. The Texas Congress approves the resolution on June 23, and a special convention accepts it on July 4.

March 3: Florida is admitted to the Union as the twenty-seventh state.

JAMES K. POLK

1845

March 4: Inauguration of Polk as the eleventh president.

March 28: Mexico breaks off diplomatic relations with the United States in protest over the annexation of Texas.

June 15: Polk orders Gen. Zachary Taylor and a U.S. Army contingent to occupy a defensive point "on or near the Rio Grande" River in preparation for a Mexican declaration of war.

December 29: Texas is admitted to the Union as the twenty-eighth state.

1846

May 13: Congress declares war on Mexico, beginning the Mexican War. Hostilities had broken out in April and continue until 1848.

President John Tyler

December 28: Iowa is admitted to the Union as the twenty-ninth state.

1847

February 23: The American victory at the Battle of Buena Vista ends the resistance of the Mexican army in northern Mexico.

September 14: U.S. forces capture Mexico City.

1848

March 10: The Senate ratifies the Treaty of Guadalupe Hidalgo, ending the Mexican War. Under the terms of the settlement the United States receives most of Mexico's North American territory.

May 29: Wisconsin is admitted to the Union as the thirtieth state.

1849

March 3: Polk signs an act establishing the Department of the Interior.

ZACHARY TAYLOR

1849

March 5: Inauguration of Taylor as the twelfth president.

1850

April 19: Congress ratifies the Clayton-Bulwer Treaty, in which the United States and Great Britain pledge to maintain the neutrality of a Central American Isthmian canal should one ever be constructed.

July 9: Taylor dies of coronary thrombosis. He is the second president to die in office.

MILLARD FILLMORE

1850

July 10: Inauguration of Fillmore as the thirteenth president.

September 9: California is admitted to the Union as the thirty-first state. The territories of Utah and New Mexico are established in separate acts. The act establishing the territory of New Mexico also defines the borders of the state of Texas.

September 18: Fillmore signs the Fugitive Slave Act, amending the act of 1793.

September 20: Fillmore signs act abolishing the slave trade in the District of Columbia.

Compromise of 1850: As a consequence of the American conquest of Mexico's North American territory, congressional and national debate over the issue of the territorial expansion of slavery intensified in the late 1840s. Originally proposed by Senator Henry Clay of Kentucky as an "omnibus bill," the five separate acts of the compromise were signed by Fillmore between September 9 and 20, 1850. California was admitted to the Union as a free state, and the territories of Utah and New

Daguerreotype, circa 1849, of President and Mrs. James K. Polk (center) and friends, including Secretary of State James Buchanan (blurred figure at far left), Buchanan's niece, Harriet Lane (next to Buchanan), and, to Polk's immediate left, eighty-one-year-old Dolley Madison (courtesy of the George Eastman House)

Mexico were organized without mention of slavery. A more stringent Fugitive Slave Law was passed, and the slave trade in the District of Columbia was abolished.

FRANKLIN PIERCE

1853

March 4: Inauguration of Pierce as the fourteenth president.

December 30: The Gadsden Purchase Treaty is concluded between the United States and Mexico. The United States annexes a tract of land south of the Gila River and gives Mexico $10 million in return. The treaty lands contain what experts consider the best railroad route from Texas to California.

1854

May 30: Pierce signs the Kansas-Nebraska Act. The act repeals the Missouri Compromise of 1820 and allows citizens of each territory to decide for themselves whether to admit slavery.

October 9: Meetings between U.S. minister to Spain Pierre Soulé, U.S. minister to Great Britain James Buchanan, and U.S. minister to France John Y. Mason begin at Ostend, Belgium, and Aix la Chapelle, Prussia, that result in the issuance of the Ostend Manifesto. The manifesto urges the United States to offer Spain $120 million to purchase Cuba and to be prepared to take the island by force if Spain refuses to sell. After the secret document is leaked to the press, the Pierce administration is severely criticized for appearing prepared to go to war to extend slavery's dominion.

1857

March 3: Pierce signs the Tariff Act

of 1857, lowering tariff rates about 20 percent.

JAMES BUCHANAN

1857

March 4: Inauguration of Buchanan as the fifteenth president.

March 6: The Supreme Court hands down its decision in the case of *Dred Scott* v. *Sandford*, declaring that black people whose ancestors were sold as slaves are not U.S. citizens and therefore have no right to sue in federal court, that the slave Dred Scott's residence in a free state does not dissolve his master's claim to him as property, and that the congressional ban on slavery expressed in the Missouri Compromise of 1820 is unconstitutional.

August 24: The failure of the New York City branch of the Ohio Life Insurance and Trust Company is said to begin the eighteen-month Panic of 1857. Underlying the subsequent wave of bank failures are the problems of railroad overexpansion, state-bank overspeculation, a decline in gold prices prompted by the ten-year gold rush in California, and the end of the Crimean War, which lowers the European demand for American exports.

1858

February 2: Buchanan recommends to Congress the admission of Kansas to the Union as a slave state under the Lecompton constitution.

May 11: Minnesota is admitted to the Union as the thirty-second state.

August 21-October 15: Abraham Lincoln and Stephen A. Douglas engage in a series of celebrated debates in a campaign for a U.S. Senate seat from Illinois. Douglas wins the election, but in the debate at Freeport, Lincoln forces Douglas to admit that the viability of slavery required local assent. That admission, known as the Freeport Doctrine, costs Douglas southern support and damages his hopes for the presidency in 1860.

1859

February 14: Oregon is admitted to the Union as the thirty-third state.

October 16: Abolitionist John Brown's abortive raid on the federal arsenal at Harpers Ferry, Virginia, antagonizes proslavery Southerners and inspires antislavery Northerners.

1860

November 6: Abraham Lincoln is elected as the sixteenth president.

December 20: South Carolina secedes from the Union, the first state ever to do so. Mississippi follows on January 9, 1861, Florida on January 10, Alabama on January 11, Georgia on January 19, Louisiana on January 26, and Texas on February 1.

1861

January 29: Kansas is admitted to the Union as the thirty-fourth state (under the free-soil Wyandotte constitution).

February 4: Delegates from the seven seceded states meet in Montgomery, Alabama, and form the provisional government of the Confederate States of America. Jefferson Davis, former U.S. senator from Mississippi, is elected provisional president on February 9.

ABRAHAM LINCOLN

1861

March 4: Inauguration of Lincoln as the sixteenth president.

April 12: Confederate forces at Charleston, South Carolina, bombard Fort Sumter in Charleston Harbor rather than permit its reprovisioning by federal forces, beginning the Civil War. U.S. troops in the fort surrender on April 13. On April 15 Lincoln issues a proclamation calling on the states to

President Zachary Taylor

supply seventy-five thousand militiamen to suppress the "insurrection."

April 19: Lincoln issues a proclamation ordering a blockade of the ports of all seceded states.

May 6: Arkansas secedes from the Union. North Carolina follows on May 20, Virginia on May 23, and Tennessee on June 8. Tennessee is the last of the eleven states to secede from the Union and join the Confederate States of America.

July 21: Confederate forces rout Union forces at the Battle of Bull Run, Manassas Junction, Virginia.

August 6: Lincoln signs the Confiscation Act, emancipating slaves forced to take part in the insurrection against the United States.

1862

February 16: Union forces under Ulysses S. Grant dislodge Confederate forces from Fort Donelson on the Cumberland River in Tennessee. The victory at Fort Donelson is the first great Union victory of the war.

February 25: Lincoln signs the first Legal Tender Act, providing for the issuance of $150 million in "greenback" currency to finance the Civil War.

April 6-7: Union and Confederate forces fight to a stalemate at the Battle of Shiloh, Tennessee.

April 16: Lincoln signs an act abolishing slavery in the District of Columbia.

April-July: The Virginia Peninsular

President Millard Fillmore (photograph by Mathew B. Brady)

Left: President Franklin Pierce (photograph by Mathew B. Brady; Library of Congress); right: President James Buchanan (photograph by Mathew B. Brady; National Archives)

Campaign under Union general George McClellan ends with the withdrawal of Union troops after defeats or standoffs in the Battle of Fair Oaks, the Seven Days' Battles, and battles at Mechanicsville, Gaines' Mill, White Oaks Swamp, and Malvern Hill.

May 20: Lincoln signs the Homestead Act, offering 160 acres of public land to adults who can prove five years of continuous residence on a piece of land and pay a small fee.

June 19: Lincoln signs an act prohibiting slavery in U.S. territories.

July 2: Lincoln issues a proclamation calling for three hundred thousand three-year volunteers to put down the Confederate rebellion.

July 2: Lincoln signs the Morrill Act for the establishment of land-grant agricultural colleges.

July 22: Lincoln submits the first draft of the Emancipation Proclamation to his cabinet. After consultation he decides to delay issuing the proclamation.

August 29-30: Union forces are defeated at the Second Battle of Bull Run.

September 14-19: Confederate forces under Gen. Robert E. Lee are forced to retreat after the Battle of Antietam, Maryland. On September 17, the famed "bloodiest single day" of the Civil War, some 26,000 men are killed or wounded. Union casualties on that day number 2,100 dead and 10,300 wounded; Confederate casualties number 2,700 dead and 11,000 wounded.

September 22: Lincoln issues the preliminary Emancipation Proclamation, freeing all slaves within areas "in rebel-

"The First Reading of the Emancipation Proclamation": President Abraham Lincoln and his cabinet, portrait by Francis B. Carpenter, 1864

lion against the United States" as of January 1, 1863.

1863

January 1: Lincoln issues the Emancipation Proclamation.

March 3: Lincoln signs the Conscription Act, inaugurating a military draft for the first time in U.S. history. Four days of antidraft riots in New York City kill about one thousand from July 13 to 16.

May 2-4: Confederate victory at the Battle of Chancellorsville, Virginia, kills or wounds about 10,600 Confederates.

June 20: West Virginia is admitted to the Union as the thirty-fifth state. Unionists in the Appalachian region of Virginia had seceded from the state and applied for statehood in 1862.

July 1-3: The Union victory at Gettysburg, Pennsylvania, repels the Confederacy's most threatening invasion of the North and signals a turning point in the war in favor of the Union.

July 4: Confederate forces surrender at Vicksburg, Mississippi, on the Mississippi River. When Port Hudson, Louisiana, falls to the Union on July 9, the Union takes control of the entire Mississippi Valley, splitting the Confederacy in two.

November 19: Lincoln delivers the Gettysburg Address during a battlefield memorial service.

November 23-25: Union forces defeat the Confederates at the Battle of Chattanooga, Tennessee, and prepare for an invasion of Georgia.

1864

March 9: Lincoln commissions Ulysses S. Grant a lieutenant general and gives him command of all Union armies. Grant takes charge of the Army of the Potomac.

May 7: Union forces under Gen. William Tecumseh Sherman set out on a campaign to win Atlanta, Georgia. They occupy the burning city on September 2.

June 7: Lincoln is nominated by the National Union party (the Republican party's adopted name) for a second term as president.

June 15-18: Battle of Petersburg, Virginia. After this indecisive battle, Union forces under Gen. Ulysses S. Grant besiege Confederate forces under Gen. Robert E. Lee in Petersburg for nine months.

June 28: Lincoln signs an act repealing the Fugitive Slave Act of 1850.

October 31: Nevada is admitted to the Union as the thirty-sixth state.

November 8: Lincoln is reelected president of the United States, defeating former Union commander George McClellan by more than four hundred thousand popular votes out of about four million cast.

November 14: Sherman's army begins its "March to the Sea."

1865

February 17: Union forces capture Columbia, South Carolina.

March 4: Lincoln is inaugurated to his second term as president.

April 1: The Battle of Five Forks, Virginia, General Lee's last assault of the Civil War, results in a Confederate retreat.

April 2: Confederate forces evacuate Petersburg and Richmond, Virginia. The Union army occupies Petersburg on April 3.

April 9: At Appomattox Courthouse, Virginia, General Lee surrenders to General Grant all Confederate forces under his command, ending the Civil War in Virginia. Later in April Gen. Joseph E. Johnston surrenders all Confederate forces on the lower Atlantic slope to General Sherman. In early May Gen. Edmund Kirby Smith surrenders all Confederate forces in the Trans-Mississippi region to Gen. E. S. Canby. Smith's troops are the last significant Confederate force to surrender to the Union in the Civil War.

April 14: Lincoln is shot by actor John Wilkes Booth while attending a play at Ford's Theater, Washington, D.C. He dies on the morning of April 15, the third president to die in office and the first to die by assassination.

ANDREW JOHNSON

1865

April 15: Inauguration of Johnson as the seventeenth president.

May 29: Johnson issues a proclamation of amnesty for all former Confederates who take an oath of allegiance to the Union, except civil, diplomatic, and military leaders.

December 18: Congress declares ratified the thirteenth amendment to the Constitution, abolishing slavery in all areas of the United States.

1866

February 19: Johnson vetoes the Freedman's Bureau Act. Congress passes another version, which Johnson also vetoes. Congress overrides that veto on July 16.

March 27: Johnson vetoes the Civil Rights Act of 1866. Congress overrides the veto on April 9.

November 6: National elections give a coalition of "Radical" and moderate Republicans control of both houses of Congress.

1867

March 1: Nebraska is admitted to the

Left: President Andrew Johnson; right: President Ulysses S. Grant

Union as the thirty-seventh state.

March 2: Congress passes the Tenure of Office Act and the Reconstruction Act of 1867 over Johnson's vetoes of the same day.

March 30: The Alaska Purchase Treaty is concluded between the United States and Russia.

November 25: The House Judiciary Committee recommends the impeachment of Johnson.

1868
March 26: Johnson is acquitted on impeachment charges by a Senate vote of 35 to 16, one vote short of the two-thirds majority necessary to convict.

July 28: Congress declares ratified the fourteenth amendment to the Constitution, granting all native and naturalized Americans status as citizens of the United States and prohibiting the states from depriving any citizen of life, liberty, or property without due process of law; apportioning representation in the House of Representatives on the basis of the proportion of a state's adult males granted the right to vote; excluding all former Confederate leaders from service in the federal government; and repudiating the Confederate debt.

ULYSSES S. GRANT

1869
March 4: Inauguration of Grant as the eighteenth president.

1870
March 28: Congress declares ratified the fifteenth amendment to the Constitution, prohibiting the abridgment "on account of race, color, or previous condition of servitude" of the right to vote.

May 31: Grant signs the First Enforcement Act, aimed against the Ku Klux Klan, which establishes heavy penalties against persons who infringe others' voting rights under the fourteenth and fifteenth amendments.

1871
April 20: Grant signs the Second Enforcement Act, authorizing the suspension of the writ of habeas corpus when combinations of private persons successfully defy the fifteenth amendment.

October 17: Grant suspends the writ of habeas corpus in nine South Carolina counties. Federal troops occupy South Carolina.

1872
March 1: Grant signs an act establishing Yellowstone National Park, the first national park.

September 4: The Crédit Mobilier scandal breaks in the press.

1873
February 12: Grant signs the Coinage Act, dubbed by critics the "Crime of '73," which establishes gold as the sole monetary standard in the United States.

March 4: Grant is inaugurated to his second term as president.

September 18: The failure of the investment house of Jay Cooke and Company precipitates the Panic of 1873. The primary reason for the panic and the subsequent five-year depression is railroad overspeculation.

1875
January 14: Grant signs the Specie Resumption Act, providing for the resumption of U.S. Treasury specie payment as of January 1, 1879.

March 1: Grant signs the Civil Rights Act of 1875, granting all U.S. citizens the right of equal access in public places.

May 1: A Treasury Department investigation of the "Whiskey Ring" scandal begins.

1876
June 25: U.S. forces under General George Custer are annihilated by Sioux Indians at the Battle of the Little Big Horn in Montana Territory.

August 1: Colorado is admitted to the Union as the thirty-eighth state.

RUTHERFORD B. HAYES

1877
March 4: Inauguration of Hayes as the nineteenth president.

April-July: Wage cuts by several prominent eastern railroads prompt a series of strikes that result in the shutdown of the nation's rail system for a week in July. Hayes orders federal troops to suppress labor unrest in West Virginia; riots and other violence kill more than one hundred people nationwide.

1878
February 28: Congress passes the Bland-Allison Act over Hayes's veto. The act requires the Department of the Treasury to purchase a minimum of $2 million worth of silver at market prices every month.

1879
March 1: Hayes vetoes the Chinese Immigration Restriction Act.

JAMES A. GARFIELD

1881
March 4: Inauguration of Garfield as the twentieth president.

July 2: Charles J. Guiteau shoots Garfield in a Washington, D.C., railroad station.

September 19: Garfield dies from the wounds he received in July. He is the fourth president to die in office and the second to die by assassination.

CHESTER A. ARTHUR

1881
September 20: Inauguration of Arthur as the twenty-first president.

1882
May 6: Arthur signs the Chinese Exclusion Act, suspending Chinese immigration to the United States for a period of ten years.

Left: Rutherford B. Hayes; right: President Chester A. Arthur

1883

January 16: Arthur signs the Civil Service Reform Act, providing for a bipartisan commission to formulate and administer examinations for federal government positions.

GROVER CLEVELAND

1885

March 4: Inauguration of Cleveland as the twenty-second president.

1886

June 29: Cleveland signs an act legalizing the incorporation of national trade unions.

1887

February 4: Cleveland signs the Interstate Commerce Commission Act, establishing the nation's first regulatory agency.

1888

June 13: Cleveland signs an act establishing the Department of Labor.

1889

February 9: Cleveland signs an act establishing the Department of Agriculture.

BENJAMIN HARRISON

1889

March 4: Inauguration of Harrison as the twenty-third president.

November 2: North Dakota and South Dakota are admitted to the Union as the thirty-ninth and fortieth states.

November 8: Montana is admitted to the Union as the forty-first state.

November 11: Washington is admitted to the Union as the forty-second state.

1890

July 2: Harrison signs the Sherman Anti-Trust Act, prohibiting "every contract, combination in the form of trust or otherwise, or conspiracy, in restraint of trade among the several states, or with foreign nations."

Left: President James A. Garfield; right: President Grover Cleveland

July 3: Idaho is admitted to the Union as the forty-third state.

July 10: Wyoming is admitted to the Union as the forty-fourth state.

July 14: Harrison signs the Sherman Silver Purchase Act, requiring the Department of the Treasury to purchase 4.5 million ounces of silver at market prices every month.

October 1: Harrison signs an act establishing the National Weather Bureau as an office of the Department of the Interior.

October 6: Harrison signs the McKinley Tariff Act, raising tariff rates 49.5 percent to establish reciprocity with foreign nations.

1891

September 18: Harrison issues a proclamation opening nine hundred thousand acres of Indian land in Oklahoma Territory to settlement. The "Sooner" invasion follows.

1892

May 5: Harrison signs the Chinese Exclusion Act, extending the provisions of the original act of 1882 by ten years.

GROVER CLEVELAND

1893

March 4: Inauguration of Cleveland as the twenty-fourth president.

June 27: A stock market crash brings on the Panic of 1893.

November 3: Cleveland signs an act repealing the Sherman Silver Purchase Act.

1894

May 11: The Pullman strike begins. A general strike of western railroads fol-

President Benjamin Harrison addressing a New York City audience from the site of George Washington's inauguration as president, centennial celebration, April 30, 1889

lows on June 26. On July 2 President Cleveland orders troops to Chicago, to enforce a federal injunction prohibiting interference with interstate commerce.

August 27: The Wilson-Gorman Tariff Act becomes law. The act lowers tariffs to 39.9 percent and also provides for the first graduated income tax in American history (the Supreme Court declares the income tax provisions of the law unconstitutional in 1895).

1896

January 4: Utah is admitted to the Union as the forty-fifth state.

May 18: The Supreme Court hands down its decision in the case of *Plessy* v. *Ferguson*, sustaining a Louisiana "Jim Crow car law" on the basis of the principle "separate but equal."

WILLIAM MCKINLEY

1897

March 4: Inauguration of McKinley as the twenty-fifth president.

July 24: McKinley signs the Dingley Tariff Act, establishing the highest tariff rates—57 percent on average—up to that time.

1898

February 15: The explosion of the U.S. battleship the *Maine* killing 260 sailors intensifies calls for war with Spain over Cuba. McKinley asks Congress to declare war on April 11, and Congress complies on April 25. In the December 10 peace treaty Spain relinquishes all claims to Cuba and cedes Puerto Rico, Guam, and the Philippines to the United States in return for $20 million.

July 8: McKinley signs a joint congressional resolution annexing Hawaii.

1901

March 4: McKinley is inaugurated to his second term as president.

September 6: McKinley is shot by Leon F. Czolgosz at the Pan-American Exposition in Buffalo, New York. He dies on September 14, the fifth president to die in office and the third to die as a result of assassination.

THEODORE ROOSEVELT

1901

September 14: Inauguration of Roosevelt as the twenty-sixth president.

October 17: Roosevelt entertains black leader Booker T. Washington in the White House, attracting widespread criticism in the South.

December 16: The Hay-Pauncefote Treaty is concluded between the United States and Great Britain, establishing the sole U.S. right to construct, maintain, and administer a Central American Isthmian canal. The treaty supercedes the Clayton-Bulwer Treaty of 1850.

1902

March 10: A federal antitrust suit against the Northern Securities Company begins. Roosevelt greatly increases antitrust prosecutions under the terms of the Sherman Anti-Trust Act.

May 12: A coal mine strike by the United Mine Workers prompts a federal investigation of coal mine conditions beginning on June 7 and, in October, direct presidential intervention to stop the strike.

1903

February 14: Roosevelt signs an act establishing the Department of Commerce and Labor.

November 3: After the nation of Colombia fails to ratify a U.S.-sponsored treaty providing for a six-mile-wide canal zone across the Isthmus of Panama, a "revolution" begins in Panama. Roosevelt recognizes the independence of Panama on November 6. The Hay-Bunau-Varilla Treaty providing for the canal zone is signed by the United States and Panama on November 18. Construction of the Panama Canal is completed in 1914.

1904

December 6: Roosevelt issues his fourth State of the Union Address, containing what becomes known as the "Roosevelt Corollary" to the Monroe Doctrine: "In the Western Hemisphere the adherence of the United States to the Monroe Doctrine may force the United States, however reluctantly, in flagrant cases of . . . wrongdoing or impotence, to the exercise of an international police force."

1905

March 4: Roosevelt is inaugurated to his second term as president.

August 5: Roosevelt begins meetings in Portsmouth, New Hampshire, with representatives of Russia and Japan to negotiate an end to the Russo-Japanese War. The combatants sign a peace treaty in Portsmouth on September 5.

1906

June 29: Roosevelt signs the Hepburn Act granting the Interstate Commerce Commission power to regulate railroad rates.

June 30: Roosevelt signs the Pure Food and Drug Act and the Meat Inspection Act. Publication the previous year of Upton Sinclair's "muckraking" novel *The Jungle* prompted a presidential commission investigation of the meat-packing industry.

December 10: Roosevelt is awarded

President William McKinley (fifth from right) watches with staff members and colleagues as Secretary of State William R. Day reenacts the signing of the protocol ending the Spanish-American War, one week after the actual signing took place on August 12, 1898 (Library of Congress)

the Nobel Peace Prize for his service in ending the Russo-Japanese War.

1907

October 22: Bank failures prompt the Panic of 1907. Personal loans made by banker J. P. Morgan to New York banks bolster a congressional appropriation of Treasury Department bailout funds to avert a deeper depression.

November 16: Oklahoma is admitted to the Union as the forty-sixth state.

WILLIAM HOWARD TAFT

1909

March 4: Inauguration of Taft as the twenty-seventh president.

August 5: Taft signs the Payne-Aldrich Tariff Act, lowering many tariffs but leaving many others unchanged.

1912

January 6: New Mexico is admitted to the Union as the forty-seventh state.

February 14: Arizona is admitted to the Union as the forty-eighth state.

1913

February 25: Congress declares ratified the sixteenth amendment to the Constitution, granting Congress the power to lay and collect income taxes.

March 4: Taft signs an act separating the Departments of Commerce and Labor.

WOODROW WILSON

1913

March 4: Inauguration of Wilson as

President Theodore Roosevelt inspecting the Panama Canal worksite

the twenty-eighth president.

April 11: At the suggestion of Postmaster General Albert S. Burleson, the Wilson administration undertakes a policy of segregation of black persons in federal service. A program of segregation, demotions, and discharges in several government departments ensues. Wilson acknowledges the policy on June 23 and, under severe criticism from nearly all quarters, later reverses it.

May 31: By proclamation Wilson declares ratified the seventeenth amendment to the Constitution, providing for the direct election of U.S. senators by popular vote.

October 3: Wilson signs the Underwood Tariff Act, reducing tariff rates to their lowest level since the Civil War and also instituting the first U.S. income tax under the provisions of the sixteenth amendment.

December 23: Wilson signs the Glass-Owen Act, creating the Federal Reserve System.

1914

June 28: The assassination of Austrian archduke Franz Ferdinand in Sarajevo, Serbia, starts the process that leads to the outbreak of World War I a month later, when Austria declares war on Serbia. Germany declares war on Russia on August 1 and on France on August 3. Britain declares war on Germany on August 4. Montenegro declares war on Austria on August 5, Serbia declares war on Germany on August 6, Austria declares war on Russia on August 6, Montenegro declares war on Germany on August 8, and Britain and France declare war on Austria on Au-

President William Howard Taft (photograph by H. E. French)

gust 12. Wilson issues a proclamation of American neutrality on August 4.

August 15: The Panama Canal is officially opened to traffic.

September 26: Wilson signs the Federal Trade Commission Act, designed to discourage unfair trade practices in interstate commerce.

October 15: Wilson signs the Clayton Anti-Trust Act, supplementing the provisions of the Sherman Anti-Trust Act of 1890.

1915

January 28: Wilson signs an act establishing the U.S. Coast Guard.

May 7: A German U-boat sinks the British luxury liner *Lusitania*, prompting international outrage and a statement by President Wilson to issue several letters of protest to the German government.

1916

April 18: Wilson issues an ultimatum to the German government after the sinking of the unarmed French vessel the *Sussex*, in which he declares that the United States will sever diplomatic relations with Germany if Germany refuses to change its submarine policy. The German government apologizes for the incident.

July 11: Wilson signs the Good Roads Act, establishing a Bureau of Roads in the Department of Agriculture and offering federal aid to state highway commissions.

July 17: Wilson signs the Federal Farm Loan Act, establishing twelve farm loan banks offering long-term credit.

September 1: Wilson signs the Child Labor Act, prohibiting the interstate shipment of the products of child labor. The Supreme Court declares the act unconstitutional on June 3, 1918.

September 3: Wilson signs the Adamson Eight-Hour Act, mandating the eight-hour day for railroads operating in interstate commerce.

1917

February 3: Wilson severs diplomatic relations with Germany over the issue of unrestricted submarine warfare.

March 4: Wilson is inaugurated to his second term as president.

April 2: Wilson delivers a war message to Congress, declaring that "the world must be made safe for democracy." Congress declares war on Germany on April 6, beginning U.S. military involvement in World War I.

May 18: Wilson signs the Selective Service Act, authorizing the registration for the draft of all men between the ages of twenty-one and thirty.

June 26: The first troops of the American Expeditionary Forces land in France.

1918

January 8: In an address to Congress, Wilson lists the "fourteen points" of his program for European peace.

May 16: Wilson signs the Sedition Act, establishing penalties for making false statements interfering with the American war effort and for using "disloyal" language in reference to the government. The act results in the imprisonment of Socialist party leader Eugene V. Debs and others.

July 18-August 6: Eighty-five thousand U.S. troops participate in the Second Battle of Marne, turning back the final German offensive of World War I.

September 26-November 11: American forces numbering more than 1.2 million participate in the Meuse-Argonne Offensive, severing the main supply lines of the German army and prompting the German government to ask for a cease-fire.

December 13: Wilson arrives in Paris to participate in the Paris Peace Conference.

1919

January 29: Congress declares ratified the eighteenth amendment to the Constitution, prohibiting the manufacture, sale, or transport of alcohol in the United States.

June 28: The Allied and Axis nations conclude the Treaty of Versailles, establishing the terms of peace with Germany. President Warren G. Harding signs the treaty on August 25, 1921.

1920

August 26: By proclamation Wilson declares ratified the nineteenth amendment to the Constitution, prohibiting the denial of suffrage rights on the basis of sex.

December 10: Wilson is awarded the Nobel Peace Prize.

WARREN G. HARDING

1921

March 4: Inauguration of Harding as the twenty-ninth president.

May 27: Harding signs the Emergency Tariff Act, raising tariffs on a variety of agricultural products.

August 9: Harding signs an act establishing the Veterans Bureau.

October 26: Harding delivers a speech to a segregated audience of whites and blacks in Birmingham, Alabama, on the virtues of racial integration.

December 23: Harding pardons Eugene V. Debs and others convicted under the wartime Sedition Act and other acts.

President Woodrow Wilson speaking in support of the Treaty of Versailles, September 13, 1919 (Library of Congress)

1922

February 6: The Five-Power Treaty is concluded between the United States, Great Britain, France, Italy, and Japan. The treaty establishes limitations on the parties' naval forces according to the ratio 5:5:3:1.75:1.75.

May 26: Harding signs an act creating the Federal Narcotics Control Board.

September 21: Harding signs the Fordney-McCumber Tariff Act, raising tariffs on a variety of manufactured goods.

1923

August 2: Harding dies of apoplexy. He is the sixth president to die in office.

Harding administration scandals: Many of President Harding's cabinet officials were unscrupulous opportunists who took advantage of their positions to engage in a variety of illegal activities. The worst of the scandals, most of which became public knowledge during the administration of Calvin Coolidge, was the "Teapot Dome" affair, which concerned Secretary of the Interior Albert Fall's illegal sale of American oil reserve lands.

CALVIN COOLIDGE

1923

August 3: Inauguration of Coolidge as the thirtieth president.

December 6: Coolidge delivers his first State of the Union Address, the first to be broadcast on radio.

1924

March 7: Coolidge issues a proclamation raising tariffs on wheat and wheat products.

May 15: Coolidge vetoes the Soldiers' Bonus Act. Congress overrides the veto on May 19.

May 26: Coolidge signs the National Origins Act. The act bans East Asian immigration, reduces the quota of European immigrants from 3 percent to 2 percent of the nation's population, and bases the quota percentages on the figures of the 1890 census, closing out many potential southern and eastern European immigrants. A subsequent act of 1929 establishes a limit on immigration of 150,000 per year.

June 2: Coolidge signs an act reducing income taxes by 25 percent and increasing estate taxes.

1925

March 4: Coolidge is inaugurated to his second term as president.

1926

February 26: Coolidge signs the Revenue Act, reducing personal income and inheritance taxes.

July 2: Coolidge signs an act creating the Army Air Corps.

1927

February 23: Coolidge signs the Radio Control Act, creating the Federal Radio Commission.

February 25: Coolidge vetoes the McNary-Haugen Farm Relief Act.

June 11: Coolidge presents the Distinguished Flying Cross to Charles A. Lindbergh, who had completed the first solo nonstop airplane flight from New York to Paris on May 20-21.

1928

May 29: Coolidge signs a Revenue Act, reducing income taxes.

December 21: Coolidge signs the Boulder Dam Act, appropriating $165 million for the construction of a dam on the Colorado River at the Nevada-Arizona border.

HERBERT HOOVER

1929

March 4: Inauguration of Hoover as the thirty-first president.

June 15: Hoover signs the Agricultural Marketing Act, creating a revolving fund of $500 million for low-interest farm loans.

July 24: Hoover issues a proclamation declaring the Kellogg-Briand Pact in effect in the United States. The previous year, representatives of fifteen countries concluded a treaty renouncing war as a means of solving international disputes. Forty-seven other countries soon joined the pact.

October 24: Stock Market prices fall sharply on "Black Thursday." A prominent group of investors agrees to purchase a large volume of stocks in an attempt to restore confidence in the market.

October 29: The Stock Market crashes, beginning the Great Depression. Several factors combine to create the nation's worst-ever economic collapse: a chronic agricultural surplus during the 1920s; an overuse of credit in the securities industry; high tariffs, which discourage world trade; and a growing decline in consumer purchasing power head the list. By early 1930 approximately four million Americans are without jobs. The slide continues for the remainder of Hoover's presidency. Unemployment peaks at 25 percent in early 1933. Nearly 25 percent of the nation's banks fail during the Hoover years.

December 2: Hoover delivers his first State of the Union address, claiming that the nation's business was fundamentally sound and pledging to lower taxes and raise tariffs.

1930

May 28: Hoover vetoes an act to provide pensions for veterans of the Spanish-American War, the Philippine Insurrection, and the Boxer Rebellion. Congress overrides the veto on June 2.

June 17: Hoover signs the Smoot-

Left: President Warren G. Harding; right: President Calvin Coolidge (courtesy of Underwood and Underwood)

Hawley Tariff Act, raising tariffs on agricultural and manufactured goods and starting a worldwide tariff war that dampens international trade.

June 26: Hoover vetoes an act to provide pensions for veterans of World War I.

December 20: Hoover signs an act appropriating $116 million for public works and an act appropriating $45 million for drought relief.

1932

January 22: Hoover signs the Reconstruction Finance Corporation Act, capitalizing the corporation at $500 million and authorizing it to issue up to $2 billion in tax-exempt bonds to assist banks, insurance corporations, railroads, and farm mortgage associations. On July 21 Hoover signs an act upping the bond-issue limit to $3 billion.

July 11: Hoover vetoes an act to provide unemployment relief.

July 22: Hoover signs the Federal Home Loan Bank Act.

July 28: Hoover calls out the U.S. Army to suppress the seventeen-thousand-man "Bonus Army" uprising in Washington.

1933

February 6: Congress declares ratified the twentieth amendment to the Constitution, fixing as of October 15, 1933, the start of the terms of the president and vice-president on January 20 and the opening of sessions of Congress on January 3.

FRANKLIN D. ROOSEVELT

1933

March 4: Inauguration of Roosevelt as the thirty-second president.

March 5: Roosevelt issues a proclamation declaring a four-day national "bank holiday" to begin on March 6.

March 9: Roosevelt signs the Emer-

President Herbert Hoover

gency Banking Relief Act, calling in outstanding gold and gold certificates for deposit in the U.S. Treasury.

March 12: Roosevelt broadcasts on radio his first "fireside chat."

March 31: Roosevelt signs the Civilian Conservation Corps Reconstruction Relief Act, creating an employment agency for public works that by 1941 had given more than 2 million young Americans jobs.

April 19: Roosevelt declares that the United States is off the gold standard.

May 12: Roosevelt signs the Federal Emergency Relief Act, appropriating $500 million in state and local matching funds.

May 13: Roosevelt signs the Agricultural Adjustment Act, implementing a system of cash subsidies and parity prices for the relief of farmers. The Supreme Court declares the act unconstitutional in 1936. Congress subsequently develops legislation that survives court challenges.

May 18: Roosevelt signs the Tennessee Valley Authority Act, appropriating funds for the construction of dams and power plants in the Tennessee Valley region.

June 16: Roosevelt signs the National Industrial Recovery Act, establishing the National Recovery Administration to regulate industrial output and prices and to guarantee the right of workers to bargain collectively and to receive a minimum wage. The act also establishes the Public Works Administration, which spends nearly $4 billion on public works. The Supreme Court declares the NRA provisions of the act unconstitutional in 1935.

The "Big Three" at Yalta, Soviet Crimea: British prime minister Winston Churchill, President Franklin D. Roosevelt, and Soviet premier Joseph Stalin, February 1945 (courtesy of the Franklin D. Roosevelt Library)

June 16: Roosevelt signs the Banking Act of 1933, also known as the Glass-Steagall Act, creating the Federal Deposit Insurance Corporation and separating commercial from investment banking.

August 5: Roosevelt appoints a National Labor Board, chaired by New York senator Robert F. Wagner, to settle labor relations disputes.

November 16: The United States recognizes the government of the Union of Soviet Socialist Republics.

December 5: Congress declares ratified the twenty-first amendment to the Constitution, repealing the eighteenth amendment prohibiting the manufacture, sale, or transport of alcohol in the United States.

1934

June 6: Roosevelt signs the Federal Securities Exchange Act, establishing the Securities and Exchange Commission to regulate trading in securities.

June 28: Roosevelt signs the Federal Housing Act, establishing the Federal Housing Administration to insure loans for family and small-business construction.

1935

April 8: Roosevelt signs the Emergency Relief Appropriations Act, creating the Works Progress Administration, which employs more than 8.5 million workers and spends about $11 billion before going out of existence in 1943.

June 26: Roosevelt issues an executive order establishing the National Youth Administration.

July 5: Roosevelt signs the Wagner

Act, creating a new National Labor Relations Board empowered to certify unions, to administer union elections, and to guarantee the right of workers to organize and bargain collectively.

August 14: Roosevelt signs the Social Security Act, creating the Social Security System.

August 30: Roosevelt signs the Revenue Act of 1935, implementing surtaxes on upper individual incomes and highly valued estates, sharply raising tax rates on upper incomes, and establishing higher taxes for most business corporations.

1937

January 20: Roosevelt is inaugurated to his second term as president.

March 9: During a fireside chat Roosevelt explains his plans to reorganize the Supreme Court by expanding its membership. Opponents denounce the plan as an attempt to "pack" the court. The House and Senate never vote on the proposed legislation.

October 5: Roosevelt delivers his "quarantine" speech, promising a "concerted effort" to "quarantine" German and Japanese aggression.

1938

May 17: Roosevelt signs the Naval Expansion Act. A series of acts expanding the American military follows during the next six years.

June 25: Roosevelt signs the Fair Labor Standards Act, raising the minimum wage of workers engaged in interstate commerce from twenty-five cents to forty cents an hour and limiting the workweek to 44 hours of regular-time pay plus overtime.

September 26: Roosevelt makes appeal to European leaders for an equitable solution to the Czechoslovakian crisis. Czechoslovakia cedes the Sudetenland to Germany on September 30.

1939

April 14: Roosevelt asks the leaders of Germany and Italy not to attack or invade nations in Europe and the Middle East.

September 1: Germany invades Poland, beginning World War II. Great Britain and France declare war on Germany on September 3. Roosevelt issues a proclamation of American neutrality on September 5. On November 4 he signs the Neutrality Act authorizing the export of arms to belligerents on a "cash and carry" basis.

1940

September 16: Roosevelt signs the Selective Training and Service Act, authorizing the first peacetime draft in American history.

1941

January 20: Roosevelt is inaugurated to his third term as president.

March 11: Roosevelt signs the Lend-Lease Act.

June 22: Germany invades the Soviet Union.

August 9-12: Roosevelt secretly meets with British prime minister Winston Churchill off the coast of Newfoundland. Their meetings produce the Atlantic Charter, which calls for a postwar order based on the principles of freedom and self-determination. On January 1, 1942, representatives of twenty-six nations sign the United Nations declaration, endorsing the principles of the Atlantic Charter.

November 7: In announcing the U.S. issue of Lend-Lease aid to the Soviet Union, Roosevelt declares the defense of the Soviet Union vital to the interests of the United States.

President Harry S Truman addressing a convention of the National Association for the Advancement of Colored People, June 29, 1947 (photograph by Abbie Rowe; National Park Service)

December 7: Japanese air forces attack the U.S. naval fleet at Pearl Harbor, Hawaii, beginning U.S. involvement in World War II. Roosevelt asks Congress to declare war on Japan on December 8, and Congress responds the same day. Germany and Italy declare war on the United States on December 11, and again Congress replies in kind on the same day.

1942

January 24-27: The Battle of Macassar Strait begins the Pacific war.

March 18: Roosevelt issues an executive order establishing the War Relocation Authority, which interns 110,000 Japanese and Japanese-Americans for the course of the war.

April 10: American and Philippine forces surrender the island of Bataan to the Japanese. The infamous "death march" follows. More than ten thousand American and Filipino prisoners die on the march.

June 3-6: The Battle of Midway brings the first major American victory in the Pacific war.

November 8: Allied forces invade North Africa.

November 12-15: The Battle of Guadalcanal.

1943

February 2: German forces surrender Stalingrad to the Soviet Union, beginning their long retreat back to Germany.

September 3: Allied forces invade Italy.

November 28-December 1: Roosevelt meets with Prime Minister Churchill and Soviet premier Joseph Stalin in Teheran, Iran. The Teheran Conference finalizes plans for the Allied invasion of France in the early summer of 1944.

1944

January 11: Allied air offensive against Germany begins.

June 6: Allied invasion of France—D day.

June 16: U.S. air offensive against Japan begins.

September 12: Allied forces enter Germany.

December 16-26: German forces attack the Allies in the Battle of the Bulge, the last great German offensive of the war. An Allied counterattack led by U.S. general George S. Patton repels the German army.

1945

January 20: Roosevelt is inaugurated to his fourth term as president.

February 3: Roosevelt confers with Churchill and Stalin at Yalta, Crimea, Soviet Union. At the Yalta Conference the three leaders agree on terms for a postwar European settlement.

April 12: Roosevelt dies of a cerebral hemorrhage at Warm Springs, Georgia. He is the seventh president to die in office.

HARRY S TRUMAN

1945

April 12: Inauguration of Truman as the thirty-third president.

May 8: Germany surrenders unconditionally to the Allies.

July 17-August 2: Truman meets with Churchill (new British prime minister Clement Attlee replaces Churchill on July 28) and Stalin at Potsdam, Germany, to finalize terms of peace with Germany.

August 5: The United States drops an atomic bomb on Hiroshima, Japan. A second bomb is dropped on Nagasaki on August 9.

August 14: Japan surrenders unconditionally to the United States. Formal surrender occurs on September 1.

1946

March 25: First meeting of the United Nations Security Council begins at Hunter College, New York. The U.N. General Assembly begins its first meeting at Flushing Meadows Park, New York, on October 23.

October 28: Truman appoints the first Atomic Energy Commission.

1947

May 22: Truman signs an act granting $400 million in U.S. aid to Greece and Turkey. The aid package implements the Truman Doctrine, pledging the United States to defend anticommunist governments everywhere in the world.

June 20: Truman vetoes the Taft-Hartley Act. Congress overrides the veto on June 23. The Taft-Hartley Act bans the closed union shop and places other limitations on union activity.

July 26: Truman signs an act merging the Department of War and the Department of the Navy into the Department of Defense.

1948

April 3: Truman signs an act establishing the Economic Cooperation Administration, which administers more than $5.3 billion in U.S. aid during the first year of the "Marshall Plan."

President Dwight D. Eisenhower conferring with Secretary of State John Foster Dulles and Charles E. Bohlen, U.S. ambassador to the Soviet Union, during the Geneva Summit, July 18, 1955 (courtesy of the Associated Press)

June 26: Truman orders an airlift for the relief of citizens in West Berlin, Germany. The Soviet Union had quarantined West Berlin on June 24. The Russians give up the blockade on May 12, 1949.

1949

January 20: Truman is inaugurated to his second term as president.

April 4: North Atlantic Treaty Organization Treaty concluded between the United States and eleven other nations. The U.S. Senate ratifies the treaty on July 21, and Truman signs it on July 25.

1950

June 25: North Korean forces invade the Republic of South Korea, beginning the Korean War. United Nations forces land at Inchon, South Korea, on September 14 to begin a counterattack. The war lasts until 1953 and ends in a stalemate.

1951

February 26: Congress declares ratified the twenty-second amendment to the Constitution, limiting future presidents to two terms.

1952

January 9: Truman delivers his seventh State of the Union Address, in which he calls for the passage of a comprehensive Civil Rights program.

DWIGHT D. EISENHOWER

1953

January 20: Inauguration of Eisenhower as the thirty-fourth president.

April 1: Eisenhower signs an act creating the Department of Health, Education, and Welfare.

July 27: Representatives of the United Nations, North Korea, and the Peoples Republic of China sign an armistice at Panmunjom, Korea, ending the Korean War.

1954

April 22: Army-McCarthy hearings begin. The hearings expose Senator Joseph McCarthy's underhanded anticommunist tactics and earn him a Senate condemnation on December 2.

May 17: The Supreme Court hands down its decision in the case of *Brown v. The Board of Education of Topeka*, declaring unconstitutional the segregation of public schools on the basis of the principle "separate but equal."

1956
July 27: Egypt seizes the Suez Canal. Israel attacks Egypt on October 29. British and French troops follow on November 5. Eisenhower issues a statement deploring the British-French action. A United Nations cease-fire goes into effect on November 7.

1957
January 20: Eisenhower is inaugurated to his second term as president.

1959
January 3: Alaska admitted to the Union as the forty-ninth state.

August 21: Hawaii admitted to the Union as the fiftieth state.

September 15: Soviet president Nikita Khrushchev begins a visit to the United States, the first Russian leader to do so. Eisenhower and Khrushchev meet at Camp David, Maryland, September 25-27.

1960
February 1: A "sit-in" to integrate a Greensboro, North Carolina, lunch counter spurs similar sit-ins across the United States in the spring and summer.

May 1: Khrushchev announces to the Supreme Soviet that an American U-2 spy plane has been shot down. The news reaches the West on May 5. At first President Eisenhower denies the existence of a spy-plane program violating Soviet airspace, then he is forced to admit it when the pilot appears on Soviet television.

May 6: Eisenhower signs the Civil Rights Act of 1960.

1961
January 3: Eisenhower announces that the United States has severed diplomatic relations with Cuba.

JOHN F. KENNEDY

1961
January 20: Inauguration of Kennedy as the thirty-fifth president.

March 1: Kennedy issues an executive order creating the Peace Corps. He signs an act of Congress making the organization permanent on September 22.

April 3: Congress declares ratified the twenty-third amendment to the Constitution, granting residents of the District of Columbia the right to vote in federal elections.

April 17-20: Anti-Castro exiles attempt an invasion of Cuba at the Bay of Pigs. President Kennedy assumes responsibility for the failed invasion.

May 5: Alan B. Shepard, Jr., takes America's first spaceflight, a suborbital journey lasting fifteen minutes, in Project Mercury's *Freedom* 7. On May 25 Kennedy delivers a special message to Congress in which he pledges the nation to land a man on the moon and return him safely to Earth "before this decade is out." John Glenn becomes the first American to orbit the Earth on February 20, 1962.

August 13: The government of East Germany begins constructing the Berlin Wall.

October 30: The Soviet Union sets off what is believed to be the largest nuclear explosion in history—estimated in excess of fifty megatons—in a remote region of the Soviet Arctic.

President John F. Kennedy signing the Nuclear Test Ban Treaty, October 8, 1963 (photograph by Abbie Rowe; National Park Service)

1962

February 8: The U.S. Military Assistance Command is organized in the Republic of South Vietnam.

October 22: Kennedy announces to the American people that the U.S. military is undertaking an air and naval quarantine of Cuba, beginning the Cuban Missile Crisis. On October 16 the United States received intelligence data indicating the introduction of medium-range ballistic missiles on the island. On October 25 and 26 Russian vessels approaching Cuba are turned back by the American navy. Khrushchev announces the withdrawal of the missiles on October 28.

1963

June 19: Kennedy sends a special message to Congress proposing an omnibus civil rights bill.

July 25: The Nuclear Test Ban Treaty is concluded between the United States, the Soviet Union, and Great Britain. The treaty prohibits atmospheric, underwater, and outer-space testing of nuclear weapons. Kennedy signs the treaty on October 8.

August 28: Two hundred thousand people gather in the "March on Washington" to demonstrate in favor of federal civil rights action. A speech by Martin Luther King, Jr., "I Have a Dream," highlights the march. President Kennedy meets with leaders of the march during the day.

August 30: The United States and the Soviet Union install a direct telephone link—dubbed the "hot line"—between the rival executive offices. The hot line is designed to improve communication in times of crisis.

November 1-2: A military coup overthrows the government of South Vietnamese president Ngo Dinh Diem.

November 22: Kennedy is shot while riding in a motorcade in Dallas, Texas, and is pronounced dead a few hours later. Kennedy is the eighth president to die in office and the fourth to die as a result of assassination.

LYNDON B. JOHNSON

1963

November 22: Inauguration of Johnson as the thirty-sixth president.

1964

February 4: Congress declares ratified the twenty-fourth amendment to the Constitution, prohibiting the levy of poll taxes.

March 16: Johnson delivers a special message to Congress announcing his "War on Poverty."

July 2: Johnson signs the Civil Rights Act of 1964, which guarantees, among many things, equal access to public accommodations and equal employment opportunity without regard to race.

August 7: Johnson signs a joint congressional resolution empowering the president to repel armed attacks on the U.S. military by any means necessary. On August 4 the United States had undertaken a bombing raid on North Vietnamese oil depots in retaliation for attacks on U.S. destroyers in the Gulf of Tonkin. The "Gulf of Tonkin Resolution" signals the beginning of a stepped-up U.S. presence in Vietnam.

August 30: Johnson signs the Economic Opportunity Act, creating the Office of Economic Opportunity for job training and public works recruitment.

September 2: Johnson signs the Housing Act, authorizing $1.1 billion for federal housing construction.

October 31: Johnson delivers a campaign speech in which he promises the establishment of a "Great Society" under a renewed Democratic administration.

1965

January 20: Johnson is inaugurated to his second term as president.

February 7: Johnson orders air strikes against North Vietnam. The first U.S. combat troops land in South Vietnam on March 8. By July 28 U.S. forces number 125,000.

July 30: Johnson signs the Medicare Act, implementing a program of federal medical insurance.

August 10: Johnson signs the Voting Rights Act.

September 9: Johnson signs an act establishing the Department of Housing and Urban Development.

October 22: Johnson signs the Highway Beautification Act.

November 8: Johnson signs the Higher Education Act, authorizing $165 million for scholarships to needy college students.

1966

January 31: Johnson announces the renewal of U.S. bombing raids on North Vietnam after a thirty-seven-day hiatus.

May 15: More than ten thousand antiwar demonstrators march outside the White House. Johnson announces on June 30 that the United States will continue to escalate the conflict until North Vietnam ends its subversion of South Vietnam.

July 4: Johnson signs the Freedom of Information Act.

October 16: Johnson signs an act establishing the Department of Transportation.

President Lyndon B. Johnson greeting civil rights leaders Ralph Abernathy and Martin Luther King, Jr., after signing the Voting Rights Act, August 10, 1965 (courtesy of the Lyndon Baines Johnson Memorial Library)

1967

January 10: Johnson delivers his fourth State of the Union Address, the first such address broadcast on all three American commercial television networks.

February 10: Congress declares ratified the twenty-fifth amendment to the Constitution, establishing a comprehensive plan for presidential succession.

April 4: Johnson signs a $12.2 billion appropriations act for military operations in Southeast Asia.

June 13: Johnson appoints Thurgood Marshall as an associate justice on the Supreme Court. Marshall is the first black to serve on the court.

July 13: U.S. troop strength in South Vietnam reaches 480,000. Soon after the troop level reaches its all-time high: 520,000.

September 27: Johnson signs the Food Stamp Act, establishing the food stamp program.

October 3: Johnson signs the Vocational Rehabilitation Act.

October 11: Johnson signs an act appropriating $170 million in aid to the Appalachian region.

November 7: Johnson signs an act creating the Corporation for Public Broadcasting.

November 20: Johnson signs an act creating the National Commission on Product Safety.

President and Mrs. Richard M. Nixon on the Great Wall of China, February 24, 1972 (courtesy of the Nixon Presidential Materials Project)

November 21: Johnson signs the Air Quality Act.

1968

January 30: North Vietnamese and Viet Cong forces launch the Tet Offensive, the largest coordinated North Vietnamese offensive of the Vietnam War. The vigor of the offensive contradicts U.S. military opinion that the North is tiring of war.

March 31: Johnson announces a halt to most of the bombing of North Vietnam and also indicates that he will not be a candidate for the Democratic presidential nomination in 1968.

April 4: Civil rights leader Martin Luther King, Jr., is assassinated in Memphis, Tennessee.

June 5: Robert F. Kennedy, front-runner for the 1968 Democratic presidential nomination and the brother of the late president, is assassinated in Los Angeles, California.

July 1: The United States, the Soviet Union, and fifty-five other nations conclude the Nuclear Non-Proliferation Treaty, pledging to limit the spread of nuclear weapons and nuclear weapons technology.

August 20-21: Troops of the Soviet Union occupy Czechoslovakia.

October 2: Johnson signs an act establishing a national system of urban and rural trails. The first trails created under the act are the Appalachian Trail and the Pacific Crest Trail.

RICHARD M. NIXON

1969

January 20: Inauguration of Richard Nixon as the thirty-seventh president.

May 14: In a nationally televised address, Nixon proposes the gradual and mutual withdrawal of all foreign troops from South Vietnam.

May 29: Nixon issues an executive order establishing the Council on Environmental Quality.

July 20: Neil Armstrong and Buzz Aldrin of the U.S. spacecraft *Apollo 11* land and walk on the moon.

November 3: In a nationally televised address, President Nixon calls on the "silent majority" of Americans to support his Vietnam War policy.

1970

April 1: Nixon signs an act banning cigarette advertising on radio and television.

April 30: Nixon announces the deployment of U.S. troops in Cambodia.

May 4: Four students are killed and eight wounded during antiwar demonstrations at Kent State University, Kent, Ohio. On May 16 two student protesters are killed at Jackson State College, Jackson, Mississippi.

December 31: Nixon signs the Clean Air Act of 1970.

1971

June 10: Nixon ends the U.S. embargo on trade with the People's Republic of China.

June 28: Daniel Ellsberg, a Johnson administration Defense Department official, publicly admits turning over a copy of the Pentagon Papers, a classified report on U.S. government involvement in the Vietnam War, to the *New York Times*.

June 30: Congress declares ratified the twenty-sixth amendment to the Constitution, granting American citizens of at least eighteen years of age the right to vote.

August 15: Nixon issues an executive order freezing wages and prices for ninety days.

September 3: White House aides later dubbed the "plumbers unit" break into the office of the psychiatrist of Daniel Ellsberg in an effort to locate information that will discredit him. The plumbers operation is later exposed during the Watergate investigation.

October 23: The United Nations General Assembly votes to seat the People's Republic of China and to expel Nationalist China.

December 18: The United States devalues its dollar as part of a ten-nation agreement to restructure currency exchange rates.

1972

February 7: Nixon signs the Federal Election Campaign Act, requiring all campaign contributions to be reported.

February 14: Nixon issues an executive order ending the U.S. trade embargo with the People's Republic of China that has existed since the establishment of the People's Republic in 1949.

February 22: Nixon confers with People's Republic premier Chou En-Lai in Peking during a visit to China. Nixon is the first president to visit China since the establishment of the Communist government in 1949.

April 3: Nixon issues an executive order devaluing the dollar by 8.37 percent.

May 22: Nixon confers with Soviet president Leonid I. Brezhnev during a visit to the Soviet Union. On May 26 the two leaders sign the Strategic Arms Limitation Treaty (SALT) to limit the growth of nuclear weapon and ballistic missile stockpiles in both countries.

June 17: Five men are arrested during a burglary of the Democratic party national headquarters in the Watergate Hotel complex in Washington, D.C. On June 19 the Federal Bureau of Investigation announces that it will investigate the burglars' connections to the Committee to Reelect the President, a Nixon administration campaign organization. The break-in signals the beginning of the Watergate scandal.

June 29: The Supreme Court declares the death penalty unconstitutional.

August 12: The last U.S. ground troops depart from South Vietnam. Significant numbers of support personnel and a substantial air presence remain in the country. The United States continues the strategic bombing of North Vietnam.

December 30: Nixon announces an end to the strategic bombing of North

President Gerald R. Ford in the Oval Office on the morning he pardoned Richard Nixon (photograph by David Hume Kennerly; courtesy of the White House)

Vietnam and also the resumption of peace talks.

1973

January 15: Nixon orders a halt to all military action against North Vietnam.

January 27: A cease-fire agreement is concluded between the United States, South Vietnam, North Vietnam, and the provisional government of the Viet Cong (which occupies portions of South Vietnam). U.S. troops complete their withdrawal from South Vietnam on March 29.

February 7: The U.S. Senate establishes a select committee to investigate charges of illegal activity during the presidential campaign of 1972.

April 30: Attorney General Richard G. Kleindienst, White House chief of staff H. R. Haldeman, and White House chief of domestic affairs John D. Ehrlichman resign, and White House counsel to the president John Dean is fired in connection with the growing Watergate scandal.

May 18: Attorney General Elliot Richardson names Archibald Cox special prosecutor in connection with the Watergate scandal.

June 16-25: Soviet president Leonid Brezhnev visits the United States and confers with Nixon.

July 16: Former aide Alexander Butterfield reveals the existence of a White House taping system.

October 3: The first major energy shortage in American history reaches a crisis point. Nixon announces a mandatory gasoline rationing program.

October 10: Vice-President Spiro Agnew resigns from office after pleading no contest to a variety of corruption charges. He is the second vice-president to resign. Gerald Ford is confirmed and sworn in as vice-president on December 6.

October 14: U.S. District Court judge

John Sirica orders Nixon to relinquish the "Watergate tapes." Nixon offers a set of transcripts as a compromise.

October 20: Attorney General Elliot Richardson resigns rather than enforce Nixon's order to fire Special Prosecutor Archibald Cox for refusing to compromise on the issue of the Watergate tapes. Assistant Attorney General William Ruckelshaus follows. William Rehnquist, third in line in the Department of Justice, finally fires Cox. Leon Jaworski is appointed special prosecutor on November 5.

November 26: District Court judge John Sirica orders Nixon to turn over the Watergate tapes. Nixon refuses to comply.

1974

January 2: Nixon signs an act limiting the speed limit on federal and state highways to 55 m.p.h.

January 4: Nixon refuses to comply with a subpoena, issued by the Senate Select Committee, for Watergate-related tapes and documents.

February 6: The U.S. House of Representatives authorizes the Judiciary Committee to begin impeachment hearings against President Nixon. The hearings begin on May 9.

March 1: Seven former presidential aides are indicted in connection with the Watergate cover-up: John Mitchell, H. R. Haldeman, John D. Ehrlichman, Charles Colson, Robert C. Mardian, Kenneth Parkinson, and Gordon Stracham.

April 11: The Judiciary Committee subpoenas tapes and records of White House conversations relating to the Watergate cover-up.

April 30: Nixon releases an edited transcript of White House conversations pertaining to Watergate. The published transcript becomes a national bestseller.

June 3: The Supreme Court rules that women must receive equal pay for equal work.

July 24: The Supreme Court votes 8-0 to require Nixon to hand over the Watergate tapes subpoenaed by the Judiciary Committee. The president complies on July 30. On July 27 and July 30, the committee hands down three articles of impeachment against Nixon. The articles recommend prosecution in the Senate for obstruction of justice, abuse of presidential power, and contempt of Congress. On August 5, a transcript of a June 23, 1972, tape is released to the press. The transcript reveals that Nixon directed the Federal Bureau of Investigation to halt its investigation of the Watergate break-in.

August 9: Nixon resigns the presidency. He is the first president to resign from office.

GERALD R. FORD

1974

August 9: Inauguration of Ford as the thirty-eighth president.

September 8: Ford grants Nixon a complete and unconditional pardon for all offenses he may have committed during his presidency.

November 23-24: Ford and Soviet president Leonid Brezhnev confer on arms limitation issues in Vladivostok, Soviet Union.

1975

April 16: The government of Cambodia surrenders to Communist-led rebel forces.

April 30: The government of South Vietnam surrenders unconditionally to

Left to right: Egyptian president Anwar Sadat, President Jimmy Carter, Israeli prime minister Menachem Begin, and Rosalyn Carter at Camp David, Maryland, September 1978 (courtesy of the Carter Family)

the provisional government of the Viet Cong.

July 17-19: Joint *Apollo-Soyuz* space mission results in the first rendezvous between U.S. and Soviet spacecraft.

July 28: Ford signs a seven-year extension of the Voting Rights Act of 1965.

1976

May 28: A treaty to limit the size of underground nuclear explosions is concluded between the United States and the Soviet Union.

July 2: The Supreme Court rules that the death penalty does not constitute cruel and unusual punishment, reversing its decision of June 29, 1972.

JIMMY CARTER

1977

January 20: Inauguration of Carter as the thirty-ninth president.

January 21: Carter pardons all Vietnam War draft resisters.

April 18: In a televised address, Carter declares the fight for American energy self-sufficiency "the moral equivalent of war" and recommends policies to limit energy use.

May 1-2: More than one thousand antinuclear-energy protesters occupy the construction site of a nuclear power plant at Seabrook, New Hampshire.

June 29: The Trans-Alaska oil pipeline is opened.

June 30: Carter declares his opposition to construction of the B-1 bomber.

August 4: Carter signs an act creating the Department of Energy.

August 10: The Panama Canal Treaty is concluded between the United States and Panama. The agreement transfers the canal from U.S. to Panamanian control.

1978

February 14: The United States agrees to sell jet fighters to Saudi Arabia, Egypt, and Israel.

May 11: Iranian troops put down large-scale Muslim fundamentalist demonstrations against the Shah of Iran.

June 12: Carter pledges the United States not to use nuclear weapons against nations that do not possess them or do not have access to them through allies.

September 6: Carter meets with Egyptian leader Anwar El-Sadat and Israeli leader Menachem Begin at Camp David, Maryland.

October 6: Congress extends the ratification period for the Equal Rights Amendment by thirty-nine months.

October 13: Carter signs the Civil Service Reform Act.

October 15: Carter signs an energy policy reform act.

December 1: Carter issues an executive order reserving 56 million acres of Alaskan wilderness from development.

1979

January 1: The United States and the People's Republic of China establish formal diplomatic relations.

February 1: Iranian spiritual leader Ayatollah Ruholla Khomeini returns to Iran after fifteen years of exile. The government of the Shah falls during the next week. On February 9 the Ayatollah takes control of the country.

March 26: Peace treaty concluded between Israel and Egypt.

June 18: The SALT II Treaty limiting the accumulation of nuclear warheads and ballistic missiles is concluded between the United States and the Soviet Union. The U.S. Senate never ratifies the treaty, but the United States adheres to its stipulations for the remainder of the Carter administration.

July 17: Nicaraguan president Anastasio Somoza resigns from office. The Sandinista Popular Front assumes control of the Nicaraguan government.

September 27: Carter signs an act creating the Department of Education.

November 4: Islamic fundamentalists and students storm the U.S. embassy in Teheran, Iran, taking sixty-six Americans hostage. The militants release thirteen black and female hostages on November 19.

December 21: Carter signs an act granting $1.5 billion in loan guarantees to the Chrysler Corporation.

December 27: The president of Afghanistan is executed, and a Soviet-sponsored rebel government takes control of the country. In retaliation, on January 4 Carter announces a U.S. embargo of sales of technology and a drastic reduction in grain sales to the Soviet Union.

1980

April 22: In response to Carter's request, the U.S. Olympic Committee votes to boycott U.S. participation in the 1980 Summer Olympics, to be held in Moscow, Soviet Union.

April 25: An Iranian hostage rescue mission is aborted when helicopters collide in the Iranian desert, killing eight U.S. soldiers. In protest against Carter's decision to order the raid, Secretary of State Cyrus Vance resigns on April 28.

1981

January 18: An agreement for the release of U.S. hostages in Iran is con-

President Ronald Reagan soliciting congressional support for his tax-cut bill, July 1981 (photograph by Bill Fitz-Patrick; courtesy of the White House)

cluded between the United States and Iran. Iran releases the hostages on January 20, after Ronald Reagan is sworn in as president.

RONALD REAGAN

1981

January 20: Inauguration of Reagan as the fortieth president.

April 12: The U.S. "space shuttle" *Columbia* lifts off on its maiden flight.

April 24: Reagan lifts a fifteen-month embargo on U.S. grain sales to the Soviet Union established by President Carter in retaliation for the Soviet invasion of Afghanistan.

June 16: Secretary of State Alexander Haig announces a decision to sell arms to the People's Republic of China.

July 7: Reagan nominates Sandra Day O'Connor to the Supreme Court. She is the first woman to be nominated to the court. The Senate later confirms the nomination.

August 4: Reagan signs an act reducing income taxes by 5 percent as of October 1, 1981, another 10 percent as of July 1, 1982, and another 10 percent as of July 1, 1983.

August 10: Reagan authorizes neutron bomb production, reversing a 1978 decision of President Carter.

August 19: U.S. Navy fighters shoot down two Libyan jets over international waters in the Gulf of Sidra.

October 8: Reagan lifts a Carter administration ban on the commercial reprocessing of nuclear fuel.

1982

June 30: The deadline passes for ratification of the Equal Rights Amendment with only thirty-five of the neces-

George and Barbara Bush and their dog Millie in the Oval Office, January 27, 1989

sary thirty-eight states consenting to the amendment.

August 20: Two hundred U.S. Marines land in Beirut, Lebanon, as part of a multinational force to oversee the withdrawal of forces of the Palestine Liberation Organization. A car bomb destroys the U.S. headquarters and kills 241 on October 23. The Marines begin to withdraw from Lebanon on February 7, 1984.

1983

April 18: The U.S. embassy in Beirut, Lebanon, is destroyed by a car bomb. Sixty-three die in the explosion.

May 24: Reagan signs an act appropriating $625 million for development of the MX mobile missile.

September 1: A Soviet military fighter shoots down a civilian South Korean airliner violating Soviet airspace, killing all 269 passengers and crew.

October 25: U.S. forces invade Grenada a week after a coup by pro-Cuban Marxists overthrows the legitimate leftist government. Hostilities end by November 2.

1984

March 20: The U.S. Senate rejects a school prayer amendment to the Constitution by a vote of fifty-six to forty-four.

April 26: Reagan visits China.

June 11: The Supreme Court rules that evidence obtained illegally may be admitted at a trial if it can be proven that the evidence inevitably would have been obtained legally.

July 17: Reagan signs an act requiring states to raise the drinking age to twenty-one by October 1, 1986, or face a 5 percent cut in federal highway funds.

September 20: The U.S. embassy in Beirut, Lebanon, is car-bombed, killing twenty-three.

1985

January 20: Reagan is inaugurated to his second term as president.

May 5: Reagan visits a military cemetery in Bitberg, West Germany. The visit creates a scandal because former Nazi soldiers are buried there.

September 9: Reagan announces U.S. economic sanctions against South Africa.

November 20-21: Reagan and Soviet president Mikhail Gorbachev meet in Geneva, Switzerland.

December 12: Reagan signs the Gramm-Rudman Budget Control Act.

1986

March 20: The U.S. House of Representatives votes down a $100 million bill to aid the Nicaraguan Contra forces.

April 14: U.S. fighter planes bomb Tripoli, Libya, in retaliation for the explosion in a West German discotheque the U.S. says Libya sponsored.

September 29-October 2: Congress overrides a presidential veto to enact anti-Apartheid economic sanctions against the nation of South Africa.

October 11-12: Reagan and Soviet president Mikhail Gorbachev meet in Reykjavik, Iceland, to discuss nuclear arms issues. Reagan nearly agrees to scuttle his "Star Wars" missile defense initiative in return for cuts in NATO and Warsaw Pact long-range nuclear missiles, but at the last minute he nixes the agreement.

1987

May 5-August 3: A joint congressional committee holds hearings on the Iran-Contra arms scandal, implicating many high officials in the Reagan administration, including National Security Advisor John Poindexter and Lt. Col. Oliver North of the National Security Agency, in dealings involving sales of U.S. missiles to the Iranian government and diversion of profits from those sales to accounts funding the military effort of antigovernment Contra forces in Nicaragua. No evidence that Reagan knew about the diversion of funds is uncovered.

October 14-16: The Dow Jones average on the New York stock exchange falls a record 261.43 points, including a largest-ever one-day drop of 108.35 points on October 16.

December 8: The Intermediate-range Nuclear Treaty is concluded between the United States and the Soviet Union, abolishing an obsolete class of Europe-based nuclear weapons and, more important, establishing precedents for on-site mutual inspection of weapons sites and further cuts in U.S.-Soviet nuclear missiles.

1988

December 21: A Pan American passenger jet flying over Lockerbie, Scotland, explodes, killing all 259 people aboard and several residents of Lockerbie. Experts find the explosion is the result of a bomb planted in the luggage compartment of the plane.

1989

January 20: Inauguration of George Bush as the forty-first president.

Fear in National Politics

by JAMES A. DUNLAP III

When one thinks of fear in national politics such episodes as the Red Scare of 1920 or the McCarthy era come immediately to mind. Closer examination reveals that fear has been an integral part of the American political mosaic since the colonial period. Only the circumstances surrounding fear have changed over the past three hundred years.

Seventeenth-century America saw its share of political events shaped wholly or in part by fear. In 1676 young Virginia settlers challenged Governor Sir William Berkeley's land and Indian policies during Bacon's Rebellion. The younger planters feared both Indian attack and an intransigent colonial government. Vigilante action against local Indian tribes soon pitted the forces of Nathaniel Bacon, a member of the House of Burgesses, and Berkeley, forcing the governor to flee to the Eastern Shore. Bacon's band burned Jamestown, but their leader's unexpected death took the wind out of the movement's sails. Berkeley reestablished power and rounded up the remaining Baconites, executing twenty-three. Bacon's serious challenge to the status quo prompted Berkeley to remark that maintaining control in the colony was a difficult matter given "a people where six parts of seven at least are poor, indebted, discontented and armed." Berkeley himself left office the following year.

A similar situation occurred in New England as an offshoot of the Glorious Revolution in the mother country. In 1688 Catholic King James II abdicated to Protestant William of Orange, who became monarch with his wife, Mary. After the Glorious Revolution in England, New England Puritans overthrew Governor Edmund Andros. Andros, an appointee of James II, had run roughshod over already-cherished colonial prerogatives regarding taxation and the sanctity of the Puritan church. Fearing that their officials stood to do the bidding of the Church of Rome, Puritans took to the streets to force a new governor and royal charter.

New England was also the locus of America's most notorious reign of fear, the Salem witch hysteria of 1692. Generally recognized by modern historians as a product of simmering conflicts between generations of Massachusetts families, of rivalries between town and country and the mass hysteria whipped up by fears of the supernatural, the episode resulted in the hangings of a score of accused women and men.

Later colonial developments also had fear as a crucial ingredient. The 1754 French and Indian War pitted English settlers against French traders, with Indians holding the balance of power. French emissaries warned the Iroquois that Englishmen intended to take Indian land and make them slaves. American settlers fled before the advance of the French and Indians with fears of the loss of access to the Mississippi and Ohio River valleys and imminent French rule. Calls for union in the face of the threat were accompanied by the exhortation "join or die." Two years after the start of hostilities the British crown committed army regulars to the conflict in the New World. The expense of waging war across the Atlantic spurred measures to increase Crown revenues by taxation in the colonies, hastening the American Revolution.

Taxation provided the unifying cause for the colonists that war had not.

President George Washington reviewing troops preparing to suppress the Whiskey Rebellion, 1794 (painting attributed to Frederick Kemmelmeyer; courtesy of the Metropolitan Museum of Art)

The Sugar Act of 1764, providing for import duty collection by a new vice-admiralty court, prompted protests against the taxation policies of the Crown. New Yorkers objected to the tax, designed to raise revenues rather than provide funds for the administration of the colony, because no representatives from New York sat in Parliament. The Stamp Act of the following year hit much closer to home, uniting newspaper editors, lawyers, and tavern owners in an outcry against British tyranny. Throughout the colonies stamp dis tributors were hung in effigy. Massachusetts lieutenant governor Thomas Hutchinson's house was picked clean by an angry mob. The Sons of Liberty, a coalition of shopkeepers and artisans, instilled fear into the hearts of tax men and Tories with vigilante action. Fears of further taxation by England prompted the formation of the Stamp Act Congress, America's first colonial assembly. Parliament, though it viewed the meeting as a "dangerous tendency," repealed the Stamp Act in 1766.

Colonial prerogatives were further insulted by the duties, especially those on tea, imposed by the 1767 Townsend Act. Local committees enforced non-importation, publishing the names of those not in compliance and boycotting their businesses. Unrest over British control reached a fever pitch in 1770 with the Boston Massacre, proof positive that another colonial fear—that of a hostile standing army—could only result in tyranny and death. The Tea Act of 1773 resulted in mob action over continued fears of economic oppression when colonists disguised as Indians tossed tea valued at ten thousand pounds sterling into Boston Harbor. The resulting "Intolerable" Acts only reinforced fears of continued British rule.

Colonial leaders injected their exhortations to fight for national independence with appeals to fear. *Common Sense* author Thomas Paine railed against King George III as the royal brute of Britain. John Adams expressed fears of British plans to enforce imperial control and to destroy civil liberties in the colonies. Benjamin Franklin noted from Europe the corrupt state of Old World regimes. Paine's rabble-rousing combined with the reason of some of the finest minds in Western history to produce a revolution that established the United States of America.

The new nation experienced its own share of political events based on fear. Shays's Rebellion of 1786-1787 was America's first full-fledged scare. Mob rule was directed not against the Crown, but against the government of the United States. Five hundred Massachusetts farmers, reeling from debt, foreclosures, and hard times, joined with Revolutionary War veteran Daniel Shays in a defiant challenge to federal authority. Demanding the issue of paper money, Shays and his followers attacked the government arsenal at Springfield. The Continental Congress authorized the use of thirteen hundred troops to augment a force of four thousand led by merchants from eastern Massachusetts, a force that eventually prevailed over the rebels in early 1787. Many Americans feared a radical division of private property and pushed for a stronger national government and a replacement for the Articles of Confederation: the Constitution.

George Washington, the nation's first chief executive, was forced to deal with still more unrest. In 1794 farmers in western Pennsylvania protested the federal government's tax on whiskey. Those farmers, in the Whiskey Rebellion, feared a loss of livelihood with the tax on their distilled corn. Shipping corn to eastern markets in bulk was too expensive, and the new federal excise roused fears similar to those prior to the Revolution. Outraged farmers met in convention in Pittsburgh to blast the Federalist tax policies of Alexander Hamilton, Washington's Treasury secretary. An angry President Washington denounced the meeting as an illegal gathering and appeared at the head of a thirteen-thousand-man army sent to put down the insurrection. In the face of that heavy show of force the rebels dispersed. Only two were convicted of treason, and they were later pardoned by Washington. Still, the action stirred up more political animosity. Thomas Jefferson and other anti-Federalists feared the aggrandizement of the central government even more than popular revolt. Washington noted his fear of such political differences in his 1796 Farewell Address with a denunciation of the divisive effects of party politics.

Such was the influence of Mr. Hamilton in Congress, that, without any recommendation from the President, they passed a bill to raise an army, not a large one, but enough to overturn the then Federal Government. Nor did I adopt this idea of an alien or sedition law. I recommended no such thing in my speech. Congress, however, adopted these measures. . . . I knew there was need enough for both, and therefore I consented to them.

—*Letter of John Adams to the editor of the* Boston Patriot, *1808, ten years after President Adams signed the Alien and Sedition Acts*

Jefferson's fears of government power were realized during the administration of Federalist president John Adams. The Alien and Sedition Acts of 1798 had the effect of stifling the Federalists' political opposition. The combined acts were directed mainly at recent emigrants from Europe, mainly those who would be sympathetic to Jefferson's Republican party. Fearing they would be written out of political contention, Jefferson and James Madison authored the Virginia and Kentucky Resolutions, in which the Republicans announced that they were "duty-bound to interpose" against aggrieving federal laws, giving fuel to secessionist arguments for later generations of politicians that feared federal power.

The election of 1800 pitted the Republican forces of Jefferson and those of Federalist John Adams. That the nation was able to engineer a peaceful transition of power amid naked plays on political fear is the true miracle of the Jeffersonian revolution. To the Republicans, the Federalists had themselves

Cartoon by Alexander Anderson satirizing the effects on New England merchants of the U.S. embargo on trade with Great Britain implemented during President Thomas Jefferson's second term (courtesy of the New York Public Library)

established the revolutionary bugbears they had sworn to prevent: a large standing army, heavy taxes, and a federal government that subverted individual liberties. Republicans also feared involvement in the European war on the side of the British. On the other hand, Federalists characterized Jefferson as an atheist and a political fanatic who also was a drunkard, an enemy of religion, and the father of mulatto children. Timothy Dwight, president of Yale University, warned that the election of Jefferson would make "our wives and daughters the victims of legal prostitution; soberly dishonored; speciously polluted." At least one New England newspaper predicted civil war, "with murder, robbery, rape, adultery, and incest . . . openly taught and practiced."

The election, a close one among Jefferson, Adams, Aaron Burr, and Charles Cotesworth Pinckney, resulted in an electoral tie between Jefferson and Burr. In the House of Representatives, Federalist congressmen threw their support to Burr. The House faced a choice between Jefferson, the alleged "brandy-soaked defamer of churches," and Burr, "whose public principles," according to Hamilton, had "no other spring or aim than his own aggrandizement." With Hamilton's reluctant support, Jefferson was elected president on the thirty-sixth ballot on February 17, 1801. Burr, who received the second-highest number of votes, became vice-president.

Jefferson's presidential tenure saw many issues revolving around fear. His avowed goal of reducing the size and power of the central government was shelved to purchase Louisiana. Eastern Federalists, appalled that the Constitution had been reduced to a "blank paper," feared eventual political alliances against them by the burgeoning South and West. Some even suggested a confederacy of New York, New Jersey,

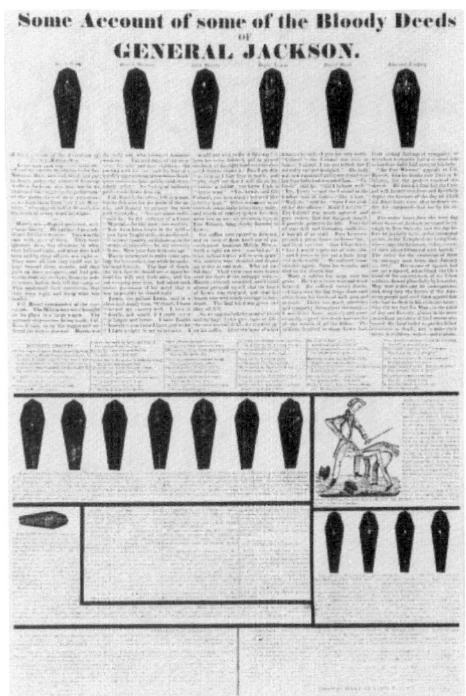

Some Account of some of the Bloody Deeds of GENERAL JACKSON.

"Coffin Handbill," published during the presidential campaign of 1828, recounting military executions carried out under candidate Gen. Andrew Jackson's command during the War of 1812

New England, and Canada "exempt from the corrupt and corrupting influence of the aristocratic Democrats of the South."

Nor was Jefferson helped by the Burr-Hamilton affair, in which the vice-president killed Alexander Hamilton in a duel near Weehawken, New Jersey. Burr soon led an unsuccessful plot to detach the western portion of the United States and was placed on trial for high treason. He was acquitted in 1807 and promptly left for self-imposed exile in Europe. Burr was the inspiration for the Twelfth Amendment, ratified in 1804, that revamped the electoral process and separated the offices of presidency and vice-presidency.

As chief executive, Jefferson often faced political dilemmas that forced choices between practicality and ideology. Those dilemmas often were accompanied by fear. As the U.S. Navy and merchant fleet got caught up in the Napoleonic Wars, Jefferson declared an embargo that forbade land and seaborne commerce with foreign nations. The embargo was a disaster for Jefferson and brought widespread unemployment, economic hardship, and a fall in agricultural prices. New Englanders deprived of trade led the outcry. Fearing federal power, Massachusetts and Connecticut threatened to interpose by nullifying the embargo and laws drawn up to enforce it. The embargo was lifted in 1809 after the election of Jefferson's successor, James Madison.

The lengthy Republican reign known as the Era of Good Feelings was, unfortunately, also marred by the politics of fear. Most notable was the bitterly divisive War of 1812. Madison's war message to Congress cited British interference with American trade, a blockade of the Eastern Seaboard, impressment of American sailors, and British-inspired Indian attacks that spared "neither age nor sex." Facing a far more powerful foe, the United States suffered reverses in Canada and along the Great Lakes. On August 24, 1814, British forces invaded Washington, D.C., and burned public buildings, including the executive mansion, while Madison fled to Virginia and Maryland. In December 1814 the United States accepted a treaty that assured the status quo antebellum.

That same month Federalists met at the Hartford Convention to denounce "Mr. Madison's War." New England states had, in fact, hindered the war effort by refusing to pay taxes on supply troops and by boycotting war loans. At Hartford delegates from five New England states met in secrecy and adopted resolutions designed to reduce significantly the power of the central government. Again the concept of interposition against "deliberate, dangerous and palpable infractions of the Constitution" manifested itself. Delegates sought to restrict the federal power to declare war, regulate commerce, and admit new states. They also sought to limit the presidency to one term and to abolish

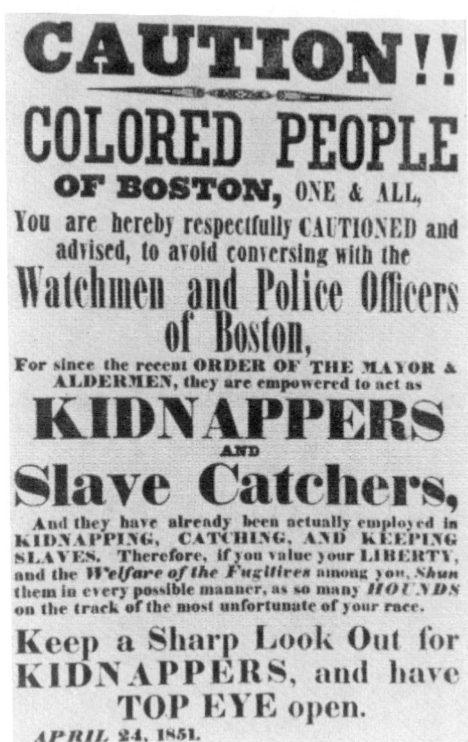

Poster addressed to certain citizens of Boston, April 24, 1851 (Library of Congress)

the three-fifths compromise in the Constitution. But bad timing doomed the Hartford Convention. News of the signing of the Treaty of Ghent and Andrew Jackson's galvanizing victory in the Battle of New Orleans undermined the Federalist effort, and left them open to ridicule. Worse, the Federalists were branded as traitors, and the party never recovered from the blunder.

The Panic of 1819, an economic disaster that revealed deep political and sectional divisions in the United States, further shattered the Era of Good Feelings. The panic was followed by a three-year depression marked by bank failures, the halving of farm prices, widespread joblessness, and the collapse of western land prices. The panic so shocked South Carolina's John C. Calhoun that he abandoned his nationalist "War Hawk" views to become the South's leading spokesman for states' rights. It set off several rounds of fear-inspired politics including struggles over stay laws to protect debtors and sectional arguments over the relative benefits of tariffs. Resentments against banks, property qualifications for voting, and privileged interests would continue for another generation.

God knows that I detest slavery, but it is an existing evil, for which we are not responsible, and we must endure it, till we can get rid of it without destroying the last hope of free government in the world.

—Letter of President Millard Fillmore to Senator Daniel Webster, October 23, 1850

In 1820 the issue of slavery arose during the deliberations over statehood for Missouri. To Thomas Jefferson the slavery crisis was a "fireball in the night." Central to the Missouri crisis was the expansion of slavery into new territories as the United States made its inexorable way to the Pacific. Described by John Quincy Adams as the "title page to a great tragic volume," the Missouri Compromise admitting Missouri as a slave state and Maine as a free state and extending a demarcation line across the continent served only to delay more controversy on the issue. Slavery would remain America's leading political bugbear for the next forty years.

The Jacksonian era was also rife with the politics of fear. In 1824 the presidential election featured a four-way race among Andrew Jackson, John Quincy Adams, Henry Clay, and William Crawford. Jackson received the highest number of popular votes but not an electoral majority. In the House of Representatives, Clay threw his support to Adams with the comment that killing twenty-five hundred Englishmen in New Orleans hardly qualified one for the presidency. Later Adams named Clay secretary of state, prompting the cry "corrupt bargain" from the Jacksonians. The tag would follow Adams through the one-term presidency that briefly delayed the rise of Jackson.

The subsequent election of Jackson

in 1828 served as a wellspring for the politics of fear. Jackson's detractors were legion, and the 1828 campaign centered on the background of "Old Hickory." Prominently displayed were handbills showing the coffins of deserters supposedly executed at Jackson's command. Unruly crowds at the inauguration ceremony instilled fears of mob rule among eastern aristocrats.

Jackson's pointed claims to be the representative of the common man instilled fear into the hearts of the "better sort." One central political episode during Jackson's tenure revolved around that class issue. Jackson's 1832 veto of the bill rechartering the Second Bank of the United States pitted the common man's president against eastern monied interests represented by bank chairman Nicholas Biddle. Biddle scoffed that Jackson's experience as an Indian scalper hardly indicated that the president would have his way with the bank. Jackson did prevail, however, by couching the issue in terms of a struggle between honest farmers and mechanics, and privileged speculators and bankers bent on maintaining an unfair advantage.

Another hotly contested controversy involved Jackson and Calhoun over the tariff issue. South Carolinians, in the throes of a prolonged depression, objected to federal tariffs enacted in 1828 and 1832. Calhoun maintained that a protective tariff was detrimental to southern economic well-being. Far more was at stake, however. White South Carolinians faced a black majority in the state and feared that the high tariff would damage its hold on the institution of slavery, already weakened by the fall in cotton prices, soil exhaustion, and out-migration. Calhoun's fears were not eased by the bloody Nat Turner revolt of 1831, which happened to follow the founding of William Lloyd Garrison's abolitionist newspaper, the *Liberator*. Jackson placed union above section and stared down Calhoun's threat.

Politicians during Jackson's tenure displayed a fascination with fear that usually centered on privilege. Aversion to Freemasonry spawned the Anti-Masonic Party in the 1830s. In 1826 the author of a scandalous exposé of the Fraternal Order of Freemasons disappeared in New York State. Subsequent investigations revealed that almost all New York state legislators were Freemasons. Aversion to secrecy and privilege drove the Anti-Masons to major third-party status.

Jackson himself served as the impetus for the founding of a new political party, the Whigs. Political foes labeled

THE CRIME AGAINST CHARLES SUMNER

In 1856 the exploding issue of slavery inspired fear and violence not only among combatants in the Kansas Territory but also between a senator and a representative in Washington. In May, Massachusetts senator Charles Sumner, a longtime antislavery advocate, gave a speech later known as "The Crime Against Kansas" in which he blasted slavery, the South, and South Carolina senator A. P. Butler in often lewd and insulting language. Absent from the Senate, Butler was unable to respond to Sumner's charges.

Butler's nephew, South Carolina representative Preston Brooks, avenged the insult shortly there-thereafter in the Senate chamber where he viciously attacked Sumner with a walking stick. Sumner, badly beaten, was absent from the Senate for three years. The "caning" earned Brooks the undying admiration of the Southland but stirred anew northern fears of a slaveholder's conspiracy. The Brooks-Sumner affair further convinced northern public opinion that southerners treated everyone as they treated their slaves—with violence and impunity.

Cartoon depicting the 1856 assault of Massachusetts senator Charles Sumner by South Carolina representative Preston Brooks from the perspective of the North

the president "King Andrew I," a tyrant and usurper of power. Several factions united in the single aspect of opposition to Jackson. Fearing Jackson's power as that "of an absolute and highly despotic temper," the Whigs took their name from the party in seventeenth-century England that challenged the authority of the Crown. The Whigs soon appropriated Jacksonian techniques and elected two presidents. Both William Henry Harrison and Zachary Taylor were war heroes in the Jackson mold. Both also died while in office, leaving the presidency to men less committed to Whig ideals.

The period that directly preceded the American Civil War was riddled with the politics of fear. As the impending secession crisis of 1860 bore down, the two sections squared off with extreme visions of one another. The South saw the North as a nation of abolitionists. The North saw the South as a nation of slaveholders with every white person holding the chains of bondage. Seen in retrospect, secession came after protracted wrangling over the politics of territorial expansion during which both sides systematically exploited the emotion of fear.

Manifest Destiny's unyielding drive west took slave culture into the Mexican province of Texas. By 1836 Anglo settlers gained their independence from Mexico and petitioned for annexation to the United States as a slave state. Antislavery forces blocked the annexation for a time. They feared a slaveholders' conspiracy to expand the peculiar institution into new territory. The Texas question proved the central issue of the election of 1844. Democrat James K. Polk won the election and presided over the 1845 annexation and the resulting war with Mexico.

Mexico took great exception to the annexation of Texas and moved to protect its historical integrity. Manifest Destiny at this juncture meant the possibility of gaining virtually all of Mexico's northern territory. The brief war ended with most of Mexico's northern provinces in American hands. But southern desires for land beyond the Rio Grande were blunted by northern fears of the slaveholders' conspiracy. Fears of the expansion of slavery into new territories brought the issue to the forefront of national politics as the captured lands later organized for statehood.

The controversy surrounding the Wilmot Proviso illustrates the phenomenon. In 1846 House Democrat David Wilmot attached an amendment to one of President Polk's appropriations bills. Wilmot's amendment barred slavery from any territory gained as a result of the Mexican War. The proviso created a furor across the nation. Southerners denounced the move as treason. Northerners feared competition between free labor and slave labor in the new territories. The Wilmot Proviso failed to get beyond the Senate but raised fears of a deep-rooted future struggle over slavery.

America's next bout of fear came in 1850 as the western territory of California petitioned for entry into the union as a free state. The admission of a new free state would upset the existing balance of fifteen slave and fifteen free states. Henry Clay hoped to allay the fears of both sides with the Compromise of 1850, in which California entered as a free state. In return, the South received a more stringent Fugitive Slave Law. The Compromise of 1850 did not ease sectional tensions, however. The Fugitive Slave Law served only to heighten fears in the North. Highly publicized and emotional, fugitive slave cases stirred up untold resentment in the North. The image of innocent blacks being chased by southern slave catchers served as the inspiration for Harriet Beecher Stowe's *Uncle Tom's Cabin*, the epitome of antislavery literature.

In only four years the slavery issue resurfaced, this time in the vast Nebraska Territory. Stephen A. Douglas proposed the organization of Nebraska Territory into the states of Kansas and Nebraska. The slavery issue would be decided in each state by the settlers themselves, in a process known as popular sovereignty. The Kansas-Nebraska Act implementing the Douglas Plan implied the repeal of the Missouri Compromise and raised new fears of southern designs on the territories. Northern politicians denounced the act as a gross violation of a sacred pledge to limit slavery to the South. They feared that popular sovereignty would perpetuate the institution and block the migration of free labor into the territories. The Kansas-Nebraska controversy helped spawn the Republican party, as antislavery Democrats and Whigs split off to form a new political alliance. Bloodshed also erupted in Kansas, as popular sovereignty soon broke down into election fraud and violence. In 1856 the struggle earned the tag "Bleeding Kansas" as a civil war erupted between proslavery and antislavery forces there. One particularly zealous antislavery band was led by John Brown. Massachusetts senator Charles Sumner endured a celebrated caning at the hand of South Carolina representative Preston Brooks, the result of Sumner's giving an inflammatory and insulting Senate-floor speech against Kansas slavery and Brooks's senator-uncle.

In 1857 the slavery issue reached the Supreme Court in the landmark *Dred Scott* case. Unfortunately, the Court's decision did not diminish fear over the issue. In the case a slave, Dred Scott, petitioned for his freedom on the grounds that his sojourn with his master in free territory above the Missouri Compromise line had ended his bondage. The Court rejected the argument, ruling that as a slave Scott was not a citizen and as such could not sue. The Court also ruled that the Missouri Compromise was unconstitutional in that it deprived slaveholders of their property without due process of law as outlined in the Fifth Amendment. The *Dred Scott* decision fell far short of the final settlement of the slavery issue envisioned by Chief Justice Roger B. Taney.

Reconstruction-period photograph, apparently defaced, of members of the Ku Klux Klan (courtesy of the Rutherford B. Hayes Library)

It only enhanced sectional hostility, as southerners celebrated the decision as vindication of their cause and northerners feared a "slave power" conspiracy to legalize slavery throughout the United States.

John Brown's 1859 raid on the federal arsenal at Harper's Ferry, Virginia, served for many southerners as the dreaded culmination of two generations of abolitionist agitation. With his raid Brown hoped to instigate a general slave uprising in the South. He failed in that effort and was captured, tried, and hanged. Still, Brown became a martyr to the antislavery cause. To slaveholders he represented the embodiment of servile insurrection.

The 1860 election caused the final fracture in the first American Union. The election of Republican Abraham Lincoln proved too much for South Carolina Democrats to bear. Fearing a "Black Republican" chief executive, South Carolina seceded on December 20, 1860. Months later, the first shots of the Civil War rang out at Fort Sumter, marking the beginning of the Civil War. The four-year ordeal ended with the realization of the white South's two great fears, military defeat and emancipation.

The Reconstruction period between 1865 and 1877 provided ample manifestations of the politics of fear. Aside from the struggle between the victors and the vanquished, another struggle, between President Andrew Johnson and Congress, ensued as well. Johnson's Reconstruction policies allowed the election of former Confederates to high office and the enactment of Black Codes creating de facto southern slavery in 1866. The codes greatly restricted the economic leverage and movement of former slaves. Northern Republicans feared both the return of a powerful southern Democratic party and a new form of slavery. Congressional "radicals" eventually won out over Johnson and nearly succeeded in removing him from office. Radical Reconstruction, with its military districts, disfranchisement of former Confederates, and new Republican-dominated southern state governments, proved a vastly different arrangement than Johnson would have preferred.

Reconstruction fueled fears for the remainder of the nineteenth century and beyond. Exploitation of fear became a finely honed skill in the South. Southern politicians highly exaggerated the "horrors" of "black rule" for generations as pretexts for the white political unity, the disfranchisement of blacks, and the rigid adherence to racial segregation that marked southern life until well into the 1960s.

In the South, Ku Klux Klan terror instilled fear in blacks and white Republicans. Violent intimidation campaigns restored conservative white rule to many parts of the South, especially in the Carolinas and Mississippi. In Mississippi intimidation by white "rifle clubs" eliminated the Republican electorate by

Striking steelworkers at the Carnegie Mills in Homestead, Pennsylvania, 1892

A disputed Kansas state election in 1893 resulted in an armed takeover of the statehouse by Kansas Republicans, who warned Populist "insurgents" to stay away (courtesy of the Kansas State Historical Society).

THE RED SCARE

One casualty of America's war to make the world safe for democracy was some measure of American democracy itself. During the war, the Woodrow Wilson administration suppressed antiwar dissent and capitalized on Americans' suspicions of foreigners and radicals. Fear of disloyalty did not end with the Armistice in 1918. Continued hysteria over radicalism resulted in the Red Scare of the 1920s, one of the most fervid episodes of fear-inspired political action in American history. Central to the Red Scare episode were the Palmer raids of 1920, in which suspected communists, anarchists, and other radicals were arrested in a campaign led by U.S. attorney general A. Mitchell Palmer. Some 250 alien radicals were deported as a result of the raids.

Asked if mass arrest and deportation of anarchists would protect the U.S. government, Palmer hotly replied that, if left to the radicals, "there wouldn't be any such thing [as American government] left. In place of the United States government we should have the horror and terror of bolshevik tyranny such as is destroying Russia now. Every scrap of radical literature demands the overthrow of the existing government. . . . Their manifesto further embraces the various organizations in this country of men and women obsessed with discontent, having disorganized relations to American society. These include the I.W.W.'s [the Syndicalist union the Industrial Workers of the World], the most radical socialists, the misguided anarchists, the agitators who oppose the limitations of unionism, the moral perverts and the hysterical neurasthenic women who abound in communism."

1875. South Carolina's "red shirts" propelled conservative Wade Hampton to the governorship in 1876 through a campaign of violence designed both to destroy the state's Republican party and to oust federal troops guarding the statehouse.

By 1877 northerners were weary of attempts to realign southern society and were more concerned with fears of their own. The Compromise of 1877 ending Reconstruction was followed closely by the nation's worst railroad strikes. Workers in Baltimore, Pittsburgh, and Chicago reacted to wage cuts with a widespread strike that paralyzed the Midwest. President Rutherford B. Hayes, reluctant to continue backing Reconstruction with armed force, sent federal troops into battle with the strikers. The fear of class revolt in the North warranted far more attention than the protection of black rights in the South.

The remainder of the nineteenth century featured several episodes that centered on the issue of fear, as society buffeted America's "better sort" from below and above. Farmers and immigrant workers agitated for a greater realization of the American dream. In doing so they instilled fear into the hearts and minds of America's middle class.

Farmers' alliances called into question the prevailing mood of laissez-faire. Seeking relief from the steady decline of farm prices and the monopolistic practices of big business, the farm movement culminated in the People's, or Populist, party. That third party made an impressive bid for the presidency in 1892. In 1896 the Populists fused with the Democrats and rallied around the issue of silver coinage as the panacea for the farmers' ills. The Populists were both ridiculed as "hayseed socialists" and feared as "dangerous classes." Promising a "full dinner pail," the Republicans denounced Democrat William Jennings Bryan as an anarchist and won the election handily.

During the same period, America's

Cartoon by Rollin Kirby that appeared during the 1932 presidential campaign

"old immigrants" responded to the "new immigrants" with virulent opposition. Classic struggles between capital and labor at Haymarket Square in Chicago (1886), Homestead, Pennsylvania (1892), and among Pullman sleeper-car workers in Chicago (1894) resulted in violent confrontations. Fearing anarchy, authorities employed an arsenal that included court injunctions, a sympathetic press, professional strikebreakers, state militia, and federal troops. Equating labor organization with radicalism, government and business combined to ensure "law and order." That meant, above all, protecting private property and maintaining production.

Concentrated capital instilled its own brand of fear and resulted in attempts to rein in the power of corporations and railroads. In 1887 Congress passed the Interstate Commerce Act to regulate railroad rates. Three years later Congress approved the Sherman Antitrust Act outlawing conspiracies in the restraint of trade. Both were landmark reforms that became fully operational only in the twentieth century. The regulatory urge continued through the Progressive Era's hold on the politics of the 1910s.

With Woodrow Wilson the Progressive Era reached its zenith. Zeal abroad matched activism at home during World War I. America's involvement in that conflict brought crucial developments in the politics of fear. The 1917 Bolshevik Revolution saw communism emerge as a major generator of fear in America. Apprehension over a changing world order pushed fear to new heights.

American socialists and pacifists, as well as German- and Irish-Americans, opposed the war. Wilson appointed newspaperman George Creel to combat antiwar sentiment through the Committee on Public Information. The Creel Committee churned out propaganda playing on fear. Touting the war effort as a crusade to make the world safe for democracy, the committee's efforts included articles, films, and recruiting advertisements. Liberty Bond drives were so conducted as to make nonbuyers appear traitorous. The campaign for "100% Americanism" had its ugly side with an anti-German and antiimmigrant bias. Americans were harassed and fired from jobs over the loyalty issue. In June 1917 the Espionage Act banned socialist publications. In 1919 leader Eugene V. Debs was sentenced to ten years under sedition provisions in the act. Constitutional rights of free speech were routinely denied during a war fought ostensibly to safeguard democracy.

There are biological and cultural reasons why there should be no mixing of Oriental and Caucasian blood.

—Letter of Secretary of Commerce Herbert Hoover to President Calvin Coolidge concerning pending legislation on immigration quotas, April 18, 1924

The period immediately following World War I also saw a resurgence of the Ku Klux Klan with a new nativist fla-

FEAR AND F.D.R.

Upon assuming the presidency on March 4, 1933, Franklin D. Roosevelt immediately tried to calm the fears of the public. In his inaugural address he dealt directly with the issue: "Let me first assert my firm belief that the only thing we have to fear is fear itself—nameless, unreasoning, unjustified terror which paralyzes needed efforts to convert retreat into advance. . . . I shall ask Congress for the one remaining instrument to meet the crisis—broad executive power to wage a war against the emergency, as great as the power that would be given me if we were in fact invaded by a foreign foe. . . . The people of the United States have not failed. In their need they registered a mandate that they want direct, vigorous action. They have asked for discipline and direction under leadership. They have made me the present instrument of their wishes. In the spirit of the gift, I take it."

vor. The new Klan was anti-immigrant, anti-Catholic, and anti-Jewish, with activity centering in the Midwest rather than the South. Fear of immigrants reached such a stage that Congress passed sweeping legislation in 1921, 1924, and 1927 that severely restricted the immigration of Europeans and Asians.

The 1920s ended with the Wall Street crash that brought the Great Depression, another watershed of American fear. Through the haze of economic dislocation, unemployment, bank failures, and overall anxiety, Americans turned to a politician who told them they had nothing to fear but fear itself. Democrat Franklin D. Roosevelt projected an attitude of smiling confidence. His radio-broadcast fireside chats were a key component of New Deal efforts to ease fears and restore confidence. Unfortunately, the New Deal did not end the Great Depression. The economy rebounded fully only after America assumed its massive production role in World War II.

World War II for America was another patriotic exercise. Americans were rewarded for their war effort with superpower status, an unscathed mainland, and unchallenged economic superiority. Still, fear remained a central component in American life. The war ended with the atomic destruction of two of Japan's major cities. The United States and the Soviet Union, once allies in the fight against Nazi fascism, faced off across Eastern Europe and around the world. At home Americans faced fear once again. Again the bugbears were communism from without and subversion from within. At stake early on was the nation's monopoly over nuclear weapons.

Buffeted by those fears, Harry Truman, president after the death of Roosevelt, was forced to protect his political position at home by ferreting out alleged Communists in government with the Federal Employee Loyalty Program. Congress passed legislation in a similar vein, including the Taft-Hartley Act of 1947, which banned Communists from labor union leadership, and the McCarran Internal Security Act of 1950, which made it illegal to advocate a Communist government. The House Un-American Activities Committee probed alleged communism in the motion picture industry and developed a spy and perjury case involving Alger Hiss, a prominent New Deal Democrat.

Wisconsin senator Joseph McCarthy was the most ardent of the fearmongers. McCarthy claimed to have uncovered Communist activity in the State Department and whipped up hysteria that coincided with the Chinese Communist revolution and the bitterly fought Korean War. The Wisconsin senator revealed the enormous power of television during broadcast hearings into alleged Communist activity in the U.S. Army.

In that episode McCarthy's allegations were proved a hoax, but only after lives and careers were irreparably damaged.

The American desire to contain communism led to the Cold War and to hot shooting wars in Korea and Vietnam in the 1950s, 1960s, and 1970s. Fear of communism continued as a major American bugbear, and communism was blamed for the civil rights movement, Vietnam War protest, and campus unrest. The arms race and its attending tensions and fears were alleviated somewhat in the 1970s with détente between the United States and the Soviet Union. The Ronald Reagan era brought renewed vigor to the fear of communism between 1981 and 1989, with the Republican chief executive publicly denouncing Russia as the "evil empire." Fear of communism has cooled considerably since late 1989 because of dramatic and widespread changes in the communist world. One by one the countries of Eastern Europe have thrown off Stalinist rule.

Reagan supporters say that massive American defense budgets brought the changes. The Soviets, they say, could not match American defense spending in their inefficient economy. Persistent efforts to keep up with the United States wrecked the Soviet economy, bringing on the major changes of *glasnost* and *perestroika* as well as the crumbling of repressive governments in the satellite nations.

Another major American fear in recent times has stemmed from nuclear weapons and nuclear power generation. Early fears centered on the loss of America's nuclear monopoly. Those fears resulted in the 1953 execution of Julius and Ethel Rosenberg, American radicals accused of passing atomic secrets to the Soviets. Later, after the Soviet Union obtained nuclear capability, fear of the arms race took precedent. The most notable example of nuclear-arms fear was the 1962 Cuban missile crisis. Two years after the communist revolution in Cuba, U.S. spy planes photographed Soviet missile sites on the island. President John F. Kennedy placed U.S. forces on full alert and ordered a naval blockade of Cuba. With the United States and the Soviet Union "eyeball to eyeball," Soviet premier Nikita Khruschev blinked first and agreed to remove the missiles, but not before America was convulsed with the fear of nuclear annihilation.

Federal Civil Defense Agency guidelines, 1950

Fear of nuclear war has gone hand in hand with fears of nuclear contamination either from accidents at nuclear power stations or their attendant hazardous wastes. This fear is a component of the consumer advocacy and antipollution efforts begun in the 1960s. Nuclear fear was realized in 1979 at the Three Mile Island nuclear power station near Harrisburg, Pennsylvania. An accident in one of the plant's reactors resulted in a partial core meltdown that released radioactive steam and water. The contamination forced the shutdown of the plant and a costly cleanup. The nuclear power industry came under seige from consumer opposition that delayed or canceled plant start-ups with protracted court battles.

The 1970s saw a new figure added to the American pantheon of fear—the Muslim fanatic. First the greedy oil sheikh entered during the 1973 Arab oil

FEAR AND WILLIE HORTON

The presidential administration of Ronald Reagan saw its share of fear-inspired politics, surrounding such issues as abortion, violent crime, and international terrorism. Critics maintain that Reagan's successor, George Bush, gained office in part because he pandered to fears engendered during Reagan's presidency. In the 1988 presidential campaign, Bush branded his opponent, Michael Dukakis, a "card-carrying" member of the American Civil Liberties Union. Bush also reflected white fears of blacks and violent crime in a series of campaign advertisements featuring Willie Horton, a black man and convicted murderer who raped a white woman while on furlough from a prison in Massachusetts, Dukakis's home state.

Bush relentlessly pursued Dukakis on the issue, claiming that Dukakis allowed "murderers out on vacation to terrorize innocent people. . . . Democrats can't find it in their hearts to get tough on criminals. . . . What did the Democratic governor of Massachusetts think he was doing when he let convicted first-degree murderers out on weekend passes, even after one of them brutally raped a woman and stabbed her fiance? . . . I think Governor Dukakis owes the American people an explanation of why he supports this outrageous program." The winning strategy in the Republican campaign against the diminutive Dukakis was articulated by Bush campaign director Lee Atwater: "We'll strip the bark off that little bastard and make Willie Horton his running mate."

embargo. Led by Saudi Arabia, Arab oil-producing countries halted the shipment of oil to retaliate for massive American military aid to Israel in the 1973 Arab-Israeli war. An energy crisis ensued, creating shortages of gasoline and fuel oil that disrupted the life-styles of Americans accustomed to inexpensive fuel.

In 1979 the glowering visage of the Ayatollah Ruholla Khomeini became the locus of fear after a revolution toppled the U.S.-backed Shah of Iran and seized the American embassy in Tehran. The Ayatollah's bearded countenance became the very symbol for kidnapping and terrorism in the Middle East, and for America's traditional fear of the exotic, the foreign, and the unknown. More recently, Iraqi leader Saddam Hussein emerged as the ultimate Middle Eastern villain after his invasion of Kuwait in August 1990. President George Bush compared Saddam to Hitler as he led a United Nations coalition of nations in employing economic sanctions and then a huge armed force to drive out the Iraqis.

In the 1980s Reaganism acted as an engine of fear with attacks on liberals and the encouragement of right-wing evangelicals. Issues centering on fear included abortion, violent crime, the budget deficit, international terrorism, toxic waste, global warming, acid rain, high cholesterol, and cancer. The ultimate health hysteria arose over Acquired Immune Deficiency Syndrome (AIDS), a disease that combined the volatile elements of sex and certain death. That AIDS was first discovered among homosexual males did nothing to lower the fear quotient.

Under Reagan's successor, George Bush, national and foreign policy has been driven by the fear of drugs. Drug testing has become nearly commonplace in the work force. Local, state, and federal authorities regularly conduct highly publicized raids on drug dealers. South American "drug cartels" have supplanted Communist dictatorships as dreaded foreign powers. Fear of the cocaine derivative known as "crack" justified the American invasion of Panama and the overthrow of Panamanian leader Manuel Noriega. Then Bush proved he was not a "wimp," as some had labeled him in the 1988 election, by flying to Cartagena, Colombia, for a "drug summit" in a nation ruled by so-called drug lords.

Critics say George Bush gained his office by pandering to the fears of white America. Bush branded his opponent, Democrat Michael Dukakis, a "card-carrying" member of the American Civil Liberties Union, a liberal organization resented by many middle-class Americans.

Recent events show that fear in American politics exhibits no sign of letting up. Indeed, key events of the early 1990s fall dramatically into the American tradition.

Secession Movements in American History

by WILLIAM PISTON

Although the word "secession" has become virtually synonymous with the establishment of the Confederacy in 1861, secession as a political theory or tactic has a much longer and more complex history in the American experience. Secession may be defined as the actual, attempted, or threatened withdrawal from the body politic of a subgroup that previously acquiesced to membership in the larger political organization, with the intention of establishing an autonomous government involving population and territory encompassing part of the former whole.

Such a precise definition makes it possible to separate secession movements from revolutions and filibustering. By this definition the war between Britain and its American colonies that began in 1775 was a secession movement, not a revolution, as the founding fathers ultimately sought autonomy for the thirteen colonies, not a revolutionary restructuring of the British domestic political system. In contrast, the overthrow of the Bourbon monarchy in France in the late eighteenth century was a true political revolution. Attempts by Native Americans to resist the tide of white expansion were neither secessionist nor revolutionary, because Native Americans never accepted the political sovereignty of the U.S. government. The Texas Revolution in 1836 was a secessionist movement within the context of Mexican history, but the admission of Texas to the Union in 1845 represented expansion in the context of American history. American intrigue, sponsorship, or tacit approval of nineteenth-century rebellions or filibusterings in the Floridas, the Caribbean, Mexico, and Latin America likewise represented expansion (however unsavory) rather than secession, because they did not involve areas considered previously to be part of the United States.

Ironically, the first attempt to secede from the United States occurred in Vermont in 1777, when American independence was by no means assured and the Second Continental Congress still governed the nation pending adoption of the Articles of Confederation. Prior to the American Revolution, settlers from Massachusetts, New York, and New Hampshire moved into the fertile region bounded on the east by the Connecticut River and on the west by the strategic Lake Champlain system, which constituted the traditional colonial invasion route to Canada. Conflicting land titles divided the inhabitants roughly into two groups, those acknowledging the authority of New York and those acknowledging the authority of New Hampshire. But many sought a government of their own, and the Revolution gave them the opportunity they needed.

The Allen brothers—Levi, Ira, and Ethan—were the largest landholders in a section of the disputed territory known as the Hampshire Grants. Ethan Allen won fame by leading the "Green Mountain Boys," a local militia unit, to victory against the British at Fort Ticonderoga in New York in May 1775. But in 1777 he and his brothers led a political movement that declared the Hampshire Grants and neighboring lands to be an independent region known as Vermont.

The Allens left Vermont's exact status conveniently and deliberately vague, allowing them to negotiate with both the British and the Continental Congress. Initially Vermont's inhabitants preferred American recognition, and they petitioned Congress for statehood in 1779. Representatives of New York and New Hampshire, however, successfully pressured Congress to deny recognition and cut off supplies to troops raised from the region. In response, some of Vermont's leading settlers formed the so-called Arlington Junto. Headed by Thomas Chittenden and Ira and Ethan Allen, it was composed of men who stood to gain socially, politically, and economically from an autonomous Vermont.

It is of definite moment that you should properly estimate the immense value of your national union to your collective and individual happiness . . . watching for its preservation with jealous anxiety; discountenancing whatever may suggest even a suspicion that it can in any event be abandoned, and indignantly frowning upon the first dawning of every attempt to alienate any portion of your country from the rest or to enfeeble the sacred ties which now link together the various parts.

—*President George Washington, Farewell Address,* American Daily Advertiser, *September 19, 1796*

In July 1780 representatives from Vermont approached the Continental Congress, threatening to make a separate peace with the British. While the move was largely a negotiating tactic meant to secure statehood, many Vermonters preferred colonial status under Britain rather than submission to the authority of New York or New Hampshire. In October, Ethan Allen held not-so-secret meetings with the British while other members of the Arlington Junto approached frontier communities within the acknowledged boundaries of New York and New Hampshire, hinting at the advantages of union with Vermont. When the legislatures of those states threatened to invade Vermont and divide it between them, the de facto government in Vermont responded in June 1781 by declaring certain areas of New York and New Hampshire annexed to their independent republic.

George Washington's victory at Yorktown in October 1781 ultimately settled the issue. With the British threat diminished, New York and New Hampshire began serious military preparations to reassert their authority over Vermont. Faced with that threat but encouraged by Washington's personal pledge to back Vermont statehood, the Vermont legislature rescinded its annexations. Tempers in New York and New Hampshire cooled as well. While frictions did not entirely disappear, the settlers in Vermont maintained their autonomy until they achieved statehood on March 4, 1791.

The government that admitted Vermont was the government of the Constitution, which went into effect in March 1789. Under both the Constitution and the earlier Articles of Confederation, the central government faced the vexing problem of resolving conflicting land claims resulting from the states' old colonial charters. Eventually the states were persuaded to cede their western lands to the national government. That took time, however, and the reluctance of Virginia and North Carolina to give up their claims caused such ill feeling with settlers living west of the Appalachian Mountains that some observers feared a breakup of the Union.

Many of the revolutionary generation feared that a country the size of the United States could not remain a single viable republic. Although in the 1780s and 1790s the nation did not extend beyond the Mississippi River or even embrace the Gulf of Mexico, the severe limitations of transportation in the late eighteenth century made effective government beyond the mountains difficult. Moreover, prior to the acquisition of New Orleans in 1803, the Spanish (and later, very briefly, the French) could threaten the economy of the West by denying settlers use of the Mississippi, for that great river offered the settlers the only cost-effective way of shipping their goods to market.

Fear of separation was widespread, if bewilderingly diverse. Henry Lee of Virginia warned President Washington that the western settlers would seize Spanish New Orleans if the government could not acquire it by negotiation. But Rufus King of Massachusetts countered that possession of New Orleans would make the overmountain settlers so independent of the seaboard population that secession would inevitably follow. From South Carolina, Charles Pinckney announced that procrastination would lead the westerners to swear allegiance to Spain. In January 1787 Thomas Jefferson wrote Madison about the trans-Appalachian settlements: "If they declare themselves a separate people, we are incapable of a single effort to retain them."

Talk of a "western conspiracy" was rife in the late 1790s, tarnishing the reputations of two heroes of the Revolution. George Rogers Clark, the captor of Vincennes, was unjustly accused of using his position as an Indian agent to unite the western settlements in a secessionist movement. John Sevier, a militia leader at Kings Mountain, worked with settlers in the overmountain counties of North Carolina to form a separate state of Franklin in December 1784. When Congress denied the state admission to the Union and North Carolina acted forcefully to reassert its authority, Sevier, elected governor of Franklin, approached Spanish officials with requests for a loan. While he contemplated a defensive alliance with Spain against North Carolinian aggression, he sought statehood, not independence. His efforts collapsed in 1789.

Some of Sevier's friends in the state of Franklin movement went further. Together with James White, a wealthy North Carolina land speculator, they became involved in 1786 in an attempted settlement at Muscle Shoals, in present-day Alabama. Their unofficial sponsor was the Spanish minister to the United States, Diego de Gardoqui, who hoped to keep America weak by promoting sectional tensions.

Charles Willson Peale's portrait of James Wilkinson, first territorial governor of Louisiana, who narrowly escaped federal indictment in connection with Aaron Burr's disunionist schemes in western America, 1805-1806 (Independence National Historical Park)

The Spanish, in turn, were manipulated by James Wilkinson, a hard-drinking former brigadier general under George Washington who possessed a knack for intrigue and personal aggrandizement. Wilkinson played both ends against the middle. He gained great popularity in the West by advocating statehood for the Kentucky region and free navigation of the Mississippi, but he also convinced Spanish officials that he was working for disunion and collected a handsome annual stipend for his efforts. Returning to the U.S. Army in 1791, he eventually became the senior officer but continued to accept

"The Hartford Convention or Leap No Leap": 1815 cartoon by William Charles depicting "Massachusetts" trying to lure "Connecticut" and "Rhode Island" into secession while a Federalist party leader prays for success

bribes for alleged services to Spain.

After the purchase of Louisiana in 1803, Wilkinson became governor of the new territory, and he soon became involved with an old friend, Aaron Burr, in grandiose schemes for an empire in the West. In addition to attempting to extort money from the Spanish and the British, their labyrinthine conspiracies involved, at one point or another, plans for a revolution in Mexico, colonization west of the Mississippi, and the detachment of some or all of the western states from the Union. Burr was tried and acquitted of treason in 1807. Wilkinson narrowly escaped indictment. Despite their comic-opera dimensions, the intrigues of Wilkinson and Burr testify to the fear of a western secession that characterized much of the late eighteenth and early nineteenth century.

The issue of secession was not limited to the West. Indeed, it plagued the earliest administrations under the Constitution. As secretary of the Treasury under President Washington, Alexander Hamilton proposed that the federal government assume the burden of debt that the states had incurred fighting for independence. Representatives of those states that had already paid their debts via state taxation protested that their constituents would in effect be taxed twice in order to pay the debts of the others. Those favoring Hamilton's scheme countered that it would benefit the country as a whole by placing the new nation on a sound financial base. A few politicians and their cronies, who had purchased state securities at low prices, stood to gain personally from debt assumption. Men on both sides of the issue threatened secession in the halls of Congress.

Congress enacted Hamilton's plan without incident in 1790, but the idea of secession resurfaced in 1798. By that time the followers of Hamilton (Federalists) and Jefferson (Democratic-Republicans) had coalesced into distinct political factions, giving rise to the first American two-party system. When Federalists secured passage of the Alien and Sedi-

JEFFERSON REFLECTS ON THE HARTFORD CONVENTION

In the *Anas,* or "Notes," that Thomas Jefferson wrote as a supplement to his autobiography, the former president looked back from the perspective of 1818 upon the political rivalries that threatened the American Union during the War of 1812:

> Federalism and monarchism have languished from that moment, until their treasonable combinations with the enemies of their country during the late war, their plots of dismembering the Union, and their Hartford convention, have consigned them to the tomb of the dead; and I fondly hope, we may now truly say, "we are all republicans, all federalists."

tion Acts in an attempt to suppress opposition to the administration of John Adams, many of Jefferson's followers advocated secession. Jefferson counseled patience and the crisis passed, but not before a new and explosive political doctrine was introduced into the American political equation—nullification. Believing the Alien and Sedition Acts unconstitutional but finding no remedy in a Supreme Court dominated by Federalist justices, Jefferson and James Madison penned resolutions passed by the state legislatures of Kentucky and Virginia that asserted the right of state governments to declare acts of Congress null and void within their boundaries. The federal government ignored the resolutions, but the issue of states' rights remained crucial and divisive for the next six decades.

The triumph of Jefferson's followers in the elections of 1800 so alarmed some Federalists that a secessionist movement sprang up in New England, the party's stronghold. After Hamilton's death, Senator Thomas Pickering of Massachusetts assumed a position of leadership within the Federalist party. Adamantly opposed to Jefferson's foreign policy and outraged by the Louisiana Purchase, Pickering openly advocated secession by 1804 and continued to do so for the next ten years. He envisioned a peaceful separation of the New England states, perhaps joined by New York and New Jersey, with the ultimate dividing line determined by the presence or absence of slavery. Like many contemporaries, he also believed geography made a western secession likely.

Pickering attracted a small group of hard-core Hamiltonians discontented with a government they considered dangerously liberal. Known as the Essex Junto, they contemplated a government that limited suffrage to substantial property holders and elected senators and the executive to lifelong terms.

The Essex Junto also led New England opposition to the War of 1812. In October 1814 the Massachusetts state legislature called a convention to meet at Hartford, Connecticut, in December to discuss remedies for New England's problems. The region's economy had been wrecked not only by the war but also by the federal government's earlier embargo policies.

The Hartford Convention adopted resolutions calling for seven amendments to the Constitution designed to limit the political power of the Democratic-Republicans. But in the public mind the entire convention expressed the will of the minority of delegates who favored secession. News of its activity spread simultaneously with news of the signing of the Treaty of Ghent and Gen. Andrew Jackson's victory over the British at New Orleans. The Federalist party acquired the stigma of disloyalty and soon became extinct as a political force. One of the nation's first two political parties perished over the issue of secession.

Like the Kentucky and Virginia resolutions, the Hartford Convention raised the specter of nullification, the concept that a state or group of states could sus-

Antitariff cartoon dating from the period of the nullification controversy (United States Telegraph, *October 19, 1832)*

pend federal laws within their jurisdiction. The concept nearly led to secession and war in 1832 in South Carolina. Senator John C. Calhoun led the state's opposition to protective tariffs, which were generally regarded as disadvantageous to the slaveholding states. During the administration of President Andrew Jackson, a majority in Congress embraced protectionism as a permanent policy. South Carolinians reacted by calling a special state convention in November 1832 that declared the federal tariff acts of 1828 and 1832 unconstitutional and therefore null and void within the state's boundaries.

When Jackson denounced nullification as treason, some of the nullifiers discussed secession. As other southern states offered only sympathy without promise of cooperative action, secessionist tempers soon cooled. Jackson's masterful carrot-and-stick policy—a reduction of the tariff balanced by preparations for military coercion—averted a crisis. South Carolina rescinded its nullification ordinance.

Increasingly secession was identified with the issue of slavery, but not always from a purely southern perspective. While slaveholders and other white southerners saw secession as a means of escaping alleged northern domination and abolitionist intrigues, residents of free states sometimes advocated secession as a means of forestalling a "Slave Power Conspiracy" they thought threatened the nation's democratic institutions.

Some New England Federalists, angered by the constitutional provision allowing southern states to count three-fifths of their slaves for purposes of representation, predicted a breakup of the Union over the admission of Louisiana as a slave state in 1812. Seven years later, as debate began over the admission of Missouri, not only southern

A CHANGE OF POLICY

July 9, 1850: Vice-President Millard Fillmore read the message written by the members of the cabinet in the Zachary Taylor administration: "Sir: The . . . painful duty devolves on us to announce to you that Zachary Taylor . . . is no more." Fillmore wrote a quick reply: "I have no language to express the emotions of my heart. The shock is so sudden and unexpected that I am overwhelmed. . . . I . . . shall appoint a time and place for taking the oath of office" at the "earliest moment."

For supporters of the Compromise of 1850, Taylor's death and Fillmore's ascension meant the possibility of preserving the American Union. Taylor, though a slaveholder, had favored the admission of California and New Mexico as free states without making concessions to the southern slave interest. Fillmore, a New Yorker who had never held slaves, supported the efforts of Senator Henry Clay and others to engineer a series of measures to manage America's expansion while also placating the South. Leaders on both sides of the argument threatened secession over the matter.

As Fillmore took the presidential oath before a joint session of Congress the next day, biographer Robert J. Rayback reports, "faces in the audience were distorted. Some tried to keep the mask of grief over their fears, and others struggled to conceal their joy for they were beginning to suspect that a revolution was in the offing." According to the terms of the compromise, California was admitted to the Union as a free state, but New Mexico remained a territory, and a tougher fugitive slave law gave southerners legal muscle for enforcement of their rights in every state of the Union. Taylor's death made it possible.

slaveholders but also northern abolitionists counseled secession if their views did not prevail. In each case, however, advocates of secession were in a distinct minority, even within their respective groups.

The expansion of slavery rather than the question of its status in existing states became the crucial issue. When Texans broke away from Mexico to form an independent republic in 1836, a few New England politicians, including former president John Quincy Adams, predicted secession by the free states if Texas won admission to the Union. Threats of secession by both northern and southern states helped to delay the admission of Texas until 1845.

Slavery, however, was not the issue in the Oregon Territory in 1849, when local Democrats, resentful of the political ascendancy of the Whig party, began discussing a Pacific republic. Talk of secession persisted until at least 1853. Secession also had adherents in California between 1848 and 1850. A California republic existed briefly, at least in the minds of some residents, during the American war with Mexico. California became part of the United States under the Treaty of Guadalupe Hidalgo in 1848. But for some settlers the vast distance between the Pacific Coast and the eastern states, at a time when no transcontinental railroad existed, made a separate Pacific republic appear attractive and practical. Secessionist talk persisted after the gold rush swelled the population at an incredible rate. Fueled by local frustrations when California's application for admission to the Union stalled in 1850, secessionist sentiment subsided when California entered as a free state that same year. The dream of a Pacific republic would be revived, however, during the Civil War.

The crisis that led to the actual breakup of the Union in 1860 had its immediate origins in the question of the

Antebellum congressional leaders Henry Clay (seated, center), John C. Calhoun (standing, center), and Daniel Webster (standing, right) figure prominently in "Union," William Pate's 1852 engraving celebrating the achievement of the Compromise of 1850.

disposition of land acquired during the Mexican War. Debate began with the Wilmot Proviso in 1846, an amendment to an appropriations bill that called for the exclusion of slavery in any territory acquired from Mexico. Congress rejected the proviso, but not before southerners warned of secession should it pass into law.

With the war's end in 1848 and the acquisition of the vast territory known as the Mexican Cession, talk of secession if slavery were excluded from the region approached a fever pitch among southern politicians at the state, local, and national levels. A bipartisan convention of southerners meeting in Mississippi in October 1849 called for a convention to meet in Nashville in 1850 to work out a strategy by which southern rights might be secured.

The Nashville Convention held two sessions. The first met in June. Only nine of the slaveholding states sent representatives, and in a nine-day session they took no action before adjourning beyond the adoption of high-sounding resolutions, for the nation's attention was riveted on Congress, where Henry Clay and Stephen Douglas utilized their talents to securing a compromise that would avert secession. Their proposals eventually became law, forming the Compromise of 1850. A key provision, "popular sovereignty," allowed settlers in the territories to determine whether slavery would be permitted where they lived. During a second session in November the Nashville Convention condemned the compromise as insufficient protection for slavery but offered no alternatives.

Far more ominous was the work at the state level of a few determined secessionists, the self-proclaimed fire-eaters. Many historians believe that with better

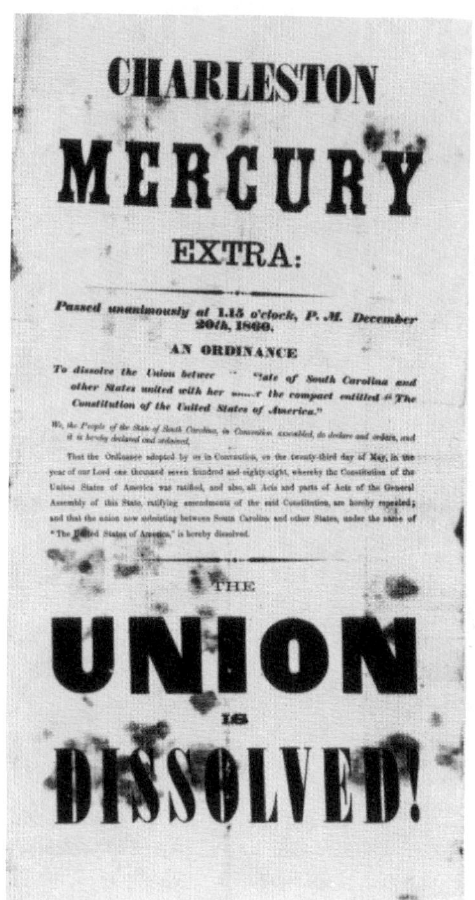

CHARLESTON

MERCURY

EXTRA:

Passed unanimously at 1.15 o'clock, P. M. December 20th, 1860.

AN ORDINANCE

To dissolve the Union between the State of South Carolina and other States united with her under the compact entitled "The Constitution of the United States of America."

We, the People of the State of South Carolina, in Convention assembled, do declare and ordain, and it is hereby declared and ordained,

That the Ordinance adopted by us in Convention, on the twenty-third day of May, in the year of our Lord one thousand seven hundred and eighty-eight, whereby the Constitution of the United States of America was ratified, and also, all Acts and parts of Acts of the General Assembly of this State, ratifying amendments of the said Constitution, are hereby repealed; and that the union now subsisting between South Carolina and other States, under the name of "The United States of America," is hereby dissolved.

THE

UNION

IS

DISSOLVED!

Announcement of secession, Charleston, South Carolina, December 1860 (Library of Congress)

luck, or more astute political timing, those men might have taken South Carolina, Mississippi, and perhaps Georgia out of the Union in 1850.

Sectional tensions mounted over the next decade, but secessionist sentiment was not limited to the South. Outraged by a perceived growth in the "Slave Power" as reflected in the proslavery Lecompton Constitution and the Dred Scott Decision, abolitionists in 1857 called a meeting in Cleveland, Ohio, where representatives of the free states might consider disunion. Because of the national economic depression, however, the meeting never took place.

Historians continue to debate the degree to which the final secession movement in the South represented the desires of the majority of whites. There is no question, however, that a relatively small group of active disunionists achieved influence disproportionate to their number by splitting the Democratic party and assuring the election of the Republican candidate, Abraham Lincoln, in November 1860. It is worth remembering that even in the act of separation, the southern states that formed the Confederacy followed different time schedules and procedures.

I am truly sorry that South Carolina will secede about the 20th & the other cotton states will, in all probability, speedily follow. The contagion of disunion is fast spreading in North Carolina and Virginia & even in Maryland to a considerable extent. They are proceeding rashly & precipitately & will afford no opportunity of trying the question at the Ballot Box in the North whether the people will or will not agree to redress these grievances. The Black Republicans say nothing & I fear do nothing to arrest the impending catastrophe. These remarks are strictly private.

—Letter of President James Buchanan to Hiram Swarr, December 10, 1860

Between December 1860 and February 1861, South Carolina, Mississippi, Florida, Alabama, Georgia, Louisiana, and Texas passed ordinances of secession in special state conventions called by their respective state legislatures. As the U.S. Constitution had been adopted via state conventions rather than referenda, plebiscites were not held.

Only after the fall of Fort Sumter in April 1861 and Lincoln's subsequent call for troops did a special convention meeting in Virginia, a state that had previously rejected disunion, vote for an ordinance of secession. A referendum held in May endorsed the convention's decision, but Confederate troops actually entered the state on April 27, at the invitation of the secession convention.

Arkansas acted in a parallel fashion, withdrawing in May. Prior to any vote,

Jefferson Davis, U.S. senator and cabinet member and president of the Confederate States of America from 1861 to 1865 (photograph by Mathew B. Brady; National Archives)

Governor Henry Rector ordered the state militia to seize federal property. He also allowed Confederate forces to enter Arkansas on his authority.

The governor of North Carolina, John Ellis, began confiscating federal property that same month. Only after federal forts on the coast and the arsenal at Fayetteville were in his hands did he summon the state legislature. The lawmakers promptly summoned a convention, which passed an ordinance of secession before the month ended.

In Tennessee, where voters had previously rejected calling a convention to consider secession, the state legislature overcame strong Unionist sentiment by declaring the state an independent republic. Governor Isham Harris concluded a military alliance with the Confederacy, making an official referendum held on June 8 meaningless.

Secessionist, if not Confederate, sentiment also existed along the Pacific Coast from Oregon to California. Three congressmen were implicated in a plot to establish an independent republic in the West. Some prosouthern newspapers advocated independence openly, as a means of avoiding the coming fratricide.

I . . . consider that . . . the Union is unbroken; and to the extent of my ability I shall take care . . . that the laws of the Union be faithfully executed in all the States. Doing this I deem to be only a simple duty on my part; and I shall perform it as far as practicable. . . . I trust this will not be regarded as a menace, but only as the declared purpose of the Union that it will . . . defend and maintain itself.

In doing this there needs be no bloodshed or violence.

—President Abraham Lincoln, First Inaugural Address, March 4, 1861

Fernando Wood was another advocate of secession. Mayor of New York City, Wood's unheeded call that the city establish its independence and treat evenly with both sides offered a small dose of comedy before the nation was enshrouded in blood.

During the war the Confederate government placed great hopes in a "Northwest Conspiracy." An indeterminate number of disaffected Democrats joined the so-called Copperhead movement, advocating a negotiated peace with the South. A portion of these joined secret organizations, such as the Sons of Liberty and the Knights of the Golden Circle, cooperating with Confederate agents in the Midwest to attempt to create a separate nation north of the Ohio River. Clement L. Vallandigham, leader of the Sons of Liberty, frightened the Lincoln administration so badly that he was forcibly exiled, but the number of northerners actually committed to secession in the Northwest was small.

As a counterpoint to the Northwest Conspiracy, there exists the legend of the Free State of Jones in Mississippi. Like many upland dwellers in the South, most residents of Jones County opposed disunion. Some fought for the federal armies. But no evidence exists that the county passed its own ordinance of secession from the Confederacy during the Civil War.

Presidents and the Civil War

by STEPHEN R. WISE

The American Civil War, like all wars, exerted an ironic mixture of negative and positive effects on the people who fought it. More than six hundred thousand soldiers and civilians died in the conflict, and great areas of the Southern half of the United States were destroyed. All the while, substantial peace movements in both North and South brought pressure for a cease-fire to bear upon the combatants, creating doubt in the minds of leaders who wanted to believe the cause was just. The war also abolished slavery, starting a process of transformation of the United States from a union to a democratic nation. While the devastated South remained economically backward for generations and arguably still suffers from the effects of the war, the North emerged in a position to take its place among the world's leading centers of industrialization and urbanization.

The war also produced its small share of success stories. Several future presidents—Grant, Hayes, and Garfield especially—won political success as a direct result of the recognition they received for military leadership. Other future chief executives—Arthur, Cleveland, Benjamin Harrison, McKinley—found that the war opened avenues of achievement. Former presidents still alive when the war came—Van Buren, Tyler, Fillmore, Pierce—reacted to it in diverse ways. An elderly Van Buren spoke out in favor of the Union, Tyler ended his quixotic political life as a Confederate, Fillmore established himself as a hometown cheerleader for the boys in blue, and Pierce played the game of politics but at the expense of his local reputation. Buchanan, president during the first phase of Southern secession, became one of the war's forgotten men. Lincoln, America's greatest president, might never have known greatness in another age.

VAN BUREN: FOR THE UNION

At the start of the Civil War there were five living former presidents. The oldest was the eighth president, Martin Van Buren. Known as the "Little Magician" for his ability to weather political storms, he tried during his presidency to compromise on the question of slavery's expansion. When that alienated both sides, he turned against expansion. Repudiated by his own Democratic party for refusing to annex Texas, Van Buren lost his bid for reelection in 1840. In 1848 he ran as the candidate of the Free Soil party and was again defeated.

The attack upon our flag and the capture of Fort Sumter by the Secessionists could be regarded in no other light than as the commencement of a treasonable attempt to overthrow the federal government by military force.

—Martin Van Buren, statement giving his support to a "Union committee" in Kinderhook, New York, April 1861

In 1856 Van Buren voted for Democrat James Buchanan, feeling that a Republican victory would lead to civil war. Disappointed with Buchanan's performance, he came to regret his vote. In 1860, again fearing the consequences of

John Tyler, circa 1860 (courtesy of the Chicago Historical Society)

a Republican victory, he voted for Stephen A. Douglas, but once the war began he gave his full support to the Union. Before fighting broke out, former president Franklin Pierce asked Van Buren to help organize a convention of ex-presidents to mediate the crisis. Since Pierce was working without President Lincoln's knowledge, Van Buren declined.

On July 24, 1862, while the war still raged, Van Buren died at his home in Kinderhook, New York. Upon learning of his death, Lincoln wrote, "That while suffering with disease and seeing his end approaching, his prayers were for the restoration of the authority of the government of which he had been head, and for peace and good will among his fellow citizens."

TYLER: FOR THE CONFEDERACY

The only former president from a Southern state alive in 1861 was Virginian John Tyler. Succeeding to the presidency as the nation's tenth chief executive following the death of William Henry Harrison, Tyler soon lost the backing of the Whig party when he carried out a program that favored a Southern states-rights party dedicated to the annexation of Texas. Nominated for the presidency by Southern Democrats in 1844, Tyler withdrew in favor of national Democratic candidate James K. Polk. Three days before he left office, Tyler signed Texas into the Union and allowed Polk to handle the consequences.

Retiring after his presidency, Tyler kept abreast of regional and national politics. A strict constitutionalist, he firmly backed the concept of secession, though he believed it would lead to war and ultimately victory by the North. In 1859 he thought he might be a dark horse candidate for the Democratic presidential nomination. When that failed to materialize, he backed John C. Breckinridge's candidacy, even though he found it distasteful to be in league with Southern fire-eaters.

BURIAL OF A PRESIDENT

The former president lay in state under the nation's flag in the Capitol, and thousands of citizens filed by, paying their last respects. Congress spent an entire day in eulogy. Dignitaries including the nation's current president crowded into the church where the funeral was held. After the ceremony a procession of 150 carriages followed the hearse to the cemetery. Only the location of the cemetery—Richmond, Virginia—and the year of the ceremony—1862—reveal the special nature of the proceedings. The former president was John Tyler, and in death he had been honored by the Confederate government of President Jefferson Davis. Tyler had been preparing to serve as a representative in that government. He is the only president to serve the Confederacy and the only president buried under a "foreign" flag.

During the secession crisis Tyler worked behind the scenes to set up a peace conference sponsored by Virginia that became the Washington Peace Conference of February 1861. Elected president of the conference, he soon realized that a spirit of compromise was not strong. When the conference failed Tyler immediately became a secessionist. He attended Virginia's secession convention and supported the state's decision to leave the Union. He later served on a Virginia commission that formed a treaty of alliance with the Confederacy and was appointed to the Provisional Confederate Congress. Too ill to journey to Montgomery, the first Confederate capital, he later joined the government when it reconvened in Richmond.

In November 1861 Tyler was elected to the Confederate House of Representatives from Virginia's Third District. He went to Richmond to attend the first Confederate Congress but died in the Exchange Hotel on January 18, 1862, before he could take his seat. His casket was draped in the Stars and Bars of the Confederacy, and he was buried in Richmond on January 26 at Hollywood Cemetery, next to the tomb of President James Monroe.

FILLMORE: "UNION CONTINENTAL"

Millard Fillmore succeeded to the presidency in 1850 on the death of Zachary Taylor. Fillmore was inaugurated at the height of congressional debate over the territory gained from the Mexican War. Unlike Taylor, he refused to risk war over slavery and signed the five bills that became known as the Compromise of 1850. But his attempts to enforce the compromise soon incurred the wrath of both the North and the South. Denied the presidential nomination in 1852 by a splintering Whig party, Fillmore became the 1856 presidential candidate for the Southern Whigs, who had formed the American or Know-Nothing party. In the 1856 election Fillmore received only eight electoral votes.

Millard Fillmore as commander of the Buffalo, New York, volunteer militia company the "Union Continentals," September 1862

After Abraham Lincoln's election in 1860, a group of New York merchants called upon Fillmore to go to South Carolina in an attempt to avert the state's secession. Fillmore refused, believing that reconciliation could only come from the Republican party, a political organization he distrusted. Fillmore was also distressed when Buchanan did not take immediate action against South Carolina, leaving to Lincoln the task of resolving the crisis at Fort Sumter. Fillmore believed the Union to be sovereign and secessionists to be traitors. When Lincoln passed through Buffalo, New York, on his way to Washington, Fillmore entertained the president-elect, but no record remains of what was said between the two.

After the firing on Fort Sumter and Lincoln's call for volunteers, Fillmore led a giant pro-Union demonstration in Buffalo. He went on to pledge and raise money for the families of volunteers. He formed a militia company of over-aged men from the city's prominent

THE REAL FUN OF BEING A SOLDIER

Too old to participate actively but too young to remain on the sidelines, Millard Fillmore of Buffalo, New York, organized a company of "home guards," the Union Continentals, at the start of the Civil War. Described in the newspapers as a group of "large, portly grandfathers with grey heads," the Continentals, a ceremonial unit, helped raise recruits and relief funds and kept the spirits of Buffalo citizens high. Commander Fillmore would march at the head of the Continentals "looking like an emperor." While seeing off the city's first Union volunteers, Fillmore cried, "Old Guard, attention! Three cheers for the Buffalo volunteers!" He also led the Continentals to Buffalo's Central Presbyterian Church, where he read George Washington's Farewell Address, with its inspiring call for perpetual union. In November 1862, having established the Continentals as a significant public force for goodwill, Fillmore retired from command and devoted himself to other causes. He remained strong for the Union and lived well into the Reconstruction period.

families called the "Union Continentals." As commander of the company, Fillmore used it to inspire volunteers and raise relief funds. He also vigorously lobbied for increased defenses at Buffalo should Great Britain enter the war against the North.

In spite of his public zeal, Fillmore was deeply troubled by the war, and as the conflict dragged on, he became convinced that the Republicans were not only responsible for the war but also for its continuation. In February 1864, while making the opening speech at a relief fair, he lashed out at Republican leadership and called for reconciliation with the South. The speech exposed him to attacks from the Republican press and party, and when he backed George B. McClellan for the presidency in 1864, he was unfairly linked to the pro-South Copperhead movement and at times declared a traitor. After Lincoln's reelection, and with the North's subsequent military victories, the attacks by the press subsided, but the public did not forget. After Lincoln's assassination Fillmore's home was defaced because some thought he had failed to display proper mourning decorations. Fillmore was not home at the time, and when he did return he draped his home in respect for Lincoln and later served as an escort for Lincoln's coffin when the funeral train passed through Buffalo.

After the war, as passions cooled, Fillmore was restored to his position within the Buffalo community. He met Gen. William T. Sherman and later President Andrew Johnson when they visited the city in 1866. He spent much of his time trying to help Buffalo become a center of culture and learning and served as chairman in an unsuccessful attempt to raise money for a Civil War monument honoring the city's soldiers and sailors. He continued his work with charitable organizations until he died on March 8, 1874.

PIERCE: SOUTHERN APOLOGIST

Fillmore was followed in the presidency by Franklin Pierce. The antiabolitionist New Hampshire native was nominated by a united Democratic party to enforce the Compromise of 1850 and keep peace between the North and South. The inexperienced and indecisive Pierce added fuel to the sectional dispute through his advocacy of positions favorable to the South, including support for a Southern transcontinental railroad route and for the Lecompton constitution allowing slavery in the Kansas Territory. His cabinet included three Southerners, including his personal friend and the future Confederate president, Jefferson Davis. His support of the Lecompton constitution cost Pierce the 1856 Democratic nomination. Though he had been ineffective in carrying out his pro-South, anti-Republican program, he did keep the two wings of the Democratic party together and passed the alliance on to his successor, James Buchanan.

In 1860 Pierce was suggested as a candidate who could hold the Democratic party together, but he refused to consider nomination, preferring that the call go to someone else who could run on a compromise platform. During the secession crisis Pierce worked hard to avert war. He thought the Confederate attack on the *Star of the West,* an unarmed ship dispatched by President Buchanan carrying supplies and reinforcements to Fort Sumter was "foolish and ill-advised," and was sickened by not only Southern secession and Northern coercion, but also by the emerging aggressiveness of the South. After the firing on Fort Sumter, Pierce attempted to organize a conference of former presidents to mediate the crisis, but when Martin Van Buren refused to join, he dropped the matter.

Though pro-Union and active in war relief, Pierce quickly became critical of President Lincoln's methods of handling the rebellion, especially when Lincoln allowed the suspension of such constitutional guarantees as the writ of habeas corpus. His views soon resulted in a letter from Secretary of State William Seward asking Pierce if he were conspiring with the secret pro-South society known as the Knights of the Golden Circle, which was plotting the government's overthrow. Outraged by the false accusation, Pierce demanded and received an apology from Seward.

The affair with Seward embittered Pierce. He continued to condemn the Lincoln administration, which he felt was controlled by abolitionists. He especially attacked the Emancipation Proclamation, which he felt was freeing a race incapable of coping with freedom and would lead to a bloody slave revolt throughout the Confederacy. Pierce even favored Southern victories as a way of returning the Democrats to power in the North; he felt a negotiated peace could be made that would bring the nation back together. On July 4, 1863, he made a speech to a Democratic rally in Concord, New Hampshire, in which he denounced Lincoln's war policies and called the war fearful, fruitless, and fatal. At the end of his speech he called upon his fellow citizens to join him in raising money for the sick and wounded. Just then word passed through the crowd of the Union victory at Gettysburg. Pierce never recovered his popularity. Then, when a letter he had written to Jefferson Davis in 1860 was published in the newspapers, the former president was seen as not only anti-Republican but also as a traitor.

Even so, there were some at the 1864 Democratic convention who considered Pierce as a possible presidential candidate, but he was never a serious contender. During the last year of the war respect for Pierce continued to dwindle, and after the deaths of his wife and close friend Nathaniel Hawthorne, he turned to drink and became a recluse. He was deeply troubled by Lincoln's as-

---

Without discussing the question of right, of abstract power to secede, I have never believed that actual disruption of the Union can occur without bloodshed; and if, through the madness of northern Abolitionists, that dire calamity must come, the fighting will not be along Mason's and Dixon's line merely. It will be within our own borders, in our own streets, between the two classes of citizens to whom I have referred. Those who defy law and scout constitutional obligations will, if we ever reach the arbitrament of arms, find occupation enough at home.

—*Letter of Franklin Pierce to Senator Jefferson Davis, January 6, 1860*

President James Buchanan (center) and his cabinet, circa 1859 (left to right): Jacob Thompson, Lewis Cass, John B. Floyd, Howell Cobb, Isaac Toucey, Joseph Holt, and Jeremiah Black (National Archives)

sassination, but he mourned privately, and when it was reported that his house did not show the required mourning flag, a mob marched on the residence. Pierce met them at the door and turned them away.

Pierce continued to live in Concord after the war. Veterans' organizations recalled only his wartime opposition and not his efforts to raise relief funds. He died at home on October 8, 1869, a nearly forgotten man.

BUCHANAN: MEDIATOR

Pierce was followed to the presidency by James Buchanan. Buchanan, a Pennsylvanian, viewed himself as a breakwater between the North and the South, but by 1860 his position was breaking apart. Support of the proslavery Lecompton constitution cost him Northern backing, and his inability to halt the rise of the Republican party resulted in Southern defections. During the secession crisis Buchanan was often dominated by Southern cabinet members, and his actions were indecisive. He did not believe in the right of secession, but he also did not believe that the federal government had the right to use force against its own citizens. In 1859 he informed his party that he would not seek reelection and continued his work to mediate the two sides. Finally, as Southerners resigned from his cabinet and were replaced with Northerners, Buchanan began to show more resolve, but when Lincoln won the 1860 election, Buchanan decided it best to wait and allow Lincoln to carry out national policy against the seceded Southern states.

Under threat of assassination Buchanan accompanied Lincoln to the 1861 inauguration. He later pledged his full support to the maintenance of the Union and gave money to outfit a local military unit. Still, many in the North felt he had willingly supported the

President Lincoln and Union officers at Antietam, Maryland, October 3, 1862 (Library of Congress)

Southern cause. He was accused of conspiring with the Southern members of his cabinet to establish the Confederacy, and during the war it was claimed that he tried to gain foreign recognition for the seceded states. The charges were untrue, but Buchanan felt it futile to rebut them while the war was ongoing. Death threats also plagued the former president, and fellow Masons volunteered to provide him protection.

My dear sir, if you are as happy in entering the White House as I shall feel on returning to Wheatland, you are a happy man indeed.
—Comment of outgoing president James Buchanan to President-elect Abraham Lincoln, March 4, 1861

Buchanan agreed with many of Lincoln's wartime policies but felt the Republican party had singled him out for attack, blaming him for not doing more to stop the crisis. Toward the end of the war he put much of his energy into writing a book that, when published in 1866, defended his actions during the secession crisis. Once the war ended, passions cooled, and though scars remained, Buchanan enjoyed a quiet life until his death on June 1, 1868.

LINCOLN: FROM UNION TO NATION

Buchanan's successor, Abraham Lincoln, confronted the greatest crisis ever faced by an American president. Born in Kentucky and raised in Illinois, Lincoln was a self-made politician who had been a member of the Whig party until its disappearance from the political scene. He then joined the infant Republican party and gained national attention for his unsuccessful senatorial campaign against Stephen A. Douglas in 1858. At the 1860 Republican convention he was the favorite son of the Illinois delegation. Promoted as an alternative to Seward and Chase, he won the nomination and, thanks to a split in the

LINCOLN MOUNTS THE PARAPET

Late in the afternoon of July 11, 1864, a Confederate army under the command of Lt. Gen. Jubal Early threatened Fort Stevens on Washington, D.C.'s northern defense line. Early got there nearly in time to surprise the North's capital without a proper garrison, but as his tired men drew up opposite the fort, Union reinforcements were arriving on Washington's docks. The Union men rushed to protect the fort and prepared to meet the rebels in battle the next morning.

The next day, as Confederate troops approached Fort Stevens, Union general Horatio G. Wright invited a special unexpected guest, President Abraham Lincoln, to review his troops—not thinking he would accept. Without hesitating, the president—six feet four inches of man and eight inches of stovepipe hat—mounted the fort's parapet and stood in the midst of enemy fire. When an officer standing only three feet from Lincoln was hit, a horrified Wright begged the president to come down. Ignoring the general, Lincoln remained exposed until a young captain, future U.S. chief justice Oliver Wendell Holmes reflexively yelled, "Get down, you damned fool, before you get shot." The warning amused the president, but he did climb down. Lincoln is the only president to have been exposed to hostile military fire while in office.

Democratic party, won the presidency with a majority of electoral votes but a minority of the popular vote.

Lincoln came to office believing that slavery was constitutionally protected where it existed, but he also believed that the federal government could and should deny its expansion. He thought secession illegal and refused to negotiate with the seceded states for fear of giving them a legitimacy that could lead to interference by foreign powers. To Lincoln the war was a domestic rebellion that should be handled by the federal government. In carrying out his program of restoring the Union, he used all powers commanded by the presidency. Taking a liberal interpretation of presidential emergency powers, he undertook actions widely viewed as unconstitutional, including blockading the Southern coast, suspending the writ of habeas corpus, authorizing the raising and outfitting of armies, and emancipating slaves via the Emancipation Proclamation; all of that he accomplished without congressional approval.

A common man, Lincoln held the interests of soldiers and his constituents close to his heart. Though deeply saddened by the human cost of the war, he continued an aggressive war policy despite tremendous battle casualties. Throughout the war he displayed a remarkable understanding of military strategy and was not averse to removing popular generals who were unable to meet the Union's goals. By late 1864 Lincoln finally formed a formidable team with Gen. Ulysses S. Grant and Gen. William T. Sherman, who eventually brought the conflict to a successful conclusion. Lincoln also became the only sitting president to endure enemy fire, when on July 11 and 12, 1864, he mounted the parapet at Fort Stevens on the outskirts of Washington, D.C., to view Confederate skirmishers.

In the sphere of foreign affairs Lincoln also showed a remarkable facility. He was able to deflect serious repercussions from the Trent affair, a diplomatic scandal, and managed to keep both Great Britain and France from interfering in the war. In domestic affairs Lincoln and the Republicans pushed through labor reform legislation, the 1862 Homestead Act, and an act for the establishment of land grant colleges. His masterful handing of the slavery issue also demonstrated his ability to walk a delicate political line. Careful not to enrage the loyal slave states, Lincoln ignored repeated requests to abolish slavery until the fall of 1862; even then the Emancipation Proclamation only freed slaves within areas still held by the Confederacy.

Throughout the war Lincoln proved a genius at handling party and national politics. He carefully took control of the Republican party and subordinated potential rivals. He also encouraged Democrats to join his administration. In 1864 he won the nomination of a combination of Republicans and War Democrats called the National Union party and emerged victorious in the general election against the Democratic peace party ticket headed by George B. McClellan.

Lincoln also pursued a course that placed Reconstruction firmly in his hands. Like the question of slavery and the war effort, Lincoln believed this all-important policy should be directed by the chief executive. During the war Lincoln developed a plan to establish loyal governments within the rebelling states. Those governments were then to serve as a base for the reconstructed Southern states. Both Lincoln and his vice-president, Andrew Johnson, believed in a policy of reconciliation toward the South and wanted to restore the rebellious states to the Union as soon as possible. Toward the end of the war, when Northern victory was assured, Lincoln made speeches calling for a mild Reconstruction, but the possibility that he might carry out his plan was ended on April 14, 1865, when he was assassinated at Ford's Theater in Washington by John Wilkes Booth.

ANDREW JOHNSON ISSUES A PASS

While he was serving as military governor of Tennessee, Andrew Johnson worked diligently to restore the state to full membership in the Union. He not only helped Unionists but also families who had supported the Confederacy. One day the beautiful widow Carter of Franklin, Tennessee, requested a pass to transport six barrels of salt from federally occupied Nashville through Confederate lines to her home. Johnson approved the request because he thought six barrels of salt too small an amount to help the Confederacy and because, as he put it, "Mrs. Carter is a lovely woman." A month later Carter returned with another request to transport salt—this time twelve barrels. Johnson balked, saying he could only issue permits for six barrels at a time. So Carter requested two permits, and the smitten Johnson complied.

ANDREW JOHNSON: SOUTHERN UNIONIST

Active in local politics from an early age, Andrew Johnson joined the Democratic party and quickly became a spokesman for his East Tennessee constituents. After ten years in the Tennessee legislature he served as governor of that state from 1853 to 1856, when he was elected to the U.S. Senate. A believer in states' rights and the constitutionality of slavery, Johnson supported the candidacy of John C. Breckinridge in the 1860 presidential election, though he remained a firm Unionist. In June 1861, when Tennessee seceded, Johnson refused to give up his Senate seat, the only Southern senator from a seceded state to do so. Branded a traitor by Confederates and a hero by his followers in East Tennessee, Johnson continued to serve in the Senate until federal armies captured much of central and western Tennessee and Lincoln called upon him to lead his state back into the Union.

In March 1862 Lincoln appointed Johnson military governor of Tennessee, and at the same time Johnson was commissioned a brigadier general in the

President Andrew Johnson (in profile, seated in the front row on the rostrum), his cabinet, spectators, and soldiers during the Grand Review of Union troops, Washington, D.C., May 22-23, 1865 (National Archives)

volunteer army. Using both his military and political positions, Johnson established a loyal government in his home state. When the Republicans joined with the War Democrats for the 1864 election, Johnson was a popular and logical choice for vice-president. The day before the inauguration, on March 3, 1865, Johnson resigned his military commission. Six weeks later, upon Lincoln's death, he became the nation's seventeenth president.

At first, Johnson, caught up in the hysteria that followed Lincoln's assassination, called for retribution against the rebellious Southerners, but he soon moderated his views and tried to implement a reconstruction of reconciliation. Because of his mild policies, Johnson soon became embroiled in a power struggle with the Radical Republicans, who in February 1868 brought a resolution of impeachment against the president. Avoiding conviction by one vote, Johnson completed his term and managed to extend additional grants of amnesty to former Confederates.

GRANT: GENERAL, PRESIDENT

Ulysses S. Grant followed Johnson in the White House. Christened Hiram Ulysses, Grant had his name changed due to an error in his West Point application, which his demanding father secured for him. Graduating twenty-first out of thirty-nine cadets in the class of 1843, Grant was assigned as a brevet second lieutenant to the Fourth Infantry Regiment. He was initially stationed at Jefferson Barracks, Missouri, and later served at Camp Salubrity in Natchitoches, Louisiana, and took part in the occupation of Texas. While in Texas he was promoted to second lieutenant and with the Fourth Regiment fought in the Mexican War.

Though Grant felt that the Mexican War had been provoked by U.S. politicians, he proved an able staff officer and fighter. Grant and the Fourth first fought under Gen. Zachary Taylor in the battles of Palo Alto, Resaca de la Palma, and Monterrey. With the regiment Grant was transferred to Gen. Winfield Scott's command and participated in the siege of Veracruz. He was made quartermaster for the regiment and went on to serve in the battles of Cerro Gordo, Churubusco, Molino del Rey, Chapultepec, and the assault and capture of Mexico City. For his actions at Molino del Rey, Grant was brevetted a first lieutenant, and for his conduct at Chapultepec he received a brevet to captain.

Promoted to first lieutenant in September 1847, Grant served in the occupation of Mexico City before being assigned to garrison duty at Sacketts Harbor, New York; Detroit, Michigan; and Fort Columbus, New York. When the Fourth Regiment was moved west, Grant was assigned to duty at Benicia, California; Columbia Barracks, Oregon; Fort Vancouver, Oregon; and Fort Humboldt, California. While at Fort Humboldt he was promoted to captain.

Duty in the remote western garrisons separated Grant from his beloved wife Julia and children. Attempts to raise money through business ventures to bring his family to California failed. Despondent, Grant reportedly turned to drink, which soon affected his career. On July 31, 1854, he resigned his captaincy and returned to his family near St. Louis, Missouri. Further business ventures failed, and eventually Grant and his family moved to his parents' home in Galena, Illinois, where he took a clerking position at his younger brother's leather store.

When the Civil War broke out he offered his services to the War Department and later to Gen. George B. McClellan, who was commanding the federal army in Ohio, but found no success in gaining a commission. After helping to train local volunteers, Grant, with the aid of the local congressman, Elihu B. Washburne, received a commission as the colonel of the Twenty-first Illinois Volunteer Infantry Regiment. From June to August his regiment guarded the St. Joseph Railroad. Promoted to brigadier general, Grant was given the command of Ironton, Missouri, on August 7, Jefferson City, Missouri, on August 17, and the District of Southwestern Missouri on September 1, with his headquarters at Cape Girardeau. The district was later expanded to include southern Illinois and western Kentucky, and his headquarters was relocated to Cairo, Illinois.

In command of that district, Grant organized and carried out on September 6 the seizure of Paducah, Kentucky, and led an unsuccessful attack against Belmont, Missouri, on November 7.

GRANT AND LINCOLN

On March 8, 1864, Gen. Ulysses S. Grant, a Union hero for his exploits against Confederate forces in the western theater, arrived in Washington, D.C., and prepared for his first meeting with President Abraham Lincoln. After checking in at the Willard Hotel, Grant had dinner and then went to the White House, where the president was holding his customary Tuesday night open-house session in the East Room. When the general arrived, the crowd around Lincoln parted. The president grasped Grant's hand and exclaimed, "Why here is General Grant! Well, this is a pleasure I assure you."

Grant, embarrassed by the commotion, was then given a turn around the room by Mrs. Lincoln. So many people wanted to meet him that he literally had to stand on a sofa so he could be seen. The following day, in a calmer, private ceremony, Lincoln personally commissioned Grant a lieutenant general. Three days later he appointed Grant general in chief of U.S. armies.

During January 1862 he directed demonstrations against the Confederates at Columbia, Missouri, and Fort Henry, Tennessee, and then organized a joint army and navy expedition that captured Fort Henry and Fort Donelson in February 1862. His successful attack resulted in the capture of 14,623 Confederate soldiers, his promotion to major general on February 16, and the nickname "Unconditional Surrender" Grant. Placed in command of the District of West Tennessee on March 5, Grant experienced difficulties with his superior, Maj. Gen. Henry Halleck, and was ordered to remain at Fort Henry while Maj. Gen. Charles Smith moved the field army along the Tennessee River. When an injury forced Smith to give up command, Grant returned and took over the advance on Corinth, Mississippi. While waiting for reinforcements at Pittsburg Landing before moving on Corinth, Grant's army was surprised at the Battle of Shiloh, on April 6-7. Barely holding on during the first day of the battle, Grant reorganized his command and, with the arriving army of Maj. Gen. Don Carlos Buell, launched counterattacks the next day that drove the Southerners back to Corinth.

After Shiloh, General Halleck took personal command of Buell's and Grant's forces for the advance on Corinth. Halleck placed Grant directly under his control by making him his second in command, during which time Grant commanded Halleck's right wing and reserve. After the occupation of Corinth, Grant again became the active district commander, when Halleck returned to his headquarters at St. Louis and Buell's command was sent to move on Chattanooga, Tennessee.

Initially Grant was under orders to protect the railroads in western Tennessee, but when the Confederates invaded Kentucky in September 1862 he made plans to move against the Southern forces that remained in northern Mississippi. On September 19 forces under his operational command attacked Iuka, Mississippi, but failed to trap the Confederates. When the Confederates launched an unsuccessful counterattack on Corinth, October 3-4, Grant directed units in an attempt to catch the retreating enemy, but they slipped away and Grant called off the pursuit.

In October, after the Battle of Corinth, Grant was given command of the Department of the Tennessee, which included the Army of the Tennessee and other units along the Mississippi River. At the same time Grant asked and received permission from now commander in chief Halleck to "fight the enemy when you please." With this new operational freedom, Grant began his Vicksburg campaign, which lasted from November 4, 1862, to July 18, 1863. During that time Grant initiated several moves against the Confederate stronghold, including an unsuccessful advance on Oxford, Mississippi, in November and December 1862 and a descent of the Mississippi to Young's Point and defeat at the battle of Chickasaw Bluffs in December and January. Grant took personal command of the Vicksburg operations when he joined his field army at Miliken's Bend on January 29, 1863. He then attempted to turn Vicksburg's defenses by Williams Canal, Yazoo Pass, Steele's Bayou, and Lake Providence. All of those operations ended in failure.

By early April 1863 Grant prepared another plan to take Vicksburg. Working closely with the navy, he moved his army through the swamps west of Vicksburg and on April 30 landed his men at Bruinsburg, Mississippi. Grant had planned to move against Vicksburg with reinforcements from New Orleans, but when those forces did not materialize, he decided to continue with the forces at hand. Taking a tremendous risk, he severed his supply lines and moved his army inland. With the soldiers living off the land, Grant moved to gain a position between the two Confederate forces at Jackson and Vicksburg. At the battles of Port Gibson, Raymond, Jackson, Champion Hill, and Big Black, Grant de-

Gen. Ulysses S. Grant at City Point, Virginia, 1864 (Library of Congress)

feated his opponents and maneuvered the main Confederate force back to Vicksburg. Initially Grant tried to take the city by assault, but when that attack failed he opened siege operations. On July 4, 1863, he captured Vicksburg and its 31,500 defenders. For his victory Grant was promoted to major general.

After Vicksburg's capture, Grant dispatched part of his army to drive off a Confederate relief force that had been forming at Jackson. His forces reoccupied Jackson on July 16. For the next few months Grant organized expeditions to raid Confederate railroads and industrial sites and undertook an inspection tour of his department.

In October 1864, after the Union disaster at Chickamauga, Grant was made commander of the Military Division of the Mississippi, which gave him control over the area between the Allegheny Mountains and the Mississippi River, except New Orleans, and control of the Armies of the Ohio, Cumberland, and Tennessee. His first task was to save the Union forces in Chattanooga. Grant personally went to Chattanooga and took over operations, directing the movements that resulted in the victory at Missionary Ridge on November 23-25, 1863. For that victory and his previous service Grant received the thanks of Congress and a gold medal on December 17.

On March 9, 1864, President Lincoln commissioned Grant a lieutenant general, and on March 12, 1864, he made Grant commander in chief of the armies of the United States. Working with Lincoln, Grant designed an overall plan to end the war. He directed the Union armies to begin a coordinated advance on all fronts, with the main assaults going against Atlanta and Richmond. Though he preferred to stay in the West, Grant bowed to political reality and made his headquarters with the Army of the Potomac. From that post he supervised the advance on Richmond and the attack against Gen. Robert E. Lee's Confederate Army of Northern Virginia. During the campaign Grant oversaw the battles of the Wilderness, Spottsylvania, North Anna, Tolopotomy, Bethesda Church, and Cold Harbor, the assault on Petersburg, and the siege of Richmond and Petersburg.

Grant's dogged determination inspired his army to fight on despite heavy casualties, and by April 1865 their hard work was rewarded when the Confederates were forced to evacuate Richmond and Petersburg. At the same time his strategy was working on other fronts. The federal armies in the West had taken Atlanta and moved through Georgia and the Carolinas. Important seaports such as Mobile and Wilmington had been taken and a major victory won at Nashville, which virtually eliminated the main Confederate western army. Pursuing Lee, Grant cornered his force at Appomattox Courthouse, Virginia, where Lee surrendered on April 9, 1865. Grant then returned to Washington and continued to serve as commander of the U.S. Army. He was promoted to general on July 25, 1866, the first officer to hold that rank since George Washington.

Grant oversaw the army's demobilization and the postwar reorganization, which placed occupation troops in the South. During President Andrew Johnson's administration he was caught between the Radicals and the president when he was ordered to replace Edwin Stanton as secretary of war. Grant managed to extradite himself from a difficult situation and remained commander of the army until he was nominated to the presidency by the Republicans in 1868.

HAYES: "BEST YEARS"

Grant was followed in the White House by two Ohioan presidents who had also served as generals in the Civil War. The first was Rutherford B. Hayes. Well educated, Hayes attended Kenyon College and Harvard Law School before becoming a lawyer in Lower Sandusky, Ohio. He later moved his office to Cincinnati, where he became active in politics, first as a Whig and later as a moderate Republican. When the Civil War broke out Hayes was active in recruiting, and in June 1861 he enlisted in the Twenty-third Ohio Volunteer Infantry Regiment. Commissioned a major, Hayes was with the regiment when it was sent into the Kanawha Valley to secure for the Union the western portion of Virginia.

As a major he participated in the September 10, 1861, battle of Carnifix Ferry. After the battle, because of his legal experience, Hayes was briefly detached from his regiment to serve as judge advocate, but when he was promoted to lieutenant colonel on October 24 he returned to the regiment and commanded it during the April-May 1862 federal attack against the Virginia and Tennessee Railroad. Hayes's men spearheaded an attack that drove the Confederates out of Princeton, Virginia (later West Virginia), and on to Giles Courthouse before Confederate resistance hardened and drove the attackers back.

After the unsuccessful attack on the railroad, Hayes, thinking that he would not be promoted to colonel of the Twenty-third, considered leaving to take command of one of the new regiments being raised in Ohio. Loyalty to his regiment kept him with the unit. In August 1862 the regiment was with the units termed the Kanawha Division that were transferred to the Army of Virginia. The men from West Virginia arrived too late to participate in the Second Bull Run campaign, but they did form a division in the Ninth Corps during the Antietam campaign. On September 14, 1862, during the Battle of South Mountain, Hayes directed the Twenty-third Ohio against Confederate positions at Fox Gap. Showing extreme bravery while leading a charge, Hayes was wounded in the left arm and was forced to leave his command.

On October 24, 1862, during his convalescence, Hayes received his promotion to colonel. He rejoined his regiment in late November. By that time the Twenty-third Ohio, with the rest of the Kanawha Division, had returned to West Virginia to take up their previous duties chasing guerrillas and garrisoning towns. Hayes continued as commander of the Twenty-third until March 1863, when he was given command of the First Brigade, Third Division, Eighth Corps, Middle Department. With the creation of the Department of West Virginia from the Middle Department in June, Hayes continued his command, which was redesignated First Brigade, Scammon's Division, Department of West Virginia. With that unit he participated in resisting and eventually defeating John Hunt Morgan's July 1863 raid into Indiana and Ohio.

Hayes's command was again retitled in April 1864, as the First Brigade, Second Division, Department of West Virginia, and the colonel led that brigade during Gen. George Crook's raid on the Virginia and Tennessee Railroad. At the Battle of Cloyd's Mountain on May 9, 1864, Hayes again led an attack against a well-defended Confederate position. He then pushed on, brushing aside Confederate cavalry led by John Hunt Morgan until he reached the railroad at Dublin, Virginia. There Hayes assisted in the destruction of a portion of the railroad and the New River Railroad Bridge; then, with the rest of Crook's command, he withdrew into West Virginia.

In late May 1864, with Crook's Army of the Kanawha, Hayes's brigade was ordered to join Maj. Gen. David Hunter's army for an advance down the Shenandoah Valley. The two commands combined at Staunton, Virginia, on May 21, 1864, and began their march toward Lynchburg. During the campaign Hayes expressed disapproval of unnecessary destruction and was especially appalled at the burning of the Virginia Military Institute. Hayes and his command participated in the June 16-18, 1864, Battle of Lynchburg, and with the rest of Hunter's command retreated into West Virginia, where they were out of position to resist the following Confederate attack on Washington.

When the Confederates pulled back from Washington, Hunter attempted to use Crook's command to trap the retreating Southerners. Missing their enemy, Crook's army was counterattacked on July 23 at Kernstown. Outmanned, the federals pulled back. Hayes led his brigade in covering the retreat, which eventually took the men back to Harpers Ferry. There, in early August, Crook's command became part of Maj.

HAYES AND THE ENEMY

On September 14, 1862, as a Union army moved to attack Confederate general Robert E. Lee's divided forces around Harpers Ferry, Virginia, Rutherford B. Hayes led the Twenty-third Ohio against Confederate defenders at Fox Gap. Having driven the enemy from behind a stone wall, Hayes ordered another advance, but as he finished issuing the command he was struck in the right arm by a bullet. Refusing to leave the battlefield, he had a soldier tie a handkerchief around the wound. He was forced to lie down, but he kept on issuing orders. He also struck up a conversation with a wounded Confederate who was lying nearby. "You came a good ways to fight us," Hayes commented. The rebel replied, "You came a good ways to fight us." Fearing he might die of his wound, Hayes gave the Confederate a message to deliver to his wife. But he lived and became, with Revolutionary War veteran James Madison, one of only two presidents to be wounded in battle.

Brig. Gen. Rutherford B. Hayes, 1864

Gen. Philip Sheridan's Army of the Shenandoah. Designated the Seventh Corps, Hayes's brigade remained the same but was now termed the First Brigade, Second Division, Seventh Corps.

On August 10, 1864, Sheridan began his advance. Later in the month Hayes learned that he had been nominated to the U.S. House of Representatives from his Cincinnati, Ohio, district. He accepted the nomination but refused to leave the army to campaign. Shortly after, on September 3, Hayes and his command fought at the inconclusive Battle of Berryville. Sixteen days later, at Opequon, or Third Winchester, Hayes's brigade led the attack on the Confederate left that eventually drove the Southerners from the field. During the battle Hayes's division commander was wounded and Hayes took over the Second Division, Eighth Corps. In that position, on September 22, at the Battle of Fisher's Hill, he again led a flank attack that broke the Confederates.

With the Confederate army momentarily in check, Hayes regretfully participated in Sheridan's devastation of the Shenandoah Valley. In mid October the army returned to quarters at Cedar Creek, and it was there that Hayes learned he had won his congressional election. What exuberance he may have felt from the news was quickly lost when the army was surprised on October 19 by a Confederate attack. Hayes's division was outflanked and momentarily routed. During the flight Hayes's horse was killed, throwing him to the ground and knocking him unconscious. Recovering, he managed to escape capture and rally a portion of his division, which was held in reserve during Sheridan's dramatic counterattack.

After the victory of Cedar Creek, Sheridan placed his army in winter quarters. On December 9, 1864, Hayes was promoted to brigadier general. On December 24 he turned command of the division over to the returning former division commander and reverted to the command of the First Brigade, Second Division, Department of West Virginia.

Hayes continued to command his brigade when it was redesignated the First Brigade, First Division, Department of West Virginia in January 1865, and he returned to divisional command with the First Division, Department of West Virginia on February 25. In March he was awarded the brevet of major general. In April he was briefly detached to organize a mixed division of cavalry and infantry for an attack on Lynchburg, but when Richmond fell the expedition was called off. On May 20, 1865, with the war winding down, Hayes submitted a letter of resignation. He requested that it take effect on June 8, four years after his first enlistment. In June he attended the Army Grand Review in Washington and visited Richmond. He then returned to Ohio before going to Washington in December to take his seat in Congress.

GARFIELD: SOLDIER-POLITICIAN

Hayes's successor was fellow Ohioan James A. Garfield. The last president born in a log cabin, Garfield came from a poverty-stricken background and through ambition and hard work overcame a deprived childhood and gained a college education. He joined the Republican party and in 1859 was elected to the Ohio senate. An influential speaker, Garfield aided in the recruitment of the Forty-second Ohio Volunteer Infantry Regiment, in which he was commissioned lieutenant colonel on August 21, 1861. A few months later he was promoted to colonel. His ability to master military manuals soon made up for his lack of martial background. A strict disciplinarian, he was soon given command of the Eighteenth Brigade, Army of the Ohio.

In early January 1862 Garfield led his inexperienced brigade into eastern Kentucky against an equally green Confederate force that was being recruited at Paintsville, Kentucky. With 1,550 men, Garfield forced the 2,240 Confederates under Brig. Gen. Humphrey Marshall out of Paintsville and to a defensive position at Middle Creek near Prestonburg, Kentucky. Following the Confederates, on January 10 Garfield's men opened the battle of Middle Creek by attempting to turn the enemy's right flank. Ineffective fighting went on until late afternoon when Union reinforcements ended a Confederate counterattack and forced the Southerners from the field.

For the next two months Garfield and his command attempted to pacify the area and encourage the populace to support the Union cause, but their work was hindered by Confederate raids and guerrilla activity originating from the Southern position at Pound Gap, on the Virginia and Kentucky border. In order to stop the attacks, Garfield led a detachment against Pound Gap and on March 15, 1862, launched an attack intended to trap his enemy. The Confederates fled before Garfield's men were able to complete their envelopment. The bloodless victory ended the Confederate threat, and by the end of March, Garfield and the majority of his command were transferred to Gen. Don C. Buell's Army of the Ohio.

Brig. Gen. James A. Garfield, 1862 or 1863 (photograph by Mathew B. Brady; Library of Congress)

For his work in Kentucky, Garfield was promoted to brigadier general and was given command of the Twentieth Brigade, Sixth Division, Army of Ohio, on April 5, 1862. With that unit he arrived at Shiloh on the second day of the battle, April 7, 1862, and briefly participated in the pursuit of the Confederates as they pulled away from the battlefield. His command then joined in Halleck's advance against Corinth. During the Corinth campaign Garfield became critical of West Point officers, an opinion that he would retain throughout the war. After the fall of Corinth at the end of May, Garfield's brigade was assigned to the repair of railroads, during which time he fell ill. By the end of July he was forced to take a furlough.

While at home in Ohio, Garfield was nominated to the U.S. House of Representatives from the Nineteenth District, a seat he won in the November election. Also in September, Garfield, his health restored, journeyed to Washington to seek a combat command. While in the capital he stayed with the secretary of the Treasury, Salmon P. Chase. The two became close friends, and Garfield soon became a protégé of the famous Ohio politician. Possibly because of his tie to Chase, and because of the fact that he was not a graduate of West Point, Garfield was named to serve on Maj. Gen. Fritz-John Porter's court-martial board on November 17, 1862. With the rest of the officers presiding over the trial, Garfield voted to cashier Porter from the army.

On January 14, 1863, Garfield was ordered to the Army of the Cumberland. He wanted a field command but eventually accepted the position of chief of staff to Maj. Gen. William S. Rosecrans, the army's commanding officer. Some viewed Garfield as a spy sent from Washington, but in time he overcame suspicions and put his energy into refitting the army for the next campaign. Though he was personally very fond of Rosecrans, he chafed at his commander's inactivity and often wrote Chase about the general. As chief of staff, Garfield helped prepare and participated in Rosecrans's brilliant Tullahoma campaign from June 23 to July 3, 1863, which forced the Confederates out of Chattanooga and into Georgia. At the following battle of Chickamauga, on September 19-20, 1863, Garfield and Rosecrans were driven from the battlefield, but when the two realized that a portion of the army had not left, Garfield volunteered to ride to the sound of the guns and report back on the situation. Returning to the front, he found Maj. Gen. George Thomas with a portion of the army still holding their position. Garfield relayed messages to Rosecrans and assisted Thomas. Garfield was so impressed by Thomas's work that he urged the general to stay and continue the battle, but that night Thomas pulled his men back to Chattanooga.

After Chickamauga, Garfield was ordered to Washington. On the way he was to stop in Louisville to confer with

---

I can never begin to describe the horrors I have witnessed. Hun[dreds] and even thousands of dead were lying around, and a great many thousands were wounded. The cannon balls fell thick around me, but I was mercifully spared.

—Letter of Brig. Gen. James A. Garfield to Mary Garfield, his sister, describing the Battle of Shiloh, April 11, 1862

Secretary of War Edwin Stanton. Thomas urged Garfield to defend Rosecrans, but before the meeting orders arrived in Chattanooga removing Rosecrans and replacing him with Thomas. Garfield conferred with Stanton and then continued to Washington, where he campaigned for the Republicans in the Maryland elections. Promoted to major general on September 19, he requested permission to return to the army but was persuaded by President Lincoln to give up his military career and take his seat in Congress. On December 5, 1863, while wearing his uniform, the first-term representative was introduced to Congress. On the same day he resigned his commission from the army.

ARTHUR: ON THE HOME FRONT

Succeeding Garfield to the presidency was Chester A. Arthur, a Vermont-born, New York politician who had been placed on the ticket to satisfy the Stalwarts. Arthur was the first president since Lincoln who had not served in the army during the Civil War. At the start of the war he served as engineer in chief of the state of New York, a militia position he secured by helping Edwin D. Morgan win reelection in the 1860 New York gubernatorial campaign. The position was purely honorary; Arthur had no training as an engineer.

When war broke out Morgan added to Arthur's duties by making him assistant quartermaster for the state of New

York. His office was in New York City, where he oversaw the outfitting of state units and the quartering and feeding of the military units that passed through the city. It was a tremendous task, and Arthur carried it out with rigid formality and honesty. He was soon promoted to quartermaster general of New York and took on the duty of outfitting all state regiments raised for the war and keeping the state's militia units ready for emergency use.

While carrying out his quartermaster duties Arthur asked to be relieved from serving as the state's chief engineer, but Governor Morgan refused, and Arthur soon went to work to improve New York's fortifications. He formed a board of engineers and, using their recommendations, laid out a defense plan. His first priority was to improve the seacoast fortifications around New York City. He then moved to strengthen and protect the state's approaches from Canada. The state's militia was given specialized training in the operation of heavy seacoast guns and prepared to take up positions should a foreign power threaten the state.

Arthur wanted to serve in the army. Early in the war he was elected colonel of the Ninth New York Regiment, and later he was asked to take command of the Metropolitan Brigade, but Governor Morgan refused to release him and Arthur declined. Arthur's brother did serve in the army, and his wife, a native of Virginia, had relatives in the Confederate army.

With the 1862 election of Democrat Horatio Seymour to the governorship of New York, Arthur's service to his state ended. On January 1, 1863, he left office and returned to private life. A year later he began a law practice that specialized in war claims and other war-related business, quickly amassing a huge fortune. He remained active in politics, and after the war President Ulysses S. Grant appointed him to run the New York Custom House.

New York militiaman Chester A. Arthur, circa 1862 (Library of Congress)

CLEVELAND: RELUCTANT DRAFTEE

Independent and determined, the reforming Cleveland was the first Democrat elected to the presidency since James Buchanan. When the Civil War broke out, Cleveland supported the actions of President Lincoln, including Lincoln's decision to suspend the writ of habeas corpus. Throughout the war, however, Cleveland remained a staunch War Democrat.

Two of Cleveland's brothers served in the army, leaving him with the task of supporting his mother and two sisters. In 1863 he was drafted, but because of his family needs he hired a substitute for $150. The man Cleveland hired, George Brenske (sometimes spelled Benninsky), served in the Sixty-sixth New York Volunteer Infantry Regiment but saw no action. He eventually hurt his back and served as a hospital orderly in Washington before being discharged.

As president, Cleveland fought against claims by Northern veterans and incurred the wrath of the influential Union veteran organization, the Grand Army of the Republic, when he vetoed a bill that would have allowed Civil War veterans to collect disability payments, including old age pensions.

BENJAMIN HARRISON: FROM LIEUTENANT TO GENERAL

Grandson of President William Henry Harrison, Benjamin Harrison practiced law in Cincinnati and in 1854 moved to Indianapolis, where he continued in the legal profession and became active in Republican politics. In July 1862, after being elected reporter of the Supreme Court of Indiana, Harrison volunteered to recruit a regiment of infantry from Indianapolis. Commissioned a second lieutenant in the Seventieth Indiana Volunteer Infantry, he began raising volunteers. Recruiting was stimulated when word of the Confederate invasion of Kentucky reached Indiana. As the size of the regiment grew, so did Harrison's rank. He was soon promoted to captain and then colonel. The regiment was filled out by August 12, and on the next day it was sent to Kentucky to assist in repelling the Confederate threat.

Harrison's regiment moved to Louisville before going on to Bowling Green, Kentucky. There, with one eye on the Confederates, Harrison went to work training his regiment. A tough and rigid disciplinarian, he quickly gained a reputation as a drillmaster. His work was not initially appreciated by his men, but in time they realized the value of his relentless precision. By mid September the Seventieth Indiana was assigned duty guarding railroads and attacking Southern guerrillas.

In October 1862, as the Confederates pulled back to Tennessee, Harrison's command became part of Ward's Brigade, Dumont's Division, Army of the Cumberland, and in November it moved south through Kentucky to Gallatin, Tennessee. On the march Harrison gained the respect of his men by carrying the belongings of tired soldiers and allowing others to use his horse. For the next year Harrison and the Seventieth Indiana served as railroad guards. During that period Harrison spent his time reading military manuals and drilling his regiment. His fine work did not go unrecognized, and from August to November 1863 he was given command of the Second Brigade, Third Division, Reserve Corps, Army of the Cumberland before returning to regimental command.

At the beginning of 1864, when Maj. Gen. William T. Sherman began preparing for his advance on Atlanta, Harrison again received a temporary brigade command. He was given control of the First Brigade, First Division, Eleventh Corps, Army of the Cumberland from January 12 to April 16, 1864. Later, when the Eleventh Corps merged with the Twelfth Corps to form a new Twentieth Corps, the brigade was redesignated the First Brigade, Third Division, Twentieth Corps, Army of the Cumberland, and Harrison returned to commanding the Seventieth Indiana.

During the Atlanta campaign Harrison and his regiment had their baptism by fire. On May 15, 1864, at Resaca, Georgia, he led his regiment in a fierce charge that overran a Confederate fort, capturing four cannons. During the battle his commander was wounded, and Harrison assumed command of the brigade for the rest of the day.

Over the next two months Harrison continued to lead the Seventieth, at New Hope Church and Golgotha Church, and in late June he again became the commander of the First Brigade, Third

Division, Twentieth Corps, Army of the Cumberland. As brigade commander Harrison was instrumental in repelling the July 20, 1864, Confederate attack at Peachtree Creek. Considered a hero of the battle, he was recommended for the rank of brigadier general by his army commander, Maj. Gen. Joseph Hooker.

After the capture of Atlanta, Harrison requested and received a furlough. He left his command for Indiana in late September 1864. While at home he assisted in campaigning during the fall elections for the Union party. Once the elections were over he attempted to return to his brigade, but due to the movement of the Confederate army into Tennessee he was unable to reach Atlanta. He was then assigned to Chattanooga, where he trained new regiments being readied to resist the Confederate attack. Harrison's expertise at training earned him handsome dividends. He organized and was given command of the First Brigade, Provisional Division, Army of the Cumberland in December 1864. He led that brigade at the Battle of Nashville, where it participated in the attack against the Confederate right flank on December 15, 1864. Then, following the route of the Confederates on the next day, the brigade pursued the Southerners into Alabama. For his actions at Nashville he was brevetted a brigadier general.

After Nashville, Harrison received orders to rejoin Sherman's forces at Savannah, Georgia. Arriving at Hilton Head, South Carolina, on March 2, 1865, Harrison tried to catch Sherman's army as it advanced through South Carolina, but he was unable to reach it. After spending a few weeks training men near Coosawhatchie, South Carolina, he took a transport to Wilmington, North Carolina, and eventually joined his brigade on December 5, 1864, at Raleigh, North Carolina. Made commander of the First Brigade, Third Division, Twentieth Corps, Army of Georgia in April, Harrison was present for the surrender of the Confederate Army of the

Brig. Gen. Benjamin Harrison (left) with generals William Ward and John Coburn, heroes of the Battle of Peachtree Creek during the Union campaign to capture Atlanta (photograph by Mathew B. Brady; courtesy of the Harrison Memorial Home)

Tennessee and then participated in the march from Raleigh to Washington. As the command moved through Richmond on May 20, 1865, he received his brevet to brigadier general. The army continued on, and on May 24, 1865, Harrison led his brigade, containing the Seventieth Indiana, in the Army Grand Review at Washington. After that Harrison remained in camp outside the capital until he received his discharge on June 8, 1865.

Harrison ran for the presidency in the 1888 election. Using his reputation as a tough fighter in the Civil War, he promised to continue civil service reform and to gain pensions for Northern Civil War veterans. Though he lost the popular vote, Harrison was elected by a majority in the electoral college. He found national politics to be more difficult than the battlefield. Forced to accept a tariff he thought too high, Harrison was also unable to continue civil service reform, and his pension program nearly bankrupted the Treasury.

McKinley: The Last Civil War President

William McKinley entered Allegheny College in Meadeville, Pennsylvania, in 1860. After leaving college because of poor health, he taught school and then enlisted as a private in the Twenty-third Ohio Volunteer Infantry Regiment, the same unit in which Rutherford B. Hayes served. During the war Hayes called McKinley "one of the bravest and finest officers in the army."

McKinley's military career followed that of his regiment. He underwent training at Camp Chase, Columbus, Ohio, and in July saw service in West Virginia in operations against Southern guerrillas. He fought at the battle of Carnifix Ferry on September 10, 1861. Promoted to commissary sergeant on April 15, 1862, he undertook the often thankless but essential tasks of distributing rations, handling fodder for the regiment's horses, and supervising the distribution of supplies. In that position he served with the regiment during the unsuccessful advance against the Virginia and Tennessee Railroad and the resulting running fight at Giles Courthouse in April and May 1862.

McKinley accompanied the Twenty-third Ohio when in August 1862 it and other units from West Virginia were sent to join Gen. John Pope's Army of Virginia. Arriving too late for the Second Bull Run campaign, McKinley continued his commissary duties as the regiment fought at the Battle of South Mountain on September 14, 1862. Two days later, during the Battle of Antietam, McKinley bravely drove a supply wagon into the midst of the fighting to deliver food and coffee to his regiment. For his actions he was recommended for a Medal of Honor.

In October 1862 the Twenty-third Ohio returned to West Virginia and was assigned to garrison duty and antiguerrilla operations. During that period McKinley was promoted to second lieutenant and later to first lieutenant. For a year McKinley and the regiment protected bridges, roads, and loyal civilians. In July 1863 the regiment joined in the pursuit of Brig. Gen. John Hunt Morgan's command, which raided into Indiana and Ohio from July 2 to July 26, 1863.

McKinley then served in Brig. Gen. George Crook's raid against the Virginia and Tennessee Railroad, which resulted in the battle of Cloyd's Mountain on May 9, 1864, and the eventual destruction of the railroad at Dublin, Virginia. In June, McKinley and the regiment were involved in Maj. Gen. David Hunter's abortive advance on Lynchburg, Virginia, and the July 23 battle of Kernstown.

Promoted to captain on July 25, McKinley started Maj. Gen. Philip Sheridan's Valley campaign with the Twenty-third Ohio, but in early September he was detached from the regiment for duty on Brig. Gen. George Crook's staff. At the battle of Opequon on September 19 he braved enemy fire to carry orders to the front, and at Cedar Creek on October 19, while Crook's command was retreating, he worked hard to rally the demoralized men and assisted in working an artillery piece against the Confederate attack. McKinley was brevetted a major on March 13, 1865, for his services during the campaigns in West Virginia and the Shenandoah Valley. He was mustered out of the army on July 26, 1865.

McKinley, who won the presidency in 1896, was the last Civil War veteran to occupy the White House. With a new nationalism apparent in the country, his administration helped the nation look away from the divisions of the Civil War and toward a united outlook. The president would never see the product of that new nationalism, because shortly after winning reelection he was assassinated by Leon Czolgosz at the Pan American Exposition in Buffalo, New York. He died on September 14, 1901.

MEMORIES OF THE WAR

The three presidents who followed McKinley were too young to serve in the Civil War, but all felt its effects. Theodore Roosevelt grew up in a divided household. His mother's family were Bullochs from Savannah, Georgia, and two of his mother's brothers fought for the South. In his parents' household lived his maternal grandmother and mother's sister. All were staunch Confederates, and on one occasion his mother flew the Confederate flag to celebrate a Southern victory. Roosevelt's father was a Republican Stalwart, but because of the division within the family he did not volunteer for service in the war. Experts have speculated that the young Roosevelt was deeply disturbed by the family conflict, which may have helped create his martial spirit and caused him to insist on forming the Rough Riders during the Spanish-American War.

Maj. William A. McKinley

Roosevelt's vice-president and presidential successor, William Howard Taft, was not as affected by the war as his predecessor. With its strong New England ties, Taft's family was pro-Republican; his father was a Cincinnati lawyer and judge during the war years. Later, Taft's father would become attorney general and secretary of war during Ulysses S. Grant's presidential administrations. As president, Taft initiated the construction of one of the war's greatest memorials when he requested Congress to fund the Lincoln Memorial.

The final president to have memories of the war was Woodrow Wilson. Wilson's father, a Presbyterian minister, had a church in Augusta, Georgia, and was extremely active in backing the Confederacy. Declaring slavery to be divinely sanctioned, the elder Wilson was prominent in forming the Presbyterian Church of the Confederacy, and after the war he refused to have contact with his brothers who were officers in the Northern army.

One of Woodrow Wilson's earliest memories is of a man standing at the gate to his parents' house shouting that Lincoln had been elected and that "There'll be war." Wilson later recalled his father's church being turned into a hospital and its grounds used to house Northern prisoners from the battle of Chickamauga. He also remembered seeing Robert E. Lee and, later, Jefferson Davis, when the latter was taken through Augusta as a prisoner of war.

The war delayed Wilson's education. He did not start school until 1865, when he was nine years old. The late start did not hinder his development. He went on to become a historian and president of Princeton University. He remained a loyal southerner, but he was never a believer in the "Lost Cause." Instead, he claimed in 1880, "because I love the South, I rejoice in the failure of the Confederacy." To Wilson the North's victory brought the nation together and readied it for new greatness. Wilson's election as the first southern president since the Civil War gave proof that the American nation had transcended its bitter conflict.

Scandals in the Highest Office

by PHILIP COCKRELL

"Power corrupts, and absolute power corrupts absolutely." Acton's maxim has become a cliché. But its common use does not vitiate its wisdom. The government of the United States contains no single office in which absolute power resides, but the executive branch does wield extensive authority. Not surprisingly, the presidents and their appointees have been involved in scandals as long as the government has existed. Some are better known than others. The scandals of Teapot Dome and Watergate, for example, are better known than the Eaton affair of Andrew Jackson's first term or the Whiskey Ring scandal of Ulysses S. Grant's presidency. Almost every presidential administration has been touched by scandal, but seldom has the president personally involved himself in the wrongdoing. In any event, certain administrations are famous (or infamous) for their indiscretions.

ANDREW JACKSON, PEGGY EATON, AND THE PETTICOAT WAR

In the first major American presidential scandal the president took what later generations have considered the side of justice. In defending the virtue of Peggy Eaton, the unusual wife of his secretary of war, John Eaton, Jackson severely hampered the workings of his cabinet and courted political disaster. But he also displayed the sense of honor and loyalty that won him the presidency in the first place.

Born Peggy O'Neill, the secretary of war's wife was the daughter of a Washington tavern keeper. As was the practice of the day, Mr. O'Neill's tavern also served as a boardinghouse, and government officials lodged there when Congress met. Boardinghouses were often seedy places, though some were quite respectable. O'Neill's probably inhabited the middle ground. In an age when taverns served as community centers of a sort, Peggy was raised in her father's establishment and developed a fairly open-minded point of view. Rumor had it that before her marriage at age sixteen to navy lieutenant John Timberlake, she had already broken several hearts. Marriage hardly changed her. Timberlake spent much of his time at sea and most of the rest of it intoxicated. During one of his frequent absences, Peggy met widower Eaton, senator from Tennessee, a friend of Jackson's, and thereafter a regular boarder at the O'Neill place. He quickly developed a friendship with the family and even helped Mr. O'Neill financially, recommending that Jackson lodge at the tavern. Soon he was escorting Peggy to Washington social functions, calling her "the smartest little woman in America." Washington society did not agree. At the behest of his wife, James Monroe banned Peggy from White House social functions during his presidency.

In April 1828 word came that John Timberlake had died at sea. Jackson, maneuvering toward the presidency and wanting Eaton as a member of his cabinet, advised the Tennessee senator to marry the widow. He did, and early in 1829 he became Jackson's secretary of war. The common tavern keeper's daughter was now the wife of a powerful cabinet member. But, according to the wives of the others in Jackson's cabinet, she was still not a member of

GEORGE AND SALLY

George Washington's reputation was rudely blemished when, on March 30, 1877, the *New York Herald* published a letter, dated September 12, 1758, from Washington to Sally Fairfax, written while he was stationed at Fort Cumberland on the Virginia frontier. At the time the letter was written, Fairfax was married to one of Washington's close friends, and Washington was seriously considering making a proposal of marriage to Martha Custis. The letter to Mrs. Fairfax contained scarcely veiled expressions of Washington's ardor for her and implied that he was not entirely committed to Martha.

Washington resigned his commission in the Virginia militia in December and married Martha Custis in January 1759. The Washingtons frequently visited the Fairfax home, and whether Mr. Fairfax or Mrs. Washington knew of George's feelings for Sally is uncertain. Equally uncertain is the degree to which Sally encouraged George's pursuit, though it seems she always kept him at a respectable public distance. Sally Fairfax eventually moved to England with her husband.

I do not claim the right to interfere in the domestic relations or personal intercourse of any member of my Cabinet. . . . But from information and from my own observation I am fully impressed with the belief that you and your families have, in addition to the exercise of your and their undoubted rights, taken measures to induce others to avoid mrs Eaton. . . . I will not part with major Eaton and those of my cabinet who cannot harmonize with him had better withdraw, for harmony I must and will have.

—Memorandum of President Andrew Jackson to his cabinet, circa June 1830 [?], concerning the Peggy Eaton "Petticoat War"

proper society. The wives refused to acknowledge Mrs. Eaton at White House parties and did not invite her to events they sponsored. They suspected that the Eaton marriage was motivated by carnal attraction rather than true love.

Jackson had recently weathered rumors of the same type that tyrannized the Eatons. In 1791 he had married Rachel Robards, the former wife of Lewis Robards, a jealous and abusive man who had obtained a divorce from her on the grounds that she had "eloped . . . with another man." That man, Jackson, a good friend of Rachel's family, had merely escorted Rachel from her unloving husband's home to the home of her parents. When he heard the news of the divorce, Jackson immediately proposed marriage, and Rachel accepted. All went well until December 1793, when the couple learned that in 1791 Robards had not actually been granted a divorce, only the right to sue for one. The real divorce came through more than two years later, meaning that Jackson and his wife were not legally married. Technically, the Jacksons had been living in adultery. They moved quickly to legitimize their relations and married again in 1794.

Jackson remained sensitive regarding the issue of his marriage for the rest of his life. The famous duel between Jackson and Charles Dickinson stemmed from Dickinson's insults regarding Mrs. Jackson's "adultery." Later, during the presidential campaign of 1828, supporters of Jackson's rival John Quincy Adams dug up the issue to impugn Jackson's character. Rachel died soon after Jackson's election but before his inauguration, and the new president attributed the death in part to stress caused by the marriage controversy during the campaign.

When the Eaton scandal surfaced,

"The Rats Leaving a Falling House": 1831 cartoon by Edward Williams depicting cabinet officers John Eaton, John Berrien, John Branch, and Samuel Ingham resigning from the Andrew Jackson administration in the wake of the Peggy Eaton "petticoat war"

Jackson, still bitter over the recent loss of his beloved Rachel, rallied to his secretary of war's side. A delegation of congressmen called on Jackson to ask him to remove Eaton from his cabinet, but the president sent them away, thundering, "I did not come here to make a cabinet for the ladies of this place, but for

President Ulysses S. Grant, as Caesar, refuses the pleas of destitute Civil War veterans: "No! I make it a rule only to receive" (Matt Morgan, October 1872)

the nation." Tensions continued to mount. Jackson thought of delaying the traditional dinner for the president and his cabinet until the argument exhausted itself, but a full-scale "petticoat war" had developed. Jackson seated Peggy next to him at the dinner; she, in turn, wore a low-cut dress that only made matters worse.

By the second year of Jackson's presidency the petticoat war had divided the cabinet and hampered the function of the executive branch. Vice-President John C. Calhoun and his wife, Floride, led the fight on the side of virtue. Relations between Jackson and Calhoun, already strained because of Calhoun's sectionalist effort to "nullify" federal tariff legislation in his home state of South Carolina, reached the point where the two would not speak to each other. When news was revealed of then-senator Calhoun's past attempt to have then-general Jackson censured for invading Spanish Florida in 1818, Jackson publicly broke with his vice-president. Secretary of State Martin Van Buren, to a certain extent taking advantage of the situation, sided with Jackson and the Eatons and even invited them to his home. Members of government found themselves having to take sides in the matter, and both factions hardened into intransigence.

Van Buren finally resolved the matter. In early 1831 he and Eaton resigned from the cabinet, and at Van Buren's suggestion Jackson demanded the resignations of the other cabinet members. Jackson was so impressed with Van Buren's loyalty that he made him his running mate in the next election. In 1832 Calhoun resigned the vice-presidency, a weaker national figure after the defeat of nullification. Eaton went on to serve as governor of Florida and U.S. minister to Spain before dying in 1856. Peggy retained a penchant for controversy. At the age of sixty she married a nineteen-year-old dancing instructor, who took her for all her money. She died lonely and penniless,

GROVER CLEVELAND'S FIRST CHILD?

During the presidential campaign of 1884 a disreputable Buffalo, New York, newspaper, the *Evening Telegraph,* published a story entitled "A Terrible Tale," claiming that Democratic candidate Grover Cleveland had fathered an illegitimate child.

The Republican press exploited the story for all it was worth. Soon cartoons appeared in which the baby in question screamed "Ma, Ma, where's my Pa!" Cleveland's advisers scrambled to end the controversy. When asked by a prominent friend what he could do to fix things up, Cleveland answered, "Tell the truth." That turned out to be sound advice, for the truth exonerated the candidate.

The truth was that in 1874, Cleveland had been one of several admirers of an attractive young widow named Maria Halpin. On September 14, 1874, she gave birth to a son she claimed Cleveland had fathered. Under the circumstances, Cleveland could not be certain that he indeed was responsible, but he recognized the possibility and agreed to provide for the child. He also wished to confine potential embarrassment, since several other men who might have been involved were married. Halpin began to drink heavily and to neglect the child, so Cleveland had him placed in a prominent orphanage. He continued to support the boy until a well-to-do family from New York adopted him.

Cleveland's frankness paid off. He won the Democratic presidential nomination and in the general election defeated Republican James Blaine—a man, it was said, who had been "delinquent in office but blameless in public life." More voters were repelled by revelations of Blaines's public indiscretions, it seemed, than by Cleveland's private one.

ninety-three years of age, in 1879.

ULYSSES S. GRANT: A SCANDALOUS PRESIDENCY

Ulysses S. Grant was a good general mostly due to the efficiency of his military subordinates. He proved a poor president mostly due to the greed of his political subordinates. Grant was never personally involved in the scandals that wracked his administrations. In fact, he most likely was unaware that members of his administration were using their positions to make money. Due to the practices of the Grant men, the Grant years are sometimes referred to as the "Era of Good Stealings."

In the early 1870s the Union Pacific Railroad was fast building transcontinental lines. The Crédit Mobilier Company, a subsidy of Union Pacific managed by Representative Okes Ames of Massachusetts, undertook much of the construction, channeling federal subsidies to Union Pacific. Other federal subsidies went to companies controlled by Crédit Mobilier. By padding construction budgets and charging Union Pacific exorbitant fees, Crédit Mobilier officials and stockholders took in enormous sums for themselves. When members of Congress discovered the setup, Ames distributed $33 million worth of Crédit Mobilier stock to selected officials at below market value or with payment deferred. Since dividends ran as high as 340 percent, the deals were difficult to turn down.

During Grant's reelection campaign the scandal went public. A congressional investigation implicated Vice-President Schulyer Colfax, and he was dropped from the ticket. Then it became known that the new vice-presidential nominee's wife had purchased two thousand dollars worth of the stock, although the nominee, Henry Wilson, had made the company refund the investment and re-

During the presidential campaign of 1884, Republicans questioned Democrat Grover Cleveland's ethics on personal, not political grounds (Frank Beard, The Judge, *September 27, 1884)*

fused to collect the profit after he realized that Crédit Mobilier officials expected legislative favors. The affair shook Grant and the country, but since most of the wrongdoing had taken place before Grant assumed office, he avoided harm.

In 1874 and 1875 the Whiskey Ring was exposed. An investigation begun in June 1874 by Secretary of the Treasury Benjamin Bristow revealed that a large group of distillers and Internal Revenue Service agents led by John McDonald, supervisor of the IRS bureau in St. Louis, Missouri, had been distorting liquor production reports and pocketing money that would have gone to pay taxes. The practice of skimming liquor money from IRS coffers was hardly new (it began during the Lincoln administration), but Grant, probably under the influence of his personal secretary, Orville E. Babcock, who, it turned out, probably took a bribe from McDonald to have the investigations halted, was slow to respond to the scandal. After Bristow supervised the arrest of 350 agents and officials in May 1875, Grant naively advised him to go to McDonald—the "one honest man in St. Louis on whom we can rely"—for the whole story. Bristow was embarrassed to tell the president

---

It was my fortune, or misfortune, to be called to the office of the Chief Executive without any previous political training. From the age of 17 I had never even witnessed the excitement attending a presidential campaign but twice antecedent to my own candidacy, and at but one of them was I eligible as a voter. . . . It is but reasonable to suppose that errors of judgment must have occurred. . . . It is not necessarily evidence of blunder on the part of the executive because there are these differences of views. Mistakes have been made, as all can see and I admit.

—President Ulysses S. Grant, eighth State of the Union Address, December 5, 1876

Members of both parties feared having their dirty linen aired during investigations of Harding administration scandals, 1924 (cartoon by McCutcheon; courtesy of the Chicago Tribune*)*

that McDonald was a prime suspect in the case. The president took a hard line when it came to prosecuting the cases, however, opposing all grants of immunity in return for testimony. McDonald went to jail and wrote a book about the ring. Bristow estimated that at the height of the scam between twelve and fifteen million gallons of whiskey went untaxed every year.

Grant found it difficult to believe that his personal secretary was part of the scandal. He submitted a deposition in favor of Babcock that was read at the secretary's trial, which began in February 1876. Babcock won his acquittal.

New accusations charged Grant's eldest son and his brother with crimes in connection with the Whiskey Ring. Some in the press claimed that even the president himself was involved. Grant instructed his attorney general to put the reporters who made the charges before a grand jury to prove their accusations. The charges melted away.

My God, this is a hell of a job! I have no trouble with my enemies. . . . But my damn friends, . . . they're the ones that keep me walking the floor nights.

—*Quote attributed to President Warren G. Harding in* The Autobiography of William Allen White *(1946)*

HARDING, COOLIDGE, AND THE TEAPOT DOME

The administration of Warren G. Harding was as infamous for scandal as Grant's. Harding looked the part of a president, but he was proof of the maxim that a man of mediocre talent could rise to the White House. Like Grant, Harding had trouble picking friends he could trust. The worst trouble they got him into involved the Teapot Dome. Lucky for Harding, he died before the news broke.

The scandal derived its name from a small mountain in Wyoming that was shaped like a teapot. Underneath the mountain lay a naval oil reserve deposit that until 1920 had been protected by the government from private development. That year, however, Congress passed the Oil Leasing Act, opening previously protected lands. By means of an executive order, in 1921 the Department of the Navy transferred control of its oil reserve lands to the Department of the Interior, which leased drilling rights to private businesses. Secretary of the Interior Albert Fall awarded the first contract at Teapot Dome a few months later.

Fall and the Department of the Interior awarded more contracts in 1922. Alarmed by the increasing development of public lands, conservationists persuaded Progressive party leader Senator Robert M. LaFollette of Wisconsin to instigate a congressional inquiry into the private drilling program. The Public Lands Committee, the committee charged with the investigation, subpoenaed numerous documents from cabinet officials and private contractors. The amount of material obtained was so massive that the committee studied it for sixteen months before opening public hearings. President Harding died before the committee uncovered the indiscretions of his friend Fall.

The interior secretary originally appeared before the committee to answer questions about improvements made to his ranch. He testified that he had received the money for the improvements as a loan from Edward McLean, publisher of the *Washington Post.* McLean denied making the loan, so Fall changed his story. The money had come from "other sources," but he would not say who those other sources were. Now certain that Fall was concealing the truth, the committee began to scrutinize his personal accounts.

Then drilling contractor Edward Doheny told the committee that he had given Fall the money for the ranch improvements and five months later had received a contract to drill for oil on public land. He tried to dissipate the burgeoning scandal by reporting that he and Fall had been close friends for more than thirty years. That revelation made the exchange more understandable, but it hardly diminished the stain of corruption.

New president Calvin Coolidge entered the fray in 1924, when he ordered the Department of Justice to investigate the Teapot Dome business. Because the attorney general was a longtime friend of Fall's, Congress asked the president to appoint special counsel; Coolidge agreed, and after a few difficulties secured a two-member team. Meanwhile, Congress also began to pressure the president to fire Navy Secretary Edwin Denby because of his role in delivering the oil reserve lands to Fall's Interior Department. Denby had done nothing wrong, but he resigned under pressure later in the year. The Public Lands Committee ended its hearings and reported that the drilling done in the navy oil reserve lands was "essentially corrupt."

Criminal courts took three years to pass judgment on Fall, Doheny, and the others involved in the scandal. Finding that a conspiracy existed between the Interior Department and the drilling companies, the courts canceled the leases. The defendants challenged the findings, but in every case the Supreme Court upheld the decisions of the lower courts. Fall went to jail for accepting a bribe from Doheny; interestingly, Do-

WARREN HARDING'S PERSONAL SCANDALS

In 1927, the publication of Nan Britton's *The President's Daughter* called the President Warren Harding's personal morality into question. In her book Miss Britton claimed she had been infatuated with Harding from the time she was a teenager when he was a married man in his forties. The affair, Britton wrote, produced a child in 1919 and continued into the Harding presidency. Britton's last visit to the White House occurred, she claimed, in January 1923, when, as usual, the president met her in an Oval Office closet. Britton described Harding as "loyal," "sensitive," "loving," and "passionate."

That Harding was passionate was further confirmed in 1964, when a series of letters he wrote to Carrie Phillips, the wife of a business associate, were uncovered. The letters indicated in graphic terms the extent to which Harding's desire for Phillips was fulfilled. Apparently Harding conducted the affairs with Britton and Phillips simultaneously, and he made sure not only that his wife remained in the dark, but also that his two mistresses were unaware of each other.

President Richard Nixon offers edited transcripts of selected "Watergate tapes" to the House Judiciary Committee, April 29, 1974 (courtesy of UPI)

heny was not convicted of bribing Fall.

NIXON AND WATERGATE

For almost fifty years the Teapot Dome scandal enjoyed the dubious distinction of being the most corrupt scandal in the annals of American government. But the Watergate affair, which began in 1972, far surpassed the Teapot Dome affair and led eventually to the resignation of President Richard M. Nixon in the first such action in U.S. history.

Nixon began his second term of office after a landslide victory over George McGovern with a "clear mandate" from the people, but he was not to enjoy the fruits of victory for long. Disturbing revelations of possible scandal appeared even before the election. During the reelection campaign, on June 17, 1972, five members of Nixon's Committee to Reelect the President (CREEP) were caught burglarizing the Democratic National Committee headquarters at the Watergate hotel complex in Washington. An investigation revealed that the CREEP men had broken in once before. Former attorney general John Mitchell, chairman of CREEP, denied that the committee had directed the break-ins. President Nixon also denied knowing about the plans of the burglars.

While Nixon was publicly disavowing the break-in, he was privately conspiring with top aides to cover it up. He was worried that a Federal Bureau of Investigation (FBI) inquiry would uncover illegal campaign contributions received by CREEP. A veteran of the political wars and something of a traditionalist when it came to campaigning, he also feared that a serious investigation would uncover other irregularities, some of which he was sure he knew nothing about. On June 23 he authorized a White House attempt to cover up the FBI investigation. The affair became further muddled when it was revealed that acting FBI director L. Patrick Gray had destroyed potentially incriminating documents taken from the safe of CREEP operative E. Howard Hunt by

BILLYGATE

Jimmy Carter's "redneck" brother, Billy, proved an asset during the 1976 presidential campaign. Billy became a popular national symbol for the "good-ol'-boy" with his easygoing style and beer-drinking antics. The fact that Jimmy had such an unaffected brother indicated to the public that the candidate's claims to be different from run-of-the-mill politicians might be genuine.

By 1980, however, Billy had become a political liability. First came several run-ins with the American press. Once he embarrassed his brother by urinating on the side of a building in full view of several journalists. His drinking, which seemed quaint during the campaign, turned into a real problem as the Carter presidency wore on. Then the story of a genuine scandal appeared in the newspapers. Billy allegedly violated a federal statute by accepting a $200,000 loan from the Libyan government. Jimmy was embarrassed to see Billy appear on television shaking hands and smiling with his new benefactors, considered state terrorists by the federal government.

Congress investigated, and Republicans, remembering the Watergate scandal during President Richard Nixon's administration, dubbed the affair "Billygate." During his reelection campaign in 1980, the president came under intense criticism for his failure to control the actions of his injudicious brother.

White House counsel John Dean. CREEP also funneled large amounts of "hush money" to the Watergate defendants to pay their legal fees and to buy their silence. The defendants were also promised presidential pardons if they agreed to serve short prison terms without telling what they knew.

Using these means, Nixon and his aides were able to keep the Watergate matter quiet for the remainder of the campaign. The break-in trial began at about the time of the president's second inauguration. U.S. District Court judge John J. Sirica presided over the case. Hunt, who along with G. Gordon Liddy of CREEP was charged with directing the break-in, and four of the burglars pleaded guilty and were provisionally given maximum sentences. Liddy and James McCord, leader of the break-in team, pleaded not guilty but were also convicted and provisionally sentenced. Sirica was convinced the seven were hiding something or someone. On February 2, 1973, he ordered a further investigation. In response, the Senate created the Select Committee on Presidential Campaign Activities, chaired by a tough old country lawyer, Senator Sam Ervin of North Carolina.

While the Ervin Committee was gearing up, pressure mounted on the Watergate defendants to come clean. In sentencing the group provisionally, Sirica had in effect dangled a carrot of leniency before them; he made it clear that all they had to do to win reduced sentences was to cooperate with prosecutors. McCord, a former CIA agent, was the first to break. In a letter to Sirica that the judge made public on March 23 he indicated that his orders had come from high up in the administration and that the Watergate defendants had committed perjury in the trial. Sirica postponed McCord's sentencing, and McCord offered to go before the Ervin Committee with his story.

Then pressure mounted within the administration. On April 27, Gray resigned as acting director of the FBI after confessing to his role in the cover-up. Three days later, chief of staff H. R. Haldeman, chief of domestic affairs John Erlichman, counsel John Dean, and Attorney General Richard Kleindienst resigned. Attorney General designate Elliot Richardson agreed to appoint a special prosecutor to investigate the growing scandal. Also, at about this time Dean realized that Haldeman decided to tell what he knew.

The Ervin Committee started its hearings on May 17, and chinks began to appear in the White House armor. McCord testified, and then, much more dramatically, so did counsel John Dean, who, in saving his own skin, related an amazing story of his and others' roles in an extensive White House effort to frustrate the FBI investigation. Most important, Dean testified that Nixon had known all along of the cover-up and had encouraged it. Then CREEP chairman John Mitchell, along with Haldeman and Erlichman, also gave testimony, much of it in contradiction to Dean's. The situation was becoming more and more confusing when a minor figure, White House record keeper Alexander Butterfield, testified that the president had routinely recorded his Oval Office conversations.

The special prosecutor, Archibald Cox, subpoenaed Nixon to get the tapes, Nixon refused to turn them over, and a court battle ensued. Cox won that battle in October, and Nixon responded with what has gone down in history as the "Saturday Night Massacre." He ordered Attorney General Richardson to fire Cox; Richardson resigned instead. Nixon then turned to the deputy attorney general, William D. Ruckelshaus, who also refused to fire Cox and resigned. Eventually the number-three man at Justice, Robert Bork, did the deed. The firing created an uproar and convinced many that much of the scandal still remained to be revealed. Four days later House Judiciary Committee chairman Peter Rodino announced that the committee would begin impeachment hearings against the president.

Nixon went on television several times in an attempt to gain public support, but his impassioned denials gradually lost credibility. In January the impeachment hearings began; on July 24 the Supreme Court decided that new special prosecutor Leon Jaworski was entitled to the tapes Nixon had withheld from Cox. The tapes revealed that on June 23, 1972, Nixon agreed to the suggestions of chief of staff Haldeman and authorized the cover-up, which he had been denying he knew about until March 1973. On July 27, 29, and 30 the Judiciary Committee voted to recommend three articles of impeachment to the full House; Nixon, his support in Congress now exhausted, resigned on August 9.

The American people were not destined to learn much more of the former president's involvement in Watergate. One of the first acts new president Gerald Ford performed was to pardon his disgraced predecessor. Although the nation was outraged, Ford justified his action by declaring that it was time to put Watergate in the past. "Our long national nightmare is over," he stated. Many of the former president's aides were not so fortunate. A total of twenty-five Nixon appointees spent time in prison as a result of Watergate offenses.

REAGAN AND THE IRAN-CONTRA AFFAIR

The administration of President Ronald Reagan began with great promise, but soon advisers and appointees began to mire themselves in indiscretions. Most of the scandals involved influence peddling, and the many indictments of Reagan administration officials recalled the times of President Harding. The president, as usual, was not involved in any of those matters, but beginning in the winter of 1986 his name came up in connection with a particularly confusing kind of scandal, dubbed by the press the Iran-Contra affair.

The matter began when Lt. Col. Oliver North, a Marine associated with the National Security Council, resigned under fire, accused of misusing government funds. That opened a Pandora's Box of scandal. As the matter unwound, terrorists, outlaw nations, secret bank accounts, and counterrevolutionaries appeared in active roles. An infuriated Congress, which during the early years of the Reagan administration had often seemed impotent, saw an opportunity to exercise its constitutional muscle and at the same time strike a blow against Reagan. It called for an investigation of the whole business.

The background to the situation was as messy as the affair itself. The installation in 1979 of a radical Moslem government ruled by the Ayatollah Khomeini had alienated the United States. Under the Ayatollah, Iran sponsored terrorist acts around the world, causing the United States to brand it an "outlaw nation." Meanwhile, Lebanon, torn by civil war between religious factions, became one of the stages upon which the U.S.-Iranian drama was played. Americans living in Lebanon, many of them teachers and clerics, became targets for Iran-supported terrorists who vented their rage by taking western hostages. Reagan took a vehement stand against the hostage-taking, publicly refusing to bargain for their release.

Thus, many Americans felt betrayed when news broke that the administration had sold arms to Iran for the purpose of buying the release of certain hostages. Given the U.S. declaration of neutrality in the Iran-Iraq war, even the legality of the weapons sales seemed questionable. Then, even more startling news filtered out.

Meanwhile, Congress was threatening the administration's efforts to maintain financial support for the Nicaraguan Contra movement. In 1986 Congress approved only a "humanitarian" aid package for the movement, denying the Contras the military aid they had received in the past. Congress had also passed laws designed to prevent federal funds from going to the Contras through other avenues. Reagan and his advisers put together a plan to circumvent the congressional restrictions. A strange (and in some ways an ingenious) network administered by National Security Adviser Robert "Bud" McFarlane (which continued under his successor, Adm. John Poindexter) and coordinated by Oliver North funneled money

Former Texas senator John Tower submits the Tower Commission report on the Iran-Contra Affair to President Ronald Reagan, February 26, 1987 (courtesy of UPI/Bettmann Newsphotos)

from the Iran arms sales to the Contras. The Iran money was transferred to Swiss bank accounts and combined with money raised by North and Poindexter from private sources for the same purpose. North obtained the private money by presenting a slide show dramatizing the plight of the Nicaraguan people and the Contras to sympathetic groups. Then the money went to Contra leaders.

I don't care if I have to go to Leavenworth; I want the hostages out.

—Quote attributed to President Ronald Reagan in Michael Ledeen, Perilous Statecraft *(1988)*

Members of Congress maintained that the actions of North and his cohorts were illegal. Naturally the question of the president's involvement arose. But Reagan cooperated with Congress by ordering an independent inquiry chaired by former Texas senator John Tower. The Tower Commission report fingered North, Poindexter, and a host of underlings but found no evidence incriminating the president. Dissatisfied with the Tower Report's failure to incriminate Reagan, Congress ordered its own Judiciary Committee investigation in the spring of 1987. Meanwhile, Reagan appeared on television and admitted to the "arms for hostages" arrangement, declaring that "mistakes were made"; popular support for the president remained strong. Citing a poor memory, Reagan continually denied any knowledge of the Iran-Contra link.

Televised committee hearings, at which North testified in uniform that he had only followed orders, made him a pop-culture hero. North further asserted that he had been set up as a scapegoat and that others had cynically used his sense of patriotism to their advantage. Other witnesses insisted that the business was transacted without presidential knowledge.

Robert McFarlane got his date with the committee postponed by attempting suicide. When he finally did appear, committee members grilled him thoroughly about Reagan's involvement. Both he and Poindexter refused to implicate the president, and Poindexter pointedly admitted responsibility for the affair. Like the Tower report, the congressional hearings produced no smoking gun. The indicted went to court and nearly all were acquitted or given suspended sentences. Afterward Poindexter and McFarlane claimed that Reagan possessed information that would shed light on the mechanics of the exchanges. Reagan continued to claim ignorance and poor memory.

Who Was President When What Was Invented

by THOMAS L. CONNELLY

One may choose to measure the success of a president not only by what he accomplishes himself, but also by what others accomplish under his leadership. Because free enterprise spurs innovation, the United States has led the world in invention for much of its history. To the extent that the presidents have tried to keep enterprise free of government interference, they deserve some credit for the nation's success. That's the American way. But not all invention is the product of the lone tinkerer or the corporate research lab. To support projects too large for loners or inappropriate for the competitive business world, sometimes the politicians feel they must get involved. As in the case of the "military-industrial complex"—which often produces inventions having as great an impact on the civilian world as the military—government and business frequently work together. Many modern inventions—publicly or privately funded—are the products of years of cooperative research. Even in this age of high technology, however, there is still room for flashes of individual inspiration.

The following is a survey of American inventors and inventions great and small.

WASHINGTON

1790

Oliver Booth of Poughkeepsie, New York, fits long blades onto a sailboat and becomes the first ice sailor.

1793

Eli Whitney invents the cotton gin, a machine that separates cotton seed from fiber. The southern cotton industry experiences explosive growth. Whitney patents his device in 1794.

JEFFERSON

1807

The first successful commercial steamboat, the *Clermont*, is constructed by Robert Fulton of New York.

MONROE

1817

Seth Hunt patents a machine for the manufacture of pins. John Ireland patents an improved model in 1832.

1818

Moses Rogers of Savannah, Georgia, constructs the first transatlantic steamer, the *Savannah*, which takes its maiden voyage from Savannah to Liverpool, England, in 1819.

1823

Rev. Samuel Read Hall, a Congregational minister and founder of the Concord (Vermont) Academy, patents a planed, black-painted pine board for use in school instruction—the first "blackboard."

JACKSON

1829

The Case Company constructs the first practical steam tractor. The Burger oil tractor follows in 1889, the Froelish gasoline tractor in 1892, the Caterpillar tractor designed by Benjamin Holt in 1905, and the Ford Motor Company tractor in 1907.

1830

D. Hyde patents a version of the fountain pen.

1831

Virginian Cyrus McCormick builds his first horse-drawn reaping machine. Large-scale production of the McCormick Reaper begins in Chicago in 1847.

1836

American railroads inaugurate the use of sleeping cars. The first dining cars are introduced in 1840.

Samuel Colt of Hartford, Connecticut, invents the revolver. The gun meets with little success until the U.S. Army orders large quantities to supply troops during the Mexican War.

VAN BUREN

1837

Massachusetts-born Samuel F. B. Morse develops a telegraph system that enters widespread American use in the 1840s and 1850s. Morse patents his device in 1840.

Thomas Davenport, of Brandon, Vermont, patents a rotary electric motor, the forerunner of the motors used in modern electric appliances.

1840

William Howe of Spencer, Massachusetts, patents a triangular-truss support system for bridges. The Howe truss makes large railroad bridges practical.

TYLER

1841

Loring Coes of Worcester, Massachusetts, invents the monkey wrench.

1842

Georgia physician Crawford W. Long becomes the first doctor to use ether as a general anesthesia in surgery. In 1844 Dr. Horace Wells of Hartford, Connecticut, becomes the first physician to publicize the anesthetic effect of nitrous oxide. The first widely publicized anesthetic success occurs in 1846, when W. Morton and J. Warren of the Massachusetts General Hospital use ether during an operation on a patient with a neck tumor.

1844

Charles Goodyear of New Haven, Connecticut, patents a process for improving the strength and stability of rubber—"vulcanizing" it.

POLK

1845

Alexander Cartwright, one of the founders of the Knickerbocker Baseball Club of New York, codifies the rules of baseball. The first game played under the Cartwright rules pits the Knickerbockers against the New York Nine in Hoboken, New Jersey. The Knickerbockers lose by a score of 23 to 1.

1846

Elias Howe patents a modern "Improvement in Sewing Machines" to make the first sewing machine capable of combining the action of two needles on opposite sides of the fabric.

1847

Robert W. Thompson patents the rubber pneumatic tire.

Richard M. Hoe patents the rotary printing press.

1848

Charles Burton of New York City builds the first baby carriage. A folding model is introduced in Paris in 1909.

TAYLOR

1849

Walter Hunt patents the modern safety pin.

Abraham Lincoln, sixteenth president of the United States, patents a device for buoying marine vessels over shoals.

FILLMORE

1851

Isaac Singer of Pittstown, New York, founder of the Singer Sewing Machine

Company, markets the first household sewing machine.

John Gorrie patents an ice-making machine.

PIERCE

1853

H. L. Emery of Albany, New York, invents the automatic hay baler.

BUCHANAN

1858

Ezra J. Warner of Waterbury, Connecticut, patents the manual can opener.

Boston detective E. T. Holmes invents the first practical burglar alarm. Windows and doors are connected to an electrical source; if an entrance is breached, a spring trips, completing the connection and setting off an alarm.

1859

At Titusville, Pennsylvania, the first "oil rush" occurs, the result of the construction by Edwin L. Drake of the first oil well.

1860

B. Tyler Henry of Connecticut invents the first successful repeating rifle, marketed by the New Haven Repeating Arms Company, later known as the Winchester Company.

Nehemiah Dodge patents the first railroad air-brake system.

LINCOLN

1861

John Charlton of Philadelphia invents the postcard.

1862

Richard J. Gatling patents a rapid-fire machine gun widely used during the American Civil War.

1863

Ebenezer Butterick invents the tissue-paper dress pattern.

1864

George M. Pullman of Chicago patents the Pullman railroad sleeping car.

ANDREW JOHNSON

1866

William Arthur "Candy" Cummings of the Brooklyn Excelsiors [?] becomes the first baseball pitcher to throw a curveball. Debate still rages over whether the curve actually curves.

1867

The city of New York constructs the first elevated railway system.

1868

Sylvester Marsch builds the first ascending "rack" railroad, the Mount Washington line in New Hampshire. Inclines on the line reach up to thirty degrees.

C. Latham Sholes, Carlos Glidden, and Samuel W. Soule patent the first practical typewriter.

GRANT

1869

New York-born George Westinghouse invents an automatic railroad air-brake system. Air brakes first appear on American locomotives in 1872.

1872

Silas Noble and James P. Cooley patent a machine for the manufacture of wooden toothpicks.

Robert A. Cheeseborough patents the substance known as "petroleum jelly," marketed under the name "Vaseline."

1873

Joseph Glidden of De Kalb, Illinois, invents barbed wire and patents the invention the next year.

Oscar Levi Strauss invents dungaree blue jeans.

Chester Greenwood of Farmington, Maine, invents earmuffs. He patents the invention in 1877.

1876

Alexander Graham Bell patents the first workable telephone system.

Melville R. Bissel patents the carpet sweeper.

The first wind-powered (windmill) electrical generators go into operation in the midwestern United States.

The National League of Baseball Clubs begins operations. The American League starts business in 1901.

HAYES

1877

Thomas Edison invents the wax-cylinder phonograph. He patents the invention the next year.

1878

Thomas Edison invents an incandescent lamp, which he patents in 1880. A Britisher, Joseph Swan, invents a similar lamp at about the same time. Edison and Swan sue each other for patent violations, then establish a company together to market the lamps in 1883.

George Eastman of Waterville, New York, invents the dry-plate photographic process. He invents and markets the first celluloid roll film in 1889.

1879

James J. Ritty of Dayton, Ohio, invents the cash register.

The first "supermarkets" appear in U.S. cities. Supermarkets are introduced into Great Britain in 1909 and into France in 1927. The owner of the Oklahoma City Humpty Dumpty supermarket invents the supermarket cart in 1937 when he attaches wheels and a basket onto metal folding chairs.

1880

Thomas Edison develops a "talking doll" that uses a record of the human voice.

ARTHUR

1884

American-born Hiram Maxim invents the automatic machine gun in England.

George Eastman patents a variety of photographic paper-strip film.

CLEVELAND

1885

W. L. Bundy invents the industry time clock, for which he receives a patent in 1888.

1886

John Pemberton of Atlanta, Georgia, develops the formula for Coca-Cola syrup.

Elihu Thompson patents an apparatus for electric-arc welding.

1887

Player pianos appear in the western United States.

1888

In Richmond, Virginia, Frank W. Sprague constructs the first operational electric tramway line.

Marvin Chester Stone of Washington, D.C., invents the paper drinking straw. His estate invents a machine to mass-produce the straws in 1905.

Harold P. Brown and Dr. A. E. Kennerly, researchers at the Edison Company, fashion an electric chair for criminal executions. The first human electrocution takes place at the Auburn, New York, prison in 1890. The victim was a murderer named William Kemmler.

John J. Loud patents the ballpoint pen.

BENJAMIN HARRISON

1889

George Blickenderfer invents the portable typewriter, designed to be carried around in a case. He receives a patent for his invention in 1892.

A team led by Thomas Edison invents the first sound motion picture camera, the kinetograph. In 1892 the team invents a kinetoscope to view sound films produced by the kinetograph.

William Gray of Hartford, Connecticut, patents the first coin-operated telephone system.

Charles M. Hall of Oberlin, Ohio, patents a process for manufacturing aluminum.

1890

Frustrated by an ice cream shortage caused by a lack of Sunday deliveries, a Wisconsin retail merchant named Smithson invents the ice cream sundae, replacing the lost ice cream with syrups, fruit, and whipped cream.

Whitecomb Judson invents the zipper. Machines to manufacture zippers go into operation in 1905, but only in 1912, after improvements are introduced by Sundback, a Swede, does the use of zippers become widespread.

1892

James Naismith, a professor at the YMCA Training School in Springfield, Massachusetts, invents the game of basketball.

CLEVELAND

1893

Henry D. Persky of Denver, Colorado, invents "shredded wheat" cereal.

1895

The Baltimore & Ohio Railroad introduces the electric locomotive into service.

William G. Morgan, a gymnastics professor at the Holyoke, Massachusetts, YMCA, invents the game of volleyball.

Michael J. Owens invents an automatic glassblowing machine, making possible the development of the bottled drinks industry.

1896

The first widely popular newspaper comic strip, the *Yellow Kid* by R. F. Outcault, appears in the *New York Tribune*.

MCKINLEY

1899

Dr. George F. Grant of Boston patents a version of the wooden golf tee.

1900

John Moses Browning of Ogden, Utah, invents the semiautomatic pistol for the Winchester Company.

THEODORE ROOSEVELT

1901

Iowa-born Thaddeus Cahill develops an electric typewriter, but only forty of the machines, which retail for $3,925, are sold. The first successful electric typewriter, the "Electromatic" designed by R. G. Thomson of the International Business Machines Company, reaches the market in 1933.

Maine-born Alvin Orlando Lombard designs the first tractor treads to move cut trees to his father's sawmill. Bulldozers and army tanks later use tractor treads of similar design.

King Camp Gillette patents the first double-edged safety razor.

Alva J. Fisher invents the electric washing machine.

Miller Reese Hutchinson develops the first electroacoustic hearing aid.

1902

W. H. Walker patents a process to manufacture the synthetic fiber acetate rayon.

1903

At Kitty Hawk, North Carolina, Wilbur and Orville Wright of Dayton, Ohio, make the first sustained and controllable powered airplane flights.

G. C. Beidler develops the process of photocopying, which he patents in 1906. The Rectigraph Company markets the first photocopying machine in 1907.

1904

Harry D. Weed of Canastota, New York, invents chains that fit on automobile tires to improve traction in snowy weather.

An American named Rubel develops the "offset" printing process.

1905

The Vick Chemical Company of North Carolina introduces Vick's Magic Croup Salve—later renamed VapoRub.

1906

The Gabel Company markets the first jukebox—an acoustic model called the "Automatic Entertainer." Electric jukeboxes first appear in 1926.

Thomas Hunt Morgan begins modern genetic studies by employing the fast-breeding fruit fly *Drosophila* to study heredity.

1907

Iowan Lee DeForest invents the triode vacuum tube. The tube becomes crucial to the development of radio, television, radar, and computers.

J. M. Splanger invents the electric vacuum cleaner.

1908

The Ford Motor Company, led by Henry Ford, inaugurates assembly-line mass production in its Detroit automobile factory.

The U.S. Army adopts the first military aircraft—the Wright Model A. The first pilots trained by the Wright brothers to fly the craft crash it.

TAFT

1909

The General Electric Company markets the first electric toaster.

Belgian-born Hendrick Baekeland invents the first thermostating phenoplastic resin—plastic. Later it is marketed in America under the name Bakelite.

1910

American Eugene Ely becomes the first airplane pilot to take off from a sea vessel. Ely learns how to land on a ship in 1911.

Fred Osius, Chester A. Beach, and L. H. Hamilton market the first practical electric motor for use in small home appliances. They mount it in sewing machines and in milkshake mixers.

The Holt Company develops the first self-propelled gasoline-powered combine harvester.

1911

Willis Carrier invents the air conditioner.

Charles Kettering designs the first practical automobile self-starter, which makes its initial appearance on the 1912 General Motors Cadillac.

1912

The electric dishwasher enters the market in the United States. Calgon dishwashing detergent appears in 1932. Automatic dishwashers follow in 1940.

WILSON

1913

The Indian motorcycle company introduces an electric starter, the first ever produced for a motorcycle, on its Hendee Special.

Crossword puzzles designed by Arthur Wynne begin to appear in the *New York World*.

The Domelre Company of Chicago markets the first electric refrigerator. The Kelvinator follows in 1918 and the Frigidaire in 1919.

Virgil D. White of Ossipee, New Hampshire, builds the first snowmobile by fitting a Ford Model T automobile chassis with tractor treads in the rear and snow skis in the front.

1914

Thomas Edison invents the alkaline storage battery.

Electric traffic lights appear in the streets of Cleveland, Ohio.

Mary Phelps Jacob patents a wireless brassiere.

1915

Detroit blacksmith and wagon maker August Fruehauf invents the tractor trailer, laying the foundation for the development of the trucking industry.

Engineers at the Corning Glass Works of New York develop heat- and chemical-resistant "Pyrex" glass.

The Kraft Company markets the first processed cheese product, which meets with success because it keeps nearly indefinitely.

1916

Automatic windshield wipers first appear on a variety of American automobiles.

A loudspeaker public-address system is demonstrated at a conference of the National Educational Association in Madison Square Garden.

Dr. Joseph Goldberger demonstrates that the disease pellagra, common in the agricultural South, is caused by dietary deficiency, not infection.

Margaret Sanger founds the first birth-control clinic in Brooklyn, New York.

1917

The Curtiss Company constructs an "aerial torpedo" for the U.S. Navy. It is essentially a pilotless biplane equipped with a load of explosives and a timing device that causes its wings to drop off when it reaches its target.

1918

Drs. Harvey Cushing and Walter Dandy develop the techniques of modern neurosurgery.

1919

The American Telephone & Telegraph Company introduces the first dial telephones in Norfolk, Virginia.

1920

Two Racine, Wisconsin, companies introduce electric hair dryers on the market. The Racine Universal Motor Company calls its model the "Race," and the Hamilton Beach Company calls its the "Cyclone." Sears, Roebuck & Company markets the first helmet-style automatic hair dryer in 1951.

HARDING

1921

Kimberly-Clark Company of Neenah, Wisconsin, markets the first feminine hygienic napkin brand, Kotex.

1922

C. K. Nelson of Onawa, Iowa, patents the first chocolate-coated ice cream bar, the Eskimo Pie.

Clarence Birdseye establishes the Freezing Company to market the first practical industrial freezing process.

George Frost installs a radio in his Ford Model-T automobile. It is the first radio ever installed in a car. The Motorola Corporation markets the first factory-made car radios in 1929.

COOLIDGE

1923

Russian-American Vladimir Kosma develops the first video camera, which converts light images captured by a lens into reconvertible electrical signals.

1924

Kimberly-Clark Company of Neenah, Wisconsin, introduces Kleenex—the first disposable paper handkerchief brand.

Maj. D. A. Turner of the U.S. Army Medical Corps invents the gas chamber for human execution. The first victim is Gee Jon, a Chinese murderer. He dies after inhaling hydrocyanide gas for six minutes.

1925

Dick Drew, a laboratory assistant for the 3M Company of St. Paul, Minnesota, invents cellulose adhesive tape.

1926

A workable power-steering system is installed on a Pierce-Arrow automobile, but power steering is widely adopted only in the 1950s.

The first continuous hot-strip steel mill goes into operation in Butler, Pennsylvania.

The first truck-mounted concrete mixers appear on American roads.

1927

The first public demonstration of television in the United States occurs when scientists from Bell Laboratories send images of Secretary of Commerce Herbert Hoover across telephone lines from Washington, D.C., to New York City.

Philip Drinken of Harvard University designs the first "iron lung." He uses two household vacuum cleaners to produce the alternating positive and negative pressure necessary to induce breathing.

1928

Walt Disney introduces the animated character Mickey Mouse to U.S. filmgoing audiences.

Kellogg Cereal Company introduces Rice Krispies on the market.

The Pioneer Company inaugurates the first transcontinental bus service. Pioneer sells out to Greyhound the following year.

HOOVER

1929

Warren Alvin Harrison of Orange, New Jersey, develops the first quartz-resonator electric clock.

Bell Laboratories beams the first color television signals through telephone lines from Washington, D.C., to New York.

1930

Stewardesses make their first appearance on American airplanes.

W. L. Semon of the B. F. Goodrich Company develops polyvinyl chloride—PVC plastic.

The Postum Company of Springfield, Massachusetts, begins selling the first prepackaged frozen foods. Only with the advent of television after World War II do frozen dinners become widely popular.

1931

The Du Pont company produces nylon fiber. Du Pont first markets the product in 1938.

Miles Laboratories of Elkhart, Indiana, markets the Alka-Seltzer effervescent tablet for the relief of headaches and nausea.

The first electric shaver, the Schick Dry Shaver, enters the market.

1932

Harold Clayton Urey employs a process of isotopic separation to obtain "heavy water," which contains molecules of deuterium instead of hydrogen. Heavy water later finds a use as a moderator in nuclear reactors.

Czech-born Bell Laboratories engineer Karl Jansky builds the first radio telescope. Constructed of wood and brass, the rotating telescope is mounted on Jansky's Ford Model T automobile. With it Jansky becomes the first person to detect space-based radio emissions.

Physicist Ernest O. Lawrence designs the first practical cyclotron, or atomic particle separator. Recording the paths of subatomic particles derived by colliding atoms will reveal new information about the structure of matter.

Chicago chemist Egloff develops a high-grade gasoline that is made from cottonseed. It proves too expensive to succeed in the U.S. market.

FRANKLIN D. ROOSEVELT

1933

The Boeing company markets the first commercial airliner, the 247, a ten-passenger model capable of crossing the United States in less than twenty hours. The vehicle carries too few passengers to prove successful.

Charles Darrow invents the board game "Monopoly."

Ruth Wakefield of Whitman, Massachusetts, invents the "Toll House" chocolate-chip cookie. The Western world gives thanks.

Edwin Armstrong develops the process of "frequency modulation" radio transmission. "FM" radio becomes popular in the 1950s.

Baltimore electrical engineer William Kouwenhoven and physician O. R. Langworthy develop an electric defibrillator to combat the problem of ventricular fibrillation during surgery. They attach electrodes directly to the heart and deliver brief shocks to restore regular heartbeat. Later they develop an external version in which the defibrillator is placed directly on the chest.

1934

Engineers for the B. F. Goodrich Company develop the first "pressure suits" for use by high-altitude aircraft pilots.

The Durex Company markets the first men's contraceptive made from latex.

In Texas, the first launderette opens.

1935

The twenty-one-passenger Douglas DC-3 becomes the first commercially successful passenger airliner.

R. K. Hopkins develops the technique of electroslag welding. The process prevents impurities from entering the weld, greatly improving its strength when placed under stress.

Former clockmaker Laurens Hammond of Chicago invents the electromagnetic organ, using cogwheels left over from his clockmaking firm, which had failed during the first year of the Great Depression.

1936

The first thermostat-controlled electric irons go on sale in the United States. The thermostats reduce the likelihood of scorching fabrics.

The first vitamin pills, called "Vitamin Plus," enter the U.S. market.

1937

Engineers in the Kitchen-Aid division of the Hobart Manufacturing Company of Troy, Ohio, develop the first electric coffee grinder.

Earl Hass establishes the Tampax Company to market the first widely used feminine hygienic tampon.

Bell Laboratories mathematician George Stibitz invents the binary calculator, the "base-two" forerunner of early computers.

The General Motors Corporation installs "Hydromatic" transmission in many of its Oldsmobile automobiles, establishing automatic transmission as a staple of U.S. automobile production.

1938

Chester Carlson produces the first xerographic image. In 1944 the nonprofit Memorial Battelle Institute of Columbus, Ohio, agrees to develop Carlson's process. Battelle transfers the rights to xerography to the Haloid Company in 1947. The Haloid Company markets the first xerographic machine in 1948. In 1959 the company, renamed Xerox, markets the Xerox 914, the first widely used xerographic machine.

Electric garbage disposal units first appear under kitchen sinks in the United States.

Du Pont engineer Roy J. Plunkett discovers polytetrafluorethylene. Beginning in 1948 Du Pont markets the substance as Teflon.

1939

Researchers at the Massachusetts Institute of Technology design and build a solar-powered home. The two-room structure features a 410-square-foot roof-mounted solar panel that heats a tank of water. The water is piped through the walls to heat the home.

New York publisher Simon and Schuster markets the first "Pocket Book," a paperback book designed to be carried in a pants or coat pocket.

1940

Researchers at Columbia University isolate the radioactive isotope uranium 235. They also demonstrate that U-235 is more "fissionable" than its heavier cousin U-238 and thus more practical for use as the explosive component in nuclear weapons.

Maurice and Richard McDonald open a hamburger restaurant in Pasadena, California. They convert it into a self-service establishment in 1948 and begin setting up "McDonald's" branches throughout Southern California. In 1952 a restaurant equipment manufacturer, Ray Kroc, offers to sell McDonald's franchises throughout the United States. In 1962 Kroc purchases the McDonalds' share of the franchise business for $2.7 million.

1941

Researchers E. Seaborg and E. McMillan of the University of California isolate the radioactive element plutonium and demonstrate that it would yield more energy in fission than uranium 235.

Albert Coons devises the technique of immunofluorescence to identify blood-bound disease organisms, "labelling" pneumonia antibodies with a fluorescent dye, injecting the labeled antibodies into the bloodstream, and watching to find out what it is they attack.

1942

The Kodak Company develops infrared photographic film.

The U.S. government inaugurates production of synthetic rubber in response to the World War II-induced shortage of the natural substance.

Scientists at the University of Chicago under the direction of Enrico Fermi construct the first atomic pile, producing the first controlled, sustained nuclear fission reaction.

General Electric engineers design a "Launcher, Rocket, AT, M-1"—the first bazooka.

1943

The U.S. Army becomes the first military force to deploy the napalm bomb, a metal container filled with a thickened mixture of gasoline and benzene and equipped with a fuse.

The first operational reactor goes on line in Oak Ridge, Tennessee. It produces plutonium for use in atomic weapons.

1944

An International Business Machines Corporation team led by Howard Aiken develops the Mark I, the first IBM Automatic Sequence Controlled Calculator. The ASCC is the first calculating machine containing a clock to synchronize calculations and a temporary memory system.

TRUMAN

1945

Designed and built during a three-year period by the U.S.-sponsored Manhattan Project, the first nuclear-fission bombs are exploded in New Mexico and Japan.

Earl W. Tupper, a former chemist with the Du Pont company, develops a line of flexible plastic boxes and other items he calls Tupperware. He sets up the "Tupperware party" system to sell the containers.

1946

The first mobile telephone system is installed in the police-car fleet of St. Louis, Missouri.

While researching shortwave electromatic emissions for the Raytheon Company, Percy Le Baron Spencer discovers that the microwaves with which he was working have melted a candy bar in his pocket. Raytheon markets the first microwave oven in 1947.

General Electric researchers Vincent J. Schaefer and Irving Langmuir produce rainfall by "seeding" clouds with carbon dioxide crystals.

In Chicago, the first drive-in bank goes into operation.

Chemist Frank Willard Libby develops the technique of carbon-14 dating.

1947

The B. F. Goodrich Company markets the first tubeless automobile tire.

With U.S. Air Force colonel Chuck Yeager at the controls, the Bell X-1 experimental rocket plane becomes the first aircraft to exceed the speed of sound.

J. L. Heid of Lake Wales, Florida, produces the first frozen orange juice concentrate.

Peter Goldmark of Columbia Broadcasting Systems invents the long-playing phonograph record.

Working for American Telephone & Telegraph's Bell Laboratories, John Bardeen, Walter Brattain, and William Shockley develop the transistor, a low-power, low-priced electric switch. In 1956 they win the Nobel Prize in physics for their efforts. "Transistor radios" appear on the market in 1955.

Yale University students are observed tossing flat, round cans the Frisbee Company of Bridgeport, Connecticut, uses to can pork. The Wham-O Manufacturing Company of San Gabriel, California, subsequently markets a plastic model of the cans, which it calls the "Frisbee."

Peter Hodgson of New Haven, Connecticut, hires a Yale University student to package balls of a soft synthetic substance developed by General Electric Company researchers investigating substitutes for rubber. Hodgson names the substance Silly Putty.

The Kerr-McGee Corporation constructs the first offshore oil-drilling platform.

1948

Edwin Herbert Land markets the first instant-development camera, the Polaroid Model 95.

James Brunot of Newton, Connecticut, invents the board game "Scrabble."

Francis Rogallo takes the first flight in an aircraft of his design he calls the Rogallo Wing. Later the wings become known as hang gliders.

International Business Machines Corporation develops the first true automatic information processor, or computer. Known as the Selective Sequence Electronic Calculator, it is the first machine capable of solving problems on the basis of stored data—a "software program."

1950

Ralph Schneider founds the Diner's Club, which offers members a card they can use to dine on credit in a group of New York restaurants. Bank of America of New York issues the first bank credit card, the BankAmericard, in 1958.

Dr. Richard Lawler of Chicago performs the first kidney transplant.

1951

Americans Eckert and Mauchly design the Univac I, the first computer containing a magnetic-tape memory unit. The first Univac was installed in the U.S. Office of Census Taking.

1952

The United States explodes the first nuclear-fusion (hydrogen) bomb.

Former U.S. soldier George Jorgensen becomes the first person to undergo a "sex change" operation. She changes her name to Christine.

Jonas Salk develops a vaccine against polio. The first mass polio vaccination program is set up in Pittsburgh, Pennsylvania, schools in 1954.

EISENHOWER

1953

Remington Rand Corporation markets the first ribbon-based computer printer. International Business Machines Corporation introduces dot-matrix printing in 1957.

The first nuclear power reactor goes into operation in the United States.

The development of a "heart-lung" machine makes possible the first open-heart surgery, at Jefferson Medical College in Philadelphia.

1954

The Boeing company markets the first commercial jetliner, the 707, which carries 179 passengers at a speed of 566 miles per hour.

FORTRAN, the first advanced computer programming language, is devised by John Backus.

A team of Boston surgeons carries out the first successful kidney transplant using a living donor.

Bell researchers develop the silicon photovoltaic cell, which converts sunlight directly into electricity.

1955

The Ford Motor Company introduces an automatic door-lock system as an option on a variety of its automobile models.

The U.S. Navy launches the first nuclear-powered submarine, the *Nautilus*.

Leskell develops the technique of echography, in which sound waves are used to produce images. The technique, also known as "ultrasound," proves especially useful in prenatal examinations after it becomes widely available in the late 1970s.

Les Paul and Mary Ford develop techniques for making "multitrack" tape recordings.

1956

A team led by Alexander Poniatoff, founder and president of the Ampex Corporation, develop a reel-to-reel videotape recorder. In 1958 Ampex develops the first color video recorder. European and Japanese firms develop videocassette recorders in the early 1970s.

Bell Laboratories introduces the first visual telephone system.

U.S. physicians begin using hemodialysis machines to cleanse the blood of impurities left behind by malfunctioning kidneys.

New York's Bank of America installs a computer to handle thirty-two thousand of its accounts, inaugurating the age of computerized banking.

1957

Stokes and Smolens of the University of Pennsylvania develop the technique of plasmapheresis, by which donated blood is immediately separated into plasma and corpuscles and the latter returned to the donor.

Portable oxygen resuscitators make their appearance in the United States. The resuscitators make it possible to revive injured patients before they get to the hospital.

1958

The United States explodes the first neutron bomb.

The Mattel Corporation markets the Barbie doll. Barbie's boyfriend, Ken, appears in 1961.

The Goodyear Company builds ten examples of the first inflatable airplane. Constructed of rubberized nylon, the planes can be inflated with an ordinary vacuum cleaner.

Harvard researcher John Enders develops a measles vaccine.

1959

The *Savannah*, the first commercial nuclear-powered ship, named after the world's first transatlantic steamer of a century and a half before, sails for the first time.

The Obie Construction Company of Pittsburgh, Pennsylvania, markets the first house plans featuring a built-in fallout shelter. By that time add-on shelters had been available for several years.

Jack S. Kilby of the Texas Instruments Corporation patents the integrated circuit, a (usually) silicon-based electronic "chip" containing transistors, resistors, and capacitors. The first "silicon chips" are used in hearing aids in 1964. Soon after they find a place in computer systems.

International Business Machines Corporation markets the 1401, the first mass-produced computer. The 1401 features an "iron-core" memory and a "card-punch" data-retrieval system.

1960

Digital Equipment Corporation markets the first minicomputer, the PDP 1.

The National Aeronautics and Space Administration launches the first weather research satellite, the *Tiros I*, built by the Radio Corporation of America.

The Food and Drug Administration approves the first contraceptive "pill." The pill had been developed in the 1950s by Gregory Pincus and Dr. John Rock.

KENNEDY

1961

Bell Aerosystems Company demonstrates the first workable "rocket belt."

Jean Nidetch of Queens, New York, founds Weight Watchers, Inc.

1962

The National Aeronautics and Space Administration launches the Telstar, the first practical telecommunications satellite, designed by the American Telephone & Telegraph Corporation.

Drs. Donald A. Malt and J. McKhan perform the first surgical limb reimplant, on a twelve-year-old boy whose arm had been severed at the shoulder.

LYNDON JOHNSON

1963

Dr. Thomas Starlz of Denver, Colorado, performs the first spleen transplant.

Professor James D. Hardy of Jackson (Mississippi) University Hospital performs the first lung transplant. In 1964 Hardy transplants the heart of a chimpanzee into a human patient, who lives for three hours.

The first nuclear breeder reactor, a fission reactor that produces more fissionable material than it consumes, goes into operation in the United States.

Roche Laboratories introduces the prescription tranquillizer Valium to great public acclaim.

A group of physicians led by J. D. Hardy perform the first human lung transplant.

Physicians F. D. Moore and Thomas E. Starlz perform the first human liver transplant.

1964

Researchers at New York's Corning Glass Works develop photochromic spectacle lenses. The lenses darken when exposed to sunlight and clear when the light dims.

Houston surgeon Michael DeBakey replaces a section of diseased aortic valve in a human patient with a section of tubing made from the synthetic fiber Dacron.

1965

Dr. Edwin Land, founder of the Polaroid Company, invents polarizing sunglasses.

BASIC, the first easy-to-learn computer programming language, is devised by a Dartmouth College team led by John Kemeny and Thomas Kurtz.

The city of Chicago installs a computer to help direct the flow of traffic.

1966

Kodak introduces a throwaway flash unit for its Instamatic cameras.

1967

R. M. Dolby devises a noise reduction system to reduce background hiss on magnetic tape recordings.

Cleveland surgeon Rene Favaloro develops the coronary bypass operation.

1968

The world's largest-ever production aircraft, the C-5A, is test-flown by the Lockheed Aircraft Company. Constructed for the U.S. Air Force, the plane weighs 380 tons, is 251 feet long, and has a wingspan of 222 feet. It is capable of carrying a payload of 57 tons.

Dr. Denton Cooley of Texas Children's Hospital performs the first human heart-lung transplant.

NIXON

1969

The largest-ever commercial jetliner, the Boeing 747, capable of carrying 490 passengers, takes its first flight.

International Business Machines Corporation introduces the "floppy disk" for computer data storage.

Astronauts Neil Armstrong and "Buzz" Aldrin of the National Aeronautics and Space Administration mission *Apollo 11* land and walk on the moon.

1970

Neurologist George Cotzias treats patients with Parkinson's disease with L-dopa, which replaces lost dopamine in the brain.

In Vietnam, the U.S. military introduces guided missiles designed to seek out targets that are illuminated by laser beams emitted from "controller" airplanes.

1971

Intel Corporation markets the Intel 4004, the first microprocessor, an extremely small silicon chip containing 2,300 transistors. Soon Intel produces chips containing as many as 225,000 or more transistors. The microprocessor proves crucial to the development of large-memory computer systems and "personal" computers.

1972

American engineer Noland Buschnel invents the first video game, Pong. He forms the Atari company to market the game.

P. C. Lauterbur, a professor of chemistry at the State University of New York at Stony Brook, develops the technique of magnetic resonance imaging, by which a computer projects a map of the water molecules in tissue that is obtained through the manipulation of magnetic fields. The technique produces extremely clear structural images of animal tissue.

Jack S. Kilby, J. D. Merryman, and J. H. Van Tassel of the Texas Instruments Corporation develop the first pocket calculator.

The National Aeronautics and Space Administration launches the *Landsat I* satellite, the first of a generation of "earth resources technology" satellites carrying sophisticated camera-radio systems capable of taking extremely detailed photographs and beaming them back to earth.

1973

California cross-country cycling enthusiasts fabricate the first "mountain bikes."

Push-through tabs appear on soft-drink cans. The tabs remain attached to the cans, cutting down on litter.

FORD

1974

The National Aeronautics and Space Administration launches the first geosynchronous-orbit weather research satellite, the *SMS I*.

1975

The U.S. government develops a low-light television camera that can detect a person up to eleven miles away, but it proves too sensitive to changes in temperature and humidity to have practical application.

1976

Seymour Cray designs the first supercomputer, the Cray I. The machine is capable of performing 150 million calculations per second. The second-generation Cray X/MP is capable of performing 400 million calculations per second. The Control Data Systems Cyber 205 surpasses the Cray with a figure of 700 million calculations per second.

The National Aeronautics and Space Administration *Viking 1* and *Viking 2* explorers land on the surface of the planet Mars and analyze its soil.

The Singer Company markets the first sewing machine equipped with a microprocessor.

CARTER

1977

The Bell Telephone Company becomes the first company to utilize optical fiber cables to transmit television signals.

The *Gossamer Condor* designed by Paul McCready is the first human-powered airplane to fly successfully, negotiating a figure-eight course of one mile in length.

1978

Several companies install microprocessors in washing machines.

Solar-powered electronic calculators appear on the U.S. market.

1979

The Waste Conversion Company of Seattle, Washington, markets a system to convert poultry excrement, twenty percent of which consists of undigested poultry feed, back into food for the chickens.

1980

Paul McCready designs and builds the first solar-powered aircraft, the *Gossamer Penguin.*

REAGAN

1981

The American firm Laser Color develops an electronic slide reproducer that "screens" a document with three monochromatic laser beams and transforms the residual light produced into electromagnetic pulses stored on diskettes. The images recorded can be reproduced on computer screens.

Bell Laboratories markets the first cellular radio-telephone system. "Car phones" proliferate in the 1980s.

The U.S. National Aeronautics and Space Administration launches the first reusable "space shuttle," the *Columbia.*

1982

Prompted by an incident in which an unknown criminal amputated the beaks of about thirty pelicans, a team of California doctors headed by Robert Hooks and Rick Woerpel design artificial beaks for the birds, the first ever constructed.

The 3M Company develops the Scotchcast, a waterproof fiberglass and polyurethane limb cast.

Kodak introduces the disc-camera. The film is packaged on a small flat disc.

1983

Harold A. Adler patents an "animated" play ball for dogs and cats. The ball contains a small motor that is activated by a radio transmitter placed on the animal's collar. Every time the pet approaches, the ball rolls away.

International Business Machines Corporation markets the first successful holographic "bar code" scanner for use in grocery store cash register systems.

1985

The Coca-Cola Company introduces "new Coke," a revised version of its original soft-drink product. Massive public protest results in the reintroduction of the old formula, dubbed "Coca-Cola Classic," a few months later.

Memorable First Ladies

by SUZANNE LINDER

Long before women could serve in government or even vote for the candidates of their choice, a select group of women enjoyed extraordinary political influence. They were the wives of the presidents, a diverse group who varied widely in their interests and abilities. Even in times when women could claim little if any public authority, the first ladies could express their ideas to the nation's chief executives.

With the expansion of the social role of American women has come an extension of the participation of first ladies in politics as well as in setting fashions, promoting culture, and supporting social causes. Twentieth-century presidential wives have tended to assume a more positive responsibility than their eighteenth- and nineteenth-century counterparts. Some, such as Eleanor Roosevelt, have actively contributed to their husbands' administrations. Even if they did not take part in governmental activities, most of the recent first ladies have assumed some sort of personal promotional cause. Nancy Reagan, for example, sponsored the "Just Say No" antidrug campaign, and Barbara Bush has developed a special interest in adult literacy. Because of the first ladies' access to power and their command of the public's attention, their advocacy has made a difference.

Whatever a modern first lady chooses to do, she knows that when her husband enters office, she does too. It is traditional in America to consider a good wife a political asset. The stories of memorable first ladies illuminate the influence of women on the presidency.

MARTHA WASHINGTON

George Washington considered his wife "a quiet wife, a quiet soul." She eased his life with common sense and aristocratic graciousness. That she was also beautiful and efficient must have helped her in traversing the uncharted course of being the original first lady of the United States.

At only five feet tall, Martha Washington could fit under her husband's arm. Large hazel eyes, wide brows, and a strong, curved nose might have made her a striking beauty had not her timidity produced a gentle charm. Being slightly plump only made her more attractive in the eyes of contemporaries.

The daughter of John and Frances Jones Dandridge, Martha grew up on the family plantation on the Pamunkey River in Virginia. Although her father was a prosperous planter, her girlhood days were not spent in idleness. Her morning began at six with a lesson in reading and writing followed by practice in music, sewing, knitting, spinning, weaving, and cooking. By the time of her presentation at the court of the governor in Williamsburg when she was fifteen, she was an accomplished needlewoman, musician, and mistress of all the housewifely arts.

At eighteen Martha married Col. Daniel Parke Custis. Of their children, the first two sons died in early childhood, but John and young Martha (called Jacky and Patsy) survived. In July 1757 Colonel Custis died, leaving Martha a wealthy widow with 150 slaves, a town house in Williamsburg called Six Chimneys, a plantation known as White House, and a fortune of forty-five thousand pounds sterling, which she held in trust for her children.

The attractive Mrs. Custis did not lack suitors. After a reasonable interval she chose Col. George Washington as her second husband, and they married on January 6, 1759. Although historians have speculated that she was not the love of his life, Washington once remarked that his marriage was the event of his life "most conducive to happiness."

The Washington estate, Mount Vernon, eventually included about eight thousand acres and three hundred slaves. The mistress of such an estate required outstanding administrative skills. Her duties included everything from planning menus and supervising the cooking to planting the vegetable and herb gardens. At one time she directed the operation of sixteen spinning wheels and had a special house for looms, wheels, flaxbrakes, and other tools. Martha also made wine, cordials, medicines, perfumes, and even tooth powder.

In the years between 1768 and 1775 the Washingtons entertained about two thousand guests ranging from relatives and intimate friends to passersby put up at nightfall. Guests praised Mount Vernon for its warm hospitality and plentiful food.

When the Revolution took George Washington away from home, his wife followed him to the battlefront. Afterward she told her grandchildren that she had "heard the opening and closing shot of almost every important campaign in the war." The roads were bad and the weather often cold, but Mrs. Washington journeyed to the general's headquarters, keeping house, mending his clothes, nursing the sick, and knitting socks for the soldiers. The rude hut at Valley Forge was far removed from the comforts of Mount Vernon, but she did not complain. She spent eight winters bringing comfort to her husband wherever he happened to be. Her courageous spirit also encouraged the officers and enlisted men.

The outspoken Bostonian Mercy Warren knew Mrs. Washington when she was with the patriot army in Massachusetts. Warren wrote, "The complacency of her manners speaks at once of the benevolence of her heart, and her affability, candor, and gentleness qualify her to soften the hours of private life, or to sweeten the cares of a hero, and smooth the rugged pains of war."

Martha Washington, portrait by Charles Willson Peale, 1772 (courtesy of the Mount Vernon Ladies' Association)

Martha herself did not escape pain relating to the conflict. Her beloved son Jacky died of camp fever in 1781. With Jacky's death she lost her last remaining child, for Patsy had died at age seventeen of epilepsy. George Washington formally adopted Jacky's two youngest children, George Washington Parke Custis and Eleanor "Nellie" Parke Custis. The grandchildren enlivened Mount Vernon in the years following the war.

When Washington became president of the United States Martha fulfilled the duties of first lady in a gracious and distinguished manner. The president and his wife had the awesome responsibility of establishing precedents that would

PARTY PRECEDENT

During their years as America's first couple, George and Martha Washington intended almost everything they did to set a precedent for the future. One object of the president's initial concern involved the question of his and his wife's accessibility to the public. After consulting with friends such as Alexander Hamilton and John Adams, Washington decided to place an advertisement in New York newspapers announcing his "general calling hours": he would accept social calls on Tuesday and Friday afternoons between two and three o'clock; persons with business for the president could call on any day of the week except Sunday. Washington also decided to hold men-only "levées" on Tuesday afternoons and to have his wife preside at Friday-evening "drawing rooms," which both men and women could attend.

Martha Washington faced a sort of social test on the occasion of the first drawing room gathering. As Mary Caroli puts it, many of the partygoers turned out "to evaluate the hostess's efforts to entertain graciously without seeming to carve a superior niche for herself." Martha did well. During the festivities she remained seated "in queenly fashion" while her husband mingled and made introductions. As the end of the evening drew near, the guests wondered whether they should wait for the hostess to depart—as would have been proper at a court function in the mother country—or, in tribute to American democratic aspirations, leave when they wanted. Martha resolved the potentially awkward situation by standing and announcing, "The General always retires at nine, and I generally precede him." She walked out, and the party ended. —ed.

endow their positions with dignity and stateliness while maintaining principles of democracy.

Martha Washington proved equal to the task. Although she never excelled in conversation, she had a talent for dealing with people. Her simple manners and uninsistent dignity put people at ease. Washington biographer James Thomas Flexner found that throughout her husband's political years she proffered appreciative friendship to all, and no man or woman ever wrote of her with enmity.

Wealth and fame did not alter Martha's basic humility. After her husband completed his terms in office and they returned to Mount Vernon, she wrote to a friend, "I am again fairly settled down to the pleasant duties of an old fashioned Virginia housekeeper, steady as a clock, busy as a bee, and cheerful as a cricket."

In her long and full life, Mrs. Washington coped with the loss of two husbands and four children. She endured the hardships of war and the challenge of administering a large household. In later life she undertook the care of two of her grandchildren. Finally, she served as first lady with charm, grace, strength, and dignity. Most amazing of all, she did it all without making a single enemy. No better woman than this "quiet soul" could have filled the position.

ABIGAIL ADAMS

Descended from a long line of Congregational ministers, Abigail Smith was the epitome of the New England Puritan woman: intelligent, strong, and resourceful. She once said, "If we have not wealth, we have what is better—integrity." Her strength of character served as her greatest asset. Yet her personal philosophy was not repressive. She wrote she was "a mortal enemy to anything but a cheerful countenance and a merry heart."

In contrast to Martha Washington, who began her wedding journey adorned with pearls and diamonds, riding in a coach and six with liveried postilions, after Abigail Smith married John Adams on October 25, 1764, he mounted his horse and swung his little bride up behind him, and they rode off together to their home in Braintree, Massachusetts. They began their married life in a sturdy brick and clay farmhouse with walls sheathed in unpainted wood.

John Adams was a lawyer, a rather unprestigious occupation at the time. Mrs. Adams was able to help him build a profitable practice, since she was related to many socially prominent families near Boston. Although she had no formal schooling, she had studied at home and was well educated. Because she was articulate and tactful, many said that she was a better statesman than her husband and that her influence greatly contributed to his success.

During the first ten years of their marriage John and Abigail had four children: Abigail (called Nabby), John Quincy, Charles, and Thomas. When the Revolution broke out, Adams went away to serve in the Continental Congress, and, except for a few scattered months, the couple was separated for the next ten years. Mrs. Adams made the farm at Braintree support the family. The war swept close to her home, and there were still unfriendly Indians beyond her fields. She met the challenge with courage, giving the minutemen her pewter spoons to be melted into bullets, helping to make coats for the soldiers, nursing the sick, and rearing four children alone. In 1777 she wrote to her husband, "We are in no wise dispirited here. If our men are all drawn off and we should be attacked, you would find a race of Amazons in America."

Abigail Adams's experience in self-reliance during the war must have influenced her opinions regarding the status of women. She was ahead of her time when she wrote her husband, who was working on a code of laws for the new nation, "I desire you would remember the ladies, and be more generous and favorable to them than your ancestors. Do not put such unlimited power into the hands of husbands. Remember all men would be tyrants if they could."

Mrs. Adams also spoke out against slavery. She said she wished there were not a slave in the province, for "it always seemed a most iniquitous scheme to me to fight ourselves for what we are robbing the Negroes of, who have as good a right to freedom as we have!"

Her opinions were soon to find a wider audience than Braintree. In 1784 she journeyed to Paris to join her husband, who was representing the United States at the French court. She found the Paris opera shocking at first. Girls dancing in the thinnest silk and gauze, showing their garters and drawers, prompted Abigail to write, "I felt my delicacy wounded and I was ashamed to be seen looking at them." However, she admitted that repeatedly seeing the dancers wore off the disgust, and she acknowledged, "I see them now with pleasure."

She spent only about a year in Paris, because her husband became the first American ambassador to Great Britain, a difficult position since animosities from the Revolution were still running strong. King George III understandably had a hostile attitude, and Adams was never noted for congeniality. Abigail, charming, calm, and cheerful, acted as a buffer between the two. By putting aside personal feelings, she won the admiration of the English with straightforward good humor and intelligence.

In 1788 the Adamses returned to America, where even further responsibility awaited. Adams became the first vice-president, an office that enabled him to set precedents as presiding officer in the Senate.

When George Washington retired after two presidential terms, Adams became, by a slender majority, the second president of the United States. Mrs. Adams became the first first lady to live in the presidential residence in Wash-

Portrait of Abigail Adams by Mather Brown, 1785

ington, D.C. The executive mansion was unfinished, and the town was little more than a wilderness. What roads existed were either mired in mud or buried in dust, and many streets and avenues had yet to be surveyed. Abigail only with great difficulty secured enough wood to heat the structure, in which not a single room was finished. With no outbuildings available, she hung her wash in the great unfinished audience room. She managed to entertain in the Oval Room, made habitable by red upholstered furniture she had brought from France.

O how they lament Mrs. A's absence. . . . She is a good counsellor! If she had been here, Murray would never have been named or his mission instituted. This ought to gratify your vanity enough to cure you.

—*Letter of President John Adams to Abigail Adams, his wife, concerning an unpopular appointment he made without benefit of her advice*

After his presidency the Adamses retired to Quincy, the new name of Braintree. Abigail wrote, "For myself and my family, I have few regrets. At my age, and with my bodily infirmities, I shall be happier at Quincy. Neither my habits, nor my education or inclination, have led me to an expensive style of living, so on that score I have little to mourn over." For fourteen years she was able to lead a tranquil and retired life, but she did not live to see her son, John Quincy, elected president in 1824.

Abigail Adams is remembered for many firsts. She was the wife of the first American ambassador to Great Britain and the first vice-president of the United States. She was the only woman in history to be the wife of one president and the mother of another. She is, however, outstanding not only because of her relationships with her husband and son but because of her own personality and intelligence. She was ahead of her time in speaking out for equality for women and blacks. She ran her household independently and supported her family for many years while her husband was away. When the time came, she took an active part in her husband's career. She once wrote, "I leave to posterity to reflect upon the times past." Posterity has remembered Abigail Adams with respect, admiration, and honor.

DOLLEY MADISON

One biographer has called Dolley Madison "the nation's hostess." She not only fulfilled that role for her husband, James Madison, but for Thomas Jefferson as well. Jefferson was a widower when he became president in 1801, as was his vice-president Aaron Burr. Since Dolley Madison was wife of the secretary of state, she often presided at social functions in the executive mansion.

Jefferson had long been acquainted with Dolley's family. Her mother, Mary Coles, was a great belle, and Jefferson was said to have been one of Mary's admirers. Dolley's grandmother, Lucy Winston Coles, was from that Virginia family known for generations of beautiful Winston women.

From her mother's family, Dolley learned gracious southern hospitality and charm and how to appreciate a comfortable life-style. On the other hand, her father, John Payne, was a Quaker who freed his slaves and moved to Philadelphia, where he encountered financial difficulties. From him Dolley learned discipline and dedication to duty. Despite the Quaker restrictions, her life was unusually full of affection and consideration for other people. Dolley's understanding of her fellow human beings proved one of the secrets of her future success.

At twenty-two Dolley married an earnest young Quaker lawyer, John Todd. They had two sons. In 1793, however, John and the youngest baby died of yellow fever. A beautiful young widow of twenty-five, Dolley returned to her mother's home in Philadelphia, the nation's capital at that time. A friend of the family, Aaron Burr, brought the forty-three-year-old James Madison to call. He was neither tall nor impressive looking, but he had already gained prestige for his work in writing the Constitution, and his hostess put him at ease. She brought out his sense of humor and gentle charm. Her overflowing geniality and genuine interest in people complemented his serious, intellectual nature. They were married September 5, 1774, at Harewood, the Virginia home of Dolley's sister Lucy Washington.

When James Madison became president in 1809, Mrs. Madison had the duty of renovating the interior of the executive mansion with the help of an architect and a five-thousand-dollar appropriation from Congress. Unfortunately, her decorations were destined for oblivion. On June 18, 1812, Congress declared war on Great Britain. In August 1814 British troops invaded Washington. On August 23, within sound of cannon fire, she wrote to her sister, "My husband left me yesterday to join General Winder. . . . He desires

Gilbert Stuart's 1804 portrait of Dolley Madison (courtesy of the Pennsylvania Academy of Fine Arts)

that I should be ready at a moment's warning to enter my carriage and leave the city."

When word came that the British were approaching, Mrs. Madison managed to save a carriage full of government documents, including an original copy of the Declaration of Independence. She also insisted that Gilbert Stuart's portrait of George Washington be broken out of its frame and preserved. As she left the capital city by one road, the British entered by another, on their way to burn the president's house.

A hurricane hastened the departure of the British, and shortly the government returned to Washington. On September 13 Francis Scott Key came to see President Madison. At his wife's request the president gave Key permission to ask the British admiral then attacking Fort McHenry to release a friend, Dr. Beane. After watching the battle from the deck of a British ship, Key was greatly relieved to see the American flag still flying at dawn. He wrote the words to "The Star-Spangled Banner," later

POLITICAL GRACES TOO

James Madison's wife, Dolley, established a reputation for superior social graces during her years as White House hostess for President Thomas Jefferson, a widower, and for her husband. She also exhibited an astute political consciousness. Aware that her predecessor Abigail Adams had attracted criticism for seeming to favor her husband's supporters over his detractors at social gatherings, Dolley tried to treat everyone who attended White House parties with equal good cheer. A friend remarked, "It is impossible to know what Mrs. Madison is thinking, because she tried to be all things to all men."

When the time came for her husband to run for reelection, Dolley tried to soothe legislators discontented with the president's policy of war with Great Britain, going so far as to invite "a large body" of Madison's opponents to dinner. She also called on legislators' families in their own homes, a practice that Washingtonians interpreted as an expression of presidential humility.

As a hostess, Dolley managed to impress the regal-minded and the egalitarian alike, retaining President Jefferson's practice of seating dinner guests without regard to rank or station but also requiring female guests to curtsy in front of the president before finding a seat. Biographer Maud Wilder Goodwin remarks that Dolley was "brilliant in the things she did not say or do." —ed.

the American national anthem. Without Dolley Madison's help, Key might never have been inspired to write the poem.

Madison considered moving the capital back to Philadelphia, but Dolley persuaded him to keep it in Washington. James Hoban, the original White House architect, directed the rebuilding of the mansion. Workmen painted the blackened walls white to cover traces of the fire, and people soon began calling it "The White House."

Dolley Madison exhibited a special interest in children. In 1815 she participated in founding a home for orphans. She cut out garments to provide clothing for the children in the institution. She owned a colorful parrot, and Washington children loved to watch her feed it. She also began one of the longest-lasting White House traditions. Her son, John Payne Todd, told her that the children of ancient Egypt used to roll colorful hard-boiled eggs against the bases of the pyramids. Dolley personally dyed hundreds of eggs and invited the children of Washington to an egg rolling on the Monday after Easter. Egg rolling at the nation's capital became an American tradition. In her later years Dolley, an energetic little lady dressed in black, visited schools to inspire the children with patriotism.

After Madison's terms as president the couple returned to Montpelier, their home in Virginia, where for twenty years Dolley cared for the aging Madison and his mother, who lived to be ninety-seven. Following Madison's death Dolley returned to Washington. Although no longer young or wealthy, she still gave the impression of beauty.

The capital cordially welcomed the charming Mrs. Madison. Congress placed in trust for her the funds appropriated for the purchase of her husband's letters. Congressmen gave her the franking privilege and voted her a seat on the floor of the House. At the time of her death, the *Washington Daily Intelligencer* of July 14, 1849, called her "one who touched all hearts by her goodness and won the admiration of all by the charm of dignity and grace."

SARAH POLK

If Sarah Childress had been born a century later, she probably would have enjoyed an outstanding personal career. In the early nineteenth century, however, few avenues were open to women. Sarah married James K. Polk on New

Year's Day 1824 and shared his career instead.

The Polks began in a small law office in Columbia, Tennessee. James Polk served in the state legislature, then in Congress for seven terms. Eventually he became Speaker of the House. Next he served as governor of Tennessee, and finally in 1844 he received the Democratic nomination for president, the first "dark horse" candidate chosen by a nominating convention. Just as she had always helped in her husband's work, Sarah worked with Polk in the presidential campaign, studying newspapers, cutting and filing clippings, writing to political leaders, and answering letters.

Mrs. Polk attended the Moravian Institute at Salem, North Carolina (later known as Salem College), where she completed her education. The Moravians offered excellent academic training in a highly disciplined and religious atmosphere.

When Polk became president, his wife continued to act as his confidential secretary. The Polks had no children, and Sarah enjoyed working in an official capacity. She took charge of the president's papers and reminded him of his appointments. Each day she read the nation's most important newspapers and magazines and selected articles she thought the president should see. Because she had worked with him throughout his career, she had a good grasp of affairs of state. Polk once remarked, "None but Sarah knew so intimately my private affairs."

In addition to acting as presidential secretary the first lady served as an outstanding White House hostess. Although she banned hard liquor, card playing, and dancing in the mansion, she held two state receptions each week and gave many state dinners in addition to informal parties and musicals.

Henry Clay, Speaker of the House, once told Mrs. Polk, "I must say that in my travels . . . I have heard but one opinion of you. All agree in commending in the highest terms your excellent administration of the domestic affairs of the White House." Clay continued by remarking that as a Whig, he could not comment as positively about the Democratic administration of her husband.

Sarah Polk at about the time of her husband's presidency, from 1845 to 1849 (Library of Congress)

Despite Clay's reservations, history has confirmed James Polk's achievements. As president Polk wanted to extend the boundaries of the United States to the Pacific by annexing Texas, settling the boundary of Oregon with Great Britain, and obtaining New Mexico and California from Mexico. Although he found it necessary to lead the country into war with Mexico to obtain that last objective, he was able to realize his goals. In doing so, he probably worked himself to death. James Polk died on June 15, 1849, only a few months after leaving office. Sarah was a widow at forty-five. She threw herself into the direction of the Polk cotton plantation in Mississippi until losses sustained in the Civil War prompted her to sell it.

The early feminist leader and educator Frances E. Willard admired Mrs. Polk and led a successful effort to have a portrait of her placed in the White House. Upon the death of the former first lady on August 14, 1891, Willard

Would you dance in so public a place as this [the White House]? I would not. To dance in these rooms would be undignified, and it would be respectful neither to the house nor to the office. How indecorous it would seem for dancing to be going on in one apartment, while in another we are conversing with dignitaries of the republic or ministers of the gospel.

—*Remark of Sarah Polk, wife of President James K. Polk, explaining her prohibition of dancing in the White House (Anson and Sarah Nelson,* Memorials of Sarah Childress Polk, *1892)*

wrote that the portrait, placed in the White House by cooperation of both northern and southern women, served as an example of renewed understanding between the sections. She said, "Well might the church bells toll for one always loyal to our Lord, and the flags be placed at half mast for a patriot who dignified the name 'American.' "

LUCY HAYES

Among America's first ladies Lucy Webb Hayes was the first graduate from an established collegiate institution. She attended Cincinnati's Wesleyan Female College, the first chartered college for women in America, and graduated with highest honors in 1852. The next December she married a promising young lawyer, Rutherford B. Hayes. When Hayes served in the Civil War, Lucy spent two winters in camp with him. She was there to nurse him back to health when he was wounded, and she worked in camps and hospitals throughout the war. The soldiers of her husband's regiment adored her.

She was in many ways typical of the "new woman" of the late nineteenth century. She was an educated person concerned about reforming social conditions and asserting feminine rights within the context of the times and an ardent advocate of woman suffrage and temperance.

Lucy Webb Hayes and President Rutherford B. Hayes, 1877 (courtesy of the Rutherford B. Hayes Presidential Center)

Her interest in temperance sparked national debate. The press dubbed her "Lemonade Lucy" because she discontinued serving alcohol at the White House. After an official dinner, Secretary of State William Evarts declared, "It was a brilliant affair; the water flowed like champagne."

President and Mrs. Hayes expanded the White House conservatory so that instead of serving after-dinner drinks they could lead their guests on healthful walks among exotic plants. Once a rumor circulated that a White House steward had slipped Santa Croix rum into some oranges served at dinner, thus providing a "Life Saving Station." President Hayes, however, insisted, "The joke of the Roman punch oranges was not on us, but on the drinking people. My orders were to flavor them *rather strongly* with the same flavor that is found in Jamaica rum!"

Members of the National Women's Christian Temperance Union were delighted with White House policy. They raised money for a full-length portrait of Lucy Hayes that depicted her as an

MORAL EXPEDIENCY?

Evidence suggests that "Lemonade Lucy" Hayes's ban on serving alcohol in the White House was motivated as much by political expediency as moral fervor. As a youth, Lucy's husband, Rutherford B. Hayes, enjoyed an occasional social drink of wine, and in his political career he never advocated prohibition. Lucy actually did serve wine at her first White House dinner, then she developed the temperance policy as a response to criticism from teetotalers.

Mary Caroli suggests that since the advent of the Hayes presidency occurred during "a powerful surge in temperance sentiment," Hayes and his wife "realized that refusing to serve alcohol in the White House could win votes without causing any personal inconvenience." The president once remarked, "There is a good deal of dissipation here. . . . Disgraceful things were done by young men made reckless by too much wine. Hence the necessity for our course is obvious and is commended in unexpected quarters. . . . We shall stick to it." In explaining the decision, Lucy commented, "it is true I shall violate a precedent; but I shall not violate the Constitution, which is all that, through my husband, I have taken the oath to obey." —ed.

idealized American matron. Furthermore, temperance at the executive mansion proved not only politically expedient but economical as well.

Not that the Hayes family needed to economize—they were the richest occupants of the White House in the nineteenth century. They lived generously but not extravagantly. Mrs. Hayes dressed fashionably in simple but elegant dresses of rich material with genuine lace. The *American Register* of Paris reported, "The administration of Mrs. Hayes receives quite as much attention as does that of her husband. Her beauty and simplicity have taken the blasé society of Washington by storm."

Lucy and Rutherford Hayes had one daughter and seven sons, three of whom died in early childhood. The second-oldest living son, Webb, acted as his father's confidential secretary. Both President and Mrs. Hayes devoted the hour after dinner each night to helping the two youngest children, Scott and Fanny, with their lessons. The family attended church together and played croquet on the White House lawn. Lucy enjoyed planning parties for young people. When Congress passed a law closing the Capitol grounds to children because they were ruining the grass, she invited them to use the White House lawn for Easter Monday egg rolling, and the tradition has persisted to the present.

Another trend Mrs. Hayes encouraged was that of trying to make the White House interior better reflect its history. She consulted Librarian of Congress Ainsworth R. Spofford about how to achieve the goal. She and Spofford decided to expand the collection of portraits of former presidents and first ladies. President Hayes was delighted with the idea. He and Mrs. Hayes began the first significant art collection at the White House.

Lucy Hayes also commissioned an unusual set of china. Produced by the Haviland Company of New York, the set featured American flowers, vegetables, and wildlife. Tomatoes, sweet potatoes, corn, and cactus adorned soup bowls, and fruit plates exhibited persimmons, pecans, and blueberries. Dinner plates showed deer in the forest, canvasback ducks in flight, and aged buffalo. At its introduction in 1880, guests reacted to the china with admiration or distaste, but seldom with indifference. Painted china was very popular during the Hayes administration, and if the nature china proved a little extreme, it was nevertheless very American.

Lucy Webb Hayes was the epitome of the late-nineteenth-century matron. She was strongly family oriented but fashionable in both personal dress and home decor. She followed her husband to war and supported his career, yet she also took an interest in social reform and woman's rights. Along with President Hayes she contributed to improving the landscaping of the White House grounds. She was interested in preserving White House history but did not object to the installation of two new inventions, the typewriter and the telephone. As first lady, Lucy Hayes exemplified many of the best attributes of the women of late-nineteenth-century America.

FRANCES CLEVELAND

When President Grover Cleveland married Frances Folsom on June 2, 1886, in the Blue Room of the White House, roses, smilax, lilies, pansies, and other flowers from the greenhouses adorned every level space while garlands of greenery and fresh flowers hung in swags from the picture molding. In the dining room the centerpiece was a giant three-masted ship made of flowers and christened the *Hymen*, for the Greek god of marriage.

The bride wore an elegant corded satin gown draped in India silk and decorated with real orange blossoms. The upstairs maids testified that the dress could "stand upright on the floor without support." As the portly president and his beautiful young bride came down the stairs, the Marine Band, resplendent in dress red and blue and under the direction of John Philip Sousa, struck up the wedding march.

By marrying the president, Frances Folsom at twenty-one became the youngest first lady and the first to marry a president in the White House. A member of the mansion staff recalled that on the day of her wedding, "She tripped up the steps and swept through the great entrance like a radiant vision of young springtime . . . from that instant every man and woman of them all was a devoted slave, and remained such." None, however, was more devoted than her husband.

Grover Cleveland had been law partner and friend to Frances's father, Oscar Folsom. After Folsom died in a carriage accident, Cleveland remained a close friend of the family and a beloved "Uncle Cleve" to Frances, whom he affectionately called "Frank." Cleveland waited for her to grow up. At the time of their marriage he was forty-nine and weighed nearly three hundred pounds. Reporters hounded them on their honeymoon, observing through binoculars and popping out of bushes to ask questions. In order to enjoy some privacy away from the White House, Cleveland purchased a large house situated on twenty-three acres near the present-day Washington Cathedral. He remodeled the ugly old house into a picturesque Queen Anne villa with porches on two levels painted dark green. The shingled roof was red. Frances Cleveland called her home "Oak View," but newsmen who could only see it from the road persisted in calling it "Red Top."

The young Mrs. Cleveland excelled as a hostess. At that time it was customary each year to hold a few full-scale public receptions open without invitation. Other evening receptions were smaller, with guests numbering in the hundreds rather than the thousands. Mrs. Cleveland added Saturday receptions to her busy schedule so that working women could attend.

Cleveland was first elected president in 1884. In 1888 Benjamin Harrison defeated him, and he returned to the practice of law. The Clevelands' first child, Ruth, was born while her father was out of office. After he returned to Washington for a second term in 1893, the second daughter, Esther, became the only president's child to be born in the White House. The Clevelands later had three other children.

Mrs. Cleveland kept busy with the two children during her husband's second term, but she found time to refurbish the Red Room in a style called "modern Romanesque." A center of interest was a kerosene oil lamp made of cut glass with a deeply ruffled silk shade that looked like a hoopskirt and glowed with a rosy light. Mrs. Cleveland also freshened the decor of the family quarters with wallpaper and paint.

Frances Folsom Cleveland claimed many unique distinctions. She was the youngest first lady, the first to marry a president in the White House, and the only president's wife to give birth there. She was also the only first lady to reenter private life and then return to the White House after four years.

Five years after Grover Cleveland's death in 1908, she married Princeton University professor Thomas J. Preston, Jr. She died October 29, 1947, at the age of eighty-three. History will remember her as a vision of springtime in white satin who married the president of the United States in the Blue Room filled with flowers.

Frances Cleveland, 1886 (Library of Congress)

EDITH WILSON

Toward the end of his presidency, after he had suffered a stroke, Woodrow Wilson talked about writing a book on government when he retired. Although he was never able to complete the book, he did write a moving dedication to his second wife, Edith Bolling Wilson, "who has shown me the full meaning of life."

Wilson was lonely and burdened with responsibility when he met Edith Galt in March 1915. His first wife had died less than a year before. The three Wilson daughters were adults with lives of their own.

One chilly spring afternoon Wilson returned to the White House after playing golf with his friend and physician, Cary Grayson. As the two men approached the elevator in the second floor hall, the doors opened, and they met Helen Bones, the president's cousin and hostess, with her friend Edith Bolling Galt. The women had been for a walk in Rock Creek Park. Edith had been hesitant to return to the White House because of her windblown appearance and muddy shoes. However, Helen insisted, and Edith later recalled that she thought, "At least I'm disheveled in a suit by Worth."

After freshening up, the women met the president and Dr. Grayson for tea in front of an open fire. Wilson was immediately taken with the tall, radiant widow, sixteen years his junior, with the beautiful face and full, curved figure. Edith was a descendant of Indian princess Pocahontas and Virginia pioneer John Rolfe. She grew up in a fine southern family in Wytheville, Virginia. Her first husband, Washington jeweler Norman Galt, had died in 1908. By May 1915 President Wilson had proposed marriage, and in September Edith agreed. They were married on December 18, 1915. Edith Wilson became a true helpmate to her husband.

Each morning she accompanied President Wilson to his study to go over the business of the day. At first she was not particularly interested, but she accommodated her husband by reading and discussing whatever he wished. She learned government codes and often decoded messages for him and encoded his replies. Her knowledge of

President Woodrow Wilson and Edith Bolling Wilson, 1916 (Library of Congress)

government business proved very valuable in times to come.

Mrs. Wilson also provided the diversion her husband needed during the tense years of World War I. She played golf with enough skill that she sometimes beat both her husband and Dr. Grayson. They even played golf in the snow with black golf balls specially made for the president. The presidential couple enjoyed almost daily drives in the Pierce Arrow touring car, but they put the car aside for a carriage to save gasoline during the war.

Edith volunteered her services to the Red Cross and saw that the White House complied with wheatless days, meatless days, and other regulations for saving food and fuel. Sheep grazed on the lawn to save the labor of grass mowing. The sheep provided about two pounds of wool to be auctioned in each state, bringing a grand total of $52,823 to be given to the Red Cross. She also helped correspond with families whose sons were missing in action.

I studied every paper, sent from the different Secretaries or Senators, and tried to digest and present in tabloid form the things that, despite my vigilance, had to go to the president. I, myself, never made a single decision regarding the disposition of public affairs. The only decision that was mine was what was important and what was not, and the very important decision of when to present matters to my husband. . . .

Woodrow Wilson was first my beloved husband whose life I was trying to save, fighting with my back to the wall—after that he was president of the United States.

—*Edith Bolling Wilson,* My Memoir *(1938)*

When World War I ended, President Wilson decided to attend the peace negotiations at Versailles in order to present his Fourteen Points personally. The Wilsons stayed at the elegant Murat Palace in Paris. During delays in the business of the conference they visited the British royal family. They also traveled to Rome at the invitation of King Victor Emmanuel III, where they found the Quirinale Palace to be much better heated than drafty Buckingham Palace.

Woodrow Wilson put his heart into the Versailles negotiations, determined to secure a just peace and the establishment of the League of Nations. When the U.S. Senate refused to accept the league, Wilson took his case to the people. He began a speaking tour across the country in the hope of stimulating the public to demand acceptance of the league. His health could not withstand the demands of the situation. In Colorado he collapsed. After returning to Washington he suffered a stroke that left him partially paralyzed.

One of the president's doctors told Mrs. Wilson that taking problems to him would be like turning a knife in an open wound. So Mrs. Wilson placed herself between the president and the outside world. She screened all business and brought to his attention only the most pressing items. She read the papers, summarized or simply read him their contents, and asked him what he wanted to do. His mind was clear, and with her help he gradually improved, although he never fully recovered.

It is doubtful that Edith Wilson realized the enormous influence her censorship by selection had on the government. However, she was certainly aware of her heavy responsibility. The fact that she had previously worked closely with her husband helped. Because the president had discussed the details of government with her constantly, she had a good idea of his opinion on most subjects. She saw him through the most difficult period of his career.

In the dedication to the book he never finished, Wilson left a tribute to the wife who had become his helpmate in every way: "Her heart is not only true but wise; her thoughts are not only free but touched with vision . . . her unconscious interpretation of faith and duty makes all the way clear; her power to comprehend makes work and thought alike easier and more near to what it seeks."

As first lady, Edith Bolling Wilson met the demands of a situation unique in American history when she took the responsibility of making governmental decisions in order to shield her ill husband. Woodrow Wilson died in 1924, but Mrs. Wilson lived to attend the inauguration of President John Kennedy. She died on December 28, 1961, at her beautiful town house in Washington, D.C.

GRACE COOLIDGE

The woman in the White House portrait by Howard Chandler Christy is dressed in a simple red silk dress, which accents her long dark hair, softly waved around her face and pinned in braids around her head. Her white collie, Rob Roy, looks up adoringly. With regal bearing, Grace Coolidge commands the large canvas with an expression kind, soft, and sensual yet mysterious and distant. The observer can see why Calvin Coolidge was extravagant about his wife's clothes in spite of the fact that his penchant for economy reduced the national debt by two billion dollars in three years.

The president liked vivid colors and big hats with fancy trimmings. He sometimes went shopping and brought home pretty things for his wife to try. Mrs. Coolidge's secretary, Mary Randolph, described the first lady's wardrobe: "There were gorgeous lamés with long court trains of gold lace—a *robe de style* of bright pink taffeta, the skirt bordered by a deep flounce of silver lace, and with a spray of silk flowers appliquéd across the front."

Grace Coolidge was not accustomed to extravagance. She was born Grace Anna Goodhue in Burlington, Vermont, January 3, 1879. After graduating from the University of Vermont in 1902 she became a teacher in the Clarke School for the Deaf in Northampton,

Grace Coolidge, portrait by Howard Chandler Christy (the White House)

Massachusetts. There she met Calvin Coolidge. After their marriage at her home in Burlington on October 4, 1905, they rented half of a double house in Northampton. Even when Coolidge became governor of Massachusetts, their life-style changed very little. The state did not provide an executive mansion, so Mrs. Coolidge and their two sons remained in the same home in Northampton while Coolidge commuted from Boston on weekends.

In the summer the family returned to Coolidge's father's farm in Plymouth, Vermont. Even after he became vice-president, he still wore a wide-brimmed straw hat and chopped wood, milked cows, and pitched hay just as he had done as a boy. The Coolidge boys, John and Calvin, Jr., helped with the farm chores.

The family was at the farm on August 3, 1923, when word came that President Warren G. Harding had died. Grandfather Coolidge, a notary public, administered the oath of office to his son.

In the White House Grace Coolidge displayed a gift for making friends. Her unpretentious, gracious manner won support for her taciturn husband. Mrs. Coolidge liked to tell the story of a society woman who sat next to the president at a dinner party. "You must talk to me, Mr. Coolidge," the woman said. "I made a bet today that I could get more than two words out of you."

"You lose," replied Coolidge.

Grace Coolidge not only made friends with adults, she also knew how to make friends with children. At an Easter Monday egg rolling she delighted her visitors by carrying a baby raccoon and outfitting her dogs with Easter bonnets. Her white collie looked festive in a black veil.

The Coolidge family also experienced tragedy while in the White House. In the summer of 1924 John and Calvin were home from school, and the house was filled with young people. Sixteen-year-old Calvin played tennis without socks and developed a blister on his right toe. It became infected, and blood poisoning ensued. He died on July 7, 1924. "You know," the president told a friend, "I sit here thinking of it, and I just can't believe it has happened."

Mrs. Coolidge spent the remainder of the summer in near seclusion in New England. After the November election in which Coolidge won the presidency she decided to refurbish the White House. She appointed an advisory committee of art and antique experts. Unfortunately, politics interfered and delayed the work. Then engineers discovered that the mansion was badly in need of structural repair. Between March and September 1927 workmen replaced deteriorating wooden beams with steel and reconstructed the third floor. The "sky parlor," a sun room built on the roof of the south portico, became a favorite of Mrs. Coolidge's.

When she returned to the repaired White House in September 1927, Mrs. Coolidge brought a coverlet she had crocheted as a gift for the house. It bore representations of the American eagle and the presidential shield. Her name appeared in the design along with the dates of her husband's administration: August 8, 1923, to March 4, 1929.

Calvin Coolidge chose not to run for reelection in 1928. The couple returned to Northampton, Massachusetts, where Mrs. Coolidge continued her active interest in the Clarke School for the Deaf. She died July 8, 1957. In the White House her lovely portrait in the red dress reminds visitors of the time when she brought color and grace to the mansion.

ELEANOR ROOSEVELT

Historian William E. Leuchtenburg called Franklin D. Roosevelt the "First Imperial President" because he greatly increased the power of the American chief executive. If that is true then perhaps Eleanor Roosevelt should be called the "Imperial First Lady." She not only supported the work of her husband, but she made the position of first lady a career unto itself. She became, according to one journalist, a "Cabinet Minister without portfolio—the most influential woman of our times."

Eleanor Roosevelt probably never dreamed that she would be influential and famous. A shy, awkward child who had to struggle with poor posture, protruding teeth, and clumsiness, she possessed little self-confidence. She had lost both parents by the age of ten, and the grandmother who took over her care was strict and somewhat unsympathetic. Although she loved to visit her uncle, President Theodore Roosevelt, and his lively family at Oyster Bay, New York, she was seldom allowed to do so. But she shared her uncle's unbounded energy and later developed a concern for the welfare of the masses that followed the spirit of his politics.

A reluctant debutante, Eleanor Roosevelt never felt that she really belonged in the New York social scene. She was much happier as a volunteer worker in a settlement house in the slums. She visited children in tenements and learned firsthand of the problems of the poor. Her handsome cousin, Franklin Roosevelt, accompanied her once and exclaimed, "My God! I didn't know people lived like that." Eleanor knew, though, and throughout her life she continued to share her perceptions with Franklin.

They were married March 17, 1905. Her Uncle Theodore gave her away. For the next eleven years she was either pregnant or recovering from childbirth. She had five children by 1910 and two more in 1914 and 1916. Sara Delano Roosevelt, Franklin's mother, thoroughly dominated family life at Hyde Park, the Roosevelt home in New York. Eleanor's shyness and insecurity increased with the domination of her mother-in-law and her sense of inadequacy in meeting Franklin's expectations.

Eleanor Roosevelt once said that "back of tranquility lies always conquered unhappiness." When she could not find happiness in her marriage and family, she built a life of her own, a life of dedication to service.

Since Franklin Roosevelt was crippled due to polio suffered at age thirty-nine, his movement was limited. In a way his handicap forced Eleanor to overcome her shyness, to become his eyes and ears, and in some cases, his representative. Rexford Tugwell, a close friend and adviser of President Roosevelt, wrote, "No one who ever saw Eleanor Roosevelt sit down facing her husband, and . . . say to him, 'Franklin, I think you should' . . . or, 'Franklin, surely you will not' . . . will ever forget the experience."

A CRUCIAL EVENT

Eleanor Roosevelt was a shy youngster who suffered under the burden of a domineering father and the taunts of friends who described her as an unattractive "granny." Marriage to her distant cousin, up-and-coming politico Franklin Roosevelt, hardly improved matters. The newlyweds lived with Franklin's overbearing mother, who dominated the household and spared the bride little criticism. Moreover, Eleanor was so intimidated by Franklin's urbane friends that she sometimes begged her husband to let her stay at home while he went out by himself. Having six children between 1905, the year of her marriage, and 1916 also tended to keep her tied down and isolated.

Life began to change for Eleanor as she approached her thirtieth birthday. First, she and Franklin got out of his mother's house when President Woodrow Wilson made him assistant secretary of war in 1913. During World War I she found a measure of fulfillment working with the wives of other Washington officials to operate canteens for servicemen stationed in the capital. The crucial event, however, occurred in late 1918, when Eleanor discovered a cache of letters Franklin had exchanged with Eleanor's former social secretary, Lucy Mercer, that clearly indicated the two were conducting an affair. "The bottom dropped out of my own particular world," she later remembered. She offered Franklin a divorce, which he refused, promising to end the relationship with Lucy.

Eleanor accepted the compromise, but, as biographer Nathan Miller writes, "the relationship between them was never the same. Eleanor could forgive but not completely forget, and she nursed her wound, never letting it completely close, for the remainder of her life. She became more independent: less a reflection of her husband and with her own life to live." Franklin eventually reestablished his relationship with Lucy. —ed.

As first lady, Eleanor Roosevelt broke all traditions. She shocked White House ushers by running the elevators herself and by driving her own car. In the first year of her husband's administration she traveled thirty-eight thousand miles. The next year the figure was forty-two thousand. Reporters soon lost track of her journeys, which took her as far afield as Pacific war zones.

In 1938 Mrs. Roosevelt earned more than one hundred thousand dollars from speaking and writing, more than the president's salary. She wrote a newspaper column as well as articles for magazines. Her radio program rated along with those of the favorite actors and actresses of the day. She held her own weekly news conferences, especially for women reporters. Once she visited a Baltimore prison to observe salvage work being done by the prisoners and left the White House early without informing her husband. The president called his wife's secretary and asked where Eleanor was. "She is in prison, Mr. President," said the secretary. "I'm not surprised," he replied, "but what for?"

In May 1933, at the height of the Depression, a "Bonus Army" composed of irate, desperate veterans demanding payment of pension bonuses not yet due descended on Washington. It was a potentially explosive situation. In a previous Bonus March four deaths had resulted. The president sent Eleanor to the camp of the veterans. Louis Howe, the president's adviser, drove her to the gate, then sent her alone into the mess hall. The first lady spoke simply but with sincerity and affection. She won over the veterans and concluded the visit by leading them in singing "There's

Eleanor Roosevelt in the White House, 1933 (the White House)

a Long, Long Trail Awinding," a song familiar on the battlefields. By early June more than twenty-six hundred bonus marchers had enrolled in the Civilian Conservation Corps, and the crisis ended. President Herbert Hoover had sent in the army to disperse the bonus marchers; Roosevelt had only to send his wife.

After Franklin Roosevelt's death, Eleanor accepted appointment as U.S. delegate to the United Nations General Assembly, where she served as chairperson of the Commission on Human Rights of the Economic and Social Council. She pioneered in developing international standards for human rights. She became a champion of minority groups and the underprivileged.

Due to her high profile, criticism was inevitable. People either loved her or hated her, but they could not ignore her. The little girl whose family undermined her confidence by calling her an "ugly duckling" realistically accepted herself and the world, yet resisted conformity. She identified with the underprivileged, was problem-centered rather than self-centered; she appreciated people in a fresh and spontaneous way. In spite of the fact that she was not exceptionally brilliant, talented, or artistic, her love of humanity and her energy for service enabled her to make a truly significant contribution to American life. She found personal fulfillment in spite of an unhappy childhood and a troubled marriage.

Eleanor Roosevelt elevated the position of first lady into a distinct career stamped with her own individuality. Many people agreed with the journalist who called her the most influential woman of her time.

JACQUELINE KENNEDY

President John F. Kennedy's admirers spoke of the time of his brief presidency as "Camelot," referring to the popular musical of that name based on the leg-

Jacqueline and John Kennedy in Houston, Texas, November 21, 1963 (courtesy of UPI / Bettmann Archive)

end of King Arthur. Jacqueline Bouvier Kennedy fit the Camelot image with her beauty, grace, and regal bearing. She had enjoyed a fashionable education and became the leading debutante of 1948. Since she had been trained in the social graces since childhood, she felt comfortable in the highest circles both at home and abroad.

Women in many countries copied Jacqueline Kennedy's elegant clothes and distinctive hairdo. Her favorite hat style, the pillbox, became a popular standard. Although she was only thirty-one when she became first lady, she brought distinction to the position.

The Kennedy children, Caroline and John, Jr., were the youngest children of a president to live in the White House since the turn of the century. The lively preschoolers amused the nation with their antics. The Kennedys established a nursery and first grade in the executive mansion so that their children could have playmates and schooling without the security risks of leaving the White House

Decorating of the mansion was a special project of Mrs. Kennedy. In February 1962 she appeared in a nationally televised tour of the house that showed the work of restoration begun under her direction. The White House Historical Association, a nonprofit organization dedicated to the historical interpretation of the mansion, in cooperation with the National Geographic Society, sponsored a full-color guidebook describing the architecture, furnishings, and history. *The White House: An Historic Guide* was so successful that its earnings provided a continual source of funds for restoration work.

Before the Kennedy era Washington was not known for its cultural attractions. Jacqueline Kennedy invited the

ALL IN THE SERVICE OF THE STATE

Nikita Krushchev really liked Jackie Kennedy. During the Vienna summit between the Russian premier and President John F. Kennedy held in June 1961, he so openly admired her that the American president was almost forced to take second place. When photographers asked Krushchev and Kennedy to pose shaking hands, Krushchev remarked, "I'd rather shake hands with her." At dinner he moved his chair close to Jackie's, complimented her on her dress, and started telling her jokes.

The conversation turned to the Russian space program, and Krushchev told Jackie that one of the dogs the Russians had sent into orbit had recently given birth to a litter of puppies. Jackie casually asked, "Why don't you send me one?" Two months later the Soviet ambassador hand-delivered a little puppy named Pushinka to Jackie at the White House. When the president asked her what it was doing there, Jackie replied, "I'm afraid I asked Krushchev for it in Vienna. I was just running out of things to say." —ed.

best artists in ballet, drama, music, and literature to the White House. She abolished the tiring custom of receiving lines at official functions. Instead, the Kennedys circulated informally. Mrs. Kennedy also replaced the huge banquet table with smaller, round tables seating ten or twelve each. Cheerful fires glowed in the old fireplaces in cool weather, and in summer guests often moved into the gardens. White House parties became enjoyable gatherings dominated by young, fashionable, talented people.

Jacqueline Kennedy's influence was not limited to the White House. In 1961 she accompanied the president on a trip to Europe. Huge crowds gathered to greet the popular couple. Her fluency in French, Spanish, and Italian proved a valuable asset in meeting foreign dignitaries and speaking to crowds. The president once introduced himself by saying, "I am the man who accompanied Jacqueline Kennedy to Paris." In 1962 Mrs. Kennedy toured Pakistan and India without the president. She charmed both the leaders and their people wherever she went.

The assassination of President Kennedy on November 22, 1963, brought an end to "Camelot." The young widow responded to the tragedy with exceptional grace. She studied reports of Abraham Lincoln's funeral and with the president's brothers planned a fitting tribute complete to the last detail, when three-year-old "John-John" saluted his father's casket.

Jacqueline Kennedy later married Greek shipping magnate Aristotle Onassis. Following his death she pursued a career in publishing in New York City. She will be remembered for her work in redecorating the White House, for stimulating interest in the arts, and for bringing style and grace to the position of first lady. Perhaps, as one British newspaper said, she gave the American people one thing they had always lacked—majesty.

Forgotten Leaders: Careers of the Vice-Presidents Who Never Served as President

by THOMAS L. CONNELLY

Forty-three men have served the United States as vice-president (not counting Vice-President Dan Quayle), but only fourteen have moved on to the highest office. Probably not even many professional historians can name all the others, but many of the forgotten vice-presidents enjoyed prominent political careers before attaining national office; others led the way in business and legal circles. Although the vice-presidency itself carries little responsibility, winning the office requires almost as much skill and as much luck as winning the presidency.

The following is a survey of the careers of the vice-presidents who never attained the presidency.

AARON BURR

Aaron Burr of New York served as vice-president from 1801 to 1805, during Thomas Jefferson's first administration. Born in Newark, New Jersey, in 1756, he was a grandson of Jonathan Edwards, the fire-eating Calvinist preacher who led the religious Great Awakening of the early eighteenth century. Burr certainly possessed little of the Calvinist ethos of self-restraint his grandfather embodied. A reputed womanizer, in politics Burr was an erratic schemer who relied more on his quick wit than on strong ethics to win success. His massive ego proved his worst enemy and caused his political downfall.

A power in New York state politics by 1790 and U.S. senator from New York from 1791 to 1797, Burr was the first of several Democratic-Republican vice-presidential nominees from New York who balanced presidential tickets featuring a Virginian in the top spot. Because the Constitution did not require the electoral college to cast separate votes for president and vice-president, Jefferson and Burr tied for the lead in the election of 1800.

Thanks in part to Alexander Hamilton's aggressive campaign effort against him, Burr lost a race for the New York governorship in 1804. The embittered loser seemed thereafter to sever his connection to reality. Prompted by Hamilton's press insults during the gubernatorial campaign, he challenged the founder of federalism to a duel. Although Hamilton opposed dueling, especially when it involved him, he did not think he could refuse and survive politically. The two met at Weehawken, New Jersey, on July 11, 1804. Hamilton refused to fire on his opponent; Burr shot with deadly accuracy.

Indicted for murder, Burr fled to the western United States, where he got involved in some shady dealings. Historians still dispute what it was he was doing, but some evidence indicates that he was working to sever Louisiana from the United States and establish a separate republic with him as its leader. Other evidence suggests he was involved in an attempt to conquer Mexico.

After two years of preparation in

Left: Aaron Burr, vice-president during Thomas Jefferson's first term, from 1801 to 1805 (portrait by Gilbert Stuart, circa 1794; New Jersey Historical Society); right: George Clinton, vice-president under Jefferson from 1805 to 1809 and under James Madison from 1809 until Clinton's death in 1812 (portrait by Ezra James, circa 1812; New York State Historical Association)

1805 and 1806, Burr's plans collapsed. He was tried for treason in 1807 by Chief Justice John Marshall. Found not guilty, he fled to Europe to avoid lesser charges. He returned to New York and his law practice in 1812, but his political career was over. Burr died in New York in 1836.

GEORGE CLINTON

George Clinton of New York served as vice-president from 1805 to 1812, during Thomas Jefferson's second presidential term and during the first three years of James Madison's first term. He was the first vice-president to die in office.

Clinton came to his position with vast military and political experience. Born in Little Britain, New York, in 1739, he ran away from home at the age of sixteen to serve on a privateer, the *Defiance.* During the French and Indian War he served in his father's regiment during Col. John Bradstreet's expedition against Fort Frontenac. After the war, Clinton became an attorney in New York City. In 1775 he won election to the Second Continental Congress. In the summer of 1776 he was serving as a commander in the New York militia and thus was not in Philadelphia when the Declaration of Independence was signed. He became a brigadier general in the Continental army in 1777, but he returned to politics that same year as governor of New York, a position he held from 1777 to 1795 and from 1801 to 1804.

ELBRIDGE GERRY

James Madison served the last year of his first presidential term without a vice-president. During the campaign of 1812 he designated Elbridge Gerry of Massachusetts to replace the deceased George Clinton. Gerry died in 1814, making the unlucky Madison the only president who had two vice-presidents who died in office.

A prominent Massachusetts Democratic-Republican, Gerry was born in

Left: Elbridge Gerry, vice-president during James Madison's second term, from 1813 until Gerry's death in 1814 (portrait by James Bogle; National Historical Park); right: Daniel D. Tompkins, vice-president during James Monroe's two presidential terms, from 1817 to 1825

Marblehead in 1744. He graduated from Harvard College in 1762, entered the law profession, and served in the Continental Congress from 1776 to 1785. He attended the Constitutional Convention in 1787 but refused to sign the resulting document. He did accept election to two terms in the U.S. House, beginning in 1789.

Elected governor of his state in 1810, Gerry is best known for the bill he sponsored during his gubernatorial term that gave members of his party electoral advantages over their Federalist opponents in several voting districts. The tactic of apportioning districts to give greater representation to one political party later became known as "gerrymandering."

DANIEL D. TOMPKINS

New Yorker Daniel D. Tompkins served as vice-president from 1817 to 1825, during both of James Monroe's terms as president. A liberal Democratic-Republican, he was born in present-day Scarsdale in 1774, became a lawyer, and in 1804 served briefly in the New York state legislature before gaining appointment to the state supreme court that same year. In 1807 he was elected governor of New York, and he served as governor until he became vice-president. Tompkins distinguished himself in the governorship, instigating among other reforms the abolition of slavery in the state. The governorship, however, also hurt him. During the War of 1812 the New York legislature refused to appropriate funds to meet the rising cost of defending the state, so Governor Tompkins borrowed the money himself, putting up his own property as collateral. When the war was over, neither the state nor the federal government offered to repay the loans, and Tompkins's estate was threatened. Litigation and controversy surrounding the loans dogged him through his terms as vice-president. Finally, in 1824 the U.S. Congress agreed to pay the debts, but the strain of the fight took its toll. Tompkins became an alcoholic, at times presiding drunkenly over the Senate. He died in 1825, a few months after leaving office.

JOHN C. CALHOUN

John C. Calhoun of South Carolina, the first inhabitant of national office not

Left: John C. Calhoun, vice-president under John Quincy Adams from 1825 to 1829 and under Andrew Jackson from 1829 until Calhoun's resignation in 1832 (from a miniature by John Trumbull; courtesy of the Yale University Art Gallery); right: Richard M. Johnson, vice-president under Martin Van Buren, from 1837 to 1841

born in Virginia, Massachusetts, or New York, served as vice-president from 1825 to 1832, during the presidential term of John Quincy Adams and for most of Andrew Jackson's first term. He was the second vice-president, after George Clinton, to serve in the administrations of two presidents.

Calhoun was born in Abbeville, South Carolina, in 1782, graduated from Yale College in 1804, became a lawyer, and quickly established himself as a political leader in his native state. He was elected to the state legislature in 1808 and to the U.S. House of Representatives in 1810. In the House he took a position on the Foreign Affairs Committee, soon after assumed the chairmanship, and emerged as a leading proponent of war with Great Britain in 1812. Calhoun left the House in 1817 to serve as President James Monroe's secretary of war. The vice-presidency followed in 1825.

Calhoun also became the first vice-president to resign from office. He clashed with President Jackson over the tariff issue, which was vital to Calhoun's Deep South constituency, and over other matters, one of which involved the supposed immorality of the wife of Jackson's secretary of war. In 1832 Jackson rejected the "nullification" doctrine Calhoun had developed to combat what he considered the usurpation of states' rights by the federal government and then bypassed the vice-president for renomination in favor of Martin Van Buren of New York. After the election of 1832 Calhoun resigned the vice-presidency to accept a seat in the U.S. Senate from South Carolina. He served in the Senate until 1844, when he accepted the job of secretary of state under President John Tyler, then returned to the Senate after Tyler's term ended the next year. He remained in the Senate until his death in 1850.

RICHARD M. JOHNSON

Richard M. Johnson of Kentucky was the first politician to have served in both the U.S. House of Representatives and the Senate before winning the vice-presidency. He served in the second spot during the presidential administration of Martin Van Buren, from 1837 to 1841.

Johnson was born in present-day Louisville, Kentucky, in 1780, became a lawyer in 1802, won election to the Kentucky state legislature in 1804, and served in the U.S. House from 1807 to 1819. During the War of 1812 he won military fame as the commander of a regiment of Kentucky volunteers in the frontier army of Gen. William Henry Harrison, participating in the Battle of the Thames, in which Harrison's forces decisively defeated the Shawnee Indian Confederacy. The Shawnee chief, Tecumseh, was killed during the battle, and popular opinion gave Johnson personal credit for striking the blow.

In 1819 Johnson left the House for the Senate, then returned to the House in 1829. He remained there until he accepted the call of his party to the vice-presidency. His nomination was controversial, however. Only the personal lobbying effort of outgoing president Jackson secured Johnson, a loyal Jacksonian, a place on the national ticket. Many Democrats opposed Johnson because his common-law wife was a former slave and the couple had several mulatto children. To win more support for the party in the South in 1840, the Democrats declined to renominate Johnson, although he appeared on the ticket in many states anyway. After Van Buren lost the election, Johnson returned to Kentucky, where he served briefly in the state legislature before retiring from politics. Johnson died in 1850.

GEORGE M. DALLAS

George M. Dallas of Pennsylvania served as James K. Polk's vice-president throughout Polk's presidential term from 1845 to 1849. Born in Philadelphia in 1792, he was the son of Alexander J. Dallas, James Madison's secretary of the Treasury. The future vice-president graduated from the College of New Jersey (Princeton), gained admission to the Pennsylvania bar in 1813, and took a position as secretary to Albert Gallatin, U.S. minister to Russia. After his service in Russia he returned to the practice of law in Philadelphia, taking a position as solicitor for the Bank of the United States. He also served as deputy attorney general of Pennsylvania in 1817, then won election as Philadelphia's mayor in 1819. He again returned to his law practice before accepting President Andrew Jackson's appointment as U.S. district attorney for eastern Pennsylvania in 1829.

Dallas was elected to the U.S. Senate in 1831 as a loyal supporter of President Jackson, but he resigned only two years into his term to accept the attorney generalship of Pennsylvania. In 1837 he was appointed U.S. minister to Russia by President Martin Van Buren. After leaving the ministerial position in Russia in 1839, he practiced law in Philadelphia before accepting the call of the Democratic party in 1845. As vice-president, Polk strongly supported the president during the war with Mexico and reversed his traditional support of high tariffs to back the president's antitariff position.

Dallas returned to Philadelphia after Polk's term was up in 1849. His tariff reversal had made him so unpopular in Pennsylvania that to consider a return to politics seemed impractical. He practiced law until President Franklin Pierce appointed him U.S. minister to Great Britain in 1856. There he remained until the conclusion of James Buchanan's presidential term in 1861. Dallas, for whom the city in Texas is named, died in 1864.

WILLIAM RUFUS DE VANE KING

William Rufus de Vane King of Alabama holds the distinction of serving the briefest term as vice-president—twenty-five days. He died before he as-

Left: George M. Dallas, vice-president in the administration of James K. Polk, from 1845 to 1849 (engraving by Thomas B. Welch); right: William Rufus de Vane King, vice-president under Franklin Pierce for twenty-five days in March 1853

sumed his duties in the administration of Franklin Pierce.

King was born in Sampson County, North Carolina, in 1786 and graduated from the University of North Carolina in 1803. He was admitted to the North Carolina bar in 1806 and served in the state legislature from 1807 to 1809. In 1810 he served as city solicitor for Wilmington, North Carolina, and in 1811 he won election to the U.S. House of Representatives.

King resigned his House seat in 1816 to serve briefly as secretary of the U.S. legation to Naples and then as secretary of the U.S. legation to Russia. He settled in Alabama upon his return to the United States in 1818 and stood successfully for one of that new state's U.S. Senate seats in 1819. He served in the U.S. Senate until 1844, when he accepted President John Tyler's appointment as U.S. minister to France. As French minister, King worked long and hard to deter France from opposing the Mexican War.

King returned to the United States in 1846 and stood for election to the Senate again in 1848. In 1850 he was made Senate president pro tem. As the election of 1852 approached, King supported his friend James Buchanan, a fellow bachelor, for the presidency. Franklin Pierce won the nomination and picked King for the vice-presidency to satisfy Buchanan's supporters. During the presidential campaign the sixty-seven-year-old King's tuberculosis, from which he had suffered for years, worsened. After his election he journeyed to sunny Cuba to find relief, but he grew steadily weaker—too weak, in fact, to return to the United States to take the vice-presidential oath. He thus became the only vice-president ever to take the oath of office in a foreign country. Toward the end of March 1853 he was able to return to his adopted hometown of Cahaba, Alabama, but he never made it to Washington.

JOHN C. BRECKINRIDGE

Kentuckian John C. Breckinridge served as vice-president under James

John C. Breckinridge, vice-president under James Buchanan, from 1857 to 1861 (portrait by Nicola Marshall, 1881, after an unidentified artist; courtesy of the Filson Club, Louisville, Kentucky)

Buchanan from 1857 to 1861. By the time of his election as the youngest vice-president he had carved a niche as a prominent member of the national Democratic party. By the end of Buchanan's term he had emerged as a leader in the burgeoning movement to sever the South from the United States.

Born in Lexington in 1821, Breckinridge graduated from Danville's Centre College in 1839 and was admitted to the Kentucky bar in 1840. He practiced law in Lexington until the outbreak of the Mexican War. As a major in the Third Kentucky Volunteers, Breckinridge distinguished himself in battle. After the war he returned to Kentucky and won election to the state House of Representatives in 1849. Two years later he went to Washington as a member of Kentucky's national House delegation.

During his two House terms Breckinridge emerged a staunch defender of southern slavery, but unlike some southern Democrats, he spoke out against the expansion of slavery into the territories. Union-minded Democrats both North and South thought him the ideal candidate to accompany Pennsylvanian James Buchanan on the national ticket in 1856.

Despite Breckinridge's loyalty to the Union, however, when the Democrats finally split in 1860, he took the side of the South. After a rump of northern Democrats nominated Stephen Douglas of Illinois for the presidency, southern Democrats nominated Breckinridge. He placed second in electoral votes to Abraham Lincoln and carried eleven states, but he did poorly in the North.

The Kentucky legislature elected the former vice-president to a seat in the U.S. Senate, but when a state convention voted to keep Kentucky in the Union, Breckinridge accepted a commission in the Confederate army and in December was expelled from the Senate. During the first three years of the Civil War he served on the western front, becoming a division commander of the Army of the Tennessee. In January 1865 he became the last Confederate secretary of war.

After the end of the war and the assassination of Lincoln, Breckinridge fled the United States, living in Europe for two years. In 1867 he returned to the States and resumed his law practice in Lexington, where he died in 1875.

HANNIBAL HAMLIN

The first Republican vice-president, Hannibal Hamlin of Maine served under Abraham Lincoln from 1861 to 1865. Born in Paris Hill, Maine, in 1809 (the year of Lincoln's birth), Hamlin started out as a Maine Democrat. Denied a college education because of the death of his father, he worked as copublisher of a local weekly newspaper, the *Jeffersonian*, before selling his interest and entering into the study of law. Admitted to the Maine bar in 1833, he won election to the Maine legislature in 1835 and was reelected for five successive terms. He served as speaker of the Maine House in 1837, 1839, and 1840.

Hamlin lost his first try for a U.S. House seat in 1840 and then won in 1842 and 1844. In national politics he took a staunch antislavery position, opposing the annexation of Texas and the Mexican War and actively supporting the failed Wilmot Proviso, which would have outlawed slavery in the territories gained from Mexico.

Hamlin declined a third House term to run for the U.S. Senate, and he won the vote of the Maine legislature in 1848 to fill an unexpired term. He won a term by general election beginning in 1851 and then resigned in January 1857 to assume the position of the first Republican governor of Maine. He quickly resigned the governorship, however, to assume another seat in the U.S. Senate, that time as a Republican. When Lincoln called in 1861 he again left the Senate.

Hamlin and Lincoln never met until after they were elected to national office in November 1860, but they remained on friendly terms throughout Lincoln's first term. Early in Lincoln's presidency Hamlin urged the chief executive to make a strong statement against slavery, and the vice-president's wish was fulfilled when Lincoln issued the Preliminary Emancipation Proclamation in September 1862.

Lincoln and the Republicans passed Hamlin by when the time came to nominate a vice-presidential candidate in 1864. They wanted someone with stronger Unionist credentials. After leaving national office Hamlin served as collector of the Port of Boston in 1865 and 1866 before winning election to the Senate for a term beginning in 1869. He won reelection in 1876 and then resigned his seat to take the position of U.S. minister to Spain in 1881. He left that position after one year and retired from public life. Hamlin died in 1891.

Hannibal Hamlin, vice-president in Abraham Lincoln's first administration, from 1861 to 1865

SCHUYLER COLFAX

Schuyler Colfax of Indiana served as vice-president from 1869 to 1873, during the first presidential term of Ulysses S. Grant. Colfax was born in New York City in 1823 and moved to Indiana with his mother and stepfather in 1836. When his stepfather was elected auditor of St. Joseph County in 1841, he made Colfax his deputy. While serving as deputy auditor the young man developed an interest in journalism and for two sessions worked as a senate reporter for the *State Journal.* In 1845 he founded the *St. Joseph Valley Register*, serving also as its editor. The paper took strong positions in favor of northern Whig principles, and Colfax emerged as a leader of the Indiana Whig party. He served as a delegate at the Whig national conventions of 1848 and 1852 and ran a strong but losing campaign for the U.S. House of Representatives in 1851.

After the passage of the Kansas-Nebraska Act in 1854, Colfax helped organize the Indiana Republican party. As a Republican he won a U.S. House seat for the term beginning in 1855. In Congress he strongly supported the antislavery stand of the Republicans, opposing the admission of Kansas to the Union

Left: Schuyler Colfax, vice-president during Ulysses S. Grant's first term, from 1869 to 1873 (engraving by H. W. Smith); right: Henry Wilson, vice-president during Grant's second term, from 1873 until Wilson's death in 1875 (engraving by Alexander H. Ritchie)

as a slave state, and also favored the passage of temperance legislation. He won seven successive campaigns for reelection to Congress, serving as House Speaker from 1863 to 1869, until he gave up his seat to run for vice-president on the Grant ticket.

The Crédit Mobilier scandal marred Colfax's vice-presidential term. In 1872 it was revealed that while he was serving as Speaker of the House he purchased twenty shares of Crédit Mobilier stock at considerably below market value. Many in Congress who had made similar purchases had worked to thwart congressional investigation of the Mobilier dealings, and Colfax suffered from the association. Although he was never formally charged in connection with the scandal, the Republican convention of 1872 refused to renominate the Indianan to the vice-presidency.

After serving out his term Colfax retired to the lecture circuit. In Minnesota in 1885 he died of a heart attack while on the way to a speaking engagement.

HENRY WILSON

Henry Wilson of Massachusetts served as vice-president from 1873 to 1875, during Ulysses S. Grant's second presidential term. Born Jeremiah Jones Colbath to a poor farm family in Farmington, New Hampshire, in 1812, he changed his name when he turned twenty-one to that of the subject of a biography he had read. From the age of ten he was indentured to a farmer.

After he worked off his apprenticeship he moved to Natick, Massachusetts, to learn shoemaking, earning twenty dollars a month. After he saved enough money he attended several New England academies and taught school during several winter seasons. Continuing financial hardship, however, forced him back to Natick and shoemaking; by 1839 he owned his own shop.

During the period in which Wilson consolidated his position as a shoemaker, he also emerged as a strong stump speaker and a prominent local leader of the Whig party. He won election to the state House of Representa-

Left: William Almon Wheeler, vice-president in the administration of Rutherford B. Hayes, from 1877 to 1881 (engraving by George E. Perine); right: Thomas A. Hendricks, vice-president during the first nine months of Grover Cleveland's first term, until Hendricks's death in 1885

tives in 1840 and was reelected in 1842. In 1844 he began serving the first of two one-year terms in the Massachusetts Senate. In 1848 he purchased a newspaper, the *Republican*, which furthered his position in favor of the territorial restriction of slavery. Also in 1848 he helped form the Massachusetts Free Soil party.

Elected as a Free Soil member of the Massachusetts House in 1850, Wilson went on to chair the national Free Soil convention in 1852. He lost a race for the U.S. House that year and a race for Massachusetts governor the year after. When the Free Soil party disintegrated in Massachusetts, Wilson joined the American (Know-Nothing) party; he won election to the U.S. Senate as a Know-Nothing in 1854. He served in the Senate, first as a Know-Nothing and then as a Republican, from 1855 to 1873, when he left congressional service to accept the call of the national Republican party as President Grant's running mate.

A pair of strokes hampered Wilson's performance during his vice-presidential service. He died at midterm, in 1875.

WILLIAM ALMON WHEELER

When William Almon Wheeler was suggested as the vice-presidential nominee on the Republican ticket for 1877, presidential nominee Rutherford B. Hayes responded, "Who is Wheeler?" He was an unglamorous individual who quietly advanced himself in New York state political circles. Born in Malone, New York, in 1819, Wheeler attended the University of Vermont in the late 1830s. He gained admission to the New York bar in 1845 and began practicing law. In 1846 he was appointed district attorney for Franklin County, New York, and he held the position through 1849. He served his state as a representative from 1850 to 1851 and as a senator from 1858 to 1859.

In 1860 Wheeler won election as a Republican to the U.S. House of Representatives. He served a term beginning in 1861 and returned to private life. He won another election to the House in 1868 and served from 1869 to 1877, when Hayes called him to the vice-presidency.

Wheeler served a typically uneventful term as vice-president. He retired after leaving office and died in 1887.

THOMAS A. HENDRICKS

Born in 1819 near Zanesville, Ohio, Thomas A. Hendricks served as vice-president during the first nine months of Grover Cleveland's first presidential term, in 1885. When he was a year old he and his family moved to Indiana, and Hendricks eventually graduated from Hanover Academy and began to prepare himself for a law career. He gained admission to the Indiana bar in 1843 and entered into practice in Shelbyville.

Hendricks began his political career as a Democratic member of Indiana's state legislature in 1848 and then won election to the U.S. House of Representatives in 1850. He served two terms in the House beginning in 1851 but lost his second bid for reelection. After Hendricks left the House, President Franklin Pierce appointed him commissioner of the General Land Office, a position he filled through 1859.

In 1860 Hendricks stood as the Democratic nominee for the governorship of Indiana, but the state party, like the national, was divided between proponents and opponents of compromise with the South. The Republican candidate won the election. Hendricks returned to the practice of law, this time in Indianapolis, but in 1863 rode the wave of mid-Civil War anti-Union sentiment to a seat in the U.S. Senate. Senator Hendricks assumed a leadership role among the small contingent of Civil War Democrats, opposing the Republicans' plans for Reconstruction and also working against passage of the civil rights constitutional amendments. He was a leading candidate for the Democratic presidential nomination in 1868 before the convention settled on a dark-horse candidate to break a deadlock. Upon completion of his senatorial term he left Congress to run, again unsuccessfully, for Indiana governor.

The former senator returned to Indianapolis and his law practice until 1872, when he ran again for the governorship of the state. Largely due to his local-option stand on temperance, he won the election, one of only two Democratic state officials elected that landslide-Republican year. He was the first Democrat elected governor of a northern state after the Civil War. Toward the end of his four-year gubernatorial term he made a run for the vice-presidency on the presidential ticket with Samuel Tilden, lost that close election, and once again returned to Indianapolis and the law.

A member of the Indiana delegation to the Democratic national convention in 1884, Hendricks was proposed as the party's presidential nominee, an honor he declined. He did accept the unanimous nomination of his party to the vice-presidency on the ticket with Grover Cleveland. By the time he assumed office he was in poor health. He died the day after attending a homecoming reception in Indianapolis.

LEVI P. MORTON

Benjamin Harrison's vice-president was New York banker Levi P. Morton, who served through the whole of Harrison's presidential term from 1889 to 1893. Morton was born in Shoreham, Vermont, in 1824 and entered into business at the age of fifteen in Hanover, New Hampshire. He opened a dry goods store in Boston in 1850 and moved to New York City in 1854. In 1863 he began his banking career as founder of L. P. Morton & Company. A successor bank, Morton, Bliss & Company, brought Morton to the forefront of the eastern banking establishment. In 1873 Morton's British subsidiary, Morton, Rose & Company, was appointed a financial agent for the U.S. government.

Morton entered formal political service as a Republican member of the U.S.

Left: Levi P. Morton, vice-president in the Benjamin Harrison administration, from 1889 to 1893; right: Adlai Stevenson, vice-president in Grover Cleveland's second administration, from 1893 to 1897 (photograph by Pach Brothers)

House of Representatives for a single term beginning in 1879. Upon completion of the term President James A. Garfield appointed him U.S. minister to France, a position he held throughout the Garfield-Chester A. Arthur presidency. Out of office for four years upon the ascension of Grover Cleveland and the Democrats to national office in 1885, Morton won the Republican vice-presidential nomination in 1888 and emerged victorious on the ticket with Harrison. In 1892 he ran again for vice-president, but the Harrison ticket lost.

In 1895 Morton began serving a two-year term as governor of New York. After that he established the Morton Trust Company, the last of the major financial services organizations in which he played a prominent role; then he retired from active professional life. Morton died in 1920, at the age of ninety-six.

ADLAI STEVENSON

Grover Cleveland's second-term vice-president was Adlai Stevenson of Illinois, grandfather of the Democratic leader of the 1950s. Born the son of Christian County, Kentucky, slaveholders in 1835, Stevenson attended Center College in Danville and moved with his family to Bloomington, Illinois, in 1852. In Illinois he studied law and was admitted to the bar in 1859. He served as master in chancery for the Illinois circuit court for four years beginning in 1860 and was a democratic presidential elector for Gen. George McClellan in the presidential election of 1864. He served as U.S. district attorney for the state of Illinois for four years beginning in 1865 and formed a law partnership in Bloomington after leaving office.

Stevenson practiced law in Bloomington until he won a seat as a Democrat in the U.S. House of Representatives for a term beginning in 1875. He lost his bid for reelection, won another term beginning in 1879, then lost again. After Grover Cleveland won the presidency in 1885, Stevenson took the position of U.S. first assistant postmaster general. Before the end of his presidential term

Left: Garret A. Hobart, vice-president during the first three years of William McKinley's first term, from 1897 until Hobart's death in 1899 (engraving by H. B. Hall's Sons); right: James S. Sherman, vice-president under William Howard Taft from 1909 until Sherman's death in 1912

Cleveland nominated Stevenson to the Supreme Court of the District of Columbia, but the Republican Senate refused to confirm the appointment.

The ousted politician returned to Bloomington to practice law before accepting the nomination of the Democratic party to the vice-presidency on the Cleveland ticket in 1893. He served an uneventful term, went back to the law, and returned to politics as the vice-presidential nominee on the unsuccessful presidential ticket of William Jennings Bryan in 1900 and as an unsuccessful gubernatorial candidate in Illinois in 1908. Stevenson died in 1914.

GARRET A. HOBART

Garret A. Hobart of New Jersey served as vice-president during the first three years of William McKinley's first presidential term. Hobart was born in Long Branch, New Jersey, in 1844 and graduated from Rutgers College in 1863. He taught school for several months and then entered into the study of law in Paterson. He was admitted to the bar in 1866 after clerking a session for the Paterson grand jury in 1865.

After serving a term as a Paterson city councilman from 1871 to 1872 and as counsel of Passaic County's Board of Freeholders in 1872, Hobart entered the New Jersey state assembly in late 1872. He served as an assemblyman until 1875, including as speaker during the 1874 session, and in the state senate from 1876 to 1882, the final year as senate president. Meanwhile he took the position of chairman of the state Republican party in 1880, and he served in that capacity through 1891, taking time out to run unsuccessfully for a seat in the U.S. Senate in 1884. He served as a member of the Republican National Committee during the convention of 1884 and as chairman of the committee during the conventions of 1892 and 1896. He also maintained an extensive law practice and memberships on several corporate boards.

Hobart won the vice-presidential nomination on the McKinley ticket on the first ballot. He is one of the few vice-presidents ever to cast a tie-breaking vote on a major piece of legislation, voting after the Spanish-American War against legislation that would have granted the Philippines independence on the same terms as Cuba. He was unable, however, to serve out his term. Home in Paterson, Hobart died in 1899.

CHARLES W. FAIRBANKS

Charles W. Fairbanks of Indiana served as vice-president during the elected term of President Theodore Roosevelt, from 1905 to 1909. He was born in a log cabin in Unionville, Ohio, in 1852 and graduated from Ohio Wesleyan College in 1872. After graduation he took a job as manager of the Pittsburgh, Pennsylvania, branch of the Western Associated Press and then moved to the Cleveland branch. In Cleveland he also studied at Cleveland Law School. He was admitted to the Ohio bar in 1874 and began his practice in Indianapolis, Indiana, later that year.

Fairbanks built a prominent practice as a railroad attorney and soon emerged as a Republican political leader in Indianapolis. He managed the unsuccessful presidential campaign of his friend Walter Q. Gresham in 1888 and served as the keynote speaker for the Republican national convention in 1896. In 1897 he won election to the U.S. Senate and won reelection in 1903. In the Senate he strongly supported the Republican positions in favor of a protective tariff and against free silver; President Theodore Roosevelt made him the Republican vice-presidential nominee in 1904.

In 1908 Fairbanks received attention as a potential presidential nominee but faded from contention after a strong showing on the first convention ballot. He returned to his law practice and also served on several honorary and public service commissions and as a director on the boards of many prominent corporations. In 1916 he again received mention as a possible Republican candidate for president; that year he accepted the vice-presidential slot on the unsuccessful ticket with Charles Evans Hughes. Fairbanks retired from public life after that campaign. He died in Indianapolis in 1918.

JAMES S. SHERMAN

James S. Sherman of New York served as vice-president during the presidential term of William Howard Taft from 1909 to just days before the election of 1912. He died of Bright's disease, the same disease that killed Chester A. Arthur a few years after the conclusion of his presidential term.

Sherman was born in Utica, New York, in 1855 and in 1878 graduated from Hamilton College in Clinton, New York, where he excelled in debate. In 1880 he received a bachelor of laws degree from Hamilton College in Utica and gained admission to the New York bar.

In 1884, at the age of twenty-eight, Sherman won election as Utica mayor. He entered the U.S. House in 1886 and was reelected nine times, skipping only the term from 1891 to 1893. In the House he gained a reputation as a behind-the-scenes Republican power who took a special interest in Indian affairs as chairman of the House committee. In 1908 he accepted a first-ballot nomination to the vice-presidency and campaigned strongly for the victorious ticket.

Sherman won renomination to the vice-presidency in 1912 but did not survive the campaign. Taft lost the election.

THOMAS MARSHALL

Woodrow Wilson's vice-president, Thomas Marshall of Indiana, served during the whole of the president's two terms. Born in 1854 in Manchester, Indiana, Marshall graduated from Wabash College in 1873 and was admitted to the Indiana bar in 1875. He started his law practice in Columbia City and soon emerged as a leader in the profession. He developed an interest in Democratic politics and ran a losing campaign for county prosecuting attorney in

Thomas Marshall, vice-president under Woodrow Wilson, from 1913 to 1921

1880. From 1896 to 1898 he served as chairman of the Democratic committee in his congressional district.

Marshall's sudden political rise in 1908 occurred because of a deadlock at the Indiana Democratic nominating convention. The factions agreed upon him as a compromise candidate for governor that year. He won the election and set about implementing a progressive program encompassing legislation in child labor, employer liability, food quality, railroad taxation, wages, and other areas. As the election of 1912 approached he earned increasing mention as a possible candidate for the presidency. At the convention he did receive a favorite-son nomination from the Indiana delegation, but Woodrow Wilson won the battle handily, then picked Marshall for the second spot on the ticket.

Marshall, though not a career politician, was probably one of the most talented men ever to occupy the frustrating job of vice-president. He handled himself with dignity, presiding over cabinet meetings when Wilson was negotiating peace in France and remaining in the background during the period of Wilson's recovery from a stroke. He is perhaps best known for an episode that occurred in connection with his role as Senate president. After listening to one member give an overlong and overblown address on "What This Country Needs," Marshall interjected, "What this country needs is a really good five-cent cigar." Another time he illustrated the status of the vice-president with a little fable: "Once there were two brothers. One ran away to sea, the other was elected vice-president, and nothing was ever heard of either of them again."

After leaving office Marshall moved to Indianapolis and resumed the practice of law. He died in 1925.

CHARLES DAWES

A banker, politician, and diplomat, Charles Dawes of Illinois was born in Marietta, Ohio, in 1865. He served as vice-president during the elected presidential term of Calvin Coolidge, from 1925 to 1929. Dawes attended school in Marietta, earning a degree in engineering from Marietta College, and then earned a bachelor of laws degree from the Cincinnati Law School in 1886. He moved to Nebraska and opened a law office, quickly earning recognition for fighting on the side of agricultural interests in the debate over the legality of the Interstate Commerce Act. He developed an interest in financial matters (in Lincoln, Nebraska, he struck up a friendship with William Jennings Bryan) and published a book, *The Banking System of the United States and Its Relation to the Money and Business of the Country,* in 1894, the same year he moved to Chicago. Dawes also acquired interests in several midwestern gas companies, purchased real estate, and developed an association with Republican party politics, at the 1896 Republican national convention playing an instrumental role in securing the votes of the Illinois delegation for William McKinley. The victorious McKinley made Dawes U.S. comptroller of the currency in 1898.

Left: Charles Gates Dawes, vice-president in Calvin Coolidge's elected administration, from 1925 to 1929; right: Charles Curtis, vice-president in Herbert Hoover's administration, from 1929 to 1933 (courtesy of the Kansas State Historical Society)

Dawes resigned his comptroller's position in 1901 to run for the U.S. Senate, but he lost the election. That behind him, he went back to business, organizing the Central Trust Company (later City National Bank and Trust Company) in 1902 and serving as its president until 1921. In that position Dawes worked on several major merger and acquisition deals and in the process developed friendships with many leading American businessmen.

When the United States entered World War I, Dawes obtained a commission in the Army Corps of Engineers as head of the General Purchasing Board. He also served as a member of the Military Board of Allied Supply. When the war ended he worked as a member of the U.S. Liquidation Commission to disperse the military equipment in Europe he had helped accumulate in the two previous jobs.

Back in the United States, Dawes earned public admiration for his testimony to the U.S. House Committee on War Expenditures in 1921. Replying to the suggestion that he had paid too much for material sent to Europe, he countered, "Men were standing at the front to be shot at. We had to get them food and ammunition. Why man alive! We had a war to win!" At another point he exclaimed, "Helen Maria [a mild frontier expletive]! I would have paid horse prices for sheep if sheep could have pulled artillery to the front!" From then on he was known as "Hell 'n' Maria Dawes."

In spite of Dawes's support for the Treaty of Versailles, President Warren G. Harding appointed him director of the newly created Bureau of the Budget. After resigning from that position he wrote a book, *The First Year of the Budget of the United States* (1923), explaining how he cut expenditures by one-third. From there he moved to a position as chairman of a committee—known as the Dawes Committee—that restructured German war reparations in 1924 (he won the 1925 Nobel Peace Prize for the effort), and then into the vice-presidency.

John Nance Garner, vice-president during Franklin D. Roosevelt's first two administrations, from 1933 to 1941 (courtesy of the Garner Memorial Museum)

After his vice-presidential term Dawes served as U.S. ambassador to Great Britain from 1929 to 1932 and briefly as chairman of the Reconstruction Finance Corporation in 1932. In retirement he turned back to writing, publishing *Notes as Vice President* in 1935, *How Long Prosperity?* in 1937, and two books in 1939: *Journal of Reparations* and *Journal as Ambassador to Great Britain*. Dawes died in 1951.

CHARLES CURTIS

Charles Curtis of Kansas served as vice-president from 1929 to 1933, during the presidential term of Herbert Hoover. He was born in North Topeka, Kansas, in 1860, attended local schools and worked in the summers as a horse-racing jockey, clerked in a law office, and gained admission to the Kansas bar in 1881.

Curtis entered politics as prosecuting attorney for Shawnee County, Kansas, from 1885 to 1889. As prosecutor he initiated enforcement of the county prohibition law with the result that eighty-eight saloons were closed within his first few weeks. Remaining a Republican in spite of the strong trend toward Populism in Kansas, he won election to the U.S. House in 1893 and prevailed in seven successive reelection campaigns.

In the House, Curtis, one-quarter Kaw Indian, served on the Indian Affairs Committee and on the committee that drafted the Gold Standard Act of 1900. In 1907 he won election to the U.S. Senate. There he supported the regular Republican policies of President William Howard Taft. Owing to election technicalities he lost his bid for reelection in 1912, then he won the other Kansas Senate seat for the term beginning in 1915. He was reelected in 1920 and again in 1926, but he resigned from the Senate midway into his third term to run for vice-president on the Hoover ticket.

Curtis's vice-presidency passed uneventfully. After going down to defeat with Hoover in 1932, he served out his term and retired from public life. Remaining in Washington, he resumed the practice of law and died in 1936.

JOHN NANCE GARNER

John Nance Garner served as vice-president during the first two of Franklin D. Roosevelt's four presidential terms. He was born in Red River County, Texas, in 1868 and attended Vanderbilt University for one year before dropping out to read law in a Clarksville, Texas, office, gaining admission to the Texas bar in 1890. He settled into a law practice in Uvalde, Texas, and soon after entered Democratic party politics. In 1894 he was appointed to fill an unexpired term as Uvalde county judge. He was elected in his own right in 1895 but went down to defeat in 1897. The next year he entered the state legislature, where he secured the passage of a bill that would have divided Texas into five states (as provided in the Tyler annexation resolution) had the Texas governor not vetoed it.

In 1903 Garner moved on to the U.S. House. He won sixteen successive reelection bids, serving as House Speaker during his final term, and left office only to accept the vice-presidential nomination. In the House he exhibited sound leadership and loyal adherence to Democratic principles characterized by an anti-protective-tariff stance, support for an increased role for the federal government in agriculture and public works, and a disdain for the growing dominance of business in American society.

At the 1932 Democratic national convention Garner claimed a significant amount of support in early ballots but gave up his presidential hopes to support Franklin Roosevelt's effort to defeat Alfred Smith. Roosevelt made him the vice-presidential nominee in return. The ticket easily defeated the Republican incumbents, Herbert Hoover and Charles Curtis.

His active House career little prepared Garner for the idleness of the vice-presidency, but he discharged what duties he had with good humor. He generally supported the New Deal and broke with Roosevelt only over the president's effort to reorganize the Supreme Court.

Garner opposed Roosevelt's bid for a third term in 1940 and mounted a brief challenge for the top job before the convention. For that and because he desired a more liberal running mate, Roosevelt dropped him from the ticket. After serving out his term Garner retired from public life. He served on the boards of several banks, invested in real estate, and ran an impressive ranch in Uvalde, where he died, at the age of ninety-nine, in 1967.

HENRY A. WALLACE

Franklin D. Roosevelt's second vice-president, Henry A. Wallace of Iowa, served during the whole of the president's third term, from 1941 to 1945.

President Franklin D. Roosevelt and Vice-President-elect Henry A. Wallace, Election Day, November 7, 1940 (courtesy of the Franklin D. Roosevelt Library)

He was born in 1888 on a farm near Orient, Iowa, and graduated from Iowa State College in 1910. After graduation he took a position as associate editor for *Wallace's Farmer*, a weekly agricultural journal founded by his grandfather and at the time edited by his father. After his father's death in 1924 Wallace succeeded to the editorship. Aside from his editorial duties he also accomplished a fair amount of farming and agricultural research on his own, developing in 1915 the first of a series of "hog-corn ratio" charts that attempted to forecast trends in those markets. He also hybridized higher-yielding strains of corn and developed methods to forecast corn yields based on rainfall and temperature. He authored several books on agricultural science and economy, in 1927 served as chairman of the agricultural round table at the International Institute of Politics at Williamstown, Massachusetts, and in 1929 served as a U.S. delegate to the International Conference of Agricultural Economists in England.

Wallace was initially drawn to politics because he believed that government should do what it could to lower domestic and foreign barriers to American agricultural exports. Convinced by the mid 1920s that the Republican party, which his grandfather and father had supported, was unwilling to do that, he supported Alfred Smith and the Democratic party in the presidential election of 1928. Four years later he served as one of Franklin Roosevelt's principal agricultural policy advisers during the presidential campaign, and Roosevelt made him secretary of agriculture in the new administration.

Wallace served in the Cabinet during a period of nearly revolutionary change in the outlook of the federal government in relation to agriculture. The 1933 Agricultural Adjustment Act gave the Department of Agriculture power to work out marketing agreements, sponsor crop-adjustment and production-control plans, and institute soil and other conservation projects. The fact that the Supreme Court declared the original Agricultural Adjustment Act unconstitutional in 1936 only made it possible to enact replacement legislation that in the long run proved more pervading and included programs for government-sponsored crop storage and crop insurance. The relationship between the federal government and farmers engendered during the New Deal remains fundamentally the same in modern times.

A split between Roosevelt and Vice-President John Nance Garner over the issue of a third Roosevelt presidential term created a vacancy in the vice-presidential slot. Roosevelt picked Wallace for the job, and the agricultural secretary resigned his position after winning the nomination in a heated convention contest.

Occupied by the war in Europe, Roosevelt made Wallace chairman of a new Board of Economic Defense (later the Board of Economic Warfare) and of the War Production Board. The vice-president also made goodwill tours of Latin America in 1943 and of the Soviet Union and China in 1944. Wallace's disagreements with Reconstruction Finance Corporation chairman Jesse Jones over war-material allocations led Roosevelt to abolish the Board of Economic Warfare in mid 1943. Furthermore, Wallace spoke strongly of the need for postwar international cooperation in a way that caused some in the administration to view him as too far to the left to do Roosevelt good as he attempted to win a fourth term. Accordingly, at the convention Wallace found himself replaced by Harry S Truman.

Wallace campaigned strongly for the president in spite of his rejection and in early 1945 was nominated to succeed Jesse Jones as secretary of commerce. His advocacy of a cooperationist foreign policy, however, began to interfere with his ability to cooperate with other members of the administration. He especially clashed with Roosevelt's successor as president, Harry S Truman, who took a hard-line stance regarding the Soviet Union. In a September 1946 speech given during a Madison Square Garden political rally, Wallace opposed the views of Secretary of War James Byrnes so strongly that Truman asked for Wallace's resignation.

Wallace accepted an editor's position with the liberal journal the *New Republic* and began an outspoken campaign against cold war politics. In 1948 he ran for president on the Progressive party ticket but did poorly. After his run for the presidency Wallace retired from public life. He authored several more agricultural books and spoke extensively on the lecture circuit. He died in 1965.

ALBEN W. BARKLEY

Harry S Truman's vice-president was Kentuckian Alben W. Barkley, who served the president during his entire elected term, from 1949 to 1953. Born near Lowes, Kentucky, in 1877, Barkley graduated from Marvin College in Clinton, Kentucky, 1897, studied for a year

President Harry S Truman and vice-presidential nominee Alben Barkley at the 1948 Democratic National Convention (courtesy of University of Kentucky Special Collections)

in the graduate school at Emory University in Atlanta, briefly returned to Marvin to teach, then entered the University of Kentucky Law School. In 1901 he graduated from law school and gained admission to the Kentucky bar.

Barkley entered into the practice of law in Paducah, Kentucky, and began to involve himself in local politics. He served as prosecuting attorney for McCracken County from 1905 to 1909 and as judge of the McCracken County court from 1909 to 1913. In 1912 he ran successfully as a Democrat for a seat in the U.S. House of Representatives. In Congress through 1927, he supported the progressive program of the Wilson administration and generally opposed the laissez-faire programs of the Harding and Coolidge administrations.

Barkley won a seat in the U.S. Senate in 1926 and served in the Senate from 1927 until his inauguration as vice-president. In the Senate he gained recognition as a champion of prohibition repeal and authored the Twenty-First Amendment repealing prohibition in 1933. Barkley served as Senate majority leader from 1937 to 1947 and as minority leader from 1947 to 1949. He loyally supported Roosevelt's New Deal and war policies and continued that support when Truman succeeded Roosevelt in office.

Truman, remembering his own isolation as vice-president, kept Barkley better informed and more involved than had been traditional for vice-presidents up to that time. Barkley served as an ex officio member of the newly created National Security Council and sat down with the president for regular briefings.

Barkley made a brief unsuccessful run for the Democratic presidential

Lyndon B. Johnson's vice-president, Hubert Humphrey (right), campaigning for president in New York City, October 1968

nomination to succeed Truman and then won back his Senate seat in 1955. By that time his health was precarious. Barkley died, aged seventy-eight, in 1956.

HUBERT HUMPHREY

Hubert Humphrey was born in Wallace, South Dakota, in 1911. He served as vice-president during Lyndon B. Johnson's elected presidential term, from 1965 to 1969. Humphrey attended the Denver College of Pharmacy in 1932 and 1933, worked as a pharmacist for several years, went back to school and earned a degree in political science from the University of Minnesota, and earned a master's degree from Louisiana State University in 1940. He moved to Minneapolis, Minnesota, and taught political science at Macalester College until 1944, resigning to help organize Minnesota's Democratic Farmer-Labor party.

In 1945 Humphrey was elected mayor of Minneapolis, at thirty-four the youngest in the city's history. At the 1948 Democratic national convention he gained national attention for his forthright advocacy of a strong civil rights plank in the party platform. The year before he had helped found the liberal political advocacy group Americans for Democratic Action. He entered the U.S. Senate in 1949.

In the Senate Humphrey steadily moved to the forefront of the liberal wing of his party until by 1960 he felt ready to make a run for the presidency. He dropped out early in the face of strong campaigns by colleagues John F. Kennedy and Lyndon B. Johnson. He took the position of majority whip in the Senate after the 1960 election and championed, albeit unsuccessfully, much of the liberal legislation proposed by the Kennedy administration.

After President Kennedy's assassination, Humphrey worked closely with Lyndon Johnson to push a liberal civil rights bill and other measures through Congress. Humphrey's constant sup-

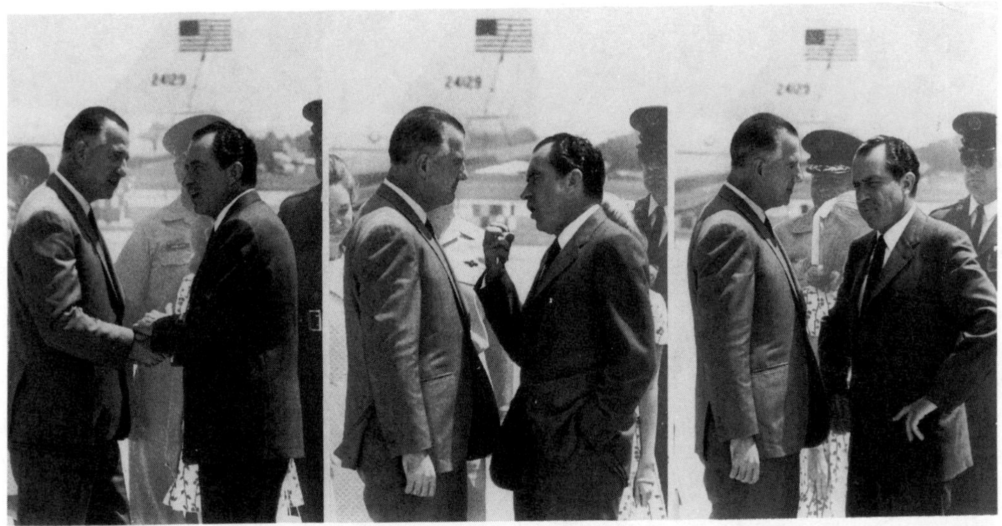

President Richard M. Nixon and Vice-President Spiro Agnew (courtesy of Thomas L. Connelly)

port and political savvy proved crucial as Johnson struggled to create the "Great Society."

President Johnson awarded Humphrey with the vice-presidential nomination in 1964, and the ticket won a landslide victory over the Republicans in the general election. More Great Society legislation followed, with Humphrey behind the president every step of the way. Unfortunately, the vice-president also supported Johnson's Vietnam policy, even as U.S. troop levels in Southeast Asia escalated and public disapproval of the war mounted. In late 1968, after a heartbroken Johnson withdrew his candidacy for another term as president, Humphrey emerged as the Democratic standard-bearer. Hemmed in by his support of the administration's stand in Vietnam, he watched as antiwar candidates Eugene McCarthy and then Robert Kennedy diverted his support. McCarthy faded as Kennedy advanced, then Kennedy was assassinated. Humphrey emerged with his party's presidential nomination.

Humphrey waged a fierce campaign in which he maintained his loyalty to the Johnson line on Vietnam. He also called for an increased national commitment to Johnson's domestic legacy, but the public seemed not to notice. Meanwhile, Republican presidential candidate Richard M. Nixon ran as a newly matured man of peace. Nixon won one of the closest presidential elections in American history.

After losing the 1968 presidential race Humphrey prepared for another try for a Senate seat while serving as a professor of social science at the University of Minnesota. He reentered the Senate in 1971 and made another run for the presidency in 1972. By then he appeared too conservative for the party liberals he helped strengthen in the 1960s. George McGovern won the nomination and lost badly to Nixon.

Humphrey served the remainder of his Senate term and won reelection. He died during the second year of that term, in 1978.

SPIRO T. AGNEW

Maryland native Spiro T. Agnew was born in Baltimore in 1918, attended Johns Hopkins University, dropped out to sell insurance and attend night classes at the University of Baltimore Law School, served with distinction during World War II, and finally graduated with a bachelor of laws degree and gained admission to the Maryland bar in 1947. He served as vice-president during Richard M. Nixon's first presidential

Future vice-president Nelson Rockefeller (left) with future president Ronald Reagan, August 19, 1972 (courtesy of the Nixon Presidential Materials Project)

term and the first few months of the second, from 1969 to 1973.

Agnew developed a lucrative and influential law practice before entering politics as a Republican. He was elected Baltimore County executive in 1963 and served in that job until 1967. Then he won election to the governor's post, winning both kudos and criticism for his law-and-order stance against rioters after the 1968 assassination of civil rights leader Martin Luther King, Jr. Anxious to run with a moderate southerner, Nixon chose him in 1968, and he resigned his governorship when the ticket emerged victorious.

As vice-president, Agnew distinguished himself primarily as a hard-line point man for the president's policies and as an increasingly virulent critic of the press, the anti-Vietnam War left, and student dissidents. He won fame for his ability to formulate old ideas in creative new ways, more notable for their sound than sense. Once he called members of the press "nattering nabobs of negativism," and another time he referred to antiwar students and intellectuals as an "effete corps of impudent snobs." Those rhetorical flourishes and Agnew's generally hostile attitude allowed Nixon often to appear above the political fray.

Agnew tried to soften his image during the reelection campaign in 1972, but allegations of personal corruption that emerged after the election tainted his victory and forced him to resign the vice-presidency in disgrace. Federal prosecutors disclosed that Agnew was a target of an investigation of a bribery scandal that reached back to his days as county executive. Investigators also alleged that Agnew had continued to accept cash payments transferred in paper grocery bags even while vice-president. The vice-president struck a deal: to avoid prosecution he agreed to resign from office and plead no contest to one count of income tax evasion. In his 1980 memoir *Go Quietly . . . Or Else* Agnew maintained his innocence, claiming that he resigned out of fear that White House Chief of Staff Alexander Haig would have him murdered if he stayed.

After his resignation Agnew founded a business consulting firm.

NELSON A. ROCKEFELLER

Nelson A. Rockefeller of New York

Left to right: Rosalyn Carter, Walter Mondale, Jimmy Carter, and Joan Mondale in the White House in the last days of the Carter presidency, January 1981 (courtesy of the Carter family)

served as vice-president after Gerald R. Ford, Vice-President Spiro T. Agnew's successor in the Nixon administration, succeeded Nixon to the presidency. Rockefeller is the only vice-president to gain the office under the terms of the Twenty-Fifth Amendment to the Constitution.

Rockefeller was born in Bar Harbor, Maine, in 1908, the grandson of billionaire oilman John D. Rockefeller. He graduated from Dartmouth College in 1930 and worked actively in his family's business and financial empire, particularly as a director of the Rockefeller Center from 1931 to 1958, as its president from 1938 to 1945, and as its chairman from 1945 to 1953.

Rockefeller served as assistant secretary of state during World War II and as chairman of the International Development Advisory Board during the Truman administration. During the Eisenhower administration he served as chairman of the President's Advisory Committee on Government Organization and then as undersecretary of health, education, and welfare until 1958. That year he won the first of four terms as governor of New York.

As New York governor Rockefeller established a distinguished record as a leader of the liberal wing of the Republican party. He ran unsuccessfully for the party's presidential nomination in 1960, again in 1964, and again in 1968. He resigned as governor in 1973 to chair a Commission on Critical Choices for America, but went back into government service when Ford called him to the vice-presidency in late 1974. Constantly under criticism from Republican conservatives, Rockefeller announced in 1975 that he would not be a candidate for the vice-presidency in 1976. Ford instead nominated hard-liner Robert Dole and lost his bid for reelection.

Rockefeller retired from politics after serving as vice-president. He died in 1979.

WALTER F. MONDALE

Walter F. Mondale of Minnesota served as vice-president during the presidential administration of Jimmy Carter, from 1977 to 1981. He was born in Ceylon, Minnesota, in 1928, graduated in 1951 from the University of Minnesota, served in the Korean War, and graduated in 1956 from the University of Minnesota Law School. By then he had developed a keen interest in politics and had worked as a manager in Hubert Humphrey's successful senatorial campaign in 1948.

After entering the law profession Mondale got into politics on his own. He served as Minnesota's attorney general from 1960 to 1964 and accepted an appointment to fill Humphrey's Senate seat after Humphrey took the vice-president's chair in 1965. He won two successive terms on his own.

In the Senate Mondale established a solidly liberal voting record, especially in the areas of housing, education, and racial relations. He briefly ran for the Democratic presidential nomination in 1976 but in the end accepted Jimmy Carter's offer of the vice-presidency.

Mondale was probably the most involved vice-president in American history. He breakfasted with the president every day it was possible, attended all cabinet meetings, served on the National Security Council, endured a punishing diplomatic and political traveling schedule, and gave Carter constructive and often decisive advice. He took a trip to China in 1979. He also served (less and less effectively) as a liaison between the president and Congress. With Carter he lost decisively to Ronald Reagan and George Bush in the election of 1980.

Mondale won the 1984 Democratic presidential nomination and ran an exhausting and futile campaign to prevent Ronald Reagan from winning a second presidential term. He made history by nominating a woman, Geraldine Ferraro, to the vice-presidential slot. Mondale and Ferraro ended up losing to Reagan and George Bush by more than sixteen million popular votes and the largest electoral margin in history. The Democrats carried only one state—Minnesota—and the District of Columbia. Mondale retired from politics after the defeat.

After the Presidency: What Happened in the Lives of the Former Presidents

by MICHAEL D. SENECAL

For most of the presidents the nation's highest office has served as the consummation of active political life. Only two presidents have gone on to serve in elective office: John Quincy Adams for a long and distinguished term in the House of Representatives, and Andrew Johnson, briefly, in the Senate. William Howard Taft served as chief justice of the Supreme Court after his presidential term. Only Herbert Hoover's failed presidency interrupted his long life of successful public service. Three former presidents—Washington, Grant, and Eisenhower—served the country in largely symbolic military capacities after their terms: Washington as commander in chief of American forces during the period of the quasi war with France, Grant as a general on the retired list (with full pay) during the last months of his life, and Eisenhower as a restored five-star general of the army.

A few presidents worked in the private sector after serving their terms. Both Benjamin Harrison and William Howard Taft worked as law instructors—Harrison at Stanford University and Taft at Yale. Harrison also enjoyed a lucrative law practice. Grover Cleveland became a chaired professor of public affairs at Princeton and then chairman of the Board of Trustees of that university. Washington, Jefferson, Madison, and Jackson worked their plantations; Rutherford B. Hayes owned several midwestern farms; and Lyndon B. Johnson lived and worked on his Texas ranch.

Eight presidents—William Henry Harrison, Zachary Taylor, Abraham Lincoln, James A. Garfield, William McKinley, Warren G. Harding, Franklin D. Roosevelt, and John F. Kennedy—never had a chance to become former presidents.

Most of the former presidents have spent time writing and talking about politics and public affairs. Many have traveled. Some have served as consultants for their successors. One, Democrat Jimmy Carter, engaged in several valuable diplomatic episodes in service of Republican Ronald Reagan. Carter has also worked as an advocate of the homeless for the Habitat for Humanity organization. Gerald Ford, Carter's immediate predecessor, has made a fortune as a director of major corporations and as a business and legal consultant.

Whatever else the former presidents decide to do, they also, for better or for worse, must take their places as part of the nation's legacy, subjected to the pressures of celebrity and historical judgment, called upon to make judgments of their own and to lend their names and reputations, and, most of all, consigned to reflect on what they did or did not do and what could have or should never have happened.

WASHINGTON
Left office March 4, 1797
Died December 14, 1799

George Washington's health, which had remained fairly strong during the years of the American Revolution, began to decline during the 1780s. Shortly before he was elected president he suffered a severe attack of malaria, a malady that troubled him until his death. During his presidential years he suffered from respiratory infections, including two severe

Portrait of George Washington drawn by Charles Balthazar Julien Fevret de Saint-Mémin, November 1799

attacks of pneumonia in 1790.

Washington was the center of attention at the inauguration of his successor, John Adams. He carried himself with his customary air of extreme formality and wore a black velvet suit, gold buckled slippers, yellow gloves, and a powdered wig. He held a cocked hat decorated with an ostrich plume and wore a sword encased in a white leather scabbard. Adams, in contrast, wore a simple suit and no wig; he carried no sword; and he dispensed with the marshals and honor guards that had accompanied Washington during his inaugurations. Much to Adams's chagrin, the outgoing president commanded the attention; after the ceremony a doting crowd followed him to the door of his residence. A day later Adams remarked in a letter to his wife, "Your dearest friend never had a more trying day than yesterday. A solemn scene it was indeed."

Remaining in Philadelphia only long enough to arrange the transport of his and his wife's effects, the sixty-five-year-old Washington retired to Mount Vernon intent on resuming his often-interrupted life as an independent farmer. He quickly readjusted to the routines of plantation living, overseeing much-needed repairs around his estate and playing host to a stream of visiting well-wishers. Political responsibilities never went away entirely. On July 4, 1798, President Adams commissioned Washington a lieutenant general and made him commander in chief of American military forces. The "quasi-war" with France that stimulated Adams to make the appointment remained just that, however, and Washington never had to face active duty.

In retirement the former president got into the habit of making a daily inspection on horseback of the farms of Mount Vernon. His health remained stable until late 1799. On December 12 a storm of snow and freezing rain engulfed Mount Vernon just after the president set out on his daily tour. For five hours Washington rode through the storm, returning to record in his plantation journal the morning and evening temperatures as thirty-three and twenty-eight degrees. His secretary, Tobias Lear, recalled that Washington's head and neck were wet when he got home.

The next day three inches of snow lay on Mount Vernon's lawns. Washington had developed a severe sore throat and did not take his daily tour. He grew worse. On the early morning of December 14 an overseer who had experience in veterinary medicine was summoned. In the fashion of the day the overseer "cupped and bled" Washington of a pint of blood. Several other doctors were summoned from nearby communities, and they bled Washington three more times. Other remedies were administered. The doctors "blistered" Washington's skin, applying hot irons to form blisters that were intended to bring infection to the surface. Calomel and other "purges" were administered to make him throw up the infection. They gave him gargles of substances such as vinegar, sage tea, and molasses. None of it worked. Washington's respiratory tract was seriously congested. A young physician, Dr. Elisha Dick of Alexandria, suggested performing a tracheotomy. The older doctors rejected that advice and instead bled Washington again.

Shortly before midnight on December 14 the sixty-seven-year-old Washington died. Originally the death was attributed to pneumonia. Recent researchers have suggested that he died either of diphtheria or a streptococcus infection of the throat.

JOHN ADAMS
Left office March 4, 1801
Died July 4, 1826

John Adams left the presidency as disappointed at not receiving another term as Washington had been happy not to accept one. The fact that Adams's supreme foe, Thomas Jefferson, had been elected in his place made the New Englander all the more bitter. In his last few days in office he did what he could to lessen the shock of transition to Jeffersonian democracy, appointing a group of Federalists to the newly established U.S. Circuit Courts of Appeal. He turned down a suggestion that he appoint himself to a vacancy on the Supreme Court, instead choosing staunch Federalist John Marshall.

Then, alone in the still-unfinished White House (his wife was already home in Quincy, Massachusetts), Adams awaited Inauguration Day. Perhaps remembering how Washington had overshadowed his own moment of triumph, Adams decided he would not be overshadowed in the same way going out as he had been coming in. Early on the morning of March 4, he summoned his coach and started on the five-hundred-mile journey to Quincy without attending Jefferson's inauguration.

The sixty-five-year-old Adams left office one of the healthiest of the early presidents. The average age of the first fifteen presidents who died of natural causes is seventy-one. Adams lived

Portrait of John Adams by Gilbert Stuart, 1825 (courtesy of the New York Public Library)

more than twenty-five years beyond the last year of his term of office and died at the age of ninety. Before retirement he appears not to have experienced much bad health except for bouts with what modern medicine would call depression. He had the usual "fevers" and like many of his friends and colleagues was troubled by bad teeth, but he had every reason to expect a long and comfortable retirement, and that is what he got.

The trip to Quincy took fourteen days. On the way the unannounced former president attracted little public attention, sometimes passing through towns without even drawing open the curtains of his coach. Only when Adams reached Boston did his spirits rise. In the Massachusetts capital the public greeted him with great affection, and members of the legislature presented a commemorative address. The hometown reception was even more exhilarating. Then Adams settled into retirement in his Quincy estate, Old House.

Soon his feelings of bitterness returned. Adams had a vain streak and could not shake the belief that the public had made a mistake by turning him out of office. A few months after arriving home he wrote a friend, "If I were to go over my life again, I would be a shoemaker rather than an American statesman." He wished he could resume his law practice, but a vocal cord impediment made it difficult for him to speak. To another friend he wrote, "The only consolation I shall want will be that of employment. Ennui, when it rains on a man in large drops, is worse than one of our north-east storms; but the labors of agriculture and amusement of letters will shelter me."

Adams indeed turned to the "labors of agriculture and amusement of letters" for shelter. He worked hard at domestic life, every morning lighting his own fire with flint and steel, putting on his work clothes, and tackling the chores. Although he received few guests, he enjoyed the company of his wife and his children and grandchildren. While he read widely and variously, he devoted most of his energies to correspondence, taking great pleasure in devising thoughtful responses to the sometimes hundreds of letters he received each year. Writing letters kept him connected to the outside world and gave him the opportunity to exercise his creative faculties. Modern critics still consider many of Adams's letters valuable as literature and philosophy.

Adams also kept abreast of politics. Never much of a partisan, he opposed the Jefferson administration on personal grounds. Jeffersonian rhetoric, he thought, encouraged lazy thinking about democracy. Toward the end of Jefferson's administration he wrote, "He [Jefferson] must know he leaves the country much worse than he found it, and that from his own error and ignorance." But Adams also supported Jefferson's Louisiana Purchase and, in a haphazard series of letters written to the *Boston Patriot* between 1808 and 1813, Jefferson and Madison's policy of embargo and war against Britain. As the years passed Adams abandoned the Federalist party as did the rest of the country. As a Massachusetts elector in the presidential election of 1820 he voted to reelect James Monroe.

Adams also reconciled with Jefferson. With the encouragement of mutual friend Dr. Benjamin Rush of Philadelphia, the old foes inaugurated an affectionate and lasting correspondence in late 1811. The two hundred Adams-Jefferson letters present two men of towering intellect who diverged in the details of politics but shared a love of liberty, a respect for property, and an insatiable curiosity about life and the life of the mind. The two discussed politics and political philosophy, history and literature, economics, religion, science, agriculture and industry, education, and whatever else came to mind, not only revealing much about their own lives and their society but also making a grand contribution to American literary history.

As the years passed Adams grew frail. His wife, Abigail, died in 1818. In 1821 he was surprised and delighted to be selected as a delegate to revise the Massachusetts Constitution of 1779, a document he had almost single-handedly written. At the 1821 convention he spoke in favor of retaining the property requirement for suffrage without attracting much support. Never conventional in his religious beliefs, he also favored severing the connection between the state and the Congregational church, a position most of his colleagues were not yet ready to accept.

In February 1825 Adams enjoyed the unique privilege of learning of his son's election to the presidency. He wrote a congratulatory letter: "Never did I feel so much solemnity as upon this occasion. The multitude of my thoughts, and the intensity of my feelings are too much for a mind like mine, in its ninetieth year. May the blessings of God Almighty continue to protect you to the end of your life, as it has heretofore protected you in so remarkable a manner from your cradle!"

As the fiftieth anniversary of the signing of the Declaration approached, the townspeople of Quincy asked Adams, along with Jefferson and Charles Carroll one of only three surviving signers of the document, to give a toast at the local celebration. A bedridden Adams had to decline. He died on July 4, fifty years to the day after the founding of the nation. With family and friends gathered, at about noon he had awakened from his coma and uttered three words: "Thomas Jefferson survives." But Jefferson had died just a few hours before.

JEFFERSON
Left office March 4, 1809
Died July 4, 1826

A beaming Thomas Jefferson could hardly conceal his pleasure at attending the inauguration of his successor, James Madison. The president had turned down the requests of eight state legislatures to run for a third term and during the inauguration festivities overshadowed Madison in the same way outgoing president Washington overshadowed incoming John Adams in 1797. With Madison's permission, Jefferson remained in the White House for a week after the change of administrations to collect his belongings.

Perhaps the sixty-five-year-old Jefferson wanted to delay his arrival at Monticello. Money problems of the sort that commonly plagued cash-poor Virginia planters hampered his enjoyment of retirement. He left the White House about $24,000 dollars in debt and could rely on only a few thousand in a good year from his wheat and tobacco crops. The good years were rare. In 1815, the year after British troops burned the Capitol, he sold his entire 6,500-volume library to the federal government for $23,950 to replace the destroyed Library of Congress. But Jefferson doggedly maintained his lavish life-style, and his debts continued to accumulate.

Portrait of Thomas Jefferson by Thomas Sully, 1821 (American Philosophical Society)

During the Panic of 1819, with agricultural prices falling, the frustrated former president wrote, "To owe what I cannot pay is a constant torment." He had to sell land piece by piece to keep afloat. He was not very efficient as a plantation-keeper, either. Of his more than two hundred slaves, only about one-third actually worked the fields. The rest worked as house servants and artisans.

Like Washington and Adams before him, however, Jefferson adjusted to the routines of life in retirement, managing not to worry excessively about money. He was a man of many interests. He attended to the business of his plantation, performed scientific and agricultural experiments (Jefferson served as president of the American Philosophical Society from 1797 to 1815), worked as an architect, read widely, received a constant stream of visitors he felt obligated to entertain, and kept up a voluminous correspondence. Once he computed that he wrote an average of 1,267 letters a year and asked, "Is this life? At best

Portrait of James Madison by Asher B. Durant, 1833 (courtesy of the New-York Historical Society)

it is but the life of a millhorse, who sees no end to his circle but death. To such a life, that of cabbage is paradise."

Jefferson regarded the renewal of his association with John Adams with as much pleasure as did Adams. What took even more of his time during the last years of his life, however, was his stewardship of the University of Virginia. In 1816 he convinced the Virginia legislature to authorize the establishment of the institution and name him chairman of the development commission. Two years later that commission, which also claimed former president James Madison and President James Monroe as members, approved a site for the university at Charlottesville, only four miles from Monticello, and made Jefferson rector.

Jefferson designed the campus for the university, led fund-raising efforts, hired the workmen to build the campus, developed the curriculum, and recruited the seven-member faculty. His friend John Adams gave wise counsel through the mail every step of the way. The institution opened in March 1825 to wide praise. Controversy developed during the first term over the unruly behavior of some of the students.

Meanwhile financial matters pressed Jefferson. At about the time of the opening of the university the possibility that Jefferson might actually lose Monticello became acute. He asked the Virginia legislature to permit him to sell a significant portion of the estate by lottery, and friends came forward with thousands in gifts. "Not a cent of this," he wrote characteristically, "is wrung from the taxpayer; it is the pure unsolicited offering of love." The state eventually granted permission to hold the lottery, but Jefferson delayed arranging it, believing incorrectly that the charity had cleared up his problem.

By the time the university opened Jefferson was in poor health. For his entire adult life he had been hampered by digestive tract ailments; diarrhea combined with crippling rheumatism made his final year difficult. By June 1826 he had weakened considerably and could not get out of bed. On July 2 he lapsed into unconsciousness. At about seven in the evening of the third he rallied briefly and asked, "Is it the fourth?" His doctor replied, "It soon will be." With that Jefferson went back to sleep. Eighty years of age, he died on July 4, a few hours before the death of John Adams.

MADISON
Left office March 4, 1817
Died June 28, 1836

Sixty-six-year-old James Madison remained in Washington for a month after attending the presidential inauguration of his friend James Monroe. Then this second member of the "Virginia Triumvirate" retired with his wife to their estate, Montpelier, not far from the estate of Madison's mentor, Thomas Jefferson. Jefferson had a letter waiting for him when he arrived: "I sincerely congratulate you," wrote the third president, "on your release from incessant labors, carroding [*sic*] anxieties, active enemies & interested friends, &, on your return to your books & farm, to tranquility and independence. A day of these is worth ages of the former." Doubtless the war-weary Madison agreed.

Like Adams and Jefferson, Madison was destined to live a long life. At Montpelier he attended to the business of his plantation (Madison hired an overseer only during the last months of his life), entertained guests, and read and studied. In 1821 he began preparing his "Notes on the Federal Convention of 1787"; it first appeared in the 1840 edition of his papers. Like Jefferson, Madison was never free from financial worry. In 1826, shortly before Jefferson's death, Madison wrote his friend, "Since my own return to private life . . . , such have been the unkind seasons, and the ravages of insects, that I have made but one tolerable crop of tobacco, and but one of wheat; the proceeds of both of which were greatly curtailed by mishaps in the sale of them. And having no resources but in the earth I cultivate, I have been living very much throughout on borrowed means." Jefferson certainly understood that.

Madison greatly enjoyed a series of visits with his Virginia neighbor. He would drive the thirty miles to Monticello and spend several days in relaxing conversation. His family looked forward to those occasions when Jefferson returned the visits. Madison also helped Jefferson found the University of Virginia, serving on the original Board of Regents and taking over as rector upon Jefferson's death.

He also kept a keen eye on the political scene. Madison blamed much of his lack of success in farming to the debilitating effect of slavery on the southern economy. In 1832 he observed with trepidation the effort of South Carolina to nullify federal tariff legislation. In a letter he referred to nullification and secession as "twin heresies" and declared they "ought to be buried in the same grave." He could see that slavery contained the potential to destroy the Union. In 1833 he became president of the American Colonization Society and worked to resettle slaves in the African nation of Liberia, without much success. As he passed eighty years of age Madison's health declined, and he retired to bed. Early on the morning of June 28, 1836, he had trouble swallowing his breakfast. A niece asked, "What is the matter, Uncle James?" Madison, eighty-five, replied, "Nothing more than a change of mind, my dear," and then he died.

MONROE
Left office March 4, 1825
Died July 4, 1831

James Monroe spent much of his brief retirement worrying about money. Like his Virginia predecessors Thomas Jefferson and James Madison, Monroe left the presidency in debt and never got out.

After attending the inauguration of his successor, John Quincy Adams, Monroe remained in Washington for ten days to care for his ailing wife. Back at his estate, Oak Hill (designed by Jefferson), the former president decided to petition the government for financial assistance. He believed the government owed him compensation for his years as U.S. minister to France (1794-1797), for losses he incurred in the sale of a French residence, for presents and gratuities he gave Spanish officials during his mission to Spain in 1805, for commissions on loans he secured for the government, and in payment for loans he made himself. Monroe wrote letters to Jefferson, Madison, John Quincy Adams, and other influential friends appealing for assistance, but Congress did nothing. Meanwhile creditors pressured him. One, fur trader and financier John Jacob Astor, wrote him a polite but firm letter: "Permit me to congratulate you on your Honourable retirement. . . . Without wishing to cause you any Inconvenience on account of the loan which I so long made to you I would be glad if you would put it in a train of sittlement [*sic*] if not the whole let it be a part with the interest due."

John Quincy Adams in 1848, daguerreotype by Philip Haas (courtesy of the Phelps Stokes Collection, Metropolitan Museum of Art)

Congress delayed. Monroe started selling land. His plantation at Ash Lawn went first. Other land—in Virginia, in Kentucky—followed. Finally, in 1831 Oak Hill had to go. Monroe had no place to call home. By then, however, he had moved away. After the death of his wife on September 30, 1830, Monroe moved to New York City to live with his daughter and son-in-law in a modest home near the Bowery. He took a daily walk to the docks, and passersby greeted him without knowing who he was. After he moved he appeared in public only once, at a rally to celebrate the dethronement of Charles X of France.

In New York Monroe's health grew precarious. Apparently he suffered from tuberculosis. In a letter to his doctor he wrote, "I am free from pain, but my cough annoys me much, both day and night." By the time Monroe died, aged eighty-five, on July 4, 1831 (he was the third president to die on the anniversary of American independence), he had no estate to leave to his successors.

JOHN QUINCY ADAMS
Left office March 4, 1829
Died February 23, 1848

Like his father, John Quincy Adams had difficulty accepting that the people wanted another president. He had, he believed, discharged his duties with honesty and efficiency and could only attribute his defeat to "skunks of party slander who have been squirting round the country the vile stench with which they sought to perfume the atmosphere of the Union." Adams had even more difficulty accepting that the people wanted Andrew Jackson instead: he thought the Tennessean unschooled, unprincipled, and unprepared for the responsibilities of office. Jackson disliked Adams too. Old Hickory believed that the campaign by Adams's supporters to call into question the virtue of Jackson's wife had shortened her life. When he arrived in Washington, three weeks before his inauguration, the president-elect refused to pay the customary courtesy call to the outgoing president. That was bad enough. Then, when Adams learned that Jackson had not reserved a place for him at the inaugural ceremonies, Adams decided he could take no more. During the evening of March 3 he stole out of the White House and rode unrecognized through the streets of Washington to his family's temporary residence on Meridian Hill. At the end of April he received news that his son George had tragically died while aboard ship. In June the family moved back to Quincy, to Old House, Adams's late father's residence.

Back home the sixty-two-year-old former president thought he would concentrate on writing. Adams had long been an enthusiastic poet and planned to write more; he also began to think about writing a biography of his father. In commemoration of his father's memory he also took up two of the old man's habits: reading and smoking. He made himself sick from smoking but adjusted to that sooner than he did to reading and rereading the classics.

Unexpected salvation came Adams's way in early 1830. A delegation of neighbors called on him to ask if he considered standing for election to the House of Representatives beneath the dignity of a former president. Adams replied that he would never hesitate to serve the public in a meritorious capacity. In November 1830 he defeated his nearest challenger by a vote of eighteen hundred to four hundred; on December 5, 1831, he began his second career in elective politics.

Adams entered the House easily the most accomplished member of that body. He assumed the chairmanship of the Committee on Manufactures and set about business as if he were no more experienced than the greenest freshman. He rarely missed a vote and each year gained in respect and power. In 1836 he settled on the issue that determined his political course for the rest of his career. The House had voted in a "gag rule" prohibiting members from submitting antislavery petitions on the floor. From that moment Adams fought, almost single-handedly at first, for the repeal of the gag rule. Finally, in December 1844, the House passed his rescinding motion. More and more the issue of slavery occupied Adams's political energies. He fought long and hard, albeit unsuccessfully, against the admission of Texas to the Union. In 1846 he voted against the declaration of war with Mexico. Earlier, in 1841 he had argued successfully before the Supreme Court to win the freedom of a group of blacks unlawfully transported as slaves on the Spanish ship *Amistad*.

"Old Man Eloquent," as he became known to his House colleagues, died in the saddle. On February 21, 1848, the eighty-year-old congressman suffered his second stroke, while seated at his place in the House chamber. He had just emitted a resounding No! vote to a proposal to decorate a group of Mexican War veterans. His fellows bore him to the Speaker's chamber, where he whispered, "This is the end of the earth" and either "I am composed" or "I am content." Two days later Adams breathed his last.

Andrew Jackson in 1845, daguerreotype probably by Daniel Adams (courtesy of the George Eastman House)

JACKSON
Left office March 4, 1837
Died June 8, 1845

Seventy-year-old Andrew Jackson was in such poor shape when he left the presidency there were those who wondered how he had made it to the end of his term. But he had suffered most of his life and was used to it by then. As a thirteen-year-old prisoner of war during the American Revolution he had contracted smallpox and malaria. As a rising Nashville, Tennessee, politician in 1806, he took a bullet in the rib cage, the result of a duel with Charles Dickinson. The bullet entered his left lung, and for the rest of his days Jackson battled chronic lung infections, abscesses, and hemorrhages. Another gun battle in 1813 earned him a bullet that shattered a bone in his left arm; he rejected the advice of doctors to have the arm amputated, preferring to live with the pain for the rest of his life. As he got older Jackson developed chronic diarrhea and intestinal cramps; those plagued him with greater intensity after he left the presidency. In retirement he developed a blinding cataract in his right eye and suffered from dropsy.

After attending the inauguration of his handpicked successor, Martin Van Buren, and remaining in the White House as a guest of the new president for the night, the widower Jackson spent two days in a friend's house across the street (later known as Blair House, the residence of the vice-presidents) before journeying to his Nashville plantation, the Hermitage. Jackson quickly settled into retirement, making necessary repairs to his home and farm and handling the correspondence chores that occupied much of the time of all the early presidents. Van Buren kindly helped him achieve the state of relaxation he deserved when he sent him a present accompanied by the following note: "My dear friend, I have sent you . . . a quarter cask of excellent sherry, which has been ordered for me by old friend, Capt. Nicholson. I find it to be of superior quality, and beg you to accept it, and shall feel most highly honored to be occasionally remembered by yourself and friends in the use of it."

In retirement Jackson encountered the same money problems that threatened the other plantation presidents. Having to cover the debts of his irresponsible son, Andrew Jackson, Jr., who lived at the Hermitage with his wife, Sarah, strained Jackson's finances even more. Jackson loved Sarah dearly, and she acted as hostess at the Hermitage, doting on her father-in-law to compensate for the stress her husband caused. Jackson borrowed from friends to cover his obligations.

More than any of the other early presidents except his immediate predecessor, Jackson kept abreast of politics. He frequently wrote Van Buren with advice and campaigned in Tennessee for the New Yorker during his unsuccessful reelection bid in 1840. Van Buren failed even to carry Jackson's home state. Mortified, Jackson wrote the defeated president: "The Democracy of the United States has been shamefully beaten, but I trust, not conquered. I still hope there is sufficient virtue in the unbought people of the Union, to stay the perjury, bribery, fraud, and imposition upon the people by the vilest system of slander, than ever before has existed, even in the most corrupt days of ancient Rome, who will unight [*sic*], and by their moral force check this hydra of corruption in its bud, or our republican system is gone."

Van Buren disappointed Jackson by taking a stand against Texas annexation as the election of 1844 approached, so Old Hickory searched for an alternative candidate more to his liking. The alternative turned out to be fellow Tennessean James K. Polk, a strong annexation advocate and with Jackson's endorsement the new Democratic nominee.

By the time of Polk's inauguration in 1845 Jackson's health was declining. He grew increasingly feeble, thanks in part to his doctors' habit of "bleeding" him in times of crisis, and was often in such pain that he could not lie flat in bed. On June 2, 1845, a doctor performed an operation on Jackson to drain fluid that had accumulated in his abdomen. On the morning of June 8 the president fell unconscious. House servants cried, "Oh, Lord! Old Massa's dead!" and Jackson revived long enough to promise all his friends—"both white and black": "Oh, do not cry. Be good children, and we shall all meet in heaven." Late that afternoon the seventy-eight-year-old Jackson died.

VAN BUREN
Left office March 4, 1841
Died July 24, 1862

Martin Van Buren was one of the most

active of the former presidents. On March 4, 1841, he attended the inauguration of his successor, William Henry Harrison. He had hoped to experience a second inauguration himself, but the Panic of 1837, not his fault, ruined his chance. Van Buren's mentor, Andrew Jackson, might have survived the panic crisis, but Van Buren had never been able to command that type of loyalty. "Tippecanoe" Harrison, meanwhile, was a popular military figure more in the homespun mold of Jackson than Jackson's dour Yankee successor.

The fact that during his term of office Van Buren had purchased a large estate in Kinderhook, New York, did not mean that he was preparing for retirement. He had every intention of serving that second term—four years later. In fact, the Missouri legislature nominated him for president soon after Harrison's inaugural. Harrison's death on his thirty-first day of office intensified Van Buren's ambitions. The Whigs stood divided under former Democrat John Tyler, who ascended to the presidency upon Harrison's death and was only nominally a Whig. After the congressional elections in 1842 Van Buren began a six-month trek across the nation, conferring with leaders along the way, giving a few strategically chosen speeches, and stopping for a long visit with Old Hickory at his estate. On the way home Van Buren made one of the few errors of his political career, an error that cost him his chance at another presidential term.

Disillusioned by Harrison's death and Tyler's intransigence, the Whigs all but swore to nominate their leader, Henry Clay, for president in 1844. Clay and Van Buren seemed poised for competition. Van Buren thought it prudent to meet with Clay in the latter's Kentucky home. One issue dominated their two-day conversation: the issue of Texas annexation. Northern politicians of both parties opposed annexation because it promised to extend the dominion of slavery. Southerners generally support-

Martin Van Buren after his presidency (Library of Congress)

ed annexation for the same reason. Van Buren and Clay decided to try to keep the issue from dominating the campaign (and threatening the party system) by refusing to discuss it until late in the race. Furthermore, they both decided that taking a stand in favor of annexation would cost them more northern support than either could afford to lose. In early April 1844, as the party nominating conventions approached, they issued letters opposing annexation.

Unfortunately for Van Buren, by then much of the Democratic party had rallied around former standard-bearer Andrew Jackson in favor of annexation. Van Buren promptly lost Jackson's support for the nomination. Jackson's pick, James K. Polk, won the nomination and the election.

Van Buren still would not retire. He moved toward a genuine antislavery position in the four years after his disappointing nomination rejection, even supporting the 1846 Wilmot Proviso, which would have banned territorial slavery had it passed the Senate. In 1848 he accepted the nomination of the Free

Soil party for president. Whether he thought he could actually win or merely wanted to make sure the Democrats could not win is a matter of conjecture. In the end the Free Soil ticket drew enough votes away from the Democrats to secure a Whig victory.

Finally the sixty-six-year-old political veteran went home to Kinderhook. He enjoyed retirement, working in his garden and fishing, and then he took a tour of Europe from 1853 to 1855, becoming the first former president to cross the Atlantic. Van Buren returned to the States in time to serve as a presidential elector for James Buchanan in 1856, and he endorsed Stephen A. Douglas for president in 1860. He died, aged seventy-nine, in Kinderhook on July 24, 1862.

TYLER
Left office March 4, 1845
Died January 18, 1862

The first vice-president to succeed to the presidency upon the death of the president experienced one of the most quixotic retirements of any chief executive. He spent most of it vainly trying to get back into politics, never succeeding until he became a supporter of the southern Confederacy. He was the only former president to take a place in the rebel government.

After alienating his original party, the Democrats, by running as a Whig for vice-president in 1840 and then alienating the Whigs by refusing to adopt their policies, Tyler had nowhere to go except home to Sherwood Forest, his Virginia estate, when he left office. He took up country living with his second wife, Julia (with whom he had seven children, matching the total he achieved with his first wife), and began thinking about attaining the presidency again in 1848. He even went so far as to travel to New York City to drum up support for his bid, but the local *Herald* reported that he was visiting to promote the Whig candidacy of Zachary Taylor. In 1852 and again in 1856 Tyler hoped against hope that deadlocked Democratic conventions would turn to him as a compromise candidate. In 1860 Tyler first promoted radical proslavery Virginian Henry Wise for president (and his own son, Robert, as vice-president), then vainly hoped that the Democrats would choose him. That failed to happen. After Abraham Lincoln's election to the presidency Tyler called a peace conference of the states. He suggested that the seceding states adopt a constitution identical to that of the United States but including provisions recognizing slavery, and invite the rest of the states to secede and adopt the new constitution. When the confused meeting broke up, Tyler began to call for Virginia to secede.

After Virginia left the Union, Tyler accepted a seat in the Provisional Congress of the Confederacy, but at seventy years of age he was too ill to journey to Montgomery, Alabama, the Confederate capital, to take office. When the Confederacy moved the seat of its government to Richmond, Virginia, and elected a new Congress, Tyler again won a seat. In early January 1862 he made his way to Richmond to renew his political life, but he fell ill before he could assume his duties. Bedridden on January 18, Tyler, seventy-one, informed his physician, "Doctor, I am going." The attendant replied, "I hope not, sir." Tyler said, "Perhaps, it is best," took a sip of brandy, smiled at his wife, and passed away.

POLK
Left office March 4, 1849
Died June 15, 1849

Only fifty-three years old when he left office, James K. Polk thought he could look forward to at least a quarter-century of retirement, but he was destined to enjoy barely three months of the leisurely life, the briefest of any former president. A detail man, he had worked hard during his four years and was very tired after the inauguration of Zachary Taylor, his successor. But he did not rest. Instead he consented to the wishes of Democratic leaders and took a farewell tour of the southern states.

Polk reached New Orleans on March 21 to find the city in the grip of an epidemic of Asiatic cholera. No one knows for sure, but he probably contracted the disease. When he finally returned home to Nashville, Tennessee, a few days later he was complaining of "a derangement of the stomach and bowels." He grew progressively weaker and died on June 15. Polk had been the youngest man to win election to the presidency and died at a younger age than any other former president.

President James K. Polk, 1849 (Library of Congress)

FILLMORE
Left office March 4, 1853
Died March 8, 1874

President Millard Fillmore's support of the Compromise of 1850 cost him the allegiance of the northern wing of the Whig party and ruined his chance for nomination to the presidency in 1852. After he attended the inauguration of his successor, Democrat Franklin Pierce, he wanted to return to his home in Buffalo, New York, but his wife's illness prevented the couple from leaving. They took up residence in the Willard Hotel in Washington, where Abigail Fillmore died on March 30. That was the first of several tragedies that darkened Fillmore's long and otherwise fruitful retirement.

After his wife's death, Fillmore returned to Buffalo. Thinking he might be the man to unite the Whigs for the presidential election of 1856, he undertook an extensive tour of the South and Midwest in the spring and summer of 1854. Soon after he arrived home in June, his daughter, Mary, died. Her death grieved Fillmore and intensified his desire to return to political office.

Fillmore had come to feel, however, that the Whigs could no longer support a national presidential bid. (Indeed, by nomination season in 1856 the Whigs no longer existed as a party.) He began to look elsewhere for political support and found what he was looking for in the American (Know-Nothing) party, the nativist amalgam that attracted him largely because of its reluctance to take a formal stand on the slavery issue. As 1855 dawned he let friends know he would accept the Know-Nothing nomination, then in the spring he and his son left on a year-long tour of Europe. In Rome in February 1856, he received word of his nomination.

Fillmore polled a surprisingly large number of ballots in the November election—more than eight hundred thousand—but he placed third behind Democrat James Buchanan and Republican John Fremont and carried only one state, Maryland. He realized his political career was over. "I profess to belong to no party but my country," he wrote after the election, "and am taking no part in politics."

For a short while Fillmore experienced some financial difficulty, caused mostly by his extensive touring before the 1856 election. In 1858 he married a wealthy widow, Caroline McIntosh, and his financial worries were over.

The former president remained out-

Left: Millard Fillmore, circa 1870; right: President Franklin Pierce, 1857

side politics until the Civil War started. He then spoke at recruitment rallies in his hometown. He spent most of his time after the war serving the city of Buffalo, as founder of the Buffalo Historical Society, founder of the Buffalo Fine Arts Academy, and as a patron of the Buffalo Young Men's Association. In February 1874 he suffered a stroke. A second stroke followed two weeks later. Fillmore died on March 8, 1874, at the age of seventy-four.

PIERCE
Left office March 4, 1857
Died October 8, 1869

Franklin Pierce bore no ill will toward James Buchanan, the man who succeeded him as president. He invited Buchanan to stay in the White House before his term began. But in his personal life things were much worse. His wife, Jane Pierce, could not shake the depression she suffered after the death of the couple's son, Bennie, shortly before Pierce took office. Bennie was their third child, and all of them had died. After the Pierces moved their belongings back into the family home in Concord, New Hampshire, they began an eighteen-month tour of Europe that Pierce hoped would heal his and his wife's wounds.

The Pierces returned to the United States in 1859. The former president discovered that friends were attempting to maneuver him into the Democratic presidential nomination in 1860. His taste for politics gone, Pierce recommended an alternate: Jefferson Davis of Mississippi, later president of the Confederacy. That recommendation came back to haunt him. After the Democrats split and the Republicans won the election, Pierce spoke out more frequently against the federal attempt to restrict slave property. Always more of a friend of the Union than an opponent of slavery, he took a stronger and stronger stand against the war and the Republican party as battle casualties mounted. All of this alienated his New Hampshire neighbors greatly. By 1863 he could claim few Yankee supporters. One, his lifelong friend Nathaniel Hawthorne, dedicated his last book, *Our Old Home*, to Pierce, remarking to his publisher that "if Pierce is so exceedingly unpopular, there is so much the more need that an old friend should stand by him."

Meanwhile personal tragedy struck again. Jane Pierce died, leaving the former president alone and nearly friendless. He began to drink heavily and spent much of the remaining years of his life in an alcoholic stupor. Early in the morning of October 8, 1869, Pierce died at the age of sixty-four.

BUCHANAN
Left office March 4, 1861
Died June 1, 1868

Sixty-nine-year-old James Buchanan was heartily tired of the presidency when he gave it up on March 4, 1861. He remained in Washington long enough to chair two meetings of his former cabinet to advise incoming president Abraham Lincoln concerning the situation at Fort Sumter in South Carolina, then he happily retired to Wheatland, his estate outside Lancaster, Pennsylvania. The first few months of his retirement went well: Buchanan relaxed as he had not in years. As the war heated up, however, criticism of his administration mounted. People blamed him for failing to solve the crisis before it came to blows. Buchanan had to call in the local Masonic lodge to provide security against threats to burn down his house.

Discouraged by such contrary public opinion, Buchanan set about defending his administration. He began penning his memoir, *Mr. Buchanan's Administration on the Eve of the Rebellion,* which appeared in 1866. By that time northerners had other villains to rake over the coals, and the book entered the market largely unnoticed. After the end of the Civil War, Buchanan's life grew quiet. He joined the Presbyterian church in 1865 and took sick in May 1868. Aged seventy-eight, Buchanan died on June 1.

ANDREW JOHNSON
Left office March 4, 1869
Died July 31, 1875

Sixty-year-old Andrew Johnson left the presidency a disgraced politician who had survived the previous year's impeachment proceedings by one vote. President-elect Ulysses S. Grant let it be known that he would refuse to ride with him in the inaugural carriage or even to speak with him, so, instead of attending the ceremony, on inauguration day Johnson finished his business, gathered up his papers, blessed his staff and servants, and walked out. He went to Baltimore, where enthusiastic crowds greeted him. A month later he began the journey back to his adopted hometown, Greeneville, Tennessee.

Johnson was determined to return to national politics. He stumped hard for a U.S. Senate seat in 1871, but President Grant and his Republican allies let the Tennessee legislature know that Johnson was not wanted in Washington. He campaigned for a U.S. House seat in 1872, but he lost that race too. In 1873 he contracted Asiatic cholera and seemed for awhile on the verge of death. He recovered, but he never regained his full vigor.

In 1875 Johnson won his Senate seat after a difficult battle in which the Tennessee legislature cast more than fifty ballots. On March 5, 1875, he took his seat in Washington, the second former president (John Quincy Adams was the first) to win elective office.

He had not long to serve. On March 22 Johnson gave his only floor speech, against the corruption of the Grant administration and the injustice of its Reconstruction policy. On the way home after the end of the session, he reminisced to friends about politics: "More than a hundred times I have said to myself, what course may I pursue so that the calm historian will say one hundred years from now, 'He pursued the right course?' "

Probably still weak from his bout with cholera, Johnson suffered a stroke while visiting his daughter in late July 1875. He regained consciousness long enough to request that no doctor be called. Johnson lingered for two days, then

Ulysses S. Grant finishing his memoirs at Mt. McGregor, New York, 1885 (Library of Congress)

died, aged sixty-six, on July 31.

GRANT
Left office March 4, 1877
Died July 23, 1885

He wanted to serve as president for a third term, but the nation had experienced enough of Ulysses S. Grant. Grant's two terms had been marked by scandal. The corruption had been so acute that the House of Representatives had taken the unprecedented step of passing a resolution asking Grant not to seek reelection again. Grant got the message and issued a statement: "It may happen in the future history of the country that to change an Executive because he has been eight years in office will prove unfortunate, if not dangerous." But he promised not to accept a third Republican nomination unless doing so appeared "an imperative duty—circumstances not likely to arise."

Grant's statement cleared the way for the nomination of Rutherford B. Hayes, who won the presidency after an unprecedented electoral battle with Democrat Samuel J. Tilden. After attending Hayes's inauguration, Grant and his wife moved back home to Galena, Illinois, and, with not much else to do, prepared for a world tour. They were gone for two years. The newspapers wondered where they got the money. Exactly how the trip was financed remains unexplained. Finally the Grants had visited nearly every place they could possibly visit and prepared to return to the States. "I am both homesick and dread going home," wrote the former president. "I have no home but must establish one when I get back; I do not know where." After arriving in San Francisco, the Grants toured the United States, keeping the president's name in the headlines and in the minds of Republican conventioneers. Just before the 1880 nominating convention they settled back in Galena. Grant still wanted that third term.

The balloting turned into a war of attrition between Grant and James G. Blaine. After several days of stalemate the party settled on a dark-horse candidate, James A. Garfield. Grant could no longer hope to return to office. "My friends have not been honest with me," he complained. "They should not have placed me in nomination unless they felt perfectly sure of my success." After campaigning for Garfield, who succeeded in winning the presidency, Grant and his wife were faced with financial difficulty. Grant landed a job as president of the Mexican Southern Railroad, headquartered in New York but actually little more than an idea that backers felt needed Grant's prestige to succeed. Grant did succeed in raising some funds for the railroad, but most of the money went to pay his salary and expenses. In 1884 the company went bankrupt.

Meanwhile Grant had already decided to go into business with his son, who in return for $100,000 of his father's money gave Grant a position with his firm, Grant & Ward. But Ward used the firm's stock as loan collateral, and when the loans went bad, the company went under.

Grant was then in desperate need of assistance. He rejected the idea of a congressional pension but accepted an honorary army commission and an annual salary of $13,500. He decided to write his memoirs to earn an estate. Just as he was starting the book he began to experience pains in his throat, and doctors diagnosed the problem as throat cancer. For a year Grant labored heroically to finish his two-volume history so that his family would have a source of income after his death. He finished the second volume at the beginning of July 1885 and wrote a letter to his doctor: "There is nothing more I should do to it [the book] now, and therefore I am not likely to be more ready to go than at this moment." Later in July he wrote, "I do not sleep though I sometimes doze a little. If up I am talked to and in my efforts to answer cause pain. The fact is I think I am a verb instead of a personal pronoun. A verb is anything that signifys to be; to do; or to suffer. I signify all three." Early in the morning of July 23, 1885, Grant died, aged sixty-three.

Lucy Webb Hayes, Rutherford B. Hayes, and journalist William Henry Smith, 1889

HAYES
Left office March 4, 1881
Died January 17, 1893

In his letter accepting the Republican presidential nomination in 1876, Rutherford B. Hayes declared that he would not accept renomination. He was happy to retire after completing his term. He wrote to a friend, "Nobody ever left the Presidency with less regret, less disappointment, fewer heartburnings, or more general content with the results of his term (in his own heart, I mean) than I do."

After attending the inauguration of his successor, James A. Garfield, Hayes and his wife returned home to Spiegel Grove, their estate in Fremont, Ohio. "We wish to get as completely back into private life as we can," Hayes wrote in a letter, "to keep out of public observation enough to show the truth that we have no hankering after the pleasures we have left." Hayes owned several farms in Ohio, Minnesota, North Dakota, and West Virginia; he soon encountered the cash-flow problems experienced by many "land-poor" farmers.

The former president managed to get by, however, and devoted his remaining years to good causes. He served as a director of the George Peabody Educational Fund and the John F. Slater Fund, both of which supported black education. As president of the Slater fund he personally granted a scholarship to future civil rights leader W. E. B. Du Bois. He served as a trustee of Ohio State University and several other midwestern colleges. As president of the National Prison Association he spoke out in favor of prison reform, including placing greater emphasis on rehabilitation. As he got older he seemed to grow more liberal in his thinking. Al-

President Chester Arthur

though he never went so far as to advocate radical social reform, he did come to believe that industrialization contributed to national decline. He began to speak out in favor of limitations on inheritances and wrote in his diary, "We ought not to allow a permanent aristocracy of inherited wealth to grow up in this country." In 1888 he wrote, "Vast accumulations of wealth in a few hands are hostile to labor. Their tendency is to break down fair competition, to build up monopoly, to corrupt politics, to bribe conventions, legislative bodies, courts and juries, to debauch society; and churches are not beyond the reach of their baneful influence."

Hayes continued to keep a full schedule of appointments into the 1890s, partly to fill the gap created by the death of his wife, Lucy, in 1889. He traveled throughout the country to participate in conferences and to speak before organizations whose causes he supported. Aged seventy, he died at Spiegel Grove on January 17, 1893.

ARTHUR
Left office March 4, 1885
Died November 18, 1886

Fifty-four-year-old Chester A. Arthur knew he was a dying man when he left the presidency. Doctors had diagnosed his condition as Bright's disease, at that time an invariably fatal kidney ailment. Arthur had succeeded in keeping the disorder hidden from the public. When during his term he was too sick to work, the White House told the press he was suffering from a cold. He knew that if he were reelected he probably would not survive the full four years.

Arthur was of two minds about the renomination. He had been tremendously honored to receive the vice-presidential nomination in 1880 and had surprised most observers by achieving a sound and efficient presidential administration under trying circumstances. Not known as a reformer during his prepresidential career, he had signed the Civil Service Reform Act in 1883, eliminating hundreds of federal patronage jobs and alienating the Stalwart faction of the Republican party, the faction that had won him the vice-presidency in the first place. Arthur could not count on their support again but would have liked to have defeated them on his own. He would not fight for the nomination, he decided, but would accept it in the unlikely event that it came his way. That never happened. Arthur even went so far as to discourage his supporters from promoting his cause at the convention. In the election of 1884, Republican nominee James G. Blaine lost to Democrat Grover Cleveland. Arthur attended the inauguration and left for his comfortable home in New York City. He resumed the practice of law, officially at least, but his health prevented him from keeping regular hours at his firm. He had not much else in his life to engender enthusiasm for living. His wife, Nell, had died slightly less than two months before Arthur assumed the vice-presidency.

Arthur spent most of his time in bed,

rallied briefly in early November 1886, then suffered a cerebral hemorrhage and died on November 18. He had lived twenty months beyond the inauguration of Cleveland and died at the age of fifty-six.

BENJAMIN HARRISON
Left office March 4, 1893
Died March 13, 1901

Benjamin Harrison did not enjoy his term as president but tried hard to win renomination in 1892. His wife, Caroline, was opposed to his decision to seek reelection, but Harrison was adamant: "If Blaine [Harrison's secretary of state] and some of those who I thought were my political friends had not turned upon me, I should retire from office with no thought of allowing my name to be used in the nominations. But no Harrison has ever run from a fight, Caroline, and there is going to be a fight." Harrison won the Republican nomination after a protracted battle with Blaine and then lost the general election to Grover Cleveland. Two weeks before the election, Caroline died.

After attending Cleveland's inauguration, Harrison, fifty-nine, lonely and depressed, returned to Indianapolis, his hometown, and plunged into professional life. Soon he was back on his feet. He set up a law practice that established him as a leader in the legal profession. He wrote articles for national magazines on politics and current events. In 1894 he accepted an offer from Stanford University to give a series of law lectures. He married Mary Dimmick in 1896, and less than a year later the couple had a daughter. In 1897 Harrison published a book, *This Country of Ours*. A memoir, *Views of an Ex-President*, followed in 1901.

Before the Republican convention in 1896 Harrison issued a statement declaring he would not accept another nomination to the presidency. That ended speculation that he might follow Grover Cleveland and serve two non-successive presidential terms. Harrison campaigned for William McKinley in several states, and the Republicans emerged victorious.

Harrison had one more political role to play. In 1898 the nation of Venezuela hired him to represent it in a boundary dispute with Great Britain. The former president threw himself into the task, preparing an eight-hundred-page brief and giving twenty-five hours of oral arguments during a five-day hearing. Great Britain won the dispute.

After his service to Venezuela, Harrison and his wife took a European tour and settled into retirement, spending summers in a mountain cabin in New York and the business year in Indianapolis. Harrison enjoyed good health almost to the end. Early in March 1901 he contracted a cold that turned into pneumonia. He died on March 13 at the age of sixty-seven.

CLEVELAND
Left office March 4, 1897
Died June 24, 1908

After attending the inauguration of his successor, William McKinley, Grover Cleveland's wife Frances settled into the Clevelands' new estate in Princeton, New Jersey, near the university. Cleveland let her go alone. The first thing he did as a former president was to take a two-week hunting and fishing trip. Back home the first months of retirement were spent relaxing, preparing for a child, and growing accustomed to college society. In October the third of five Cleveland children—two boys and three girls—was born. Princeton's student body "adopted" the baby and, ribbing his father's rotundity, predicted that he would one day play center for the football team. Cleveland and his wife rarely missed the Princeton eleven's Saturday contests.

In 1899 Cleveland accepted the Henry Stafford Little Lectureship in Public Affairs at Princeton, and his lectures—two a year—were well attended. In 1901 he became a trustee of the university and in 1904 president of

Frances and Grover Cleveland and children during the former president's service as a Princeton University trustee from 1897 to 1907

the Board of Trustees. As trustee Cleveland came into conflict with the university's president, Woodrow Wilson, who attempted to introduce curricular innovations that Cleveland and his fellow traditionalists thought too trendy. Generally the board prevailed.

Retirement was satisfying. A reporter for the *Chicago Record* wrote, "Ex-President Cleveland is living a quiet, dignified life at Princeton in a congenial atmosphere and apparent contentment. He has plenty of time for study and reflection. . . . He can accept consultation cases from New York firms and corporations that pay big fees and thus make an income sufficient for his wants; he can receive a sufficient amount of deference, adulation, and honor to satisfy his pride and keep his name before the public, and can have all the fun he needs watching the pranks of the students—all this without going out of Princeton; and what more can an ex-President ask for?"

The ex-president asked for, and got, lots of time for fishing and hunting to go along with his quiet collegiate life. He was the first president to make the outdoors an object of his dedication and even published a nature book—*Fishing and Hunting Sketches*—in 1906. That was the second of his three books. The first, *Presidential Problems*, appeared in 1904, and the third, *Good Citizenship*, in 1908. By then he was an old man. Cleveland suffered from rheumatism and acute indigestion and in his last years spent weeks at a time in bed. Aged seventy-one, he died on June 24, 1908.

THEODORE ROOSEVELT
Left office March 4, 1909
Died January 6, 1919

After winning election to the presidency in 1904, Theodore Roosevelt announced he would not be a candidate for another term in 1908. He came to regret making that announcement. He told William Jennings Bryan, "When you see me quoted in the press as welcoming the rest I will have, take no stock of it. . . . I will confess to you that I like my job. The burdens . . . will be laid aside with a good deal of regret." The reluctant retiree, only fifty years old when his term was up, settled for what he thought was the next best thing to another presidential term for himself—a term for his friend, Secretary of War William Howard Taft. Roosevelt engineered Taft's nomination and electoral victory, invited his portly successor into the White House weeks early, and bade him a fond farewell after attending the inauguration ceremony. He slipped out a side door of the capitol and took a train to Sagamore Hill, his New York estate.

Unsure of what to do with himself, Roosevelt took a job as a contributing editor for the *Outlook*, a small-circulation monthly, and pledged to contribute one article a month on a topic of his choice. The position gave him a center of gravity, as it were: an office from which to pursue his many interests. Then he began to plan an African safari, something he had long wanted to undertake. To fund his safari he signed a fifty-thousand-dollar contract with *Scribner's Monthly* to produce a series of articles about it. He intended it to be more than a pleasure jaunt and hired more than two hundred porters to carry supplies sufficient to maintain a yearlong scientific investigation. The party, which included Roosevelt's son Kermit, collected hundreds of plant and animal samples and donated them to the Smithsonian Institution. They shot five elephants, seven hippos, nine lions, and thirteen rhinos. Roosevelt, isolated from the world except by way of his communications to *Scribner's*, did not see his wife for a year. On the way back to the States he toured the capitals of Europe and learned of a rift in the Republican party and of his successor's seemingly lackluster performance as president. He lectured at Oxford University and served as American representative at the funeral of British king Edward VII. Back home in June 1910, Roosevelt was treated by the citizens of New York City to a parade. His *Scribner's* articles were collected into a book, *African Game Trails*, which was published in 1910 and sold more than one million copies.

Theodore Roosevelt on his African safari, 1909-1910

Roosevelt published another book in 1910—a book with more political character than his safari writings. The book, *The New Nationalism*, contributed considerably to growing speculation that the former president would seek another term. Roosevelt encouraged a liberal Republican insurgency against the regular party and finally declared his candidacy for the Republican nomination in February 1911. Taft won the call after a hard battle, whereupon Roosevelt's supporters called for a national convention of "progressives." That convention formed a party, the National Progressive or "Bull Moose" party (thus dubbed after Roosevelt had declared himself "as fit as a bull moose" and ready for another term) and nominated Roosevelt for the presidency. The Republican party had split.

The campaign pitted Roosevelt against Taft and the Democratic nominee, Woodrow Wilson, former president of Princeton University and governor of New Jersey. Wilson's progressive credentials were at least as impressive as Roosevelt's, and he enjoyed the backing of a regular party organization.

Roosevelt was indeed still "fit as a bull moose." During a campaign stop in Milwaukee, Wisconsin, an attacker shot him in the chest; but he refused medical attention until he had given the one-hour address he came to give. In the election Taft never had much of a chance, and Roosevelt fared poorly as well. The Republican split put Wilson in office with about 43 percent of the popular vote and a decisive electoral-vote victory.

Roosevelt quickly got back to business. As president of the American Historical Association he gave an address on "History as Literature" before the association's annual meeting in 1913. That essay and several others were published as a book. That same year Roosevelt also published his autobiography and the next year another book on his African travels.

Meanwhile, his most spectacular adventure nearly cost him his life. In October 1913 he and son Kermit sailed for South America, where Roosevelt intended to give a series of lectures on natural history. He could not turn down the offer of the American Museum of Natural History to explore the Paraguay River. On that trip he heard of the unexplored River of Doubt in Brazil; the Brazilian government agreed to sponsor a major expedition of that uncharted and hazardous territory. It turned into a terrible ordeal. Roosevelt suffered from attacks of malaria and dysentery, boats were lost in the raging river, and three men died. One drowned; another went insane, killing a third member of the party before disappearing into the jungle. Roosevelt lost fifty-seven pounds on the trip and was never again in very good health. The Brazilian government renamed the river Rio Roosevelt in his honor. In 1914 the explorer published an exciting account of the expedition, entitled *Through the Brazilian Wilderness.*

The former president lived a considerably more sedate life after returning from Brazil. He continued to write, turning his literary attention to the problem of America's role in the burgeoning world war. With his wife he took a long but safe vacation to the British West Indies. He let it be known that he would accept the Republican nomination for president in 1916 but ended up campaigning for Charles Evans Hughes (a future chief justice of the Supreme Court) after declining another nomination by the National Progressive party. After the United States entered World War I he asked President Wilson to commission him a division commander; Wilson declined. In July 1918 his son Quentin was killed in France while on an air patrol behind German lines.

In November 1918 Roosevelt entered Roosevelt Hospital in New York City for treatment of rheumatism. He was also hampered by recurrent bouts with malaria and infections contracted on the Brazil trip. He died on January 6, 1919, at the age of sixty.

TAFT
Left office March 4, 1913
Died March 8, 1930

William Howard Taft entered the presidency as Theodore Roosevelt's handpicked successor and left as the object of Roosevelt's biting criticism. Roosevelt's third-party candidacy not only doomed Taft to defeat in his reelection bid but also embarrassed him. He finished a distant third to Roosevelt and the victorious Democrat, Woodrow Wilson.

Taft was destined to enjoy his postpresidential years much more than he did his years as chief executive. He ended up compiling one of the more-distinguished records of the former presidents.

After attending Wilson's inauguration, Taft and his wife took a train to Augusta, Georgia, where the deposed president enjoyed a relaxing golfing holiday at Augusta National Golf Club (later a favorite haunt of Dwight D. Eisenhower). They then made their way to New Haven, Connecticut, where Taft took up duties as Kent Professor of Law at Yale University. In addition to his teaching responsibilities, he assumed the presidency of the American Bar Association and gave speeches around the country. A series of lectures Taft gave at the University of Virginia was published as *The Presidency: Its Duties, Its Powers, Its Opportunities and Its Limitations* in 1916. That same year another series of lectures, given at Columbia University, was published as *Our Chief Magistrate and His Powers.*

William Howard Taft during his Yale professorship, from 1913 to 1921

Also in 1916 Taft hit the road to campaign for unsuccessful Republican presidential candidate Charles Evans Hughes. In 1918 a celebrated reconciliation with Theodore Roosevelt took place. The two had not spoken civilly since Roosevelt had thwarted Taft's presidential candidacy in 1912. The old friends ran into each other at a restaurant in Chicago and had a nice talk. Roosevelt later remarked, "I've seen old Taft, and we're in perfect harmony on everything."

In June 1921 President Warren G. Harding appointed Taft to the position he had hoped for throughout his political life: chief justice of the Supreme Court. He wrote, "The truth is that in my present life I don't remember that I ever was president." In his ten years on the court Taft wrote 253 opinions, about one-sixth of the total. He quickly gained a reputation for efficiency and consistency and maintained that reputation throughout his tenure.

Generally Taft took a constructionist stance as chief justice. In *Truax* v. *Corrigan* (1921) the court invalidated a provision of the Clayton Antitrust Act that had prohibited the issuance of court injunctions to halt peaceful labor picketing. In *Bailey* v. *Drexel Furniture Co.* (1922) the court prohibited Congress from levying taxes on the produce of child labor for the purpose of discouraging such labor, declaring unconstitutional the Wilson administration's Child Labor Tax Act of 1919. The chief justice loquaciously wrote, "The good sought in unconstitutional legislation is an insidious feature because it leads citizens and legislators of good purpose to promote it without thought of the serious breach it will make in the ark of our covenant or the harm which will come from breaking down recognized standards." In *Myers* v. *United States* (1926), Taft's most famous case, the court in part pronounced unconstitutional the Tenure of Office Act of 1867, the act that nearly forced President Andrew Johnson out of office.

Taft lightened his schedule in his final years as chief justice. By February 1930 a combination of heart disease, high blood pressure, and a bladder inflammation forced him to tender his resignation. He failed rapidly after he

President and Mrs. Woodrow Wilson, 1921 (courtesy of the Firestone Library, Princeton University)

left the court and died on March 8, 1930, aged seventy-two.

WILSON
Left office March 4, 1921
Died February 3, 1924

Woodrow Wilson left the presidency a broken man, his dreams for peace and democracy shattered, he thought, by base values of nationalism and self-interest. On a speaking tour to promote U.S. entry into his League of Nations, he had collapsed in a nervous breakdown. Back in Washington a week later, he suffered an incapacitating stroke. The public and most of Congress remained unaware of his critical condition, and Wilson's second wife, Edith Galt, became a surrogate executive, screening presidential duties to conserve her husband's strength and will. Wilson's dream of American participation in the League of Nations dissolved as he struggled to regain his health.

Briefly he considered a third run for the presidency, and friends felt too sorry for him to tell him bluntly that they would never let that happen. He ended up watching as the nation "returned to normalcy" and elected Republican Warren G. Harding to the presidency. Without attending Harding's inauguration, Wilson and his wife left the White House on March 4, 1921, and settled in a Washington home.

The former president briefly tried a law partnership with his former secretary of state, but his poor health and lack of enthusiasm quickly turned the concern into a financial failure. He thought about writing a book but never got beyond writing much more than the dedication to his wife. He settled into the routine of an invalid. Wilson enjoyed a brief return to the national spotlight in the form of a radio address to the nation on Armistice Day 1923. Unable to memorize the speech and prevented by failing eyesight from reading it, he was prompted by his wife, who

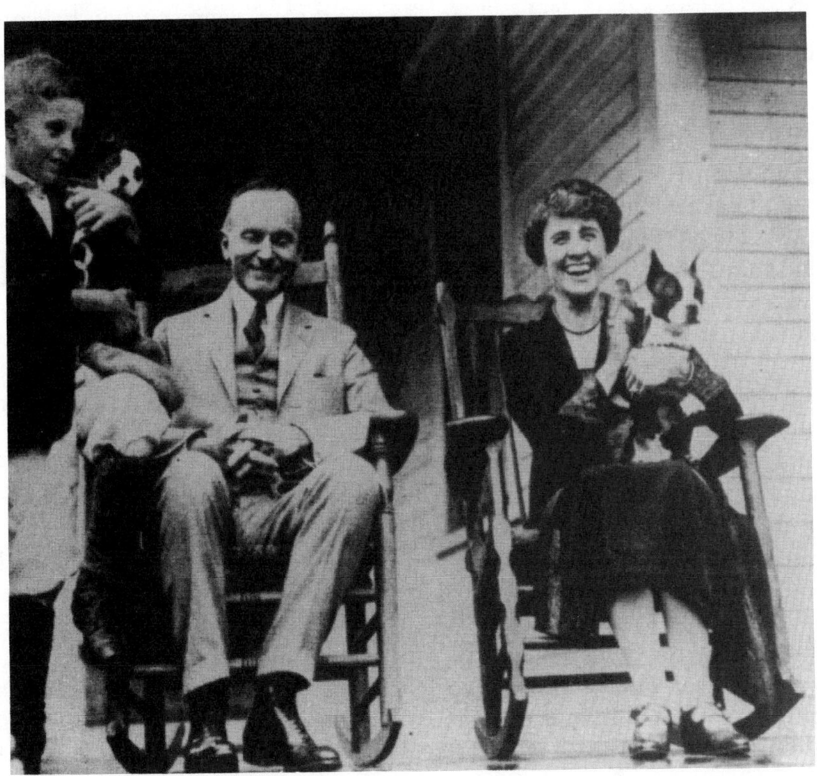

Calvin and Grace Coolidge, with son John and the family pets, one week after the former president's term ended on March 4, 1929 (Library of Congress)

could be heard in the background: "Memories of that happy time are forever marred and embittered for us," Wilson said, "by the shameful fact that when the victory was won . . . we withdrew into a sullen and selfish isolation which is manifestly ignoble because it is manifestly dishonorable. The only way in which we can worthily give proof of our appreciation of the high significance of Armistice Day is by resolving to put self-interest away and once more formulate and act upon the highest ideals and purposes of international policy." The day after Wilson gave the address a crowd of twenty thousand gathered outside his Washington home to show its appreciation.

After that Wilson faded slowly away. By early 1924 he was on his deathbed. On February 2 his doctor spoke with reporters: "Mr. Wilson realizes his fight is over. He is making a game effort. It almost breaks one down. He is very brave. He is just slowly ebbing away." Wilson died on the morning of February 3, aged sixty-seven.

COOLIDGE
Left office March 4, 1929
Died January 5, 1933

Fifty-six-year-old Calvin Coolidge left office one of the most popular chief executives in American history, destined, it appeared, for a fulfilling retirement. The president and his wife attended the inauguration of Herbert Hoover and left immediately afterward for home in Northampton, Massachusetts. At the train station Coolidge bade the nation farewell: "Good-bye, I have had a very enjoyable time in Washington."

At home Coolidge settled into the quiet life. He oversaw the publication in magazine installments of his autobiography, written before he left the White House. He accepted an offer to write a daily newspaper column, "Thinking

Things Over with Calvin Coolidge." He took a position on the Board of Directors of the New York Life Insurance Company and in 1931 gave insurance tips in a national radio address. In 1932 he campaigned unsuccessfully to reelect Hoover to the presidency.

The Depression that stymied Hoover's reelection bid also took its toll on Coolidge. As the nation spiraled into economic chaos, experts and nonexperts alike began to fault what they had previously approved. Coolidge grew bitter. He wrote, "I feel I no longer fit with these times. Great changes can come in four years. These socialistic notions of government are not of my day. . . . It has always seemed to me that common sense is the real solvent for the nation's problems at all times, common sense and hard work. When I read of the newfangled things that are now popular I realize that my time in public affairs is past. I wouldn't know how to handle them if I were called upon to do so." He was not in the best of health and actually never had been. A lifelong sufferer from asthma, he complained increasingly of breathing difficulties and fatigue as 1932 wore on. On January 5, 1933, he went to his office as usual but went home for lunch at ten in the morning. He went upstairs to shave at around noon. His wife found him there lying on his back, dead from coronary thrombosis. Coolidge was sixty-one.

HOOVER
Left office March 4, 1933
Died October 20, 1964

Herbert Hoover left the presidency in disgrace and died one of the nation's most-revered former chief executives. He took a while to get back into circulation. After straining to remain civil during the inauguration of his successor, Franklin D. Roosevelt, Hoover left for home in Palo Alto, California, with his wife. Feeling isolated, he moved to the Waldorf Astoria Hotel in New York City in 1934. About that time he began to speak out against what he considered the "fascistic" tendencies of Roosevelt's New Deal. Hoover continued his criticism of Roosevelt in an address to the Republican national convention in 1936 and campaigned for unsuccessful Republican presidential candidate Alf Landon. Hoover spoke to every Republican convention from 1936 through 1952.

The former president toured Europe in 1938. In Germany he met Adolph Hitler; later he told a friend that Hitler was "partly insane." In Poland he became one of the first Americans to speak out against Nazi persecution of the Jews. After World War II began Hoover resumed a role in which he had found much fulfillment twenty years earlier—as a relief administrator. At various times he served as chairman of the Commission for Polish Relief, of the Finnish Relief Fund, and of the Belgian Relief Fund. During the war Hoover also experienced a personal tragedy. His wife, Lou, died in 1944.

The death of Franklin Roosevelt in 1945 cleared the way for Hoover to reenter government service. In May President Harry S Truman invited Hoover to the White House. The former president had not set foot in Washington since leaving on Roosevelt's inauguration day. In 1946 Truman appointed Hoover coordinator of food relief in all areas affected by World War II. In 1947 Truman established a commission to study ways to streamline the executive branch of the federal government and made Hoover its chairman. The "Hoover Commission" undertook a nearly two-year-long study of the problem and drew up an extensive list of recommendations, many of which were enacted in the Reorganization Act of 1949.

Hoover performed the same type of service in the administration of Dwight D. Eisenhower. Eisenhower made Hoover chairman of a twelve-member Commission on Government Operations. This "Second Hoover Commission" recommended the establishment of the

Herbert and Lou Henry Hoover, Stanford, California, 1940 (Breton W. Crandall Photograph Collection)

Department of Health, Education, and Welfare.

Eighty years old in 1954, Hoover remained active for another decade, writing, speaking, and fulfilling his responsibilities as a loyal Republican. He had difficulty backing Richard Nixon for the presidency in 1960, replying when someone asked him how he felt about Nixon's nomination, "How do you think I feel? I'm among those who persuaded him to run for Congress in the first place."

As the 1960s dawned, Hoover grew feeble. His eyesight and hearing declined. He remained vigorous enough to endorse Barry Goldwater for president in 1964, then he died, three weeks later, on October 20, 1964. He was ninety and had lived longer than any other president except John Adams.

TRUMAN
Left office January 20, 1953
Died December 26, 1972

A reporter asked Harry Truman what he did on his first day home in Independence, Missouri, after his term as president. "I took the suitcases up to the attic," he replied. Then the sixty-eight-year-old Democrat became a public man again. He spent the years of the Eisenhower administration as the titular head of the Democratic party and wasted no opportunity to promote his views on the state of the nation. He campaigned vigorously for Adlai Stevenson in 1956 (after advocating the nomination of Averell Harriman) and constantly criticized Eisenhower for his lack of leadership. In 1960 Truman would have preferred nearly anyone to John Kennedy as the Democratic presidential nominee, but when Kennedy won the honor he fell in behind the ticket. Why? a reporter asked. "I'm a Democrat, and I follow the law," replied Truman.

He slowed down in the 1960s. Truman continued to speak out in favor of what he considered to be the policies of the Democratic party, but he appeared increasingly out of touch. Once a pioneer in the cause of federal support for civil rights, for example, he railed against the freedom rides and other forms of "outside agitation."

By 1964 Truman was so feeble he could not attend the Democratic national convention. But he still had a long way to go. Even though his political positions became more or less irrelevant, successive presidents courted "Give 'em Hell Harry." He stood for an age in which politicians spoke their minds and not what they thought would win the election. Even President Richard Nixon—never one of Truman's favorites—visited Independence to play the piano in the old man's memorial library. His health steadily declined until finally he could not take his famous "morning constitutional" around the block. Truman died in a Kansas City hospital on December 26, 1972, at the age of eighty-eight.

EISENHOWER
Left office January 20, 1961
Died March 28, 1969

Dwight D. Eisenhower earned a well-

Harry S Truman in the White House with President John F. Kennedy, January 21, 1961 (National Park Service)

Dwight D. Eisenhower advising President Lyndon B. Johnson, Palm Springs, California, 1968 (courtesy of the Dwight D. Eisenhower Library)

Lyndon and Lady Bird Johnson, circa 1971 (courtesy of the Lyndon Baines Johnson Memorial Library)

deserved reputation as a president of leisure. He did little to alter that reputation in retirement. But he deserved the rest. As commander of allied forces he had served his country through one of its greatest crises; as president he kept the peace and presided over a period of unprecedented economic growth. He also played a lot of golf, both during and after its presidency. In 1968, at the age of seventy-eight, he shot a hole-in-one.

At home in Gettysburg, Pennsylvania, he worked to complete his memoirs. The first volume, *Mandate for Change, 1953-1956*, appeared in 1965; the second, *Waging Peace, 1956-1961*, appeared in 1966. Eisenhower published an anecdotal volume, *At Ease: Stories I Tell to Friends*, in 1967. He tried to stay clear of Republican party squabbles and reluctantly endorsed Barry Goldwater for president in 1964. He supported Democrat Lyndon B. Johnson's Vietnam War policy.

In poor health when he left office in 1961, Eisenhower suffered a succession of heart attacks during his retirement years. By August 1968, one month after his vice-president, Richard Nixon, gained the Republican nomination for the presidency, Eisenhower suffered his seventh heart attack. From then on he was an invalid. He died, aged seventy-nine, on March 28, 1969.

LYNDON B. JOHNSON
Left office January 20, 1969
Died January 22, 1973

President Richard Nixon said, "He thought he could win. I think President Johnson died of a broken heart. I really do." Johnson left the presidency in 1969 after experiencing some of the highest highs and the lowest lows of any president. Assuming office after the assassination of John F. Kennedy, Johnson rallied the nation and the Congress to pass the Civil Rights Act of 1964. Winning election in his own right that year, he engineered passage of the Voting Rights Act of 1965 and inaugurated his vision of a "Great Society." That vision required the same idealism abroad as at

Richard M. Nixon during an NBC "Meet the Press" television interview, 1988 (photograph by Roger Sandler)

home, but the Vietnam War divided the nation more deeply than it had been divided since the days of the Civil War, severely damaging Johnson's legacy. At the height of the nation's upheaval over the war, he announced his retirement from politics.

Johnson was a shattered man when he left office. He had spent his entire life trying to gain power and had to give it all up. With his wife he retired to his ranch in Texas. There he penned a lackluster memoir, *The Vantage Point* (1971), gave a series of television interviews to journalist Walter Cronkite, and tended to business. Mostly he tried to keep to himself. Gregarious as no president was before him, Johnson out of office became a recluse.

The former president suffered his second heart attack (the first came in 1955) in April 1972. His health was not robust after that. He suffered a third attack on January 22, 1973, aged sixty-four and died on the way to the hospital. President Nixon had notified him of the impending cease-fire in Vietnam the day before his death.

NIXON
Left office August 9, 1974

Richard Nixon is the only president who was forced to resign from office. He has spent much of the time since his presidency trying to establish his credibility as an elder statesman of the nation, and to some extent he has succeeded.

One month after Nixon's resignation, President Gerald Ford pardoned the former president. Nixon concentrated on regaining his health after the stress of the Watergate scandal, then started his rehabilitation process. He has spoken out often in reference to political and public issues and has written seven books, including *RN: The Memoirs of Richard Nixon* (1978) and *In the Arena* (1989). He retains the quality of resiliency that brought him political success in the first place. In 1990 Nixon oversaw the dedication of his presidential library.

Gerald and Betty Ford with Chinese premier Deng Xiaoping, March 1981

Jimmy Carter with wife Rosalyn (left) and Habitat for Humanity colleagues, New York City

FORD
Left office January 20, 1977

Disappointed at losing to Jimmy Carter in the presidential election of 1976, Gerald Ford attended the inauguration of his successor and then left with his wife for a new life in Palm Springs, California. The Fords have also spent much time at the vacation resort of Vail, Colorado. One of the most physically active presidents, in retirement Ford has often appeared in public as a celebrity-golf hopeful, sometimes to his own chagrin, as errant shots and comedian Chevy Chase reinforced his image as a klutz. He serves on the boards of several major corporations and has given lectures across the nation, enriching himself to an extent unusual for a former president.

Ford attempted a political comeback in 1980 but lost the Republican presidential nomination to Ronald Reagan. Reagan briefly considered having Ford nominated for the vice-presidency, but Ford wanted Reagan to guarantee him a substantive role in the new administration, actually a kind of "co-presidency," and Reagan balked.

CARTER
Left office January 20, 1981

Jimmy and Rosalyn Carter attended the inauguration of Ronald Reagan and left immediately to greet the released American hostages from Iran, who had been flown to West Germany. Then the couple went home to Plains, Georgia. They took a tour of China and Japan later in 1981.

Both husband and wife secured fortunes by writing memoirs. Jimmy Carter campaigned for Democratic presidential candidate Walter Mondale, Carter's vice-president, in 1984, to no avail.

The former president has busied himself most prominently as director of the Carter Presidential Center and Library in Atlanta, Georgia. Carter teams have supervised several foreign elections—in Panama, for example—and have won praise for their effort to secure peace settlements in third-world military conflicts such as the civil war in Ethiopia. The Carters also volunteer for the Habitat for Humanity, an organization that constructs low-cost residential housing in the United States and other countries.

REAGAN
Left office January 20, 1989

Ronald Reagan and his wife Nancy retired to Bel Air, California, at the conclusion of Reagan's presidential term. The former president attracted some criticism for embarking on a heavily compensated lecture tour of Japan soon after leaving office. In 1990 he became the first former president to travel to the site of the Berlin Wall to congratulate East and West on its destruction.

Results of American Presidential Elections

Year	Presidential Candidate	Party	Votes Electoral	Votes Popular
1789	George Washington		69	
	John Adams		34	
	others		35	
	votes not cast		4	
1792	George Washington	Federalist	132	
	John Adams	Federalist	77	
	George Clinton	Dem.-Rep.	50	
	Thomas Jefferson	Dem.-Rep.	4	
	Aaron Burr	Dem.-Rep.	1	
	votes not cast		3	
1796	John Adams	Federalist	71	
	Thomas Jefferson	Dem.-Rep.	68	
	Thomas Pinckney	Federalist	59	
	Aaron Burr	Dem.-Rep.	30	
	others		48	
1800	Thomas Jefferson[1]	Dem.-Rep.	73	
	Aaron Burr	Dem.-Rep.	73	
	John Adams	Federalist	65	
	Charles C. Pinckney	Federalist	64	
	John Jay	Federalist	1	
1804	Thomas Jefferson	Dem.-Rep.	162	
	Charles C. Pinckney	Federalist	14	
1808	James Madison	Dem.-Rep.	122	
	Charles C. Pinckney	Federalist	47	
	George Clinton	Federalist	6	
	votes not cast		1	
1812	James Madison	Dem.-Rep.	128	
	DeWitt Clinton	Federalist	89	
	votes not cast		1	
1816	James Monroe	Dem.-Rep.	183	
	Rufus King	Federalist	34	
	votes not cast		4	
1820	James Monroe	Dem.-Rep.	231	
	John Quincy Adams	Dem.-Rep.	1	
	votes not cast		3	
1824	John Quincy Adams[2]	Dem.-Rep.	84	113,122
	Andrew Jackson	Dem.-Rep.	99	151,271
	William H. Crawford	Dem.-Rep.	37	40,856
	Henry Clay	Dem.-Rep.	41	47,531
1828	Andrew Jackson	Dem.-Rep.	178	642,553
	John Quincy Adams	Natl.-Rep.	83	500,897

1832	Andrew Jackson	Democratic	219	701,780
	Henry Clay	Natl.-Rep.	49	484,285
	John Floyd	no party	11	n.a.
	William Wirt	Anti-Masonic	7	100,715
	votes not cast		2	
1836	Martin Van Buren	Democratic	170	764,176
	William Henry Harrison	Whig	73	550,816
	Hugh Lawson White	Whig	26	146,107
	Daniel Webster	Whig	14	41,201
	W. P. Magnum	no party	11	
1840	William Henry Harrison	Whig	234	1,275,390
	Martin Van Buren	Democratic	60	1,128,854
1844	James K. Polk	Democratic	170	1,339,494
	Henry Clay	Whig	105	1,300,004
1848	Zachary Taylor	Whig	163	1,361,393
	Lewis Cass	Democratic	127	1,223,460
1852	Franklin Pierce	Democratic	254	1,607,510
	Winfield Scott	Whig	42	1,386,942
1856	James Buchanan	Democratic	174	1,836,072
	John C. Fremont	Republican	114	1,342,345
	Millard Fillmore	American	8	873,053
1860	Abraham Lincoln	Republican	180	1,865,908
	John C. Breckinridge	Southern-Dem.	72	848,019
	John Bell	Constl. Union	39	590,901
	Stephen A. Douglas	Democratic	12	1,380,202
1864	Abraham Lincoln	Union	212	2,218,388
	George B. McClellan	Democratic	21	1,812,807
1868	Ulysses S. Grant	Republican	214	3,013,650
	Horatio Seymour	Democratic	80	2,708,744
	votes not counted		23	
1872	Ulysses S. Grant	Republican	286	3,598,235
	Horace Greeley[3]	Dem., Lib. Rep.		2,834,761
	Thomas A. Hendricks	Democratic	42	
	B. Gratz Brown	Dem., Lib. Rep.	18	
	Charles J. Jenkins	Democratic	2	
	David Davis	Democratic	1	
	votes not counted		17	
1876	Rutherford B. Hayes[4]	Republican	185	4,034,311
	Samuel J. Tilden	Democratic	184	4,288,546
1880	James A. Garfield	Republican	214	4,446,158
	Winfield S. Hancock	Democratic	155	4,444,260
1884	Grover Cleveland	Democratic	219	4,874,621
	James G. Blaine	Republican	182	4,848,936
1888	Benjamin Harrison	Republican	233	5,443,892
	Grover Cleveland	Democratic	168	5,534,488
1892	Grover Cleveland	Democratic	277	5,551,883
	Benjamin Harrison	Republican	145	5,179,244
	James B. Weaver	Populist	22	1,024,280

1896	William McKinley	Republican	271	7,108,480
	William Jennings Bryan	Dem., Populist	176	6,511,495
1900	William McKinley	Republican	292	7,218,039
	William Jennings Bryan	Dem., Populist	155	6,358,345
1904	Theodore Roosevelt	Republican	336	7,626,593
	Alton B. Parker	Democratic	140	5,082,898
1908	William Howard Taft	Republican	321	7,676,258
	William Jennings Bryan	Democratic	162	6,406,801
1912	Woodrow Wilson	Democratic	435	6,293,152
	Theodore Roosevelt	Progressive	88	4,119,207
	William Howard Taft	Republican	8	3,486,333
1916	Woodrow Wilson	Democratic	277	9,126,300
	Charles Evans Hughes	Republican	254	8,546,789
1920	Warren G. Harding	Republican	404	16,133,314
	James M. Cox	Democratic	127	9,140,884
1924	Calvin Coolidge	Republican	382	15,717,553
	John W. Davis	Democratic	136	8,386,169
	Robert M. LaFollette	Progressive	13	4,814,050
1928	Herbert Hoover	Republican	444	21,411,991
	Alfred E. Smith	Democratic	87	15,000,185
1932	Franklin D. Roosevelt	Democratic	472	22,825,016
	Herbert Hoover	Republican	59	15,758,397
1936	Franklin D. Roosevelt	Democratic	523	27,747,636
	Alfred M. Landon	Republican	8	16,679,543
1940	Franklin D. Roosevelt	Democratic	449	27,263,448
	Wendell L. Willkie	Republican	82	22,336,260
1944	Franklin D. Roosevelt	Democratic	432	25,611,936
	Thomas E. Dewey	Republican	99	22,013,372
1948	Harry S Truman	Democratic	303	24,105,587
	Thomas E. Dewey	Republican	189	21,970,017
	J. Strom Thurmond	States' Rights	39	1,169,134
1952	Dwight D. Eisenhower	Republican	442	33,936,137
	Adlai E. Stevenson	Democratic	89	27,314,649
1956	Dwight D. Eisenhower	Republican	457	35,585,245
	Adlai E. Stevenson	Democratic	73[5]	26,030,172
1960	John F. Kennedy	Democratic	303	34,221,344
	Richard M. Nixon	Republican	219[6]	34,106,671
1964	Lyndon B. Johnson	Democratic	486	43,126,584
	Barry Goldwater	Republican	52	27,177,838
1968	Richard M. Nixon	Republican	301	31,785,148
	Hubert H. Humphrey	Democratic	191	31,274,503
	George Wallace	Am. Indep.	46	9,901,151
1972	Richard M. Nixon	Republican	520[7]	47,170,179
	George M. McGovern	Democratic	17	29,171,791

1976	Jimmy Carter	Democratic	297	40,830,763
	Gerald R. Ford	Republican	240[8]	39,147,793
1980	Ronald Reagan	Republican	489	43,904,153
	Jimmy Carter	Democratic	49	35,483,883
1984	Ronald Reagan	Republican	525	54,455,074
	Walter F. Mondale	Democratic	13	37,577,137
1988	George Bush	Republican	426	48,886,097
	Michael S. Dukakis	Democratic	111	41,809,074

---

1. Election decided in House of Representatives because of an electoral vote tie.

2. Electoral vote decided in House of Representatives because no candidate won an electoral vote majority.

3. Greeley died after the popular election but before the electoral vote tabulation. Democratic and Liberal Republican electors scattered their presidential votes among four other men.

4. Election decided by fifteen-member congressional Electoral Commission after electoral vote dispute caused by Florida, Louisiana, Oregon, and South Carolina each returning two sets of electoral votes.

5. One electoral vote from Alabama cast for Walter F. Jones.

6. Harry F. Byrd received fifteen electoral votes.

7. One electoral vote from Virginia cast for John Hospers.

8. One electoral vote from Washington cast for Ronald Reagan.

Sources: *America Votes,* volume 18, edited by Richard M. Scammon and Alice V. McGillivray (Washington, D.C.: Congressional Quarterly, 1989); *Guide to U.S. Elections,* second edition, John L. Moore, editor, Mary Ames Booker and H. Amy Stern, assistant editors (Washington, D.C.: Congressional Quarterly, 1985).

Presidential Candidates Not Receiving Electoral Votes

YEAR	PRESIDENTIAL CANDIDATE	PARTY	POPULAR VOTE	VICE-PRESIDENTIAL CANDIDATE
1840	James G. Birney	Liberty	6,797	Thomas Earle
1844	James G. Birney	Liberty	62,103	Thomas Morris
1848	Martin Van Buren	Free Soil	291,501	Charles Francis Adams
	Gerrit Smith	Liberty	2,545	Charles C. Foote
1852	John P. Hale	Free Soil	155,210	George W. Julian
1872	Charles O'Connor	Straight-Out	18,602	John Quincy Adams
	James Black	Prohibition	3,371	John Russell
1876	Peter Cooper	Greenback	75,973	Samuel F. Cary
	Green Clay Smith	Prohibition	6,743	Gideon T. Stewart
1880	James B. Weaver	Greenback	305,997	Benjamin Chambers
	Neal Dow	Prohibition	9,674	Henry A. Thompson
1884	Benjamin F. Butler	Greenback	175,096	Absolom M. West
	John P. St. John	Prohibition	147,482	William Daniel
1888	Clinton B. Fisk	Prohibition	249,813	John A. Brooks
	Alson B. Streeter	Union Labor	146,602	Charles E. Cunningham
1892	John Bidwell	Prohibition	270,770	James B. Cranfill
	Simon Wing	Socialist Labor	21,163	Charles H. Matchett
1896	John M. Palmer	Natl. Dem.	133,435	Simon Bolivar Buckner
	Joshua Levering	Prohibition	125,072	Hale Johnson
	Charles H. Matchett	Socialist Labor	35,356	Matthew Maguire
	Charles E. Bentley	Prohibition	19,363	James Southgate
1900	John C. Woolley	Prohibition	209,004	Henry B. Metcalf
	Eugene V. Debs	Socialist	86,935	Job Harriman
	Wharton Barker	Populist	50,340	Ignatius Donnelly
	Joseph F. Malloney	Socialist Labor	40,900	Valentine Remmel
1904	Eugene V. Debs	Socialist	402,489	Benjamin Hanford
	Silas C. Swallow	Prohibition	258,596	George W. Carroll
	Thomas E. Watson	Populist	114,051	Thomas H. Tibbles
	Charles H. Corregan	Socialist Labor	33,156	William W. Cox
1908	Eugene V. Debs	Socialist	420,380	Benjamin Hanford
	Eugene W. Chafin	Prohibition	252,821	Aaron S. Watkins
	Thomas L. Hisgen	Independence	82,537	John T. Graves
	Thomas E. Watson	Populist	28,376	Samuel Williams
	August Gilhaus	Socialist Labor	14,018	Donald L. Munro
1912	Eugene V. Debs	Socialist	900,369	Emil Seidel
	Eugene W. Chafin	Prohibition	207,972	Aaron S. Watkins
	Arthur E. Reimer	Socialist Labor	29,374	August Gilhaus

1916	Allan L. Benson	Socialist	589,924	George R. Kirkpatrick
	J. Frank Hanly	Prohibition	221,030	Ira Landrith
	Arthur E. Reimer	Socialist Labor	15,284	Caleb Harrison
1920	Eugene V. Debs	Socialist	913,664	Seymour Stedman
	Parley P. Christensen	Farmer-Labor	264,540	Maximilian S. Hayes
	Aaron Sherman Watkins	Prohibition	188,391	David L. Colvin
	James E. Ferguson	American	47,812	William J. Hough
	William W. Cox	Socialist Labor	30,418	August Gilhaus
	Robert C. Macauley	Single Tax	5,960	R. G. Barnum
1924	Herman P. Faris	Prohibition	54,833	Marie C. Brehm
	William Z. Foster	Communist	38,080	Benjamin Gitlow
	Frank T. Johns	Socialist Labor	28,368	Verne L. Reynolds
	Gilbert O. Nations	American	24,215	Charles H. Randall
	William J. Wallace	Commonwealth	2,919	John C. Lincoln
1928	Norman M. Thomas	Socialist	266,453	James H. Maurer
	William Z. Foster	Communist	48,170	Benjamin Gitlow
	William F. Varney	Prohibition	34,489	James A. Edgerton
	Verne L. Reynolds	Socialist Labor	21,608	Jeremiah Crowley
	Frank E. Webb	Farmer-Labor	6,390	Will Vereen
1932	Norman M. Thomas	Socialist	883,990	James H. Maurer
	William Z. Foster	Communist	102,221	James W. Ford
	William D. Upshaw	Prohibition	81,916	Frank S. Regan
	William H. Harvey	Liberty	53,199	Frank B. Hemenway
	Verne L. Reynolds	Socialist Labor	34,028	John W. Aiken
	Jacob S. Coxey	Farmer-Labor	7,431	Julius B. Reiter
1936	William Lemke	Union	892,492	Thomas C. O'Brien
	Norman M. Thomas	Socialist	187,785	George A. Nelson
	Earl Browder	Communist	79,211	James W. Ford
	David L. Colvin	Prohibition	37,668	Alvin York
	John W. Aiken	Socialist Labor	12,790	Emil F. Teichert
1940	Norman M. Thomas	Socialist	116,827	Maynard C. Krueger
	Roger W. Babson	Prohibition	58,685	Edgar V. Moorman
	Earl Browder	Communist	48,548	James W. Ford
	John W. Aiken	Socialist Labor	14,883	Aaron M. Orange
1944	Norman M. Thomas	Socialist	79,000	Darlington Hoopes
	Claude A. Watson	Prohibition	74,733	Andrew Johnson
	Edward A. Teichert	Socialist Labor	45,179	Arla A. Albaugh
1948	Henry A. Wallace	Progressive	1,157,057	Glen H. Taylor
	Norman M. Thomas	Socialist	138,973	Tucker P. Smith
	Claude A. Watson	Prohibition	103,489	Dale Learn
	Edward A. Teichert	Socialist Labor	29,038	Stephen Emery
	Farrell Dobbs	Socialist Workers	13,614	Grace Carlson
1952	Vincent Hallinan	Progressive	140,416	Charlotta A. Bass
	Stuart Hamblen	Prohibition	73,413	Enoch A. Holtwick
	Eric Hass	Socialist Labor	30,250	Stephen Emery
	Darlington Hoopes	Socialist	20,065	Samuel H. Friedman
	Douglas MacArthur	Constitution	17,200	Harry F. Byrd
	Farrell Dobbs	Socialist Workers	10,312	Myra T. Weiss
1956	T. Coleman Andrews	Constitution	108,055	n.a.
	Eric Hass	Socialist Labor	44,300	Georgia Cozzini
	Enoch A. Holtwick	Prohibition	41,937	Edward M. Cooper
	Farrell Dobbs	Socialist Workers	7,797	Myra T. Weiss
	Darlington Hoopes	Socialist	2,044	Samuel H. Friedman

1960	Orval E. Faubus	States' Rights	209,314	John G. Crommelin
	Eric Hass	Socialist Labor	47,522	Georgia Cozzini
	Rutherford L. Decker	Prohibition	44,087	E. Harold Munn
	Farrell Dobbs	Socialist Workers	40,166	Myra T. Weiss
1964	Eric Hass	Socialist Labor	45,187	Henning A. Blomen
	Clifton DeBerry	Socialist Workers	32,701	Edward Shaw
	E. Harold Munn	Prohibition	23,266	Mark Shaw
	John Kasper	States' Rights	6,953	J. B. Stoner
1968	Henning A. Blowen	Socialist Labor	52,591	George Sam Taylor
	Dick Gregory	Freedom & Peace	47,097	none
	Fred Halstead	Socialist Workers	41,930	Paul Boutelle
	Eugene McCarthy	Independent	25,552	various
	E. Harold Munn	Prohibition	14,915	Rolland E. Fisler
1972	John G. Schmitz	Am. Indep.	1,090,673	Thomas J. Anderson
	Benjamin Spock	People's	78,751	Julius Hobson
	Louis Fisher	Socialist Labor	53,811	Genevieve Gunderson
	Linda Jenness	Socialist Workers	37,423	Andrew Pulley
	Gus Hall	Communist	25,343	Jarvis Tyner
	Evelyn Reed	Socialist Workers	13,878	Andrew Pulley
	E. Harold Munn	Prohibition	12,818	Marshall E. Uncepher
1976	Eugene McCarthy	independent	756,691	various
	Roger MacBride	Libertarian	173,011	David Bergland
	Lester Maddox	Am. Indep.	170,531	William Dyke
	Thomas J. Anderson	American	160,773	Rufus Shackelford
	Peter Camejo	Socialist Workers	91,314	Willie Mae Reid
	Gus Hall	Communist	58,992	Jarvis Tyner
	Margaret Wright	People's	49,024	Benjamin Spock
	Lyndon LaRouche	U.S. Labor	40,043	R. W. Evans
	Benjamin C. Bubar	Prohibition	15,934	Earl F. Dodge
	Jules Levin	Socialist Labor	9,616	Constance Blumen
	Frank P. Zeidler	Socialist	6,038	J. Q. Brisben
1980	John Anderson	independent	5,720,060	Patrick Lucey
	Ed Clark	Libertarian	921,299	David Koch
	Barry Commoner	Citizens	234,294	LaDonna Harris
	Gus Hall	Communist	45,023	Angela Davis
	John R. Rarick	Am. Indep.	41,268	Eileen M. Shearer
	Clifton DeBerry	Socialist Workers	38,737	Matilde Zimmerman
	Ellen McCormack	Right to Life	32,327	Carroll Driscoll
	Maureen Smith	Peace & Freedom	18,116	Elizabeth Barron
	Deirdre Griswold	Workers World	13,300	Larry Holmes
	Benjamin C. Bubar	Statesman	7,212	Earl F. Dodge
	David McReynolds	Socialist	6,898	Diane Drufenbrock
	Percy L. Greaves	American	6,647	Frank L. Varnum
	Andrew Pulley	Socialist Workers	6,272	Matilde Zimmerman
1984	David Bergland	Libertarian	228,314	James A. Lewis
	Lyndon LaRouche	independent	78,807	Billy M. Davis
	Sonia Johnson	Citizens	72,200	Richard Walton
	Bob Richards	Populist	66,336	Maureen Salaman
	Dennis L. Serrette	Ind. Alliance	46,852	Nancy Ross
	Gus Hall	Communist	36,386	Angela Davis
	Mel Mason	Socialist Workers	24,706	Matilde Zimmerman
	Larry Holmes	Workers World	15,329	Gloria La Riva
	Delmar Davis	American	13,161	Traves Brownlee
	Ed Winn	Workers League	10,801	various
	Earl F. Dodge	Prohibition	4,242	Warren C. Martin

1988	Ron Paul	Libertarian	432,179	Andre V. Marron
	Lenora B. Fulani	New Alliance	217,219	Joyce Dattner
	David E. Duke	Populist	47,047	Floyd C. Parker
	Eugene McCarthy	Consumer	30,905	Florence Rice
	James C. Griffin	Am. Indep.	27,818	Charles J. Morsa
	Lyndon LaRouche	Econ. Recovery	25,562	Debra H. Freeman
	William Marra	Right to Life	20,504	Joan Andrews
	Ed Winn	Workers League	18,693	Barry Porster
	James Warren	Socialist Workers	15,604	Kathleen Mickells
	Herbert Lewin	Peace & Freedom	10,370	Vikki Murdock
	Earl F. Dodge	Prohibition	8,002	George Ormsby
	Larry Holmes	Workers World	7,846	Gloria La Riva
	Willa Kenoyer	Socialist	3,882	Ron Enrenreich
	Delmar Dennis	American	3,475	Earl Jeppson
	Jack Herer	Grassroots	1,949	Dana Beal

Sources: *America Votes,* volume 18, edited by Richard M. Scammon and Alice V. McGillivray (Washington, D.C.: Congressional Quarterly, 1989); *Guide to U.S. Elections,* second edition, John L. Moore, editor, Mary Ames Booker and H. Amy Stern, assistant editors (Washington, D.C.: Congressional Quarterly, 1985).

Books by the Presidents Published During Their Lifetimes

The job of the presidency is such that almost everything the president writes becomes a potential subject for historical analysis; and anything of interest to historians is liable to be published. In addition to the official documents every president has generated, scholars have published editions of the letters, essays, speeches, and other writings of many of the presidents. Much of this material was never intended for public eyes, but its value as historical evidence is said to supersede the rights of presidential privacy, even in the opinion of most of the presidents. A complete compilation of published presidential writings would run to nearly book length; consult Fenton S. Martin and Robert U. Goehlert's *American Presidents: A Bibliography* (1987) and Frank L. Schick, Renee Schick, and Marc Carroll's *Records of the Presidency: Presidential Papers and Libraries from Washington to Reagan* (1989) for the most complete lists.

Some of the presidents, especially those of the twentieth century, also wrote works intended for publication. Limiting the list to books the presidents intended for publication omits certain well-known writings, such as *The Autobiography of Thomas Jefferson,* first published in 1914; but it also conveys a view of the presidents as literary men of their times. See the Martin and Goehlert bibliography cited above for lists of posthumously published presidential writings.

JOHN ADAMS

A Defence of the Constitutions of Government of the United States of America, 3 volumes. London: C. Dilly, 1787-1788. Volume 1, New York: H. Gaine, 1787; Philadelphia: Hall & Sellers, 1787; Boston: Edmund Freeman, 1787. 3 volumes, Philadelphia: William Cobbett, 1797.

Discourses on Davila. A series of papers, on political history. Boston: Russell & Cutler, 1805.

THOMAS JEFFERSON

Notes on the State of Virginia. Paris, 1784-1785; London: J. Stockdale, 1787; Philadelphia: Prichard & Hall, 1788.

JAMES MADISON

A View of the conduct of the executive, in the foreign affairs of the United States, connected with the mission to the French republic, during the years 1794, 5, & 6. Philadelphia: Benj. Franklin Bache, 1797.

JOHN QUINCY ADAMS

Dermont MacMorrogh, or, The Conquest of Ireland; an historical tale of the twelfth century. Boston: Carter, Hendree, 1832.

The Lives of James Madison and James Monroe, fourth and sixth presidents of the United States. Buffalo: G. H. Derby, 1850.

JAMES BUCHANAN

Mr. Buchanan's Administration on the Eve of the Rebellion. New York: Appleton, 1865.

ULYSSES S. GRANT

Personal Memoirs of U. S. Grant, 2 volumes. New York: C. L. Webster, 1885-1886.

GROVER CLEVELAND

Presidential Problems. New York: Century, 1904.

Fishing and Hunting Sketches. New York; Outing Publishing Co., 1906.

Good Citizenship. Philadelphia: H. Altemus, 1908.

BENJAMIN HARRISON

This Country of Ours. New York: Scribners, 1897.

Views of an Ex-President. Indianapolis: Bowen-Merrill, 1901.

WILLIAM MCKINLEY

The Tariff in the Days of Henry Clay, and Since. New York: Henry Clay Publishing Co., 1896.

THEODORE ROOSEVELT

The Naval War of 1812. New York: Putnam's, 1882.

Hunting Trips of a Ranchman: Sketches of Sport on the Northern Cattle Plains. New York & London: Putnam's, 1885.

Life of Thomas Hart Benton. Boston & New York: Houghton, Mifflin, 1886.

Gouverneur Morris. Boston & New York: Houghton, Mifflin, 1888.

Ranch Life and the Hunting Trail. New York: Century, 1888.

The Winning of the West: An Account of the Exploration and Settling of Our Country from the Alleghanies to the Pacific, 4 volumes. New York & London: Putnam's, 1889-1896.

New York. New York & London: Longmans, Green, 1891.

Hero Tales from American History, by Roosevelt and Henry Cabot Lodge. New York: Century, 1895.

The Rough Riders. New York: Scribners, 1899.

African Game Trails: An Acccount of the African Wanderings of an American Hunter-Naturalist. New York: Scribners, 1910.

The New Nationalism. New York: Outlook Publishing Co., 1910.

History as Literature. New York: Scribners, 1913.

Theodore Roosevelt: An Autobiography. New York: Macmillan, 1913.

Life-histories of African Game Animals, 2 volumes. New York: Scribners, 1914.

Through the Brazilian Wilderness. New York: Scribners, 1914.

America and the World War. New York: Scribners, 1915.

Fear God and Take Your Own Part. New York: George H. Doran, 1916.

The Foes of Our Own Household. New York: George H. Doran, 1917.

National Strength and International Duty. Princeton: Princeton University Press, 1917.

WILLIAM HOWARD TAFT

Four Aspects of Civic Duty. New York: Scribners, 1906.

Our Chief Magistrate and His Powers. New York: Columbia University Press, 1916.

WOODROW WILSON

Congressional Government: A Study in American Politics. Boston: Houghton, Mifflin, 1885.

The State: Elements of Historical and Practical Politics. A Sketch of Institutional History and Administration. Boston: Heath, 1889.

An Old Master, and Other Political Essays. New York: Scribners, 1893.

Mere Literature, and Other Essays. Boston & New York: Houghton, Mifflin, 1896.

George Washington. New York & London: Harper, 1897.

A History of the American People, 5 volumes. New York & London: Harper, 1902.

Woodrow Wilson's Case for the League of Nations, Compiled with His Approval by Hamilton Foley. Princeton: Princeton University Press, 1923.

CALVIN COOLIDGE

The Autobiography of Calvin Coolidge. New York: Macmillan, 1929.

HERBERT HOOVER

Principles of Mining: Valuation, Organization and Administration: Copper, Gold,

Lead, Silver, Tin and Zinc. New York: Hill, 1909.
American Individualism. New York: Doubleday, Page, 1922.
The Challenge to Liberty. New York & London: Scribners, 1934.
America's First Crusade. New York: Scribners, 1942.
The Problems of Lasting Peace, by Hoover and Hugh Gibson. Garden City, N.Y.: Doubleday, Doran, 1942.
The Basis of Lasting Peace. New York: Van Nostrand, 1945.
Memoirs, 3 volumes. New York: Macmillan, 1951-1952.
The Ordeal of Woodrow Wilson. New York: McGraw-Hill, 1958.
An American Epic, 3 volumes. Chicago: Regnery, 1959-1961.
Fishing for Fun—And to Wash Your Soul. New York: Random House, 1963.

FRANKLIN D. ROOSEVELT

The Happy Warrior, Alfred E. Smith: A Study of a Public Servant. Boston & New York: Houghton Mifflin, 1928.

HARRY S TRUMAN

Year of Decisions. Garden City, N.Y.: Doubleday, 1955.
Years of Trial and Hope. Garden City, N.Y.: Doubleday, 1956.
Mr. Citizen. New York: Geis, 1960.

DWIGHT D. EISENHOWER

Crusade in Europe. Garden City, N.Y.: Doubleday, 1948.
The White House Years: Mandate for Change, 1953-1956. Garden City, N.Y.: Doubleday, 1963.
The White House Years: Waging Peace, 1956-1961. Garden City, N.Y.: Doubleday, 1965.
At Ease: Stories I Tell to Friends. Garden City, N.Y.: Doubleday, 1967.

JOHN F. KENNEDY

Why England Slept. New York: Funk, 1940; London: Hutchinson, 1940.
Profiles in Courage. New York: Harper, 1956.

LYNDON B. JOHNSON

The Vantage Point: Perspectives of the Presidency, 1963-1969. New York: Holt, Rinehart & Winston, 1971.

RICHARD M. NIXON

Six Crises. Garden City, N.Y.: Doubleday, 1962.
RN: The Memoirs of Richard Nixon. New York: Grosset & Dunlap, 1978.
The Real War. New York: Warner, 1980.
Leaders. New York: Warner, 1982.
Real Peace: Strategy for the West. Boston: Little, Brown, 1984.
No More Vietnams. New York: Arbor, 1985.
1999: Victory Without War. New York: Simon & Schuster, 1988.
In the Arena: A Memoir of Victory, Defeat & Renewal. New York: Simon & Schuster, 1990.

JIMMY CARTER

Why Not the Best? Nashville, Tenn.: Broadman, 1975.
Keeping Faith: Memoirs of a President. New York: Bantam, 1982.
The Blood of Abraham. Boston: Houghton Mifflin, 1985.
Everything to Gain: Making the Most Out of the Rest of Your Life, by Carter and Rosalyn Carter. New York: Random, 1987.
An Outdoor Journal: Adventures and Reflections. New York: Bantam, 1988.

RONALD REAGAN

Where's the Rest of Me? The Autobiography of Ronald Reagan, by Reagan and Richard G. Hubler. New York: Karz, 1965.
An American Life: The Autobiography. New York: Simon & Schuster, 1990.

GEORGE BUSH

Looking Forward: An Autobiography, by Bush and Victor Gold. Garden City, N.Y.: Doubleday, 1987.

Basic Reference Sources for the Study of the Presidency

What follows is a brief list of readily available material pertinent to presidential studies:

1. Bibliographies
2. Journals
3. Indexes and Registers of Presidential Papers
4. Published Documents
5. General Works
6. Biographical and Historical Sources

The section on published documents lists the major scholarly editions of presidential papers, letters, and other writings; the section on biographical and historical sources lists the major biographies of the presidents and a selection of analytical writings. The sections on published documents and biographical and historical sources are organized by president in the order in which the presidents served their terms.

1. Bibliographies

Davison, Kenneth E. *The American Presidency: A Guide to Information Sources.* Detroit: Gale, 1983. One-volume compilation of aids to presidential research; books and articles on the presidency, first ladies, presidential elections, presidential documents, and libraries and museums; and brief lists of books and articles relating to each president.

Martin, Fenton S., and Robert U. Goehlert. *The American Presidency: A Bibliography.* Washington, D.C.: Congressional Quarterly, 1987. Definitive compilation of books and articles on the presidency arranged under the following headings: Perspectives on the Presidency; The Presidency and the Law; The Organization of the Presidency; The Presidency and Presidents; The President and Government; The President and the Media; The Presidency and Foreign Affairs; The Presidency and the World; The Presidency and Society; The Selection of Presidents; Presidential Elections; Problems of the Presidency; and Extra-Presidential Topics.

Martin and Goehlert. *American Presidents: A Bibliography.* Washington, D.C.: Congressional Quarterly, 1987. Definitive compilation of books and articles on the presidents, organized by president in the order in which the presidents served their terms, under the following headings: Biographies; Private Life; Public Career; and Presidential Years. Also lists the complete publications of each president.

2. Journals

Abraham Lincoln Quarterly, 1940-1952.
Presidential Studies Quarterly, 1972- .

3. Indexes and Registers

Index to the George Washington Papers.

Washington, D.C.: Library of Congress, Manuscript Division, 1964.

Index to the Thomas Jefferson Papers. Washington, D.C.: Library of Congress, Manuscript Division, 1976.

Index to the James Madison Papers. Washington, D.C.: Library of Congress, Manuscript Division, 1965.

Index to the James Monroe Papers. Washington, D.C.: Library of Congress, Manuscript Division, 1963.

Index to the Andrew Jackson Papers. Washington, D.C.: Library of Congress, Manuscript Division, 1967.

Calendar of the Papers of Martin Van Buren, compiled by Elizabeth Howard West. Washington, D.C.: U.S. Government Printing Office, 1910.

Index to the William Henry Harrison Papers. Washington, D.C.: Library of Congress, 1960.

Index to the John Tyler Papers. Washington, D.C.: Library of Congress, Manuscript Division, 1961.

Index to the Zachary Taylor Papers. Washington, D.C.: Library of Congress, Manuscript Division, 1960.

Index to the Franklin Pierce Papers. Washington, D.C.: Library of Congress, Manuscript Division, 1962.

James Buchanan and Harriet [Lane] Johnston: A Register and Index to Their Papers in the Library of Congress. Washington, D.C.: Library of Congress, Manuscript Division, 1979.

Index to the Abraham Lincoln Papers. Washington, D.C.: Library of Congress, Manuscript Division, 1960.

Index to the Andrew Johnson Papers. Washington, D.C.: Library of Congress, Manuscript Division, 1963.

Index to the Ulysses S. Grant Papers. Washington, D.C.: Library of Congress, Manuscript Division, 1965.

Index to the James A. Garfield Papers. Washington, D.C.: Library of Congress, Manuscript Division, 1973.

Index to the Chester Arthur Papers. Washington, D.C.: Library of Congress, Manuscript Division, 1961.

Index to the Grover Cleveland Papers. Washington, D.C.: Library of Congress, Manuscript Division, 1965.

Index to the Benjamin Harrison Papers. Washington, D.C.: Library of Congress, Manuscript Division, 1964.

Index to the William McKinley Papers. Washington, D.C.: Library of Congress, Manuscript Division, 1963.

Index to the Theodore Roosevelt Papers. Washington, D.C.: Library of Congress, Manuscript Division, 1970.

Index to the William Howard Taft Papers, 6 volumes. Washington, D.C.: Library of Congress, Manuscript Division, 1972.

Index to the Woodrow Wilson Papers, 3 volumes. Washington, D.C.: Library of Congress, 1973.

Index to the Calvin Coolidge Papers. Washington, D.C.: Library of Congress, Manuscript Division, 1965.

Historical Materials in the Herbert Hoover Library. West Branch, Iowa: Herbert Hoover Presidential Library, 1985.

Historical Materials in the Franklin D. Roosevelt Library. Hyde Park, N.Y.: Franklin D. Roosevelt Library, 1985.

Historical Materials in the Harry S Truman Library. Independence, Mo.: Harry S Truman Library, 1984.

Historical Materials in the Dwight D. Eisenhower Library. Abilene, Kan.: Dwight D. Eisenhower Library, 1984.

Historical Materials in the John Fitzgerald Kennedy Library. Boston: John Fitzgerald Kennedy Library, 1986.

LBJ: A Bibliography Prepared by the Staff of the LBJ Library. Austin, Tex.: University of Texas Press, 1984.

Historical Materials in the Gerald R. Ford Library. Ann Arbor, Mich.: Gerald R. Ford Library, 1986.

4. PUBLISHED DOCUMENTS

GEORGE WASHINGTON

The Diaries of George Washington, 6 volumes, Dorothy Twohig, general editor. Charlottesville: University Press of Virginia, 1976-1979.

The Papers of George Washington, 6 volumes to date, W. W. Abbot, general editor. Charlottesville: University

Press of Virginia, 1983- .

The Writings of George Washington from the Original Manuscript Sources, 1745-1799, 39 volumes, John C. Fitzpatrick, general editor. Washington, D.C.: U.S. Government Printing Office, 1931-1944.

JOHN ADAMS

The Adams-Jefferson Letters: The Complete Correspondence between Thomas Jefferson and Abigail and John Adams, 2 volumes, edited by Lester J. Cappon. Chapel Hill: University of North Carolina Press, 1959.

The Papers of John Adams, 8 volumes to date, Robert J. Taylor, general editor, volumes 1-6; Gregg L. Lint, general editor, volumes 7-8. Cambridge, Mass.: Belknap Press of Harvard University Press, 1977- .

THOMAS JEFFERSON

The Adams-Jefferson Letters: The Complete Correspondence of Thomas Jefferson and Abigail and John Adams, 2 volumes, edited by Lester J. Cappon. Chapel Hill: University of North Carolina Press, 1959.

The Garden and Farm Books of Thomas Jefferson, edited by Robert C. Baron. Golden, Colo.: Fulcrum, 1987.

Jefferson's Parliamentary Writings: "Parliamentary Pocket-Book" and A Manual of Parliamentary Practice, edited, with an introduction, by Wilbur Samuel Howell. Princeton: Princeton University Press, 1988.

The Papers of Thomas Jefferson, 24 volumes to date, Julian P. Boyd, general editor, volumes 1-20; Charles T. Cullen, general editor, volumes 21-23; John Catanzariti, general editor, volume 24. Princeton: Princeton University Press, 1950- .

JAMES MADISON

Debates on the Adoption of the Federal Constitution, 5 volumes. Salem, N.H.: Ayer, 1987.

James Madison on Religious Liberty, edited, with an introduction, by Robert S. Alley. Buffalo, N.Y.: Prometheus, 1985.

The Papers of James Madison, 17 volumes to date, William T. Hutchinson and William M. E. Rachal, general editors, volumes 1-7; Rachal and Robert A. Rutland, general editors, volume 8; Rutland, general editor, volumes 9-10; Rutland and Charles F. Hobson, general editors, volumes 11-13; Rutland and Thomas A. Mason, general editors, volumes 14-15; Mason, J. C. A. Stagg, and Jeanne K. Sisson, general editors, volume 16; Rutland and Mason, general editors, Presidential Series volume 1. Volumes 1-10, Chicago: University of Chicago Press, 1962-1977; volumes 11-16, Charlottesville: University Press of Virginia, 1977-1984; Presidential Series, Charlottesville: University Press of Virginia, 1984- .

JAMES MONROE

The Writings of James Monroe, Including a Collection of His Public and Private Papers Now for the First Time Printed, 7 volumes, edited by Stanislaus Murray Hamilton. New York & London: Putnam's, 1898-1903.

JOHN QUINCY ADAMS

Diary of John Quincy Adams, 2 volumes, Robert J. Taylor, general editor, David Grayson Allen, associate editor. Cambridge, Mass. & London: Belknap Press of Harvard University Press, 1981.

Memoirs of John Quincy Adams, Comprising Portions of His Diary from 1795 to 1848, 12 volumes, edited by Charles Francis Adams. Philadelphia: Lippincott, 1874-1877.

Writings of John Quincy Adams, 7 volumes, edited by Worthington Chauncey Ford. New York: Macmillan, 1913-1917.

ANDREW JACKSON

Legal Papers of Andrew Jackson, edited by James W. Ely, Jr., and Theodore Brown, Jr.; consulting editor, William J. Harbison. Knoxville: University of Tennessee Press, 1987.

The Papers of Andrew Jackson, 2 volumes to date, Sam B. Smith and Harriet Chappelle Owsley, general editors, volume 1; Harold D. Mosser and Sharon Macpherson, general editors, volume 2. Knoxville: University of Tennessee Press, 1980- .

MILLARD FILLMORE

The Millard Fillmore Papers, 2 volumes, edited by Frank Severance. Buffalo, N.Y.: Buffalo and Erie County Historical Society, 1907.

JAMES K. POLK

Correspondence of James K. Polk, 7 volumes to date, Herbert Weaver, general editor, volumes 1-4; Wayne Cutler, general editor, volumes 5-7. Nashville: Vanderbilt University Press, 1969- .

The Diary of James K. Polk During His Presidency, 1845-1849, 4 volumes, edited by Milo Milton Quaife. Chicago: McClurg, 1910.

ABRAHAM LINCOLN

The Collected Works of Abraham Lincoln, 9 volumes, Roy P. Basler, general editor. New Brunswick, N.J.: Rutgers University Press, 1953-1955.

ANDREW JOHNSON

The Papers of Andrew Johnson, 7 volumes to date, Leroy P. Graf and Ralph W. Haskins, general editors, volumes 1-6; Graf, general editor, volume 7. Knoxville: University of Tennessee Press, 1967- .

RUTHERFORD B. HAYES

Diary and Letters of Rutherford Birchard Hayes, 5 volumes, edited by Charles R. Williams. Columbus: Ohio State Archaeological and Historical Society, 1922-1926.

JAMES A. GARFIELD

The Diary of James A. Garfield, 4 volumes, edited by Harry James Brown and Frederick D. Williams. East Lansing: Michigan State University Press, 1967-1981.

The Works of James Abram Garfield, 2 volumes, edited by Burke A. Hinsdale. Boston: Osgood, 1882-1883.

GROVER CLEVELAND

Letters of Grover Cleveland, 1850-1908, edited by Allan Nevins. Boston & New York: Houghton Mifflin, 1933.

THEODORE ROOSEVELT

American Bears: Selections from the Writings of Theodore Roosevelt, edited, with an introduction, by Paul Schullery. Boulder: Colorado Associated University Press, 1983.

Selections from the Correspondence of Theodore Roosevelt and Henry Cabot Lodge: 1884-1918, 2 volumes. New York & London: Scribners, 1925.

WOODROW WILSON

Papers of Woodrow Wilson, 40 volumes, Arthur S. Link, general editor. Princeton: Princeton University Press, 1966-1986.

FRANKLIN D. ROOSEVELT

Churchill and Roosevelt: The Complete Correspondence, 3 volumes, edited by Warren F. Kimball. Princeton: Princeton University Press, 1984.

FDR: His Personal Letters, 4 volumes, edited by Elliott Roosevelt. New York: Duell, Sloan & Pearce, 1947-1950.

Public Papers and Addresses of Franklin D. Roosevelt, 13 volumes, edited by Samuel I. Rosenman. New York: Random House, 1938-1950.

Roosevelt and Churchill: Their Secret Wartime Correspondence, edited by Francis L. Loewenheim, Harold D. Langley, and Manfred Jonas. New York: Saturday Review Press, 1975.

HARRY S TRUMAN

The Autobiography of Harry S. Truman, edited by Robert H. Ferrell. Boulder: Colorado Associated University Press, 1980.

Dear Bess: The Letters from Harry to Bess Truman, 1910-1959, edited by Ferrell. New York: Norton, 1983.

Off the Record: The Private Papers of Harry Truman, edited by Ferrell. New York: Harper & Row, 1980.

DWIGHT D. EISENHOWER

The Eisenhower Diaries, edited by Robert H. Ferrell. New York: Norton, 1981.

Letters to Mamie, edited by John S. Eisenhower. Garden City, N.Y.: Doubleday, 1978.

Ike's Letters to a Friend, 1941-1958, edited, with an introduction, by Robert Griffith. Lawrence: University Press of Kansas, 1984.

The Papers of Dwight David Eisenhower, 9 volumes, edited by Alfred D. Chandler, Jr. Baltimore: Johns Hopkins University Press, 1970-1978.

RICHARD M. NIXON

The White House Transcripts: Submission of Recorded Presidential Conversations to the Committee on the Judiciary of the House of Representatives. New York: Bantam, 1974.

5. GENERAL WORKS

Armbruster, Maxim Ethan. *The Presidents of the United States and Their Administrations from Washington to Nixon*. New York: Horizon, 1969.

Boller, Paul F., Jr. *Presidential Anecdotes*. Harmondsworth, U.K. & New York: Penguin, 1982.

Clark, James C. *Faded Glory: Presidents Out of Power*. New York: Praeger, 1985.

DeGregorio, William A. *The Complete Book of U.S. Presidents*, second edition. New York: Dembner, 1989.

Goebel, Dorothy Burne, and Julius Goebel, Jr. *Generals in the White House*. Garden City, N.Y.: Doubleday, Doran, 1945.

Haas, Irvin. *Historic Homes of the American Presidents*. New York: David McKay, 1976.

Jones, Cranston. *Homes of the American Presidents*. New York: McGraw-Hill, 1962.

Kane, Joseph Nathan. *Facts About the Presidents: A Compilation of Biographical and Historical Data*. New York: Wilson, 1959.

Leish, Kenneth W., ed. *The American Heritage Pictorial History of the Presidents of the United States*, 2 volumes. New York: Simon & Schuster, 1968.

Martin, Asa E. *After the White House*. State College, Penn.: Penns Valley, 1951.

Perling, J. J. *President's Sons: The Prestige of Name in a Democracy*. New York: Odyssey, 1947.

Quinn, Sandra L., and Sanford Katner. *America's Royalty: All the Presidents' Children*. Westport, Conn.: Greenwood, 1983.

Schick, Frank L., Renee Schick, and Mark Carroll. *Records of the Presidency: Presidential Papers and Libraries from Washington to Reagan*. Phoenix, Ariz.: Oryx, 1989.

Taylor, Tim. *The Book of Presidents*. New York: Arno, 1972.

Whitney, David C. *The American Presidents*, seventh edition. Englewood Cliffs, N.J.: Prentice-Hall, 1990.

6. SELECTED BIOGRAPHICAL AND HISTORICAL SOURCES

GEORGE WASHINGTON

Alden, John Richard. *George Washington: A Biography*. Baton Rouge: Louisiana State University Press, 1984.

Cunliffe, Marcus. *George Washington: Man and Monument*. Boston: Little, Brown, 1958.

Ferling, John E. *The First of Men: A Life of George Washington*. Knoxville: University of Tennessee Press, 1988.

Flexner, James T. *George Washington: A Biography*, 4 volumes. Boston: Little, Brown, 1965-1972.

Freeman, Douglas Southall. *George Washington: A Biography*, 7 volumes. New York: Scribners, 1948-1957.

McDonald, Forrest. *The Presidency of George Washington*. Lawrence: University Press of Kansas, 1974.

Reuter, Frank T. *Trials and Triumphs: George Washington's Foreign Policy.* Fort Worth: Texas Christian University Press, 1983.

Schwartz, Barry. *George Washington: The Making of an American Symbol.* New York: Free Press, 1987.

Wright, Esmond. *Washington and the American Revolution.* London: English Universities Press, 1957.

JOHN ADAMS

Bowen, Catherine Drinker. *John Adams and the American Revolution.* Boston: Little, Brown, 1950.

Brown, Ralph Adams. *The Presidency of John Adams.* Lawrence: University Press of Kansas, 1975.

Burleigh, Ann Husted. *John Adams.* New Rochelle, N.Y.: Arlington House, 1969.

Smith, Page. *John Adams,* 2 volumes. Garden City, N.Y.: Doubleday, 1962.

Shaw, Peter. *The Character of John Adams.* Chapel Hill: University of North Carolina Press, 1976.

THOMAS JEFFERSON

Brodie, Fawn. *Thomas Jefferson: An Intimate History.* New York: Norton, 1974.

Cunningham, Noble E., Jr. *In Pursuit of Reason: The Life of Thomas Jefferson.* Baton Rouge: Louisiana State University Press, 1987.

Malone, Dumas. *Jefferson and His Time,* 6 volumes. Boston: Little, Brown, 1948-1981.

McDonald, Forrest. *The Presidency of Thomas Jefferson.* Lawrence: University Press of Kansas, 1976.

Peterson, Merrill D. *Thomas Jefferson and the New Nation: A Biography.* New York: Oxford University Press, 1970.

JAMES MADISON

Brant, Irving. *James Madison,* 6 volumes. Indianapolis: Bobbs-Merrill, 1941-1961.

Ketcham, Ralph. *James Madison: A Biography.* New York: Macmillan, 1971.

Moore, Virginia. *The Madisons: A Biography.* New York: McGraw-Hill, 1979.

Rutland, Robert A. *James Madison: The Founding Father.* New York: Macmillan, 1987.

Rutland. *The Presidency of James Madison.* Lawrence: University Press of Kansas, 1990.

JAMES MONROE

Ammon, Harry. *James Monroe: The Quest for National Identity.* New York: McGraw-Hill, 1971.

Cresson, W. P. *James Monroe.* Chapel Hill: University of North Carolina Press, 1946.

Styron, Arthur. *The Last of the Cocked Hats: James Monroe and the Virginia Dynasty.* Norman: University of Oklahoma Press, 1945.

JOHN QUINCY ADAMS

Bemis, Samuel Flagg. *John Quincy Adams and the Foundations of American Foreign Policy.* New York: Knopf, 1949.

Bemis. *John Quincy Adams and the Union.* New York: Knopf, 1956.

Falkner, Leonard. *The President Who Wouldn't Retire: John Quincy Adams, Congressman from Massachusetts.* New York: Coward-McCann, 1967.

Hargreaves, Mary W. M. *The Presidency of John Quincy Adams.* Lawrence: University Press of Kansas, 1985.

Hecht, Marie B. *John Quincy Adams: A Personal History of an Independent Man.* New York: Macmillan, 1972.

ANDREW JACKSON

Curtis, James C. *Andrew Jackson and the Search for Vindication.* Boston: Little, Brown, 1976.

James, Marquis. *The Life of Andrew Jackson.* Indianapolis: Bobbs-Merrill, 1938.

Latner, Richard B. *The Presidency of Andrew Jackson: White House Politics 1829-1837.* Athens: University of Georgia Press, 1979.

Remini, Robert V. *Andrew Jackson and the Course of American Democracy, 1833-1845.* New York: Harper & Row, 1984.

Remini. *Andrew Jackson and the Course of American Empire, 1767-1821.* New York: Harper & Row, 1977.

Remini. *Andrew Jackson and the Course of American Freedom, 1822-1832.* New York: Harper, 1981.

Schlesinger, Arthur M. *The Age of Jackson.* Boston: Little, Brown, 1946.

MARTIN VAN BUREN

Curtis, James C. *The Fox at Bay: Martin Van Buren and the Presidency 1837-41.* Lexington: University of Kentucky Press, 1970.

Lynch, Dennis Tilden. *An Epoch and a Man: Martin Van Buren and His Times,* republished. Port Washington, N.Y.: Kennikat, 1971.

Niven, John. *Martin Van Buren: The Romantic Age of American Politics.* New York: Oxford University Press, 1983.

Remini, Robert V. *Martin Van Buren and the Making of the Democratic Party.* New York: Columbia University Press, 1959.

Wilson, Major L. *The Presidency of Martin Van Buren.* Lawrence: University Press of Kansas, 1984.

WILLIAM HENRY HARRISON

Cleaves, Freeman. *Old Tippecanoe: William Henry Harrison and His Times.* New York: Scribners, 1939.

Goebel, Dorothy Burne. *William Henry Harrison: A Political Biography.* Indianapolis: Indiana Library and Historical Department, 1926.

Peterson, Norma Lois. *The Presidencies of William Henry Harrison and John Tyler.* Lawrence: University Press of Kansas, 1989.

JOHN TYLER

Chidsey, Donald Barr. *And Tyler Too.* New York: Thomas, Nelson, 1978.

Chitwood, Oliver Perry. *John Tyler: Champion of the Old South.* New York & London: Appleton-Century, 1939.

Morgan, Robert J. *A Whig Embattled: The Presidency under John Tyler.* Lincoln: University of Nebraska Press, 1954.

Peterson, Norma Lois. *The Presidencies of William Henry Harrison and John Tyler.* Lawrence: University Press of Kansas, 1989.

Seager, Robert II. *And Tyler Too: A Biography of John and Julia Gardner Tyler.* New York: McGraw-Hill, 1963.

JAMES K. POLK

Bergeron, Paul H. *The Presidency of James K. Polk.* Lawrence: University Press of Kansas, 1987.

McCormac, Eugene I. *James K. Polk: A Political Biography.* Berkeley: University of California Press, 1922; republished, New York: Russell & Russell, 1965.

McCoy, Charles A. *Polk and the Presidency.* Austin: University of Texas Press, 1960.

Sellers, Charles Grier, Jr. *James K. Polk, Jacksonian.* Princeton: Princeton University Press, 1957.

Sellers. *Polk, Continentalist, 1843-1846.* Princeton: Princeton University Press, 1966.

ZACHARY TAYLOR

Bauer, Karl Jack. *Zachary Taylor: Soldier, Planter, Statesman of the Old Southwest.* Baton Rouge: Louisiana State University Press, 1985.

Hamilton, Holman. *Zachary Taylor: Soldier in the White House,* 2 volumes. Indianapolis: Bobbs-Merrill, 1941-1951.

McKinley, Silas Bent, and Silas Bent. *Old Rough and Ready: The Life and Times of Zachary Taylor.* New York: Vanguard, 1946.

Nichols, Edward J. *Zach Taylor's Little Army.* Garden City, N.Y. Doubleday, 1963.

Smith, Elbert B. *The Presidencies of Zachary Taylor and Millard Fillmore.* Lawrence: University Press of Kansas, 1988.

MILLARD FILLMORE

Rayback, Robert J. *Millard Fillmore: Biography of a President.* Buffalo: Stewart, 1959.

Smith, Elbert B. *The Presidencies of Zach-*

ary Taylor and Millard Fillmore. Lawrence: University Press of Kansas, 1988.

FRANKLIN PIERCE

Nichols, Roy Franklin. *Franklin Pierce: Young Hickory of the Granite Hills*. Philadelphia: University of Pennsylvania Press, 1931.

JAMES BUCHANAN

Klein, Philip S. *President James Buchanan*. University Park: Pennsylvania State University Press, 1962.

Smith, Elbert B. *The Presidency of James Buchanan*. Lawrence: University Press of Kansas, 1975.

ABRAHAM LINCOLN

Anderson, Dwight G. *Abraham Lincoln: The Quest for Immortality*. New York: Knopf, 1982.

Donald, David. *Lincoln Reconsidered: Essays on the Civil War Era*. New York: Knopf, 1956.

Oates, Stephen B. *Abraham Lincoln: The Man Behind the Myths*. New York: Harper & Row, 1984.

Oates. *With Malice Toward None: The Life of Abraham Lincoln*. New York: Harper & Row, 1977.

Randall, J. G. *Lincoln the President*, 4 volumes. New York: Dodd, Mead, 1945-1955.

Sandburg, Carl. *Abraham Lincoln: The Prairie Years and the War Years*, 6 volumes. New York: Harcourt, Brace & World, 1926-1939.

Strozier, Charles B. *Lincoln's Quest for Union: Public and Private Meanings*. New York: Basic Books, 1962.

Thomas, Benjamin P. *Abraham Lincoln*. New York: Knopf, 1952.

ANDREW JOHNSON

Castel, Albert. *The Presidency of Andrew Johnson*. Lawrence: University Press of Kansas, 1979.

Lomask, Milton. *Andrew Johnson: President on Trial*. New York: Farrar, Straus, 1960.

Milton, George Fort. *The Age of Hate: Andrew Johnson and the Radicals*. New York: Coward-McCann, 1930.

ULYSSES S. GRANT

Carpenter, John A. *Ulysses S. Grant*. New York: Twayne, 1970.

Catton, Bruce. *Grant and the American Military Tradition*. Boston: Little, Brown, 1954.

Catton. *Grant Moves South*. Boston: Little, Brown, 1960.

Catton. *Grant Takes Command*. Boston: Little, Brown, 1969.

Grant, Major General Ulysses S. III. *Ulysses S. Grant: Warrior and Statesman*. New York: Morrow, 1968.

McFeely, William S. *Grant: A Biography*. New York: Norton, 1981.

RUTHERFORD B. HAYES

Barnard, Harry. *Rutherford B. Hayes and His America*. New York: Russell & Russell, 1967.

Eckenrode, Hamilton James. *Rutherford B. Hayes: Statesman of Reunion*. New York: Dodd, Mead, 1930.

Hoogenboom, Ari. *The Presidency of Rutherford B. Hayes*. Lawrence: University Press of Kansas, 1988.

Williams, Charles Richard. *The Life of Rutherford Birchard Hayes: Nineteenth President of the United States*, 2 volumes. Columbus: Ohio State Archaeological and Historical Society, 1928.

JAMES A. GARFIELD

Doenecke, Justus D. *The Presidencies of James A. Garfield and Chester A. Arthur*. Lawrence: University Press of Kansas, 1981.

Leech, Margaret, and Harry J. Brown. *The Garfield Orbit*. New York: Harper & Row, 1978.

Peskin, Allan. *Garfield: A Biography*. Kent, Ohio: Kent State University Press, 1978.

Taylor, John M. *Garfield of Ohio: The Available Man*. New York: Norton, 1970.

CHESTER A. ARTHUR

Doenecke, Justus D. *The Presidencies of*

James A. Garfield and Chester A. Arthur. Lawrence: University Press of Kansas, 1981.

Howe, George F. *Chester A. Arthur, A Quarter-Century of Machine Politics.* New York: Dodd, Mead, 1934.

Reeves, Thomas. *Gentleman Boss: The Life of Chester Alan Arthur.* New York: Knopf, 1975.

GROVER CLEVELAND

Lynch, Dennis Tilden. *Grover Cleveland: A Man Four-Square.* New York: Horace Liveright, 1932.

McElroy, Robert. *Grover Cleveland: The Man and the Statesman: An Authorized Biography.* New York: Harper, 1923.

Merrill, Horace S. *Bourbon Leader: Grover Cleveland and the Democratic Party.* Boston: Little, Brown, 1957.

Nevins, Allan. *Grover Cleveland: A Study in Courage.* New York: Dodd, Mead, 1932.

Tugwell, Rexford G. *Grover Cleveland.* New York: Macmillan, 1968.

Welch, Richard E., Jr. *The Presidencies of Grover Cleveland.* Lawrence: University Press of Kansas, 1988.

BENJAMIN HARRISON

Sievers, Harry J. *Benjamin Harrison,* 3 volumes. Volumes 1 and 2, New York: University Publishers, 1952-1959; volume 3, Indianapolis: Bobbs-Merrill, 1968.

Socolofsky, Homer E., and Allan Spetter. *The Presidency of Benjamin Harrison.* Lawrence: University Press of Kansas, 1987.

WILLIAM MCKINLEY

Gould, Lewis L. *The Presidency of William McKinley.* Lawrence: University Press of Kansas, 1981.

Leech, Margaret. *In the Days of McKinley.* New York: Harper, 1959.

Morgan, H. Wayne. *William McKinley and His America.* Syracuse, N.Y.: Syracuse University Press, 1963.

Olcott, Charles S. *The Life of William McKinley,* 2 volumes. Boston: Houghton Mifflin, 1916.

Spielman, William Carl. *William McKinley: Stalwart Republican: A Biographical Study.* New York: Exposition Press, 1954.

THEODORE ROOSEVELT

Blum, John M. *The Republican Roosevelt,* second edition. Cambridge, Mass.: Harvard University Press, 1977.

Hagedorn, Hermann. *The Roosevelt Family of Sagamore Hill.* New York: Macmillan, 1954.

Harbaugh, William H. *The Life and Times of Theodore Roosevelt,* revised edition. New York: Oxford University Press, 1975.

McCullough, David. *Mornings on Horseback.* New York: Simon & Schuster, 1981.

Morris, Edmund. *The Rise of Theodore Roosevelt.* New York: Coward, McCann & Geoghegan, 1979.

Pringle, Henry F. *Theodore Roosevelt: A Biography.* New York: Harcourt, Brace, 1956.

Roosevelt, Nicholas. *Theodore Roosevelt: The Man as I Knew Him.* New York: Dodd, Mead, 1967.

WILLIAM HOWARD TAFT

Anderson, Donald F. *William Howard Taft: A Conservative's Conception About the Presidency.* Ithaca, N.Y.: Cornell University Press, 1973.

Anderson, Judith Icke. *William Howard Taft: An Intimate History.* New York: Norton, 1981.

Coletta, Paolo E. *The Presidency of William Howard Taft.* Lawrence: University Press of Kansas, 1973.

Pringle, Henry F. *The Life and Times of William Howard Taft: A Biography,* 2 volumes. New York: Farrar & Rinehart, 1939.

WOODROW WILSON

Baker, Ray Stannard. *Woodrow Wilson: Life and Letters,* 8 volumes. Garden City, N.Y.: Doubleday, Page, 1927-1939.

Smith, Gene. *When the Cheering Stopped: The Last Years of Woodrow Wilson.* New

York: Morrow, 1964.

Tribble, Edwin, ed. *A President in Love: The Courtship Years of Woodrow Wilson and Edith Bolling Galt.* Boston: Houghton Mifflin, 1981.

Walworth, Arthur C. *Woodrow Wilson*, third edition. New York: Norton, 1978.

Weinstein, Edwin A. *Woodrow Wilson: A Medical and Psychological Biography.* Princeton: Princeton University Press, 1981.

WARREN G. HARDING

Adams, Samuel Hopkins. *Incredible Era: The Life and Times of Warren Gamaliel Harding.* Boston: Houghton Mifflin, 1939.

Downes, Randolph C. *The Rise of Warren Gamaliel Harding, 1865-1920.* Columbus: Ohio State University Press, 1970.

Russell, Francis. *The Shadow of Blooming Grove: Warren G. Harding in His Times.* New York: McGraw-Hill, 1968.

Sinclair, Andrew. *The Available Man: The Life Behind the Mask of Warren Gamaliel Harding.* New York: Macmillan, 1965.

Trani, Eugene P., and David L. Wilson. *The Presidency of Warren G. Harding.* Lawrence: University Press of Kansas, 1977.

CALVIN COOLIDGE

McCoy, Donald R. *Calvin Coolidge: The Quiet President.* New York: Macmillan, 1967.

Silver, Thomas Barton. *Coolidge and the Historians.* Durham, N.C.: Carolina Academic Press for the Claremont Institute, 1982.

White, William Allen. *A Puritan in Babylon: The Story of Calvin Coolidge.* New York: Macmillan, 1938.

HERBERT HOOVER

Burner, David. *Herbert Hoover: A Public Life.* New York: Knopf, 1979.

Fausold, Martin L. *The Presidency of Herbert Hoover.* Lawrence: University Press of Kansas, 1985.

Hinshaw, David. *Herbert Hoover: American Quaker.* New York: Farrar, Straus, 1950.

Lyons, Eugene. *Herbert Hoover: A Biography.* Garden City, N.Y.: Doubleday, 1964.

Nash, George H. *The Life of Herbert Hoover: The Engineer.* New York: Norton, 1983.

Smith, Richard Norton. *An Uncommon Man: The Triumph of Herbert Hoover.* New York: Simon & Schuster, 1984.

FRANKLIN D. ROOSEVELT

Alsop, Joseph. *FDR, 1882-1945: A Centenary Remembrance.* New York: Viking, 1982.

Bishop, Jim. *FDR's Last Year, April 1944-April 1945.* New York: Morrow, 1974.

Burns, James MacGregor. *Roosevelt: The Soldier of Freedom.* New York: Harcourt Brace Jovanovich, 1970.

Burns. *Roosevelt: The Lion and the Fox.* New York: Harcourt Brace & World, 1956.

Davis, Kenneth. *FDR: The Beckoning of Destiny.* New York: Putnam's, 1972.

Freidel, Frank. *Franklin D. Roosevelt*, 4 volumes. Boston: Little, Brown, 1952-1973.

Miller, Nathan. *The Roosevelt Chronicles.* Garden City, N.Y.: Doubleday, 1979.

Ward, Geoffrey C. *Before the Trumpet: Young Franklin Roosevelt, 1882-1905.* New York: Harper & Row, 1985.

HARRY S TRUMAN

Cochran, Bert. *Harry Truman and the Crisis of the Presidency.* New York: Funk & Wagnalls, 1973.

Donovan, Robert J. *Conflict and Crisis: The Presidency of Harry S. Truman, 1945-1948.* New York: Norton, 1979.

Donovan. *Tumultuous Years : The Presidency of Harry S. Truman, 1949-1953.* New York: Norton, 1982.

Ferrell, Robert H. *Harry S. Truman and the Modern American Presidency.* Boston: Little, Brown, 1983.

Miller, Merle. *Plain Speaking: An Oral Biography of Harry S Truman.* New

York: Berkeley, 1974.

Miller, Richard Lawrence. *Truman: The Rise to Power*. New York: McGraw-Hill, 1986.

McCoy, Donald R. *The Presidency of Harry S. Truman*. Lawrence: University Press of Kansas, 1984.

Steinberg, Alfred. *The Man from Missouri: The Life and Times of Harry S. Truman*. New York: Putnam's, 1962.

Truman, Margaret. *Harry S Truman*. New York: Morrow, 1973.

DWIGHT D. EISENHOWER

Ambrose, Stephen E. *Eisenhower: President and Elder Statesman, 1952-1969*. New York: Simon & Schuster, 1984.

Ambrose. *Eisenhower: Soldier, General of the Army, President-Elect, 1896-1952*. New York: Simon & Schuster, 1983.

Greenstein, Fred I. *The Hidden-Hand Presidency: Eisenhower as Leader*. New York: Basic Books, 1982.

Lyon, Peter. *Eisenhower: Portrait of the Hero*. Boston: Little, Brown, 1974.

Neal, Steve. *The Eisenhowers: Reluctant Dynasty*. Garden City, N.Y.: Doubleday, 1978.

Richardson, Elmo. *The Presidency of Dwight D. Eisenhower*. Lawrence: University Press of Kansas, 1979.

JOHN F. KENNEDY

Blair, Joan, and Clay Blair, Jr. *In Search of JFK*. New York: Berkeley/Putnam's, 1976.

Goodwin, Doris Kearns. *The Fitzgeralds and the Kennedys: An American Saga*. New York: Simon & Schuster, 1987.

Manchester, William. *Portrait of a President: John F. Kennedy in Profile*. Boston: Little, Brown, 1962.

Parmet, Herbert S. *Jack: The Struggles of John F. Kennedy*. New York: Dial, 1980.

Parmet. *JFK: The Presidency of John F. Kennedy*. New York: Dial, 1983.

O'Donnell, Kenneth P., and David F. Powers. *Johnny, We Hardly Knew Ye: Memories of John Fitzgerald Kennedy*. Boston: Little, Brown, 1972.

Schlesinger, Arthur M. *A Thousand Days: John F. Kennedy in the White House*. Boston: Houghton Mifflin, 1965.

Sorensen, Theodore C. *The Kennedy Legacy*. New York: Macmillan, 1969.

Wills, Garry. *The Kennedy Imprisonment: A Meditation on Power*. Boston: Little, Brown, 1982.

LYNDON B. JOHNSON

Bornet, Vaughn Davis. *The Presidency of Lyndon B. Johnson*. Lawrence: University Press of Kansas, 1983.

Caro, Robert A. *The Years of Lyndon Johnson: Means of Ascent*. New York: Knopf, 1990.

Caro. *The Years of Lyndon Johnson: The Path to Power*. New York: Knopf, 1982.

Dugger, Ronnie. *The Politician: The Life and Times of Lyndon Johnson: The Drive for Power, From the Frontier to Master of the Senate*. New York: Norton, 1982.

Goldman, Eric F. *The Tragedy of Lyndon Johnson*. New York: Knopf, 1969.

Harwood, Richard, and Haynes Johnson. *Lyndon*. New York: Praeger, 1973.

Kearns, Doris. *Lyndon Johnson and the American Dream*. New York: Harper & Row, 1976.

Steinberg, Alfred. *Sam Johnson's Boy: A Close-Up of the President from Texas*. New York: Macmillan, 1968.

RICHARD M. NIXON

Ambrose, Stephen E. *Nixon: The Education of a Politician, 1913-1962*. New York; Simon & Schuster, 1987.

Ambrose. *Nixon: The Triumph of a Politician, 1962-1972*. New York: Simon & Schuster, 1990.

Brodie, Fawn M. *Richard Nixon: The Shaping of His Character*. Cambridge, Mass.: Harvard University Press, 1983.

Kornitzer, Bela. *The Real Nixon: An Intimate Biography*. New York: Rand McNally, 1960.

Kutler, Stanley I. *The Wars of Watergate: The Last Crisis of Richard Nixon*. New York: Knopf, 1990.

Lurie, Leonard. *The Running of Richard Nixon*. New York: Coward, McCann & Geoghegan, 1972.

Mazo, Earl, and Stephen Hess. *Nixon: A Political Portrait*. New York: Harper & Row, 1968.

Morris, Roger. *Richard Milhous Nixon: The Rise of an American Politician, 1913-1952*. New York: Holt, 1990.

Parmet, Herbert. *Richard Nixon and His America*. Boston: Little, Brown, 1990.

Schell, Jonathan. *Observing the Nixon Years: "Notes and Comment" from the* New Yorker. New York: Pantheon, 1989.

Schell. *The Time of Illusion*. New York: Knopf, 1975.

White, Theodore. *Breach of Faith: The Fall of Richard Nixon*. New York: Atheneum, 1975.

Wills, Garry. *Nixon Agonistes: The Crisis of the Self-Made Man*. Boston: Houghton Mifflin, 1970.

GERALD R. FORD

TerHorst, Jerald F. *Gerald Ford and the Future of the Presidency*. New York: Third Press, 1974.

Vestal, Bud. *Jerry Ford Up Close*. New York: Coward, McCann & Geoghegan, 1974.

JIMMY CARTER

Glad, Betty. *Jimmy Carter: In Search of the Great White House*. New York: Norton, 1980.

Kucharsky, David. *The Man from Plains: The Mind and Spirit of Jimmy Carter*. New York: Harper & Row, 1976.

Mazlish, Bruce, and Edwin Diamond. *Jimmy Carter: An Interpretative Biography*. New York: Simon & Schuster, 1979.

Stroud, Kandy. *How Jimmy Won: The Victory Campaign from Plains to the White House*. New York: Morrow, 1977.

Wooten, James. *Dasher: The Roots and the Rising of Jimmy Carter*. New York: Summit, 1978.

RONALD REAGAN

Barrett, Laurence I. *Gambling With History: Ronald Reagan in the White House*. Garden City, N.Y.: Doubleday, 1983.

Boyarski, Bill. *Ronald Reagan: His Life and Rise to the Presidency*. New York: Random House, 1981.

Cannon, Lou. *Reagan*. New York: Putnam's, 1982.

Dugger, Ronnie. *On Reagan: The Man and His Presidency*. New York: McGraw-Hill, 1983.

Edwards, Anne. *Early Reagan: The Rise to Power*. New York: Morrow, 1987.

Mayer, Jane, and Doyle McManus. *Landslide: The Unmaking of the President 1984-1988*. Boston: Houghton Mifflin, 1988.

Van der Linden, Frank. *The Real Reagan*. New York: Morrow, 1981.

Wills, Garry. *Reagan's America: Innocents at Home*. Garden City, N.Y.: Doubleday, 1987.

GEORGE BUSH

King, Nicholas. *George Bush: A Biography*. New York: Dodd, Mead, 1980.

Contributors

Robert B. Bennett, Jr.	*St. Augustine, Florida*
Edward D. C. Campbell, Jr.	*Virginia State Library and Archives*
Philip Cockrell	*University of South Carolina*
Thomas L. Connelly	*University of South Carolina*
Scott Derks	*Columbia, South Carolina*
James A. Dunlap III	*Spartanburg, South Carolina*
Richard Gamble	*University of South Carolina*
Suzanne Linder	*University of South Carolina*
William Piston	*Southwest Missouri State University*
Miles S. Richards	*University of South Carolina*
Katherine H. Richardson	*Columbia, South Carolina*
Michael D. Senecal	*Columbia, South Carolina*
Stephen R. Wise	*U.S. Marine Corps Museum, Parris Island, South Carolina*

Index